Cognitive Effects of Multimedia Learning

Robert Z. Zheng
University of Utah, USA

INFORMATION SCIENCE REFERENCE

Hershey · New York

Director of Editorial Content:	Kristin Klinger
Director of Production:	Jennifer Neidig
Managing Editor:	Jamie Snavely
Assistant Managing Editor:	Carole Coulson
Typesetter:	Jeff Ash
Cover Design:	Lisa Tosheff
Printed at:	Yurchak Printing Inc.

Published in the United States of America by
Information Science Reference (an imprint of IGI Global)
701 E. Chocolate Avenue, Suite 200
Hershey PA 17033
Tel: 717-533-8845
Fax: 717-533-8661
E-mail: cust@igi-global.com
Web site: http://www.igi-global.com

and in the United Kingdom by
Information Science Reference (an imprint of IGI Global)
3 Henrietta Street
Covent Garden
London WC2E 8LU
Tel: 44 20 7240 0856
Fax: 44 20 7379 0609
Web site: http://www.eurospanbookstore.com

Library of Congress Cataloging-in-Publication Data

Cognitive effects of multimedia learning / Robert Zheng, editor.

p. cm.

Includes bibliographical references and index.

Summary: "This book identifies the role and function of multimedia in learning through a collection of research studies focusing on cognitive functionality"--Provided by publisher.

ISBN 978-1-60566-158-2 (hardcover) -- ISBN 978-1-60566-159-9 (ebook)

1. Media programs (Education) 2. Learning, Psychology of. I. Zheng, Robert.

LB1028.4.C64 2009

371.33--dc22

2008024195

British Cataloguing in Publication Data
A Cataloguing in Publication record for this book is available from the British Library.

If a library purchased a print copy of this publication, please go to http://www.igi-global.com/agreement for information on activating the library's complimentary electronic access to this publication.

Table of Contents

Section I
Multimedia Learning: Cognitive Perspectives

Chapter I
Renae Low, University of New South Wales, Australia
Putai Jin, University of New South Wales, Australia
John Sweller, University of New South Wales, Australia

Chapter II
Peter E. Doolittle, Virginia Tech, USA
Krista P. Terry, Radford University, USA
Gina J. Mariano, Virginia Tech, USA

Chapter III
Anne E. Cook, University of Utah, USA
Robert Z. Zheng, University of Utah, USA
Jacquelyn W. Blaz, University of Utah, USA

Chapter IV
Stephen K. Reed, San Diego State University, USA

Section II
Multimedia Learning: Affective Perspectives

Section III
Teaching and Learning with Multimedia

Detailed Table of Contents

Section I
Multimedia Learning: Cognitive Perspectives

Chapter I

Renae Low, University of New South Wales, Australia
Putai Jin, University of New South Wales, Australia
John Sweller, University of New South Wales, Australia

This chapter describes human cognitive architecture within an evolutionary framework. The framework can be used as a base for cognitive load theory that uses human cognitive architecture to provide testable hypotheses concerning instructional design issues. Human cognition can be characterized as a natural information processing system. The core of such systems can be described using five principles: (a) information store principle, (b) borrowing principle and reorganizing principle, (c) randomness as genesis principle, (d) narrow limits of change principle, and (e) environment organizing and linking principle. These five principles lead directly to the instructional effects generated by cognitive load theory. Some of these effects are concerned with multimedia learning. The particular ones discussed in the chapter are the split-attention, modality, redundancy, element interactivity, and expertise reversal effects.

Chapter II

Peter E. Doolittle, Virginia Tech, USA
Krista P. Terry, Radford University, USA
Gina J. Mariano, Virginia Tech, USA

This chapter addresses the role that working memory capacity (WMC) plays in learning in multimedia environments. It focuses on how individual differences in attentional control, affect cognitive performance in general, and cognitive performance in multimedia environments, in particular. The authors conducted a study that examined the effects of WMC on learning in a multimedia environment. Results of this study indicated students with high WMC recalled and transferred significantly more information than students with low WMC. Ultimately, the chapter provides evidence that individual differences in working memory capacity should be taken into account when creating and implementing multimedia instructional environments.

Chapter III

  Anne E. Cook, University of Utah, USA
  Robert Z. Zheng, University of Utah, USA
  Jacquelyn W. Blaz, University of Utah, USA

This chapter focuses on issues dealing with the definition and measurement of cognitive load in multimedia and other complex learning activities. The chapter is broken into three main sections: defining multimedia learning and describing its effects on cognitive load; describing theoretical definitions of cognitive load; and mapping definitions of cognitive load onto commonly used measurement techniques. The chapter concludes with a discussion of how research on multimedia learning and cognitive load could be advanced by carefully considering issues of construct validity, and by including the use of convergent measurement techniques.

Chapter IV

  Stephen K. Reed, San Diego State University, USA

The chapter discusses a theoretical framework for designing multimedia in which manipulation, rather than perception, of objects plays the predominant role. The framework is based on research by cognitive psychologists and on Engelkamp's (1998) multimodal model of action-based learning. Although the assumptions of Engelkamp's model should be helpful for instructional design, they are not complete enough to include the additional demands of multimedia learning. These additional demands can result in unintended actions, involve sequences of related actions, and require reflection about domain-specific knowledge. Actions can be performed on either physical or virtual manipulatives, but virtual manipulatives exist in idealized environments, support continuous transformations of objects, and allow for dynamic linking to other objects, symbols, and data displays. The use of manipulatives in the Building Blocks and Animation Tutor projects provide illustrations.

Chapter V

  Katharina Scheiter, University of Tuebingen, Germany
  Eric Wiebe, North Carolina State University, USA
  Jana Holsanova, Lund University, Sweden

The chapter uses a semiotics approach to provide a definition of visualizations as a specific form of external representation. It then discusses the differences between verbal and visual representations in how they represent information, and finally, how meaning is achieved when learning with them. Also included in the chapter is the discussion of basic perceptual and cognitive processes relevant to learning with visualizations. This background is used to specify the instructional functions that visualizations have either as self-contained instructional messages or as text adjuncts. Moreover, the role of individual differences in processing visualizations is highlighted. The chapter ends with methodological suggestions concerning the important role of interdisciplinary research and assessment methods in this area.

Chapter VI

This chapter introduces eye tracking as a method to observe how the split of visual attention is managed in multimedia learning. The chapter reviews eye tracking literature on multirepresentational material. A special emphasis will be devoted to recent studies which were conducted to explore viewing behavior in learning from dynamic vs. static visualizations and the matter of pacing of presentation. It is argued that the learners' viewing behavior is affected by design characteristics of the learning material. Characteristics like the dynamics of visualization, or the pace of presentation, only slightly influence the learners' visual strategy while user interaction (i.e., learner controlled pace of presentation) leads to a different visual strategy compared to system-paced presentation. Taking viewing behavior as an indicator of how split attention is managed the harms of a split source format in multimedia learning can be overcome by implementing a user interaction that allows the learner to adapt the material to perceptual and individual characteristics.

Chapter VII

Multiformat and modality interfaces have become popular and effective tools for presenting information in training and instructional systems. Technological innovation, however, has far surpassed researchers' understanding of how and under what circumstances these technologies are useful towards information gathering. Some recent research has begun to characterize the cognitive mechanisms that may be responsible for the comprehension and memory advantages typically seen with multimedia learning as well as the role of individual differences in this process. Other work has defined effective pedagogical practices, such as instructional content and organization, for producing engaging and effective learning experiences. This chapter attempts to bridge these two research areas, provides concrete design recommendations for current instructional practice, and directions for future research.

The Web is emerging as a quintessential multimedia environment for complex learning, particularly in ill-structured domains. This chapter explores the cognitive load considerations associated with several constructs of deep and extended learning on the Web. Also examined, is how adjunct online tools and the role of learner motivation may help ameliorate cognitive load concerns when immersed in Web environments. The need for a reconceptualization of Cognitive Load Theory is proposed for more ill-structured conceptual arenas. The reconceptualization emphasizes support for the development of flexible knowledge assembly skills through processes of organic, reciprocal, and deep Web learning.

Section II
Multimedia Learning: Affective Perspectives

Although research on cognitive effects and their implications for instructional design is rich, research on the effects of motivation in a multimedia learning context is surprisingly scarce. Since one of the major goals of providing multimedia instruction is to motivate students, there is a need to examine motivational elements. This chapter focuses on four major motivation theories–expectancy-value theory, self-efficacy, goal-setting and task motivation, and self-determination theory–and two motivation models–ARCS model and the integrated model of cognitive-motivational processes –that are derived from multimedia research, and reviews the literature on motivation in multimedia learning contexts. Suggestions are made with respect to motivation features and how they can be incorporated in multimedia learning resources to optimize learners' experience.

Chapter X

This study investigates students' engagement with a multimedia enhanced problem-based learning (PBL) environment, Alien Rescue. Alien Rescue is a PBL environment for students to learn science. Fifty-seven sixth-grade students were interviewed. Analysis of the interviews, using the constant comparative method, showed that students were intrinsically motivated and that there were 11 key elements of Alien Rescue that helped evoke students' motivation: authenticity, challenge, cognitive engagement, competence, choice, fantasy, identity, interactivity, novelty, sensory engagement, and social relations. These elements can be grouped into five perspectives of the sources of intrinsic motivation for students using the PBL environment: problem solving, playing, socializing, information processing, and voluntary acting; with problem solving and playing contributing the highest level of intrinsic motivation. The findings are discussed with respect to designing multimedia learning environments.

Section III
Teaching and Learning with Multimedia

This chapter examines the cognitive demands of student-centered learning, from and with, Web-based multimedia. In contrast to externally-structured directed learning, during student-centered learning the individual assumes responsibility for determining learning goals, monitoring progress toward meeting goals, adjusting or adapting approaches as warranted, and determining when individual goals have been adequately addressed. These tasks can be particularly challenging in learning from the World Wide Web, where billions of resources address a variety of needs. The individual, in effect, must identify which tools and resources are available and appropriate, how to assemble them, and how to manage the process to support unique learning goals. The chapter focuses on the applicability of current cognitive principles to Web-based multimedia learning and implications for research.

This chapter presents a review of research on the use and role of interactive simulations for learning. Contemporary theories of learning, instruction, and media, suggest that learning involves a complex relationship and dependency between a learner's prior knowledge, a learner's motivation, the context, the task, and the resources (e.g., simulations) provided to and used by the learner to support or enable the task. Given this perspective, and data from an evolving research program, simulations are best used to help learners construct knowledge and make meaning by giving them control over phenomena modeled by the simulation. Several theoretical frameworks have guided this research program: dual coding theory, mental models, and constructivist learning theory. An overall result of this research is that learning should be based on experience, such as that derived from interacting with a simulation, and supported with explanations. This is counter to traditional educational wisdom where explanations rule instructional strategies.

Chapter XIII

The role and promotion of transfer in multimedia instructional environments is an oft-neglected concept in instructional multimedia research. However, while most instructional multimedia research does not focus specifically on transfer, the majority of basic multimedia research conducted uses retention and transfer as dependent measures. The purposes of this chapter are to (a) provide a review of the current state of the transfer literature, (b) provide a synthesis of the existing literature on the evidence for transfer in multimedia instructional environments, and (c) provide a series of strategies for constructing and using multimedia for the purpose of fostering transfer. The significance of proactively creating multimedia instructional environments that fosters transfer, lays in the benefits of creating knowledge that may be generalized and applied in the "real world." Specifically, knowledge that may be generalized, applied, or transferred broadly, facilitates the learner's ability to solve problems of all types. In addition, and unfortunately even under the best of conditions, fostering transfer is challenging; thus, a proactive stance in fostering transfer is necessary to increase the likelihood of generating knowledge transfer.

This chapter discusses an emerging theme in supporting effective multimedia learning: developing scalable, cognitively-grounded tools that customize learning interactions for individual students. The theoretical foundation for expected benefits of customization and current approaches in educational technology that leverage learner prior knowledge is discussed. Followed by a description of the development of a customized tool for science learning, called CLICK, that uses automatic techniques to create knowledge models that can be fed into cognitively-informed pedagogical tools. CLICK leverages existing multimedia resources in educational digital libraries for two purposes. To generate rich representations of domain content relevant for learner modeling that are easily scaled to new domains and disciplines, and also to serve as a repository of instructional resources that support customized pedagogical interactions. The potential of the CLICK system is discussed along with initial comparisons of knowledge models created by CLICK and human experts. Finally, the chapter discusses remaining challenges and relevant future extensions for effective customization tools in educational technology.

Multimedia environments can benefit learning as well as offer significant capacity to serve research purposes. The authors reviewed current hypermedia learning models, specifically focusing on how they integrate motivational elements into their frameworks. The goal-tracing methodology was proposed to identify traces of learners' use of cognitive tools that reflect their goal orientations. By applying data mining techniques to these data, the authors show how it is possible to identify goal patterns together with study tactic patterns. The authors propose that future research could benefit substantially by merging trace methodologies with other methods for gathering data about motivation and learning.

The first part of this chapter explores how narrative can be used as a cognitive aid in educational video games. It discusses how narrative is currently used in games, and how that modality of presentation, when combined with instruction, is complimentary to the way we comprehend, store, and retrieve information. The second part of the chapter reviews the cognitive prerequisites needed in the minds of players to adequately attend to, and leverage, the instructional aspects of games. To this end, it offers suggestions for how to instill a functional game-schema in the minds of novice players so that they can be productive in the game environment. The focus on the interplay of narrative and game schema construction in this chapter is also meant to serve as a model for a holistic approach to games research in which a game's cognitive prerequisites are explicitly studied alongside the more traditional pedagogical measures.

Advanced digital storybooks offer, in addition to an oral rendition of text, the possibility of enhancing story content through the use of video. In three experiments effects of added video with accompanying music and sound on language comprehension and language acquisition were tested in a group of second language learners from low educated families. Three questions were posed. Do video additions positively influence young children's story understanding over and above still images when listening to a storybook? How does video add to language acquisition; through added information or through the appraisal of helpfulness of the added information? Do these extra information sources benefit all young children to the same extent or especially children with insufficient prior knowledge?

To learn by means of analogies, students have to see surface and deep structures in both source and target domains. Educators generally assume that students, presented with images, texts, video, or demonstrations, see what the curriculum designer intends them to see, that is, pick out and integrate information into their existing understanding. There is however, evidence that students do not see what they are supposed to see, which precisely inhibits them to learn what they are supposed to learn. In this extended case study, which exemplifies a successful multimedia application, three classroom episodes are used (a) to show how students in an advanced physics course do not see relevant information on the computer monitor, (b) to exemplify teaching strategies designed to allow relevant structures to become salient in students' perception allowing them to generate analogies and thereby learn, and (c) to exemplify how a teacher might assist students in bridging from the multimedia context to the real world.

Preface

Given the increasing presence of multimedia in K-12 schools, higher education, and professional training settings, it is appropriate to study the impact of multimedia on learning. This edited book represents works in multimedia that include both theoretical and empirical research. Its purpose is to explicate the phenomenon related to multimedia learning and provide a better understanding of how multimedia effects learning affectively and cognitively.

One of the heavily studied topics with respect to multimedia learning is human information processing capacity. Over the last 20 years, much of the research in multimedia learning has been informed by the work of memory research, particularly the research on working memory by Baddeley and his colleagues (1986; 1999; Baddeley & Hitch, 1974). For example, Cognitive Load Theory (Sweller & Chandler, 1991, 1994; Sweller, van Merrienboer, & Pass, 1998) and Cognitive Theory of Multimedia Learning (Mayer, 2001) consider the impact of limited capacity of working memory in learning.

Recently, research has focused on human cognitive architecture and multiple representations, including manipulation, in multimedia learning environments (Reed, 2006). This book includes a collection of works that focuses on multimedia learning and working memory, cognitive architecture and instructional design, and cognitive demands of multimedia learning in a Web-based environment. Readers will find an array of interesting topics ranging from theoretical framework for designing manipulative multimedia, to cognitive functionality of multimedia through the lens of semiotics. Other topics explore cognitive mechanisms involving visual and non-visual information representations, as well as the complex relationship among learners' prior knowledge, motivation, context, and task in a simulation learning environment.

Although much is known about the cognitive aspects of multimedia, little research has been done to understand the affective aspects in multimedia learning (Astleitner & Wiesner, 2004; Keller, 1987). This book contains two chapters on motivation with the first chapter focusing on the motivational theories and models of multimedia learning, followed by a chapter on case study that investigates students' engagement with multimedia enhanced problem-based learning. Both chapters identify the intrinsic and extrinsic motivational factors related to multimedia learning.

There has been a tremendous amount of interest among researchers and educators who see multimedia as a viable tool for teaching and learning. Researchers are interested in understanding how multimedia contributes to deeper learning and knowledge transfer, when and what external representations should be used to promote such deeper learning, how multimedia should be designed to facilitate information distribution among the external representations in order to better assist learners' cognitive learning, and so forth. Readers will find in this book, chapters that focus on the practical aspects of multimedia learning. The topics covered include: knowledge transfer in multimedia learning consisting of both vertical and horizontal knowledge transfers, use of multimedia to facilitate students' research through a goal-tracing methodology, development of scalable, cognitively-grounded multimedia learning tools customized for individual students, integration of multimedia to support linguistically challenged students, and use of multimedia to facilitate analogical learning in a high school physics course.

THE CONTRIBUTION OF THIS BOOK

This book addresses pressing needs in multimedia learning and cognition by, (a) identifying the role and function of multimedia in learning; (b) bringing together research in multimedia study with a focus on cognitive functionality; and (c) bridging the theories with practices in multimedia by focusing on the effective use of multimedia in teaching and learning. The book targets educators globally, with an emphasis on diverse aspects of multimedia learning and cognition. A major contribution of this book is to bring together multimedia learning theories and practices with an emphasis on cognitive effects in multimedia learning. Thus, the book is significant both theoretically and practically. At the theoretical level, it contributes to the knowledge base in multimedia research. It enhances our understanding of the cognitive functionality related to multimedia learning. At the practical level, the book provides an array of instructional strategies in multimedia learning, ranging from knowledge transfer and goal tracing, to scalable, multimedia learning tools which, among others, readers will find beneficial in the design and development of multimedia learning.

The book also reflects the collective effort of multimedia learning theorists and practitioners who challenge the traditional theoretical boundaries pertaining to multimedia and cognition, identify parameters critical to multimedia design, and propose theoretical frameworks that would lead to new research and practice in multimedia learning. Fortunately, we are able to bring together a group of excellent authors who represent various perspectives in multimedia learning and cognition from a broad range of academic institutions and research organizations–from private to public comprehensive and from state and national to international. This book thus appeals to readers from the United States to the international educational community. Researchers and educators will find this book a useful companion as they discover helpful information representing new perspectives on cognitive effects in multimedia learning.

THE ORGANIZATION OF THIS BOOK

The three sections of this book are organized to maximize the value for the readers as they move from the theoretical to the practical and from a focus on cognitive and affective, to specific issues of teaching and learning with multimedia.

Section I presents a theoretical perspective on multimedia learning and cognition. It contains eight chapters that cover a wide range of topics on multimedia and cognition that include cognitive architecture, working memory, manipulation, visualization, specialty, and deep learning in multimedia.

In **Chapter I**, Renee Low, Putai Jin, and John Sweller, University of New South Wales, Australia, analyze human cognitive architecture within an evolutionary framework. Using the framework as a basis for understanding cognitive load involved in learning, the authors argue that human cognition can be characterized as a natural information processing system which operates on five principles described as: (a) *information store principle*, (b) *borrowing principle and reorganizing principle*, (c) *randomness as genesis principle*, (d) *narrow limits of change principle*, and (e) *environment organizing and linking principle*. The authors propose that instructional design need to consider these five principles in terms of their effects on cognitive load in learning.

In **Chapter II**, the concept of control attention in multimedia learning is discussed by Peter E. Doolittle, Virginia Tech University, Krista P. Terry, Radford University, Gina J. Mariano, Virginia Tech University, who address the role of working memory capacity (WMC) that plays in multimedia environments. Specifically, the authors examine the relationship between individual differences, working memory and attentional control in learning. In their findings, the authors discover that students with high WMC perform better than those with low WMC in terms of attentional control measured by recall and transfer tests. The authors thus suggest that individual differences in working memory capacity should be taken into consideration when creating and implementing multimedia instructional environments.

Chapter III raises an important issue related to cognitive load research–the measurement of cognitive load. Anne E. Cook, Robert Z. Zheng, and Jacquelyn W. Blaz, University of Utah, review the existing approaches to cognitive load measurement by, (a) defining multimedia learning and describing its effects on cognitive load; (b) describing theoretical definitions of cognitive load; and (c) mapping definitions of cognitive load onto commonly used measurement techniques. The authors propose using convergent measures to gauge cognitive load, which would allow researchers to map different constructs of cognitive load onto their respective behavioral, affective, and physiological components. This would also allow researchers to understand the associations and dissociations among different aspects of cognitive load.

Chapter IV presents a relevant topic in multimedia research, that is, manipulating multimedia materials, which has been, for some reason, understudied. Stephen K. Reed, San Diego State University, discusses a theoretical framework by Engelkemp (1998) who sees manipulation or haptic learning as a different encoding system that requires a different approach in terms of defining research parameters. Reed points out that although the assumptions of Engelkamp's model should be helpful for instructional design, they are not complete enough to include the additional demands of multimedia learning. Thus, he explores the instructional use of manipulative multimedia where the ability to integrate schematic knowledge is highlighted, compared to the ability to recall from action phrases based on which Engelkamp's theory is formed.

In **Chapter V**, Katherina Scheiter, University of Tuebingen, Germany, Eric Wiebe, North Carolina State University, and Jana Holsanova, Lund University, Sweden, use a semiotics approach to provide a definition of visualizations as a specific form of external representation. The authors discuss the differences between verbal and visual representations and how each represents information; and how meaning is achieved when learning with them. The authors then discuss basic perceptual and cognitive processes relevant to learning with visualizations, which is further used to specify the instructional functions that visualizations have either as self-contained instructional messages, or as text adjuncts. Moreover, the role of individual differences in processing visualizations is highlighted.

Chapter VI continues the discussion of visualization, but with a different focus–the management of visual split attention in multimedia learning. Florian Schmidt-Weigand, University of Kassel, Germany, explores the viewing behavior in learning from dynamic vs. static visualizations as well as issues related to the pacing of visual presentation. The author concludes that the negative effect of visual split attention can be reduced by implementing a user interaction that allows the learner to adapt the material to perceptual and individual characteristics.

In **Chapter VII**, Tad T. Brunyé, U.S. Army NSRDEC, Comsumer Research & Cognitive Science and Tufts University, Tali Ditman, Tufts University and Massachusetts General Hospital, Jason S. Augustyn, U.S. Army NSRDEC, Consumer Research & Cognitive Science, and Caroline R. Mahoney, U.S. Army NSRDEC, Consumer Research & Cognitive Science and Tufts University, offer a discussion on the cognitive mechanisms that accounts for the advantages associated with multimedia learning. The authors are specially interested in knowing (a) what effects, if any, do format and modality manipulations have on eventuating memory form and function; (b) which working memory mechanisms are involved in the processing, manipulation, and integration of multiformat and multimodality information; (c) how does the effectiveness of manipulations vary as a function of learning material types; and (d) what, if any, individual differences predict the success of various media combinations? The authors conclude that multimedia is advantageous to learning because well-designed multimedia aligns with the structure and capacity of human working memory. They claim that complementing images when well designed, reduce cognitive loads and allow resources to be devoted to higher-level integration which facilitates mental model development. Finally, multimedia is more engaging and more likely to accommodate different cognitive and learning styles.

The section concludes with **Chapter VIII** on the application of multimedia in Web learning. Mike DeSchryver and Rand J. Spiro, Michigan State University, explore the cognitive load considerations associated with several constructs of deep and extended learning on the Web. They also examine how adjunct online tools and the role of learner motivation may help ameliorate cognitive load concerns when immersed in Web environments. The authors propose a need for a re-conceptualization of Cognitive Load Theory for more ill-structured conceptual arenas. The reconceptualization emphasizes support for the development of flexible knowledge assembly skills through processes of organic, reciprocal, and deep Web learning.

Section II deals with issues of affective aspects in multimedia learning. The section contains two chapters that introduce motivational theories, explore motivational factors associated with multimedia learning, and suggest ways to incorporate motivational features into multimedia learning resources to optimize the learners' experience.

In **Chapter IX**, Renee Low and Putai Jin, University of New South Wales, Australia, focus on four major motivation theories–expectancy-value theory, self-efficacy, goal-setting and task motivation, and self-determination theory–and two motivation models–the ARCS model and the integrated model of cognitive-motivational processes. The authors analyze and discuss motivational determinants in effective multimedia learning from social-cognitive perspectives. Important aspects covered pertaining to motivation in multimedia learning include: (a) theoretical development; (b) motivational features and design of multimedia instruction; (c) learner characteristics; (d) self-regulated learning strategies and motivational training; and (e) evaluating quality of motivational features in multimedia learning resources.

Chapter X introduces a case study conducted by Min Liu, University of Texas Paul Toprac, Southern Methodist University, and Timothy T. Yuen, University of Texas. Liu et al. offers a unique perspective on looking at learners' motivational determinants, by situating them in a problem-based multimedia learning environment. Their findings reveal 11 key elements that help evoke learners' motivation: authenticity, challenge, cognitive engagement, competence, choice, fantasy, identity, interactivity, novelty, sensory engagement, and social relations.

Section III presents research studies and conceptual papers on teaching and learning with multimedia. It entails chapters that focus on new perspectives pertaining to the use of multimedia in various educational settings.

The section opens with a theoretical investigation in **Chapter XI** by Michael J. Hannafin, Richard E. West, University of Georgia, and Graig E. Shepherd, of University of Wyoming, on the cognitive demands in a user-centered, Web-based multimedia environment. The chapter starts with a discussion on perception, encoding, and retrieving processes related to multimedia learning, followed by an examination on the cognitive styles and strategies, as well as self-regulation involved in such learning. Finally, the authors elaborate on the cognitive demands in student-centered multimedia learning, by putting in perspective the issues discussed above. Other important issues being mentioned include metacognition, locus of knowledge, beliefs and conceptual change, prior experience, system knowledge, and so forth.

Chapter XII presents a review of research on the use of interactive simulations for learning. Lloyd P. Rieber, University of Georgia, considers the relationship between presentation and interaction. The issues of mental model, constructivist learning, and universal design related to simulation learning, are discussed. The author supports his discussion with three empirical studies demonstrating that learning should be based on experience, such as that derived from interacting with a simulation, and supported with explanation.

In **Chapter XIII**, Gina J. Mariano, Peter E. Doolittle, and David Hicks, Virginia Tech, consider the role of transfer in multimedia instructional environments. The authors reviewed the functionality of transfer and its impact on deep learning. Based on a review of 22 studies, the authors concluded that while transfer is often found in the multimedia learning research, it has yet to become a variable of interest. The authors suggest future research should focus on a coherent agenda that explores the use of multimedia to proactively foster transfer, as well as the development of metacognition within a multimedia learning environment.

In **Chapter XIV**, Kirsten R. Butcher, University of Utah, Sebastian de la Chica, Faisal Ahmad, Qianyi Gu, Tamara Summer, and James H. Martin, University of Colorado at Boulder, discuss an emerging theme in supporting effective multimedia learning; developing scalable, cognitively-grounded tools that customize learning interactions for individual students. They describe the development of a customized tool for science learning, called CLICK, which uses automatic techniques to create knowledge models that can be fed into cognitively-informed pedagogical tools.

In **Chapter XV**, Mingming Zhou and Philip H. Winne, of Simon Fraser University, Canada, introduce a goal-tracing methodology to identify students' goal patterns together with their study tactic patterns. The goal-tracing method provides a bridge to join students' perceptions about goals, with traces that reveal how the students seek goals. Using a multimedia learning tool called gStudy, the authors are able to gain insights into students' implicit goals, their motivation, and metacognition in learning.

In **Chapter XVI**, Alan D. Koenig, University of California–Los Angeles, and Robert K. Atkinson, Arizona State University, explore how a narrative can be used as a cognitive aid in educational video games. It discusses how narrative is currently used in games, and how that modality of presentation, when combined with instruction, is complimentary to the way humans comprehend, store, and retrieve information. The authors offer suggestions for how to instill a functional game-schema in the minds of novice players so that they can be productive in the game environment. They also propose a model for a holistic approach to games research in which a game's cognitive prerequisites are explicitly studied alongside the more traditional pedagogical measures.

In **Chapter XVII**, Marian J.A.J. Verhallen and Adriana.G. Bus, Leiden University, The Netherlands, offer a new perspective on how to use multimedia to enhance language comprehension and language acquisition skills for second language learners. The authors support their discussion with empirical data from three experiments. They conclude that multimedia such as animated digital storybook, promotes the young linguistically disadvantaged to become more engaged in and therefore investigate more mental effort in learning.

Finally, in **Chapter XVIII**, Wolff-Michael Roth, University of Victoria, Canada, describes a naturalistic case study designed to investigate knowing and learning in a real classroom setting where students use computer simulation tools to learn about Newtonian motion. The study purports to show the mediatory role of the instructor and teaching strategies in digital simulation learning. It reveals how teacher assistance may help students in bridging the gap from the multimedia context to the real world, and how teaching strategies may allow relevant structures to become salient in students' perception, which allow them to generate analogies and thereby learn.

REFERENCES

Astleitner, H., & Wiesner, C. (2004). An integrated model of multimedia learning and motivation. *Journal of Educational Multimedia and Hypermedia, 13(1), 3-21.*

Baddeley, A. D. (1986). *Working memory.* Oxford, England: Oxford University Press.

Baddeley, A. D. (1999). *Essentials of human memory.* Hove, England : Psychology Press.

Baddeley, A.D., & Hitch, G.J. (1974). Working memory, In G.A. Bower (Ed.), *The psychology of learning and motivation: advances in research and* theory, 8, 47-89, New York: Academic Press.

Engelkamp, J. (1998). *Memory for actions.* Hove, England: Psychology Press.

Keller, J. M. (1987). Motivational design and multimedia: Beyond the novelty effect. *Strategic Human Resource Development Review, 1*(1), 188-203.

Mayer, R. E. (2001). *Multimedia learning.* New York: Cambridge University Press.

Reed, S. K..(2006). Cognitive architectures for multimedia learning. *Educational Psychologist, 41*(2), 87-98.

Sweller, J., & Chandler, P. (1991). Evidence for cognitive load theory. *Cognition and Instruction, 8*(4), 351-362.

Sweller, J., & Chandler, P. (1994).Why some material is difficult to learn. *Cognition and Instruction, 12*(3), 185-233.

Sweller, J., Van Merrienboer, J. J. G., & Pass, F. G. W. C. (1998). Cognitive architecture and instructional design. *Educational Psychology Review, 10*(3), 251-296.

Acknowledgment

This volume represents the collective wisdom of many who voluntarily spent hundreds of hours putting together a series of chapters that provide excellent overview of the theories and practice in multimedia learning. I would like to express my deepest gratitude and sincere appreciation to all these authors for their outstanding contribution.

My appreciation also goes to our reviewers who provide insightful input and suggestions. I thank all of our authors for their own expert assistance. I would also like to thank the following reviewers in particularly for their hard work, generous donation of their time, and their attention to detail: Louis Berry, University of Pittsburgh; Laura Dahl, University of Utah; Markus Deimann, Erfurt University; Jill Flygare and John Kircher, University of Utah; and Matthew McAlack, Philadelphia Biblical University. My special thanks go to Richard Hoffman and Elizabeth McCadden at the University of Utah who assisted in proof-reading the chapters.

I feel exceptionally fortunate to work with Jessica Thompson and Julia Mosemann, editors at IGI Global, whose expertise and generous support make this project a great success. I would like to thank the publishing team at IGI Global who has demonstrated the highest level of professionalism and integrity.

I would like to thank my wife Sharon and two children Joanna and Henry for their understanding and support, and for tolerating the erratic schedule as I was working on the project. Finally, I would like to thank my mother who has always been the source of wisdom and inspiration in my life.

Robert Z. Zheng
University of Utah, USA

Section I
Multimedia Learning:
Cognitive Perspectives

Chapter I
Cognitive Architecture and Instructional Design in a Multimedia Context

Renae Low
University of New South Wales, Australia

Putai Jin
University of New South Wales, Australia

John Sweller
University of New South Wales, Australia

ABSTRACT

Our knowledge of human cognitive architecture has advanced dramatically in the last few decades. In turn, that knowledge has implications for instructional design in multimedia contexts. In this chapter, we will analyse human cognitive architecture within an evolutionary framework. That framework can be used as a base for cognitive load theory that uses human cognitive architecture to provide testable hypotheses concerning instructional design issues. Human cognition can be characterised as a natural information processing system. The core of such systems can be described using 5 principles: (a) information store principle, (b) borrowing principle and reorganizing principle, (c) randomness as genesis principle, (d) narrow limits of change principle, and (e) environment organizing and linking principle. These 5 principles lead directly to the instructional effects generated by cognitive load theory. Some of these effects are concerned with multimedia learning. The particular ones discussed in the chapter are the split-attention, modality, redundancy, element interactivity, and expertise reversal effects.

INTRODUCTION

Instructional design recommendations not based on our knowledge of human cognitive architecture are likely to be limited in their effectiveness or may even have negative consequences. In this chapter, we will use an evolutionary approach to human cognition (see Sweller 2003; Sweller 2004; Sweller and Sweller 2006). Evolution by natural selection can be used to determine categories of knowledge that humans are particularly adept at gaining because we have evolved to acquire that knowledge. Furthermore, the basic logic that underlies evolutionary biology is shared by human cognition and so can be used to analyse our cognitive processes. Those cognitive processes, in turn, determine the effectiveness of particular instructional procedures. We will begin by discussing two categories of knowledge from an evolutionary perspective.

BIOLOGICALLY PRIMARY AND BIOLOGICALLY SECONDARY KNOWLEDGE

Geary (2007) divides knowledge into biologically primary knowledge that we have evolved to acquire easily and automatically and biologically secondary knowledge that relies on primary knowledge but that we have not evolved to acquire. Examples of activities driven by primary knowledge are listening and speaking our first language, recognising faces, using general problem solving techniques and engaging in basic social relations. We have evolved over millennia to acquire massive amounts of knowledge associated with these activities easily, quickly and without conscious effort. We can acquire biologically primary knowledge simply by being immersed in a normal human society. Explicit instruction is unnecessary.

In contrast, biologically secondary knowledge tends to be associated with a more advanced stage of development of civilization. It has only been required since the rise of civilisation and so we have not evolved to acquire specific examples of biologically secondary knowledge. We can acquire such knowledge using biologically primary knowledge but it is acquired relatively slowly and with conscious effort. In contrast to biologically primary knowledge, biologically secondary knowledge requires explicit instruction and conscious effort on the part of learners. The bulk of knowledge acquired in educational institutions such as schools consists of biologically secondary knowledge.

HUMAN COGNITIVE ARCHITECTURE WHEN DEALING WITH BIOLOGICALLY SECONDARY KNOWLEDGE

There is a basic logic associated with the acquisition of biologically secondary knowledge and that logic is identical to the logic that underlies the processes of evolution by natural selection. Both are examples of natural information processing systems (Sweller & Sweller, 2006). There are many ways of describing that logic. In this chapter we will use five basic principles.

Information Store Principle

In order to function, natural information processing systems require a massive store of information used to govern activity. In the case of human cognition, long-term memory provides that store. The well-known work of De Groot (1965) and Chase and Simon (1973) on the knowledge chess masters have for board configurations taken from real games provides evidence for the importance of long-term memory for most facets of cognition, including problem solving. A genome provides the same function for evolution by natural selection.

Borrowing and Reorganising Principle

Acquiring a massive store of information requires an efficient acquisition procedure. In the case of the human cognitive system, that procedure involves borrowing and reorganising information from the long-term store of other individuals by imitating what they do, listening to what they say and reading what they write. The information obtained is combined with previous information resulting in reorganisation. Findings based on cognitive load theory provide evidence for the importance of the borrowing and reorganising principle (e.g. Sweller, 2003, 2004). How cognitive load theory suggests instruction should be organised to facilitate the borrowing of information is discussed below. During sexual reproduction, evolution by natural selection uses the borrowing and reorganising principle to allow a genome to acquire large amounts of information that is necessarily reorganised during the process.

Randomness as Genesis Principle

While information is best acquired by using the borrowing and reorganising principle, that information must be created in the first instance. In genetics, random mutation is the ultimate source of all biological variation and so is the genesis of all biological novelty. In human cognition, information is created via the randomness as genesis principle during problem solving. In order to generate a problem solving move, we must use a combination of information held in long-term memory and a random generate and test for effectiveness procedure. If at any point while solving a problem, two or more moves are available to us, and if we do not have information in long-term memory indicating which move might be best, we must randomly generate one of the moves and test to see what effect it has. To the extent to which information is not available in long-term memory, no other procedure has been

identified to generate moves other than random generate and test. That process is the ultimate source of all novel information we create just as random mutation is the ultimate source of all biological variation.

Narrow Limits of Change Principle

Since the creation of novel information requires a random generate and test procedure, mechanisms are required to ensure that randomly generated information, most of which is dysfunctional, does not destroy the functionality of the information store. Our cognitive system achieves this end by ensuring that all changes to the store are small and incremental by requiring information to first be processed by a limited capacity, limited duration working memory. Evidence for the limited capacity of working memory comes from the well-known work of Miller (1956) while evidence for its limited duration comes from Peterson and Peterson (1959). It must be emphasised that the limitations of working memory only apply to novel information to which the randomness as genesis principle applies. Changes to a genome require random mutation, are governed by the epigenetic system and also are slow and incremental.

Environmental Organising and Linking Principle

The limitations of working memory disappear when it processes organised information from long-term memory. When dealing with familiar information, working memory has neither capacity nor duration limits. Evidence for the altered characteristics of working memory when dealing with well-learned information comes from Ericsson and Kintsch's (1995) work on long-term working memory. We can hold huge amounts of familiar information in working memory for indefinite periods. That material can be used to organise information from our environment and link our activities appropriately to the environment. It provides the ultimate justification for our cognitive system. Similarly, the epigenetic system determines how information stored in DNA is used to govern biological activity.

INSTRUCTIONAL CONSEQUENCES

There are instructional consequences that follow from the manner in which our cognitive structures are organised to process information. The first and most obvious implication is that the purpose of instruction is to alter the information store – long-term memory. If nothing has changed in long-term memory, nothing has been learned. The second implication is that the best way to alter long-term memory is via the borrowing and reorganising principle. Wherever possible, we should present information to students rather than have them search for the information themselves. The third implication is that when presenting information to learners, we should organise that information in a manner that takes into account the characteristics of human cognitive architecture. For instruction to be effective, the narrow limits of change principle is paramount. Instruction has to be designed in such a way that the limitations of working memory are overcome by, for instance, minimising extraneous cognitive load. By minimising unnecessary working memory load, essential information can be stored in long-term memory and in turn, that information will increase the effective capacity of working memory via the environmental organising and linking principle. That principle permits humans to readily engage in very complex activities.

Cognitive load theory has used this architecture to devise a variety of instructional procedures. Some of those procedures are directly concerned with the presentation of information within a multimedia framework. In this chapter, we focus on three cognitive load effects concerned with aspects of multimedia presentation of information:

the split-attention effect, the redundancy effect and the modality effect.

The Split-Attention Effect

Split-attention occurs when learners have to mentally integrate two or more sources of physically or temporally disparate information and each source of information is essential for understanding the material. The working memory load imposed by the need to mentally integrate the disparate sources of information interferes with learning. Consider a conventionally structured geometry worked example consisting of a diagram and its associated solution statements (see Figure 1). The diagram alone does not communicate the solution to the problem. The statements, in turn, are incomprehensible until they have been integrated with the diagram. Learners must mentally integrate the two sources of information (the diagram and the statements) in order to understand them. This process can be cognitively demanding, especially for a novice learner, thus imposing a cognitive load that is extraneous simply because of the particular format used.

Research into split-attention was initially conducted by Tarmizi and Sweller (1988) who looked into the effectiveness of worked examples on learning geometry. Previous research had demonstrated that worked examples were highly effective for learning algebra (Cooper & Sweller, 1987; Sweller & Cooper, 1985) and in other mathematical-related domains (Zhu & Simon, 1987). However, Tarmizi and Sweller found that in comparison to conventional problem-solving strategies, worked examples did not enhance performance in geometry. They argued that the requirement due to the format of the worked examples to mentally integrate the two sources of information (diagram and textual solutions) must have imposed an increase in cognitive load that prevented cognitive resources to be used for learning. In subsequent experiments, Tarmizi

Figure 1. Conventionally structured geometry worked example consisting of a diagram and its associated solution statements

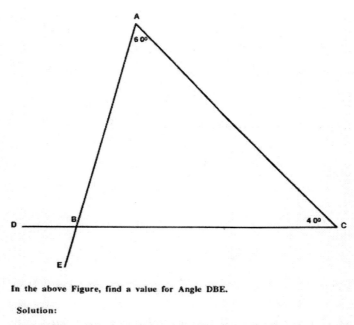

In the above Figure, find a value for Angle DBE.

Solution:

Angle ABC = 180° - Angle BAC - Angle BCA (Internal angles of a triangle
sum to 180°)
= 180° - 60° - 40°
= 80°

Angle DBE = Angle ABC (Vertically opposite angles are equal)
= 80°

and Sweller demonstrated that learners who studied integrated worked examples (see Figure 2) performed better than learners who followed a conventional problem solving strategy during acquisition.

Subsequent research sought to test the hypothesis that if multiple sources of information were integrated, the need for learners to engage in mental integration would be obviated thus freeing cognitive resources for learning. The Tarmizi and Sweller findings were replicated by Sweller, Chandler, Tierney, and Cooper (1990) in the domain of coordinate geometry, by Ward and Sweller (1990) in the domain of physics, by Chandler and Sweller (1991) using instructional materials designed for electrical apprentices, and by Sweller and Chandler (1994) and Chandler

and Sweller (1996) investigating learning in a computer environment. This line of research has been extended to language learning. In a series of experiments designed to test the split attention effect, Yeung, Jin and Sweller (1998) found that explanatory notes integrated with reading passages, by reducing cognitive load related to search for meaning, improved reading compression for both fifth grade first language pupils and inexperienced learners of English as a second language (ESL). Together, these findings in different domains generate the expectation that training conditions comparing split-attention and integrated formats will yield results demonstrating the superiority of the integrated format. This phenomenon is known as the split-attention effect.

Figure 2. Integrated worked example

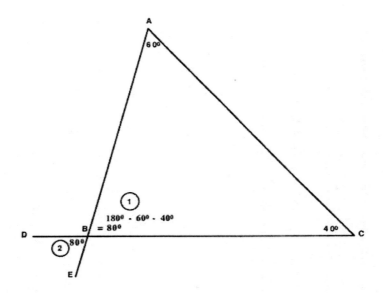

Various forms of different sources of information can lead to split-attention: text and text, text and mathematical equations, or different forms of multimedia. Any instructional material that contains more than one source of information is potentially a context for integrating split-source information. Split-attention will frequently occur in a multimedia context as there will always be at least two sources of information involved.

The split-attention studies mentioned so far deal with sources that are physically separate and have engaged learners in the visual medium only. Whether the cause of split-attention is text and a diagram, or computer and a manual, the different sources of information are physically separate in a manner that requires visual and cognitive search that imposes an extraneous load. However, physical separation is not the only form of separation that generates unnecessary cognitive load. Multiple sources of information that must be integrated before they can be understood can also be separated in time, resulting in temporal separation. The consequences of temporal rather than spatial versions of the split-attention effect

have been largely carried out by Mayer and his colleagues who have extended the effect to include sound (Mayer & Anderson, 1991, 1992; Mayer & Sims, 1994; Moreno & Mayer, 1999). This body of work demonstrates that learners who received information simultaneously, that is integrated narration and animation outperformed learners who received non-integrated instructions (narration and animation separated temporally).

In summary, the split-attention effect has been demonstrated in many studies using a wide variety of materials and participants under many conditions (see Ayres & Sweller, 2005 for a detailed review). The presence of this effect has implications for instructional design in a multimedia context where there will always be at least two sources of information.

Split-attention effect and instructional design. The split-attention effect has both theoretical and practical implications. From a theoretical perspective, the results provide evidence that minimising extraneous cognitive load benefits learning. From a practical perspective, the results provide some instructional guidelines for dealing with multiple sources of information. One guideline is that where instruction includes multiple sources of information that must be integrated in order to make sense, those sources of information should be both physically and temporally integrated in order to reduce extraneous cognitive load. This guideline should have the potential to improve multimedia instruction substantially. However, considerable care must be taken when physically integrating disparate sources of information as there are conditions under which simply integrating all text onto a diagram will have negative rather than positive effects on learning (see Ayres & Sweller, 2005).

One condition under which integrated instructions do not have positive effects on learning is when the multiple sources of information are intelligible in isolation. For example, physically integrating a diagram with statements that merely redescribe the diagram has negative, not positive effects on learning due to the redundancy effect (see next section). If all sources of information are intelligible in isolation and redundant, elimination of redundancy rather than physical integration should be undertaken. Thus, analysing the relation between multiple sources of information prior to physical integration is important.

Another condition under which integrated instructions are not beneficial is when the learning materials do not involve high element interactivity (e.g. Sweller 1994) where element interactivity refers to the number of elements that must be simultaneously processed in working memory because they interact. Low element interactivity material consists of elements that can be processed individually because they do not interact. Since the elements can be processed individually, they impose a low load on working memory and such material is described as having a low intrinsic cognitive load. In contrast, the elements of high element interactivity material, because they interact, must be processed simultaneously in working memory if the material is to be understood. Such material has a high intrinsic cognitive load. A

diagram and related text that have few interacting elements and therefore are easily understood are unlikely to impose an extraneous cognitive load due to split-attention. There is no real benefit in physically integrating the different sources of information as they can be easily learned even when presented in a split-source format.

A further factor to consider when integrating different sources of information is learner characteristics that interact with material characteristics. Material that is not intelligible in isolation and high in element interactivity for low knowledge learners may be intelligible in isolation and low in element interactivity for learners with more knowledge. For high knowledge individuals, physical integration may be harmful because of the redundancy effect (Yeung, Jin & Sweller, 1998).

The Redundancy Effect

The redundancy effect occurs when additional information presented to learners results in negative rather than positive effects on learning. It can be obtained in one of two ways. First, when identical information is presented in two or more different forms or media, such as pictures and words, or words in both auditory and written form, if one of these forms is redundant then the elimination of that form may result in enhanced learning resulting in the redundancy effect. Second, when additional information is presented in an attempt to enhance or elaborate information, if the additional explanations or elaborations are redundant then the exclusion of that additional information may enhance learning providing another example of the effect. There is overlap between these two forms in that the same information presented in a different medium may be essentially an elaboration. Nevertheless, the distinction is real in that some elaborations use the same medium while others use different media. In both instances, the effect is the same: redundant information can interfere with learning.

The redundancy effect was probably first demonstrated by Miller (1937) and subsequently by various researchers (e.g., Reder & Anderson, 1980, 1982; Solman, Singh & Kehoe, 1992). However, these researchers did not explain the effect in terms of cognitive load theory. Cognitive load theory suggests that processing redundant information with essential information increases working memory load, which interferes with the transfer of information to long term memory. Removing redundant information eliminates the requirement to process information that is not essential to learning. Consider instruction on the flow of blood in the heart, lungs, and body. Frequently, it will consist of a diagram of the heart, lungs, and body with arrows indicating the direction of the blood flowing the veins and arteries. In addition, text consisting of statements such as, "The blood entering the aorta is pumped back into the body", or "Blood from the lungs flows into the left atrium." In contrast to the geometry example given earlier, the diagram is self-contained and intelligible. It shows by means of arrows and labelling, that blood entering the aorta is pumped back into the body and that blood from the lungs flows into the left atrium. The text in this case is redundant since it merely repeats the same information albeit in a different form. In addition, when such redundant text is integrated with the diagram by being placed at appropriate locations on the diagram, the text is not only redundant, it is also unavoidable. Learners looking at the diagram are very likely to read the text as well. In contrast, if the text is below or next to the diagram rather than integrated with the diagram, it is much easier to ignore. Using the biology material mentioned earlier, Chandler and Sweller (1991) compared the performance of learners under the conditions of integrated instruction, split-attention instruction, and diagram without text instruction. The best condition was the diagram without text instruction indicating that redundant instructional material should be eliminated.

In contrast to inexperienced language learners, senior undergraduate students and high-ability ESL learners, when reading passages integrated with vocabulary explanations, found that the information about the meanings of many words was redundant but hard to ignore (Yeung, Jin & Sweller, 1998). Consequently, for those experienced learners, explanatory notes with an integrated format led to lower scores of reading comprehension in comparison with the conventional text plus a separate vocabulary list. It appears that, although explanatory notes using an integrated format within passages may be helpful for those learners with less expertise to reduce the split attention effect, this format may not be suitable for readers with high language proficiency because of the redundancy effect. Diao and Sweller (2007) further examined the redundancy effect in the context of educational multimedia designed for learners of English as a foreign language (EFL). In their study, Chinese EFL learners using simultaneous presentations of spoken and written text reported having a higher mental load and produced lower scores in both word decoding and reading comprehension than did those using materials presented in written form only. The findings support an earlier study of Japanese EFL learners (Hirai, 1999), which claimed that the listening rate was far behind the reading rate for less proficient learners. When the aim is to teach novice EFL learner to read, such poor audio-visual correspondence may cause a redundancy effect in the presentations comprising both identical auditory and written text.

Since the Chandler and Sweller (1991) findings, the redundancy effect has been demonstrated in a variety of contexts. It is not just the diagrams and redundant text that can be used to demonstrate the redundancy effect. While diagrams are frequently more intelligible than the equivalent text, there are instances where any one of diagrams, the presence of equipment, or auditory information have been found to be redundant (see Sweller 2005 for experimental evidence). In other words, what is redundant depends on what is being taught.

Redundancy effect and instructional design. As is the case with the split-attention effect, the redundancy effect has been demonstrated in many studies using a wide variety of materials and participants under many conditions. In practical terms, the redundancy effect provides a simple guideline for instructional design: eliminate any redundant material in whatever form presented to learners and any redundant activity that instruction may encourage learners to engage in. However, this guideline alone does not indicate exactly what material may or may not be redundant. This guiding principle needs to be considered in conjunction with cognitive load theory. The theory can be used to provide guidance concerning the conditions that determine redundancy and hence what material is likely to be redundant. For instance, in deciding whether text should be added to a diagram, the instructional designer needs to consider several factors. Is the diagram intelligible on its own? If so, the text may be redundant. Does the text provide essential information? If so, it is not likely to be redundant and should be retained. Is there a high level of element interactivity within the text, that is, to understand one element, one must consider many other elements at the same time? If so, as far as possible, diagrams should not be presented with the text to avoid the risk of overloading working memory. Another factor to consider is learner expertise. Whether information is high in element interactivity and whether it is intelligible on its own depends largely on the learner. Information that is intelligible for more expert learners may not make sense to novices who require additional explanatory material. In short, whether or not additional material is redundant can be determined by considering the cognitive load implications of that material in the context of learner expertise.

The Modality Effect

Studies documenting the split–attention and redundancy effects have provided evidence to indicate that the manner in which information is presented will affect how well it is learnt and remembered. Another effect that has important implications for instructional design, especially in multi-media learning is the modality effect. The modality effect occurs when information presented in a mixed mode (partly visual and partly auditory) is more effective than when the same information is presented in a single mode (either visually or in auditory form alone). For example, consider a typical geometry problem consisting of a diagram and associated statements (Figure 1). Conventionally, the diagram and the associated statements are visually presented. However, although the diagram has to be presented visually, the associated statements can be presented visually or orally. There is evidence to show that students learn better when the associated statements are narrated rather than presented visually.

According to cognitive load theory, many instructional materials and techniques may be ineffective because they ignore the limitations of human working memory and impose a heavy cognitive load. This type of load is referred to as extraneous cognitive load and has been the main concern of cognitive theorists whose focus has been on devising alternatives to those conventional instructional designs and procedures that were developed without taking into consideration the structure of human memory.

Theoretically, there are two ways in which extraneous cognitive load can be manipulated. First, instructional procedures can alleviate extraneous cognitive load by formatting instructional material in such a way that minimises cognitive activities that are unnecessary to learning so that cognitive resources can be freed to concentrate on activities essential to learning. The split attention and redundancy effects discussed above fall into this category.

The consequences of extraneous cognitive load can also be alleviated by increasing effective working memory capacity. Working memory was initially considered a single entity. More recent research has indicated that working memory may consist of multiple processors rather than a single processor (Baddeley, 1992; Schneider & Detweiler, 1987). These multiple stores, processors, channels, or streams (the terminology varies among researchers) are frequently associated with the separate processing of visual-spatial and oral material. For example, Baddeley's model of working memory (Baddeley, 1986, 1992, 1999) divides working memory into a visuo-spatial sketch pad that processes visually based information such as diagrams and pictures, and a phonological loop that processes auditory information.

There is considerable evidence to suggest that the visuo-spatial sketch pad and the phonological loop process different types of information independently, at least to some extent. If the two systems are relatively independent, the total amount of information that can be processed by working memory may be determined by the mode (auditory or visual) of presentation. It may be possible to increase effective working memory capacity by presenting information in a mixed visual and auditory mode rather than a single mode.

Low & Sweller (2005) provided a discussion of research evidence to support the notion that working memory can be subdivided into partially independent processors consisting of an auditory working memory system to deal with verbal material and a visual working memory system to deal with diagrammatical/pictorial information. Since the two processors deal with appropriate information independently to some extent, it is plausible that a mixed mode of presentation can increase the amount of information that can be processed in working memory. In a detailed review of the experimental literature, Penney (1989) provided two different lines of evidence demonstrating an appreciable increase in effective working memory capacity by employing both visual and auditory, rather than a single processor. One line of evidence shows improved ability to perform two concurrent tasks when information was presented in a partly audio, partly visual format, rather than in either single format. The other line of evidence demonstrates improved memory when information was presented to two sensory modalities rather than one. As previously indicated, the occurrence of increased working memory capacity due to the employment of a dual, rather than a single mode of presentation, is termed the modality effect. (See Low & Sweller, 2005 for a discussion of research demonstrating the modality effect).

If effective working memory can be increased by using dual-modality presentation techniques, theoretically, this procedure may be just as effective in facilitating learning as physically integrating two sources of visually presented information. The instructional version of the modality effect can be considered to stem from the spilt-attention effect. It occurs under split-attention conditions when a written source of information that must be integrated with another source of visually presented information such as a diagram, is instead presented in auditory rather than visual mode. The instructional modality effect is obtained when a dual mode presentation is superior to a visual only, split-attention presentation.

Modality effect and instructional design. The instructional predictions that flow from the experimental work on the modality effect are straightforward. Assume instruction that includes a diagram and text that are unintelligible unless they are mentally integrated. A geometry diagram and associated text provide one of many examples. From a cognitive load theory perspective, the modality effect can be explained by assuming the memory load due to a diagram (or picture) with text presentation induces a high load in the visual working memory system because both sources of information are processed in this system. In contrast, the diagram and narration version induces a lower load in visual working memory because auditory and visual information are each processed in their respective systems. Therefore, the total load induced by this version is spread between the visual and the auditory components in the working memory system. In other words, integration of the audio and visual information may not overload working memory if its capacity is effectively expanded by using a dual-mode presentation.

Using the cognitive load framework as a theoretical base, Mousavi, Low, and Sweller (1995) tested for the modality effect using split-attention geometry materials consisting of a diagram and its associated statements. It is obvious that a geometry diagram must be presented in visual form. However, the textual information could be presented in either visual (written) or auditory form. A visually presented diagram and auditorially presented text may increase effective working memory and so facilitate learning over conditions where visual working memory alone must be used to process all of the information. In a series of experiments, Mousavi et al. obtained this result. Audio-visual instructions were consistently superior to visual-visual instructions, demonstrating the modality effect. Furthermore, strong evidence was obtained indicating that the effect was due to working memory considerations, not merely due to the physical fact that auditory and visual signals can be received simultaneously while two visual signals (e.g. from a diagram and separate text) cannot be perceived simultaneously but must be attended to successively. The effect was retained even when the geometric diagram and its associated text were presented successively rather than simultaneously in both the audio-visual and visual-visual conditions. Remembering and using a previously presented statement while looking at a diagram is easier when the statement is spoken rather than written.

Tindall-Ford, Chandler, and Sweller (1997) replicated the basic, modality effect finding in another series of experiments with electrical engineering instructional materials. In addition, these experiments differentiated between materials that were low or high in element interactivity. Tindall-Ford et al. predicted that low element interactivity material with its low intrinsic cognitive load would not demonstrate the modality effect because increasing effective working memory would be irrelevant under conditions where the information that had to be processed did not strain working memory capacity. The modality effect was obtained with high but not low element interactive materials. In addition, assessment of comparative cognitive load using subjective ratings (see Paas & Van Merriënboer, 1993) indicated that cognitive load was higher under visual-visual than under audio-visual conditions, but only when the instructional material was high in element interactivity. Jeung, Chandler & Sweller (1997) found that the modality effect was enhanced when visual indicators were used to indicate to learners which parts of complex information were being referred to by the spoken text. Leahy, Chandler and Sweller (2003) demonstrated the modality principle but also found that the modality effect could only be obtained under split-attention conditions where the information of both modalities was essential for understanding. The effect was not obtained under redundancy conditions where one modality could be understood in isolation and the other was redundant in that it presented the same information in a different form.

The importance of split-attention conditions (i.e. with both sources of information essential for understanding) rather than redundancy conditions (both sources of information independently intelligible) for the modality effect can be seen from the work on the expertise reversal effect. Expertise reversal occurs when instructional techniques that are highly effective with inexperienced learners lose their effectiveness and may even have negative consequences when used with more experiences learners. Information in a dual-mode presentation may become redundant when presented to more experienced learners. Kalyuga, Chandler, and Sweller (2000) demonstrated that if experienced learners attend to redundant auditory explanations, learning might be inhibited. In a set of experiments with instructions on using industrial manufacturing machinery, inexperienced learners in a domain clearly benefited most from studying a visually presented diagram combined with simultaneously presented auditory explanations. After additional training, the relative advantage of the narration disappeared whereas the effectiveness of the diagram-only condition increased. When the same students became even more experienced after further intensive training in the subject area, the diagram-only condition was far superior to the diagram with narration condition, reversing the advantage of the dual-mode presentation previously obtained.

The modality effect is especially important in the context of multimedia learning because the instructional medium involves different presentation modes and sensory modalities. Multimedia instruction is becoming increasingly popular and findings associated with the modality effect that can be interpreted within a cognitive load framework can provide a coherent theoretical base for multimedia investigations and applications. Indeed, in a number of web-based instructional studies, Mayer and his colleagues have demonstrated that students performed better on tests of problem solving transfer when scientific explanations were presented as pictures and narration rather than as pictures and on-screen text (Mayer & Moreno, 1998; Moreno & Mayer, 1999; Moreno, Mayer, Spires, & Lester, 2001). According to the researchers, such results are consistent with dual information processing theory. When pictures and words are both presented visually, the visual processor can become overloaded but the auditory processor is unused. When words are narrated, they can be dealt with in the auditory processor, thereby leaving the visual processor to deal with the pictures only. Thus, the use of narrated animation reassigns some of the essential processing from the overloaded visual processor to the underloaded auditory processor. Unlike the earlier research that used book-based materials, the work of Mayer, Moreno and their colleagues used on-screen materials.

More recently, Brünken, Steinbacher, Plass, and Leutner (2002) replicated the modality effect in two different multimedia learning environments while using a dual-task approach to measure cognitive load. Learners' performance on a visual secondary reaction time task was taken as a direct measure of the cognitive load induced by multimedia instruction. Brünken et al. found evidence that the differences in learning outcome demonstrated by the modality effect are related to different levels of cognitive load induced by the different presentation formats of the learning material. Specifically, they found that an emphasis on visual presentation of material resulted in a decrement on a visual secondary task, indicating an overload of the visual processor. In further work, Brünken, Plass, and Leutner (2004) again reproduced the modality effect while measuring cognitive load using a dual-task methodology. In this work, the secondary task was auditory instead of visual and there was a decrement in performance on the auditory secondary task when the primary task placed an emphasis on the auditory processor.

CONCLUSION

The split-attention, redundancy, and modality effects discussed in this chapter can be explained by cognitive load theory. In turn, instructional predictions that flow from these effects provide a theoretical base leading to practical applications for e-learning and multimedia presentations. The results associated with the modality effect provide a new instructional procedure. Under split-attention conditions, rather than physically integrating disparate sources of information, learning may be facilitated by presenting a written source of information in auditory mode. While care must be taken to ensure the auditory material is essential and not redundant and that the instructional material is sufficiently complex to warrant the use of a technique that reduces cognitive load, under appropriate circumstances, the instructional gains can be large.

FUTURE RESEARCH DIRECTIONS

To this point, cognitive load theory has primarily been concerned with the borrowing and reorganising principle – how instructors should organise visual and aural information to maximise learning. Less attention has been paid to the initial creation of information where the randomness as genesis principle has primacy. Human creativity has been recognised as an important field of study for a very long time. That recognition has not been associated with a commensurate advance in knowledge. Bluntly, the field of creativity has never been integrated with our knowledge of human cognitive architecture and it can be argued, as a consequence, has been unable to generate usable information.

The cognitive architecture outlined in this chapter may have the potential to begin a rectification of this state of affairs. By accepting that the randomness as genesis principle is the source of novel information and by considering the interactions of this principle with knowledge held in long-term memory, it may be possible to generate instructional recommendations concerning human creativity. Theoretical work is commencing on this project.

REFERENCES

Ayres, P., & Sweller, J. (2005). The split-attention effect in multimedia learning. In R. E. Mayer (Ed.), *The Cambridge Handbook of Multimedia Learning* (pp. 135-146). New York: Cambridge University Press.

Baddeley, A.D. (1986). *Working memory.* Oxford, England: Oxford University Press.

Baddeley, A.D. (1992). Working memory. *Science, 255,* 556-559.

Baddeley, A.D. (1999). *Human memory.* Boston. Allyn & Bacon.

Brünken, R., Steinbacher, S., Plass, J. L., & Leutner, D. (2002). Assessment of cognitive load in multimedia learning using dual-task methodology. *Experimental Psychology , 49,* 109-119.

Brünken, R., Plass, J. L., & Leutner, D. (2004) Assessment of cognitive load in multimedia learning with dual task methodology: Auditory load and modality effects. *Instructional Science, 32,* 115-132.

Chandler, P., & Sweller, J. (1991). Cognitive load theory and the format of instruction. *Cognition and Instruction, 8,* 293-332.

Chandler, P., & Sweller, J. (1996). Cognitive load while learning to use a computer program. *Applied Cognitive Psychology, 10,* 151-170.

Chase, W. G., & Simon, H. A. (1973). Perception in chess. *Cognitive Psychology, 4,* 55-81.

Cooper, G., & Sweller, J. (1987). The effects of schema acquisition and rule automation on mathematical problem-solving transfer. *Journal of Educational Psychology, 79,* 347-362.

De Groot, A. (1965). *Thought and choice in chess.* The Hague, Netherlands: Mouton. (Original work published 1946).

Diao, Y., & Sweller, J. (2007). Redundancy in foreign language reading comprehension instruction: Concurrent written and spoken presentations. *Learning and Instruction, 17,* 78-88.

Ericsson, K. A., & Kintsch, W. (1995). Long-term working memory. *Psychological Review, 102,* 211-245.

Geary, D. (2007). Educating the evolved mind: Conceptual foundations for an evolutionary educational psychology. In J. S. Carlson & J. R. Levin (Eds.), *Psychological perspectives on contemporary educational issues* (pp. 1-99). Greenwich, CT: Information Age Publishing.

Hirai, A (1999). The relationship between listening and reading rates of Japanese EFL learners, *Modern Language Journal, 83,* 367–384.

Jeung, H., Chandler, P., & Sweller, J. (1997). The role of visual indicators in dual sensory mode instruction, *Educational Psychology, 17,* 329-343.

Kalyuga, S., Chandler, P., & Sweller, J. (2000). Incorporating learner experience into the design of multimedia instruction. *Journal of Educational Psychology, 92,* 126-136.

Leahy, W., Chandler, P., & Sweller, J. (2003). When auditory presentations should and should not be a component of multimedia instruction. *Applied Cognitive Psychology, 17,* 401-418.

Low, R., & Sweller, J. (2005). The modality principle in multimedia learning. In R. E. Mayer (Ed.), *The Cambridge Handbook of Multimedia Learning* (pp. 147-158). New York: Cambridge University Press.

Mayer, R. E., & Anderson, R. (1991). Animations need narrations: An experimental test of a dual-coding hypothesis. *Journal of Educational Psychology, 83,* 484-490.

Mayer, R. E., & Anderson, R. (1992). The instructive animation: Helping students build connections between words and pictures in multimedia learning. *Journal of Educational Psychology, 84,* 444-452.

Mayer, R. E., & Moreno, R. (1998). A split-attention effect in multi-media learning: Evidence for dual processing systems in working memory. *Journal of Educational Psychology, 90,* 312-320.

Mayer, R. E., & Sims, V. K. (1994). For whom is a picture worth a thousand words? Extensions of a dual-coding theory of multimedia learning. *Journal of Educational Psychology, 86,* 389-401.

Miller, G. A. (1956). The magical number seven, plus or minus two: Some limits on our capacity for processing information. *Psychological Review, 63,* 81-97.

Miller, W. (1937). The picture clutch in reading. *Elementary English Review, 14,* 263-264.

Moreno, R., & Mayer, R. E. (1999). Cognitive principles of multimedia learning: The role of modality and contiguity. *Journal of Educational psychology, 91,* 358-368.

Moreno, R., Mayer, R. E., Spires, H.A., & Lester, J.C. (2001). The case for social agency in computer-based multimedia learning: Do students learn more deeply when they interact with animated pedagogical agents? *Cognition and Instruction, 19,* 177-214.

Mousavi, S., Low, R., & Sweller, J. (1995). Reducing cognitive load by mixing auditory and visual presentation modes. *Journal of Educational Psychology, 87,* 319-334.

Paas, F., & Van Merrienboer, J. (1993). The efficiency of instructional conditions: An approach to combine mental-effort and performance measures. *Human Factors, 35,* 737-743.

Penney, C. G. (1989). Modality effects and the structure of short-term verbal memory. *Memory & Cognition, 17,* 398-422.

Peterson, L., & Peterson, M. J. (1959). Short-term retention of individual verbal items. *Journal of Experimental Psychology, 58,* 193-198.

Reder, L., & Anderson, J. R. (1980). A comparison of texts and their summaries: Memorial consequences. *Journal of Verbal Learning and Verbal Behaviour, 19,* 121-134.

Reder, L., & Anderson, J. R. (1982). Effects of spacing and embellishment on memory for main points of a text. *Memory and Cognition, 10,* 97-102.

Schneider, W., & Detweiler, M. (1987). A connectionist/control architecture for working memory. In G.H. Bower (Ed.), *The psychology of learning and motivation.* Vol. 21 (pp53-119). New York: Academic Press.

Solman, R., Singh, N., & Kehoe, E. J. (1992). Pictures block the learning of sight words. *Educational Psychology, 12,* 143-153.

Sweller, J. (1994). Cognitive load theory, learning difficulty, and instructional design. *Learning and Instruction, 4,* 295-312.

Sweller, J. (2003). Evolution of human cognitive architecture. In B. Ross (Ed.), *The psychology of learning and motivation* (Vol. 43, pp. 215-266). San Diego: Academic Press.

Sweller, J. (2004). Instructional design consequences of an analogy between evolution by natural selection and human cognitive architecture. *Instructional Science, 32,* 9-31.

Sweller, J. (2005). The redundancy principle. In R. E. Mayer (Ed.), *Cambridge handbook of multimedia learning* (pp. 159-167). New York: Cambridge University Press.

Sweller, J., & Sweller, S. (2006). Natural information processing systems. *Evolutionary Psychology, 4,* 434-458.

Sweller, J., & Chandler, P. (1994). Why some material is difficult to learn. *Cognition and Instruction, 12,* 185-233.

Sweller, J., Chandler, P., Tierney, P., & Cooper, M. (1990). Cognitive load as a factor in the structuring of technical material. *Journal of Experimental Psychology: General, 119,* 176-192.

Sweller, J., & Cooper, G. (1985). The use of worked examples as a substitute for problem solving in learning algebra. *Cognition and Instruction, 2,* 59-89.

Tarmizi, R., & Sweller, J. (1988). Guidance during mathematical problem solving. *Journal of Educational Psychology, 80,* 424-436.

Tindall-Ford, S., Chandler, P., & Sweller, J. (1997). When two sensory modes are better than one. *Journal of Experimental Psychology: Applied, 3,* 257-287.

Ward, M., & Sweller, J. (1990). Structuring effective worked examples. *Cognition and Instruction, 7,* 1-39.

Yeung, A. S., Jin, P., & Sweller, J. (1998). Cognitive load and learner expertise: Split-attention and redundancy effects in reading with explanatory notes. *Contemporary Educational Psychology, 23,* 1-21.

Zhu, X., & Simon, H. (1987). Learning mathematics from examples and by doing. *Cognition and Instruction, 4,* 137-166.

ADDITIONAL READING

Chase, W. G., & Simon, H.A. (1973). Perception in chess. *Cognitive Psychology, 4,* 55-81.

De Groot, A. (1965). *Thought and choice in chess.* The Hague, Netherlands, Mouton. (Original work published 1946).

Ericsson, K. A., & Kintsch, W. (1995). Long-term working memory. *Psychological Review, 102,* 211-245.

Geary, D. (2007). Educating the evolved mind: Conceptual foundations for an evolutionary educational psychology. In J. S. Carlson & J. R. Levin (Eds.), *Psychological perspectives on contemporary educational issues* (pp. 1-99). Greenwich, CT, Information Age Publishing.

Miller, G. A. (1956). "The magical number seven, plus or minus two: Some limits on our capacity for processing information." *Psychological Review, 63,* 81-97.

Penney, C. G. (1989). "Modality effects and the structure of short-term verbal memory." *Memory & Cognition, 17,* 398-422.

Peterson, L., & Peterson, M. J. (1959). "Short-term retention of individual verbal items." *Journal of Experimental Psychology, 58,* 193-198.

Sweller, J. (1994). Cognitive load theory, learning difficulty, and instructional design. *Learning and Instruction, 4,* 295-312.

Sweller, J. (2004). Instructional design consequences of an analogy between evolution by natural selection and human cognitive architecture. *Instructional Science, 32,* 9-31.

Sweller, J. (2005). The redundancy principle. In R. E. Mayer (Ed.), *Cambridge handbook of multimedia learning* (pp. 159-167). New York, Cambridge University Press.

Sweller, J., & Sweller, S. (2006). Natural information processing systems. *Evolutionary Psychology, 4,* 434-458.

Chapter II
Multimedia Learning and Working Memory Capacity

Peter E. Doolittle
Virginia Tech, USA

Krista P. Terry
Radford University, USA

Gina J. Mariano
Virginia Tech, USA

ABSTRACT

This chapter addresses the role that working memory capacity (WMC) plays in learning in multimedia environments. WMC represents the ability to control attention, that is, to be able to remain focused on the task at hand while simultaneously retrieving relevant information from long-term memory, all in the presence of distraction. The chapter focuses on how individual differences in attentional control affect cognitive performance, in general, and cognitive performance in multimedia environments, in particular. A review of the relevant literature demonstrates that, in general, students with high WMC outperform students with low WMC on measures of cognitive performance. However, there has been very little research addressing the role of WMC in learning in multimedia environments. To address this need, the authors conducted a study that examined the effects of WMC on learning in a multimedia environment. Results of this study indicated students with high WMC recalled and transferred significantly more information than students with low WMC. Ultimately, this chapter provides evidence that individual differences in working memory capacity should be taken into account when creating and implementing multimedia instructional environments.

INTRODUCTION

Attention has been demonstrated to be an essential component of learning in multimedia instructional environments. Specifically, when a student's attention is split between multiple sources of information, such as when a student's visual attention is split between an animation-based tutorial depicting the cause of lighting and a simultaneously presented text-based description of the lightning tutorial (Mayer & Moreno, 1998), learning and performance suffer. In addition, when a student's attention is seduced away from important content toward interesting, but irrelevant information, such as when a student views an animation-based tutorial with concurrent narration describing the cause of lighting that includes interesting, but irrelevant background sounds and music (Moreno & Mayer, 2000), learning and performance suffer. In contrast to these negative effects of attentional interference, as a student's attention is guided toward relevant ideas or concepts through the inclusion of signals or cues, such as when a student views an animation-based tutorial describing airplane flight with concurrent narration that emphasizes important ideas by using a slower and deeper intonation of voice (Mautone & Mayer, 2001), learning and performance improve. Also, when a student's attention is guided toward a specific goal for reading and viewing an illustrated, text-based tutorial of the cause of lighting, such as when students are told to focus on learning the steps involved in creating a stroke of lightning prior to engaging the tutorial (Harp & Mayer, 1998), learning and performance improve.

These differential effects on learning and performance in multimedia instructional environments, based on treatment variations in attention, raise the question as to whether individual differences in attention may influence individuals' learning and performance in multimedia instructional environments. There is an extensive body of literature indicating that an individual's ability to control attention affects performance on complex mental tasks (Daneman & Carpenter, 1980; Oberauer, Süß, Schulze, Wilhelm, & Wittmann, 2000; Unsworth & Engle, 2007). In this literature, attentional control is a component of working memory capacity (WMC; Kane, Bleckley, Conway, & Engle, 2001; Kane & Engle, 2003), that is, the ability to maintain information in working memory and to effectively retrieve task relevant information from long-term memory (Feldman Barrett, Tugade, & Engle, 2004). The purpose of this chapter is to explore the relationship between attentional control and learning in a multimedia environment.

BACKGROUND

The successful completion of complex cognitive tasks requires that individuals are able to dynamically retrieve, maintain, manipulate, and update information in memory during task performance (Baddeley & Hitch, 1974). This dynamic memory model was investigated by Daneman and Carpenter (1980) who established a positive correlation between complex cognitive task completion and a measure of working memory capacity (WMC); specifically, through the positive correlation of global and local measures of reading comprehension with a working-memory span task involving both the storage and processing of information. Daneman and Carpenter's working-memory span task (i.e., reading span) required participants to read a series of sentences (processing), while maintaining a list of the last word from each sentence in memory (storage). This storage + processing working-memory span task differed from previous storage-only working-memory span tasks (e.g., digit span, word span) in that a secondary processing task, reading, provided additional working-memory load complexity. It is believed that this storage + processing working-memory span task provides a more complex memory task, and a better estimate of the cognition necessary to complete complex cognitive tasks, than the simpler storage-only span tasks (Daneman & Carpenter, 1980; Unsworth & Engle, 2007).

This genre of complex memory span task, storage + processing, has been used as a measure of working memory capacity (WMC) for the past 25 years to investigate both the constitution of WMC and the effects of individual differences in WMC on complex cognitive task performance. Investigations into the constitution of WMC have determined that high WMC is a good predictor of general fluid intelligence (Conway, Cowan, Bunting, Therriault, & Minkoff, 2002; Kane, Hambrick, Tuhoski, Wilhelm, Payne, & Engle, 2004), long-term memory activation (Cantor & Engle, 1993), attentional control (Kane et al., 2001; Rosen & Engle, 1997), resistance to proactive interference (Kane & Engle, 2000; Lustig, May, & Hasher, 2001), primary memory maintenance and secondary memory search (Unsworth & Engle, 2007), and resistance to goal neglect (Kane & Engle, 2003; Roberts, Hager, & Heron, 1994). This constitutional research has provided a general picture of WMC as based on attentional control; specifically, the ability to actively maintain information in working-memory during task completion and the ability to effectively and efficiently search long-term memory for task relevant information, especially, although not exclusively, under conditions of interference or distraction (see Feldman Barrett et al., 2004; Unsworth & Engle, 2007).

This focus on the attentional control aspect of WMC has led to a plethora of individual differences research examining the effects of individual differences in WMC – high WMC participants versus low WMC participants – on complex cognitive task performance. This research has resulted in individual difference effects, favoring participants with high WMC, for reading comprehension (Daneman & Carpenter, 1980), language comprehension (Just & Carpenter, 1992), vocabulary learning (Daneman & Green, 1986), reasoning (Conway et al., 2002; Kyllonen

& Christal, 1990; cf. Buehner, Krumm, & Pick, 2005), computer language learning (Shute, 1991), lecture note taking (Kiewra & Benton, 1988), Scholastic Aptitude Test performance (Turner & Engle, 1989), mnemonic strategy effectiveness (Gaultney, Kipp, & Kirk, 2005), and story telling (Pratt, Boyes, Robins, & Manchester, 1989). This research has demonstrated a strong, positive relationship between variations in WMC and variations in complex cognitive task performance.

Working Memory Capacity: Domain General vs Domain Specific

The constitutional and individual difference research in WMC has revealed a stable construct sensitive to individual variation. A question still under consideration is whether WMC represents a domain specific or domain general construct: Is WMC heavily mediated by task specificity, or is WMC based on general underlying processes? Support for a domain-specific WMC perspective arises from research comparing verbal and spatial measures of WMC to measures of verbal and spatial ability. Correlational studies have yielded significant, positive relationships between measures of verbal WMC and verbal ability, and measures of spatial WMC and spatial ability; however, little or no correlations have been found between verbal WMC and spatial ability, or spatial WMC and verbal ability (Daneman & Tardif, 1987; Morrell & Park, 1993; Shah & Miyake, 1996). In addition, in exploratory and confirmatory factor analysis studies, verbal WMC and verbal ability measures, and spatial WMC and spatial ability measures have yielded separate and independent factors (Friedman & Miyake, 2000; Handley, Capon, Copp, & Harper, 2002; Kane et al., 2004; Shah & Miyake, 1996). This support for a domain-specific view of WMC, however, has not gone unchallenged.

Kane et al. (2004) used a latent-variable approach to verbal and spatial WMC and examined multiple measures of verbal WMC, verbal short-term memory, verbal reasoning, spatial WMC, spatial short-term memory, and spatial reasoning. Kane et al. concluded that the extensive shared variance (70-85%) between verbal and spatial WMC tasks indicated that WMC was primarily domain general. Kane et al. also found, however, a small domain-specific factor. These results confirm other similar latent-variable examinations of WMC; that is, that verbal and spatial WMC represent a single underlying factor (Ackerman, Beier, & Boyle 2002; Oberauer et al., 2000). Additional support for a domain-general WMC perspective comes from Kane and Engle (2003) who established that general controlled-attention is responsible for the maintenance of information (e.g., goals, representations) and the avoidance of distraction (e.g., irrelevant stimuli, prepotent responses) in complex cognitive tasks. Further, research involving a wide array of tasks that demand attention-control for success (e.g., dichotic-listening task, antisaccade task, Stroop task) have demonstrated a general performance advantage for high WMC participants (Conway et al., 2001; Kane & Engle, 2003; Unsworth, Schrock, & Engle, 2004; cf. Kane, Poole, Tuholski, & Engle, 2006).

The research on the domain specificity and generality of WMC has not yet reached consensus, and as indicated by Kane et al. (2004), it may not. Kane et al., having completed a series of confirmatory factor analyses involving a one-factor (i.e., unitary WMC) domain-general model and a two-factor (i.e., verbal and spatial WMC) domain-specific model, and excluding error correlations, concluded that WMC appears to be constructed of both domain-general processes (e.g., attentional control) and domain-specific processes (e.g., storage, coding, rehearsal); although Kane et al. emphasize that WMC is primarily domain general. This support for a domain-general WMC effect helps to explain the underlying mechanism in the broad array of individual differences WMC effects.

Working Memory Capacity in Multimedia Instructional Environments

Working memory capacity is a measure of an individual's ability to control attention in order to maintain representations in working memory and to search for and retrieve relevant information from long-term memory. WMC effects have been most consistent in tasks that require information maintenance, require long-term memory search, or involve interfering or distracting stimuli (Feldman Barrett, Tugade, & Engle, 2004; Unsworth & Engle, 2007). The previously reviewed WMC tasks (e.g., reading span, operation span, counting span) and the complex cognition tasks (e.g., antisaccade, dichotic listening, reading), however, are all single-media tasks, involving only visual *or* auditory information. Conversely, multimedia tasks are generally comprised of tasks with both a visual component (e.g., pictures, animation) and a verbal component (e.g., text, narration). Further, the multimedia learning literature, as with WMC, is based upon the combination of attentional selection of stimuli, retrieval of relevant information from long-term memory, and active processing and integration of representations (see Mayer, 2001, 2005; Mayer & Anderson, 1991; Moreno & Mayer, 1999).

While it is evident that WMC and learning in multimedia instructional environments require similar processing (i.e., attention, retrieval, integration), it is unknown if individual difference effects of WMC on learning in multimedia instructional environments exist. Sanchez and Wiley (2006) examined individual difference effects of WMC on the multimedia coherence principle; that is, participants learn more from multimedia instructional environments that are devoid of seductive details – extraneous, non-relevant, words, pictures, sounds or music (Harp & Mayer, 1998; Mayer & Jackson, 2005; Moreno & Mayer, 2000). Sanchez and Wiley (2006) provided high and low WMC participants with an expository text addressing the causes of ice ages in a non-illustrated, relevantly illustrated, or irrelevantly illustrated format. On measures of recall (i.e., "what causes ice ages?") there was no main effect for WMC, high WMC participants did not recall more causes of ice ages than low WMC, and no main effect for illustration format, participants in the relevant illustration performed no better or worse than participants in the no illustrations or irrelevant illustrations groups. There was, however, an interaction effect such that low WMC participants performed more poorly in the irrelevantly illustrated condition (i.e., seductive details) than high WMC participants. Also within Sanchez and Wiley (2006), on measures of inference verification (participants were provided with 25 inferential statements and asked to identify each statement as true or false) there was a main effect for WMC, high WMC participants responded more accurately to the inference statements than low WMC participants, but no main effect for illustration format, participants in the relevant illustration performed no better or worse than participants in the no illustrations or irrelevant illustrations groups. There was, however, an interaction effect such that low WMC participants performed more poorly in the irrelevantly illustrated condition (i.e., seductive details) than high WMC participants.

The results of Sanchez and Wiley (2006) indicate only partial support for a general individual differences WMC effect; that is, high WMC participants provided superior performance on the inference verification task, but not on the recall task. The results of Sanchez and Wiley also only provide partial support for the coherence effect; that is, seductive details negatively affected low WMC students, but positively affect high WMC students.

Given the partial support for an individual differences WMC effect within Sanchez and Wiley (2006), an experiment was designed to assess the individual differences WMC effect for learning in multimedia instructional environments. Specifi-cally, high and low WMC participants engaged in a tutorial on how a bicycle pump works in one of three conditions, visual animation with auditory narration (AN), visual animation with visual screen-based text (AT), or visual animation with both auditory narration and visual screen-based text (ANT). Previous research has determined that participants in the AN condition tend to outperform participants in the AT condition, the modality effect (Ginns, 2005; Mayer & Moreno, 1998), and participants in the AN condition tend to outperform the participants in the ANT condition, the redundancy principle (Kalyuga, Chandler, & Sweller, 1999; Mayer, Heiser, & Lonn, 2001). This experiment was designed to assess whether a general individual differences effect of WMC for learning in a multimedia instructional environment exists and to verify the previously supported modality and redundancy principles of multimedia learning.

MULTIMEDIA LEARNING AND WORKING MEMORY CAPACITY: A STUDY

The purposes of this experiment were to test the general individual differences WMC hypothesis, that high WMC participants would outperform low WMC participants on measures of recall and transfer after engaging in a multimedia tutorial, and validate the modality and redundancy principles. The modality principle hypothesizes that participants who engage in an animation + narration (AN) multimedia tutorial will perform better on measures of recall and transfer than participants who engage in an animation + on-screen text (AT) multimedia tutorial due to the two visual sources of information, animation and on-screen text, overloading the visual processing channel (Mayer & Moreno, 1998; Moreno & Mayer, 1999). The redundancy principle hypothesizes that participants who engage in an animation + narration (AN) multimedia tutorial will perform better on measures of recall and transfer than participants who engage in an animation + narration + on-screen text (AT) multimedia tutorial due to two visual sources of information, animation and on-screen text, overloading the visual processing channel (Kalyuga et al, 1999; Mayer et al., 2001).

Participants and Materials

To investigate the effects of working memory capacity (WMC) on multimedia learning, 113 undergraduate students (80 men and 33 women), with a mean age of 20.1 years, were taken from a larger pool of 213 participants who were administered the OSPAN working memory span test. Of these 213 participants, only those participants that scored in the upper (n = 57) or lower quartiles (n = 56) were included as participants. The experimental design was a 2 X 3 factorial design with working memory capacity (high WMC, low WMC) and multimedia group (animation + narration [AN], animation + on-screen text [AT], animation + narration + on-screen text [ANT]) as between-subject variables. Participants were randomly assigned to the AN (n = 40), AT (n = 30), or ANT (n = 43) group.

Working Memory Capacity OSPAN Task

WMC was measured using the OSPAN operation-span task (La Point & Engle, 1990; Turner & Engle, 1989). The OSPAN requires participants to solve a series of basic math problems while attempting to remember a series of unrelated words. Specifically, participants were shown a series of math-word sentences in the form of "IS (3 + 7) - 4 = 5 ? Bird" or "IS (8 − 4) / 2 = 2 ? Grass". Participants were required to read the math statement aloud and respond aloud "yes" or "no" as to whether the math statement was true or false, respectively. After reading and solving the math statement, and without pausing, participants

then read the unrelated word aloud. For example, given the second example above, the participant would say, "Is eight minus four divided by two equal to two? Yes. Grass." Participants viewed and read aloud one math-word sentence at a time on a computer screen and clicked a "Continue" button to advance to the next math-word sentence. Participants viewed and responded to a set of 2 to 6 math-word sentences before they were asked to recall the unrelated words from that set, in order, and type the words into a text box on the computer screen. The OSPAN score was determined by counting the number of words recalled for those sets in which the participant recalled all words, in order, correctly; thus, if a participant recalled *all* four words from a four math-word sentence set, in proper order, the participant would receive four points. Participants viewed 15 sets of math-word sentences, 3 sets each that contained 2 to 6 math-word sentences, for a total of 60 math-word sentences. The order of the math-word sets and the math-word sentences within each set were randomized for each participant. Potential scores ranged from 0 to 60. Participants were assigned to the high WMC group if they scored in the upper quartile and to the low WMC group if they scored in the lower quartile of the original 213 participants' scores. The mean OPSAN scores for the high WMC and low WMC groups were 29.35 (SD = 5.69) and 6.07 (SD = 2.94), respectively.

Recall and Transfer Tests

The recall test included answering the following question on the computer, "Please provide an explanation of how a bicycle tire pump works." The recall question was provided on its own screen with a response box located directly below it. The transfer test included answering four questions taken from Mayer and Anderson (1991) and included, "What could be done to make a pump more reliable - that is, to make sure it would not fail?"; "What could be done to make a pump more effective - that is, to make it move more air more rapidly?"; "Suppose you push down and pull up the handle of a pump several times but no air comes out. What could have gone wrong?"; and "Why does air enter a pump? Why does air exit from a pump?" The four transfer questions were all provided on the same computer screen such that each question was followed by its own response box.

"How Does a Bicycle Tire Pump Work?" Tutorial

The multimedia tutorials consisted of Flash® animations based on Mayer and Anderson's (1992) animation depicting the mechanics and movement of a bicycle tire pump. This depiction included a line drawing of a pump casing, a piston, an inlet valve and an outlet valve. The animation visualizes the upstroke as the piston rising, the outlet valve closing, the inlet value opening, and air entering the casing. The downstroke is visualized as the piston falling, the inlet valve closing, the outlet valve opening, and air exiting the casing (see Figure 1). The pump tutorials were presented on iMac computers with 15-inch screens and Altec Lansing headphones. Three versions of this content were constructed based on the same pump animation and verbal content such that the AN version contained the pump animation and an auditory narration of the verbal content, the AT version contained the same pump animation with on-screen text underneath the animation instead of auditory narration, and the ANT version contained the same animation, narration and on-screen text used in the AN and AT versions. Each version lasted 30 seconds.

Procedure

All data collection and media presentations were completed on wireless laptop computers. Participants first completed the OSPAN task. After completing the OSPAN task, participants then completed the basic mechanics pre-assess-

ment. Next, following a brief introduction, the participants pressed the Enter key and viewed the appropriate version of the tire pump content given their multimedia group assignment (i.e., AN, AT, or ANT). Following the viewing of the tire pump tutorial, and after pressing the Enter key, participants were given 5 minutes to complete the recall test. Finally, after the recall test was completed, and after pressing the Enter key, participants were given 15 minutes to complete the transfer test. Each data collection session lasted 45 minutes.

Recall Test

Two trained raters evaluated each participant's recall response (inter-rater reliability, $r = .96$) for the presence of 10 idea units. One point was given to participants for the inclusion of each of the following idea units: "(a) handle is pulled up, (b) piston moves up, (c) inlet valve opens, (d) outlet valve closes, (e) air enters the cylinder, (f) handle is pushed down, (g) piston moves down, (h) inlet valve closes, (i) outlet valve opens, [and] (j) air moves out through the hose" (Mayer & Anderson, 1991, p. 488).

Transfer Test

Two trained raters evaluated each participant's transfer responses (inter-rater reliability, $r = .90$) by computing the total number of valid answers, based on Mayer and Anderson (1991), across the four transfer questions. Acceptable answers to the first transfer question, "What could be done to make a pump more reliable - that is, to make sure it would not fail?" included, use airtight valve seals and have a back up system; acceptable answers to the second transfer question, "What could be done to make a pump more effective - that is, to make it move more air more rapidly?" included increase the capacity of the casing and raise the piston more quickly; acceptable answers to the third transfer question, "Suppose you push

Figure 1. Sample animation screens and accompanying verbal content from the pump tutorial (American Psychological Association; adapted with permission)

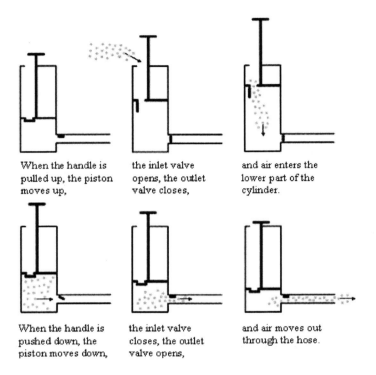

down and pull up the handle of a pump several times but no air comes out. What could have gone wrong?" included a leak in the pump and a valve stuck in the open position; and finally, acceptable answers to the forth transfer question, "Why does air enter a pump? Why does air exit from a pump?", included a vacuum or a low pressure differential and a compression or a high pressure differential.

Results

The experiment was designed to (a) evaluate the general individual differences WMC hypothesis that students with high WMC will recall and transfer more from multimedia tutorials than students with low WMC, and (b) confirm previous results related to the modality effect and redundancy effect. These two questions were analyzed using two 2 (high WMC, low WMC) X 3 (AN, AT, ANT) factorial designs based on the recall and transfer data.

Individual Differences WMC Effect

According to a general individual differences WMC approach, students with high WMC should recall and transfer more information from the multimedia tutorials than low WMC students as a result of high WMC students exhibiting better attentional control and resistance to distraction. This general individual differences WMC effect was confirmed for recall as high WMC students recalled more idea units than low WMC students (see Table 1), resulting in a significant main effect for WMC, $F(1,107) = 6.24$, $MSe = 3.60$, Cohen's $d = 0.46$, $p = .01$. Similarly, for transfer, high WMC students generated more valid transfer responses than low WMC students, resulting in a significant main effect for WMC, $F(1,107) = 5.12$, MSe = 2.02, Cohen's $d = .40$, p = .02. These results are consistent with the predications of the general individual differences WMC hypothesis; high WMC students outperformed low WMC students on recall and transfer after engaging in a multimedia tutorial.

Modality and Redundancy Effects

According to the cognitive theory of multimedia learning (see Mayer, 2001), students should recall and transfer more from multimedia tutorials comprised of animation and narration (AN) than animation and on-screen text (AT), the modality principle, and students should recall and transfer more from multimedia tutorials comprised of animation and narration (AN) than animation, narration, and on-screen text (ANT), the redundancy principle. The ANOVA for recall data resulted in no significant main effect for multimedia group (see Table 2), $F(2,107) = 2.54$, MSe = 3.60, Cohen's $d = 0.20$, p = .08. The ANOVA for transfer data also resulted in no significant main effect for multimedia group, $F(2,107) = 1.94$, MSe = 2.02, Cohen's $d = 0.06$, p = .14. These results are inconsistent with prior research (Kalyuga, Chandler, & Sweller, 1999; Mayer & Moreno, 1998; Moreno & Mayer, 1999) and do not provide support for either the modality effect or the redundancy effect.

Differential Multimedia Group Effects on Individual Differences in WMC

There were no interactions between WMC and the multimedia groups (i.e., AN, AT, ANT) for recall, $F(2,107) = 0.47$, MSe = 3.60, Cohen's $d = 0.22$, p = .62, or transfer, $F(2,107) = 0.25$, MSe = 2.02, Cohen's $d = 0.18$, p = .77. Therefore, there was no indication that multimedia group affected high and low WMC students differently.

Table 1. *Means and standard deviations for recall and transfer scores for high and low working memory capacity students in experiment 1*

	Recall		Transfer	
	M	SD	M	SD
Low WMC	6.15	2.18	3.36	1.44
High WMC	7.05*	1.61	3.97*	1.40

Note. Max recall score = 10. Max transfer score = 8.
* p < .05

Table 2. *Means and standard deviations for recall and transfer scores for students in differing multimedia groups in experiment 1*

	Recall		Transfer	
	M	SD	M	SD
AN	6.64	2.11	3.53	1.31
AT	7.08	1.87	4.05	1.52
ANT	6.08	2.10	3.41	1.41

Note. Max recall score = 10. Max transfer score = 8.
* p < .05

Discussion

General Individual Differences WMC Effect in Multimedia Learning

Theoretically, the results of the experiment demonstrate that, in general, the ability to control attention and avoid distraction, as measured by WMC, positively affects cognitive performance in a multimedia environment. Specifically, students with high WMC outperformed students with low WMC after engaging in a multimedia tutorial. These results are consistent with predictions from both the domain-general and individual differences perspectives of WMC; that is, that variances in WMC are due to a general underlying attentional mechanism, and that individual differences in WMC systematically affect cognitive performance.

The present study extends the WMC literature by addressing WMC in a multimedia instructional environment. The previous WMC research focused on complex cognitive tasks that involved only single-media instructional environments, such as reading and vocabulary learning (Daneman & Carpenter, 1980, 1983; Daneman & Green, 1986), aural comprehension (Just & Carpenter, 1992), standardized test performance (Turner & Engle, 1989), story telling (Pratt et al., 1989), and the dichotomous listening task (Conway, Cowan, & Bunting, 2001), antisaccade task (Unsworth et al., 2004), associative list task (Watson, Bunting, Poole, & Conway, 2005), baseball task (Hambrick & Oswald, 2005) and Stroop task (Kane & Engle, 2003). In each of these instructional environments, perceptual attention is focused on only a single modality, visual *or* auditory, while in a multimedia instructional environment attention must be focused on two modalities, visual *and* auditory.

The present study also extends the multimedia learning literature by identifying a specific individual difference variable of interest – working memory capacity. Previous research has identified

spatial ability (Moreno & Mayer, 1999) and prior knowledge (Cooper, Tindall-Ford, Chandler, & Sweller, 2001; Mayer & Sims, 1994; Ollerenshaw, Aidman, & Kidd, 1997) as individual difference variables that affect multimedia learning performance, to which WMC is now added. This general finding that high and low WMC systematically affects individuals differently leads to the question of how WMC differences may interact with specific multimedia learning principles. In addition, it is important that future research address which aspects of WMC (e.g., attention control, distraction avoidance, goal neglect, representation activation, knowledge search, knowledge updating) affect learning in multimedia instructional environments, and how.

The practical application of the general individual differences WMC effect relates to the generality of the benefits of learning in multimedia instructional environments. While there is significant research indicating the benefits of learning in multimedia instructional environments (see Mayer, 2005), there is emerging evidence that multimedia instructional environments may benefit some learners (e.g., high spatial ability, high prior knowledge, high WMC) more than others.

Modality and Redundancy Multimedia Learning Effects

The current experiment failed to validate previous findings regarding the modality and redundancy effects. That is there was no appreciable decrement in performance due to switching from audio narration to on-screen text, nor from adding on-screen text to audio narration. This lack of modality and redundancy effects are suprising given Ginns' (2005) meta-analysis of the modality effect in which he examined 43 relevant studies, yielding an overall weighted mean effect size (Cohen's d) of 0.72. That said, Tabbers, Marten, and van Merriënboer (2004) also failed to validate the modality effect using an explanatory multimedia presentation, providing instruction regarding the

4C/ID instructional design model. The results of the current study and that of Tabbers et al. would seem to call into question the generalizability of the modality and redundancy effects.

Differential Effects of WMC on Multimedia Learning Principles

The current study clearly finds no interactions between WMC and the modality and redundancy principles; that is, high and low WMC student were not differentially affected by the multimedia principles. These findings are in contrast to Sanchez and Wiley (2006) who found that low WMC students were more affected by seductive details (coherence effect) than high WMC. This lack of differential effect supports the conclusion that there exists a "general" individual differences WMC effect and that the generalizability of the multimedia learning principles is in question. Specifically, the current results indicate that high WMC positively affected all groups of students in similar and general ways, and that the lack of findings related to the multimedia principles held for both the treatment groups as a whole and the high and low WMC subgroups.

Overall, the current study provides support for a general individual difference WMC effect related to learning in multimedia instructional environments. This effect adds to the list of identified multimedia learning individual difference variables: prior knowledge, spatial ability, and working memory capacity. The same studies, however, found no support for the specific modality, redundancy, coherence and signaling effects tested, and no support for differential effects of WMC on multimedia learning principles.

CONCLUSION

Attention plays a significant role in multimedia learning. Recent theories of multimedia learning (see Mayer, 2001; Schnotz & Bannert, 2003)

emphasize the importance of selecting and organizing visual/auditory and verbal/non-verbal stimuli within multimedia environments. In each of these theoretical approaches, these processes of selecting and organizing are guided by the use of attentional resources. The current chapter has focused on how individual differences in attentional control affect cognitive performance, in general, and cognitive performance in multimedia environments, in particular. Attentional control, measured by working memory capacity, has been demonstrated to affect cognitive performance across a wide array of tasks, including, reading, language, and vocabulary comprehension, as well as performance on standardized tests (see Daneman & Carpenter, 1980; Just & Carpenter, 1992; Turner & Engle, 1989). Sanchez and Wiley (2006), however, examined attentional control in a multimedia instructional environment involving illustrated web pages where the illustrations were either relevant or irrelevant to the content of the web pages. Sanchez and Wiley found no general WMC effect – high WMC students did not perform significantly better than low WMC students on measures of learning – but did find that students with low WMC performed less well, cognitively, than students with high WMC when the web pages contained irrelevant graphics. These results can be explained as the low WMC students having difficulty focusing (i.e., controlling) their attention on the task goal and the elements of the multimedia environment designed to foster the successful completion of that task goal.

The Sanchez and Wiley (2006) study, however, involved only uni-modal multimedia, words and static pictures both available visually. The study reported in this chapter involved bi-modal multimedia that included visual animation and auditory narration. The results of the present study provided initial support for a general WMC effect, that is, students with high WMC recalled and transferred more than students with low WMC. This finding can be explained by high WMC students having better attentional control. This advantage in attentional control leads to better maintenance of the task goal in working memory, as well as better retrieval and integration of relevant knowledge to and from long-term memory (see Kane & Engle, 2003; Rosen & Engle, 1997).

The implications of these finding for multimedia developers and instructional designers will depend in part on the next round of research involving WMC and multimedia instruction. That is, now that it is known that low WMC individuals perform poorly in multimedia instructional environments that require elevated levels of attentional control, the arises: How can multimedia instructional environments be created that facilitate low WMC individual's cognitive performance? In addition, can these low WMC friendly environments be created such that they do not inhibit the learning of high WMC individuals? Recently, Lusk, Evans, Jeffrey, Palmer, Wikstrom, and Doolittle, (in press) determined that segmenting multimedia instruction – dividing instruction into small segments and allowing the learner control over when each segment begins – increased low WMC students' cognitive performance with out decreasing high WMC students' cognitive performance. It may be that those techniques that reduce learners' cognitive load, in general, will facilitate low WMC students' cognitive performance while not affecting the cognitive performance of high WMC.

Ultimately, the present chapter provides evidence that individual differences in working memory capacity should be taken into account when creating and implementing multimedia instructional environments.

FUTURE RESEARCH DIRECTIONS

The role of working memory capacity (WMC) within multimedia learning has been demonstrated to be significant. That said, both the Sanchez and Wiley (2006) study and the current study are only first steps in examining the relationship between WMC and multimedia learning. If student variations in WMC affect cognitive performance in multimedia learning environments, how can low WMC students' learning be scaffolded to support their learning? Reiser (2004) divides scaffolding into structuring and problematizing, where *structuring* involves reducing the complexity of the task to make the task more tenable for students and *problematizing* involves focusing students attention on aspects of the task that they might otherwise overlook. Thus, how can multimedia learning environments be structured so that low WMC students can learn successfully, while at the same time, how can multimedia learning environments be problematized so that students attend to the attributes of the learning situation that are necessary for meaningful learning?

In addition, what attributes within the multimedia learning environment have greater or lesser impact on low and high WMC students? For example, what impact do task complexity, task length, and task interactivity have on low and high WMC students engaged in a multimedia learning environment? Also, several principles of multimedia learning have been demonstrated to have a significant impact on student learning (e.g., modality principle, coherence principle, signaling principle, segmenting principle), however, these principles have not been investigated to determine if differences in WMC account for the differences resulting from the principles themselves. As a general individual difference variable, there is much work to be done to parse the effects of WMC on learning in multimedia learning environments.

REFERENCES

Ackerman, P. L., Beier, M. E., & Boyle, M. O. (2002). Individual differences in working memory within a nomological network of cognitive and perceptual speed abilities. *Journal of Experimental Psychology: General, 131,* 567–589.

Baddeley, A.D., & Hitch, G.J. (1974). Working memory, In G.A. Bower (Ed.), *The psychology of learning and motivation: advances in research and theory* (Vol. 8, pp. 47-89), New York: Academic Press.

Buehner, M., Krumm, S., & Pick, M. (2005). Reasoning = working memory ≠ attention. *Intelligence, 33,* 251-272.

Cantor, J., & Engle, R. W. (1993). Working-memory capacity as long-term memory activation: An individual-differences approach. *Journal of Experimental Psychology: Learning, Memory, and Cognition, 19*(5), 1101-1114.

Conway, A. R. A., Cowan, N., & Bunting, M. F. (2001). The cocktail party phenomenon revisited: The importance of working memory capacity. *Psychonomic Bulletin & Review, 8,* 331–335.

Conway, A. R., Cowan, N., Bunting, M. F., Therriault, D. J., & Minkoff, S. R. (2002). A latent variable analysis of working memory capacity, short-term memory capacity, processing speed, and general fluid intelligence. *Intelligence, 30,* 163-183.

Cooper, G., Tindall-Ford, S., Chandler, P., & Sweller, J. (2001). Learning by imagining. *Journal of Experimental Psychology: Applied, 7,* 68-82.

Daneman, M., & Carpenter, P. A. (1980). Individual differences in working memory and reading. *Journal of Verbal Learning and Verbal Behavior, 19,* 450-466.

Daneman, M., & Carpenter, P. A. (1983). Individual differences in integrating information between and within sentences. *Journal of Experimental Psychology: Learning, Memory, and Cognition, 9,* 561-584.

Daneman M., & Green, I. (1986). Individual differences in comprehending and producing words in context. *Journal of Verbal Learning and Verbal Behavior, 19,* 450–466.

Daneman, M, & Tardif, T. (1987). Working memory and reading skill re-examined. In M. E. Coltheart (Ed.), *Attention and performance XII: The psychology of reading* (pp. 491-508). Hove, UK: Lawrence Erlbaum.

Feldman Barrett, L., Tugade, M. M., & Engle, R. A. (2004). Individual differences in working memory capacity and dual-process theories of the mind. *Psychological Bulletin, 130*(4), 553-573.

Friedman, N. P., & Miyake, A. (2000). Differential roles for visuospatial and verbal working memroy in situation model construction. *Journal of Experimental Psychology: General, 129,* 61-83.

Gaultney, J. F., Kipp, K., & Kirk, G. (2005). Utilization deficiency and working memory capacity in adult memory performance: Not just for children anymore. *Cognitive Development, 20,* 205-213.

Ginns, P. (2005). Meta-analysis of the modality effect. *Learning and Instruction, 15,* 313-331.

Hambrick, D., & Oswald, F. L. (2005). Does domain knowledge moderate involvement of working memory capacity in higher –level cognition? A test of three models. *Journal of Memory and Language, 52,* 377-397.

Handley, S. J., Capon, A., Copp, C., & Harper, C. (2002). Conditional reasoning and the Tower of Hanoi: The role of spatial and verbal working memory. *British Journal of Psychology, 93,* 501–518.

Harp, S. F., & Mayer, R. E. (1998). How seductive details do their damage. A theory of cognitive interest in science learning. *Journal of Educational Psychology, 90,* 414-434.

Just, M., & Carpenter, P. A. (1992). A capacity theory of comprehension: Individual differences in working memory. *Psychological Review, 99,* 122-149.

Kalyuga, S., Chandler, P., & Sweller, J. (1999). Managing split-attention and redundancy in multimedia instruction. *Applied Cognitive Psychology, 13*, 351-371.

Kane, M. J., Bleckley, M. K., Conway, A. R., & Engle, R. W., (2001). A controlled-attention view of working memory capacity. *Journal of Experimental Psychology: General, 130*(2), 169-183.

Kane, M. J., & Engle, R. W. (2000). Working-memory capacity, proactive interference, and divided attention: Limits on long-term memory retrieval. *Journal of Experimental Psychology: Learning, Memory, and Cognition, 26*(2), 336-358.

Kane, M. J., & Engle, R. W., (2003). Working-memory capacity and the control of attention: The contributions of goal neglect, response competition, and task set to Stroop interference. *Journal of Experimental Psychology: General, 132*(1), 47-70.

Kane, M. J., Hambrick, D. Z., Tuhoski, S. W., Wilhelm, O., Payne, T. W., & Engle, R. W. (2004). The generality of working memory capacity: A latent-variable approach to verbal and visuospatial memory span and reasoning, *Journal of Experimental Psychology: General, 133*(2), 189-217.

Kane, M. J., Poole, B. J., Tuholski, S. W., & Engle, R. W. (2006). Working memory capacity and the top-down control of visual search: Exploring the boundaries of "executive attention." *Journal of Experimental Psychology: Learning, Memory, and Cognition, 32*, 749-777.

Kiewra, K. A., & Benton, S. L. (1988). The relationship between information-processing ability and note taking. *Contemporary Educational Psychology, 13*, 33-44.

Kyllonen, P. C., & Christal, R. E. (1990). Reasoning ability is (little more than) working-memory capacity?! *Intelligence, 14*, 389-433.

La Pointe, L. B., & Engle, R. W. (1990). Simple and complex word spans as measures of working memory capacity. *Journal of Experimental Psychology: Learning, Memory and Cognition, 16*, 1118-1133.

Lusk, D. L., Evans, A., D. Jeffrey, T. R., Palmer, K. R., Wikstrom, C. S., & Doolittle, P. E. (in press). Multimedia learning and individual differences: Mediating the effects of working memory capacity with segmentation. *British Journal of Educational Technology.*

Lustig, C., May, C. P., & Hasher, L. (2001). Working memory span and the role of proactive interference. *Journal of Experimental Psychology: General, 130*(2), 199-207.

Mautone, P. D., & Mayer, R. E. (2001). Signaling as a cognitive guide in multimedia learning. *Journal of Educational Psychology, 93*(2), 377-389.

Mayer, R. E. (2001). *Multimedia learning.* Cambridge, UK: Cambridge University Press.

Mayer, R. E. (Ed.) (2005). *The Cambridge Handbook of Multimedia Learning.* Cambridge: Cambridge Press.

Mayer, R. E., & Anderson, R. B. (1991). Animations need narrations: An experimental test of a dual-coding hypothesis. *Journal of Educational Psychology, 83*(4), 484-490.

Mayer, R. E., & Anderson, R. B. (1992). The instructive animation: Helping students build connections between words and pictures in multimedia learning. *Journal of Educational Psychology, 84*(4), 444-452.

Mayer, R. E., Heiser, J., & Lonn, S. (2001). Cognitive constraints on multimedia learning: When presenting more material results in less understanding. *Journal of Educational Psychology, 93*(1), 187-198.

Mayer, R., & Jackson, J. (2005). The case for coherence in scientific explanations: Quantitative details can hurt qualitative understanding. *Journal of Experimental Psychology: Applied, 11*(1), 13-18.

Mayer, R. E., & Moreno, R. (1998). A split-attention effect in multimedia learning: Evidence for dual processing systems in working memory.

Journal of Educational Psychology, 90(2), 312-320.

Mayer, R. E., & Sims, V. (1994). For whom is a picture worth a thousand words? Extensions of a dual-coding theory of multimedia learning. *Journal of Educational Psychology, 86*, 389-401.

Morrell, R. W., & Park, D. C. (1993). The effects of age, illustrations, and task variables on the performance of procedural assembly tasks. *Psychology and Aging, 8*, 389-399.

Moreno, R., & Mayer, R. E. (1999). Cognitive principles of multimedia learning: The role of modality and contiguity. *Journal of Educational Psychology, 91*(2), 358-368.

Moreno, R., & Mayer, R. E. (2000). A coherence effect in multimedia learning: The case for minimizing irrelevant sounds in the design of multimedia instructional messages. *Journal of Educational Psychology, 92*(1), 117-125.

Oberauer, K., Süß, H. M., Schulze, R., Wilhelm, O., & Wittmann, W. W. (2000) Working memory capacity – facets of a cognitive ability construct. *Personality and Individual Differences, 29*, 1017-1045.

Ollerenshaw, A., Aidman, E., & Kidd, G. (1997). Is an illustration always worth ten thousand words? Effects of prior knowledge, learning style, and multimedia illustrations on text comprehension. *International Journal of Instructional Media, 24*, 227-238.

Pratt, M.W., Boyes, C., Robins, S., & Manchester, J. (1989). Telling tales: Aging, working memory, and the narrative cohesion of story retellings. *Developmental Psychology, 25*, 628-63

Reiser, B. J. (2004). Scaffolding complex learning: The mechanisms of structuring and problematizing student work. *Journal of the Learning Sciences, 13*(3), 273-304.

Roberts, R. J., Hager, L. D., & Heron, C. (1994). Prefrontal cognitive processes: Working memory and inhibition in the antisaccade task. *Journal of Experimental Psychology: General, 123*, 374-393.

Rosen, V. M., & Engle, R. W. (1997). The role of working memory capacity in retrieval. *Journal of Experimental Psychology: General, 126*(3), 211-227.

Sanchez, C. A., & Wiley, J. (2006). An examination of the seductive details effect in terms of working memory capacity. *Memory & Cognition, 34*(2), 344-355.

Schnotz, W., & Bannert, M. (2003). Construction and interference in learning from multiple representation. *Learning and Instruction, 13*, 141-156.

Shah, P., Miyake, A. (1996). The separability of working memory resources for spatial thinking and language processing: An individual differences approach. *Journal of Experimental Psychology: General, 125*, 4-27.

Shute, V. J. (1991). Who is likely to acquire programming skills? *Journal of Educational Computing Research, 7*, 1-24.

Tabbers, H. K., Martens, R. O., & van Merrienboer, J. J. G. (2004). Multimedia instructions and cognitive load theory: Effects of modality an cueing. *British Journal of Educational psychology, 74*, 71-81.

Turner, M. L., & Engle, R. W. (1989). Is working memory capacity task dependent? *Journal of Memory and Language, 28*, 127-154.

Unsworth, N., & Engle, R. W. (2007). The nature of individual difference n working memory capacity: Active maintenance in primary memory and controlled search from secondary memory. *Psychological Review, 114*(1), 104-132.

Unsworth, N., & Schrock, J. C., & Engle, R. W. (2004). Working memory capacity and the antisaccade task: Individual differences in voluntary saccade control. *Journal of Experimental Psychology: Learning, Memory, and Cognition, 30*(6), 1302-1321.

Watson, J. M., Bunting, M. F., Poole, B. J., & Conway, A. R. (2005). Individual differences in susceptibility to false memory in the Deese–Roediger–McDermott Paradigm, *Journal of Experimental Psychology: Learning, Memory, and Cognition, 31*(1), 76–85.

ADDITIONAL READING

Ashcraft, M. H., & Kirk, E. P. (2001). The relationships among working memory, math anxiety, and performance. *Journal of Experimental Psychology: General, 130*(2), 224-237.

Bayliss, D. M., Jarrold, C., Baddeley, A. D., & Gunn, D. M. (2005). The relationship between short-term memory and working memory: Complex span made simple? *Memory, 13*(3/4), 414-421.

Bunting, M. F., Conway, A. R., & Heitz, R. P. (2004). Individual differences in the fan effect and working memory capacity. *Journal of Memory and Language, 51*, 604-622.

Carretti, B., Cornoldi, C., De Beni, R., & Romano, M. (2005). Updating in working memory: A comparison of good and poor comprehenders. *Journal of Experimental Child Psychology 91*, 45-66.

Chambers, B., Cheung, A. C., Madden, N. A., Slavin, R. E., & Gifford, R. (2006). Achievement effects of embedded multimedia in a Success for all Reading program. *Journal of Educational psychology, 98*(1), 232-237.

Duff, S. C., & Logie, R. H. (2001). Processing and storage in working memory span. *Quarterly Journal of Experimental Psychology, 54A*(1), 31-48.

Dutke, S., & Rinck, M. (2006). Multimedia learning: Working memory and the learning of word and picture diagrams. *Learning and Instruction, 16*, 526-537.

Eilam, B., & Poyas, Y. (2007). Learning with multiple representations: Extending multimedia learning beyond the lab. *Learning and Instruction, 32*, 1-11.

Fedforenk, E., Gison, E., & Rohde, D. (2006). The nature of working memory capacity in sentence comprehension: Evidence against domain-specific working memory resources *Journal of Memory and Language, 54*, 541-553.

Gemino, A., Parker, D., & Kutzschan, A. O. (2006). Investigating coherence and multimedia effects of a technology-mediated collaborate environment. *Journal of Management Information systems, 22*(3), 97-121.

Hambrick, D. Z., & Oswald, F. L. (2005). Does domain knowledge moderate involvement of working memory capacity in higher-level cognition? A test of three modes. *Journal of Memory and Language, 52*, 377-397.

Harskamp, E. G., Mayer, R. E., & Suhre, C. (2007). Does the modality principle for multimedia learning apply to science classrooms? *Learning and Instruction, 17*, 465-477.

Hoffler, T. N., & Leutner, D. (2007). Instructional animation versus static pictures: A meta-analysis. *Learning and Instruction, 32*, 1-17.

Jamet, E., & Le Bohec, O. (2007). The effect of redundant text in multimedia instruction. *Contemporary Educational Psychology, 32*, 588-598.

Jamet, E., Gavota, M., Quaireau, C. (2007). Attention guiding in multimedia learning. *Learning and Instruction, 32*, 1-11.

Logan, G. D. (2004). Working memory, task switching, and executive control in the task span procedure. *Journal of Experimental Psychology: General, 133*(2), 218-236.

Miyake, A. (2001). Individual differences in working memory: Introduction to the special section. *Journal of Experimental Psychology: General, 130*(2), 163-168.

Moreno, R. (2006). Does the modality principle hold for different media? A test of the method-affects-learning hypothesis. *Journal of Computer Assisted Learning, 22*, 149-158.

Moreno, R., & Flowerday, R. (2006). Students' choice of animated pedagogical agents in science learning: A test of the similarity-attraction hypothesis on gender and ethnicity. *Contemporary Educational Psychology, 31*, 186-207.

Oberauer, K., & Kliegl, R. (2004). Simultaneous cognitive operations in working memory after dual-task practice. *Journal of Experimental Psychology: Human Perception and Performance, 30*(4), 689-707.

Reed, S. K. (2006). Cognitive architectures for multimedia learning. *Educational Psychologist, 41*(2), 87-98.

Samaras, H., Giouvanakis, T., Bousiou, D., & Tarabanis, K. (2006). Towards a new generation of multimedia learning research. *AACE Journal, 14*(1), 3-30.

Chapter III
Measurement of Cognitive Load During Multimedia Learning Activities

Anne E. Cook
University of Utah, USA

Robert Z. Zheng
University of Utah, USA

Jacquelyn W. Blaz
University of Utah, USA

ABSTRACT

This chapter focuses on issues dealing with the definition and measurement of cognitive load in multimedia and other complex learning activities. The chapter is broken into 3 main sections: defining multimedia learning and describing its effects on cognitive load; describing theoretical definitions of cognitive load; and mapping definitions of cognitive load onto commonly used measurement techniques. The chapter concludes with a discussion of how research on multimedia learning and cognitive load could be advanced by carefully considering issues of construct validity, and by including the use of convergent measurement techniques.

INTRODUCTION

Over the last thirty years, there has been considerable interest in the areas of cognition and instruction (Ayres, 2006; Brunken, Plass, & Leutner, 2003; Sweller & Chandler, 1991, 1994; van Merrriënboer & Sweller, 2005). Specifically, researchers are interested in understanding learners' mental processes, as well as the instructional procedures and designs that best facilitate those processes, especially when learning involves multimedia, where information is processed through multiple sensory channels (Mayer & Moreno, 2003; Michas & Berry, 2000; Moreno & Mayer, 1999). One of the most studied topics in this domain has been cognitive load and modality in learning (Mayer, 2001; Mayer & Moreno, 2003; Sweller & Chandler, 1991). Based on the assumptions of working memory theory (Baddeley, 1986, 1999), the concept of cognitive load refers to learners' ability to process information given the current demands placed on working memory. As learning tasks become more complex, they demand more working memory resources, thereby increasing cognitive load. When the demand for working memory resources exceeds availability, cognitive "overload" occurs, and individuals' ability to learn and process information decreases.

Although there is a plethora of evidence concerning the effects of cognitive load on learning from multimedia and ways to effectively reduce cognitive load (Mayer, 2001; Mayer & Moreno, 2003), the central question pertaining to the study of cognitive load still remains unanswered: When, how, and at what level do we know the learner is cognitively overloaded? In other words, how do we define cognitive load, and how do we measure it, particularly in multimedia learning tasks? This chapter discusses: (1) multimedia learning and its cognitive consequences with regard to learners' information processes; (2) definitions of cognitive load; and (3) approaches to measuring cognitive load in multimedia and complex learning environments.

MULTIMEDIA LEARNING

What is Multimedia Learning?

Multimedia instruction involves presenting educational content through multiple media, primarily through visual and auditory presentations. Mayer (2001) proposed a theory of multimedia learning which relies on three major assumptions drawn from theories in cognitive psychology. First,

working memory involves two distinct systems for encoding and processing visual and auditory information (Baddeley, 1986, 1999; Paivio, 1986). Second, the processing resources devoted to each of these channels are limited, such that when demand exceeds availability, cognitive "overload" can occur (Baddeley, 1986, 1999). Third, meaningful learning occurs when individuals actively and simultaneously process information from the visual and auditory channels, and attempt to select, organize, and integrate that information in conjunction with existing mental schemas (Anderson, 1996; Kozma, 1991; Mayer & Sims, 1994; Michas & Berry, 2000; Wittrock, 1989). Because well-designed multimedia presentations organize and integrate visual and auditory information, learners are able to devote more resources to mapping this incoming information onto content retrieved from long-term memory.

A number of studies on multimedia learning have demonstrated that the appropriate use of multimedia presentations can result in the reduction of cognitive load (e.g., Mayer & Anderson, 1991, 1992; Mayer & Moreno, 2003; Mayer, Moreno, Boire, & Vagge, 1999; Mayer & Sims, 1994). For example, Tarmizi and Sweller (1988) found that when learners were required to mentally integrate two sources of information (diagrams and texts) from worked geometry examples, cognitive resources were overloaded due to learners having to split their attention between the two sources of information. However, Chandler & Sweller (1991) found that when diagrams were embedded with text (i.e., the diagram and text were integrated), learning increased. Although cognitive benefits of multimedia learning have been recognized by researchers across a wide spectrum of disciplines (see Kozma, 1994; Lee, Plass, & Homer, 2006; Mayer & Moreno, 2003), there is a concurred view among researchers that multimedia may also impede learning and increase cognitive load if not appropriately designed.

The issue of how to appropriately measure multimedia effects on cognitive load is complex, because the construct of cognitive load has been defined in a number of different ways in the research literature and may in fact involve several components. In addition, researchers have assessed multimedia effects on cognitive load with a variety of measurement techniques, in many cases without any clear indication of which aspect of cognitive load was under investigation. The goal of this chapter is to map theoretical definitions of cognitive load onto their respective measurement techniques. We first review how the construct of cognitive load has been defined, and then we address current measurement techniques in light of these definitions. We conclude the chapter with a discussion of how researchers may further refine assumptions about how multimedia presentations and other complex learning contexts differentially affect the underlying components of cognitive load by making use of convergent measurement techniques.

COGNITIVE LOAD THEORY

Theoretical Assumptions

Cognitive load refers to the demand for working memory resources during learning. Cognitive load theory (CLT) outlines the circumstances under which the results of learning may be affected (Sweller & Chandler, 1991, 1994; Paas, Renkl, & Sweller, 2003). CLT applies to a broader range of instructional contexts than Mayer's (2001) multimedia theory, but it is based on many of the same general assumptions. First, working memory resources are limited, such that individuals can only process a few novel interacting elements at a time (Baddeley, 1986, 1999; Miller, 1956). But because working memory also allows for the retrieval of information from long-term memory, including schematic structures (e.g., Piaget, 1952), individuals are able to process several (novel and previously-learned) interacting elements of information at any given point in time (Pollock,

Chandler, & Sweller, 2002). Like multimedia theory, CLT applies these assumptions about human cognition to the design of instructional contexts that do not overtax working memory resources (van Merriënboer and Sweller, 2005). CLT thus goes beyond traditional cognitive psychology theories, which have focused more on explaining and predicting cognitive processes, to describe how human cognition and instructional variables interact to impact learning.

Researchers have applied CLT with a variety of instructional approaches. For example, Paas and van Merriënboer (1994a) used worked examples to teach geometry to secondary technical school students and found that training with worked examples required less time and was perceived as demanding less mental effort than training with conventional problems. Similarly, van Merriënboer and Krammer (1990) found that partial solution (i.e., problem completion) strategies provided the necessary cognitive support to guide learners through the complex process of mastering the syntax and the logic of a programming language. Owen and Sweller (1985) compared goal-specific and goal-free approaches in instruction and concluded that the goal- specific approach "places a heavy load on cognitive processing capacity" (p. 272), whereas the goal-free approach improves the cognitive conditions in information processing. In multimedia design, Mayer and his associates demonstrated across several studies that the mode of learning can significantly influence learners' cognitive information processing (Mayer, 2001; Mayer & Moreno, 2003; Mayer & Sims, 1994; Mayer et al., 1999). They noted that optimally designed multimedia learning (see Mayer's, 2001, principles of multimedia design) can help reduce cognitive load, facilitate mental representation, and aid schema acquisition. In support of this view, Lee et al. (2006) developed a multimedia program that pre-trained learners with required prior knowledge before exposing them to more complex content and found that cognitive load was reduced for the subsequent complex learning task.

To provide a better explanation of how educators and researchers can apply the assumptions of CLT to instructional designs that lead to optimal cognitive load in learners, it is first necessary to describe the construct of cognitive load, and the various ways that it and its components have been described in the literature. In the next section, we will summarize some of the major conceptual views of cognitive load, with the goal of then tying these construct definitions to specific methods of measuring cognitive load.

Definitions and Types of Cognitive Load

CLT distinguishes among three types of cognitive load: *intrinsic load*, *extraneous* or *ineffective load*, and *germane* or *effective load*. *Intrinsic cognitive load* refers to the inherent structure and complexity of the instructional material, which increases as element interactivity increases. Element interactivity refers to the number of different types of information that learners must integrate in order to understand new information. For example, trigonometry involves a high degree of element interactivity, because learners must apply algebraic rules to the angular relationships of planar and three-dimensional figures to solve trigonometric formulas. Usually, teachers or instructional designers can do little to influence intrinsic cognitive load; thus, without any external influences, the intrinsic nature of the task may be sufficient to impede learning.

The degree to which a task influences learning, however, also depends on instructional variables. *Extraneous cognitive load*, or *ineffective load* refers to poorly designed instructional variables that may make a hard task even harder. That is, extraneous load results in the reduction of available resources. For example, instructors may unwittingly increase learners' extraneous cognitive load by presenting materials that "require students to mentally integrate mutually referring, disparate sources of information" (Sweller & Chandler,

1991, p.353). Consider the task presented in Figure 1. The learner would have to expend extra cognitive resources coordinating the information between the text and the image, which may overtax the working memory resources allocated to the processing of visual information (see previous description of Mayer's 2001 multimedia theory). Instruction like this would be likely to induce a high level of extraneous cognitive load.

Germane cognitive load, or *effective load*, on the other hand, refers to instructional variables that facilitate learning and information processing, and may actually increase the working memory resources available to perform the task at hand. Factors contributing to a task's germane load induce learners' efforts to engage in strategic processing that may facilitate construction and retrieval of schematic knowledge. That is, unlike intrinsic or extraneous load, factors related to germane load lead to a reduction in cognitive load.

Within CLT, intrinsic, extraneous, and germane load are additive; when combined, they comprise the overall construct of cognitive load.

Figure 1. An example of instruction that may induce high extraneous load

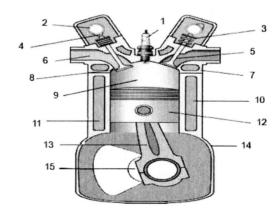

1. spark plug 2. camshaft 3. valve spring 4. cam
5. exhaust valve 6. mixture in 7. cylinder head
8. intake value 9. combustion chamber 10. cooling water
11. cylinder block 12. piston 13. connecting rod
14. crankcase 15. crankshaft

It should also be noted that this may interact with learner characteristics, such that instructional techniques may be more or less effective for learners as a function of their expertise, ability, or motivation (Paas et al., 2003). Thus, instructional variables such as task format, task complexity, use of multimedia, time pressure, and pacing of instruction could increase extraneous load if applied ineffectively, or could increase germane load if applied effectively (e.g., see Schmidt-Weigand, Chapter VI in this volume). For example, even when instructional variables are successfully applied to decrease extraneous load, van Merriënboer and Sweller (2005) argued that it may be necessary to employ practices to increase student motivation to invest in germane load. This is because instructional manipulations designed to reduce overall cognitive load are only effective if learners actually use the freed cognitive resources to engage in meaningful, effortful learning.

In empirical studies, the sum of intrinsic, extraneous, and germane load may be operationalized as either *mental load, mental effort*, or *performance* (Paas & van Merriënboer, 1994b). *Mental load* is the demand for cognitive resources expected to result from the interaction of task and subject characteristics in an instructional task. *Mental effort* refers to the actual resources allocated to the task. *Performance* refers to a learner's ability to successfully complete a task, given the components of that task. To make the issue ever more complex, Paas and van Merriënboer (1993) pointed out that even if researchers understand the influences of a particular instructional intervention on cognitive load, those influences are best interpreted in the context of actual performance on the task. Thus, they proposed a computational approach that combined measures of mental effort with measures of performance to create a new construct, *mental efficiency*. A learner's mental efficiency would be high if he/she achieved high performance scores but exerted low mental effort. Conversely, his/her mental efficiency would be low if poor performance was associated with a high degree of mental effort.

One potential problem with these conceptualizations of cognitive load, though, is that even if unintended, they imply a cumulative, static degree of resource allocation. However, many multimedia presentations are designed to instruct learners on complex concepts (e.g., Mayer's lightning presentation examples), and complex learning typically involves "not one decision, but a long series, in which early decisions condition later ones" (Quesada, Kintsch, & Comez., p.6). This dynamic nature of learning necessitates that the mental load associated with it also be viewed as a dynamic construct. That is, the general mental load of a task may be high, but the actual mental effort expended during a task may rise and fall, depending on the difficulty the learner experiences from moment to moment. Citing this issue and other problems with existing approaches to defining/measuring mental load, Xie and Salvendy (2000) proposed a framework that can capture both the dynamic and cumulative aspects of the construct. They distinguished among *instantaneous load, peak load, accumulated load, average load*, and *overall load*. *Instantaneous load* captures the fluctuations in load that may occur over time during complex learning and best reflects the dynamic aspect of complex learning, whereas *accumulated load* captures the load that "builds up" over a task and is assumed to be the total amount of load experienced at task completion. *Peak load* refers to the maximum amount of load experienced, and *average load* refers to the mean degree or intensity of load experienced per unit of time. Finally, *overall load* refers to the learner's experienced load during the task.

As outlined in the previous paragraphs, there have been numerous attempts and approaches to defining cognitive load. See Table 1 for a summary of cognitive load definitions. Xie and Salvendy (2000) put it best in their statement, "Mental workload is incompletely defined, is certainly multifaceted, and has a direct bearing on an operator's ability to maintain or reach performance level" (p. 214). Mark (2000, as cited in Shadish, Cook, & Campbell, 2001) listed four common errors in defining constructs: 1), defining constructs too generally; 2), defining constructs too narrowly; 3) misidentifying constructs; and 4) attributing a single construct to what is actually multiple constructs. We argue that each of these errors has been made in the cognitive load research literature – especially errors 1 and 4 – and that these errors raise serious concerns for measurement of cognitive load. This is because researchers in the field often generally refer to their studies as testing the effects of an instructional manipulation on cognitive load, which, as we have just described, could be defined several different ways. If researchers are not adequately defining their constructs, then it is difficult to determine whether or not the techniques chosen to measure those constructs are appropriate. Before

addressing this issue in detail, however, we first will provide a review of the most commonly used measurements in cognitive load research.

MEASURING COGNITIVE LOAD

As mentioned earlier in this chapter, questions concerning measurement of cognitive load are not new in the literature (e.g., see Brunken et al., 2003; Paas, Tuovinen, Tabbers, & Van Gerven, 2003; Paas, van Merriënboer, & Adam, 1994; Xie & Salvendy, 2000). Cognitive load measurements have, for the most part, been categorized into analytical methods, rating scales, task- and performance-based methods, and physiological techniques (Pass et al., 2003). Brunken et al. argued that these techniques can be further classified along two dimensions: objectivity and causal relation. For now, we will only address the objectivity dimension, which refers to whether

Table 1. Cognitive load construct definitions

Construct	Definition
Conceptualizations of Load as a Static, or Cumulative Concept	
Mental Load	Demand on cognitive resources expected to result from the interaction of task and subject characteristics
Mental Effort	Cognitive resources actually allocated to a task, and that measured during a task
Performance	Learner's ability to successfully complete a task
Mental Efficiency	Learner's ability to successfully complete a task, given the degree of mental effort expended during that task
Overall Load	Learner's subjective experience of load during a task
Average Load	Mean degree or intensity of load expended during a task, per unit of time
Accumulated Load	The total amount of load experienced at task completion
Conceptualizations of Load as a Dynamic, Fluctuating Concept	
Instantaneous Load	Measurement of load at any point in time; captures subtle fluctuations in load that may occur during a task
Peak Load	The maximum amount of load experienced during a task

the measurement tool relies on subjective, self-report methods, or more objective performance, behavioral, or physiological data. The causal relations dimension will be addressed at the end of this section. Note that because we are describing general categories of measures and not how specific exemplars of each category are used in empirical studies of cognitive load, this section does not provide information on the different measures' psychometric properties.

Analytical Methods

The first category of cognitive load measurement techniques, analytical methods, describes those methods that are designed to estimate cognitive load without actually empirically measuring it. These methods may employ expert opinion, task analysis, mathematical models, or computer simulations, and are designed to be predictive and/or evaluative, but not confirmative. Thus, although analytical methods may provide a good *a priori* estimate of cognitive load, they should be supported by empirical data. For example, Sweller (1988) developed a chaining production system to assess learners' cognitive load. The system describes goal-specific (i.e., mean-ends) and goal-free production rules with which the learner decides at any given problem state whether the problem can be solved. The chaining production system is used to measure goal-specific and goal-free learning by examining (a) the number of statements in working memory; (b) the number of productions; (c) the number of cycles to solution; and (d) the total number of conditions matched. The aforementioned variables often serve as a framework to determine learners' cognitive load in problem solving. For example, Sweller used the number of statements and productions to determine the average working memory and peak working memory involved in both goal-specific and goal-free learning in kinematics problem solving. Although the chaining production system has been used to measure cognitive load, it has several limitations. First, the system is narrowly limited to production related problems, specifically in mathematics and science. Secondly, it is not clear how *mental load, mental effort* and *performance* are being assessed based on the operation of the chaining production system. Finally, the system may be considered a good subjective estimate of mental load based on the number of statements and productions but is less robust in demonstrating the overall cognitive load experienced by the learners compared to other measures such as task- and performance- based measures (Brunken, Plass, & Leutner, 2004), physiological measures (Beatty & Lucero-Wagner, 2000), and ratings (Paas, 1992; Windell & Wieber, 2007).

As noted in Table 2, analytical methods fall into Brunken et al.'s (2003) subjective category. In addition, we argue that because they do not empirically measure cognitive load, analytical measures assess only the construct of *mental load*, which Paas and van Merriënboer (1994b) defined as the load expected in a given instructional task.

Rating Scales

Rating scale techniques are widely used by researchers to measure cognitive load because they are easy to use and relatively inexpensive. One of the best known instruments is Paas's (1992) cognitive load (CL) questionnaire, which was based on a measure developed by Borg, Bratfish, and Dornic (1971) for measuring perceived task difficulty. The questionnaire measures the mental effort invested and the difficulty level experienced by the learner in problem solving, as well as the learner's ability to understand the problems. Although this instrument has been shown to be very reliable and sensitive to small differences in load, it does not always correlate well with other load measures. Windell and Wieber (2007) compared the self-report measures of NASA Task Load IndeX (Moroney, Biers, Eggemeier, & Mitchell, 1992) and Short Self-report Instrument (SSI; Paas et al., 2003) which contained a single question derived from Paas's questionnaire, and found a low correlation between scores on the two instruments. In addition, when estimating perceived effort, it is not clear how factors such as task difficulty, the time required to complete a task, or attentional variables may influence learners' ratings (Brunken et al., 2003). Irrespective of the concerns mentioned above, Paas's CL questionnaire remains one of the more popular instruments used for measuring cognitive load.

Additional concerns with using rating scales to assess cognitive load is that they rely solely on self-report, which may be subject to social desirability bias, and errors in metacognitive judgments (Bray & Howard, 1980; Kaderavek, Gillam, & Ukrainetz, 2004; Wilson, 2001). Studies employing these scales also typically use between-subjects designs, which may introduce additional variability in the form of differences between groups not due to task manipulations. In Table 2, we categorized Paas' (1992) rating scale and similar instruments in Brunken et al.'s (2003) subjective category. Furthermore, we argue that rating scales only measure the learner's subjective experience of cognitive load, characterized by Xie and Salvendy (2000) as *overall load*.

Task- and Performance-Based Measures

Measures in this category are commonly used in cognitive load research, probably due to ease of implementation and analysis. They can be broken into primary and secondary task methodologies. Primary task methodologies typically include accuracy and response time on measures that assess learning of information from an instructional module. In tests of Mayer's (2001) theory of multimedia learning, for example, most studies have used accuracy scores on recall or recognition and transfer tests as the dependent variable (e.g., Lee et al., 2006; Mayer & Sims, 1994; Mayer, Mautone, & Prothero, 2002; Moreno & Duran, 2004). Researchers in the hypermedia learning

literature may also measure individuals' navigation behaviors, errors, and orientation problems (Astleitner & Leutner, 1996). Accuracy scores only tap into the *performance* aspect of cognitive load (Paas & van Merriënboer, 1994b). Response time to such tasks, however, may be argued to represent *mental effort* (Paas & van Merriënboer, 1993); as working memory resources become increasingly depleted, fewer are available for initiating and executing responses, and response times typically increase (Wickens, 1984). When response time is combined with accuracy, the result is a measure of "response speed" (Schmidt-Weigand, Chapter VI in this volume) or *mental efficiency* (Paas & van Merriënboer, 1994b; Zheng, Miller, Snelbecker, & Cohen, 2006). Unlike the analytical and rating scale methods, primary task measures fall under the objective category in Brunken et al.'s (2003) classification scheme (see Table 2).

In secondary task methods, also called dual-task methods, learners are engaged in a primary learning task but are also required to simultaneously participate in a secondary task (Brunken et al., 2004). Usually, the secondary task involves monitoring for an auditory or visual signal to which learners are instructed to respond as quickly and accurately as possible. Presumably, the secondary task utilizes the capacity "leftover" from processing on the primary task. As the primary task becomes more difficult, less capacity is available for the secondary task, resulting in increased response times and lower accuracy, or lower *mental effort, performance,* and/or *mental efficiency* (see Table 2). Brunye, Taylor, Rapp, and Spiro (2006) also demonstrated that dual-task paradigms can be used to assess the involvement of different working memory mechanisms in multimedia learning contexts (e.g., visual vs. auditory processing systems). Brunken et al. (2003) argued that one benefit of dual task methods is that they allow researchers to objectively assess load while the primary task is still in progress; in Xie and Salvendy's (2000) terminology, that is, they allow for the measurement of *instantaneous*

Table 2. Mapping construct definitions of cognitive load onto measurements of cognitive load

	Includes:	Subjective or Objective?	Mental Load	Mental Effort	Performance	Mental Efficiency	Instantaneous Load	Peak Load	Accumulated Load	Average Load	Overall Load	Attended Content
Analytical	Production Systems	Subjective	•									
	Expert Opinion	Subjective	•									
	Task Analysis	Subjective	•									
	Mathematical Models/computer Simulations	Subjective	•									
Rating	Rating Scales	Subjective		•							•	
Task- and Performance- Based	Primary Task Measures	Objective		•	•	•						
	Navigation Behaviors	Objective		•	•	•						•
	Secondary Task Measures	Objective		•	•	•	•					
Physiological	Heart Rate	Objective		•			•	•	•	•		
	Measures of Brain Activity	Objective		•			•	•	•	•		
	TEPRs	Objective					•	•	•	•		
Other	Eye Tracking Measures	Objective		•			•	•	•	•		•

load. A more practical issue is that dual task methods are typically used in within-subjects designs, which may reduce some of the individual differences variability that may be associated with between-subjects designs. Although dual task methods may be more reliable and sensitive than analytical, ratings, or primary task methods (Brunken et al., 2003, 2004), it can be difficult to determine with certainty whether outcomes on the secondary task are truly due to load associated with the primary task, or a combination of load from both the primary and secondary tasks. The secondary task may also interfere with learners' processing of the primary task, especially if the primary task is complex and cognitive capacity is limited (van Gerven, Paas, van Merriënboer, & Schmidt, 2002).

Physiological Techniques

Changes in cognitive processing may also be reflected in changes in physiological variables such as heart rate, brain activity, and pupil diameter, etc. Paas and van Merriënboer (1994a) argued heart rate was not a good measure of cognitive load. However, others have provided evidence that task-evoked pupillary responses (TEPRs; Beatty, 1982; Beatty & Lucero-Wagner, 2000) are very sensitive to changes in cognitive load in both simple (e.g., Ahern & Beatty, 1979; Kahneman & Beatty, 1966) and complex learning tasks (e.g., Just & Carpenter, 1993; van Gerven et al., 2002). Measures such as TEPRs tap into changes in autonomic nervous system functioning, which occur without learners' conscious control. As a result, physiological techniques used to measure cognitive load are more objective and may be freer of some of the measurement errors associated with rating and task- and performance-based measures. In addition, because physiological variables are typically measured with high sampling rates – hundreds of samples per second – they are sensitive to subtle fluctuations in load over the course of a task. Thus, as indicated in Table 2, they can be used

to provide measures of *instantaneous load, peak load, accumulated load,* and *average load* (Xie & Salvendy, 2000). However, drawbacks associated with physiological variables are that the equipment used to measure them is often expensive, difficult to use, and can be intrusive, and the data analysis process can be cumbersome. In addition, changes in physiological measures may be the direct result of an increase in cognitive load, but they may also reflect emotional factors, such as stress, interest, or motivation.

Eye Tracking Measures

Although eye tracking technology has been used heavily in research on reading (for a review, see Rayner, 1998) and scene perception (see Henderson, 2007; Henderson & Hollingworth, 1999), it has only recently gained popularity in the multimedia and cognitive load literatures (also see Schmidt-Weigand, Chapter VI in this volume). Briefly, eye tracking allows researchers to record learners' eye movements and fixations as they process visual information; the eye movement record yields objective information about the number and duration of fixations on particular areas of interest within a stimulus, as well as scan-paths, or the spatial pattern of fixations over time on a stimulus. Although not all eye tracking researchers analyze and report TEPRs, these variables can be easily measured with most commercially available eye trackers. In general, as cognitive processing becomes more difficult (or cognitive load increases), individuals' fixations tend to increase in both number and duration; individuals may also be more likely to return to reprocess difficult or confusing areas within a stimulus. Thus, similar to response time, use of fixation duration information may provide a measure of learners' *mental effort* (Paas & van Merriënboer, 1993). Because eye movements are recorded continuously at high sampling rates during a task, though, this technology may also yield measures of *instantaneous load, peak load, accu-*

mulated load, and *average load* (Xie & Salvendy, 2000). Finally, because analysis of eye fixation locations also provides information about specific aspects of a task that cause processing difficulty, it may also yield an *attentional* aspect of load not captured by any of the previously described measures. It is important to note, however, that eye movements are not synonymous with attention, because individuals may continue to process information long after their eyes have moved away from it (Rayner, 1998). The correspondence of eye tracking measures to individual constructs of cognitive load is presented in Table 2.

Causal Inferences and Cognitive Load

As mentioned at the beginning of the previous section, Brunken et al. (2003) rated measures of cognitive load according to dimensions of objectivity and causal relation. The latter dimension refers to whether changes in a particular variable can be directly or indirectly attributed to changes in cognitive load. Brunken et al. argued that direct causal inferences about cognitive load could be drawn from self-report ratings of stress level or task difficulty, measures of brain activity, and results of dual-performance tasks, because these variables reflect direct influences of intrinsic and extraneous load of the instructional task. They argued that only indirect causal inferences could be drawn from self-report ratings of mental effort, performance variables, and physiological measures, because changes in these measures could be due to direct influences of load, or they could be due to differences in investment of germane load, individual differences in competency levels or attentional processes, or emotional responses.

Brunken et al.'s (2003) direct/indirect classifications seem somewhat arbitrary, though, because the arguments they made about the indirect measures could also be applied to some of the measures they classified as direct. For example, ratings of task difficulty could also

be influenced by individual differences among learners, and results of dual-task methods could be due to confounds across tasks or attentional and motivational issues. Thus, without considering specific study design issues, it is difficult to determine whether a measure is directly or indirectly related to cognitive load. In addition, as we have laid out in Table 2, each individual measure may reflect only a particular aspect of cognitive load. To gain a more well-rounded view of how task manipulations influence cognitive load, researchers should use a variety of convergent measures when designing studies to investigate cognitive load. This is the topic of the next and final section of this chapter.

USING CONVERGENT MEASURES OF COGNITIVE LOAD

As indicated in the previous discussion of definitions of cognitive load, we believe researchers in the field have unwittingly made the four errors in defining constructs outlined by Mark (2000, cited in Shadish et al., 2001). Specifically, the concept of cognitive load is so general that researchers have sought out more precise definitions that may or may not capture overall "essence" of cognitive load (e.g., performance, instantaneous load, etc.). In addition, when researchers measure "cognitive load" in multimedia learning studies, they often rely on easy-to-use measures such as Paas's (1992) rating scale and performance, although it is unclear whether they are really interested in the specific constructs actually assessed by those measurements. A related problem occurs when researchers argue an instructional manipulation in a multimedia presentation is influencing cognitive load, when it actually might be influencing some aspect of cognitive load in addition to emotional or attentional variables.

Thus, it appears that there has been a failure to match specific constructs associated with cognitive load to the measurements that best capture those specific constructs. Cook and Campbell (1979) argued that constructs can be "fitted" to their measurements when supported by data related to each of the following four points: 1) testing the extent to which independent variables alter what they are intended to alter; 2) testing that the independent variable does not vary with related but different constructs; 3) dependent variables should measure the factors they are meant to measure; and 4) dependent variables should not be dominated by irrelevant factors. One way to apply these guidelines to address problems with construct validity in the multimedia learning and cognitive load literature is for researchers to use convergent measures.

The use of convergent measures of cognitive load would allow researchers to map different constructs of cognitive load onto their respective behavioral, affective, and physiological components. This would also allow researchers to understand the associations and dissociations among different aspects of cognitive load. Some instructional manipulations may, for example, influence both affective and behavioral components of cognitive load (e.g., Casali & Wierwille, 1983; Lin, Zhang, & Watson, 2003). More interesting cases, and those that would further both multimedia theory specifically and cognitive load theory in general, are those task manipulations which differentially affect behavioral, affective and/or physiological components of cognitive load. For example, Karatekin, Couperus, and Marcus (2004) argued that when TEPRs are combined with dual-task paradigms, dissociations between outcomes on the dependent variables can be used to differentiate between *mental effort* and *mental efficiency* (see also Kahneman, 1973). Work in our lab has also supported the idea of dissociations between affective and physiological measures. For example, Zheng, Cook, & Blaz (2008) gave individuals computerized presentations of multiple-rule based problems that did or did not contain descriptive graphics, and measured response time, performance, self-

reported ratings of cognitive load, and TEPRs. In preliminary analyses, TEPRs were sensitive to subtle task manipulations, whereas performance, response times, and self-report ratings were not. Thus, the instructional manipulation impacted learners' *average loads*, but it did not impact their *performance, mental effort,* or *mental efficiency.* Similarly, Yaros and Cook (2007) found that TEPRs and eye movement measures were sensitive to manipulations in the graphical presentations and story structures of hypermedia news stories, but performance-based measures were not. On a task in which subjects were instructed to behave and respond deceptively, Cook, Hacker, Webb, Osher, Kristjansson, Woltz, and Kircher (2007) found that performance-based measures were not sensitive to instructional manipulations. However, TEPRs were good indicators of individuals' overall cognitive load, and eye movement measures were more indicative of subjects' strategies to avoid being detected as deceptive. These findings provide support for our argument that convergent measures allow researchers to determine how and when instructional manipulations differentially affect learners' behavioral (e.g., performance-based measures), affective (e.g., ratings measures), and physiological responses (e.g., TEPRs). This allows us to understand how making subtle or not-so-subtle changes to instructional variables in multimedia presentations and other complex learning activities may impact different aspects of learners' cognitive load in different ways.

CONCLUSION

In summary, although there has been a great deal of work investigating influences of instructional manipulations on cognitive load, the field would still benefit immensely from more precise construct definitions of cognitive load, and better mapping of those constructs onto specific measures used to assess changes in cognitive load. In this chapter, we have attempted to outline the correspondences between the definitions and the measurements used in cognitive load research, in the hopes that future research will test the validity of these correspondences. Furthermore, identifying the associations and dissociations among different constructs associated with cognitive load may lead to refinement and advancement of both multimedia theory and cognitive load theory.

FUTURE RESEARCH DIRECTIONS

Future research on multimedia learning and cognitive load measure should be directed toward a more accurate definition of the load(s) associated with the various processes in learning. The measures of cognitive load need to be mapped onto mental activities such as mental effort, mental load, and mental efficiency involved in multimedia learning. The convergent research method proposed in this chapter provides a viable venue to such effort. However, empirical research is needed to provide further evidence of the validity and reliability of each of the individual approaches outlined in this chapter.

It is also suggested that future research should examine closely the definition and role of germane load in learning. As of yet, the concept is not well understood and may cause misunderstanding in some cases. For some, increasing germane load would mean an increase in cognitive load, and thus would negatively affect learning. That is, it is not clear to what extent the effort involved in increasing germane load might cross over to become a factor contributing to extraneous load.

For others, increasing germane load is a strategic effort to connect the new knowledge with schematic knowledge, which would eventually decrease cognitive load. These issues pose significant challenges to future research in both multimedia learning and cognitive load.

REFERENCES

Ahern S., & Beatty, J. (1979). Pupillary responses during information processing vary with Scholastic Aptitude Test scores. *Science, 205,* 1289-1292.

Anderson, J. R. (1996). *The architecture of cognition.* Mahwah, NJ: Lawrence Erlbaum Associates.

Astleitner, H., & Leutner, D. (1996). Applying standard network analysis to hypermedia systems: Implications for learning. *Journal of Educational Computing Research, 14,* 285-303.

Ayres, P. (1993). Why goal-free problems can facilitate learning. *Contemporary Educational Psychology, 18,* 376-381.

Ayres, P. (2006). Impact of reducing intrinsic cognitive load on learning in a mathematical domain. *Applied Cognitive Psychology, 20,* 287-298.

Baddeley, A. D. (1986). *Working memory.* Oxford, England: Oxford University Press.

Baddeley, A. D. (1999). *Essentials of human memory.* Hove, England : Psychology Press.

Beatty, J. (1982). Task-evoked pupillary responses, processing load, and the structure of processing resources. *Psychological Bulletin, 91,* 276-292.

Beatty, J., & Lucero-Wagner, B. (2000). The pupillary system. In J. T., Cacioppo, L. G. Tassinary, & G. G. Berntson (Eds.), *Handbook of psychophysiology* (2nd ed., pp. 142-162). Cambridge, UK: Cambridge University Press.

Borg, Bratfish, & Dornic (1971). On the problem of perceived difficulty. *Scandinavian Journal of Psychology, 12,* 249-260.

Bray, J. H., & Howard, G. S. (1980). Methodological considerations in the evaluation of a teacher-training program. *Journal of Educational Psychology, 72,* 62-70.

Brunken, R., Plass, J., & Leutner, D. (2003). Direct measurement of cognitive load in multimedia learning. *Educational Psychologist, 38*(1), 53-61.

Brunken, R., Plass, J., & Leutner, D. (2004). Assessment of cognitive load in multimedia learning with dual-task methodology: Auditory load and modality effects. *Instructional Science, 32*, 115-132.

Brunye, T. T., Taylor, H. A., Rapp, D. N., Spiro, A. B. (2006). Learning procedures: The role of working memory in multimedia learning experiences. *Applied Cognitive Psychology, 20*, 917-940.

Casali, J. G., & Wierwille, W. W. (1983). A comparison of rating scale, secondary-task, physiological, and primary-task workload estimation techniques in a simulated flight task emphasizing communications load. *Human Factors, 25*, 623-641.

Chandler, P., & Sweller, J. (1991). Cognitive load theory and the format of instruction. *Cognition and Instruction, 8*, 293-332.

Clarke, T., Ayres, P., & Sweller, J. (2005). The impact of sequencing and prior knowledge on learning mathematics through spreadsheet application. *Educational Technology, Research and Development, 53*(3), 15-24.

Cook, A. E., Hacker, D. J., Webb, A., Osher, D., Kristjansson, K., Woltz, D. J., & Kircher, J. C. (2007). Lyin' Eyes: Oculomotor Measures of Reading Reveal Deception. Manuscript under review.

Cook, D. T., & Campbell, T. D. (1979). *Quasi-experimentation: design & analysis issues for field settings.* Boston, MA: Houghton Mifflin.

Cooper, G., & Sweller, J. (1987). The effects of schema acquisition and rule automation on mathematical problem-solving transfer. *Journal of Educational Psychology, 79*, 347-362.

Henderson, J. M. (2007). Regarding scenes. *Current Directions in Psychological Science, 16*, 219-222.

Henderson, J. M., & Hollingworth, A. (1999). High-level scene perception. *Annual Review of Psychology, 50*, 243-271.

Just, M. A., & Carpenter, P. A. (1993). The intensity of dimension of thought: Pupillometric indices of sentence processing. *Canadian Journal of Experimental Psychology, 47*, 310-339.

Kaderavek, J. N., Gillam, R. B., & Ukrainetz, T. A.. (2004). School-age children's self-assessment of oral narrative production. *Communication Disorders Quarterly, 26*(1), 37-48.

Kahneman, D. (1973). *Attention and effort.* Englewood Cliffs, NJ: Prentice-Hall.

Kahneman, D., & Beatty, J. (1966). Pupil diameter and load on memory. *Science, 154*, 1583-1585.

Karatekin, C., Couperus, J. W., & Marcus, D. J. (2004). Attention allocation in the dual-task paradigm as measured through behavioral and psychophysiological responses. *Psychophysiology, 41*, 175-185.

Kozma, R. B. (1991). Learning with media. *Review of Educational Research, 61*(2), 179-211.

Kozma, R. B. (1994). Will media influence learning? Reframing the debate. *Educational Technology Research & Development, 42*, 7-19.

Lee. H., Plass, J. L., & Homer, B. D. (2006). Optimizing cognitive load for learning from computer-based science simulations. *Journal of Educational Psychology, 98*(4), 902-913.

Lin, Y., Zhang, W. J., & Watson, L. G. (2003). Using eye movement parameters for evaluating human-machine interface frameworks under normal control operation and fault detection situations. *International Journal of Human-Computer Studies, 59*, 837-873.

Marcus, N., Cooper, M., & Sweller, J. (1996). Understanding instruction. *Journal of Educational Psychology, 88*(1), 49-63.

Mark, M. M. (2000). Realism, validity, and the experimenting society. In L. Bickman (Ed.), *Validity and social experimentation: Donald Campbell's legacy* (Vol. 1, pp. 141-166). Thousand Oaks, CA: Sage.

Mayer, R. E. (2001). *Multimedia learning.* Cambridge, UK: Cambridge University Press.

Mayer, R. E., & Anderson, R. B. (1991). Animations need narrations: An experimental test of a dual-coding hypothesis. *Journal of Educational Psychology, 83*, 484-490.

Mayer, R. E., & Anderson, R. B. (1992). The instructive animation: Helping students build connections between words and pictures in multimedia learning. *Journal of Educational Psychology, 84*, 444-452.

Mayer, R. E., & Moreno, R. (1998). A split-attention effect in multimedia learning: Evidence for dual processing systems in working memory. *Journal of Educational Psychology, 90*, 312-320.

Mayer, R. E., & Moreno, R. (2003). Nine ways to reduce cognitive load in multimedia learning. *Educational Psychologist, 38*(1), 43-52.

Mayer, R. E., Moreno, R., Boire, M., & Vagge, S. (1999). Maximizing constructivist learning from multimedia communications by minimizing cognitive load. *Journal of Educational Psychology, 86*, 389-401.

Mayer, R. E., & Sims, V. K. (1994). For whom is a picture worth a thousand words? Extensions of a dual-coding theory of multimedia learning. *Journal of Educational Psychology, 86*(3), 389-401.

Mayer, R. E., Mautone, P., & Prothero, W. (2002). Pictorial aids for learning by doing in a multimedia geology simulation game. *Journal of Educational Psychology, 94*, 171-185.

Michas, I. C., & Berry, D. C. (2000). Learning a procedural task: Effectiveness of multimedia presentations. *Applied Cognitive Psychology, 14*, 555-575.

Miller, G. A. (1956). The magical number seven plus or minus two: Some limits on our capacity for processing information. *Psychological Review, 63*, 737-743.

Moreno, R., & Duran, R. (2004). Do multiple representations need explanations? The role of verbal guidance and individual differences in multimedia mathematics learning. *Journal of Educational Psychology, 96*, 492-503.

Moreno, R., & Mayer, R, E. (1999). Cognitive principles of multimedia learning: The role of modality and contiguity. *Journal of Educational Psychology, 91*, 358-368.

Moroney, W. F., Biers, D. W., Eggemeier, F. T. & Mitchell, J. A. (1992). *A Comparison of two scoring procedures with the NASA TASK LOAD INDEX in a simulated flight task.* Proceedings of the IEEE NAECON 1992 National Aerospace and Electronics Conference, New York, 2, 734-740.

Owen, E., & Sweller, J. (1985). What do students learn while solving mathematics problems. *Journal of Educational Psychology, 77*, 272-284.

Paas, F. (1992). Training strategies for attaining transfer of problem solving skill in statistics: A cognitive load approach. *Journal of Educational Psychology, 84*, 429-434.

Paas, F., Renkl, A., & Sweller, J. (2003). Cognitive load theory and instructional design: Recent developments. *Educational Psychologist, 38*, 1-4.

Paas, F., Tuovinen, J., Tabbers, H., & Van Gerven, P. W. M. (2003). Cognitive load measurement as a means to advance cognitive load theory. *Educational Psychologist, 38*, 63-71.

Paas, F., & van Merriënboer, J. J. G. (1993). The efficiency of instructional conditions: An approach to combine mental effort and performance measures. *Human Factors, 35,* 737-743.

Paas, F., & van Merriënboer, J. J. G. (1994a). Variability of worked examples and transfer of geometrical problem-solving skills: A cognitive-load approach. *Journal of Educational Psychology, 86,* 122-133.

Paas, F., & van Merriënboer, J. J. G. (1994b). Instructional control of cognitive load in the training of complex cognitive tasks. *Educational Psychology Review, 6,* 51-71.

Paas, F., van Merriënboer J. J. G., & Adam, J. J. (1994). Measurement of cognitive-load in instructional research. *Perceptual and Motor Skills, 79,* 419-430.

Paivio, A.(1986). *Mental representations: A dual coding approach.* New York: Oxford University Press.

Piaget, J. (1952). *The origins of intelligence in children* (Margaret Cook, Trans). New York: International Universities Press.

Pollock, E., Chandler, P., & Sweller, J. (2002). Assimilating complex information. *Learning and Instruction, 12,* 61-86.

Quesada, J., Kintsch, W., & Comez, E. (2005). Complex problem-solving: A field in search of a definition? *Theoretical Issues in Ergonomics Science, 6*(1), 5-33.

Rayner, K. (1998). Eye movements in reading and information processing: 20 years of research. *Psychological Bulletin, 124,* 372-422.

Schmidt-Weigand, F. (2008). The influence of visual and temporal dynamics on split attention: Evidences from eye tracking. In R. Zheng (Ed.), *Cognitive effects of multimedia learning* (Chapter Six). Hershey, PA: IGI Global Publishing.

Shadish, W. R., Cook, T. D., & Campbell, D. T. (2001). *Experimental and quasi-experimental designs for generalized causal inference.* Boston, MA: Houghton Mifflin Company.

Sweller, J. (1988). Cognitive load during problem solving: Effects on learning. *Cognitive Science, 12,* 257-285.

Sweller, J., & Chandler, P. (1991). Evidence for cognitive load theory. *Cognition and Instruction, 8*(4), 351-362.

Sweller, J., & Chandler, P. (1994). Why some material is difficult to learn. *Cognition and Instruction, 12*(3), 185-233.

Tarmizi, R., & Sweller, J. (1988). Guidance during mathematical problem solving. *Journal of Educational Psychology, 80,* 424-436.

Van Gerven, P. W. M., Paas, F., van Merrienboer, J. J. G., & Schmidt, H. G. (2002). Memory load and the cognitive pupillary response. *Psychophysiology, 41,* 167-174.

van Merriënboer, J. J. G., & Krammer, H. P. M. (1987). Instructional strategies and tactics for the design of introductory computer programming courses in high school. *Instructional Science, 16,* 251-285.

van Merriënboer, J. J. G., & Krammer, H. P. M. (1990). The "completion strategy" in programming instruction: Theoretical and empirical support. In S. Dijkstra, B. H. M. van Hout-Wolters, and P. C. van der Sijde (Eds.), *Research on instruction* (pp. 45-61). Englewood Cliffs, NJ: Educational Technology Publications.

van Merriënboer, J. J. G., & Sweller, J. (2005). Cognitive load theory and complex learning: Recent developments and future directions. *Educational Psychology Review, 17*(2), 147-177.

Wickens, C. D. (1984). Processing resources in attention. In R. Parasuraman & D. R. Davies (Eds.), *Varieties of attention* (pp. 63-102). London: Academic.

Wilson, J. (2001). Methodological difficulties of assessing metacognition: A new approach. (ERIC Document Reproduction Service No. ED460143).

Windell, D., & Wieber, E. N. (2007). *Measuring cognitive load in multimedia instruction: A comparison of two instruments*. Paper presented at American Educational Research Association Annual Conference. Chicago, IL.

Wittrock, M. C. (1989). Generative processes of comprehension. *Educational Psychologist, 24,* 345-376.

Xie, B., & Salvendy, G. (2000). Prediction of mental workload in single and multiple tasks environments. *International Journal of Cognitive Ergonomics, 4,* 213-242.

Yaros, R. A., & Cook, A. E. (2007). The use of eye-tracking hardware to assess effects in health news: Is there more than meets the eye? Unpublished manuscript.

Zheng, R., Cook, A. E., & Blaz, J. W. (2008). *Solving complex problems: A convergent approach to cognitive load measurement.* Unpublished manuscript.

Zheng, R., Miller, S., Snelbecker, G., & Cohen, I. (2006). Use of multimedia for problem-solving tasks. *Journal of Technology, Instruction, Cognition and Learning, 3*(1-2), 135-143.

ADDITIONAL READINGS

Kalyuga, S., Chandler, P., & Sweller, J. (1999). Managing split-attention and redundancy in multimedia instruction. *Applied Cognitive Psychology, 92,* 126-136.

Mayer, R. E., & Moreno, R. (1998). A split-attention effect in multimedia learning: Evidence for dual processing systems in working memory. *Journal of Educational Psychology, 90,* 312-320.

Mousavi, S. Y., Low, R., & Sweller, J. (1995). Reducing cognitive load by mixing auditory and visual presentation modes. *Journal of Educational Psychology, 87,* 319-334.

Sweller, J., & Cooper, G. (1985). The use of worked examples as substitute for problem solving in learning algebra. *Cognition and Instruction, 2,* 59-89.

Sweller, J., Mawer, R., & Ward, M. (1983). Development of expertise in mathematics problem solving. *Journal of Experimental Psychology: General, 112,* 639-661.

Van Merriënboer, J. J. G., Kester, L., & Paas, F. (2006). Teaching complex rather than simple tasks: Balancing intrinsic and germane load to enhance transfer of learning. *Applied Cognitive Psychology, 20,* 343-352.

Chapter IV
Manipulating Multimedia Materials

Stephen K. Reed
San Diego State University, USA

ABSTRACT

This chapter discusses a theoretical framework for designing multimedia in which manipulation, rather than perception, of objects plays the predominant role. The framework is based on research by cognitive psychologists and on Engelkamp's (1998) multimodal model of action-based learning. Although the assumptions of Engelkamp's model should be helpful for instructional design, they are not complete enough to include the additional demands of multimedia learning. These additional demands can result in unintended actions, involve sequences of related actions, and require reflection about domain-specific knowledge. Actions can be performed on either physical or virtual manipulatives, but virtual manipulatives exist in idealized environments, support continuous transformations of objects, and allow for dynamic linking to other objects, symbols, and data displays. The use of manipulatives in the Building Blocks and Animation Tutor projects provide illustrations.

INTRODUCTION

In his preface to *The Cambridge Handbook of Multimedia Learning* Mayer (2005) defines multimedia learning as learning from words (spoken or printed text) and pictures (illustrations, photos, maps, graphs, animation, or video). *The Cambridge Handbook* consists of 35 excellent chapters on many aspects of multimedia learning that emphasize the viewing of pictures. However,

the word "manipulation" does not appear in the index. This does not imply that the manipulation of objects is ignored in the chapters but action receives comparatively little discussion compared to perception.

The purpose of this chapter is to provide a theoretical framework for designing multimedia in which manipulation, rather than perception, of objects plays the predominant role. The term "manipulation" in this chapter refers to the movement of an object by a person. The object is typically referred to as a "manipulative" in instruction and although the chapter focuses on virtual manipulatives that exist on a computer screen, it also includes research on physical manipulatives that exist in the environment. Examples include superimposing shapes to estimate relative areas and selecting and combining parts to build an object. Clicking on navigation buttons and changing parameters in simulations are not included as examples of manipulation.

The discussed theoretical framework for using manipulatives is based on research by cognitive psychologists that should be relevant to the design of multimedia instruction. It must be emphasized that the objectives of the laboratory tasks created by cognitive psychologists often differ from the objectives of the instructional software created by instructional designers. However, at this early stage in applying cognitive psychology to instructional design, I decided not to prejudge which findings will be most helpful and so include a variety of results that potentially could influence the effectiveness of manipulatives.

I use Engelkamp's multimodal model of learning to organize these findings and refer to recent research to illustrate assumptions of his model. I next discuss applications of the model to instruction by considering some differences between the free recall of action phrases that forms the empirical basis of his model and the instructional learning of schematic knowledge. Although instruction may use physical manipulatives, there are some advantages to using virtual manipulatives that I discuss in the next section. I conclude by summarizing two multimedia projects before proposing future directions.

BACKGROUND

There are few theoretical frameworks for understanding the role that object manipulation plays in instruction. In my article on cognitive

architectures for multimedia learning (Reed, 2006) only one of the six theories incorporated action. Engelkamp's (1998) multimodal theory was designed to account for the recall of long lists of action phrases such as "saw wood", "play a flute", "blow out a candle", and "water a plant". The recall of action phrases is a very different task than the ones designed for multimedia learning but the central finding of this research is relevant. That finding – labeled the enactment effect – is that acting out phrases results in better recall than simply reading phrases (Engelkamp, 1998).

The multimodal components of Engelkamp's theory are illustrated in Figure 1. They consist of a nonverbal input (visual) and output (enactment) system and a verbal input (hearing, reading) and output (speaking, writing) system. All four of these modality-specific components are connected to a conceptual system. Engelkamp (1998) describes the many assumptions of his multimodal theory in his book *Memory for Actions*. I have listed the major assumptions (and page numbers) in Table 1 (See Appendix) and evaluate them below within the context of recent research on memory and reasoning.

1. Recall of observed actions should differ from that of performed actions because different systems are involved in encoding.

Engelkamp proposes that observations encode visual information about movement but performance encodes motor information, as is illustrated in Figure 1. One application of this idea to instruction is that observed actions can lead to performed actions such as initially observing an instructor's dance steps or tennis serve. Subsequent recall can then be influenced by both visual memories of observing the instructor and motor memories of performing the action.

One implication of this assumption is that a person should be better at recalling verb-action phrases by enacting them than by verbally encoding them or by observing another person

Figure 1. A flow chart of Englekamp's (1998) multimodal memory theory

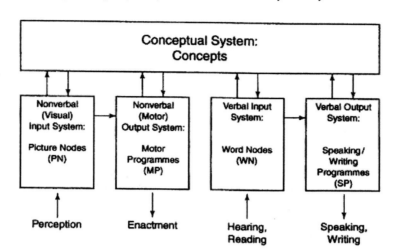

enact them. Steffens (2007) recently reported that although such results are typically found for action phrases, she did not find an advantage of enactment over observation for goal-directed actions. Students were instructed to either "Pack the backpack exactly as I instruct you" (enactment), "Watch closely how I pack the backpack" (observation), or "Listen well while I tell you what you need to pack" (verbal learning). The results of two experiments did not reveal an advantage of enactment over observation although both encoding tasks were superior to verbal learning (in which the objects were also visible). Steffins proposed that enactment creates excellent item-specific encoding that is helpful for recalling unrelated phrases but does not create relational encoding that is helpful for recalling goal-directed actions.

2. Although both sensory and motor processes exert a positive influence on retention, each of these influences should be independent of each other.

This assumption mirrors the assumptions of Paivio's (1986) dual coding theory in which two memory codes (visual and verbal for Paivio) pro-vide two opportunities for recall if the memory codes are at least partially independent. However, this assumption raises questions about when visual and motor codes are independent because the actor can usually observe her actions or because sensory experiences are often the precursors of action. For example, the coordination of perception and action is the key assumption of the theory of event encoding (Hommel, Musseler, Aschersleben, & Prinz, 2001) that integrates perception and action into a common representational framework. Sensory and motor memory codes could therefore be more coordinated than independent and discovering when each occurs is an important theoretical and applied problem.

Research by Schwartz and Black (1999) demonstrates that the extent to which visual and motor codes are coordinated depends on the task. They instructed students to tip a glass of "water" (its level indicated by a mark on the glass) until it would pour from the glass. Students did the task with a blindfold but were allowed to readjust the angle after removing the blindfold. Fifteen of the 16 participants correctly increased the angle after viewing it, indicating that their perceptual and motor codes differed. However, when asked to tilt the glass to a specified angle (such as 2 o'clock), participants did not readjust the angle after viewing it. In this task the motor and visual codes appeared to be coordinated.

3. Planning an action should lead to poorer recall than performing an action because the performance includes planning.

Engelkamp proposes that only part of the motor information should be available when the action has been planned but not yet performed. Evidence from brain-imaging studies now indicates the involvement of motor areas in the brain during the recall of enacted action phrases. In a study by Nilsson activity in the right motor cortex was strongest following encoding by enactment, intermediate following imaginary enactment, and lowest following verbal encoding (Nilsson, Nyberg, Aberg, Persson, & Roland, 2000). The stronger activation of the motor cortex following enactment should help people remember the action.

However, recent research showed that both actual manipulation and imagined manipulation of toy objects greatly increased memory and comprehension of text when compared to a control group that read the text twice without manipulation (Glenberg, Gutierrez, Levin, Japuntich, & Kaschak, 2004). Children in the second grade were initially shown commercially available toys that consisted of either a farm scene (animals, tractor, barn, hay), a house with several rooms and people (mother, father, baby), or a garage scene (gas pumps, tow truck, car wash). The children in the manipulation condition either physically manipulated the toys or imagined manipulating the toys after reading each sentence. The researchers suggested two reasons why manipulation is helpful. The first is that manipulation helps young readers map the words to the objects they represent. The second is that manipulation helps children derive inferences by constructing a mental model of the situation described in the story. Children who manipulated the objects did

better on questions about spatial relations that were not explicitly stated but could be inferred from the story.

4. Responses can be controlled either from the conceptual system or directly from the particular input system without going through the conceptual system.

This assumption reminds us that manipulation is not necessarily meaningful for students. In commenting on the mixed results of research that has used manipulatives, Thompson (1994) proposed that instructors must continually ask what they want their students to understand rather than what they want their students to do. Although the material is concrete, the concepts behind the manipulations may not be obvious because of students' ability to create multiple interpretations of actions.

Manipulation with limited understanding was observed by Moyer (2002) when she recorded how 10 teachers used manipulatives. The teachers had attended a 2-week summer institute on the use of a Middle Grades Mathematics Kit that included base-10 blocks, color tiles, snap cubes, pattern blocks, fractions bars and tangrams. They made subtle distinctions between real math that used rules, procedures, and paper-and-pencil tasks and fun math that used the manipulatives. Unfortunately, the fun math typically was done at the end of the period or the end of the week and was not well integrated with the "real" math.

5. Encoding of relational information occurs only in the conceptual system through a process of spreading activation.

The basis for this assumption is the excellent item-specific, rather than relational, encoding produced by enactment (Engelkamp & Seiler, 2003). However, research by Koriat and Pearlman-Avnion's (2003) challenges this assumption by showing that the free recall of action phrases can be clustered by either the similarity of movements or the similarity of meaning. A person who recalled the phrase "wax the car" might next recall "spread ointment on a wound" based on similar motor movements. Evidence for the creation of conceptual relations would include recalling together phrases that had similar meanings. A person who recalled the phrase "wax the car" might next recall "pour oil into the engine" because both phrases refer to cars.

Undergraduates at the University of Haifa were required to either enact each phrase (enactment instruction) or simply say the phrase aloud (verbal instruction). The enactment instructions required students to imagine the object and pantomime the described action as if the object were present. Students in the enactment condition primarily recalled together phrases based on similar movements, whereas students in the verbal condition primarily recalled together phrases based on similar meanings. The authors concluded that the different conditions influence the relative salience of different types of memory organization and their relative contributions to recall. However, as found in many other experiments, the enactment of the phrases resulted in better recall than simply reading aloud the phrases.

6. Performing an action makes it difficult to form new associations in the conceptual system because performing an action forces concentration on information relevant to the action.

This assumption provides a word of caution for instructional designers. Although there is extensive evidence for the enactment effect, too much focus on actions could distract from learning new information if attention is shifted away from concepts. Research by Shockley and Turvey (2006) demonstrated that performing an action can also reduce retrieval of old associations. Their participants were given 30 seconds to retrieve instances from a semantic category such as four-legged animals. Swinging hand-held pendulums

reduced the number of successful retrievals.

However, action can also facilitate reasoning as shown by the finding that gesturing *reduced* the cognitive demands on working memory when students explained mathematical solutions (Wagner, Nusbaum, & Goldin-Meadow, 2004). This is more likely to occur when the gestures and verbal explanation are compatible. But the mismatch between information conveyed by gesture and by speech provided useful diagnostic information, such as indicating when students were considering different solution options as they reasoned about problems.

APPLICATION TO INSTRUCTION

The assumptions of Engelkamp's multimodal theory form a theoretical foundation for thinking about the design of multimedia instruction. The enactment effect – the robust finding that acting out action phrases results in better recall than reading phrases – forms the basis for the theory and for the inclusion of manipulatives in instruction.

However, it is important to keep in mind that Engelkamp's theoretical assumptions were formulated from research on the free recall of action phrases. Instructional use of multimedia, in contrast, typically requires the learning of integrated schematic knowledge to produce a deep understanding of both procedures and concepts (Baroody, Feil, & Johnson, 2007). One consequence of using manipulatives to teach schematic knowledge is that students can perform actions that differ from the ones intended by the instructional designer. Another difference between the free-recall and instructional paradigms is that schematic knowledge usually requires the integrated learning of action sequences rather than the recall of independent actions. A third difference is that acquisition of schematic structures requires reflecting on actions rather than simply recalling them. A fourth difference is that instruction involves learning domain-specific knowledge rather than forming associations among words.

Unintended actions. One challenge for using manipulatives in instruction is that students' actions can differ from normative ones. A formative evaluation of one of the modules in the Animation Tutor software (Reed, 2005) illustrates this challenge. The design of the Dimensional Thinking module attempts to correct students' tendency to inappropriately apply proportional reasoning to area and volume For instance, many students believe that doubling the diameter of a circle will double its area and doubling the diameter of a sphere will double its volume. Attempts to correct such misconceptions with static diagrams have been largely unsuccessful (De Bock, Verschaffel, & Janssens, 2002). Brian Greer, Bob Hoffman, and I therefore designed the Dimensional Thinking module so students can virtually manipulate diagrams of circles, squares, cubes, and irregular figures to learn when proportional reasoning does and does not apply.

The module begins with a sign in the window of a pizza parlor that shows the prices of pizzas with different diameters. A 12-inch pizza sells for $6.99 and a 20-inch pizza sells for $12.99. It then raises the following question of which is the better value. A proportional reasoning solution of dividing price by diameter would reveal that the smaller pizza sells for $0.58 per inch and the larger pizza sells for $0.65 per inch. Students who use this approach should falsely conclude that the smaller pizza is a better value.

Kien Lim did a formative evaluation of the Dimensional Thinking module by assigning it to 19 freshmen in his science laboratory class at the University of Texas, El Paso. Eleven of the students initially decided that the 12-inch pizza was the better value. Later in the module students were asked to compare the relative sizes of the two pizzas by determining how many smaller pizzas would cover the area of the larger pizza (see Figure 2). They were again asked which was

the better buy. Only three of the eleven students switched from the 12- to the 20-inch pizza and one student switched from the 20- to the 12-inch pizza. The interesting aspect of the results is that those students who still claimed the 12-inch pizza was the better buy had a mean estimate of 2.26 small pizzas to cover the large one. Those students who claimed the 20-inch pizza was the better buy estimated that it would take 3.35 small pizzas to cover the large one. These two means differed significantly and indicate that although students' answers were influenced by their manipulations, underestimation of relative area was correlated with incorrect decisions.

The formative evaluation revealed that this aspect of the instruction needs to include more guidance about estimating relative area and using relative area to make best-buy decisions. The larger pizza would still be the better buy even if it were only 2.26 times as large because it costs only 1.86 times as much. Allowing students to calculate exact proportions rather than make estimates may help them make better decisions.

Action sequences. Making comparisons by dragging smaller circles over a larger circle is more typical of the use of object manipulation in instruction than is recalling a list of action phrases. This raises a different set of challenges for instructional researchers such as determining whether students can integrate action sequences and avoid interference from performing similar actions. This challenge is particularly timely because of Steffins' (2007) recent finding that enactment is not superior to observation for recalling goal-directed actions such as packing a backpack.

Edwards' (1991) research on middle-school children's learning transformation geometry is a good example of learning sequences of actions. The children used a set of simple Logo commands to slide, rotate, pivot, reflect, flip, and scale geometric forms. After gaining experience with each transformation, they played a match game the encouraged them to supimpose two congruent shapes by using as few transformations as possible.

A study that Jeffrey Johnsen and I performed some years ago illustrates the challenge that students face in learning sequences of actions (Reed & Johnsen, 1977). The task required solving the missionaries and cannibals problem by moving tokens across a "river". The intentional group was told to try to remember their moves because they would have to solve the same problem a second time. The incidental learning group did not know they would have to solve the problem twice. Students in the intentional group improved more on their second attempt than students in the incidental group and two subsequent experiments evaluated what these students had learned.

There was no significant difference between the two groups in their ability to recall what move they made at the different problem states or select the best move at a problem state. Problem solvers were not very accurate in remembering the details, perhaps because of the similarity of the problem states that differed only in the number of missionaries and cannibals on each side of the river. Instead, students in the intentional group were better at learning more generic strategies such as moving cannibals across the river during the first third of the sequence and missionaries across the river during the second third of the sequence. Learning action sequences needs to be part of a theoretical framework for the use of manipulatives.

Reflection. The intentional learners may have learned more about effective strategies because they reflected on their actions rather than simply solved the problem. Both action and reflection are important components of Piaget's theory. Action is important because knowledge for Piaget is fundamentally *operative*; it is knowledge of what to do with something under certain possible conditions. Piaget (1977) subsequently emphasized the importance of reflection in his book *Recherches sur l'abstraction réfléchissante*. According to Robert Campbell (2001), who translated the book into English as *Studies in Reflecting Abstraction,* reflection became an important part of Piaget's theory rather late in his prolific writing career.

Campbell illustrates Piaget's use of this concept through an example in which Piaget uses poker chips to teach multiplication as repeated addition. For instance, children are asked to place

Figure 2. A screen design that allows for dragging small circles over a large circle

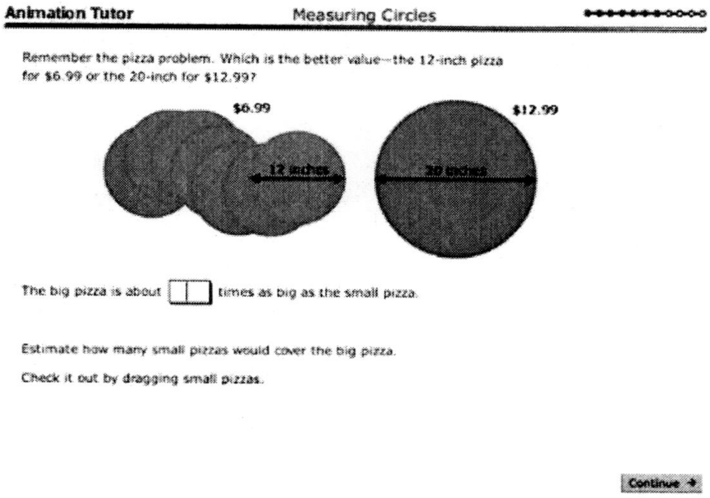

three chips in a row, followed by placing another three chips in the same row. According to Piaget, children have to perform two types of abstraction to think about multiplication as repeated addition ($2 \times 3 = 3 + 3$). The first is to recognize how many chips they are adding each time. The second is to keep track of the number of times that they add the same amount. This requires the use of *reflecting abstraction* to abstract a property of their actions. Reflecting abstraction is required to create new knowledge such as recognizing that adding 2 chips three times produces the same number of chips as adding 3 chips two times ($3 \times 2 = 2 \times 3$). Learning from manipulatives requires students to not only remember their actions, but to reflect on the consequences of their actions.

Domain-specific knowledge. Reflecting on actions, however, will not be sufficient if students lack domain-specific knowledge to guide their reflections. A study that compared learning domain-specific schemas with learning general strategies found that the more specific (schema-based) instruction was superior to general strategy instruction (Jitendra et al., 2007). The schema-based instruction taught third-grade children to solve addition and subtraction word problems by learning problem types such as change, group, and compare (Marshall, 1995). The general-strategy instruction taught a four-step procedure to read and understand the problem, plan to solve the problem, solve the problem, and check the solution. The plan step included more specific advice such as using manipulatives (counters) to act out the information in the problem. The schema-based instruction was more effective in improving students' ability to solve the word problems. However, both strategies were equally effective in improving computational skills, which the investigators attributed to the use of diagrams in the schema-based instruction and the use of manipulatives in the general-strategy instruction.

ADVANTAGES OF MANIPULATIVE SOFTWARE

Piaget and many others have studied the instructional consequences of manipulatives by using physical objects such as poker chips. However, there may be some unique advantages to using virtual manipulatives in computer-based instruction. Three advantages are that computers make it easier to create idealized environments, dynamically link materials, and produce continuous transformations of objects.

Idealized environments. One advantage of manipulating virtual objects over real objects is that virtual objects exist in idealized environments. For example, there are many advantages of using computer-based laboratory materials including portability, safety, cost-efficiency, and flexible, rapid, and dynamic data displays. As distance learning becomes more wide spread, there will be a greater need for the virtual manipulation of objects.

An example is the use of virtual objects to teach children how to design scientific experiments by isolating and testing one variable at a time (Triona & Klahr, 2003). The task required 4th- and 5th-grade students to evaluate how variables such as the length, width, wire size, and weight influence the stretching of a spring. After selecting pairs of springs and weights from a computer display, children saw a video of how far the springs stretched.

Triona and Klahr compared a group of children who trained on the instructional software with a group of children who trained with real springs and weights. Their results showed that children who trained with the virtual materials were as capable in correctly designing experiments as children who trained with the physical materials. Following training, both groups were asked to design experiments to evaluate the effects of four variables on the time it would take a ball to roll down a ramp. Only physical materials were used on this transfer task. Again, the group who had trained on virtual springs did as well as the group who had trained on real springs in designing experiments with real ramps, even though they had not interacted with physical materials during the training.

Another study compared the effectiveness of constructing and evaluating toy cars in either a real or virtual environment (Klahr, Triona, & Williams, 2007). Seventh and eighth-grade students assembled and tested the cars in order to design a car that would travel the farthest. Computer-based virtual design was again equally effective and it avoided some of the problems encountered when assembling real cars. These included real cars that did not travel straight, had wheels that were too tight, and required a long corridor for testing. The investigators concluded that their findings support the effectiveness of manipulating virtual objects for learning designing experiments. This does not imply that teachers should abandon hands-on science materials, but teachers should not assume that virtual materials are less effective.

Dynamic linking. Another potential advantage of multimedia learning environments is that actions on screen-based objects can be dynamically linked to more abstract information to establish a direct mapping between actions and mathematical structures. As discussed by Kaput (1994), a central problem of mathematics education is to create functional connections between the world of experience and the formal systems of mathematics. Instructional animations developed by Kaput allow students to observe both how changing the speed of an object is reflected in a graph and how physically manipulating the shape of the graph changes the speed of an object. Bowers and Doerr (2001) report findings from a qualitative study, using Kaput's Simcalc software, that the dynamic linking of two graphs helped prospective teachers better understand the relations among distance, rate, and time. The students could manipulate the relations in one graph to observe how the relations would change in a corresponding graph.

In contrast, a quantitative study by Thompson (1992; see also Thompson, 1994) failed to find that the dynamic linking of base-ten blocks with decimal numbers improved performance in a pretest-posttest design. However, interviews revealed that the children who used the Blocks Microworld repeatedly made references to actions on symbols as referring to actions on virtual blocks because of the dynamic linking of symbols and blocks. This contrasts with observations of other children whose operations on symbols and wooden blocks were typically thought of as separate activities.

One of the limitations in using manipulatives is that they may be introduced too late. Resnick and Omanson (1987) expressed disappointment in how seldom their students referred to Dienes blocks in a subtraction task, which they attributed to the students' automated use of symbols. Thompson proposed that students in his blocks group assimilated instruction on decimals into previously learned operations on whole numbers. He argued that "if students memorize a procedure meaninglessly, it is extremely difficult to get them to change it, even with extended, meaningful remediation" (Thompson, 1992, p. 144).

Continuous variation. The manipulation of blocks is typical of tasks using manipulatives in which students perform actions on discrete objects. However, an advantage of virtual manipulatives is that it is easier to perform actions that produce continuous variation of variables. Figure 3 shows a screen design that Bob Hoffman and I recently created to teach students about variables in algebra word problems. Students are instructed to raise and lower the height of the second bar to vary both the balance and owed interest on the Visa card. Varying this bar changes the height and amount of the Total Interest bar. It also changes values in the equation.

The purpose of this variation and dynamic linking to other objects and numbers is to demonstrate that variables can take on different values but only a single value satisfies the constraint that the total interest is $165. The use of symbols (typi-

Figure 3. A screen design that allows for the continuous variation of a variable

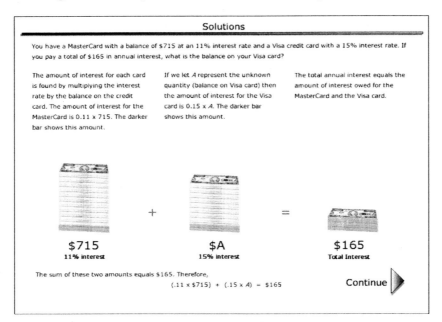

cally letters) to represent unknown quantities in algebra word problems is initially a challenge for students because letters have many other uses in mathematics classes besides the representation of unknown values (Philipp, 1992). The continuous variation of objects that are dynamically linked to variables in equations will hopefully make the concept of a variable less abstract for students.

ILLUSTRATIVE PROJECTS

The *Building Blocks* project, which is in the final stages of evaluation, provides an example of the effectiveness of instruction designed around the virtual manipulation of objects. It is an exemplary model of multimedia design and evaluation. The *Animation Tutor* project is in the initial stages of evaluation but illustrates the application of some of the ideas in this chapter to current research.

The Building Blocks project. The *Building Blocks* curriculum (Clements & Sarama, 2007) demonstrates the effectiveness of manipulatives. It is an NSF-funded curriculum development project

that has created technology-enhanced mathematics materials for children in pre-kindergarten through second grade. The materials are designed to build on children's intuitive knowledge to help them learn both spatial-geometric concepts and numeric-quantitative concepts. The project's title reflects both its literal and metaphorical goals. Building blocks are physical and virtual manipulatives that help children form cognitive building blocks by creating, copying, and combining discrete objects, numbers, and shapes to represent mathematical ideas.

The numeric concepts include verbal and object counting; number recognition, comparison, sequencing, and composition; adding, subtracting, and place value. Activities such as placing toppings on pizza support acquisition of these concepts. Geometric concepts include shape identification, composition, and construction; turns, measurement, and patterning. Combining different shapes to make pictures supports these concepts. Although both physical and virtual manipulatives are part of the curriculum, the unique advantages of software include linking virtual manipulatives to numbers, providing feedback, and guiding children along learning trajectories by moving backward or forward depending on performance.

A summative evaluation of the *Building Blocks* curriculum demonstrated its effectiveness in improving mathematical skills (Clements & Sarama, 2007). The experimental teachers inserted the *Building Blocks* activities at appropriate points during the day while the comparison teachers used the school's typical mathematics activities that included most of the same concepts covered in the experimental curriculum. The investigators measured the performance of all children at the beginning and end of the school year. Results showed that the experimental group scores increased significantly more than the comparison group scores for both number (effect size = .85) and geometric (effect size = 1.47) concepts.

These large effect sizes are a result of the extensive research (both within and outside of the project) of how children acquire numerical and geometric concepts. The summative evaluation provides empirical support for the effectiveness of computer software that uses manipulatives to improve mathematical reasoning. The *Building Blocks* project should serve as a role model for the design of future research projects.

The Animation Tutor project. The *Animation Tutor* project is another NSF-funded curriculum development project that uses computer graphics to support mathematical reasoning. It consists of eight modules that apply high-school level mathematics to topics such as population growth, chemical kinetics, safe driving distances, task completion times, average speed, and personal finance (Reed & Hoffman, in press).

Bob Hoffman, Albert Corbett, and I are conducting a study to determine whether the kinds of graphics created for the Animation Tutor will help prepare students for solving problems on the Algebra Cognitive Tutor developed at Carnegie Mellon University. The Algebra Cognitive Tutor provides effective feedback to help students learn procedures for solving algebra problems (Ritter, Anderson, Koedinger, & Corbett, 2007). Our goal is to determine whether object manipulation will reduce the amount of required tutoring by creating more effective worked examples.

High school students who have been using the Algebra Cognitive Tutor will receive one of three different types of worked examples. One example is a static graphics display that can not be manipulated, a second example is a dynamic graphics display that can be manipulated, and a third example is a verbal control that organizes quantities in a table rather than in a bar graph. Figure 3 shows the static graphics display for one of the algebra word problems. As discussed previously, the dynamic graphics display will enable to students to raise and lower the unknown quantity to see how it changes total interest in the graphics display and in the equation.

Before receiving instruction on algebra problems students will be instructed on arithmetic word problems, such as the following:

You have a MasterCard with a balance of $532 at a 21% interest rate. You also have a Visa credit card with a balance of $841 at a 16% interest rate. How much money are you paying in total annual interest?

Students in the dynamics graphics group will construct the bar representing total interest from the two bars on the left side of the equation. Manipulation requires that they click on the amount of interest in the first bar and drag a copy to the right side of the equation. Clicking will create a red border around the owed interest in the first bar and around the dragged copy. It will also highlight in red that part of the equation (0.21 x $532) that mathematically represents this amount. Students will then click on the owed interest in the second bar to drag and then stack this amount on top of the first dragged copy. Blue borders and corresponding numbers in the equation (0.16 x $841) will be used to dynamically link these quantities within the graphics and to the equation.

Each worked example will be followed by an equivalent test problem on the Algebra Cognitive Tutor in which students construct a table to represent quantities and then construct an equation for solving the problem. The Algebra Cognitive Tutor provides constructive feedback that will enable us to determine whether the three different kinds of worked examples influence the amount and type of required feedback. We will also examine whether there are performance differences during a delayed paper-and pencil test that includes all the problems.

Our planned research takes advantage of the strengths of virtual manipulatives. The continuous variation of bar graphs for the algebra problems and the dynamic linking of actions on objects to equations will hopefully encourage students to relate symbols to quantities. However, to be effective, virtual manipulation will need scaffolding to provide constructive feedback on unintended actions, coordinate action sequences, encourage reflection, and provide domain-specific knowledge. Providing such support should enable us to fulfill the potential of manipulating multimedia materials.

CONCLUSION

The manipulation of multimedia materials offers a promising method of instruction. However, we still lack a theoretical framework for understanding when and how object manipulation facilitates learning. Engelkamp's multimodal model provides a beginning of such a framework. This chapter examines its theoretical assumptions listed in Table 1 and discusses their application to multimedia learning. The first three assumptions that performing actions creates additional memory codes provide a potential explanation for instructional improvement. However, the subsequent three assumptions that performing actions can bypass the conceptual system provide

a potential explanation for the ineffectiveness of actions.

Although Engelkamp's assumptions are relevant to instructional design, they are not complete enough to include the additional demands of multimedia learning. These demands can result in unintended actions, involve sequences of related actions, and require reflection about domain-specific knowledge for successful learning. Actions can be performed on either physical or virtual manipulatives but virtual manipulatives have some advantages. They exist in idealized environments, support continuous transformations of objects, and allow for dynamic linking to other objects, symbols, and data displays. The *Building Blocks* and *Animation Tutor* programs illustrate the use of virtual manipulatives in instruction.

FUTURE RESEARCH DIRECTIONS

Much more research and development are required to fulfill the promise of multimedia materials. One issue concerns how to optimally blend directed and discovery-based instruction. Some theorists have argued that students need directed instruction based on worked examples (Kirschner, Sweller, & Clark, 2006). Other theorists have argued that students need the opportunity for carefully-scaffolded inquiry learning (Hmelo-Silver, Duncan, & Chinn, 2007). The appropriate blend of directed and inquiry learning needs to be based on formative evaluations. For example, our initial formative evaluations of the best-buy pizza problem discussed previously revealed that more guidance is required to improve decisions.

Another research issue is to explore how to best coordinate the use of virtual and physical manipulatives. As argued in this chapter, virtual manipulatives have advantages over physical manipulatives but students may also require experience with real manipulatives. Virtual reality environments are now enabling cognitive scientists to study situations that combine physical manipulatives with multimedia-produced environments. University of Iowa researchers are studying children's ability to bike across busy virtual intersections by having them peddle a stationary bike that is partially surrounded by large multimedia screens (Plumert, Kearney, & Cremer, 2007). University of Massachusetts researchers are studying young drivers' ability to attend to relevant information in virtual environments by driving a stationary car in those environments (Pollatsek, Fisher, & Pradhan, 2006). Such virtual reality environments will provide new opportunities for research and training.

Another future challenge is to place effective multimedia instruction in the schools. I argue in my book *Thinking Visually* (Reed, in press) that multimedia programs that could support spatial reasoning in mathematics and science education will not be in widespread use by the year 2020. My pessimistic prediction is based on the tremendous hurdles required to scale up successful design for widespread use in schools (Goldman, 2005). It also is based on the paucity of research-proven, multimedia programs in mathematics and science education that could be scaled up. I hope my prediction will contribute to creating a stronger commitment for creating and distributing instructional multimedia that has the potential to make dramatic improvements in learning.

ACKNOWLEDGMENT

I would like to thank Kirsten Butcher for her helpful comments on a draft of this chapter. This research was supported by NSF under Award Number SBE-0354420 to Carnegie Mellon University. Any opinions, findings, conclusions or recommendations expressed herein are those of the author(s) and do not necessarily reflect the views of the National Science Foundation or Carnegie Mellon University.

REFERENCES

Baroody, A. J., Feil, Y., & Johnson, A. R. (2007). An alternative reconceptualization of procedural and conceptual knowledge. *Journal for Research in Mathematics Education, 38*, 115-131.

Bowers, J. S., & Doerr, H. M. (2001). An analysis of prospective teachers' dual roles in understanding the mathematics of change: Eliciting growth with technology. *Journal of Mathematics Teacher Education, 4*, 115-137.

Campbell, R. L. (Ed.). (2001). *Studies in reflecting abstraction.* Hove, England: Psychology Press.

Clements, D. H., & Sarama, J. (2007). Effects of a preschool mathematics curriculum: Summative research on the Building Blocks project. *Journal for Research in Mathematics Education, 38*, 136-163.

De Bock, D., Verschaffel, L., & Janssens, D. (2002). The effects of different problem presentations and formulations on the illusion of linearity in secondary school students. *Mathematical Thinking and Learning, 4*, 65-89.

Edwards, L. D. (1991). Children's learning in a computer microworld for transformation geometry. *Journal for Research in Mathematics Education, 22*, 122-137.

Engelkamp, J. (1998). *Memory for actions.* Hove, England: Psychology Press.

Engelkamp, J., & Seiler, K. H. (2003). Gains and losses in action memory. *The Quarterly Journal of Experimental Psychology, 56A*, 829-848.

Glenberg, A. M., Gutierrez, T., Levin, J. R., Japuntich, S., & Kaschak, M. P. (2004). Activity and imagined activity can enhance young children's reading comprehension. *Journal of Educational Psychology, 96*, 424-436.

Goldman, S. R. (2005). Designing for scalable educational improvement. In C. Dede, J. P.

Honan & L. C. Peters (Eds.), *Scaling up success: Lessons learned from technology-based educational improvement* (pp. 67-96). San Francisco: Jossey-Bass.

Hmelo-Silver, C. E., Duncan, R. V., & Chinn, C. A. (2007). Scaffolding and achievement in problem-based and inquiry learning: A response to Kirschner, Sweller, and Clark (2006). *Educational Psychologist, 42*, 99-107.

Hommel, B., Musseler, J., Aschersleben, G., & Prinz, W. (2001). The theory of event coding (TEC): A framework for perception and action planning. *Behavioral & Brain Sciences, 24*, 849-937.

Jitendra, A. K., Griffin, C. C., Haria, P., Leh, J., Adams, A., & Kaduvettoor, A. (2007). A comparison of single and multiple strategy instruction on third-grade students' mathematical problem solving. *Journal for Research in Mathematics Education, 99*(1), 115-127.

Kaput, J. J. (1994). The representational roles of technology in connecting mathematics with authentic experience. In R. Bieler, R. W. Scholz, R. Strasser & B. Winkelman (Eds.), *Mathematics didactics as a scientific discipline* (pp. 379-397). Dordecht, The Netherlands: Kluwer.

Kirschner, P. A., Sweller, J., & Clark, R. C. (2006). Why minimal guidance during instruction does not work: An analysis of the failure of constructivist, discovery, problem-based, experiential, and inquiry-based tearching. *Educational Psychologist, 41*, 75-86.

Klahr, D., Triona, L. M., & Williams, C. (2007). Hands on what? The relative effectiveness of physical vs. virtual materials in an engineering design project by middle school children. *Journal of Research in Science Teaching, 44*, 183-203.

Koriat, A., & Pearlman-Avnion, S. (2003). Memory organization of action events and its relationship to memory performance. *Journal of Experimental Psychology: General, 132*, 435-454.

Marshall, S. P. (1995). *Schemas in problem solving*. New York: Cambridge University Press.

Mayer, R. E. (Ed.). (2005). *The Cambridge Handbook of Multimedia Learning*. New York: Cambridge University Press.

Moyer, P. S. (2002). Are we having fun yet? How teachers use manipulatives to teach mathematics. *Educational Studies in Mathematics, 47*, 175-197.

Nilsson, L.-G., Nyberg, L., T., K., Aberg, C., Persson, J., & Roland, P. E. (2000). Activity in motor areas while remembering action events. *Neuroreport, 11*, 2199-2201.

Paivio, A. (1986). *Mental representations: A dual coding approach*. New York: Oxford University Press.

Philipp, R. A. (1992). The many uses of algebraic variables. In B. Moses (Ed.), *Algebraic thinking, Grades K-12: Readings from NCTM's School-based journals and other publications* (pp. 157-162). Reston, VA: National Council of Teachers of Mathematics.

Piaget, J. (1977). *Recherches sur l'abstraction réfléchissante*. Paris: Presses Universitaires de France.

Plumert, J. M., Kearney, J. K., & Cremer, J. F. (2007). Children's road crossing: A window into perceptual-motor development. *Current Directions in Psychological Science, 16*, 255-263.

Pollatsek, A., Fisher, D. L., & Pradhan, A. (2006). Identifying and remedying failures of selective attention in younger drivers. *Current Directions in Psychological Science, 15*, 255-259.

Reed, S. K. (2005). From research to practice and back: The Animation Tutor project. *Educational Psychology Review, 17*, 55-82.

Reed, S. K. (2006). Cognitive architectures for multimedia learning. *Educational Psychologist, 41*, 87-98.

Reed, S. K. (in press). *Thinking Visually*. New York: Taylor & Francis.

Reed, S. K., & Hoffman, B. (in press). Animation Tutor (Version 1.0) [computer software]. New York: Taylor & Francis.

Reed, S. K., & Johnsen, J. A. (1977). Memory for problem solutions. In G. H. Bower (Ed.), *The psychology of learning and motivation, 11* 161-201. New York: Academic Press.

Resnick, L., & Omanson, S. (1987). Learning to understand arithmetic. In R. Glaser (Ed.), *Advances in instructional psychology* (41-95). Mahwah, NJ: LEA.

Ritter, S., Anderson, J. R., Koedinger, K. R., & Corbett, A. (2007). Cognitive tutor: Applied research in mathematics education. *Psychonomic Bulletin & Review, 14,* 249-255.

Schwartz, D. L., & Black, T. (1999). Inferences through imagined actions: Knowing by simulated doing. *Journal of Experimental Psychology: Learning, Memory and Cognition, 25,* 116-136.

Shockley, K., & Turvey, M. T. (2006). Dual-task influences on retrieval from semantic memory and coordination dynamcs. *Psychonomic Bulletin & Review, 13,* 985-990.

Steffens, M. C. (2007). Memory for goal-directed sequences of actions: Is doing better than seeing? *Psychonomic Bulletin & Review, 14,* 1194-1198.

Thompson, P. W. (1992). Notations, conventions, and constraints: Contributions to effective use of concrete materials in elementary mathematics. *Journal for Research in Mathematics Education, 23,* 123-147.

Thompson, P. W. (1994). Concrete materials and teaching for mathematical understanding. *Arithmetic Teacher, 40,* 556-558.

Triona, L. M., & Klahr, D. (2003). Point and click or grab and heft: Comparing the influence of physical and virtual instructional materials on elementary school students' ability to design experiments. *Cognition and Instruction, 21,* 149-173.

Wagner, S. M., Nusbaum, H., & Goldin-Meadow, S. (2004). Probing the mental representation of gesture: Is handwaving spatial? *Journal of Memory and Language, 50,* 395-407.

ADDITIONAL READING

Allen, B. S., Otto, R. G., & Hoffman, B. (2004). Media as lived environments: The ecological psychology of educational technology. In D. H. Jonassen (Ed.), *Handbook of research on educational communications and technology* (second ed., pp. 215-241). Mahwah, NJ: Erlbaum.

Barsalou, L., Simmons, W. K., Barbey, A. K., & Wilson, C. D. (2003). Grounding conceptual knowledge in modality-specific systems. *TRENDS in Cognitive Sciences, 7,* 84-91.

Feyereisen, P. (2006). Further investigation of the mnemonic effect of gestures: Their meaning matters. *European Journal of Cognitive Psychology, 18,* 185-205.

Gibbs, R. W. (2006). *Embodiment and cognitive science*. New York: Cambridge University Press.

Glenberg, A. M., & Kaschak, M. P. (2002). Grounding language in action. *Psychonomic Bulletin & Review, 9,* 558-565.

Goldin-Meadow, S., & Wagner, S. M. (2005). How our hands help us learn. *TRENDS in Cognitive Sciences, 9,* 234-241.

Linn, M. C., Lee, H., Tinker, R., Husic, F., & Chiu, J. L. (2006). Teaching and assessing knowledge integration in science. *Science, 313,* 1049-1050.

Moreno, R., & Mayer, R. E. (2007). Interactive multimodal learning environments. *Educational Psychology Review, 19,* 309-326.

Nemirovsky, R., Tierney, C., & Wright, T. (1998). Body motion and graphing. *Cognition and Instruction, 16*, 119-172.

Noice, H., & Noice, T. (2006). What studies of actors and acting can tell us about memory and cognitive functioning. *Current Directions in Psychological Science, 15*, 14-18.

Reed, S. K. (2006). Does unit analysis help students construct equations? *Cognition and Instruction, 24*, 341-366.

Richland, L. E., Zur, O., & Holyoak, K. J. (2007). Cognitive supports for analogies in the mathematics classroom. *Science, 316*, 1128-1129.

Rieber, L. P. (2003). Microworlds. In D. Jonassen (Ed.), *Handbook of research on educational communications and technology* (2nd ed., pp. 583-603). Mahwah, NJ: Erlbaum.

Rubin, D. C. (2007). The basic-systems model of episodic memory. *Perspectives on Psychological Science, 1*, 277-311.

Schwarz, C. V., & White, B. Y. (2005). Metamodeling knowledge: Developing students' understanding of scientific modeling. *Cognition and Instruction, 23*, 165-205.

Staley, D. J. (2003). *Computers, visualization, and history: How new technology will transform our understanding of the past.* Armonk, NY: M. E. Sharpe.

Steffens, M. C., Buchner, A., & Wender, K. F. (2003). Quite ordinary retrieval cues may determine free recall of actions. *Journal of Memory and Language, 48*, 399-415.

Wilson, M. (2002). Six views of embodied cognition. *Psychonomic Bulletin & Review, 9*, 625-636.

Young, M. (2004). An ecological psychology of instructional design: Learning and thinking by perceiving-acting systems. In D. H. Jonassen (Ed.), *Handbook of research on educational communications and technology* (second ed., pp. 169-177). Mahwah, NJ: Erlbaum.

APPENDIX

Major Assumptions of Engelkamp's (1998) Multimodal Theory

1. Recall of observed actions should differ from that of performed actions because different systems are involved in encoding (p. 45). Observations encode visual information about movement but performance encodes motor information (p. 37).
2. Although both sensory and motor processes exert a positive influence on retention, each of these influences should be independent of each other (p. 38).
3. Planning an action should lead to poorer recall than performing an action because the performance includes planning (p. 46). Only part of the motor information should be available when the action has been planned but not yet performed (p. 37).
4. Responses can be controlled either from the conceptual system or directly from the particular input system without going through the conceptual system (p. 35).
5. Encoding of relational information occurs only in the conceptual system through a process of spreading activation (p. 40).
6. Performing an action makes it difficult to form new associations in the conceptual system because performing an action forces concentration on information relevant to the action (p. 41).

Chapter V
Theoretical and Instructional Aspects of Learning with Visualizations

Katharina Scheiter
University of Tuebingen, Germany

Eric Wiebe
North Carolina State University, USA

Jana Holsanova
Lund University, Sweden

ABSTRACT

Multimedia environments consist of verbal and visual representations that, if appropriately processed, allow for the construction of an integrated mental model of the content. Whereas much is known on how students learn from verbal representations, there are fewer insights regarding the processing of visual information, alone or in conjunction with text. This chapter uses a semiotics approach to provide a definition of visualizations as a specific form of external representation, and then discusses the differences between verbal and visual representations in how they represent information. Finally, it discusses how meaning is achieved when learning with them. The next section discusses basic perceptual and cognitive processes relevant to learning with visualizations. This background is used to specify the instructional functions that visualizations have either as self-contained instructional messages or as text adjuncts. Moreover, the role of individual differences in processing visualizations is highlighted. The chapter ends with methodological suggestions concerning the important role of interdisciplinary research and assessment methods in this area.

INTRODUCTION

Visualizations constitute a key component in multimedia-based instruction, which can be defined as learning from text and pictures (e.g., Mayer, 2005). Despite the fact that visualizations are used more and more frequently in informal and formal educational settings, not much is understood about their semiotic properties, how humans process them, and how they can be best designed to learn from. In educational research, visualizations are often treated in a uniform manner, despite the fact that the visualizations might serve vastly different functions depending on the audience and goals. Just as bad, visualizations are treated as functionally equivalent to text. As a consequence, reviews on learning with visualizations are equivocal, with studies showing widely varying effects (negative to positive) on learning. In the current chapter, we will try to provide a more differentiated view by first reviewing the literature from different disciplinary perspectives (education, semiotics, perception, and cognition) to characterize different types of visualizations, to distinguish them from verbal representations, and to describe how information is derived from them. This approach will attempt to provide a unique approach to addressing the question of when and why visualizations are effective for learning. After some summarizing remarks, directions for future research will be outlined in the final section of this chapter. It is important to note, however, that we will not review the more mainstream literature on the effectiveness of learning with visualizations, as comprehensive reviews can be found elsewhere (e.g., Anglin, Vaez, & Cunningham, 2004; Rieber, 1994).

BACKGROUND

What are Visualizations?

Visualizations are a specific form of external representation that are intended to communicate information by using a visuo-spatial layout of this information and that are processed in the visual sensory system. According to Rieber (1990, p. 45) "visualization is defined as representations of information consisting of spatial, nonarbitrary (i.e. "picture-like" qualities resembling actual objects or events), and continuous (i.e., an "all-in-oneness" quality) characteristics". Visualizations are often best understood through the context of their use (MacEachren & Kraak, 1997). In as much as visualizations are created to communicate in a learning or problem-solving context, these visualizations are typically based on models and leverage human perceptual and cognitive abilities to efficiently and effectively convey information (Gilbert, 2005). The model and its use in the context of the visualization then drive particulars of the visualization—from the visual metaphors employed to the dynamic characteristics of elements (Bertoline & Wiebe, 2003).

External representations such as visualizations are defined with regard to their relation to the real world. "The nature of representation is that there exists a correspondence (mapping) from objects in the represented world to objects in the representing world such that at least some relations in the represented world are structurally preserved in the representing world" (Palmer, 1978, p. 266). Thus, a representation is defined through its structural correspondence to what it stands for (i.e., the referent) and is hence analogical to the referent. By means of this analogy, representations can act as a substitute for the referent and evoke similar responses as the real-world referent. Semiotics is an approach that can be used to more rigorously analyze the relationship between the signs that make up a visualization, the underlying intended instructional message of the visualization, and the learning task context in which the visualizations are being employed.

Using semiotics as a methodology, visualizations can be understood and organized in ways that better guides their creation and intended use. Peirce (1960) identified three forms of relations between the representation and the represented object: an *icon* resembles the object it depicts in terms of its criterial attributes in a given context. Criterial attributes are properties of the object that "act as discriminanda for sorting and resorting the objects in the perceptual world" (Knowlton, 1966, p. 162). An *index* refers to its object by means of a physical connection to it (e.g., a footprint as a representation of a bear). A *symbol* (or digital sign, according to Knowlton, 1966) bears no resemblance to what it stands for and is thus arbitrary (e.g., words, numbers). Knowlton (1966) further distinguishes between realistic pictures, analogical pictures, and logical pictures.

Realistic pictures resemble their referents by means of physical similarity (e.g., a picture of a tree looks like a tree we see with our eyes). This similarity is achieved by copying the real-world referent with respect to shape, details, color, or motion. From a semiotics perspective, there are at least three problems associated with the labeling of this category of visualizations. First, constructivists like Gombrich (1969) have proposed that what people perceive as being realistic in a picture is strongly affected by their preconceptions of how a representation of the real-world object should look like. Second, realistic pictures may vary largely with regard to the level of realistic detail, which is why Alessandrini (1987) suggested calling this type of pictures 'representational' rather than 'realistic'. The third problem with this labeling is that it does not help distinguishing the first from the second visualization category, namely analogical pictures.

Analogical pictures may seem realistic in the sense that the depicted objects look alike to something known from the phenomenal world. However, analogical pictures "make reference to something else – something that is in some way analogous to the portrayed object or to its manner of functioning" (Knowlton, 1966, p. 176). Thus, the objects depicted in the visualization refer to entities that are different from entities that they resemble (e.g., two lumberjacks moving a felled tree as an analogous picture for muscles

moving a bone). Resemblance to the referent is established solely through functional similarity or structural correspondence. Whereas realistic pictures can be used to represent the phenomenal world only, "analogical pictures can represent either the phenomenal or nonphenomenal world. In both cases, this is done through the bridge of the 'visual' phenomenal world" (Knowlton, 1966, p. 177). Accordingly, these pictures can represent abstract concepts, albeit not directly; rather, "they can be illustrated indirectly by showing their effects on visible objects, tangible results, specific instances, or concrete exemplars" (Alessandrini, 1987, p. 176).

Logical pictures can be thought of as highly schematized pictures, where the elements of the picture do not bear any physical resemblance to objects in the phenomenal world and are thus arbitrary (*cf.* arbitrary pictures, Alessandrini, 1987; Rieber, 1994). Accordingly, one might argue that logical pictures are symbols rather than icons. On the other hand, logical pictures, like analogical pictures, preserve the structural interrelations between these referents. Examples of logical pictures are depictions of things that are potentially visible, but where we do not know how they look like (e.g., atoms) or of things that do not exist in any tangible way (e.g., a mathematical proof). Moreover, the term logical (or arbitrary) picture is used to describe charts, diagrams, and graphs, because here the spatial layout is used to convey information on conceptual relationships. Logical may be the better term in this case since conventions for the design and layout of charts, diagrams, and graphs are often far from what would typically be considered arbitrary (Bertin, 1983).

Semiotic taxonomies like the one by Knowlton (1966) have been largely neglected in educational research (Anglin et al., 2004), although they may be very relevant to the research and development of visualizations. Research on learning with visualizations has often made generalizations across a wide range of types, which have led to the misuse of multimedia principles (Mayer, 2005). Moreover, visualizations have been incorporated in instruction with the assumption that they behave the same as verbal representations. While both text and graphics can be scrutinized through semiotic analysis, they are truly unique sign systems with differing strengths and weaknesses in communicating referents.

How Do Visual Representations Differ from Verbal Representations?

The properties that make visualizations different from verbal representations have been discussed in various disciplines. Differences between the two representational formats pertain to three aspects: (1) the features of the external representation, (2) the external representation's relation to the represented world, and (3) the relation between the external and the internal representation (i.e., the representation's meaning).

Features of the Representational Formats

Modularity. Kosslyn (1994) has suggested that verbal and pictorial representations differ with regard to their modularity. Verbal representations can be broken down in small, discrete symbols (i.e., letters), however breaking down letters into even smaller parts will not yield meaningful pieces. On the other hand, there is no discrete unit for visualizations, because they can be arbitrarily broken down in multiple ways and still yield potentially meaningful patterns.

Sequentiality. Visualizations comprise spatial relations to represent information in a two- or three-dimensional structure. Linguistic information, on the other hand, is presented in a purely sequential manner (Larkin & Simon, 1987).

Modality. Verbal representations are amodal, in that information extraction is not linked to a specific perceptual modality. That is, verbal information can be processed by the auditory system, the visual system, or even by the haptic system. On the other hand, the processing of visual representations is strongly associated with the visual modality.

The Relation between the External Representation and the Represented World

Arbitrariness. Verbal representations are said to be arbitrary in the sense that there is no inherent reason for why the word "house" denotes the thing we live in, for instance. Rather, the object could be represented by any given arrangement of letters or phonemes if a culture agreed on this. On the other hand, most visualizations are non-arbitrary in that the representation and the represented world are linked to each other by means of inherent structural correspondences or even by physical resemblance.

Notationality. In verbal representations, distinct elements are linked to real-world elements in an unambiguous and explicit way, thereby determining the semantics of the representational elements (Goodman, 1976). Moreover, for every language there are explicit rules telling us how to combine words to sentences or how to express temporal relationships, thereby determining the syntax of the representation. Goodman calls this the notationality of a representational system, which denotes the "degree to which the elements of a symbol system are distinct and are combined according to precise rules" (Anglin et al., 2004, p. 870). Visual representations are far less explicit in terms of their semantics, whereby these elements can be represented in many different ways and still be recognized, as long as the structural relations are preserved. Nevertheless, in semiotic theory there have been attempts to determine the regularities of visualizations and, therefore, to identify their underlying syntax (Kress & van Leeuwen, 1996). Logical pictures may lend themselves best to this approach since they are often notational in that there are distinct elements arranged according to specific rules or conventions (Tversky, 2003).

Parsimony. The famous saying "a picture may be sometimes worth 10,000 words" suggests that it sometimes takes 10,000 words to express what can be depicted in a picture with markedly fewer symbols. One reason for this parsimony is that spatial relations of objects are automatically implied in a picture and thus do not require any additional symbols, whereas in verbal representations spatial arrangements need to be made explicit (e.g., x is positioned above and to the right of y). According to Kosslyn (1994) visualizations are more complete than verbal representations in that they deliver information on all possible details of the object (e.g., its shape, size etc.) that is being represented through them.

Expressiveness. Contrary to verbal expressions, visualizations have limited power for expressing logical and temporal relations as well as abstractions (Maybury, 1995). For instance, to represent the concept "animal" it would not be very helpful to show a dog or a cat, as these would be interpreted as standing for the concrete animal, but not for the superordinate category. Knowlton (1966), however, notes "that it may be possible to *suggest* a concept with an iconic sign, depending, in part, on its level of realism" (p. 167). Accordingly, Schwartz (1995) demonstrated that realistic visualizations made people think more about the concrete referent of the depiction. On the other hand, schematized visualizations facilitated abstract reasoning and symbolic interpretations of the represented objects (DeLoache, 1995; Goldstone & Son, 2005; Schwartz, 1995).

Specificity. According to Stenning and Oberlander (1994) and Bernsen (1994), visualizations can be characterized by their higher specificity compared to verbal representations. That is, while language can be interpreted in multiple ways, thereby corresponding to multiple possible represented worlds, visualizations are often more constrained in that respect and reduce the number of possible worlds that can be represented through them (*cf.* graphical constraining, Scaife & Rogers, 1996).

The Relationship between Internal and External Representations

Conventionalism. The meaning of a verbal representation (i.e., what it stands for or what it signifies) is established through convention or cultural agreement. This is why Palmer (1978) referred to verbal representations as extrinsic representations, where meaning is imposed onto the representation from the outside. The meaning of the visualization is intrinsic to the representation as it is constructed based on the properties of the objects that it represents; thus, its meaning is derived from these inherent characteristics. Whereas these structural correspondences can potentially be expressed in very many ways, for some visualization forms there are established cultural rules as to how to represent the structural features of the real world, thereby constraining the multitude of options (*cf.* Gombrich, 1969; Kosslyn, 1994). As outlined before, this is particularly true for logical pictures (Tversky, 2003).

Interpretation and Reasoning. When being confronted with a verbal expression for the first time (e.g., as a child or as a second-language learner) we will not understand this expression unless we are explicitly told its meaning. Realistic visualizations, on the other hand, can be intuitively understood without making the link to the real-world referent explicit. This is even true for babies who lack experience with external representations (DeLoache, 1995; Hochberg & Brooks, 1962). Gibson (1979) has argued that this is because realistic visualizations result in optical arrays similar to those when looking at their real-world referents. Hence, information "can be directly picked up without the mediation of memory, inference, deliberation, or any other mental processes that involve internal representation" (Zhang, 1997, p. 181). Similarly, other researchers have suggested that visualizations may support inference and reasoning processes grounded in perception (Goldstone & Son, 2005; Schwartz, 1995; Stenning & Oberlander, 1994), allowing perceptual judgments to substitute for more demanding logical inferences. While these arguments are evident for realistic or representational visualizations (Alessandrini, 1987; Knowlton, 1966), logical pictures may also have specific cognitive processing benefits compared to verbal representations. Larkin and Simon (1987) have suggested that diagrammatic visualizations are often more computationally efficient for accomplishing tasks that require the processing of visuo-spatial properties (*cf.* cognitive offloading, Scaife & Rogers, 1996). In particular, visualizations reduce the need of searching for multiple information elements related to a single idea because this information is grouped (chunked) in visualizations. Thus, in visualizations related information can be processed in parallel (to a certain extent), rather than sequentially.

Internal representation. Verbal and visual representations differ in their dominant internal representation formed in long-term memory. Whereas verbal descriptions are associated with the construction of a propositional representation, non-verbal formats like visualizations are more likely to be encoded and stored as analogical representations (Kosslyn, 1994; Paivio, 1991). According to Paivio, these two internal representations are interconnected by referential links so that they can activate each other (e.g., the word "apple" activating the mental image of an apply tree). It is important to note that words and visualizations may, in principle, both yield a propositional representation as well as an analogical representation (e.g., through construction of a mental image for concrete words). The so called picture-superiority effect (i.e., better recall for pictorial than verbal information) is explained by assuming that this dual coding of information based on a single input representation is more likely to occur for pictures than for words. The picture-superiority effect can also be explained by Baggett's *bushiness hypothesis* (e.g., Baggett, 1984). It states that knowledge acquired from visual rather than verbal external representations

will be better accessible in memory because the respective nodes in memory share more associations with other nodes in the semantic network. Thus, visual concepts are assumed to be "bushier" than verbal concepts and, therefore, more salient in memory.

Bernsen (1994) mentions a number of mechanisms that help to overcome inherent weaknesses of the two representational formats, such as *focusing mechanisms* in graphics and *specificity mechanisms* in language. Thanks to focusing mechanisms (e.g., selective removal of specificity, highlighting, selective enlargement), analogous visualizations come closer to the strengths of a natural language. Thanks to specificity mechanisms in language (summaries, key points, usage of metaphor and analogy), language comes closer to the strengths of an analogous representation. Even with these mechanisms being present, visual and verbal representations will differ on a variety of dimensions, which naturally affects the way they are processed during multimedia learning. While there are elaborated models of text comprehension, no comprehensive models exist for the processing of complex visual information. In the following section, some pivotal concepts of visual perception are described as they are relevant to multimedia instruction.

Processing of Visualizations

While the research traditions in understanding text and graphic representations are equally rich, visual perception has been less well represented in educational research. Understanding the perceptual and cognitive processing of graphics is crucial to understanding the differences between text and graphic representations and how to most effectively design visualizations.

The processing of visualizations for learning and problem-solving can be understood in the context of information processing theory and, more specifically, multiple resource theory (Wickens, 2002). Using this approach, the processing of visual images contains both perceptual and cognitive elements, each of which require their own resources. In addition, there will also be resources dedicated to overarching, executive functions, guided by both short-term and long-term goals (i.e., the task). While earlier information processing models were often depicted as consisting of a number of distinct stages and functions, multiple resource theory recognizes that mental functions differ both in terms of the amount of resources required and the degree of resource overlap with other functions. Common to information processing theory, resources related to both sensory buffers and short term memory are finite while long term memory resources can be considered essentially infinite. It is the resource-limiting nature of sensory and short term memory and the ability (or lack thereof) to access relevant long term memory resources that informs much of the research in multimedia instructional design (Mayer, 2005; Sweller, van Merriënboer, & Paas, 1998).

It is useful to think of perception unique from cognition (Hochberg, 1978; Zhang, 1997). Perception can be operationally defined as those (visual) mental functions that do not require access to long-term memory. These, then, are abilities common to the normal adult and adolescent population and can be assumed when designing visual representations. Perception, therefore, involves basic processes such as discrimination based on visual properties of color, shape, texture, and orientation, form recognition and spatial arrangement.

Within perception, there is both ambient and focal vision, with the difference largely based on attention (Wickens, 2002). In terms of resources, attention is an executive function that allocates resources to processing information received by the sensory buffers. Some perceptual functions—including peripheral vision—make use of low-level processing capabilities in the brain that require little or no resources (i.e., pre-attentive or automatic processes). These ambient perceptual capabilities include supporting much of everyday

functions such as basic hand-eye motor skills or locomotion through space. All perceptual processes are actively involved in sense-making. These low level ambient functions will attempt to organize a scene as three-dimensional space, segregating foreground and background elements and determining whether these elements lie in discrete locations in depth (e.g., a planar surface) or as a continuous three-dimensional form. Elements will be grouped based on visual properties and their spatial relation to each other. While some of these properties, such as color, are pre-attentive, others (e.g., shape) may require additional attentive processing (Treisman & Gelade, 1980). The Gestalt principles of configuration are some the best known examples of active perceptual organization of a scene (Rock & Palmer, 1990). These ambient processes can be seen at work initially organizing visual information used in multimedia instruction.

Focal vision requires attention and thus more resources than ambient vision. Focal vision will make use of both bottom-up information gathered from ambient vision and top-down information provided by both ongoing focal viewing and higher level cognitive processing. Ambient visual function may provide the "gist" of a scene whereby focal vision then attends to elements initially deemed as interesting, unusual or important. Ongoing processing of this scene then guides focused vision. In addition to information being passed from ambient vision to focused vision functions, information processed at this next level may be processed further and passed to long term memory. Eye movement research informs our understanding of this ongoing process (*cf.* Henderson, 1992). While our conscious perception of a scene is of a single, unified, stable image, the underlying eye movements reveal constant saccadic movement, sampling various portions of the scene to varying degrees. The brain, employing both ambient and focal vision, engages in both real-time, transient and longer-term meaning making of what is received in the sensory buffers and creates the sense of a stable, meaningful scene.

Cognition, in this context, can be thought of those resource-driven processes that require long-term memory. For example, viewing a photograph of a lion, perception would be able to separate the lion from the surrounding background, use shading and perspective convergence to mentally orient it's three-dimensional shape in space. Prior knowledge would, however, be needed to know that this form was a lion. Further knowledge would be needed to know whether this lion was male or female, and still further specialized knowledge might allow you to use visual cues to discern the approximate age of the lion. In the context of learning, the difference between perceptual and cognitive functions becomes very important. While most perceptual capabilities can be assumed to be universally present in a population, cognitive capabilities may be much more varied (Mayer & Massa, 2003; Siegler & Alibali, 2005). While all of the students in a sixth grade classroom may know that the photograph is of a lion, they may not all know its sex or approximate age. What is important is which of these elements of prior knowledge is important for the learning task and/or whether these elements are what you hope the student will learn about. Prior knowledge is equally important with analogical or logical images, where the visual sign element must be mapped to its referent in memory. Improper scaffolding may leave a student at a lower level of processing, where the image seen is just a "red triangle" and not, say, a representation of a key biological molecule used in DNA replication (Patrick, Carter, & Wiebe, 2006).

The movement of visual information from sensory buffers to short term memory and then possibly to long term memory establishes a number of points of possible failure to encode into schemas information necessary for a learning task. Low level visual information that cannot be apprehended because it is too small or does not possess enough contrast to be segregated from surrounding elements cannot be used as part of higher level visual processing. Similarly, elements that meet the requirements of low level apprehension may still not be further processed because attention has not directed the necessary resources to this visual information; the information is not rehearsed in short term memory and not integrated into long-term memory. Finally, visual information in long term memory may not be retrieved because it is not recognized as related to the current visual processing task.

It is important not to think of these processes as rigid and linear, as there is an ongoing flow of information between all levels in both directions, with some of it happening in parallel while other elements happening in a more serial fashion. In addition, it is equally important to not make assumptions about the structure of visual information as it is stored or processed. There is no reason to believe that there is a direct, homologous relationship between the distal visualization (whether it be a physical three-dimensional object, printed graphic, or computer display) and the internally coded visual information (Scaife & Rogers, 1996). That is, that one's internal mental images, no matter how they might "look" like their corresponding real world objects, can be composed of information from multiple sources, including both real-time sensory streams and long-term memory traces of previous experiences. Ongoing cognitive and neuroscience research is continuing to unravel both the physiological and psychological basis for visual information processing and storage.

LEARNING WITH VISUALIZATIONS

If visualizations are going to be optimally deployed in instructional materials, their semiotic, perceptual, and cognitive characteristics and their relationship to textual elements need to be synthesized and operationalized. In the following sections, two issues will be addressed that are relevant to learning with visualizations. The first section aims at specifying the conditions under which visualizations will contribute to learning. The second section addresses the role of learner characteristics in visualization research.

When Do Visualizations Aid Learning?

A main issue in designing instructional materials pertains to the questions of when and how to use visualizations for conveying knowledge in a particular domain. To find an answer to these questions, one has to ask what information is to be conveyed, what the users' physical and cognitive abilities, preferences, and intentions are, and what the communicative situation is where the instruction will be used (Maybury, 1995). In the following section, we will highlight the function a visualization may have for learning and whether this function is relevant to achieving a particular learning objective. Hence, visualizations are supposed to be effective for learning only if they fulfill functions relevant to achieving a particular learning objective. In the following, we will distinguish instructional functions that visualizations may have if presented as self-contained messages (i.e., regardless of verbal information) or if they accompany verbal explanations. We will end this section with a discussion on whether visualizations can aid learning even if they are redundant to other representations.

Instructional Functions of Visualizations as Self-Contained Messages

The design of the visualization, of course, has to take the instructional context into consideration. There are several instructional functions that visualizations may have—irrespective of whether they are accompanied by verbal explanations or not.

Affect. Visualizations are often said to be motivating for students, because they can make a subject matter more interesting and appealing to students. Moreover, they can trigger specific

emotions or lead to a change in learners' attitudes (Levie & Lentz, 1982). However, there is a danger that visualizations that do not convey any information relevant to the learning objective will distract learners (*cf.* seductive details effect, Harp & Mayer, 1998).

Replace and augment real-world experience. Visualizations as instructional materials can act as an substitute to direct experience by offering highly realistic impressions of real-world objects and events, which might otherwise be too small, too large, too fast, too far away, or too dangerous to observe in reality. In that respect, visualizations do not replace real-world experience, but they may even improve this experience by providing information that would not have been accessible in the real world (i.e., 'better than reality').

Visuo-spatial reasoning. As has been outlined in the section on differences between verbal and visual representations the latter provide direct and parsimonious access to visuo-spatial information and, in case of dynamic visualizations, temporal properties of objects and events (Larkin & Simon, 1987; Rieber, 1990; Tversky, Bauer Morrison, & Betrancourt, 2002). This visuo-spatial information can also be directly used for inferences and reasoning (Goldstone & Son, 2005; Schwartz, 1995). With verbal representations, the sequential information would not only require cognitively demanding processes of searching related information, but also it would need to be internally transformed into a form more appropriate for spatial reasoning. Thus, for visuo-spatial reasoning tasks visualizations are more computationally efficient and allow for cognitive offloading (Larkin & Simon, 1987; Scaife & Rogers, 1996). This function is important in that it does not limit a visualization's capabilities to act as a memory aid; rather, it suggests that reasoning based on visualizations is a way of extending the boundaries of cognition to external representations (Zhang, 1997). External visualizations enable cognitive operations that would otherwise have to be conducted internally (e.g., mental imagery) and thereby require more cognitive effort (*cf.* supplantation, Salomon, 1979).

Instructional Functions of Visualizations as Text Adjuncts

Most often, visualizations are used in conjunction with verbal instructional materials rather than acting as self-contained messages. Analyzing the combination of text and pictures has a long tradition within semiotics and sociosemiotics (Eco, 1976; Kress & van Leeuwen, 1996), in interface design (Bernsen, 1994; Mullet & Sano, 1995) and in human–computer interaction (Maybury, 1995) and textlinguistics. The perspectives in these works differ; while some stress the differences between text and pictures with regard to their suitability for expressing specific information (Bernsen, 1994; Mullet & Sano 1995), others are more interested in the interplay between them. The latter perspective is also taken here in this section, where it is emphasized that when visualizations accompany text they have functions in addition to those mentioned before, because they interact with the verbal information in specific ways. The most prominent analysis of the instructional functions associated with such a use of visualizations as text-adjuncts in the education literature has been conducted by Levin, Anglin, and Carney (1987). In their review, the authors described five functions of visualizations as text adjuncts: decorative, representation, organization, interpretation, and transformation.

Visualizations with a *decoration function* are not related to the verbal information and are introduced only to make a text more appealing and interesting for learners. However, while they are supposed to motivate learners, the meta-analysis by Levin et al. (1987) actually revealed a negative effect of decorative visualizations (*cf.* seductive details effect, Harp & Mayer, 1998). Presenting irrelevant additional information may distract learners from processing the pivotal learning contents or it may trigger inappropriate schemas for encoding the relevant content.

Visualizations in their *representational function* depict objects and relations mentioned in a text in a way that the meaning of the text more accessible for learners by making a text more concrete. Visualizations with an *organization function* provide an organizational framework for a text (e.g., how-to-do-it diagrams) and thereby make the content more coherent by highlighting the argumentative or organizational structure of the text (Verdi, Kulhavy, Stock, Rittschof, & Johnson, 1996). According to Levin et al. (1987) this function refers to comprehensible texts, whereas the *interpretation function* of visualizations is to make texts understandable for learners that would otherwise be incomprehensible. Accordingly, these visualizations are often introduced in textbooks and multimedia instructions to clarify difficult-to-understand passages and abstract concepts within passages (e.g., pictorial analogies).

The rarest function that visualizations are used for pertains to the *transformation function*. Visualizations that follow this function are designed to improve memory performance directly "by targeting the critical information to be learned, and then (a) *recoding* it into a more concrete and memorable form, (b) *relating* in a well-organized content the separate pieces for that information and (c) providing the student with a systematic means of *retrieving* the critical information when later asked for it." (Levin et al., 1987, p. 61). Visualizations with a transformation function showed the strongest positive effects on learning outcomes in the meta-analysis conducted by the authors.

It is important to note that Levin's review is limited to prose learning, whereas most multimedia materials are concerned with a broader and deeper understanding that can be transfered to novel situations. It is thus questionable whether these recommendations can be simply applied to the design or multimedia materials. There is at least one recommendation where research seems to disagree: informational equivalence of verbal and visual representations. According to Levin et al. (1987), students who use redundant information to acquire content knowledge benefit from visualizations if these show a large information overlap with the verbally presented information. In fact, the representational, organizational, and interpretational function of visualizations presuppose that text and picture are at least partially redundant. On the other hand, multimedia learning research, has suggested to not present redundant information to learners, because this may require additional cognitive ressources for comparing and integrating the information, which are then no longer available for learning (redundancy effect; e.g., Bobis, Sweller, & Cooper, 1993).

There are at least three things that are usually ignored in this discussion in the literature on multimedia learning: First, a certain degree of overlap is necessary to allow for a coherent mental representation, where learners can draw connections between the two sources of information. Second, what is redundant information is often impossible to say. Even when deliberately trying to construct informationally equivalent (and thus fully redundant) representations, it is almost impossible to counteract the fact that visualizations often "unintentionally" convey more, albeit potentially irrelevant information than do verbal descriptions due to their higher specificity or completeness (Kosslyn, 1994; Stenning & Oberlander, 1994). Third, as has been emphasized by Ainsworth (1999, 2006) in her functional taxonomy of multiple external representations (MERs), even informationally equivalent representations may have different functional roles for learning and thus support knowledge acquisition differently. She categorizes these roles into three groups: First, visual and verbal representations may fulfill *complementary roles* in instruction by faciliating different cognitive processes, serving different learning objectives, or addressing the individual representational preferences of different learners. Second, they can *constrain interpretation* and guide learners' reasoning about a domain. Third, visual and verbal representations together might be

suited to foster a *deeper understanding* than could be achieved by using just one representational format. Thus, whenever any of these functional roles can contribute to learning, representing redundant information visually as well as verbally may be advised according to Ainsworth's taxonomy. On the other hand, if one of the representations does not contribute to learning on a functional level, it should be deleted from the instruction.

Hence, when designing multimedia materials special attention has to be paid to how to distribute information across text and graphic representations by maximizing the representations' strengths and reducing their potential weaknesses for delivering specific information aspects. This pertains to the notion of Palmer (1978) that the represented world can be depicted in many different ways and the decision about which constitutes the most appropriate representation depends on the operations that need to be performed with it and the questions that should be answered with it.

The Role of Individual Learner Characteristics in Learning with Visualizations

In order to be effective for learning, visualizations need to be designed in a way that they can be "readily and accurately perceived and comprehended" (Tversky et al., 2002, p. 258). Moreover, the effectiveness of visualizations is affected by what the learner brings to the learning task as another crucial component of the instructional context. Visualization design needs to recognize that there is no homogenous response to graphic or textual representations and how they are, or are not, used in learning. Several learner characteristics have been suggested that may affect learning with visualizations. We will follow a suggestion by Mayer and Massa (2003), who tried to disentangle cognitive abilities, cognitive style, and learning preference along the visualizer-verbalizer dimension. These dimensions account for the fact that "some people are better at processing words and some people are better at processing pictures" (Mayer & Massa, 2003, p. 833).

Cognitive Abilities

Cognitive abilities related to the processing of visualizations comprise a wide range of constructs that differ not only with regard to their specificity, but also with regard to their empirical foundations. Some constructs like pictorial competence or visual literacy are rather general, whereas the impact of visuo-spatial abilities clearly depends on the type of learning tasks students are confronted with. For the former constructs, to our knowledge, no straightforward measures exist to assess them other than by observing a person performing a task that either requires or does not require this specific ability. On the other hand, there have been many different attempts to assess visuo-spatial abilities, though their literature is still equivocal (see Carroll, 1993; Hegarty & Waller, 2005 for overviews). Thus, at the current moment it is unclear how the concepts are related to each other and how they contribute to learning with visualizations independently as well as in interaction with each other. For these reasons, we will refrain from providing a comprehensive overview and instead sketch some of concepts that are relevant in the current context. The general notion is that learners who lack the abilities to process visualizations will benefit from them to a lesser extent, demonstrated, for example, in a study of science textbook instruction by Hannus and Hyönä (1999).

Pictorial competence. DeLoache, Pierrout-sakos, and Uttal (2003) discuss the ability to use pictures from a developmental psychology perspective. According to their view, pictorial competence encompasses "the many factors that are involved in perceiving, interpreting, understanding and using pictures, ranging from the straightforward perception and recognition of simple pictures to the most sophisticated understanding of the conventions and techniques of highly complex ones" (DeLoache et al., 2003, p. 115). While basic elements of pictorial competence exist already in newborns, more complex skills are characterized by strong developmental shifts. In particular, the ability to understand the relationship between the representation and the referent; that is, to become symbol-minded, is clearly age-dependent (DeLoache, 1995). DeLoache's research suggests that pictorial competence develops during the daily interactions with pictures and their real-world referents. However, it is unclear whether this kind of familiarity is sufficient to use pictures in academic contexts. According to Pozzer and Roth (2003), "most students are familiar with photographs in general; however, appropriate instructions for how to read and analyze photographs currently are not provided to them." (p. 1092). While the concept of pictorial competency mostly refers to the interpretation of realistic visualizations, the term visual literacy denotes a more general ability of dealing with visual media of all types (e.g., video, graphics, diagrams, animation, etc.).

Visual literacy. According to Nöth (2003) this concept refers to the "the ability to decode the pictorial repertoire of the media without indexical or iconic support" (p. 186). Messaris (1994) calls it "the familiarity with visual conventions that a person acquires through cumulative exposure to visual media" (p. 3). The "visual literacy" model defined by Messaris (1994) specifies different levels of visual communication that range from simple understanding to aesthetic appreciation of visual media. Despite its popularity in discussions on computer-based instruction, there is no objective assessment tool that would allow measuring the visual literacy of students. While in reading research, illiteracy can be conceptualized as a the lack of knowledge on the syntax, semantics, and pragmatics of language, there is nothing comparable in non-notational representational systems, where the interpretation of visualizations is often subjective and context-dependent. Because of this, it has also been suggested to refrain from using the term literacy and replace it with graphicacy instead (Roth, Pozzer-Ardenghi, & Han, 2005) to get rid of the strong association between literacy and reading. The term literacy may however be adequate for logical pictures, where it can be defined as the knowledge of notational rules, allowing mapping visual features of a representation to an interpretation of the depicted part (Pinker, 1990; Shah & Hoeffner, 2002).

Domain-specific prior knowledge. There is increasing evidence that students' level of domain-specific prior knowledge moderates learning from visualizations. For instance, learners with a high level of prior knowledge are better able to direct their visual attention towards relevant information (Lowe, 2003) and are less affected by a high visual complexity of the display (Lee, Plass, & Homer, 2006). Both findings support the notion that extracting information from a visualization is both a bottom-up as well as a top-down process. In the latter case, existing mental representation guide the lower-level perceptual processes and the interpretation of information acquired through them.

Visuo-spatial abilities. According to Carroll (1993), visuo-spatial ability is not a unitary construct; rather, it comprises five different dimensions that all make up abilities in the perception of visual input: (1) Spatial visualization is "the ability to mentally rotate or fold objects in two or three dimensions and to imagine the changing of configurations of objects that would result from such manipulations" (Mayer & Sims, 1994, p. 392) without referring to one's self, (2) spatial orientation is the ability to imagine an object's appearance from different view points as the observer's body orientation changes, (3) closure speed is the ability to access representations quickly from long-term memory, (4) flexibility of closure, and (5) perceptual speed is involved in the processing of simple visual displays (e.g., quick scanning). Prior findings from other researchers have likewise established evidence for the first two dimensions (spatial visualization and orientation),

while they failed to find consistent evidence for the latter three (Hegarty & Waller, 2005).

Research on spatial visualization suggests that "high- and low-spatial abilities individuals differ in the quality of the spatial representations that they construct and their ability to maintain its quality after transforming the representations in different ways" (Hegarty & Waller, 2005, p. 141). Accordingly, spatial visualization differences have been successfully conceptualized against the background of differences in working memory resources (Shah & Miyake, 1996). The role of visuo-spatial abilities has mostly been investigated in mental animation, where learners have to infer the motion of a mechanical system from a static picture. Here it has been demonstrated that learners with high abilities perform better in this task than low-ability students (e.g., Hegarty & Sims, 1994). It seems very plausible to assume that visuo-spatial abilities will show a strong influence in other tasks involving learning with visualizations. For instance, Plass, Chun, Mayer, and Leutner (2003) demonstrated that either students with low verbal or spatial abilities showed worse performance in multimedia learning than their higher-ability counterparts when receiving visual annotations, whereas abilities played no role when students were given verbal annotations.

Cognitive Styles: Visualizers versus Verbalizers

"A cognitive style is a psychological dimension that represents consistencies in how an individual acquires and processes information" (Kozhevnikov, Kosslyn, & Shepard, 2005, p. 710). The visualizer-verbalizer dimension (Richardson, 1977) characterizes students as verbalizers, if they rely on verbal-analytical strategies when performing a task, whereas visualizers use imagery as a predominant strategy of task accomplishment. Kozhevnikov, Hegarty and Mayer (2002) revised the visualizer-verbalizer dimension and suggest a more fine-grained distinction between spatial and iconic visualizers (object visualizers according to Kozhevnikov et al., 2005). In a problem-solving task, they collected evidence for these two types of visualizers. Spatial visualizers, in a schematic interpretation, focused on the location of objects and on spatial relations between objects. This group also used "imagery to represent and transform spatial relations" (Kozhevnikov et al., 2005, p. 722), where images were processed analytically to infer their spatial interrelations. Iconic visualizers, on the other hand, in a pictorial interpretation, focused on vivid visual details like shape, size, colour and brightness, thereby processing these objects as a single perceptual unit. Interestingly, this distinction between the two groups fits nicely with research that focuses on dissociating the ways in which visual information is processed. This work shows that there are brain areas that either focus on processing shape and color information to determine an object's identity (what-system) or on processing spatial and dynamic input (where-system). Moreover, current theories of visuo-spatial working memory (Logie, 1995) make a similar distinction by relating the function of the inner scribe – as one component of visuo-spatial working memory – to the processing of spatial and movement information, whereas the other part is responsible for the processing of color and shape information (i.e., the visual cache). At this moment, however, it is highly speculative if the cognitive styles identified by Kozhevnikov et al. (2002; 2005) could be linked to a different use of these brain areas or working memory systems.

Preferences for Visual versus Verbal Information

Leutner and Plass (1998) developed a method to assess preferences for verbal or visual materials by analyzing the students' information-selection behavior. The VV-BOS (Visualizer/Verbalizer Choice Behavior Observation Scale) showed very promising psychometric properties as well as a superior validity with regard to the differential prediction of learning outcomes. Plass, Chun, Mayer, and Leutner (1998) demonstrated that students with visual preferences as assessed by the VV-BOS benefited predominantly from visual annotations, whereas students with verbal preferences gained most from verbal annotations.

Taken together, there is evidence that suggests that when investigating learning with visualizations, the students' individual differences in terms of cognitive abilities, cognitive styles, and learning preferences need to be considered. With the current state of research, it is impossible to tell their relative influence and direction, but first studies show promising results in this respect.

CONCLUSION

When developing multimedia materials, instructional designers are faced with a multitude of decisions as to which contents should be part of the instruction, which representational format to use for these contents, and how to design these contents. For improving multimedia instructions, two conclusions can be drawn from the current paper.

First, one needs to clearly understand the learning task and relevant individual differences of the learner. From this, the relative strengths and weaknesses of different representational formats can be considered and information visually encoded in accordance with the results of this analysis. Visualizations should be used whenever their instructional functions are assumed to add considerably to the effectiveness of the multimedia instruction.

Second, the use of visualizations often seems to suffer from the *resemblance fallacy* (Scaife & Rogers, 1996). While it is seductive to assume that mental imagery and distal visualizations are homologous and that processing these visualizations only involve low level perceptual processing inate to all humans, this is a grave error in instructional strategy. While perceptual processes are naturally involved in learning from visualizations, only seldom are the visualizations supposed to be taken literally. Rather, they have to be taken as representations standing for something else than what is being depicted. Identifying what is being represented based on the structural correspondences (rather than physical similarity) may cause severe difficulties for learners when studying visualizations. Thus, it should not be taken for granted that learners will extract the information from a visualization that was intended by an instructor. Rather, students need to be supported in extracting the relevant information from the visualization and guided as to how to best deploy their limited perceptual and cognitive resources. This support can be provided either by guiding learners' attention towards its relevant aspects (e.g., highlighting) or by improving students' competencies in dealing with visualizations. The latter comprises teaching to students existing conventions underlying these (logical) visualizations (e.g., how to read a graph, Pinker, 1990) or training them in developing graphicacy (Roth et al., 2005).

FUTURE DIRECTIONS

The final section of this paper is devoted to future directions in research on learning from visualizations. In particular, we wish to emphasize that more in-depth analyses are needed that shed light on the process of perceiving and interpreting instructional visualizations and on the visualization's impact on performance in a variety of tasks. We believe that respective analyses would benefit from an interdisciplinary perspective, where insights from different areas (e.g., cognitive science, education, semiotics, visual perception, human-computer-interaction, human factors) could be united.

Integrating models of visual perception and cognition. Most researchers argue for visualization's instructional effectiveness by referring to its relative ability to support higher-level cognitive processes. Accordingly, pictorial representations may support a dual coding of the information (Paivio, 1991), the construction of a mental model (e.g., Mayer, 2005), or cognitive offloading (Scaife & Rogers, 1996). These approaches pay considerably less attention to perceptual processes, thereby ignoring that these processes need to take place before higher-level cognitive processes can act upon the information that has been attended to. As a consequence, the vast literature on visual perception is largely neglected in the educational literature, even though it may provide important and novel insights into the design of effective visualizations (e.g., MacEachren, 1995). According to Anglin et al. (2004), "theory-based studies that are informed by both memory research and theories of picture perception are lacking" (p. 876).

Taxonomy research. Currently, visualizations are mostly treated as a unitary construct without taking into account the differences among them. These differences may pertain to their appearance, content, or instructional functions. Future research should attempt to develop taxonomies that will allow classifying visualizations according to these different dimensions. There have been morphological approaches that classify visualizations according to their appearance (e.g., Lohse, Biolsi, Walker, & Rueter, 1994; Twyman, 1985) however, we do not think that these taxonomies will help explaining much of the variance with regard to the instructional effectiveness of visualizations. Rather, content-oriented classifications (Bieger & Glock, 1984) or more systematic approaches to instructional functions like the one by Levin et al. (1987) seem to be more promising in this respect. The availability of such taxonomies would allow greater generalization of findings across studies than what is currently possible.

Analyzing processes and learning outcomes in parallel. While there are some theoretical assumptions on how pictorial representations are processed, most of the existing studies have refrained from empirically investigating these processes. Knowledge on how students use pictorial representations is, however, not only necessary for theory development, it is also relevant for practical reasons. For instance, for logical pictures it is often not clear whether these representations sometimes fail to improve learning because they are designed in a bad way or because students did not understand the underlying conventions. Process-oriented data may allow identifying possible misconceptions students have regarding the meaning of the visualizations and assist in developing effective teaching strategies for using them. Despite these promises of analyzing the processes of learning from visualizations, most of the studies until now have only looked at learning outcomes in isolation. Some noteworthy exceptions to this situation come from research that has applied eye tracking methodologies (e.g., Cook, Carter, & Wiebe, 2008; Lowe, 1999). This methodology provides information on the temporal and spatial resolution of visual attention by tracking the location of the eye as a person watches a visual display. It thus offers a good starting point to analyze perceptual and possibly cognitive processes when learning with visualizations. In particular, its combination with think aloud data has been shown to be very informative (van Gog, Paas, & van Merriënboer, 2005). Hence, we suggest combining the predominant outcome-oriented research strategy with a more process-oriented strategy (*cf.* Peeck, 1987).

Assessment of learning outcomes. Despite the fact that core information is often conveyed by means of visualizations in multimedia instruction, most test items are presented in words only. Moreover, in class students are typically required to provide their answers verbally. Thus, most ways of assessing what has been learned from a visualization potentially requires multiple recodings of this information by the learner to accomplish a task. In particular, non-sequential information

needs to be transformed into a sequential format to provide a verbal answer (speaker's linearization problem; Levelt, 1981). Moreover, according to the verbal overshadowing effect (Melcher & Schooler, 1996) it may well be that asking learners to provide verbal answers when assessing their learning outcomes may interfere with the "visual" knowledge stored in memory and make this information less accessible. Hence, verbal tests may inadequately reflect students' acquired knowledge. Moreover, interactions between the instructional format and the learning objective should be considered more thoroughly in future research. A larger variety of test formats might be more apt to account for the complexities underlying learning with visualizations. Accordingly, Joseph and Dwyer (1984) found positive effects for illustrated text compared to text-only versions only in a drawing test, but not in a comprehension test, suggesting that the type of test moderates the effectiveness of instruction. Furthermore, Levie and Lentz (1982) showed in their review on learning with visualizations that visualizations improved recall more in delayed tests than in immediate tests. It might be that the advantages of visualizations relate to dual coding in memory and creating more associations to other long term memory content—a pay off only seen in situations that impose higher demands on memory and understanding.

REFERENCES

Ainsworth, S. (1999). A functional taxonomy of multiple representations. *Computers and Education, 33*, 131-152.

Ainsworth, S. (2006). DeFT: A conceptual framework for considering learning with multiple representations. *Learning and Instruction, 16*, 183-198.

Alessandrini, K. L. (1987). Computer graphics in learning and instruction. In D. M. Willows & H.

A. Houghton (Eds.), *The psychology of illustration* (Vol. 2, pp. 159-188). New York: Springer.

Anglin, G. J., Vaez, H., & Cunningham, K. L. (2004). Visual representations and learning: The role of static and animated graphics. In D. Jonassen (Ed.), *Handbook of research on educational communications and technology* (pp. 865-916). Mahwah, NJ: Erlbaum.

Baggett, P. (1984). Role of temporal overlap of visual and auditory material in forming dual media associations. *Journal of Educational Psychology, 76*, 408-417.

Barthes, R. (1964). Rhétorique de l'image. *Communications, 4*, 40–51.

Bernsen, N. O. (1994). Foundations of multimodal representations: A taxonomy of representational modalities. *Interacting with Computers, 6*, 347-371.

Bertin, J. (1983). *Semiology of graphics: Diagrams networks maps* (W. J. Berg, Trans.). Madison, WI: University of Wisconsin Press.

Bertoline, G. R., & Wiebe, E. N. (2003). *Technical graphics communications* (3rd ed.). New York, NY: McGraw-Hill.

Bieger, G. R., & Glock, M. D. (1984). The information content of picture-text instructions. *The Journal of Experimental Education, 53*, 68-76.

Bobis, J., Sweller, J., & Cooper, M. (1993). Cognitive load effects in a primary school geometry task. *Learning and Instruction, 3*, 1-21.

Carroll, J. B. (1993). *Human cognitive abilities: A survey of factor-analytic studies.* New York: Cambridge University Press.

Cook, M. P., Carter, G., & Wiebe, E. N. (2008). The interpretation of cellular transport graphics by students with low and high prior knowledge. *International Journal of Science Education 30*, 241-263.

DeLoache, J. S. (1995). Early understanding and use of symbols: The model model. *Current Directions in Psychological Science, 4*, 109-113.

DeLoache, J. S., Pierroutsakos, S. L., & Uttal, D. H. (2003). The origins of pictorial competence. *Current Directions in Psychological Science, 12*, 114-118.

Eco, U. (1976). *A theory of semiotics.* Bloomington, IN: Indiana University Press.

Gibson, J. J. (1979). *The ecological approach to visual perception.* Boston, MA: Houghton Mifflin.

Gilbert, J. K. (2005). Visualization: A metacognitive skill in science and science education. In J. K. Gilbert (Ed.), *Visualization in Science Education* (pp. 9-27). Amsterdam: Springer.

Goldstone, R. L., & Son, J. Y. (2005). The transfer of scientific principles using concrete and idealized simulations. *The Journal of the Learning Sciences, 14*, 69-110.

Gombrich, E. H. (1969). *Art and illusion: A study in the psychology of pictorial representation.* Princeton, NJ: Princeton University Press.

Goodman, N. (1976). *Languages of art: An approach to a theory of symbols* (2nd ed.). Indianapolis, IN: Hackett.

Hannus, M., & Hyönä, J. (1999). Utilization of illustrations during learning of science textbook passages among low- and high-ability children. *Contemporary Educational Psychology, 24*, 95-123.

Harp, S. F., & Mayer, R. E. (1998). How seductive details do their damage: A theory of cognitive interest in science learning. *Journal of Educational Psychology, 90*, 414-434.

Hegarty, M., & Sims, V. K. (1994). Individual differences in mental animation during mechanical reasoning. *Memory & Cognition, 22*, 411-430.

Hegarty, M., & Waller, D. A. (2005). Individual Differences in Spatial Abilities. In P. Shah & A. Miyake (Eds.), *The Cambridge handbook of visuospatial thinking* (pp. 121-169). Cambridge MA: Cambridge University Press.

Henderson, J. M. (1992). Visual attention and eye movement control during reading and picture viewing. In K. Rayner (Ed.), *Eye movements and visual cognition: Scene perception and reading* (pp. 260-283). New York, NY: Springer-Verlag.

Hochberg, J. E. (1978). *Perception* (2nd ed.). Englewood Cliffs, NJ: Prentice-Hall.

Hochberg, J. E., & Brooks, V. (1962). Pictorial recognition as an unlearned ability: A study of one child's performance. *American Journal of Psychology, 75,* 624-628.

Joseph, J. H., & Dwyer, F. M. (1984). The effects of prior knowledge, presentation mode, and visual realism ons tudent achievement. *Journal of Experimental Education, 52,* 110-121.

Knowlton, J. Q. (1966). On the definition of "picture". *AV Communication Review, 14,* 157-183.

Kosslyn, S. M. (1994). *Elements of graph design.* New York, NY: W.H. Freeman.

Kozhevnikov, M., Hegarty, M., & Mayer, R. E. (2002). Revising the visualizer-verbalizer dimension: Evidence for two types of visualizers. *Cognition and Instruction, 20,* 47-77.

Kozhevnikov, M., Kosslyn, S., & Shephard, J. (2005). Spatial versus object visualizers: A new characterization of visual cognitive style. *Memory & Cognition, 33,* 710-726.

Kress, G., & van Leeuwen, T. (1996). *Reading images: The grammar of visual design.* London: Routledge.

Larkin, J. H., & Simon, H. A. (1987). Why a diagram is (sometimes) worth ten thousand words. *Cognitive Science, 11,* 65-99.

Lee, H., Plass, J. L., & Homer, B. D. (2006). Optimizing cognitive load for learning from computer-based science simulations. *Journal of Educational Psychology, 98,* 902-913.

Leutner, D., & Plass, J. L. (1998). Measuring learning styles with questionnaires versus direct observation of preferential choice behavior: Development of the Visualizer/Verbalizer Behavior Observation Scale (VV-BOS). *Computers in Human Behavior, 14,* 543-557.

Levelt, W. J. M. (1981). The speaker's linearization problem. *Philosophical Transactions of the Royal Society, Series B, 295,* 305-315.

Levie, W., & Lentz, R. (1982). Effects of text illustrations: a review of research. *Educational Communication and Technology Journal, 30,* 195-232.

Levin, J. R., Anglin, G. J., & Carney, R. N. (1987). On empirically validating functions of pictures in prose. In D. M. Willows & H. A. Houghton (Eds.), *The psychology of illustration* (Vol. 1, pp. 51-85). New York: Springer.

Logie, R. H. (1995). *Visuo-spatial working memory.* Hove, UK: Erlbaum.

Lohse, G. J., Biolsi, K., Walker, N., & Rueter, H. H. (1994). A classification of visual representations. *Communications of the ACM, 37,* 36-49.

Lowe, R. K. (1999). Extracting information from an animation during complex visual learning. *European Journal of Psychology of Education, 14,* 225-244.

Lowe, R. K. (2003). Animation and learning: Selective processing of information in dynamic graphics. *Learning and Instruction, 13,* 157-176.

MacEachren, A. M. (1995). *How maps work: Representation, visualization, and design.* New York: Guilford Press.

MacEachren, A. M., & Kraak, M.-J. (1997). Exploratory cartographic visualization: Advancing the agenda. *Computers and Geosciences, 23,* 335-343.

Maybury, M. T. (1995). Research in multimedia and multimodal parsing and generation. *Artificial Intelligence Review, 9,* 103-127.

Mayer, R. E. (2005). *The Cambridge handbook of multimedia learning.* New York, NY: Cambridge University Press.

Mayer, R. E., & Massa, L. J. (2003). Three facets of visual and verbal learners: Cognitive ability, cognitive style, and learning preference. *Journal of Educational Psychology, 95,* 833-846.

Mayer, R. E., & Sims, V. K. (1994). For whom is a picture worth ten thousand words? Extensions of a dual-coding theory of multimedia learning. *Journal of Educational Psychology, 86,* 389-401.

Melcher, J. M., & Schooler, J. W. (1996). The misremembrance of wines past: Verbal and perceptual expertise differentially mediate verbal overshadowing of taste memory. *Journal of Memory and Language, 35,* 231–245.

Messaris, P. (1994). Four aspects of visual literacy. In P. Messaris (Ed.), *Visual literacy: Image, mind and reality* (pp. 1-40). Boulder: Westview Press.

Mullet, K., & Sano, D. (1995). *Designing visual interfaces. Communication oriented techniques.* Englewood Cliffs, NJ: Prentice Hall.

Nöth, W. (2003). Press photos and their captions. In H. Lönnroth (Ed.), *Från Närpesdialekt till EU-svenska* (pp. 169–188). Tampere: Tampere University Press.

Paivio, A. (1991). Dual coding theory: Retrospect and current status. *Canadian Journal of Psychology, 45,* 255-287.

Palmer, S. E. (1978). Fundamental aspects of cognitive representation. In E. Rosch & B. B. Lloyd (Eds.), *Cognition and categorization* (pp. 259-303). Hillsdale, NJ: Erlbaum.

Patrick, M. D., Carter, G., & Wiebe, E. N. (2006). *Visual representations of DNA: A comparison of salient features for experts and novices.* Paper presented at the NARST Annual Meeting, San Francisco, CA.

Peeck, J. (1987). The role of illustrations in processing and remembering illustrated text. In D. M. Willows & H. A. Houghton (Eds.), *The psychology of illustration* (Vol. 1, pp. 115-151). New York: Springer.

Peirce, C. S. (1960). *The icons, index, and symbol (1902): Collected papers.* Cambridge, MA: Harvard University Press.

Pinker, S. (1990). A theory of graph comprehension. In R. Friedle (Ed.), *Artificial intelligence and the future of testing* (pp. 73-126). Norwood, NJ: Ablex.

Plass, J. L., Chun, D., Mayer, R. E., & Leutner, D. (1998). Supporting visualizer and verbalizer learning preferences in a second language multimedia learning environment. *Journal of Educational Psychology, 90,* 25-36.

Plass, J. L., Chun, D., Mayer, R. E., & Leutner, D. (2003). Cognitive load in reading a foreign language text with multimedia aids and the influence of verbal and spatial abilities. *Computers in Human Behavior, 19,* 211-220.

Pozzer, L. L., & Roth, W. M. (2003). Prevalence, function, and structure of photographs in high school biology textbooks. *Journal of Research in Science Teaching, 40,* 1089-1114.

Richardson, A. (1977). Verbalizer–visualizer: A cognitive style dimension. *Journal of Mental Imagery, 1,* 109–126.

Rieber, L. P. (1990). Animation in computer-based instruction. *Educational Technology Research & Development, 38,* 77-86.

Rieber, L. P. (1994). *Computers, graphics, and learning*. Madison, WI: Brown & Benchmark.

Rock, I., & Palmer, S. E. (1990). The legacy of Gestalt psychology. *Scientific American, 263*(6, Dec.), 84-90.

Roth, W.-M., Pozzer-Ardenghi, L., & Han, J. Y. (2005). *Critical graphicacy. Understanding visual representation practices in school science*. New York: Springer.

Salomon, G. (1979). Media and symbol systems as related to cognition and learning. *Journal of Educational Psychology, 71*, 131-148.

Scaife, M., & Rogers, Y. (1996). External cognition: How do graphical representations work? *International Journal of Human-Computer Studies, 45*, 185-213.

Schwartz, D. L. (1995). Reasoning about the referent of a picture versus reasoning about the picture as a referent: An effect of visual realism. *Memory & Cognition, 23*, 709-722.

Shah, P., & Hoeffner, J. (2002). Review of graph comprehension research: Implications for instruction. *Educational Psychology Review, 14*, 47-69.

Shah, P., & Miyake, A. (1996). The separability of working memory resources for spatial thinking and language processing: An individual differences approach. *Journal of Experimental Psychology: General, 125*, 4-27.

Siegler, R. S., & Alibali, M. W. (2005). *Children's thinking*. Upper Saddle River: Prentice Hall.

Stenning, K., & Oberlander, J. (1994). A cognitive theory of graphical and linguistic reasoning: Logic and implementation. *Cognitive Science, 19*, 96-140.

Sweller, J., van Merriënboer, J. J. G., & Paas, F. G. W. C. (1998). Cognitive architecture and instructional design. *Educational Psychology Review, 10*, 251-296.

Treisman, A. M., & Gelade, G. (1980). A feature integration theory of attention. *Cognitive Psychology, 12*, 97-136.

Tufte, E. R. (2001). *The visual display of quantitative information*. Graphics Press.

Tversky, B. (2003). Some ways graphics communicate. In K. Nyiri (Ed.), *Mobile communication: Essays on cognition and community* (pp. 143-156). Wien: Passagen Verlag.

Tversky, B., Morrison, J. B., & Betrancourt, M. (2002). Animation: Does it facilitate? *International Journal of Human-Computer Studies, 57*, 247-262.

Twyman, M. (1985). Using pictorial language: A discussion of the dimensions of the problem. In T. M. Duffy & R Waller (Eds.) *Designing Usable Texts* (pp. 245–312). Orlando, FL: Academic Press.

Van Gog, T., Paas, F., & van Merriënboer, J. J. G. (2005). Uncovering expertise-related differences in troubleshooting performance: Combining eye movement and concurrent verbal protocol data. *Applied Cognitive Psychology, 19*, 205-221.

Verdi, M. P., Kulhavy, R. W., Stock, W. A., Rittschof, K., & Johnson, J. T. (1996). Text learning using scientific diagrams: Implications for classroom use. *Contemporary Educational Psychology, 21*, 487-499.

Wickens, C. D. (2002). Multiple resources and performance prediction. *Theoretical Issues in Ergonomics Science, 3*, 159-177.

Zhang, J. (1997). The nature of external representations in problem solving. *Cognitive Science, 21*, 179-217.

ADDITIONAL READINGS

Biederman, I. (1987). Recognition-by-components: A theory of human image understanding. *Psychological Review, 94,* 115-147.

Blackwell, A. F., & Engelhardt, Y. (2002). A meta-taxonomy for diagram research. In M. Anderson & B. Meyer & P. Olivier (Eds.), *Diagrammatic representation and reasoning* (pp. 47-64). London: Springer.

Carney, R. N., & Levin, J. R. (2002). Pictorial illustrations still improve students' learning from text. *Educational Psychology Review, 14,* 5-26.

Doblin, J. (1980). A structure for nontextual communications. In P. A. Kolers, M. E. Wrolstad & H. Bouma (Eds.), *Processing of visible language 2* (pp. 89-111). New York, NY: Plenum Press.

Eliot, J. (1980). Classification of figural spatial tests. *Perceptual and Motor Skills, 51,* 847-851.

Eliot, J. (1987). *Models of psychological space: Psychometric, developmental, and experimental approaches.* NY: Springer.

Goldberg, J. H., & Kotval, X. P. (1999). Computer interface evaluation using eye movements: methods and constructs. *International Journal of Industrial Ergonomics, 24,* 631-645.

Goldsmith, E. (1984). *Research into illustration: An approach and a review.* Cambridge, MA: Cambridge University Press.

Groner, R., McConkie, G. W., & Menz, C. (Eds.). (1985). *Eye movements and human information processing.* Amsterdam: Elsevier.

Haber, R. N., & Wilkenson, L. (1982). Perceptual components of computer displays. *IEEE CG&A, 2,* 23-35.

Holsanova, J. (2008). *Discourse, vision, and cognition.* Amsterdam/Philadelphia: Benjamins.

Johansson, R., Holsanova, J., & Holmqvist, K. (2006). Pictures and spoken descriptions elicit similar eye movements during mental imagery, both in light and in complete darkness. *Cognitive Science, 30,* 1053-1079.

Lemke, J. L. (1998). Multiplying meaning: Visual and verbal semiotics in scientific text. In J. R. Martin & R. Veel (Eds.), *Reading science: Critical and functional perspectives of the discourses of science* (pp. 87-111). New York: Routledge.

Mandler, J., & Johnson, M. (1976). Some of the thousand words a picture is worth. *Journal of experimental Psychology: Human Learning and Memory, 2,* 529-540.

Marr, D. (1992). *Vision. A computational investigation into the human representation and processing of visual information.* New York, NY: Holt.

Massironi, M. (2002). *The psychology of graphic images: Seeing, drawing, communicating.* Mahwah, NJ: Erlbaum.

Najjar, L. J. (1998). Principles of educational multimedia user interface design. *Human Factors, 40,* 311-323.

Purchase, H. C. (1999). Informationally equivalent representations: an architecture and applications. In J. Wiles & Dartnell (Eds.), *Perspectives on Cognitive Science. Theories, experiments, and foundations* (Vol. 2). Stanford, Conneticut: Ablex Publishing Corporation.

Rayner, K. (1998). Eye movements in reading and information processing: 20 years of research. *Psychological Bulletin, 124,* 372-422.

Schnotz, W. (2002). Towards an integrated view of learning from text and visual displays. *Educational Psychology Review, 14,* 101-120.

Schnotz, W. & Kulhavy, R. W. (Eds.) (1994) *Comprehension of graphics.* New York, NY: Elsevier.

Tufte, E. R. (1997). *Visual explanations.* Cheshire, CT: Graphics Press.

Tufte, E. R. (2001). *The visual display of quantitative information.* Cheshire, CT: Graphics Press.

Underwood, G. (Ed.). (2005). *Cognitive Processes in Eye Guidance.* London, UK.: Oxford University Press.

Vekiri, I. (2002). What is the value of graphical displays in learning? *Educational Psychology Review, 14,* 261-312.

Chapter VI
The Influence of Visual and Temporal Dynamics on Split Attention:
Evidences from Eye Tracking

Florian Schmidt-Weigand
University of Kassel, Germany

ABSTRACT

This chapter introduces eye tracking as a method to observe how the split of visual attention is managed in multimedia learning. The chapter reviews eye tracking literature on multirepresentational material. A special emphasis is devoted to recent studies conducted to explore viewing behavior in learning from dynamic vs. static visualizations and the matter of pacing of presentation. A presented argument is that the learners' viewing behavior is affected by design characteristics of the learning material. Characteristics like the dynamics of visualization or the pace of presentation only slightly influence the learners' visual strategy, while user interaction (i.e., learner controlled pace of presentation) leads to a different visual strategy compared to system-paced presentation. Taking viewing behavior as an indicator of how split attention is managed the harms of a split source format in multimedia learning can be overcome by implementing a user interaction that allows the learner to adapt the material to perceptual and individual characteristics.

INTRODUCTION

"Before information can be stored (…), it must be extracted and manipulated in working memory." (Paas, Tuovinen, Tabbers, & Van Gerven, 2003, p. 64).

In multimedia learning environments, a learner often has to extract and integrate information from different sources of information like words and pictures. Empirical evidences as well as theoretical considerations led to various instructional design principles to present those different sources of information in a learner supporting fashion (e.g. Mayer, 2001, 2005; Sweller, van Merrienboer, & Paas, 1998). The attentional, perceptual, and cognitive demands of multimedia instruction, however, are mostly *inferred* from learners' performance on subsequent tasks or self-reported difficulties with the materials at hand. In order to advance theoretical approaches and to refine instructional design principles process-related but subjective measures (e.g. cognitive load) and objective but product-related measures (e.g. learning outcomes) need to be complemented with more objective *and* process-related measures (Brünken, Plass, & Leutner, 2003; Paas et al., 2003). An often suggested, well suited, albeit – in multimedia learning – seldom-used process-related observation is the learner's viewing behavior during acquisition.

The absence of studies applying, for example, eye tracking methodology in this area may at least partly be explained by a lack of satisfying theoretical understanding of how the presumably complex cognitive processes involved in multimedia learning correspond to viewing behavior. The chapter tries to take a step towards an understanding of such viewing behavior in multimedia learning environments. Before we can discuss and further investigate how a particular viewing behavior may correspond to a particular learning outcome it is necessary to explore, if and how multimedia design actually affects viewing behavior. Reviewing the eye tracking research on combined presentation of text and pictures and providing recent research results of eye tracking studies in multimedia learning the chapter aims to answer the following questions:

1. How do learners split their visual attention during learning from a multimedia instruction? And
2. Which attributes of a multimedia instruction *moderate* a learner's viewing behavior?

BACKGROUND

Currently, research on multimedia learning and instructional design is influenced by two theoretical frameworks, cognitive load theory (Sweller et al. 1998) and Mayer's (2001) cognitive theory of multimedia learning. The main aim of these theoretical approaches is to base instructional design on "how the human mind works" (Mayer, 2001, p. 41). The most central concept of human cognitive architecture in both, the cognitive load theory and the cognitive theory of multimedia learning, is working memory. The central role of working memory for the matter of understanding and learning stems from the assumption that, simply stated, working memory is the gateway between the external world and the internal cognitive entities. Meaningful learning requires the learner to select relevant information, to organize that information in a coherent structure, and to integrate this structure into existing knowledge. Working memory plays an essential role since it is here, where the selection, organization, and integration processes are assumed to take place.

Among the various models and theories of working memory (for an overview, see Miyake & Shah, 1999) consensus exists on two aspects that are relevant to multimedia learning. First, most theorists agree that working memory resources are limited, and second, in most models of working memory there are, apart from a central regulation system, two or more separate subsystems. The notion of separate subsystems comes into play whenever information is presented in different codes (e.g. words, pictures, etc.) and/or different modalities (eye, ear, etc.) as it is the case in multimedia learning. In accordance with Baddeley's (1986) working memory model cognitive load theory and the cognitive theory of multimedia learning assume different subsystems or processing channels for visual and auditory information. Visual information is processed in a visuo-spatial sketchpad; auditory information is processed in an auditory loop. The limited processing capacities of the subsystems are easily exhausted by multimedia learning material. Consequently, the commonly assumed positive effect of multi-representational material on learning – as expressed by the multimedia principle (Fletcher & Tobias, 2005; Mayer, 2001) – is complemented by a set of design principles that deal with the issue, how to overcome problems connected with the presentation of multiple information sources (Mayer, 2001, 2005).

One of these principles is the so-called modality principle: "Students learn better when words in a multimedia message are presented as spoken rather than printed text" (Mayer, 2001, p. 134). The theoretical explanations for this superiority of spoken over written text presentation in multimedia learning basically rest on the limitations of visual processing. If verbal information is added to some visualization (illustration, graph, etc.) in written form, both information sources must be processed by the visual processing channel. As we know from everyday experience, we usually cannot attend simultaneously to spatially distinct visual information sources. Physiologically, visual acuity is restricted to an area of about 1° to 2° of visual angle which on a computer monitor in 80 cm distance roughly corresponds to a circular area with a diameter of 2.5 cm (approximately corresponding to the size of a quarter dollar coin). Thus, in order to extract all information learners are forced to split their visual attention between the information sources. Consequently, before integrating both sources, the source that was attended first must be held active in working memory until the corresponding information in the second source is found and processed. The more information is held active or the more capacity is needed to search for corresponding information the more cognitive resources are occupied, resulting in a higher cognitive load. Presenting spoken rather than written text is supposed to reduce this load by *eliminating* the need to split visual attention between the two sources.

The modality principle is supported by several studies verifying that it is more beneficial for learning if text in simultaneous presentation with visualizations is presented aurally rather than visually (Brünken & Leutner, 2001; Mayer & Moreno, 1998; Moreno & Mayer, 1999; Mousavi, Low, & Sweller, 1995; Schmidt-Weigand, Kohnert, & Glowalla, 2008; Tabbers, 2002; Tindall-Ford, Chandler, & Sweller, 1997; for a review see Ginns, 2005). For example, Moreno and Mayer (1999) used a sequence of 16 animated illustrations depicting the process of lightning. The illustrations dynamically visualized e.g. the motion of cool air that becomes heated or positive charges moving up to the cloud producing a flash light. Illustrations were accompanied by an expository text describing each of the major events. Text was spoken, written inside the illustration frame or written below the illustration frame. Participants performed better on subsequent retention and transfer tests when text was spoken rather than written (modality effect). Within written text conditions, participants performed better when text was written inside rather than below the illustration frame (spatial contiguity effect).

As outlined above, these effects can be explained by differing processing demands due to a visual split attention. However, as Moreno and Mayer (1999) point out "the superiority of concurrent animation and narration over concurrent animation with on-screen text might [also] be caused by students missing part of the visual information while they are reading the on-screen text (or vice versa)" (Moreno & Mayer, 1999, p. 359). Thus, split attention entails a cognitive and a perceptual component. In fact, due to the afore mentioned physiological boundaries several theories on visual attention allocation (for an overview, see Allport, 1989) suggest that the eye itself is a limiting factor for information processing. The resources of working memory may or may not be sufficient to process all information gathered by the eye. But the eye itself is surely limited in the amount of information that can be fixated and gathered in a discrete time interval. Reconsidering the introductory quotation, information may have to be extracted and manipulated in working memory before it can be stored (Paas et al., 2003), but it also must be extracted before it can be manipulated. Tversky, Morrison, and Betrancourt (2002) refer to this notion as the *Apprehension Principle*. The structure and content of the representation must be readily and accurately perceived and comprehended.

In most studies the actual split of a learner's visual attention has mostly been inferred from subsequent learning outcomes or self-ratings of cognitive load. In order to explore, *how* a learner actually splits his or her visual attention between written text and visualizations it appears reasonable, if not necessary, to observe the *process* of allocating visual attention and cognitive ressources to split information sources. One method that is commonly associated with visual attention and cognitive processing is the measurement of eye movements. The relationship between visual attention and eye movements has been extensively investigated (cf. Rayner, 1998). In complex information processing such as reading, the link between the two is probably quite tight. For such complex tasks it is commonly assumed that there is a functional relationship between the allocation of visual attention, cognitive processing and eye movements. Before outlining these assumptions it is necessary to shortly consider particularities of eye movements.

Contrary to introspection we do not move our eyes smoothly over some static visual display (e.g. a text or a graphic) but instead make sudden jumps from one location to another. There are periods of 100 to 500 ms, called fixations, in which the eyes come to rest, interspersed with rapid eye movements of 15-40 ms (depending on the size of the eye movement), called saccades (cf. Reichle, Pollatsek, Fisher, & Rayner, 1998). During saccadic movements little visual information is acquired. Instead, the visual information necessary for reading or scene perception is acquired primarily during the fixations (cf. Just & Carpenter, 1980). Consequently, fixating a discrete area (words, sentences, objects, etc.) is commonly taken as a correlate of attentional and cognitive processes allocated to the inspected area (eye-mind assumption). That is, at the beginning of each new fixation visual attention is assumed to be allocated to the stimulus at the center of fixation. When the information within this area is sufficiently processed attention may be reallocated to a new stimulus in order to program the next saccade while the eye remains fixated. These covert shifts of attention are assumed to occur shortly before the next saccade is executed (Henderson, 1992; Reichle et al., 1998).

For the matter of split attention in multimedia learning two general aspects of a learner's viewing behavior might be of particular interest, (a) the distribution of fixations across the split information sources, and (b) the pattern of saccades from one source to the other. Unfortunately, none of the theories in the field of multimedia learnig predicts particular patterns of eye movements yet. However, applying the method of eye tracking may help gaining further insight into how much visual attention is captured by each of multiple visual information sources, how the integration of spatially separated stimuli is visually managed, and which attributes of a learning material moderate the split of visual attention.

EYE MOVEMENTS IN SPLIT ATTENTION CONDITIONS

Although eye movement studies have generated a good understanding of the processes involved in reading and in scene perception (for reviews, see Rayner, 1998; Underwood, 2005) only few experimental eye movement studies have addressed *combinations* of words and pictures in the past. Notable exceptions are studies from Hegarty on the comprehension of mechanical diagrams (Hegarty, 1992a, 1992b; Hegarty &

Just, 1993), Carroll, Young, & Guertin (1992) on the visual analysis of cartoons, d'Ydewalle and colleagues on attention allocation in subtitled television (d'Ydewalle, Praet, Verfaillie, & Van Rensbergen, 1991; d'Ydewalle & Gielen, 1992), Rayner, Rotello, Stewart, Keir, & Duffy (2001) on the integration of text and pictorial information in print advertisements, and more recently Holsanova and colleagues on newspaper reading (Holmqvist, Holsanova, & Holmberg, 2007; Holsanova, Rahm, & Holmqvist, 2006). Meanwhile, a growing number of eye tracking studies have been conducted with multimedia learning material (e.g. Ciernak, Scheiter, & Gerjets, 2007; Faraday & Sutcliffe, 1996; Folker, Ritter, & Sichelschmidt, 2005; Hannus & Hyönä, 1999; Schmidt-Weigand et al., 2008).

A common result among these eye movement studies is that people favor text over pictures. Rayner et al. (2001) investigated the pattern of viewing behavior for people looking at print advertisements. When looking at an advertisement viewers tended to read the large print first, then the smaller print and then they looked at the picture. Although some viewers did an initial cursory scan of the picture, most of them did not alternate fixations between the text and the picture part of the ad. Also the viewing behavior in subtitled television is largely text directed (d'Ydewalle et al., 1991; d'Ydewalle & Gielen, 1992). Clearly, when foreign movies are subtitled in the local language, reading subtitles is more or less obligatory. However, d'Ydewalle and colleagues (1991) found that reading subtitles is preferred even if the movie and the subtitles were both presented in the local language. Since this preference was observed no matter if the participants were familiar (Dutch) or rather unfamiliar (Americans) with subtitled television the authors conclude that either (a) reading subtitles is more efficient in following and understanding a movie or (b) processing of the visual modality is more dominant.

In learning material one may expect illustrations to attract some more visual attention because

of their functions in the learning context. Levie and Lentz (1982) distinguish four general functions: (1) attention guiding, (2) affective, (3) cognitive, and (4) compensatory functions. However, the assumed benefits of illustrations do not seem to be reflected in the learners viewing behavior. Hannus and Hyönä (1999) found that learning from illustrated textbooks is heavily driven by the text. They presented text passages from 4th-year elementary school biology books to elementary school children. The children spent 80% of their learning time on reading the texts. Furthermore, 66% of the time spent inspecting illustrations was devoted to read the figure captions! In accordance with Rayner et al. (2001) there was also little back-and-forth looking between a relevant text segment and a corresponding illustration. This viewing behavior may have been due to some text characteristics. As the authors note, in their text book passages, no reference was made in the text to any illustration.

Folker et al. (2005) used color-coding to make references between text and illustrations more explicit. Twenty students (mean age 24.3 years) read a textbook passage describing the function and the different phases of mitotic cell division. In the color-coding condition, passages of the text corresponding to structures or labels in the pictures were of the same color. Participants in this group were significantly faster in processing the material than participants who had no explicit color reference in the text (control condition). The faster processing, however, was due to fewer fixations on the picture region in the color condition while the time spent reading remained constant across conditions. Unfortunately, Folker et al. (2005) do not report the movement patterns between text and picture region. Thus, we do not know if color coding simply facilitated the processing of the illustration or if it evoked a different visual strategy.

It might well be the case that the textbook illustrations used by Hannus and Hyönä (1999) and Folker et al. (2005) were not sufficiently helpful or necessary to understand the text. In multimedia learning, however, a special emphasis is given to the *integration* of text and pictures in working memory. Hegarty (1992a, 1992b; Hegarty & Just, 1993) applied diagrams and verbal descriptions of pulley systems in order to examine such integration processes. In a study from Hegarty and Just (1993) participants viewed text and diagrams describing pulley systems. Being instructed to understand how the respective pulley system worked, viewers tended to inspect the diagram at the ends of sentences and clauses. Approximately 80% of the participants' diagram inspections occurred after reading the segment describing that particular aspect of the diagram. Thus, the participants' viewing behavior as they read text accompanied by diagrams suggests that viewers attempted to fully interpret a sentence or clause before inspecting its referent in the diagram. Hegarty (1992b) concluded that the construction of a mental model from the material was largely text directed.

In another study, Hegarty (1992a) further examined the construction process of the mental model by using a sentence-picture verification task. Participants were presented with a static diagram of a pulley system and a sentence describing a dynamic attribute of a component of the pulley system. Participants were asked to respond whether the sentence was true or false of the depicted system. Recording reaction time and inspection time, she found that differences in reaction time were largely due to differences in diagram inspection time. Both, reaction time and inspection time were highly related to the statements' difficulty (number of inferences required to verify a dynamic attribute). Concerning the strategies, participants typically read the sentence before inspecting the diagram in 98.5% of trials, suggesting that the overall strategy was to construct a representation of the text first and then verify this representation against the diagram. However, participants also reread the text during a trial, thus switching back and forth between text and diagram about three times per

trial on average. The number of re-readings was again related to the statements' difficulty, being higher the more inferences were required to verify the sentence. Hegarty interpreted these results in terms of working memory load. The higher the demands of inferring and storing the motion of the pulley system, the earlier the sentence representation decayed and had to be reactivated by re-reading.

In the Hegarty (1992a) study participants had to infer motion from a static diagram of a dynamic pulley system. Exploiting the possibilities of computer-based instruction, processes that are dynamic by nature can be depicted by dynamic rather than static visualizations. In comparison to static visualizations, the cognitive demands to process and integrate written text accompanied by *dynamic* visualizations may be different. Motion does not need to be inferred by the learner but is readily available. This direct access to dynamic information may cause a visual strategy different from the one commonly observed with static visualizations. First, the depicted information does not need to be mentally animated. And second, dynamic visual information is more transient than a static display. Therefore, learners may be inclined to attend to dynamic visualizations earlier in the integration process, being not as much text directed as with static visualizations.

Taken together, the management of split attention during learning appears to be driven by written text. But how is the visual attention to written text influenced by the presence of dynamic compared to static visualizations and/or the presence and degree of time constraints? The following sections describe a series of four experiments in which learners' eye fixations were tracked as they watched a multimedia instruction on the formation of lightning similar to the one used by Moreno and Mayer (1999). Besides eye movements, the experiments applied measures of cognitive load as well as learning outcomes. In order to explore the influence of split attention on cognitive load and learning outcome measures the experiments also entailed presentation conditions in which text was spoken. The focus, however, will be set on the learners' viewing behavior under split attention conditions.

EFFECTS OF DYNAMIC VS. STATIC VISUALIZATIONS ON SPLIT ATTENTION

The purpose of the first two experiments was to examine whether characteristics of visualizations moderate the effects of split attention on viewing behavior. By comparing dynamic with static visualizations, the experiments ask whether and to what degree the transience of visualizations affects visual attention allocation. How much attention is devoted to dynamic compared to static visualizations? How is visual attention on written text affected by the presence or absence of dynamics in visualizations? And, how do learners estimate the presence or absence of dynamics in visualizations in relation to their split of attention? To answer these questions, the experiments observed viewing behavior and collected subjective estimates of students who received one of the following four presentation formats: a multimedia instruction presenting (1) dynamic visualizations together with written text, (2) dynamic visualizations with spoken text, (3) static visualizations with written text, and (4) static visualizations with spoken text. The learning material consisted of a 16-step multimedia instruction on the formation of lightning. The content of the material was based on an animation used by Moreno and Mayer (1999). Visualizations were designed to illustrate the dynamics of the major events (cf. Figure 1).

Figure 1. Selected frames of the multimedia instruction (scenes 1 – 4)

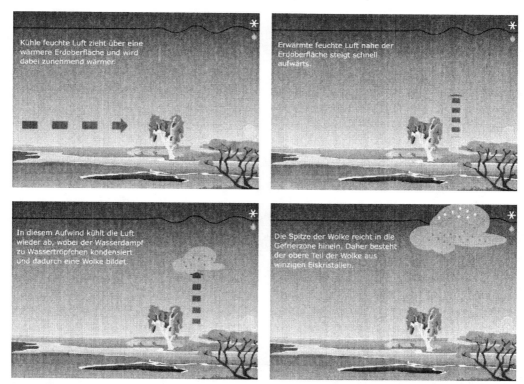

Note: The expository text is written in German since the experiments were run at Justus Liebig University, Giessen, Germany.

Both experiments confirmed that split attention during learning from the applied multimedia instruction was largely text directed. The presence of written text led learners to attend to the text before splitting their visual attention by switching back and forth between text and visualization. Overall, participants spent up to twice as much time reading than inspecting visualizations and switched on average 4 times per scene between written text and visualizations. Both, viewing time on text and visualizations as well as the number of transitions between both information sources were slightly affected by the presence vs. absence of dynamics within the visualizations. Participants spent some more time on dynamic compared to static visualizations and, thus, less time reading text. Furthermore, experiment 2 revealed that visual attention was captured by dynamic visualizations, indicated by a lower number of transitions between text and visualizations compared to static visualizations. However, the amount of initial reading after a scene change was not affected by the presentation format of the visualizations.

Experiment 2 obtained self-ratings in order to assess cognitive load. These measures allow a more detailed view on the attentional aspects of presentation format. Participants reported a higher difficulty with the learning material for written compared to spoken text presentation ("How easy or difficult was it for you to learn something about lightning from the presentation you just saw?"), confirming the afore mentioned effect of text modality. In addition, participants were asked to give subjective estimates of the following more detailed statements: (1) "I would have preferred to stop the presentation myself at certain points", (2) "I would have preferred to look at some illustrations again", (3) "I would have preferred to rewind and repeat parts of the text", (4) "I missed parts of the textual information", (5) "I missed parts of the illustrations", (6) "It was difficult for me to relate textual and pictorial information to each other", (7) "The illustration

distracted me from textual information", (8) "The textual information distracted me from the illustration", and (9) "How did you perceive the presentation pace? The pace was …". Statements 1 to 8 had to be rated on a 6-point scale from completely false, false, rather false, rather true, true to completely true. Statement 9, concerning the pace of presentation had to be answered on a 7-point scale from very slow, slow, rather slow, optimal, rather fast, fast, to very fast. The internal consistency of the statements was considerably good (Cronbach's α = .83). Correlations between single statements and overall difficulty with the material range from r = .25 to r = .51. The highest correlation is reached by statement (3) (repeat parts of the text). This correlation highlights the role of text comprehension in cognitive load.

Furthermore, the initial and constant reliance on written text, as found in numerous eye tracking studies, suggests that learners follow a visual strategy, i.e. voluntarily attending to written text. In contrast to this hypothesis, participants in the experiment reported a significantly higher agreement with statement (8) than with statement (7), i.e. they felt distracted from inspecting visualizations by the presence of written text (and not vice versa), no matter if visualizations were dynamic or static. Thus, initial reading appears to be rather automatic than intended.

Since the presentation time was limited (i.e. once the animation was started it proceeded with a constant pace), the time spent reading was lost for inspecting the visualizations. Consequently, participants rated presentation time as less appropriate in written compared to spoken text conditions (statement (9)), i.e. the split of visual attention was subjectively time consuming. Thus, the effect of split attention can be described as a distraction effect evoked by written text in a time limited presentation condition. Participants felt they needed more time to sufficiently attend to all offered information sources.

Taken together, presenting written rather than spoken text in a multimedia instruction leads to a rather automatic initial reading behavior that is, compared to spoken text presentation, perceived as a time-consuming process. Consequently, one should expect that with longer presentation duration learners devote relatively more time to visualizations than to written text. Once enough time is given to attend and integrate all information sources the harms of split attention should disappear. Furthermore, the visual strategy may change as soon as the learner can control the pace of presentation. The experiments presented in the following section were designed to test these hypotheses.

EFFECTS OF TIME CONSTRAINTS ON SPLIT ATTENTION

The main idea of these two experiments was that pacing is an additional source of cognitive load. If learners have more time to read expository text, the need to split visual attention between written text and visualizations should be less harmful. Moreover, if learning is largely text directed, as indicated by prior studies, split attention should have a larger effect on visual compared to verbal information. Finally, it is an open question how additional time is used in terms of visual attention allocation. We may expect that after reading has been successfully completed relatively more time can be spent viewing visualizations.

The purpose of the first of these experiments was to examine the influence of system-controlled pacing of instruction on effects of split attention and text modality. The learning material consisted of the same multimedia instruction as in the first two studies. Dynamic visualizations on the formation of lightning were accompanied by expository text (visualization format was not varied). The text was either presented in spoken or written format. The variation of pacing was derived in the following manner. In the fast condition, timing was set to a ratio of 120 words per minute resulting in a presentation duration of

140 s. This pace approximates a timing originally applied in Mayer and Moreno (1998) by adjusting the pace of presentation to a normal speaker's rate. Medium and slow paces were obtained by reducing the ratio successively with a factor of 0.75. Thus, the ratio was 90 words per minute for medium pace and 67.5 words per minute for slow pace resulting in durations of 187 s and 249 s respectively. These variations resulted in a 2 (spoken vs. written text) x 3 (fast, medium, and slow pace) factorial design. Results are presented for the split attention conditions, i.e. where text was written.

Overall, learners under split attention conditions showed a comparable viewing behavior at the beginning of each scene, i.e. they started with a reading sequence. However, the longer the presentation lasted relatively more time was spent inspecting visualizations. As it was expected, the absolute number of transitions between text and visualizations increased with presentation duration. However, also the *relative* number of transitions (i.e. transitions per second) increased with presentation duration. All these changes emerged in the additional time for each scene. Comparing the viewing behavior only in the time intervals of the fastest pace of presentation revealed no differences in the ratio of time spent reading to time spent inspecting visualization or in the number of transitions. Deviating viewing behavior obviously settled in the additional time given by slower pacing.

In accordance with this viewing behavior, the difference between written and spoken text presentation became more evident in a visual memory task compared to a text retention task. This difference was larger the faster the pace of presentation was. In addition, subjective cognitive load revealed that the harms of split attention (i.e. the modality effect) were apparent under serious time constraints. Overall, cognitive load dropped down for longer presentation durations. A modality effect could only be found under fast presentation.

The observed patterns of viewing behavior and its contribution to cognitive load and learning outcome can be understood in terms of particularities of reading. People are known to differ in reading speed (cf. Just & Carpenter, 1987). Reading speed reflects individual abilities (e.g. Jackson & McClelland, 1975, 1979; Just & Carpenter, 1992) but it is also adjusted to characteristics of the text (e.g. Graesser, Hoffman, & Clark, 1980) and task demands (e.g. Hartley, Stojack, Mushaney, Annon, & Lee, 1994). Concerning the specific task of reading to summarize expository text, Hyönä, Lorch, and Kaakinen (2002) identified different types of eye movement patterns. Participants read (and subsequently summarized) two expository texts (approximately 1,000 words each). 75% of their participants followed a linear reading strategy, i.e. most readers went through the texts from left to right with only few backward saccades to earlier passages, so-called regressions. Such regressions usually do not exceed 10% of the saccades occurring during reading (cf. Rayner, 1998). The linear readers in the Hyönä et al. study could be further divided into "fast linear readers" (mean reading rate: 231 words/minute) and "slow linear readers" (133 words/minute). These results confirm (a) the linear reading behavior consistently found across various reading tasks and (b) the inter-individual differences of the pace of progressing through the text. There was, however, a group of 20% of readers who followed a distinctive strategy, the "topic structure processors". With a reading rate of 139 words per minute this type of reader was rather slow. Compared to the linear readers the topic structure processors devoted additional visual attention to headings and topic-final sentences as expressed by significantly more and longer reinspective fixations. Most notably, these readers turned out to have the highest working memory span (Danemann & Carpenter, 1980) and to have written the best summaries. The worst summaries were produced by the slow readers. While the comparably slow reading rate of the topic structure processors appears due to deliberate,

probably effortful strategies for remembering and summarizing the expository texts, in the case of the slow linear readers this same rate appears to be a rather unsuccessful attempt to compensate for comprehension difficulties.

Individual differences in reading speed may interfere with the learning task in a system paced multimedia instruction for several reasons. First, the faster the pace the more likely some – especially visualized – information is missed or not sufficiently processed due to the general tendency to attend to written text first. Second, a faster pace of presentation especially challenges slow readers probably resulting in even poorer text comprehension. And third, adjusting ones reading speed to a system-controlled pacing may hinder an adjustment to the complexity of the content and the application of deliberate viewing strategies. Thus, split attention effects might at least partly be caused by a mismatch of system-paced instruction with self-paced reading. These hypotheses gain support from a final study to be reported in this chapter. In this study, learners were under control of the pace of presentation. Each of the 16 scenes lasted until participants hit the space bar to start the next scene. Text was again either written or spoken.

First of all, learning under self-paced presentation did not reveal any differences between written and spoken text presentation in terms of learning outcomes and cognitive load. That is, the learners were able to adjust the pace of presentation to be comparably successful in learning from the animation and to experience a comparable cognitive load. One may expect the higher cognitive load under split attention to be expressed in a longer time on task for written compared to spoken text presentation. Contrary to this hypothesis, the learner-paced presentation durations in written text presentation were almost identical to spoken text presentation in terms of means, variances, and ranges. Overall, the variation of system-paced presentation durations in the former experiment (140, 187, and 249 s, respectively) roughly fitted

Figure 2. Time spent reading (triangles) and time spent inspecting visualizations (circles) for each learner under written text conditions in system controlled (left panel) vs. learner controlled (right panel) presentation

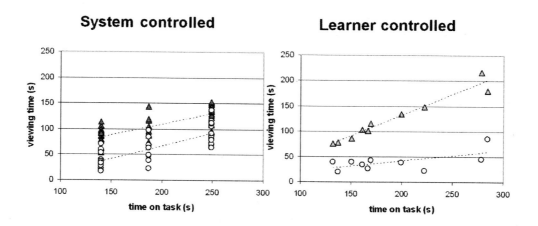

in with the range of learner-paced presentation durations (132 to 285 s). It is also notable that the average presentation duration in this experiment (183 s) was very close to the medium system-paced presentation duration of 187 s in the former experiment. Due to these similarities on the time dimension, differences in the observed viewing behavior of both experiments can be devoted to the issue of learner control. Figure 2 depicts the amounts of time each participant spent reading and inspecting visualizations under system controlled (left panel) and learner controlled (right panel) presentation. Figure 3 depicts the number of transitions for each participant in both experiments.

As can be seen in the right panel of Figure 2 time on task under learner-controlled presentation is almost exclusively driven by the time learners spent viewing text. That is, while participants in system-paced instruction used additional presentation time in favor of illustrations (Figure 2, left panel) participants in learner-paced instruction used additional presentation time exclusively for reading. Furthermore, transitions in learner-paced instruction did not systematically vary with time on task (Figure 3, right panel) while in system-

paced instruction additional presentation time lead to an increase of transitions between text and visualizations (Figure 3, left panel). Taken together, participants in system-paced instruction used additional presentation time in favor of visualizations and switches between text and visualizations while participants in self-paced instruction used additional presentation time mainly for reading. Apart from the time learners spent reading the text, they showed a highly stable fixation pattern in a self-paced instruction. Learners adjusted the pace of presentation to their individual reading speed and engaged in an otherwise systematic viewing behavior.

These results can be interpreted in the following manner. The longer the system-paced presentation duration was the more participants can be assumed to have read the written text. They really had additional time to spend on inspecting visualizations and "to look around". In learner-paced instruction, the split of visual attention between text and visualizations appears rather systematic and is comparable to the viewing behavior shown by the medium system-paced presentation group. The general strategy was to read (some portion or all of the) text, then switching to inspect the

Figure 3. Number of transitions between text and visualizations for written text conditions in system controlled (left panel) vs. learner controlled (right panel) presentation

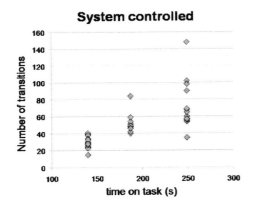 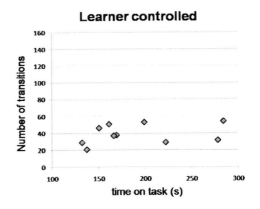

visualization, re-reading some portion of text and going back to the illustration once more. The inter-individual difference in the time spent reading almost perfectly correlated with the chosen presentation duration. Thus, an optimal fit of presentation pace to task demands in concurrent presentation of text and visualizations is apparently driven by individual reading speed.

THEORETICAL IMPLICATIONS

The findings of the studies reported in this chapter have some implications for theoretical accounts of split attention effects in multimedia learning, namely cognitive load theory (Sweller et al., 1998) and the cognitive theory of multimedia learning (Mayer, 2001). Split attention effects are usually explained in terms of limited cognitive resources. Two further resources were introduced in this chapter that may interact with the cognitive processes associated with split attention: (a) visual perception and (b) learning time. As noted earlier, due to restrictions of visual acuity our eyes have to move in order to gather all information given in a multimedia learning material. In fact, the term "split attention" may rather refer to the common insight that we cannot look at a text

and an illustration at the same time. Eye tracking studies revealed that we manage this limitation of our eyes in a fairly consistent way. Learners almost immediately look at written text and usually spend much more time reading than viewing visualizations. Some researchers concluded that text is perceived as the main medium for the acquisition of information. In this view, the observed eye movements indicate a strategic and reasonable decision made by the learners. In fact, expository text is a highly structured information source and people are used to gain much information from reading. Visualizations are usually not self-explaining and are often accompanied by written text. Reading the text first might often have been experienced as being helpful in order to understand visualized information. In one of the presented studies, however, participants felt distracted from inspecting visualizations by the presence of written text – although they spent most of their time reading! Thus, the observed viewing behavior rather indicate a preconcious attentional capture of written text.

One may conclude that due to the attentional capture of written text visualizations are not sufficiently processed. But the comparably short fixation times on visualizations may also indicate a higher computational efficiency of pictures compared to text. As Larkin and Simon (1987) point out, "sentential representations [i.e. text] are sequential while diagrammatic representations [i.e. visualizations] are indexed by location in a plane. The information displayed by [visualizations] is only implicit in sentential representations and therefore has to be computed, sometimes at great cost, to make it explicit for use" (p. 65). In other words, reading requires word-by-word fixations, lexical access, and syntactic as well as semantic processing while the information depicted by visualizations may be gathered at a glance. In accordance with this interpretation, eye movement studies on scene perception have led to the conclusion that "participants get the gist of a scene very early in the process of looking. [...] The gist of the scene is abstracted on the first couple of fixations, and the remainder of fixations on the scene are used to fill in details" (Rayner, 1998, p. 398). However, whether the 'gist of a scene' is sufficient for learning depends on the complexity of the visualization and the complexity of referential connections between the text and the visualization.

A necessary precondition for split attention effects to occur is that one source of visual information cannot be understood without the other (Sweller, 1999), i.e. both sources have to be attended in order to "get the full picture" of what is to be learned. There is evidence that the interdependence between different learning elements moderate effects of split attention, being harder to handle for learning material of high compared to low "element interactivity" (Tindall-Ford et al., 1997). Element interactivity refers to the extent to which the learning task requires the learner to hold several related chunks of to-be-learned information in working memory simultaneously. As Ginns (2005) notes, there is no objective measure of element interactivity. However, eye movements may be interpreted as an indication of this interplay between text and visualizations. In the studies reviewed in this chapter eye movements varied with the complexity of the material.

A picture in an advertisement is almost surely less complex than, for example, the diagram of a pulley system. As a result, participants in the Rayner et al. (2001) study did not look back from the picture of an ad to the text while those re-readings occurred between a pulley diagram and the accompanied text (Hegarty, 1992b). Hegarty (1992a) interpreted the number of switches between the text and the visualization in terms of working memory load. More re-readings occurred when more inferences were required. Concerning the perceptual aspects of split attention there may be less content-specific variables that moderate split attention as well. For example, dynamic visualizations may be considered as less complex than static visualizations since the depicted dynamics are readily perceivable and do not need to be inferred by the learner. Accordingly, in one of the presented studies more alternations occured between text and static visualizations compared to text with dynamic visualizations.

The presented studies also highlighted the role of learning time for the management of split attention. In contrast to the physiological restrictions of visual perception, learning time is a resource that is either set by the 'instructor' or allocated by the learner. If learning time is restricted by a system-controlled pacing of instruction, it is an obvious source of extraneous cognitive load. Consequently, the pacing of instruction moderates effects associated with split attention (cf. Ginns, 2005). In the presented studies learners perceived multimedia instructions as "faster" when verbal explanations were written rather than spoken, a higher cognitive load only occurred for fast presentation paces, and no effect of text modality occurred at all when learners controlled the pace of presentation. Given the general tendency to attend to written text first, split attention under time constraints especially impairs processing time for the pictorial information. The results of the presented eye tracking studies support this view in showing that especially visual memory proved sensitive to the modality of text presentation.

Furthermore, participants spent relatively more time viewing visualizations when the pacing of instruction was slower.

But the influence of time constraints is not restricted to visualizations. Conversely, the comparison of viewing behavior under system-paced and self-paced instruction rather highlights the prominent role of reading for split attention effects once more. The pattern of viewing behavior in self-paced instruction is fundamentally different from the one observable in system-paced instruction. Under self-paced instruction, learners spent a comparable amount of time looking at visualizations while their time on task strongly varied with the time spent reading. In the absence of extraneous load in terms of time constraints, the inter-individual differences in reading time suggest that the main source of cognitive load in the instructional material was the text. In fact, text comprehension is well recognized as a matter of managing working memory load (Graesser & Britton, 1996; Just & Carpenter, 1992). The difference between system-paced and self-paced viewing behavior may indicate a change in cognitive strategies. Reading is an inherently self-paced activity. Individual reading speed does not only reflect text comprehension abilities but also the contribution of deliberate, probably effortful, strategies for remembering expository text (Hartley et al., 1994; Hyönä et al., 2002). While under system-paced presentation reading speed has to be adapted in some way to the pace of presentation, self-paced presentation allows the learner to engage in a more elaborated processing of verbal explanation. Consequently, written text must be assumed more compatible with self-paced than with system-paced instructions. In this view, under self-paced presentation written text may also be superior to spoken text. Actually, there already exists empirical evidence for such a "reversed" modality effect (Tabbers, 2002).

PRACTICAL IMPLICATIONS

The research presented in this chapter allows suggesting how split attention effects may be overcome. In time-limited presentation, (a) the perceptibility especially for the visualization is decreased, and (b) written text comprehension is disturbed. Consequently, negative influences of split attention on learning can be avoided if both information sources are sufficiently perceptible and/or if the design of a multimedia instruction ensures not to bother a regular reading behavior.

To make sure that all information sources in a multimedia instruction are sufficiently perceptible the instructional designer must consider the split of visual attention that occurs whenever two or more visual information sources are presented concurrently. In fact, current design guidelines already recommend presenting written text near rather than far from visualizations in order to minimize split attention (spatial contiguity principle). Furthermore, guiding visual attention to appropriate referents, e.g. by color-coding, can have positive effect on visual processing (Folker et al., 2005) and cognitive load (Kalyuga, Chandler, & Sweller, 1999). Due to the fact that learners consistently attend to written text first one might be seduced to present text and visualizations sequentially rather than concurrently. Indeed, sequential presentation eliminates visual split attention, which may facilitate text comprehension. But sequential presentation also eliminates the temporal contiguity between the text and the corresponding visualization. A number of studies have shown that concurrent presentation is superior to sequential presentation of corresponding information sources ('temporal contiguity principle', Mayer, 2001; for a review, see Ginns, 2006). In his meta-analysis, Ginns (2006) also identified the complexity of learning materials as a moderator of temporal contiguity effects. Indeed, complexity in terms of referential connections between text and visualizations may require alternations between both information sources. Thus, it is recommendable to present corresponding information sources close together in space *and* time as well as to make referential connections explicit.

Reducing split attention by spatial contiguity or color-coding while the presentation is still system-paced (as it is indeed the case in many of the studied materials) always bears the risk for the learner to miss some information. This risk is probably higher for visualizations than for text and if the material is rather complex. Furthermore, system-paced presentation may interfere with individual differences in (self-paced) reading speed. An easy way to avoid these problems is learner-paced instruction. Instead of specifying a system-controlled pace that may be appropriate for an average learner, this minimal form of user interaction allows each learner to adjust the pace of presentation to his or her individual needs. Doing so, the learner can ensure to capture all information that is displayed. An individually chosen pace allows the learner to follow a regular reading behavior that is susceptible to cognitive strategies. In this view, learner-control is not only recommendable to overcome difficulties with split attention in multimedia learning but learner-paced instructions can even benefit from written text presentation.

CONCLUSION

Two main conclusions can be drawn from the eye tracking studies outlined above. First, viewing behavior in combinations of text and visualizations follows a fairly stable pattern that can be moderated by design attributes of the instruction. In general, written text drags visual attention away from inspecting visualizations. Thus, visualizations have to "compete" with the text, whenever it is written. The degree of competition is influenced by visual dynamics as well as the presence and degree of time constraints. Learners adapt to these properties of a multimedia instruction by distributing their visual attention between written text and visualizations differently. Furthermore, they are able to adjust the pace of presentation to a regular reading strategy that only varies in the time taken to read text.

Second, under less attentional competition, less time constraints, and learner control of pace, effects of split attention change, decrease, or even disappear. The competition between written text and visualizations was stronger when visualizations were dynamic rather than static and when presentation time was seriously constrained. Especially when learners are relieved from time constraints, the need to split visual attention loses much of its detrimental effects. These differential effects on cognitive load and learning outcome are associated to particularities of the viewing behavior. In general, presenting written text forces the learner to read text. When learners can follow a regular reading strategy by controlling the pace of presentation they do not suffer from written (compared to spoken) text presentation. Thus, the need to read written text may or may not interfere with extracting information from visualizations depending on how seriously reading and viewing visualizations are disturbed by the design of a multimedia instruction.

A theoretical implication of these results is that current explanations of split attention need to incorporate resources of visual perception and learning time in addition to cognitive resources. As a practical consequence, the question for an instructional designer is if the displayed information can be sufficiently extracted by an individual learner. Understanding the demands of a particular learning material on the learner's perception and accounting for individual differences by implementing user interaction appears promising to advance the design of multimedia instructions in a learner-supporting fashion.

FUTURE RESEARCH DIRECTIONS

Concerning the limitations of the presented eye tracking studies, the applied learning materials consisted of rather short presentations. A three-minute multimedia instruction on the formation of lightning can be considered to be a prototypical case of an application of dynamic visualizations. For the matter of generality, this research must be extended to broader classes of multimedia learning material. For example, the comparison of viewing behavior under system-paced and self-paced instruction led to the hypothesis that reading strategies play an important role even in split attention. Effects of a strategic behavior may be rather small in an instruction of 3 minutes length. Thus, it appears worth examining if and how visual strategies may change with the amount of content, especially the amount of text.

Visual and temporal dynamics of a multimedia presentation are only two design characteristics that may be expected to affect a learner's viewing behavior. The patterns of viewing behavior in the presented studies highlighted the role of expository text in split attention. However, one can easily imagine more complex and/or abstract pictorial information, for example electric circuits or statistical graphs that may require more processing resources for visualizations than for written text. Similarly, text difficulty depends on the text structure and the subject matter. Furthermore, multimedia learning material can differ with respect to the referential connections between text and visualizations. It can be assumed that all these characteristics of a learning material affect the learner's viewing behavior and, thus, the way split attention is managed. In order to gain a better understanding of split attention effects one direction of further research is to explore the viewing behavior with learning material that systematically varies those aspects. Such research can help estimating the relative contribution of verbal explanations in comparison to visualizations and the contribution of "element interactivity" (Tindall-Ford et al., 1997) between textual and visual information.

Finally, eye tracking offers an extensive database. There are numerous ways in which those data can be analyzed that go way beyond the level of analyses presented in this chapter. For example, in reading research viewing behavior is usually not described in the overall time spent reading a text but in terms of gaze durations or single fixations on words and the saccadic movements between these gazes or fixations (Rayner, 1998). Such analyses are accompanied by theoretical models accounting for eye movements on the same level of description (e.g. Reichle et al., 1998). These fine-grained cognitive process models can be tested by tracing the eye-movement protocol (e.g. Salvucci & Anderson, 2001). So far, there is no such interplay between theories of multimedia learning and observations of viewing behavior, i.e. current models on the integration of verbal and pictorial information do not predict the time course of visually attending to the information sources. However, models develop with the level of observations they have to account for. Further eye tracking studies may stimulate to advance current models in order to allow predictions of fixation paths based on an accurate model of the learning process.

REFERENCES

Allport, A. (1989). Visual attention. In M. I. Posner (Ed.), *Foundations of cognitive science* (pp. 631-682). Cambridge, MA: MIT Press.

Baddeley, A. (1986). *Working memory.* Oxford, UK: Clarendon Press.

Brünken, R., & Leutner, D. (2001). Aufmerksamkeitsverteilung oder Aufmerksamkeitsfokussierung? Empirische Ergebnisse zur "Split-Attention-Hypothese" beim Lernen mit Multimedia. [Split attention or focusing of attention? Empirical results on the split-attention hypothesis in multimedia learning.]. *Unterrichtswissenschaft, 29,* 357-366.

Brünken, R., Plass, J. L., & Leutner, D. (2003). Direct measurement of cognitive load in multimedia learning. *Educational Psychologist, 38,* 53-61.

Carroll, P. J., Young, R. J., & Guertin, M. S. (1992). Visual analysis of cartoons: A view from the far side. In K. Rayner (Ed.), *Eye movements and visual cognition: Scene perception and reading* (pp. 444-461). New York: Springer.

Ciernak, G., Scheiter, K., & Gerjets, P. (2007, August). *Eye movements of differently knowledgeable learners during learning with split-source of integrated format.* Paper presented at the biannual meeting of the European Association of Research on Learning and Instruction (EARLI). Budapest, Hungary.

Danemann, M., & Carpenter, P. (1980). Individual differences in working memory and reading. *Journal of Verbal Learning and Verbal Behavior, 19,* 450-466.

d'Ydewalle, G., & Gielen, I. (1992). Attention allocation with overlapping sound, image, and text. In K. Rayner (Ed.), *Eye movements and visual cognition: Scene perception and reading.* (pp. 415-427). New York: Springer.

d'Ydewalle, G., Praet, C., Verfaillie, K., & Van Rensbergen, J. (1991). Watching subtitled television: Automatic reading behavior. *Communication Research, 18,* 650-666.

Faraday, P., & Sutcliffe, A. (1996). An empirical study of attending and comprehending multimedia presentations. In *Proceedings ACM Multimedia, 96,* 265-275. Boston MA.

Fletcher, J. D., & Tobias, S. (2005). The multimedia principle. In R. E. Mayer (Ed.), *The Cambridge Handbook of Multimedia Learning* (pp. 117-133). New York: Cambridge University Press.

Folker, S., Ritter, H., & Sichelschmidt (2005). Processing and integrating multimodal material – the influence of color-coding. In: B. G. Bara, L. Barsalou and M. Bucciarelli (Eds.), *Proceedings of the 27th Annual Conference of the Cognitive Science Society 2005 (p.* 690-695). Mahwah, NJ: Erlbaum.

Ginns, P. (2005). Meta-analysis of the modality effect. *Learning and Instruction, 15,* 313-331.

Ginns, P. (2006). Integrating information: A meta-analysis of the spatial contiguity and temporal contiguity effects. *Learning and Instruction, 16,* 511-525.

Graesser, A. C., & Britton, B. K. (1996). Five metaphors for text understanding. In B. K. Britton, & A. C. Graesser (Eds.), *Models of understanding text.* (pp. 341-352). Mahwah, NJ: Erlbaum.

Graesser, A. C., Hoffman, N. L., & Clark, L. F. (1980). Structural components of reading time. *Journal of Verbal Learning and Verbal Behavior, 19,* 135-151.

Hannus, M., & Hyönä, J. (1999). Utilization of illustrations during learning of science textbook passages among low- and high-ability children. *Contemporary Educational Psychology, 24,* 95-123.

Hartley, J. T., Stojack, C. C., Mushaney, T. J., Annon, T. A. K., & Lee, D. W. (1994). Reading speed and prose memory in older and younger adults. *Psychology and Aging, 9,* 216-223.

Hegarty, M. (1992a). Mental animation: Inferring motion from static displays of mechanical systems. *Journal of Experimental Psychology: Learning, Memory, and Cognition, 18,* 1084-1102.

Hegarty, M. (1992b). The mechanics of comprehension and comprehension of mechanics. In K. Rayner (Ed.), *Eye movements and visual cognition: Scene perception and reading.* (pp. 428-443). New York: Springer.

Hegarty, M., & Just, M. A. (1993). Constructing mental models of machines from text and diagrams. *Journal of Memory and Language, 32*, 717-742.

Henderson, J. M. (1992). Visual attention and eye movement control during reading and picture viewing. In: Rayner, K. (Ed.), *Eye movements and visual cognition: Scene perception and reading.* (pp. 260-283). New York: Springer.

Holmqvist, K., Holsanova, J., & Holmberg, N. (2007, August). *Newspaper reading, eye tracking and multimodality.* Paper presented at the bi-annual meeting of the European Association of Research on Learning and Instruction (EARLI). Budapest, Hungary.

Holsanova, J., Rahm, H., & Holmqvist, K. (2006). Entry points and reading paths on newspaper spreads: Comparing a semiotic analysis with eye-tracking measurements. *Journal of visual communication, 5*(1), 65-93.

Hyönä, J., Lorch, R., and Kaakinen, J. (2002). Individual differences in reading to summarize expository text: Evidence from eye fixation patterns. *Journal of Educational Psychology, 94*(1), 44-55.

Jackson, M. D., & McClelland, J. L. (1975). Sensory and cognitive determinants of reading speed. *Journal of Verbal Learning and Verbal Behavior, 14*, 565-574.

Jackson, M. D., & McClelland, J. L. (1979). Processing determinants of reading speed. *Journal of Experimental Psychology: General, 108*, 151-181.

Just, M. A., & Carpenter, P. A. (1980). A theory of reading: From eye fixations to comprehension. *Psychological Review, 87*, 329-354.

Just, M. A., & Carpenter, P. A. (1987). *The Psychology of Reading andLlanguage Comprehension.* Newton: Allyn and Bacon.

Just, M. A., & Carpenter, P. A. (1992). A capacity theory of comprehension: Individual differences in working memory. *Psychological Review, 99*, 122-149.

Kalyuga, S., Chandler, P., & Sweller, J. (1999). Managing split-attention and redundancy in multimedia instruction. *Applied Cognitive Psychology, 13*, 351-371.

Larkin, J. H., & Simon, H. A. (1987). Why a diagram is (sometimes) worth ten thousand words. *Cognitive Science, 11*, 65-100.

Levie, W., & Lentz, R. (1982). Effects of text illustration: A review of research. *Educational Communication and Technology Journal, 30*, 195-232.

Mayer, R. E. (2001). *Multimedia learning.* Cambridge: UK: Cambridge University Press.

Mayer, R. E. (Ed.) (2005). *The Cambridge Handbook of Multimedia Learning.* New York: Cambridge University Press.

Mayer, R. E., & Moreno, R. (1998). A split-attention effect in multimedia learning: Evidence for dual processing systems in working memory. *Journal of Educational Psychology, 90*, 312-320.

Miyake, A., & Shah, P. (Eds.) (1999). Models of working memory: Mechanisms of active maintenance and executive control. New York, NY: Cambridge University Press.

Moreno, R., & Mayer, R. E. (1999). Cognitive principles of multimedia learning: The role of modality and contiguity. *Journal of Educational Psychology, 91*, 358-368.

Mousavi, S. Y., Low, R., & Sweller, J. (1995). Reducing cognitive load by mixing auditory and visual presentation modes. *Journal of Educational Psychology, 87*, 319-334.

Paas, F. G., Tuovinen, J. E., Tabbers, H., & Van Gerven, P. W. M. (2003). Cognitive load measurement as a means to advance cognitive load theory. *Educational Psychologist, 38*, 63-71.

Rayner, K. (1998). Eye movements in reading and information processing: 20 years of research. *Psychological Bulletin, 124,* 372-422.

Rayner, K., Rotello, C. M., Stewart, A. J., Keir, J., & Duffy, S. A. (2001). Integrating text and pictorial information: Eye movements when looking at print advertisements. *Journal of Experimental Psychology: Applied, 7,* 219-226.

Reichle, E. D., Pollatsek, A., Fisher, D. L., & Rayner, K. (1998). Toward a model of eye movement control in reading. *Psychological Review, 105,* 125-157.

Salvucci, D. D., & Anderson, J. R. (2001). Automated eye-movement protocol analysis. *Human-Computer Interaction, 16,* 39-86.

Schmidt-Weigand, F., Kohnert, A., & Glowalla, U. (2008). *Integrating different sources of information in multimedia learning: An eye tracking study on split attention.* Manuscript submitted for publication.

Sweller, J. (1999). *Instructional design in technical areas.* Camberwell, Australia: ACER Press.

Sweller, J., van Merrienboer, J. J. G., & Paas, F. G. (1998). Cognitive architecture and instructional design. *Educational Psychology Review, 10,* 251-196.

Tabbers, H. K. (2002). *The modality of text in multimedia instructions. Refining the design guidelines.* Unpublished doctoral dissertation, Open University of the Netherlands Heerlen.

Tindall-Ford, S., Chandler, P., & Sweller, J. (1997). When two sensory modes are better than one. *Journal of Experimental Psychology: Applied, 3,* 257-287.

Tversky, B., Morrison, J. B., & Betrancourt, M. (2002). Animation: Can it facilitate? *International Journal of Human-Computer Studies, 57,* 247-262.

Underwood, G. (Ed.) (2005). *Cognitive Processes in Eye Guidance.* Oxford, UK: Oxford University Press.

ADDITIONAL READING

Ainsworth, S., & VanLabeke, N. (2004). Multiple forms of dynamic representation. *Learning and Instruction, 14,* 241-255.

Hyönä, J., Radach, R., & Deubel, H. (Eds.) (2003). *The Mind's Eyes: Cognitive and Applied Aspects of Eye Movements.* Oxford, UK: Elsevier.

Lowe, R. K. (1999). Extracting information from an animation during complex visual learning. *European Journal of Psychology of Education, 14,* 225–244.

Lowe, R. K. (2003). Animation and learning: Selective processing of information in dynamic graphics. *Learning and Instruction, 13,* 247–262.

Narayanan, H. N., & Hegarty, M. (2002). Multimedia design for communication of dynamic information. *International Journal of Human-Computer Studies, 57,* 279-315.

Schmidt-Weigand, F. (2007). Designing text and visualizations in multimedia learning: How to overcome split-attention effects? Saarbrücken, Germany: VDM.

Underwood, G. (Ed.) (1998). *Eye guidance in reading and scene perception.* Oxford, UK: Elsevier.

Van Gompel, R. (Ed.) (2007). *Eye movements: A window on mind and brain.* Amsterdam: Elsevier.

Chapter VII
Spatial and Nonspatial Integration in Learning and Training with Multimedia Systems

Tad T. Brunyé
U.S. Army NSRDEC, Consumer Research & Cognitive Science, USA
Tufts University, USA

Tali Ditman
Tufts University, USA & Massachusetts General Hospital, USA

Jason S. Augustyn
U.S. Army NSRDEC, Consumer Research & Cognitive Science, USA

Caroline R. Mahoney
U.S. Army NSRDEC, Consumer Research & Cognitive Science, USA
Tufts University, USA

ABSTRACT

Multiformat and modality interfaces have become popular and effective tools for presenting information in training and instructional systems. Technological innovation, however, has far surpassed researchers' understanding of how and under what circumstances these technologies are useful towards information gathering. Some recent research has begun to characterize the cognitive mechanisms that may be responsible for the comprehension and memory advantages typically seen with multimedia learning, as well as the role of individual differences in this process. Other work has defined effective pedagogical practices, such as instructional content and organization, for producing engaging and effective learning experiences. This chapter attempts to bridge these two research areas and provides concrete design recommendations for current instructional practice and directions for future research.

INTRODUCTION

When I was a child, I judged how interesting books would be based upon the picture-to-page ratio. Only high ratio books would stand a chance of ending up in my backpack. Much older now, to some extent, I still adhere to this rule. In reading textbooks, I know that the ones that are more helpful to my students are those that embed pictures in the text. Perhaps not surprisingly and consistent with much research (e.g., Mayer, 2001; Paivio, 1986), smartly-combined pictures and text is inevitably a better learning medium than either format in isolation. However, it is clear that the story is not that simple. In 2006 alone, PsycINFO lists 184 multimedia publications in peer-reviewed journals, book chapters, and handbooks, demonstrating that while much is known, much is also being explored with regard to the cognitive and educational influences of multimedia across a wide range of applications. Increases in the availability of technologies with which educators, experimenters, and software companies can integrate text, images, narration, animation, and virtual reality have unfortunately not corresponded with increases in educational and cognitive psychologists' understanding of how such technologies influence learning. The application of these technologies is as broad as the research that engenders them: from the young student studying photosynthesis to the Soldier studying maps and descriptive details about an area of operation. Across these applications, educators, designers, and engineers must ensure that information gatherers are successfully processing and comprehending, and ultimately using knowledge in appropriate ways.

To address this need four questions are posed that have broad and powerful implications for both systems design and educational effectiveness: 1) what effects, if any, do format and modality manipulations have on eventuating memory form and function, 2) which working memory mechanisms are involved in the processing, manipulation and integration of multi-format and multi-modality information, 3) how does the effectiveness of manipulations vary as a function of learning material types (e.g., facts, rules, procedures), and 4) what, if any, individual differences predict the success of various media combinations?

The present chapter attempts to answer these questions by reviewing research from cognitive, educational, and human factors psychology and pointing out gaps in knowledge that can motivate subsequent experimental investigations. Three broad domains are examined for which multimedia may prove an effective learning tool: spatial learning (e.g., maps, spatial descriptions, virtual reality), procedure learning (e.g., object assembly), and declarative learning (e.g., facts, rules, information). Theoretical motivations are provided regarding how media manipulations affect human mental representation, how these effects vary with the domain of application, and how the human mind uses working memory to manipulate and integrate spatial and verbal information towards abstract and flexible final memory forms. Finally, insights are provided into how educators may predict the success of multimedia at the level of the individual student.

BACKGROUND

Defining Multimedia, Learning, and Transfer

Multimedia can be broadly defined as information sources that present more than one content format to the viewer. These formats can be presented within a single modality, such as visual (e.g., pictures and text), or across multiple modalities, such as visual and auditory (e.g., pictures and spoken narration). A great deal of multimedia research has been devoted to identifying the most useful combinations of formats for learning. While one of the most obvious learners is the classroom student, the tools and techniques gathered from cognitive and educational psychology are also important for learning in the home (e.g., self-care CD-ROMs for diabetics) and workplace (e.g., procedural and teamwork skills training for medical practitioners; Grady, Kehrer, Trusty, Entin, Entin, & Brunyé, in press; Lai, Entin, Brunyé, Sidman, & Entin, 2007; Neal, Entin, Lai, Sidman, Mizrahi, & Brunyé, 2005).

There are at least two critical components to learning. First, there must be a change in the mechanisms of behavior brought about through prior experience with a particular stimulus or set of stimuli. For instance, when first-responder medics are taught the appropriate radio communication channels and calls, they gain the ability to subsequently use these new skills on the job (i.e., Lai et al., 2007). Second, there must also be evidence of *transfer*; that is, one should be able to not only change their behavior but also apply new knowledge across a diverse set of contexts and problems (i.e., Byrnes, 1996). For instance, upon encountering a novel emergency situation with degraded communication channels, a well-trained first responder must navigate her repertoire of communication behaviors to quickly and accurately divert messages to the appropriate persons. Individuals fail to exhibit transfer when the behavioral repertoire breaks down in novel situations.

Without transfer a carpenter, for instance, may retain that "the claw of a hammer is for pulling out nails" but may not transfer the properties of the hammer (i.e., prying, slotted, strong) to novel circumstances, such as prying a stuck door or levering a heavy object. Similar distinctions between potentially inflexible declarative (fact-based) memories versus flexible and broadly transferable memories have been made in the domains of discourse processing (van Dijk & Kintsch, 1983), spatial cognition (Brunyé, Rapp, & Taylor, in press; Brunyé & Taylor, in press; Brunyé & Taylor, 2008; Brunyé, Taylor, & Worboys, 2007; Taylor, Brunyé, & Taylor, in press; Taylor & Tversky, 1992), computer programming (Klahr & Carver, 1988; Mayer, 1988), complex skills training (Broudy, 1977; Hussain, Weil, Brunyé, Sidman, Ferguson, & Alexander, 2007), and procedural learning (Brunyé, Taylor, & Rapp, in press; Brunyé, Taylor, Rapp, & Spiro, 2006).

Some of the earliest work investigating learning transfer proposed that transfer success depends solely on the degree to which the *elements* (i.e., facts and skills) of learning and testing overlap, and the extent to which this overlap exists across contexts and problems (Klausmeier, 1985; Thorndike, 1913). More recent work emphasizes the importance of both learning (media types, organizations) and learner (attentional focus, motivation, existing knowledge, creativity) characteristics towards transfer success (see Singley & Anderson, 1989). It is our belief that the most useful mental representations to be used towards transfer contain not only the necessary elements (i.e., facts, rules, procedures) as posited by Thorndike and others, but also the referential associations made possible through abstraction (i.e., Novick & Holyoak, 1991; Spiro, Feltovich, Jacobson, & Coulson, 1991) and generalization (i.e., Bjork & Richardson-Klavehn, 1989) during and after learning. In fact, much work has demonstrated the importance of reducing contextualized knowledge in favor of "learning for understanding" through such exercises as deliberate practice (Ericsson, Krampe, & Tesch-Roemer, 1993), tell-and-practice (Schwartz & Martin, 2004), monitoring knowledge and seeking feedback (Chi, De Leeuw, Chiu, & Lavancher, 1994), contrasting cases (Bransford, Franks, Vye, & Sherwood, 1989; Schwartz & Bransford, 1998), invention activities (Schwartz & Martin, 2004), generation (Lutz, Briggs, & Cain, 2003), and active mental imagery formation (Schwartz & Heiser, 2006).

Progress in Multimedia Research

The present section focuses on two characteristics of multimedia learning: representation and reference. Representational characteristics are external to the learner, and include what information is presented and how it is organized in a multimedia system towards effective learning and eventual transfer success. Referential characteristics are internal to the learner, and include associations between information sources and existing knowledge within and between working and long-term memory. One important challenge for educational and cognitive psychology is integrating fairly disparate research areas that tend to focus on either representational (i.e., content and formats) or referential (i.e., associative processes) characteristics of learning. The natural progression of multimedia research is integrating these two areas; such work will help us identify any interactive effects of media and learner variations.

In 1967, Roger Shepard published a paper investigating recognition memory for different stimulus types: words, sentences, and pictures. Three experiments demonstrated remarkably high recognition overall, with words accurately recognized 90% of the time, sentences 88% of the time, and pictures coming out on top with 98% recognition. This was not an easy task – participants learned over 600 stimuli in a single session. Soon thereafter many studies were conducted to investigate the potential learning utility of presenting images alongside conventional texts – such as in textbooks, handbooks, and instruction manuals (e.g., Allen, 1967, 1971; Baggett, 1987; Stone & Glock, 1981). In an early review of this work (Levie & Lentz, 1982), there was some general correspondence across these studies: first, memory was improved when images accompanied texts relative to when texts were presented alone (in fact no single study demonstrated memory advantages for text-alone versus text and images); and second, memory was especially improved when such images were immediately and clearly relevant to the text-based information. More recent work has included investigations of multimedia benefits in procedural learning (i.e., Brunyé, Taylor, & Rapp, in press; Brunyé, Taylor, Rapp, & Spiro, 2006; Novick & Morse, 2000; Zacks & Tversky,

2003), scientific concept learning (Mayer, 1989; Mayer, Bove, Bryman, Mars, & Tapangco, 1995), and geographical learning (Renshaw & Taylor, 2000; Reynolds, Renshaw, & Taylor, 2004). One consistent finding is that multimedia facilitates learning to a greater extent than single-formats alone. At first glance it may seem that pictures and diagrams should be employed in presentations whenever and wherever they might fit. Unfortunately the story is not quite that simple.

Indeed, some recent work has demonstrated that at least seven representational characteristics are critical in determining successful learning from multimedia systems (i.e., Mayer, 1997, 2001). These characteristics include: 1) presenting information formats closely in space, 2) presenting formats closely in time, 3) removing extraneous information, 4) promoting coherence, 5) crossing modalities such as presenting animation with narration (i.e., aural) rather than with text, 6) minimizing redundant information whether within or across formats and/or modalities, and 7) realizing the predictable effects of individual differences such as low- versus high-knowledge learners. These principles have guided much work in cognitive and educational psychology as well as decisions in the classroom and workplace, and provide clear research questions for experimentalists and design recommendations for educators. For instance, one should hold off on unwittingly inserting an animated diagram showing how to perform tracheal intubation alongside accompanying text; rather, learners should benefit more from accompanying narration rather than written text. Additional research questions might be derived from this example, for instance, regarding appropriate levels of embedded text in such animated diagrams – such as labels and brief descriptors.

Cognition and Multimedia

Whereas much research has been conducted to determine the representational characteristics that promote learning, relatively few studies have addressed the cognitive mechanisms that are responsible for learning advantages with multimedia. The question is *how*, in a cognitive sense, do these format and organizational principles facilitate understanding, retention, and transfer? Some of the earliest work providing insights into these questions was conducted by Allan Paivio at the University of Western Ontario (e.g., 1965, 1986), who was generally interested in the role of mental imagery in memory for word lists. Across multiple experiments Paivio found greater memory for concrete (e.g.,book) versus abstract (e.g., love) nouns, and attributed these differences to the ability for participants to actively form mental imagery while studying the former. This was in contrast to abstract nouns which do not directly (or without effort) evoke mental imagery. Paivio's *Dual Coding Theory* (DCT) proposed that strong associative activation of mental imagery (made possible by prior experience, retrieved as imagery) facilitates memory for words, and these two processes – one verbal (symbolic codes) and one visual (analogue codes) – were separable in memory.

More recent work done by Richard Mayer's group has led to the Generative Theory of Multimedia Learning (Mayer, 1997). This theory leverages Paivio's DCT, working memory modeling (i.e., Baddeley, 1992, 2002), and generative learning theory (i.e., Slamecka & Graf, 1978). Generative learning theory proposes that the active selection and integration of information within working memory leads to stronger associations between sources and more routes towards retrieval. Based on prior work in his own and others' labs, Mayer proposed that the learning advantages typically seen with multimedia relative to single-format presentations can be accounted for by the structure, processing characteristics, and limitations of human working memory. In essence, learning advantages are found because multimedia promotes associatively rich memories (i.e., associations between verbal and image-based information in working and long-term memory),

leverages the simultaneous and independent processing of information within multiple working memory systems, encourages learners to actively process and integrate perceptually disparate information, and does not overload the learner.

Whereas most work has focused on visual presentations such as images and text, other work has proposed theoretical foundations for integrating sound (i.e., Bishop & Cates, 2001) and even haptic information. Sound is perhaps most often used as a tool for verbatim narration of on-screen text (e.g., Mandel, 1997), but is also used as a stand-alone information source, and for error alerting. Bishop and Cates argued that without a strong theoretical foundation, "the sounds used in instructional software may not only fail to enhance learning, they may actually detract from it" (p. 6). One approach, they argued, is to integrate both information processing (i.e., Atkinson & Shiffrin, 1968; Baddeley, 1992, 2002; Phye, 1997; Sweller, 1999) and communication theory (i.e., Banathy, 1996; Shannon & Weaver, 1969). Communication theory, analogous to what we have described as the representational characteristics of the learning situation, describes how to structure presentations to facilitate acquisition. Information processing theory, as we describe above as referential characteristics of the learning situation, describes how learners process and integrate information into cohesive mental representations that are amenable to transfer success. Combining information processing and communication theory provides instructional guidelines that focus on the selection, analysis, and synthesis of information within three phases: acquisition, processing, and retrieval. During selection, learners must alert to, orient to, and maintain attention upon the instructional message (see also Posner & Peterson, 1990). During processing, learners must select relevant information, and organize and elaborate upon this information within working memory (see also Mayer, 2001). Finally, at retrieval learners use existing schemata to organize new knowledge, and construct flexible and transferable knowledge structures (see also Sweller, 1999). So how might using sound in instructional presentations help or hinder these processes? Sounds might be particularly effective at alerting and orienting attention towards a message, providing information when the visual system is overloaded or impaired (e.g., Klatzky, Marston, Giudice, Golledge, & Loomis, 2006), elaborating upon visual information especially in situations when abstract concepts (i.e., invisible effects or structures, dynamic changes, effects of time) must be conveyed, and completing obstructed signals or transmission errors. Sound may not be as effective, however, when any of these characteristics are minimized, as information redundancy may overload working memory and induce boredom and fatigue.

Haptic information is quickly gaining popularity as a mechanism for conveying information via vibration (e.g., cellular phones, game controls), force feedback (e.g., laparoscopic surgery, military robotics), and movement. In fact, in 2006, IEEE Multimedia featured a special issue on haptic user interfaces for multimedia systems; several articles addressed the success of and potential for haptic systems in conveying complex information that cannot be presented in the visual, auditory, or olfactory/gustatory senses. Examples include precise shape, contour, movement, and texture information (Kohli, Niwa, Homa, Susami, Yanagida, Lindeman, Hosaka, & Kume, 2006). Not surprisingly haptic learning is also a popular choice for the visually impaired, and haptic systems have been used successfully by some researchers for conveying spatial information during nonvisual navigation tasks (e.g., Loomis, Golledge, Klatzky, & Marston, 2007; Marston, Loomis, Klatzky, & Golledge, 2007). Haptic information appears to be most useful when it provides information that complements existing information sources that cannot themselves convey a particular information type; substituting haptic information for visual information, in contrast, may impair learning and task performance (Hale & Stanney, 2004).

Of course, as with any new modality, experience and training may help individuals become better-accustomed to new information sources and increase the scope of useful haptic applications (i.e., Chang, Satava, Pellegrini, & Sinanan, 2003; Passmore, Nielsen, Cosh, & Darzi, 2001). Indeed work with navigation suggests that properly designed systems, appropriate training, and extensive experience can lead to the development of functionally equivalent spatial memories whether the information is presented via vision, haptics, or hearing (Loomis & Klatzky, 2007).

The Influence of Action on Memory and Learning

Try to answer the following questions in as much detail as possible. What did you do this morning? What was said in the opening paragraph of this chapter? If you are like most people, it was significantly easier to answer the first question than the second one. Educational and developmental theorists have long recognized that action plays a powerful role in learning (e.g., Piaget, 1978), and it is a general finding that individuals remember more when they engage physically with their environment. For example, research has shown that people recall neutral verb phrases (e.g., "lift the cup") better when they act the phrases out than when they simply read or hear them spoken aloud (for reviews see Cohen, 1989; Engelkamp & Zimmer, 1994, Engelkamp, 1998). This "enactment effect" is large and extremely robust, yielding memory gains of 125% to 150% across a range of experimental designs and manipulations including both free recall and old/new recognition paradigms. In addition, the effect holds regardless of whether the actions are performed with physical objects or are merely pantomimed (Knopf, 1991; Engelkamp, Zimmer, & Mohr, 1994: Engelkamp & Zimmer, 1997; Zimmer, Helstrup, & Engelkamp, 2000). In an unpublished study, Augustyn, Stefanucci, and Hodgins found that the enactment effect is also obtained when individuals view a video of another person pantomiming verb phrases while hearing them read aloud.

The enactment effect improves memory by providing additional cues for retrieval and increasing depth of processing. Another route by which action can support learning emerges from people's exquisite sensitivity toward actions performed by others. Studies have shown that there is a neural system in humans whose primary function is to directly map the observation of an action onto the motor representation used to perform that action (Iacoboni et al., 1999; Butterworth, 1990; Gray et al., 1991). Essentially, the observation of an action automatically triggers a mental simulation in the observer's mind of executing that action. This "mirror neuron" system supports the ability to learn by imitation, and is analogous to a similar system discovered in other primate species (Gallese, Fadiga, Fogassi, & Rizzolatti, 1996). In fact, data linking deficiencies in the mirror neuron system to autism (Williams, Whiten, Suddendorf, & Perrett, 2001) suggest that the mirror neuron system may be central to most human social interactions. For a contrasting and compelling stance on the possibility of mirror neurons in humans, see Gernsbacher, Stevenson, & Schweigert (2007).

Single cell research in chimpanzees and functional magnetic resonance imaging studies in humans have pointed to a circuit connecting the frontal and parietal lobes of the brain as the neural instantiation of the mirror neuron system. More specifically, Iacoboni et al. (1999) found that brain activity increased in the left frontal operculum (BA 44), the right anterior parietal region (PE/PC), and the right parietal operculum when humans viewed a video-recorded action performed by another person. Researchers hypothesize that the inferior frontal activation was associated with processing the goal of the observed action whereas the parietal activity indicated simulation of the likely somatosensory feedback that would be generated if the observer executed the action. Interestingly, animal studies suggest that

activation of the mirror neuron system requires that the organism witness a goal-directed action related to an object (Rumiati & Bekkering, 2003; Umilta et al., 2001). Both the enactment effect and the discovery of the mirror neuron system highlight the important role of action in shaping human cognition (Clark, 1990) and underscore the value of including representations of human action in multimedia learning systems.

INTEGRATING AND CONSOLIDATING SPATIAL AND NON-SPATIAL INFORMATION

Whether with sounds, images, haptics, or text, one large influence on learning from multiple information sources is the overload that can be experienced when too much information is presented for a learner to process at any given time. Sweller's cognitive load theory proposes that learning and memory are facilitated when information is aligned with the form and function of human memory (Sweller, 1988, 1999). The notion is that properly structured information has the potential to reduce working memory load and "free up" the cognitive resources necessary for higher-level integration and schema acquisition. In Sweller's theory, these long-term memory schemas are what make complex problem solving, inferencing, and transfer of new information possible.

Clearly one challenge for psychologists and instructional designers is to strike a balance between presenting too little versus too much information. Such an assessment, however, can only be made after careful consideration of the nature of learning material, the time and resource constraints of the learning environment, and the capabilities, motivations, and existing knowledge of the learner. In general, with more concrete and less difficult materials, the less redundancy that is necessary to convey information. However, when time is restricted and instructors need to provide as much information as possible within a particularly small time frame, redundancy may be especially useful as it provides multiple formats towards understanding and ultimately representing information (Brunyé, Taylor, & Rapp, in press). Resource constraints also have a large impact on instructional design – how much technology is available, when is it available, and how much does it cost?

A focus on the materials and their presentation often suggests that learner characteristics take a back seat; however, careful consideration must be given to a learner's capabilities – no two students read, view, or listen to information at the same speed, have precisely the same competencies, or identical cognitive styles (i.e., Kozhevnikov, Kosslyn, & Shephard, 2005). Within this complex web of design principles, one might ask whether there are **any** general principles that information system designers can rely upon. Luckily, some can be derived from research looking at how working memory is structured, what information types use these structures, and how resources are allocated amongst these structures.

A foundation for understanding basic information processing comes out of contemporary working memory theory posited by Alan Baddeley (1992, 2002). Baddeley's working memory model maintains that human working memory is divided into at least four systems – one central executive and three slave systems – that divide cognitive resources towards the processing of different information types. In general, working memory appears to be divided into independent systems that process, in the most general sense, spatial, verbal, and episodic information. The visuospatial sketchpad is involved in processing visual information such as that found in images, diagrams, and maps (e.g., Brunyé, Taylor, Rapp, & Spiro, 2006; Garden, Cornoldi, & Logie, 2001; Gyselinck, Cornoldi, DuBois, De Beni, & Ehrlich, 2002; Kruley, Sciama, & Glenberg, 1994; Logie, 1995), understanding locations and movement through space (Brunyé & Taylor, in press; De Beni, Pazzaglia, Gyselinck, & Meneghetti, 2005),

and generating and manipulating mental imagery (Farmer, Berman, & Fletcher, 1986; Miyake, Friedman, Rettinger, Shah, & Hegarty, 2001). The articulatory and phonological subsystem appears to be involved in processing and manipulating verbal information across multiple modalities, such as auditory, visual, and tactile (Baddeley, Lewis, & Vallar, 1984; Brunyé et al., 2006; De Beni et al., 2005; Farmer et al., 1986; Goldman & Healy, 1985; Longoni, Richardson, & Aiello, 1993; Millar, 1990). The central executive and episodic buffer appear to be involved in the allocation of cognitive resources among the visuospatial and articulatory/phonological mechanisms, and the integration of multimodal information into episodic memories, respectively (Brunyé et al., 2006; Miyake et al., 2001).

One useful way of identifying the function of each of these mechanisms during multimedia learning is by using a dual-task paradigm (Brunyé & Taylor, in press; Brunyé et al., 2006; Gyselinck et al., 2002). Dual-tasking involves performing both primary and secondary tasks; typically the primary task requires participants to learn from presented stimuli, whereas the secondary task involves doing "something else" simultaneously during learning. The notion is that by carefully designing and validating the secondary task to ensure that it only taps into a particular working memory mechanism, one can assess the involvement of that mechanism towards learning. For instance, articulatory secondary tasks typically involve the repetition of simple syllable strings, such as "BA BE BI BO BU," and have been found to selectively interfere with a variety of verbal (but not non-verbal) learning scenarios (e.g., Baddeley et al., 1984; Brunyé et al., 2006; De Beni et al., 2005; Farmer et al., 1986; Goldman & Healy, 1985; Longoni et al., 1993). Visuospatial secondary tasks, in contrast, involve spatial reasoning or simple manual movement in a spatial sequence, and have been found to selectively interfere with learning visual and spatial features found in a variety of input formats and modalities (e.g., Brunyé et al., 2006; Garden et al., 2001; Gyselinck et al., 2002; Kruley et al., 1994; Logie, 1995; Miyake et al., 2001). Finally, secondary tasks targeting the central executive typically involve monitoring n-back tasks or random string production, in the form of digits, words, and finger taps (e.g., Baddeley, 1996; Baddeley et al., 1998; Brunye et al., 2006; Della Sala, Baddeley, Papagno, & Spinnler, 1995; Duff, 2000; Duff & Logie, 2001; Gyselinck et al., 2002).

To the extent that performing a given secondary task during learning causes decrements on later memory or performance tasks, one can implicate the targeted working memory mechanism in that particular learning paradigm. In a recent set of experiments in our laboratory, participants learned a series of 18 procedural assembly sequences (e.g., assembling a small toy car or sailboat) that involved the computer-aided presentation of images, text alone, or pictures and text together (Brunyé et al., 2006). While participants learned these sequences they performed either one of six secondary tasks designed to interfere with visuospatial, articulatory, and central executive resources, or they did not perform any secondary task (controls). After learning the assembly sequences, participants performed several memory tests including free recall, step order verification, format source memory, and object assembly. Several interesting findings emerged. First, learning from multimedia produced broad-based memory advantages relative to both picture-only and text-only learning, and picture-only learning outperformed text-only learning. Second, the visuospatial task selectively interfered with the processing of spatial information in images, the articulatory task selectively interfered with text comprehension, and the central executive task interfered primarily with learning from multimedia. Finally, multimedia and picture-only learning showed advantages towards transfer to object assembly, perhaps because in both cases pictures can directly provide a perceptual representation of the described (or non-described) objects.

These data provide support for existing conceptualizations of working memory (i.e., Baddeley, 2002) and multimedia learning (Mayer, 2000). The lower-level processing of incoming information appears to occur largely in independent processing mechanisms devoted to either spatial or verbal information. At a relatively higher level, central mechanisms appear to be involved in actively integrating spatial and verbal information into cohesive memory representations that can be applied successfully at test. The memory forms resulting from multimedia presentations provide the strongest foundation for free recall of declarative information (i.e., participants were able to remember more individual steps in an assembly sequence relative to when they learned with picture-only or text-only learning), verifying step order (participants were better able to identify in which order events had been presented), and assembling objects (participants performed best when required to transfer learned information to complex and novel tasks). In contrast to these positive memory/learning effects, multimedia also produced the highest levels of source memory errors; in general, participants misattributed multimedia presentations to picture-only ones. In other words, whereas memory for information necessary to perform several basic and applied memory tests was relatively strong following multimedia learning, participants' ability to remember the nature of their initial learning experiences was relatively poor. Thus, while multimedia presentations appear to lead to better learning and memory performance, learners themselves may not be aware of these benefits. This finding has large applied relevance when considering protocols using media value judgments (e.g., which format(s) do you prefer to learn from?): whereas certain media may facilitate learning, students may not acknowledge these benefits. The best insight into which formats suit learning can only be derived from objective determinations of declarative memory and transfer task performance. These findings also point to the abstract nature of mental models derived from multimedia presentations (see also Gyselinck & Tardieu, 1999; Wilson & Rutherford, 1989). Verbatim memories would be relatively easy to source monitor; the abstract nature of mental models resulting from multimedia presentations is likely the characteristic that leads to later transfer advantages relative to single-format learning, yet poor source-monitoring.

When taken together with other work investigating the working memory mechanisms involved during learning (e.g., Brunyé & Taylor, in press; De Beni, Pazzaglia, Gyselinck, & Meneghetti, 2005; Gyselinck et al., 2002; Kruley, Sciama, & Glenberg, 1994), the above findings provide important insights into general mechanisms involved during multimedia learning. First, separate processing mechanisms are involved during the comprehension of illustrations and texts. In general participants tend to use specific processing systems in rather predictable ways during learning. There are two important caveats here: first, the processing of extended spatial text appears to recruit visuospatial mechanisms, and second, whereas the mechanisms themselves might be best-conceptualized as separate and independent, they appear to pull from a common (rather than several domain-specific) resource pool (i.e., Fedorenko, Gibson, & Rohde, 2007). This resource pool is most often thought of as being limited to the extent that the processing in one can interfere with the processing in another mechanism, particularly under the conditions of high cognitive load (Brunyé, Taylor & Worboys, 2007; Paas, Renkle, & Sweller, 2003). Second, participants appear to actively integrate simultaneously presented multi-format information during learning; central integration processes appear to be involved during study itself, and the mental representations resulting from presenting images alongside corresponding text appear to be relatively comprehensive and flexible. Thus, a general pattern is that during study, learners will actively process and integrate information across formats.

The result is a broad integration of new information within both working and long-term memory; the extent to which new information is comprehended and integrated into existing memory schemata is related to whether or not a learner can successfully transfer newly-acquired information to solve complex and novel problems.

Effort Towards Comprehension

Often times it can be difficult to integrate presented information within working memory, such as when the materials are complex, confusing, or poorly presented. Some work finds, however, that the very process of resolving such difficulties can actually be beneficial towards learning. There is some work that suggests that providing individuals with basic declarative knowledge schemas early in a learning process can guide the gathering and integration of subsequent information, especially when it complements hands-on learning (e.g., Schwartz & Bransford, 1998). Yet other work shows benefits of providing information towards the end of a learning process that resolves information and aids in final consolidation (e.g., Auble, Franks, & Soraci, 1979; Novick & Morse, 2000; Wills, Soraci, Chechile, & Taylor, 2000).

In a series of unpublished studies in our laboratory we used the assembly sequence paradigm described above (i.e., Brunyé et al., 2006) to test the relative efficacy of providing final state diagrams before or after the assembly sequences (Spiro, unpublished). A total of thirty participants learned 18 toy assembly sequences in picture (6), text (6), or multimedia (6) formats; half of the participants received a final state diagram depicting the finished toy at the beginning of the sequence, and half received it at the end. Our intention was to gain insights into whether providing a schema as a foundation for later learning, or an image as a tool for disambiguation and consolidation, could be an effective learning tool and if so which formats were most facilitated by their inclusion. Overall, results from free recall and order verification tasks confirmed that receiving a final-state diagram at the end of a sequence provided the most effective learning medium. As in past work, performance on these memory tasks following multimedia learning exceeded that of both picture-only and text-only learning; further, the addition of final state diagrams at the end, but not at the beginning, of the sequences improved performance on these tasks. Further, addition of final state diagrams in text-only presentations provided the greatest benefits relative to picture-only and multimedia presentations. Figure 1 depicts accuracy on an order verification task which required determining if two presented steps of a particular assembly sequence are in the learned temporal order from left to right. Data showed a significant learning condition (picture, text, multimedia) by final state position group interaction [$F(2, 56) = 3.56$, $p < .05$, $MSE = .005$], and significant difference between groups following text [$t(28) = 3.76$, $p < .01$], but not the other two learning conditions (p's $> .05$).

What could account for such findings? Some theories suggest that effortful disambiguation of complex materials can lead to what has been labeled as an 'aha!' effect (e.g., Wills et al., 2000) – the term used to describe when a learner suddenly arrives at disambiguation. Interestingly, the 'aha!' effect produced by final state diagrams placed at the end of the sequences was strongest following text-only learning, suggesting that images provided a useful consolidation tool for otherwise ambiguous text descriptions.

Schwartz and Bransford (1998) found that hands-on experiential learning provides opportunity for learners to recognize contrasts and distinctions in a domain, which then in turn prepares the student to learn 'why' and 'how' things work together. In the above work, perhaps demonstrating the piecemeal assembly of a toy allowed students to learn how to differentiate between the component parts of the toy (i.e., hat, skis, ski poles, torso), and motivated learners to seek resolution as to how things come together as a whole. That is, early differentiation of information later motivates students to seek knowledge of how things work together as a whole, congruent with the predictions of constructivist learning theory. One question that arises, however, is how well students will be able to use the memories resulting from

Figure 1. Accuracy and standard error representing order verification performance following learning with three study conditions and with a final state diagram either at the beginning or end of each of 18 sequences (see Brunyé et al., 2006 for paradigm specifics)

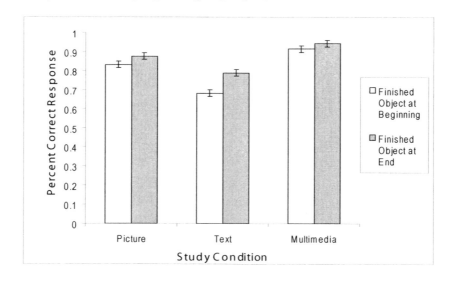

their learning experiences towards success in a variety of circumstances; that is, are the memories flexible enough to provide "transfer?"

BUILDING FLEXIBLE MEMORIES FOR TRANSFER SUCCESS

If the ultimate goal of education is to provide students with information that will allow them to transfer their knowledge to solve novel problems, one step is to understand what types of memory forms facilitate these functions. Work in discourse processing may provide some insights into these forms. Research investigating memory representations following reading has repeatedly demonstrated that memory for a discourse is often abstracted beyond the information provided by the text itself (e.g., van Dijk & Kintsch, 1983; Zwaan & Radvansky, 1998); these memory forms are often referred to as *mental models* or *situation models*. For instance, take the following passage:

A breeze ruffled the neat hedges of Privet Drive, which lay silent and tidy under the inky sky, the very last place you would expect astonishing things to happen. Harry Potter rolled over inside his blankets without waking up. One small hand closed on the letter beside him and he slept on, not knowing he was special, not knowing he was famous, not knowing he would be woken in a few hours' time by Mrs. Dursley's scream as she opened the front door to put out the milk bottles, nor that he would spend the next few weeks being prodded and pinched by his cousin Dudley ... He couldn't know that at this very moment, people meeting in secret all over the country were holding up their glasses and saying in hushed voices: "To Harry Potter - the boy who lived!"

– Harry Potter and the Sorceror's Stone, Chapter One

In just a few short sentences, one is quickly and seemingly effortlessly transported to Privet Drive, meeting Harry Potter ("the boy who lived!") for the first time. We travel back and forth in time to understand Harry's present situation, and even glimpse his past and future, and journey to other parts of the country to observe celebrations. It is apparent that understanding discourse involves not only knowing the meaning of words within sentences and linking this meaning with syntactic structure, but also requires tracking dynamic information as a story unfolds. To do this, readers go beyond a representation of the text itself to construct a mental representation of the events described within this text, known as a situation model (Johnson-Laird, 1983; van Dijk & Kintsch, 1983; Zwaan & Radvansky, 1998). This model incorporates information about time, space, causality of events, and information about protagonists' goals and emotions, integrates multiple references to the same character or object, and goes beyond explicitly stated information to incorporate inferences (Gernsbacher, 1990; Zwaan & Radvansky, 1998; Zwaan, Magliano, & Graesser, 1995). The pace of a normal conversation or the short amount of time needed to read a paragraph in a novel exemplifies the speed at which comprehenders are able to do this. This is no small feat, especially when one considers that in just one Harry Potter book, readers integrate information across hundreds of pages and even across multiple books!

The information that tends to remain in readers' abstracted models codes for elements of the story, rather than the text per se, such as characters, intentions, goals, temporal and spatial information, and causality (e.g., Rapp & Taylor, 2004; Rapp & van den Broek, 2005; Zwaan, Langston, & Graesser, 1995; Zwaan & Radvansky, 1998). There are several proposed reasons for storing information in an abstracted form; some claim that limited human information processing capacity necessitates abstracted rather than verbatim memory forms (Baddeley & Hitch, 1974; Parasuraman & Caggiano, 2002), and others propose that all final memory forms are propositional, associative, and/or schematic, as opposed to analog in format (Pylyshyn, 1981; van Dijk & Kintsch, 1983).

These mental models have been found to be particularly useful towards solving complex inferences. For instance, participants can learn about small- or large-scale environments by reading spatial descriptions; these descriptions can take on several different perspectives, such as a first-person route perspective (i.e., egocentric, intrinsic reference frame, ground-level), or a survey perspective (i.e., allocentric, extrinsic reference frame, aerial-level). Taylor and Tversky (1992) found that participants form what they termed *spatial mental models,* or abstracted memories of the described environments. These models, for instance, allow an individual to reason about a spatial relationship between two landmarks that was never explicitly described in the text, and also to switch perspectives – such as learning from the ground-level route perspective and later drawing a map or describing landmark interrelationships using canonical terms. The abilities to infer landmark interrelationships and switch perspectives have become trademark advantages of forming spatial mental models. These models are thus flexible and extensible to an array of problem solving tasks. In fact, when limited time is given for participants to form these models, or when the learning materials induce high cognitive load, later inferencing and perspective switching are both impaired (Brunyé & Taylor, 2008). When mental models are formed, they are abstracted far enough from the surface and propositional information in a text so that transferring new knowledge to complex problem sets is possible (Biederman & Shiffrar, 1987; Brunyé & Taylor, in press; Singley & Anderson, 1989). Abstracting too far, however, from the propositions contained in the text can lead to inappropriate and/or negative transfer. Negative transfer occurs when a new

problem set activates either the wrong or a faulty memory schema, the result of which is attempting to apply an incorrect solution.

Mental model theory (i.e., Johnson-Laird, 1983; van Dijk & Kintsch, 1983) has been adopted in attempting to understand the memory representations formed from multi-format and multi-modality information sources. Similar to how spatial mental models are necessary to form spatial inferences and perform perspective switching tasks following spatial description reading, mental models are needed to understand the function of a device (Glenberg & Langston, 1992; Rapp, 2005a), such as knowing how a bicycle pump or car brakes work. How can multimedia be developed to facilitate mental model formation? One popular way to combine pictures and texts is to allow the picture to depict structure and the text to describe function or process (Brunyé, Taylor, & Rapp, in press; Mani & Johnson-Laird, 1982; Winn, 1987). Pictures and diagrams can directly convey structure but not function without including complex animation or video; conversely, text can directly convey function but not structure without lengthy and complex texts. Indeed using complex diagrams to convey function and dense texts to convey structure can induce undue cognitive load and detract from learning and eventual transfer (Hegarty & Just, 1993; Hegarty & Sims, 1994; Mayer & Gallini, 1990). Just as a survey description conveys structure by detailing spatial relationships and route descriptions by detailing actions, depictions can directly convey spatial relationships and texts can directly detail actions using motion and transitive verbs (Taylor & Tversky, 1996). Some recent work demonstrates that arrows are one effective means for conveying function and process in diagrams, allowing individuals to develop more comprehensive mental models that ultimately aid knowledge transfer without inducing high cognitive load (Heiser & Tversky, 2006). For instance, attempting to describe the proper angle of movement during tracheal intubation might be rather difficult and require extended texts; arrows, in contrast, can depict such movement easily and effectively.

It is clear that the mental model metaphor is useful for understanding learning and memory, and the mental model itself is a useful tool towards transfer success; it is less clear what precise form these models take in memory. Mental models are often thought to be part of schemata, or related events, facts and concepts stored in memory in an abstracted format (Novick & Holyoak, 1991). Useful schemata are formed when an individual is able to observe and represent similarities and differences inherent to multiple events and learning experiences (Holyoak, 1984). In effect, an individual learns not only one use for a hammer (bang nail), but multiple associated use cases (pull nail, pry door) that allow analogical reasoning towards novel use (lever a stone); they also learn to contrast these associations with cases within which the tool will not suffice. This is quite different from theories of analog representational formats (e.g., Kosslyn, 1980), such as storing a mental image of a map after study, but does not preclude the possibility that schemata may store image-like representations of objects and places.

INDIVIDUAL DIFFERENCES TOWARDS LEARNING AND TRANSFER

Much of the above work makes it easy for one to assume that by delineating cognitive processes we can predict performance regardless of individual learner characteristics. Much work, however, has demonstrated that individuals vary at least in terms of prior knowledge, spatial and verbal ability, cognitive styles and learning preferences, age, social status and roles, and gender (i.e., individual differences). Each of these factors independently, additively, and interactively may play large roles in influencing what information learners will process, how this information is integrated, and ultimately which media formats best facilitate learning.

No two students walk into a learning experience with the same repertoire of knowledge, skills, motivations, or abilities. The depth and breadth of a student's existing knowledge can play a large role in how much information she or he can comprehend and later use. There are two broad categories of learners: experts and novices. Experts, by definition, can think effectively and efficiently about problems within a particular domain; they have the requisite knowledge that allows them to process, comprehend, organize, interpret, and represent information differently from novices (Glaser & Chi, 1988). How do experts perform such feats? Some say that experts have formed mental schemata that allow them to quickly recognize and organize new information into existing knowledge (Chi, 1978; Chi, Feltovich, & Glaser, 1980; Normon, 2005; Schneider, et al., 1993); others say that experts have developed high sensitivity to meaningful patterns that allow them to quickly classify incoming information and retrieve the appropriate memories to solve problems (Glaser, 1984; Robinson & Hayes, 1978; Sabers et al., 1991; Simon, 1990). In both cases, experts have developed the capacity to quickly and effectively deal with information within a particular domain. Examples of this include classifying mathematical problem sets (Hinsley et al., 1977) and diagnosing radiological charts (Lesgold, 1988). In fact, experts can become so adept at quickly recognizing and comprehending the important functional elements of domain-relevant diagrams and images (Suwa & Tversky, 1997) that they no longer benefit from the accompanying verbal information commonly found in multimedia presentations (Kalyuga, Chandler, & Sweller, 1998). Experts have also been found to use the "big idea" or larger concepts when solving problems, such as applying major principles and laws of physics towards solving a problem set (Larkin, 1983).

Relatively novice students, in contrast, will focus on the mechanics of an equation and how they can be manipulated and in what order. One way to move novices into more expert status is to teach them in a way that contextualizes their knowledge – that is, providing them with not only the knowledge of how to solve a wide array of problems, but fine-tuning that knowledge such that it is appropriately applied in a variety of contexts (Bransford & Stein, 1993). Of course, overly contextualizing knowledge can lead to negative transfer, so instructors must expose students to an array of problem sets and appropriate solutions. Those with low prior knowledge clearly need to develop, perhaps in a scaffolded (i.e., stepwise progression) manner, the organizational schemata that will guide knowledge organization in memory; these may already be present in learners with existing domain knowledge. Sometimes a lack of knowledge will cue a learner that something is amiss and prompt them to acquire the information towards a solution (e.g., Dooling & Lachman, 1971). For instance, in developing an educational software package to convey risk and treatment options for human papillomavirus (HPV), the present first author identified a common misconception that those with HPV always have perceptible symptoms that will inevitably lead to self-diagnosis. To address this issue the software presented several testimonials from individuals with targeted demographics discussing their lack of symptoms and surprise when discovering that they are infected with the virus. When learners encountered this portion of the educational program, the vast majority of them asked "so how do I know if I have HPV?" The method of presenting information in a manner that evokes this sort of question is rather simple, but the consequences are quite large and serious: informal interviews with learners revealed that those who previously held misconceptions about HPV symptoms were more motivated to seek answers to this question than those without the misconception. This is one example of how contemporary research in multimedia can be applied in conjunction with broader research in instructional strategy.

One method for early instruction of novice learners is the *contrasting cases* approach, which involves exposing students to a variety of cases in which a particular solution set may or may not be applied; in this way students learn to differentiate their knowledge and better-recognize the cues that allow them to choose the correct solution to a novel problem set (Schwartz & Bransford, 1998). Eventually, the knowledge becomes structured in such a way that the now-expert demonstrates high fluidity and automaticity within their particular domain. Novices, in contrast, can vary widely in terms of their amount of knowledge. Novices, unlike what the term might imply, are never truly *tabula rasa*. Not only do novices bring the ability to learn new materials, but also their own experiences and tacit or explicit (and often idiosyncratic) existing knowledge about a domain that can both help and hinder knowledge acquisition (Gelman, 1967; Wandersee, 1983). One critical method for preventing prior knowledge from hindering learning is to assess knowledge prior to instruction: assess preconceived notions and misconceptions, and then counter them by adapting instructional strategies to directly address identified problems (Mestre, 1994).

An abundance of existing knowledge can facilitate knowledge acquisition, but also make it difficult to understand new information especially when it is incongruent with prior knowledge (see Mestre, 1994 for a review). Consider also that prior knowledge is comprised of not only domain and content knowledge, and developmental experiences, but also an individual's social roles and cultural, ethnic, and racial affiliations.

Learners also enter an educational situation with varying spatial and verbal skill levels. Spatial skill is often divided into at least three factors: spatial visualization, spatial relations, and visuo-spatial perceptual speed (Carroll, 1993; Miyaki et al., 2001). Spatial visualization is the ability to develop, maintain, and use/manipulate accurate mental imagery (Carpenter & Just, 1986). Spatial relations is the ability to represent and quickly infer the relationships between objects, people, and landmarks in space; for instance, inferring the relative locations of landmarks in a small-scale environment. Visuospatial perceptual speed is the ability to quickly match visual patterns. Each of these factors can have large influences on learning. For instance, spatial visualization skills allow students to imagine described molecular compounds in chemistry and visualize object projectiles in physics class; students with lower spatial visualization skills may benefit highly from viewing rather than imagining such materials. Spatial visualization is demanding upon central resources and strongly tied to general intelligence measures (Hegarty & Waller, 2005; Miyaki et al., 2001). Spatial relation skills allow students to mentally transform and manipulate visualized objects, such as adding or removing an atom from a molecule, or rotating an object and knowing where it ends up relative to another object. Students with lower spatial relation knowledge may especially benefit from animation and videos to depict complex and dynamic transformations. Visuospatial perceptual speed is a relatively lower-level (Carroll, 1993) skill that allows students to quickly compare and match visual information, such as recognizing that two molecules share structure, or that several bacterial cultures are identical in shape. These three spatial skills are highly interrelated and easily measured (Carroll, 1993), none of them is typically deficient in isolation (Lohman, 1988), and they can have large influences on learning.

Verbal skill is thought to be independent of spatial skill (i.e., Eysenck, 1939; Thurstone, 1938) and is an important contributor to knowledge acquisition (Fleishman & Mumford, 1989). Understanding verbal information involves both lower-level processing such as reading ability, vocabulary and semantic skills and higher-level influences that involve the integration of information across sentences and ideas, such as referential coherence, integration (Cooke et al., 1998), inference (Graesser et al., 1994), and comprehension monitoring. Not surprisingly, the notion of verbal skills is as complex as the number of processes that appear to engender them. At the lower level, limited reading ability and vocabulary can increase cognitive load and reduce verbal and spatial integration during learning, and ultimately reduce the advantages typically seen with dual-format learning (Plass, Chun, Mayer, & Leutner, 2003). Greater low-level verbal abilities, however, allow learners to assign verbal explanations to images and quickly integrate textual information during learning (Hartman, 2001). At a higher-level, comprehension monitoring (i.e., the ability to actively monitor understanding during learning) and integration are improved in those with low verbal skills when diagrams and images, but not additional verbal information, are included in instructional systems (Cuevas, Fiore, & Oser, 2002). In fact, whereas even low verbal skill learners can acquire basic declarative knowledge with or without diagrams, only with diagrams do they form mental models that are integrated, cohesive, and can be transferred to complex problems. These findings lend support for adaptive instructional technologies that can accommodate learners with varying verbal skills, such as decreasing text length and complexity and increasing diagram use for individuals with low verbal skill.

Even when spatial and verbal skills are high, instructional systems can benefit from adapting to individual cognitive style, which characterizes consistencies in a learner's manner of information processing, such as a tendency to focus on and prefer visual or verbal information (Kozhevnikov, 2007). Early work in cognitive style identified the Verbal-Visual cognitive style dimension, which describes learners as either visualizers or verbalizers (Paivio, 1971; Richardson, 1977). Visualizers tend to focus on, rely upon, and prefer imagery-based information such as diagrams and pictures. Verbalizers, in contrast, tend to use verbal information such as found in text and spoken narration. Assessing this dimension is typically done using self-report measures such as the VVQ (Richardson, 1977), IDQ (Paivio, 1971). Other measures have used problem solving to assess the fluidity with which individuals can solve verbal and visual tasks, such as the VICS (Peterson et al., 2005). Recent work has developed measures to more accurately parse visualizers into object and spatial imagery scales (Blajenkova et al., 2006; Kozhevnikov, Hegarty, & Mayer, 2002; Kozhevnikov, Kosslyn, & Shephard, 2005), and has applied this work to instructional system design (Kozhevnikov & Thornton, 2006). In general, while spatial visualization ability positively predicts successful learning from multimedia instruction, instructional systems may also enhance these abilities in both students and learners (Kozhevnikov & Thornton, 2006). Thus, instructional systems can be designed with spatial visualization abilities in mind, but can also be viewed as a training opportunity to enhance the very skills they were designed to accommodate.

Age of learner is an additional difference that can have large effects on instructional effectiveness. Whereas most formal learning takes place in the classroom with students between the ages of 5 and 18 years, elderly learning has been a recent research focus (for a review see Van Gerven, Paas, & Tabbers, 2006). Cognitive aging refers to declining cognitive function relatively late in the lifespan, characterized by slowed cognitive speed (Salthouse, 1996) and reduced executive control (Fisk & Sharp, 2004; Hasher & Zacks, 1988). Cognitive aging can have multiple influences on an elderly individual's ability to learn, especially from computer-aided instruction (i.e., Czaja, 1996). Similar to design recommendations used for the general student audience, instructional systems for the elderly have been found to benefit from scaffolding, pacing, simple language, active voice, legible fonts, and online feedback during learning (Morrell & Echt, 1996, 1997; Rogers & Fisk, 2000). The notion is that slowed cognitive speed can be overcome by pacing and limiting the complexity and amount of information presented; reduced executive control can be overcome by limiting the number of inferences

the learner must self-generate, providing goals during problem solving and learning (Van Gerven, Paas, Van Merrienboer, & Schmidt, 2002), and offering corrections during learning to prevent interference. In fact, the design characteristics posited by cognitive load theory (Sweller, 1999) and Mayer's (2001) Generative Theory of Multimedia Learning are perfectly suited (perhaps in an amplified manner relative to younger learners) to inform instructional design for the elderly (Van Gerven et al., 2006).

The present review of individual differences in learner expertise, skill, preference, style, and age is in an attempt to emphasize the importance of adaptive instructional technologies. Because there are no general principles that completely apply to all learners, the content and organization of multimedia systems should cater to identified differences. Simple self-report questionnaires and more complex problem solving sets can complement instructional systems and provide timely measurement of individual differences. These differences can then be used, for instance, to slow or speed the pacing of content display, increase or reduce spatial and verbal content, and provide different starting points for students with varying background knowledge. Adaptive instructional technology is a current interest to many research groups, and additional research is needed to better-define the relationships between identified individual differences and structured instructional changes that will effectively target them.

CONCLUSION

Whereas educational psychologists have long been developing and testing best pedagogical practices, only recently have cognitive and educational psychologists begun to experimentally investigate the cognitive mechanisms responsible for learning advantages seen with new technologies. It appears to be the case that, generally speaking, multimedia is very advantageous for learning. This may be the result of several factors. First, well-designed multimedia aligns with the structure and capacity of human working memory. Second, visual depictions such as pictures and animations have the ability to convey abstract concepts such as motion, the effects of time, and cause and effect without the use of extended discourse. Third, complementing images with narration, or other cross-modality and cross-format manipulations, reduces cognitive load and allows resources to be devoted to higher-level integration. Fourth, higher-level integration processes that are made possible by well-designed multimedia facilitate mental model development, allowing learners to later apply new knowledge in a flexible manner towards novel problem solving. Fifth, the inherent redundancy included in many multimedia presentations can facilitate learning, especially when that redundancy is found across formats and modalities. Sixth, individual differences and cognitive styles are more likely to be accommodated with multimedia relative to single-format or modality information sources, and adaptive multimedia instructional technologies make this a more feasible and structured advantage. Finally, multimedia is more engaging for students relative to conventional learning media, especially when coupled with experiential learning.

Multimedia, however, must be designed in accordance with modern design principles, or it will induce the sort of cognitive loads that preclude effective learning and transfer. Further, our view is that the most effective multimedia instruction will be found when it is coupled with contemporary pedagogical principles. Thus, while the pictures can do the showing and the words can do the telling, learning advantages and subsequent transfer performance will only be facilitated when these formats and modalities are properly combined (visually) and properly organized (conceptually). Even then, however, individual differences in learner prior knowledge, skills, preferences and age will have large effects upon instructional system effectiveness. We urge more research in this regard.

Adaptive multimedia technologies are certainly one example of how multimedia research and development efforts can continue to progress (e.g., Rapp, 2005b). Future research should focus on modeling task and individual characteristics towards effective system design. First, there is a paucity of work attempting to delineate how multimedia content and organizations should adapt to different learning media. Much work remains to be done, therefore, in better characterizing the elements of topics (e.g., assembly skill versus fact knowledge) and which instructional formats and methods best-match these topics. One result of this work could be predictive models for educators. For example, an educator could input topic characteristics and the model generates best-practices with regard to multimedia content and structure. Second, there is little work addressing how systems should adapt to individual differences in a structured manner. Some insights can be derived from the section above, but much remains to be done for educators to better-understand how individual differences map onto multimedia design. One critical step toward this goal is to developing reliable and well-validated metrics to assess individual differences. Later work should involve determining the independent and interactive effects of each individual difference on learning from alternate input formats, modalities, and organizations. Only then will we truly be able to capture the potential of multimedia in training and education.

REFERENCES

Allen, W.H. (1967). Media stimulus and types of learning. *Audiovisual Instruction. 12*, 27-31.

Allen, W.H. (1971). Instructional media research: Past, present, and future. *AV Communications Review, 19*, 5-18.

Atkinson, R. C., & Shiffrin, R. M. (1968). Human memory: A proposed system and its control processes. In K. W. Spence & J. T. Spence (Eds.), *The Psychology of Learning and Emotion*. London: Academic Press.

Auble, P. M., Franks, J. J., & Soraci, S. A., Jr. (1979). Effort toward comprehension: Elaboration or "aha"?. *Memory & Cognition, 7,* 426-434.

Baddeley, A.D. (1992). Working memory. *Science, 255,* 556-559.

Baddeley, A. D. (1996). Exploring the central executive. *Quarterly Journal of Experimental Psychology: Human Experimental Psychology, 49,* 5-28.

Baddeley, A. D. (2002). Is working memory still working? *European Psychologist, 7,* 85-97.

Baddeley, A. D., & Hitch, G. (1974). Working Memory. In G. H. Bower (Ed.), *The psychology of learning and motivation: Advances in research and theory.* New York: Academic Press.

Baddeley, A. D., Emslie, H., Kolodny, J., & Duncan, J. (1998). Random generation and the executive control of working memory. *Quarterly Journal of Experimental Psychology, 51A,* 818-852.

Baddeley, A. D., Lewis, V. J., & Vallar, G. (1984). Exploring the articulatory loop. *Quarterly Journal of Experimental Psychology, 36,* 233–252.

Baggett, P. (1987). Structurally equivalent stories in movie and text and the effect of the medium on recall. *Journal of Verbal Learning & Verbal Behavior, 18,* 333-356.

Banathy, B. (1996). Systems inquiry and its application in education. In D. Jonassen (Ed.), *The Handbook of Research for Educational Communications Technology* (pp. 74-92). New York: Simon & Schuster MacMillan.

Biederman, I., & Shiffrar, M. M. (1987). Sexing day-old chicks: A case study and expert systems analysis of a difficult perceptual learning task.

Journal of Experimental Psychology: Learning, Memory, & Cognition, 13, 640-645.

Bishop, M. J., & Cates, W. M. (2001). Theoretical foundations for sound's use in multimedia instruction to enhance learning. *Educational Technology Research and Development, 49,* 5-22.

Bjork, R. A., & Richardson-Klavehn, A. (1989). On the puzzling relationship between environmental context and human memory. In C. Izawa (ed.), *Current Issues in Cognitive Processes: The Tulane Flowerree Symposium on Cognition* (pp. 313-344. Hillsdale, NJ: Lawrence Erlbaum.

Bransford, J. D., Franks, J. J., Vye, N. J., & Sherwood, R. D. (1989). New approaches to instruction. Because wisdom can't be told. In S. Vosniadou & A. Ortony (Eds.), *Similarity and analogical reasoning* (pp. 470-497). Cambridge, UK: Cambridge University Press.

Broudy, H. S. (1977). Types of knowledge and purposes of education. In R. Anderson, C. Shapiro, & W. E. Montagne (Eds). *Schooling and the Acquisition of Knowledge* (pp. 1-17). Hillsdale, NJ: Lawrence Erlbaum Associates.

Brunyé, T. T., Rapp, D. N., & Taylor, H. A. (in press). Representational flexibility and specificity following spatial descriptions of real world environments. *Cognition.*

Brunyé, T. T., & Taylor, H. A. (2008). Extended experience benefits spatial mental model development with route but not survey descriptions. *Acta Psychologica, 127,* 340-354.

Brunyé, T. T., & Taylor, H. A. (in press). Working memory in developing and applying mental models from spatial descriptions. *Journal of Memory and Language, doi:10.1016/j.jml.2007.08.003.*

Brunyé, T. T., Taylor, H. A., & Rapp, D. N. (in press). Repetition and dual coding in procedural multimedia learning. *Applied Cognitive Psychology, DOI: 10.1002/acp.1396.*

Brunyé, T. T., Taylor, H. A., Rapp, D. N., & Spiro, A. B. (2006). Procedural Learning: The Role of Working Memory in Multimedia Learning Experiences. *Applied Cognitive Psychology, 20,* 917-940.

Brunyé, T. T., Taylor, H. A., & Worboys, M. (2007). Levels of detail in descriptions and depictions of geographic space. *Spatial Cognition and Computation, 7(3), 227-266.*

Butterworth, G. (1990). On reconceptualising sensori-motor development in dynamic systems terms. In H. Bloch, B. I. Bertenthal (Eds.), *Sensory-motor organizations and development in infancy and early childhood (pp. 57-73).* New York, NY: Kluwer Academic.

Byrnes, J. P. (1996). *Cognitive development and learning in instructional contexts.* Boston: Allyn and Bacon.

Chang, L., Satava, R. M., Pelligrini, C. A., & Sinanan, M. N. (2003). Robotic surgery: Identifying the learning curve through objective measurement of skill. *Surgical Endoscopy, 17,* 1744-1748.

Chi, M. T. H., De Leeuw, N., Chiu, M., & Lavancher, C. (1994). Eliciting self-explanations improves understanding. *Cognitive Science, 18,* 439-477.

Chi, M. T. H., Feltovich, P. J., & Glaser, P. (1980). Categorization and representation of physics problems by experts and novices. *Cognitive Science, 5,* 121-152.

Clark, A. (1990). Embodied, situated, and distributed cognition. In W. Betchel, & G. Graham (Eds.), *A companion to cognitive science.* Malden, MA: Blackwell Publishing.

Cohen, R. L. (1989). Memory for enactment events: The power of enactment. *Educational Psychology Review, 1,* 57-80.

De Beni, R., Pazzaglia, F., Gyselinck, V., & Meneghetti, C. (2005). Visuospatial working memory and mental representation of spatial descriptions. *European Journal of Cognitive Psychology, 17,* 77-95.

Della Sala, S., Baddeley, A., Papagno, C., Spinnler, H. (1995). Dual-task paradigm: A means to examine the central executive. Annals of the New York Academy of Science, 769, 161-171.

Duff, S. C. (2000). What's working in working memory: A role for the central executive. *Scandinavian Journal of Psychology, 41,* 9-16.

Duff, S. C., Logie, R. H. (2001). Processing and storage in working memory span. *The Quarterly Journal of Experimental Psychology, 54,* 31-48.

Engelkamp, J. (1998). *Memory for actions.* Hove, UK: Psychology Press.

Engelkamp, J., & Zimmer, H. D. (1997). Sensory factors in memory for subject-performed tasks. *Acta Psychologica, 96,* 43-60.

Engelkamp, J., & Zimmer, H. D. (1994). *Human memory: A multimodal approach.* Seattle, WA: Hogefe and Huber.

Engelkamp, J., Zimmer, H. D., & Mohr, G. (1994). Memory of self-performed tasks: Self-performing during recognition. *Memory & Cognition, 22,* 34-39.

Ericsson, K. A., Krampe, R. Th., & Tesch-Roemer, C. (1993). The role of deliberate practice in the acquisition of expert performance. *Psychological Review, 100,* 363-406.

Farmer, E. W., Berman, J. V., Fletcher, Y. L. (1986). Evidence for a visuo-spatial scratchpad in working memory. *Quarterly Journal of Experimental Psychology, 38,* 675-688.

Fedorenko, E., Gibson, E., & Rohde, D. (2007). The nature of working memory in linguistic, arithmetic and spatial integration processes. *Journal of Memory and Language, 56,* 246-269.

Gallese, V., Fadiga, L., Fogassi, L., & Rizzolatti, G. (1996). Action recognition in the premotor cortex. *Brain, 119,* 593-609.

Garden, S., Cornoldi, C., & Logie, R. H. (2001). Visuo-spatial working memory in navigation. *Applied Cognitive Psychology, 16,* 35-50.

Gernsbacher, M. A. (1990). *Language comprehension as structure building.* Hillsdale, NJ: Erlbaum.

Gernsbacher, M. A., Stevenson, J. L., & Schweigert, E. K. (2007). Mirror neurons in humans? *Presentation at the annual meeting of the Psychonomic Society, Long Beach, CA.*

Glaser, R. (1984). Education and thinking. The role of knowledge. *American Psychologist, 39,* 93-104.

Glaser, R., & Chi, M. T. H. (1988). Overview. In M. T. H. Chi, R. Glaser, & M. J. Farr (Eds.), *The Nature of Expertise* (pp. Xv-xxviii). Hillsdale, NJ: Erlbaum.

Glenberg, A. M. & Langston, W. E. (1992). Comprehension of illustrated text: Pictures help to build mental models. *Journal of Memory and Language, 31,* 129-151.

Goldman, H. B., & Healy, A. F. (1985). Detection errors in a task with articulatory suppression: Phonological recoding and reading. *Memory & Cognition, 13,* 463-468.

Grady, J. L., Kehrer, R. G., Trusty, C., Entin, E. B., Entin, E. E., & Brunyé, T. T. (in press). Learning nursing procedures: The impact of simulator fidelity and student gender on teaching effectiveness. *Journal of Nursing Education.*

Gray, J. A., Feldon, J. M., Rawlings, J. N. P., Hemsley, D. R., Snith, A. D. (1991). The neuropsychology of schizophrenia. *Behavioral Brain Sciences, 14,* 1-84.

Gyselinck, V., Cornoldi, C., Dubois, V., De Beni, R., & Ehrlich, M. F. (2002). Visuospatial

memory and phonological loop in learning from multimedia. *Applied Cognitive Psychology, 16,* 665-685.

Gyselinck, V., & Tardieu, H. (1999). The role of illustrations in text comprehension: What, when, for whom, and why? In van Oostendorp, H. & Goldman, S.R. (Eds.), *The construction of mental representations during reading (pp. 195-218).* Mahwah, NJ, US: Lawrence Erlbaum Associates.

Hale, K. S., & Stanney, K. M. (2004). Deriving haptic design guidelines from human physiological, psychophysical, and neurological foundations. *IEEE Computer Graphics and Applications, 24,* 33-39.

Hegarty, M., & Just, M. A. (1993). Constructing mental models of machines from text and diagrams. *Journal of Memory & Language, 32,* 717-742.

Hegarty, M., & Sims, V. K. (1994). Individual differences in mental animation during mechanical reasoning. *Memory & Cognition, 22,* 411-430.

Heiser, J., Tversky, B. (2006). Arrows in comprehending and producing mechanical diagrams. *Cognitive Science, 30,* 581-592.

Holyoak, K. J. (1984). Analogical thinking and human intelligence. In R. J. Sternberg (Ed.), *Advances in the psychology of human intelligence, 2,* 199-230. Hillsdale, NJ: Lawrence Erlbaum.

Hussain, T., Weil, S., Brunyé, T. T., Sidman, J., & Ferguson, W. (2007). Eliciting and evaluating large-scale teamwork within a multiplayer game-based training environment. In H. F. O'Neil, & R. Perez (Eds.), *Computer Games and Team and Individual Learning* (pp. 77-104). Amsterdam: Elsevier Science.

Iacoboni, M., Woods, R. P., & Brass, M. (1999). Cortical mechanisms of human imitation. *Science, 286,* 2526-2528.

Johnson-Laird, P. N. (1983). *Mental Models: Towards a Cognitive Science of Language, Inference, and Consciousness.* Cambridge, MA: Harvard University Press.

Klahr, D., & Carver, S. M. (1988). Cognitive objectives in a LOGO debugging curriculum: Instruction, learning, and transfer. *Cognitive Psychology, 20,* 362-404.

Klatzky, R. L., Marston, J. R., Giudice, N. A., Golledge, R. G., & Loomis, J. M. (2006). Cognitive load of navigating without vision when guided by virtual sound versus spatial language. *Journal of Experimental Psychology: Applied, 12,* 223-232.

Klausmeier, H. J. (1985). *Educational psychology.* New York, NY: Harper & Row.

Knopf, M. (1991). Having shaved a kiwi fruit: Memory of unfamiliar subject-performed actions. *Psychological Research, 53,* 203-211.

Kohli, L., Niwa, M., Noma, H., Susami, K., Yanagida, Y., Lindeman, R. W., Hosaka, K., & Kume, Y. (2006). Towards effective information display using vibrotactile apparent motion. In *14th Symposium on Haptic Interfaces for Virtual Environment and Teleoperator Systems* (445-451.

Kosslyn, S. M. (1980). *Image and mind.* Cambridge, MA: MIT Press.

Kozhevnikov, M., Kosslyn, S., & Shephard, J. (2005). Spatial versus object visualizers: A new characterization of visual cognitive style. *Memory & Cognition, 33,* 710-726.

Kruley, P., Sciama, S. C., & Glenberg, A. M. (1994). On-line processing of textual illustrations in the visuospatial sketchpad: Evidence from dual-task studies. *Memory & Cognition, 22,* 261-272.

Lai, F., Entin, E. B., Brunye, T., Sidman, J., & Entin, E. E. (2007). Evaluation of a simulation-based program for medic cognitive skills training. *Studies in Health Technology and Informatics, 125,* 259-261.

Levie, W. H., & Lentz, R. (1982). Effects of text illustrations: A review of research. *Educational Communication & Technology Journal, 30,* 195-232.

Logie, R. H. (1995). *Visuo-spatial Working Memory.* Hove, UK: Lawrence Erlbaum Associates, Ltd.

Longoni, A. M., Richardson, J. T., & Aiello, A. (1993). Articulating rehearsal and phonological storage in working memory. *Memory and Cognition, 21,* 11-22.

Loomis, J. M., & Klatzky, R. L. (2007). Functional equivalence of spatial representations from vision, touch, and hearing: Relevance for sensory substitution. In J. J. Reiser, D. H. Ashmead, F. F. Ebner, & A. L. Corn (Eds.), *Blindness and brain plasticity in navigation and object perception* (pp. 155-184). New York: Lawrence Erlbaum.

Loomis, J. M., Golledge, R. G., Klatzky, R. L., & Marston, J. R. (2007). Assisting wayfinding in visually impaired travelers. In G. Allen (Ed.), *Applied spatial cognition: From research to cognitive technology* (pp. 179-202). Mahwah, N.J.: Lawrence Erlbaum.

Lutz, J., Brigs, A., & Cain, K. (2003). An examination of the value of the generation effect for learning new material. *The Journal of General Psychology, 130,* 171-188.

Mandel, T. (1997). *The elements of user interface design.* New York: Wiley.

Mani, K., & Johnson-Laird, P. N. (1982). The mental representation of spatial descriptions. *Memory & Cognition, 10,* 181-187.

Marston, J. R., Loomis, J. M., Klatzky, R. L., & Golledge, R. G. (2007). Nonvisual route following with guidance from a simple haptic or auditory display. *Journal of Visual Impairment & Blindness, 101,* 203-211.

Mayer, R. E. (1988). From novice to expert. In M. Helander (Ed.), *Handbook of Human-Com-*

puter Interaction (pp. 569-580). Amsterdam: Elsevier.

Mayer, R.E. (1989). Systematic thinking fostered by illustrations in scientific text. *Journal of Educational Psychology, 81,* 240-246.

Mayer, R.E. (1997). Multimedia learning: Are we asking the right questions? *Educational Psychologist, 32,* 1-19.

Mayer, R. E. (2001). *Multimedia Learning.* New York, NY: Cambridge University Press.

Mayer, R.E., Bove, W., Bryman, A., Mars, R., & Tapangco, L. (1995). A generative theory of textbook design: Using annotated illustrations to foster meaningful learning of scientific text. *Educational Technology Research and Development, 43*(1), 31-44.

Mayer, R.E., & Gallini, J.K. (1990). When is an illustration worth ten thousand words? *Journal of Educational Psychology, 82,* 715-726.

Mestre, J. P. (1994). Cognitive aspects of learning and teaching science. In S. J. Fitzsimmons & L. C. Kerpelman (Eds.), *Teacher Enhancement for Elementary and Secondary Science and Mathematics: Status, Issues, and Problems* (pp. 3-1 - 3-53). Washington, DC: National Science Foundation (NSF 94-80).

Millar, S. (1990). Articulatory coding in prose reading: Evidence from braille on changes with skill. *British Journal of Psychology, 81,* 205-219.

Miyaki, A., Friedman, N. P., Rettinger, D. A., Shah, P., & Hegarty, M. (2001). How are visuospatial working memory, executive functioning, and spatial abilities related? A latent-variable analysis. *Journal of Experimental Psychology: General, 130,* 621-640.

Neal, L., Entin, E., Lai, F., Sidman, J., Mizrahi, G., & Brunyé, T. (2005). Teamwork skills training for medical practitioners. *Proceedings of the 11ᵗʰ*

International Conference on Human-Computer Interaction.

Novick, L. R., & Holyoak, K. J. (1991). Mathematical problem solving by analogy. *Journal of Experimental Psychology: Learning, Memory, and Cognition, 17,* 398-415.

Novick, L.R., & Morse, D.L. (2000). Folding a fish, making a mushroom: The role of diagrams in executing assembly procedures. *Memory & Cognition, 28*(7), 1242-1256.

Paivio, A. (1965). Abstractness, imagery, and meaningfulness in paired-associate learning. *Journal of Verbal Learning & Verbal Behavior, 4,* 32-38.

Paivio, A. (1971). Imagery and verbal processes. New York: Holt, Rinehart & Winston.

Paivio, A. (1986). *Mental representations: A dual coding approach.* Oxford, England: Oxford University Press.

Paas, F., Renkl, A., & Sweller, J. (2003). Cognitive load theory and instructional design: Recent Developments. *Educational Psychologist, 38,* 1-4.

Parasuraman, R., & Caggiano, D. (2002). Mental workload. In V. S. Ramachandran (Ed.), *Encyclopedia of the Human Brain.* San Diego, CA: Academic Press.

Passmore, P. J., Nielsen, C. F., Cosh, W. J., & Darzi, A. (2001). Effects of viewing and orientation on path following in a medical teleoperation environment. *Proceedings of the 2001 IEEE Virtual Reality Conference,* (p. 209).

Phye, G. D. (1997). Learning and remembering: The basis for personal knowledge construction. In G. D. Phye (Ed.), *Handbook of academic learning: Construction of Knowledge.* San Diego: Academic Press.

Piaget, J. (1978). *Success and understanding.* London: Routledge and Kegan Paul.

Plass, J. L., Chun, D. M., Mayer, R. E., & Leutner, D. (2003). Cognitive load in reading a foreign language text with multimedia aids and the influence of verbal and spatial abilities. *Computers in Human Behavior, 19,* 221-243.

Posner, M. I., & Peterson, S. E. (1990). The attention system of the human brain. *Annual Review of Neuroscience, 13,* 25-42.

Pylyshyn, Z. W. (1981). The imagery debate: Analogue media versus tacit knowledge. *Psychological Review, 87,* 16-45.

Rapp, D. N. (2005a). Mental models: Theoretical issues for visualizations in science education. In J. K. Gilbert (Ed.), *Visualization in Science Education* (pp. 43-60). The Netherlands: Springer.

Rapp, D. N. (2005b). The value of attention aware systems in educational settings. *Computers in Human Behavior, 22,* 603-614.

Rapp, D. N., & Taylor, H. A. (2004). Interactive dimensions in the construction of mental representations for text. *Journal of Experimental Psychology: Learning, Memory, and Cognition, 30,* 988-1001.

Rapp, D. N., & van den Broek, P. (2005). Dynamic text comprehension: An integrative view of reading. *Current Directions in Psychological Science, 14,* 276-279.

Renshaw, C. E., & Taylor, H. A. (2000). The educational effectiveness of computer-based instruction. *Computers & Geosciences, 26,* 677-682.

Reynolds, K. J., Renshaw, C. E., & Taylor, H. A. (2004). Improving computer-assisted instruction in teaching higher-order skills. *Computers & Education, 42,* 169-180.

Rumiati, R. I., & Bekkering, H. (2003). To imitate or not to imitate: How the brain can do it, that is the question. *Brain and Cognition, 53,* 479-482.

Schwartz, D. L., & Bransford, J. D. (1998). A time for telling. *Cognition & Instruction, 16,* 475-522.

Schwartz, D. L., & Heiser, J. (2006). Spatial representations and imagery in learning. In R. K. Sawyer (Ed.). *The Cambridge Handbook of the Learning Sciences.* Cambridge, UK: Cambridge University Press.

Schwartz, D. L., & Martin, T. (2004). Inventing to prepare for learning: The hidden efficiency of original student production in statistics instruction. *Cognition and Instruction, 22,* 129-184.

Shannon, C. E., & Weaver, W. (1969). *The mathematical theory of communication.* Urbana, IL: The University of Illinois Press.

Singley, M. K., & Anderson, J. R. (1989). *The transfer of cognitive skill.* Cambridge, MA: Harvard University Press.

Slamecka, N.J., & Graf, P. (1978). The generation effect: Delineation of a phenomenon. Journal of Experimental Psychology: Human Learning and Memory, 6, 592-604.

Spiro, R., Feltovich, P., Jacobson, M., & Coulson, R. (1991). Cognitive flexibility, constructivism, and hypertext: Random access instruction for advanced knowledge acquisition in ill-structured domains. *Educational Technology, 31,* 24-33.

Stone, D.E., & Glock, M.D. (1981). How do young adults read directions with and without pictures? *Journal of Educational Psychology, 73,* 419-426.

Sweller, J. (1988). Cognitive load during problem solving: Effects on learning. *Cognitive Science, 12,* 257-285.

Sweller, J. (1999). *Instructional design in technical areas.* Camberwell, Victoria, Australia: ACER Press.

Taylor, H. A., Brunyé, T. T., & Taylor, S. (in press). Wayfinding and Navigation: Mental Representation and Implications for Navigational System Design. To appear in Carswell, C.M. (Ed.), *Reviews of Human Factors and Ergonomics, Volume 4.*

Taylor, H. A., & Tversky, B. (1992). Spatial mental models derived from survey and route descriptions. *Journal of Memory and Language, 31,* 261-292.

Taylor, H.A., & Tversky, B. (1996). Perspective in spatial descriptions. *Journal of Memory and Language, 35,* 371-391.

Thorndike, E. (1913). *Educational psychology: The psychology of learning.* New York: Teachers College Press.

Umilta, M. A., Kohler, E., Gallese, V., Fogassi, L., Fadiga, L., Keysers, C., & Rizzolatti, G. (2001). I know what you are doing. A neurophysiological study. *Neuron, 31,* 155-165.

van Dijk, T. A., & Kintsch, W. (1983). *Strategies of Discourse Comprehension.* New York: Academic Press.

Williams, J. H. G., Whiten, A., Suddendorf, T., & Perrett, D. I. (2001). Imitation, mirror neurons and autism. *Neuroscience and Biobehavioral Reviews, 25,* 287-295.

Wills, T. W., Soraci, S. A., Chechile, R. A., & Taylor, H. A. (2000). "Aha" effects in the generation of pictures. *Memory & Cognition, 28,* 939-948.

Wilson, J. R., & Rutherford, A. (1989). Mental models: Theory and application in human factors. *Human Factors, 31,* 617-634.

Winn, W. D. (1987). Charts, graphics and diagrams in educational materials. In D. Willows & H. Houghton (Eds.). *Knowledge acquisition from text and pictures* (pp. 125-144). North Holland: Elsevier.

Zacks, J. M, & Tversky, B. (2003). Structuring information interfaces for procedural learning. *Journal of Experimental Psychology: Applied, 9,* 88-100.

Zimmer, H. D., Helstrup, T., & Engelkamp, J. (2000). Pop-out into memory: A retrieval mechanism that is enhanced with the recall of subject-performed tasks. *Journal of Experimental Psychology: Learning, Memory, and Cognition, 26,* 658-670.

Zwaan, R. A., Langston, M. C., & Graesser, A. C. (1995). The construction of situation models in narrative comprehension: an event-indexing model. *Psychological Science, 6,* 292-297.

Zwaan, R. A., Magliano, J. P., & Graesser, A. C. (1995). Dimensions of situation-model construction in narrative comprehension. *Journal of Experimental Psychology: Learning, Memory, & Cognition, 21,* 386-397.

Zwaan, R. A., & Radvansky, G. A. (1998). Situation models in language comprehension and memory. *Psychological Bulletin, 123,* 162-185.

ADDITIONAL READING

Allen, G. L. (2007). *Applied Spatial Cognition.* Mahwah, NJ: Lawrence Erlbaum Associates.

Bransford, J. D., Brown, A. L., & Cocking, R. R. (Eds.). (1999). *How people learn: Brain, mind, experience, and school.* Washington, DC: National Academy Press.

Carpenter, P. A., & Shah, P. (1998). A model of the perceptual and conceptual processes in graph comprehension. *Journal of Experimental Psychology: Applied, 4,* 75-100.

Chandler, P., & Sweller, J. (1991). Cognitive load theory and the format of instruction. *Cognition and Instruction, 8,* 293-332.

Duffy, T. M., & Jonassen, D. H. (1991). Constructivism: New implications for instructional technology? *Educational Technology, 31,* 7-12.

Foos, P. W., & Goolkasian, P. (2005). Presentation format effects in working memory: The role of attention. *Memory & Cognition, 33,* 499-513.

Gilbert, J. K. (Ed.). (2005). Visualization in science education. Dordrecht: Springer.

Goolkasian, P., & Foos, P. W. (2002). Presentation format and its effect on working memory. *Memory & Cognition, 30,* 1096-1105.

Schnotz, W., & Kulhavy, R. (Eds.). (1994). *Comprehension of Graphics.* Amsterdam: Elsevier.

Hegarty, M., Meyer, B., & Narayanan, H. (2002). *Diagrammatic representation and inference.* Berlin: Springer-Verlag.

Hegarty, M., Shah, P., & Miyake, A. (2000). Constraints on using the dual task methodology to specify the degree of central executive involvement in cognitive tasks. *Memory & Cognition, 28,* 376-385.

Karpicke, J. D., & Roediger, H. L. (2007). Repeated retrieval during learning is the key to long-term retention. *Journal of Memory and Language, 57,* 151-162.

Karpicke, J. D., & Roediger, H. L. (2007). Expanding retrieval practice promotes short-term retention, but equally spaced retrieval enhances long-term retention. *Journal of Experimental Psychology: Learning, Memory, and Cognition, 33,* 704-719.

Kalyuga, S. (2007). Expertise reversal effect and its implications for learner-tailored instruction. *Educational Psychology Review, 19,* 509-539.

Lee, H., Plass, J. L., & Homer, B. D. (2006). Optimizing cognitive load for learning from computer-based science simulations. *Journal of Educational Psychology, 98,* 902-913.

Lovett, M., & Shah, P. (Eds.). (2007). *Thinking with data.* Mahweh, NJ: Erlbaum Associates.

Mayer, R. E. (Ed.). (2005). *The Cambridge handbook of multimedia learning.* New York: Cambridge University Press.

Mestre, J. P. (Ed.). (2005). *Transfer of learning from a modern multidisciplinary perspective.* Greenwich, CT: Information Age Publishing.

Miyake, A., & Shah, P. (Eds.). (1999). *Models of working memory: Mechanisms of active maintenance and executive control.* New York, NY: Cambridge University Press.

Nix, D., & Spiro, R. (Eds.). (1990). Cognition, education and multimedia. Hillsdale, NJ: Erlbaum Associates.

O'Neil, H. F., & Perez, R. S. (Eds.). (2007). *Computer games and team and individual learning.* Amsterdam, Netherlands: Elsevier.

Rapp, D. N. (2006). The value of attention aware systems in educational settings. *Computers in Human Behavior, 22,* 603-614.

Schnotz, W., & Kurschner, C. (2007). A reconsideration of cognitive load theory. *Educational Psychology Review, 19,* 469-508.

Shah, P., & Miyaki, A. (Eds.). (2005). *The Cambridge handbook of visuospatial thinking.* New York, NY: Cambridge University Press.

van Merrienboer, J. J. G., & Sweller, J. (2005). Cognitive load theory and complex learning: Recent developments and future directions. *Educational Psychology Review, 17,* 147-177.

van Oostendorp, H. (Ed.). (2003). *Cognition in a digital world.* Mahwah, NJ: Lawrence Erlbaum Associates.

Chapter VIII
New Forms of Deep Learning on the Web:
Meeting the Challenge of Cognitive Load in Conditions of Unfettered Exploration in Online Multimedia Environments

Michael DeSchryver
Michigan State University, USA

Rand J. Spiro
Michigan State University, USA

ABSTRACT

We claim that the Web has the potential to be a quintessential multimedia environment for complex learning, particularly in ill-structured domains. This chapter explores the cognitive load considerations associated with several aspects of deep and extended learning on the Web. We also propose the need for a reconceptualization of Cognitive Load Theory for comprehension and learning in more ill-structured conceptual arenas. This reconceptualization emphasizes the need for learning approaches that promote flexible knowledge assembly through processes of organic, reciprocal, and deep Web learning.

INTRODUCTION

The Web has the potential to become a quintessential multimedia learning environment. Both formal and informal learners are increasingly turning to the search engine as their primary source of information. For example, college students regularly use the Internet and commercial search engines (e.g., Google) before, or in lieu of, local library resources (Griffiths & Brophy,

2005; Jones, 2002; Thompson, 2003; Van Scoyoc, 2006). At the same time, the content provided to them on the Web is presented in multimedia form, often comprising various combinations of text, data, pictures, animation, audio, and video, of differing levels of interactivity. These myriad forms of information all battle for learner attention and consideration.

The second author argued that this migration away from traditional information resources to Web mediated multimedia learning environments is ushering in a revolution in thought, a New Gutenberg Revolution (2006a, b, c, d, e). He outlined how, given the dramatic increases in the speed with which information can be accessed, the increasing well directedness of search (due to more advanced search algorithms, data organization, and searcher skill), and the *de facto* assumption of "ambient findability" (Morville, 2005), the Web is becoming a more fertile knowledge landscape than man has ever known. Consequently, the Web is particularly well suited to support *deep* learning for subjects and concepts that are complex and ill-structured; the kind that we seem to be finding more and more of in the world everyday. These ill-structured domains of knowledge demonstrate an inherent *irregularity* of conceptual application across instances and contexts (for discussion of the special qualities of learning in ill-structured domains, see Spiro & DeSchryver, in press; Spiro, Vispoel, Schmitz, Samarapungavan, & Boerger, 1987; Spiro, Feltovich & Coulson, 1996).

In order to harvest information from this landscape in the most effective and meaningful ways, learners will need to explore the Web with a Post-Gutenberg Mind. This involves searching with *advanced Web exploration* techniques and an *opening mindset* that together result in advanced knowledge acquisition that goes well beyond the cursory and fact based searches most common to learning on the Web (Kuiper, Volman & Terwl, 2005). The knowledge structures acquired by a Post-Gutenberg Mind will be tailored assemblages that are contextualized, interconnected, and flex-

ible, enabling the everyday creativity necessary to succeed in a world increasingly driven by complex and rapidly changing information.

Sounds great, doesn't it? Well, as it turns out, not everyone is prepared to use the Web to learn like this right now. In fact, we do not really know precisely how deep learning on the Web occurs. As such, it is imperative that we begin to thoroughly examine the phenomenon. We need to better understand the specific ways that Post-Gutenberg learning will manifest itself. What specific affordances and aspects will enable deep Web learning of ill-structured concepts? How will they differ from the characteristics of traditional learning? How will we best prepare learners to maximize the benefits of deep learning on the Web? What will be the cognitive load considerations for learning that is of such depth and complexity?

With these questions in mind, we recently embarked on an inquiry to investigate the emergent aspects of Post-Gutenberg learning for an advanced Web learner in an ill-structured domain. In this study, we documented the decision-making, knowledge construction, and general learning reflections of an advanced Web searcher who examined the subject of climate change through deep and extended Web learning. The data were collected from a baseline mind-map of existing knowledge, extensive notes taken by the learner during each session, the parallel use of Clipmarks (an online tool that allows for portions of Web resources to be saved, tagged, annotated, updated, and retrieved in multiple ways), and corresponding updates to the mind-map. A detailed analysis of the data collected from this study has provided a better picture of what Post-Gutenberg learning may look like. And, while we do not claim any generalizability from the results of this demonstration case study (i.e., we sought to demonstrate what *is possible* not *what is*), several interesting phenomena emerged that are worthy of continued scholarly examination. (For a more detailed presentation of the theoretical implications of this study, see Spiro and DeSchryver, in preparation; for a more detailed accounting of a full list of deep Web learning aspects and their derivation, see DeSchryver and Spiro, in preparation.)

One of the primary considerations that surfaced was whether this form of advanced knowledge acquisition would be, in general, too challenging for the learner. Cognitive Load Theory has provided an excellent framework with which to address these questions (e.g., see Sweller, van Merrienboer & Paas, 1998; van Merrienboer & Sweller, 2005). Therefore, this chapter focuses on the cognitive load implications of deep Web learning in ill-structured domains that were identified during our investigation. First, we present an overview of deep Web learning. Second, we review the basic assertions of Cognitive Load Theory and suggest the need to reconceptualize cognitive load as it relates to the goals of learning in ill-structured domains and the skills needed for the requisite flexible knowledge acquisition. Finally, we discuss the cognitive load considerations for specific aspects of deep learning in ill-structured domains on the Web, the adjunct online tools that support them, and related motivational developments.

DEEP WEB LEARNING AND THE NEW GUTENBERG REVOLUTION

Post-Gutenberg learning holds the promise for increasingly complex, but cognitively manageable knowledge acquisition, through learning and instruction that better fits the contours of the world and knowledge about that world. Among other things, it may provide answers to many of the greatest challenges to learning complex and ill-structured topics by supporting the development of the type of adaptive knowledge application that is increasingly important in the world today.

The foundation of Post-Gutenberg learning is the dramatically increasing high speed of connection and access to effectively unlimited

Web resources. The former has resulted from technical advancements in hardware and software (e.g., search engine and data-mining algorithms that result in more precise results); enhanced techniques for information organization, such as tagging *en masse*; and, increased integration that advanced Web learners are demonstrating with information search, access, and evaluation (DeSchryver & Spiro, in preparation; Tremayne & Dunwoody, 2001). The seemingly unlimited nature of information available on the Web is described by Morville's (2005) notion of ambient findability, or the crossroads of ubiquitous computing and the Web, in which we can find anyone or anything from anywhere at anytime. This breadth and depth of knowledge provides a multiplicity of perspective, context, interconnectedness, and points of entry that are essential to learning complex, ill-structured concepts.

Most current Web-based learning is rather cursory and fact based (Kuiper, Volman, & Terwel, 2005), therefore new skills and approaches are needed to in order for Post-Gutenberg learning to develop. Foremost among these are the ability to search using *advanced Web exploration* techniques and with an *opening mindset* that promote more wide ranging searches that go well beyond finding facts or "answers" by using just simple Google results or embedded hyperlinks. These wide ranging searches unfold using learner-initiated, complex, reciprocally adaptive (LICRA) techniques that capitalize on the Web's affordances for deep learning by permitting maximally unfettered and externally oriented nonlinear traversals of knowledge spaces. We use "externally oriented" in the sense that the learner's next steps can be strongly influenced by the content that is encountered in Web explorations, rather than operating with more internally driven or "top-down" expectations and learner guidance, such as that provided by embedded and precompiled hyperlinks or simple sequential review of Google result lists. The learner creates their own search phrases based on information they encounter on the Web, either through employing specific ideas from the current page as new search phrases, or by conceptualizing novel search phrases based on recent activity, past experience, and the related momentum Web learning affords. These techniques result in learner controlled non-linear movement through the conceptual landscape, where the learner creates "undefined" connections between resources. In our recent investigation, this LICRA type searching led to several more conceptual breakthroughs than did the use of existing embedded hyperlinks (DeSchryver & Spiro, in preparation).

While performing these searches, learners much be prepared for discovery, complexity, change, and creativity (Spiro, 2006a) and see the Web as *open* to their exploration. When reflected in LICRA searches, openness allows the learners to see the key phrases or ideas in the current document (text, animation, audio, or video) that merit a new branching inquiry. An opening mindset also includes being open to using the Web for more than "basic" Web searches. At Google alone, searches through images, videos, blogs, scholarly materials, books, and news are separately available. Searching with these individual engines provides several unique knowledge landscapes, variant representations, and differing perspectives based on the identical search phrase. Finally, an open mindset is essential to taking advantage of the myriad opportunities for unexpected and *serendipitous* learning on the Web.

Together, these foundational components to deep Web learning undergird *virtual simultaneity*, defined as the condition "in which many things are [simultaneously] being considered in the context of each other and in which *conceptual wholes greater than the sum of the parts* can form" (Spiro, 2006e, p. 2). The simultaneity is virtual, not temporal, in the sense that it is within a functioning cognitive space. This is a core aspect for Post-Gutenberg learning, which, in concert with cognitive spreading activation, allows connections to be noticed that would not be noticed otherwise. It facilitates

multiple conceptual comparisons and contrasts, allows for increasingly complex but cognitively manageable learning, provides an acceleration of the acquisition of experience, and develops open knowledge structures that can be tailored to new contexts. The speed increases outlined above have resulted in a learning environment where virtually simultaneity is not only possible, but may be common.

While very little empirical evidence exists for this emergent learning phenomenon, our recent demonstration case study provided evidence of the type of learning we describe above. For instance, the concept of virtual simultaneity was exemplified well in an early session of the study. While learning about climate change, the subject navigated quickly through successive articles in the NY Times global warming section, scanning articles about the New Hampshire ski industry, autobahn speed limit considerations, carbon sequestration, and Pacific Islanders' concerns over rising ocean water. Though seemingly unrelated, this progression of articles one after another lead directly to the learner recognizing and documenting the importance of "selfishness" and "local recognition" as two important concepts in his understanding of climate change. We submit that the speed with which information can be accessed and the precise targetability provided by modern search engines on the Web directly facilitated such rapid conceptual development in a way that no other medium could. In this case, there was clearly a *loose* connection made among what were otherwise *heterogeneous* resources.

Two specific benefits arise from such loose associations and resultant conceptual development. First, the learner begins to appreciate the *conceptual variability* inherent to ill-structured domains. It becomes clear that though similarities exist across the disparate examples, they are not exactly the same. The nuances of New Hampshire residents' concerns with its ski industry cannot be mistaken for the concerns of Pacific Islanders'; these examples are not interchangeable. Fast nonreductive conceptual induction safeguards the conceptual rough edges that are desirable when learning concepts in ill-structured domains. These rough edges directly facilitate the second benefit: *flexible use*. When faced with situation specific need for the concept of selfishness or local recognition, the learner will be well prepared to select an appropriate prototype example (or examples) for application, based on both the similarities and differences that have been preserved among the candidates.

The development of several even more complex knowledge structures related to climate change were also apparent in our study. Among them, consider the concept of carbon markets, about which the subject had minimal prior knowledge at the onset of the study. However, during early research sessions, a complex understanding of carbon markets developed quickly, including the varying effects of mandatory and volunteer cap and trade systems; the Chicago Climate Exchange; related government inclinations (from the United States, European, and Chinese governments); and corporate interests. The subject considered the benefits and drawbacks of carbon markets, from the innovations that were directly credited to Clean Development Mechanism applications, to the inherent waste that carbon market critics argued. Ideas about why (typically anti-regulatory) US business interests are actually calling for more federal regulation in this arena were considered, and proposals that markets may not be able to cure the problem, given some assertions that climate change is the "greatest market failure" ever, were examined.

The implications of this specific example for deep learning in an ill-structured domain are twofold. First, imagine trying to gather the resources to "instruct" a learner about the topics outlined above, and then completing this task in just a few hours. Any reasonable analogous approximation of the time necessary to replicate this information with traditional resources would be *many* times

greater. Examination of a knowledge structure this complex and ill-structured cannot otherwise be accomplished without a learning environment like the Web, its specific affordances, and the skills and mindset outlined above. However, even more important was the evidence that this knowledge was later *flexibly reassembled*. In one of the final research sessions, in the context of how to change individual behavior to address climate change, the learner recombined several of the ideas about carbon markets with concepts from elsewhere (e.g., capitalism and economics) to propose the use of cap and trade systems for individual energy consumption. When considering the impact higher demand, lower supply energy may have on home energy use, the subject adapted the concept of lower effective per-unit carbon costs from carbon markets (and how mandated versus volunteer caps impact the level of incentive provided), with the profit considerations of utility companies, to propose how the adoption of a "personal" cap and trade system for home energy would differ from those currently in place in industrial carbon marketplaces. This thought experiment served to both strengthen his understanding of industrial cap and trade systems (through revisitation of the related ideas) and provided key insights into some of the economic considerations needed to better understand issues related to his inquiry into individual climate change behavior. A more detailed accounting of both learning experiences is provided in DeSchryver & Spiro (in preparation). In sum, this demonstration case study suggested a clear relationship between the way that the material about carbon markets was learned and how it was later flexibly applied.

The level of complexity varied widely for the ideas encountered by the subject over the course of our study. However, he examined several more broadly ill-structured concepts, identified their inter-relationships and integrated them into an evolving and complex knowledge structure of climate change. These included:

- The role of capitalism/consumerism in climate change
- The mixed messages of corporate climate change agendas (e.g., Wal-Mart)
- The ever-changing nature of religion as it relates to climate change, and how "religious" perspectives often differ from the theological and philosophical considerations
- The educational implications of changing climate related behavior
- The complex relationship between climate change mitigation and adaptation
- Technology as both a climate change "cause" and "cure"
- The nascent eco-biz industry and related alternative fuel considerations
- The role and impact of international agencies (e.g., IPCC) and studies (e.g., Stern Report) in climate change
- Why the US and Europe have decidedly different approaches to climate change (both individual and governmental)
- The relationship among supercomputers, modeling, and climate change
- The role of media as it relates to climate change

It is important to note the extent to which each of these ideas interconnected with the others. For instance, the concept of religion was encountered several times. The subject developed an understanding of how both personal and institutional religious considerations shape issues related to climate change in powerful ways, and cannot be disconnected from policy and personal behavioral decisions. At the same time, these ideas demonstrated irregularity across instances, a hallmark of ill-structured concepts that differentiate them from complex, but well-structured concepts. For instance, early in the study, it was determined that several key religious institutions had begun to support policies to aggressively combat climate change. After having seen multiple examples of this positive support, the *temptation to generalize*

on the part of the subject could have been very high (e.g., he could have generalized the concept that religious organizations support aggressive policies to mitigate climate change). However, a few sessions later, information about how one key religious institution had reversed its position was encountered. The ability to recognize and appreciate the irregularities that exist for concepts applied in ill-structured domains is critical, and directly facilitated by deep Web learning; learning in this way disables the temptation to overgeneralize by inculcating a mindset that "it's not that simple."

COGNITIVE LOAD THEORY

While we find the above learning outcomes impressive, it may well be that this method of learning is just *hard*, or cognitively demanding. How, then, can we ensure that more people will be able to achieve these outcomes without overwhelming cognitive demands? We will address this question through the lens of Cognitive Load Theory (CLT), a framework often utilized for just such concerns in learning.

CLT has been a leading framework for the study of human learning (e.g., see Sweller, van Merrienboer & Paas, 1998; van Merrienboer & Sweller, 2005). At the heart of CLT is a limited working memory for novel information and procedures, which demonstrates no such limitation when information is retrieved from long-term memory and related schemas (Ericsson & Kintsch, 1995). CLT assumes that long-term memory has unlimited capacity and that learning only occurs when changes in long-term memory have occurred (Kirschner, Sweller, & Clark, 2006). Cognitive load is calculated by the additive relationship among *intrinsic, extraneous,* and *germane* cognitive load (Paas, Renkl & Sweller, 2003; Sweller, van Merrienboer & Paas, 1998; van Merrienboer & Sweller, 2005). Intrinsic cognitive load is based on the fundamental characteristics of the material to be learned, most importantly, the number of elements that have to be considered simultaneously for successful learning (called *element interactivity*). Extraneous cognitive load is the *ineffective* load imposed by poor decision making related to the organization and presentation of information to be learned. Germane cognitive load is *effective*, in that it requires the "mindful engagement" of the learner with what is most essential to enhancing learning. Both extraneous and germane cognitive load are considered in CLT to be under the control of instructional designers. The ideas of CLT have been examined in a number of experiments that have confirmed the theory's predicted relationship between kind of load and success in learning for different instructional designs.

In recent years, these basic ideas have been developed and extended to incorporate the demands of "real-life" tasks and the complex learning they often represent (van Merrienboer & Sweller, 2005). For example, the role of "chunking" by experts in reducing the number of interacting elements, which results in lower effective intrinsic load, is increasingly of interest. CLT researchers have also begun to examine the effect of motivation on cognitive load in real-life learning and training contexts (e.g., see Pass, Tuovinen, van Merrienboer & Darabi, 2005).

Learning of the depth and complexity we describe in the section above has several cognitive load implications. Often, the total cognitive load is high. But, this heightened load should not always be avoided, given the potentially deleterious effects to learning from oversimplifying complex material (Feltovich, Coulson & Spiro, 2001; Spiro, Feltovich, Coulson & Anderson, 1989). It does no good to ignore *necessary* learning difficulty. When high cognitive loads for learning in ill-structured domains are encountered, they primarily derive from the nature of the material itself, or its intrinsic cognitive load. We have no choice but to acknowledge that this is the case, and work with it. Whereas, CLT has recently

expanded and developed to address complex learning by "artificially" reducing element interactivity to reduce intrinsic cognitive load, since "understanding complex information may not be necessary or even possible in the early stages of learning" (van Merrienboer & Sweller, 2005, p. 157), we do not advocate this approach for ill-structured domains.

If intrinsic cognitive load in an ill-structured domain is high, artificially reducing the complexity in early learning is dangerous in two ways. First, with respect to the local concept, early simplifications interfere with the later acquisition of complexity (Feltovich et al., 1989, 1997, 2001; Spiro, Coulson, Feltovich, & Anderson, 1988; Spiro, Feltovich, Coulson, & Anderson, 1989). Second, such simplifications inculcate a reductive mindset, in general. Instead of simplifying complex, ill-structured material, we need to learn how to deal with it. Learning in and about ill-structured domains is hard and requires mental effort. Boiling these ideas down for simple presentation makes the ideas easier to learn (and easier to teach and assess), but does not facilitate the situation specific, interconnected, context dependent, flexible assemblies of knowledge that are necessary for successful learning outcomes.

In other situations, cognitive load may appear to be higher than it actually is. We present two reasons why this is case. First, in the following section, we revisit the concept of cognitive load and explore how it must be reconceptualized in order to better apply to ill-structured concepts, deep Web learning, and the Post-Gutenberg Mind. This reconceptualization mitigates some of the cognitive load concerns by arguing that common sources of extraneous cognitive load in well-structured domains actually represent germane load in ill-structured domains. Then, in the section thereafter, we discuss how specific aspects of deep learning on the Web may further ameliorate cognitive load concerns.

COGNITIVE LOAD THEORY REVISITED

We find the evolution of CLT to be impressive in its consideration of expertise, real-life tasks, and complex learning. However, given that in its application, CLT has primarily been concerned with "relatively well-structured procedural and conceptual domains" (van Merrienboer & Sweller, 2005, p. 156), we propose that a reconceptualization is necessary in order for CLT to apply to real-life learning tasks in ill-structured domains, especially in deep Web learning. (See also Gerjets and Scheiter (2003) for their useful suggestions about the relationship between cognitive load, learner goals, and individual processing strategies in hypertext learning environments.) We present this reconceptualization with four distinct arguments. First, we highlight how ill-structured domains and well-structured domains are dissimilar and how the goals for learning in each must also necessarily differ. Second, we outline a reconceptualized germane cognitive load that is more appropriate for learning in ill-structured domains. Third, we discuss how this reconceptualization underscores our position that *what is considered extraneous cognitive load in well-structured domains is often germane in ill-structured domains*. Finally, we argue that the Web represents a quintessential environment in which to optimize the ratio of extraneous load to germane load for learning in ill-structured domains.

Learning Goals in Ill-Structured versus Well-Structured Domains

The learning goals in well-structured and ill-structured domains are not the same. This stems from the structural differences that exist between them. Well-structured material, even that which demonstrates complexity, exhibits orderliness and regularity that underscore the goals for learning. It is always possible to present essential information or known procedures for well-structured material.

Answers exist to questions posed in well-structured domains. Therefore, the primary goal for learning in well-structured domains is the construction and automation of schemas. Traditional CLT, primarily working within well-structured domains, therefore defines germane cognitive load to comprise the mental effort devoted to such schema construction and automation (van Merrienboer & Sweller, 2005).

However, the goal for learning in ill-structured domains is very different, focusing on the construction of open and flexible knowledge structures for situation specific application. This is primarily due to the *irregularity* that concepts and phenomena demonstrate across instances and applications, such that pre-specifying the conditions under which knowledge will be used is not possible. Because of this irregularity, emphasizing only the acquisition and automation of prepackaged schemas does not provide the flexible knowledge structures required; schemas alone cannot prepare learners for the wide scope of application needed, since essential information and known procedures do not exist. Since there are not specific answers with universal application to questions posed in ill-structured domains, preparing the learner for situation-sensitive development of "schemas-of-the-moment" is of utmost importance. (For a more detailed presentation of the special qualities of learning in ill-structured domains, see Spiro & DeSchryver, in press; Spiro, Vispoel, Schmitz, Samarapungavan, & Boerger, 1987; Spiro, Feltovich & Coulson, 1996.)

Germane Cognitive Load for Ill-Structured Domains

The concept of germane cognitive load must therefore be reconceptualized in order to be consistent with the learning goals for ill-structured domains. In general, we encourage mental efforts that resist oversimplification and resist reductive thinking. In this way, we advocate an emphasis on learning activities that support new constructions of indefinite numbers of situation sensitive assemblages and not retrieval of precompiled schemas or templates from long-term memory. These activities comprise a more appropriate conceptualization of germane cognitive load for ill-structured domains, and should include:

- Recognizing interconnections
- Criss-crossing the knowledge landscape
- Experiencing multiple perspectives and representations
- Testing candidate generalizations with a presumption of "it's not that simple" until proven otherwise
- Seeing patterns of context dependence
- Identifying how surprising similarities and surprising differences unfold

Recognizing that Extraneous Cognitive Load Activities in WSDs Often Appear as Germane Cognitive Load in ISDs

Based on traditional conceptions of CLT, the activities we have outlined that are crucial to learning in ill-structured domains represent extraneous cognitive load when learning in well-structured domains. As well they should. When essential information is known, or a correct procedure available (as is typically the case for well-structured material), it should be presented to learners in a way that maximizes their ability to acquire, update, and automate schemas. Criss-crossing the knowledge landscape to find essential information would increase extraneous load dramatically, wastefully, and unnecessarily.

The reverse is also true. Schema construction and automation (considered germane to learning in well-structured domains) is extraneous to the goal of flexible learning in ill-structured domains. It is equally as wasteful to construct and automate schemas in ill-structured domains as it is to criss-cross well-structured domains looking for

known information. Since tailored "in-the-moment" assemblages are most germane to learning in ill-structure domains, intact schema retrieval is minimized, and any time spent constructing intact schemas is essentially wasted. In fact, use of intact schemas tends to compartmentalize knowledge in a way that works against the goals of flexible knowledge, by blocking the ability for the learner to properly recognize the inherent interconnectedness in ill-structured domains (Spiro et al., 1991). In this way, schema construction not only represents extraneous load for learning in ill-structured domains, but also directly undermines the primary process of flexible knowledge construction.

The Web is a Quintessential Learning Environment in Which to Optimize Germane Cognitive Load for Learning in Ill-Structured Domains

Our conceptualization of germane cognitive load for ill-structured domains will also appear to represent extraneous cognitive load when considered for traditional linear media. However, with hypermedia and especially now the Web, we finally have learning environments that accommodate advanced knowledge acquisition in ill-structured domains and work to make our proposed mental efforts germane. In fact, the affordances of the Web keep extraneous load *much lower* for learning activities that are specifically relevant to ill-structured domains than they would otherwise be with traditional media.

For instance, if you accept that criss-crossing non-linear irregularly interconnected knowledge is essential to learning in ill-structured domains, what better medium exists than the Web? Consider again how long it would take for a learner to find print media in a library even closely approximating the expansive and up-to-the-minute resources outlined above for climate change. Then, imagine how long it would take to begin to recognize the intricate interconnectedness among these myriad resources. The extraneous load requirements would be overwhelming with traditional media. However, on the Web, interconnectedness is inherent. What is the optimal use of cognitive load resources to recognize interconnections among disparate information resources, card catalogs and indexes, or the instant-access, fully searchable, non-linear Web? There is no comparison. The Web is ideal for learning in this way.

COGNITIVE LOAD CONSIDERATIONS FOR SPECIFIC ASPECTS OF DEEP WEB LEARNING IN ILL-STRUCTURED DOMAINS

As we have noted, many aspects of deep Web learning in ill-structured domains that are germane might, in well-structured domains or with traditional linear media, be considered extraneous, and vice-versa. In this section, we discuss several aspects of deep Web learning in ill-structured domains and how they may help to maximize the ratio of germane cognitive load to extraneous cognitive load. Again, we present these ideas as *what is possible* for deep learning on the Web not *what is* the case for everyone. Continued research that examines these phenomena more specifically will help identify the conditions under which they apply more broadly, and how to best prepare novice learners for deep Web learning in ill-structured domains.

LICRA Searches

Learner-initiated, complex, reciprocally adaptive (LICRA) searches are a core feature to successful deep Web learning in ill-structured domains. These searches promote active involvement from the learner, require heightened attention, and emphasize the need for value determination and judgment. Given this additional effort required

to generate successful LICRA searches, it should be expected that associated cognitive loads are rather high. Indeed, traditional CLT often associates searching of any kind-- for information needed to complete a learning task, for solutions, or for referents in an explanation-- with extraneous cognitive load (Paas, Renkl, & Sweller, 2003; van Merrienboer Sweller, 2005).

However, consistent with the above account of how cognitive load applies to ill-structured domains, this effort represents *germane* cognitive load. LICRA searches are part of the learning process and cannot be viewed separately. When learners use a LICRA phrase, they create implicit interconnections among resources. The iterative nature of these searches also facilitates criss-crossing the conceptual landscape in order to construct a better sense of the whole. As a result, when compared to following embedded hyperlinks or scanning through a single list of Google results, these iterative search techniques promise an even greater payoff.

Extraneous cognitive load concerns about hypertext learning are somewhat ameliorated by LICRA searching, as well. The decision-making that is "required" by the visual cue of an embedded hyperlink may serve to increase extraneous load, especially if multiple links appear on the same page (DeStefano & LeFevre, 2007). This "interruptive" quality does not exist for LICRA searches, because they result from an internal, somewhat spontaneous, assignment of importance on the part of the learner. There is also some concern that following hyperlinks, especially for a long time or to "semantically distant information" (DeStefano & LeFevre, 2007, p. 1620) increases cognitive load and reduces comprehension. However, criss-crossing, or following links, either embedded or learner initiated, is a core feature of deep Web learning when learning in ill-structured domains. And, many forms of extraneous load associated with the criss-crossing supported by LICRA searches should be increasingly mitigated by the growing body of adjunct learning aids (see below) that help to manage and make explicit the choices and relationships that emerge while exploring the knowledge landscape. We also envision that as learners become more effective at LICRA searching, the "after-the-fact" ratio of germane to extraneous load will also optimize (i.e., more LICRA phrases will yield useful information and less will be "dead-ends").

It should be noted that there are well-structured skills that are necessary in order for learners to perform successful LICRA searches. For instance, using quotation marks to target exact phrases, employing Boolean logic, searching a specific site, using a tilde to return related items in a search, and using the "link:" phrase to determine backlinks, are all useful skills that should be taught to and practiced by Web users. We support the notion that the automation of schema for such skills is essential to good LICRA searching and should be done with the lowest possible extraneous cognitive load.

Serendipitous Learning

Serendipitous learning comprises an accidental encounter with seemingly unrelated or useless information that then becomes relevant. Such serendipitous learning is automatic, unconscious, and spontaneous in nature, inherently requires no conscious mental effort, and thus demonstrates a very low cognitive load requirement. While the value of making serendipitous connections between unrelated ideas is not new to hypertext research (e.g., Bernstein, Bolter, Joyce, and Mylonas, 1991), it has often been a form of "quasi-random" knowledge association, given the finite amount of information in closed hypertext systems or when just following links provided on a web page. However, in deep Web searches utilizing LICRA methods, serendipitous information can, and does, emerge at any time. The likelihood of the occurrence of serendipitous learning increases exponentially as the speed of access to information increases, as Web users search more efficiently,

and as the landscape of resources available becomes, for practical purposes, unlimited. This exponential increase in potential random encounters requires no additional effort on the part of the learner, but is often significant to the learning process. Our recent research demonstrated several points at which serendipitous finds resulted in significant conceptual breakthroughs and novel interconnections of information for the learner (DeSchryver & Spiro, in preparation).

Such serendipitous learning can happen at any time on the Web, including moving "backwards" in the search process. For instance, in our recent study, it was common for the learner to open several new browser tabs during LICRA searches to accommodate multilevel iterative search phrase development. Several times, after a "stopping-point" in this process was reached, and while returning to his original search results (e.g., "backing out" of the iterative searches), the subject noticed information that did not seem relevant when it was first viewed but that was particularly useful in the context of the new information he had since encountered. This new relevance may simply have occurred as a result of the accumulated context. However, the benefits of "considering," or reviewing, information multiple times within a relatively short period, need to be explored.

Resource Evaluation

The evaluation of a Web resource for authority and accuracy typically has extensive extraneous cognitive load implications. Learners are often provided with rubrics containing several questions to answer for each Web resource they encounter. For example: Is it a personal page? What type of domain is it from? Who wrote the page? Is it dated? Is it current enough? What are the author's credentials? Are sources documented? Are there links to other sources? (see Finding, 2008, for a full and much more exhaustive list). The use of such guidelines requires very high extraneous cognitive loads. And, while such rubrics may be valuable for young or introductory learners, our recent study provided evidence that this process may become fully integrated into the learning process for advanced learners.

One reason for such integration is that the Web is full of "trusted aggregators" that reduce the evaluation necessary. For instance, the New York Times has a list of articles related to climate change. At the same time, especially in extended learning on the Web, learners will visit the same sites over and over. Subsequent visits to a trusted site (including what are often visits to topically disparate sub-nodes in the site) require no additional evaluation.

However, more significantly, we submit that the integration of resource evaluation results primarily when the learner becomes adept at seeking out multiple representations of one concept while learning about it. Through recognizing the similarities and differences among the multiplicity of resources, it quickly becomes apparent which resources are trusted and which are not, without working through a guideline of static questions about each resource. In this way, resource evaluation is *fully integrated into the learning process* for the advanced learner by an often unwitting method of *triangulation*. Each site visited not only provides new information, new contexts, new representations, and new perspectives that are germane to learning, but also tightens the criteria for filtering out resources that do not reflect the quality, accuracy or credibility of acceptable sites. From a cognitive load perspective, an extraneous load requirement has been transferred to a germane learning activity.

Blogs

The nature of the information found during deep Web learning has significant implications for the learner's cognitive load. For instance, blogs now increasingly find their way into Web search results. The casual form of information typically encountered in blogs has largely been considered useless for serious knowledge inquiry (e.g., see Head, 2007). However, we found that several categories of blogs were examined during our recent study, running the gamut from factual to opinionated. Analysis of the various types of blogs that were used, as well as their interactions with the differing stages of meaningful learning (Sheull, 1990), indicated that blogs can be quite valuable to the learning process and that the related cognitive load requirements vary.

For instance, the use of blogs in early stage learning (fact-based) does not seem beneficial. The above methods for resource evaluation require more authoritative resources for fact-finding. Though many excellent factual blogs exist and were encountered by the subject during early stage learning, most were filtered out by resource triangulation methods. It seems additional extraneous cognitive load would be required to determine the credibility of facts in a blog, whereas the triangulation techniques for resource evaluation for other more authoritative factual sites require less effort. Evaluating blogs for "facts" just does not seem worth the extra mental effort at this stage in learning.

However, during latter stages in the learning process (involving more problem-solving and abstract thinking) triangulation methods for resource evaluation valued the opportunity for "idea play" that less factual blogs provided. We submit that taking into account the speed with which ideas from different blog sites can be experienced on the Web can result in a dialogical interaction among the user and multiple blog sites. In this way, the learner can agree with some authors and disagree with others; accept some points, and discount others; all the while developing his or her own ideas through arguing, counter-arguing, and the related combinatorial idea play. In this way, the voices in blog entries are *virtually synchronized* and provide great potential for deep learning of ill-structured domains on the Web. At the same time, the extraneous load associated with early (fact-based) use of blogs is minimized, since the interactions with blogs become germane during creative knowledge assemblies. Extraneous cognitive load is also further reduced by the conversational text found in most blogs that is often easier to comprehend for the learner than other, more authoritative resources. Examples of this type of learning are provided in DeSchryver and Spiro (in preparation), where the use of blogs was directly responsible for several significant conceptual breakthroughs on the part of the learner.

Adjunct Online Tools

Cognitive support tools for deep learning on the Web are widely available. From Web text highlighting to page specific sticky notes, *adjunct online tools* abound, and new ones are released regularly. The number of modern tools to support deep Web learning dwarfs those available for traditional text or lecture-based environments. The unprecedented availability of these adjunct supportive aids also has significant cognitive load implications.

External memory aids like Clipmarks (http://www.clipmarks.com) make it effortless to save whole pages as well as small segments of pages (including images and video) in a personalized database. The information contained therein can be accessed by keyword, Boolean search, or chronologically, and increases the ease with which learners can criss-cross and revisit the information. This facilitates the recognition of interconnections, multiplicities, and differing contexts that are critical to the acquisition of flexible knowledge (Spiro & Jehng, 1990). At the same time, tools such as Google History and Trailfire (or even just concerted use of the tabs available in modern browsers for individual sessions) allow users to document and easily trace their paths through the web. While keeping extraneous cognitive load low relative to navigation (e.g., you can never really get lost), these services also have the potential to dramatically support the ad-

ditional (germane) meta-cognitive activities that deep Web learning affords, by making explicit the paths of inquiry for later review, with little or no additional extraneous load.

Though not a specific tool, the functionality of *tagging* (assigning keywords to content of interest) also increases the potential benefits of deep Web learning. Most contemporary Web-based content management systems (e.g., Clipmarks), utilize this feature extensively. Tagging is a categorization activity that requires the assignment of meaning, a task that therefore represents germane cognitive load. Tagging information can represent an elaboration that fosters the encoding of long-term memories (Budiu, Pirolli, & Hong, 2007; van Merrienboer & Sweller, 2005). However, more important to learning in ill-structured domains, the application of multiple tags facilitates learner recognition of interconnections that may exist among the newly discovered information and previous information that has been similarly tagged. And, as Sinha (2005) noted, the practice of applying multiple tags to information may actually require a lower cognitive load than assigning information to a single category. She argued that upon encountering worthwhile information, multiple semantic concepts are typically activated in a learner. When forced to assign the information to one category, significant cognitive load is spent determining the *best* category, often resulting in what she called "post activation analysis paralysis" (para 16). However, the multiplicity of tagging allows learners to freedom to assign information to all related semantic concepts that are activated. She claims that it "taps into an existing cognitive process without adding much cognitive cost" (para 19).

There are also broader benefits to be accrued from tagging. For instance, Weinberger (2007) asserted that tagging *en masse*, combined with sophisticated data mining and search technologies, will facilitate better reconstructions of the implicit meaning of information on the Web. When available as part of the search process, this "meaning" will greatly focus searches for everyone, thus lowering any extraneous cognitive load related to filtering results.

The Question of Motivation

Recent developments in CLT have begun to integrate the importance of motivation, especially when considering "real-life," extended time tasks (Pass, Tuovinen, van Merrienboer & Darabi, 2005; van Merrienboer & Sweller, 2005). And, while Astleitner and Wiesner (2004) raised concern for how a high density of motivational strategies explicitly designed for instructional settings may lead to increased cognitive load, we submit that motivation in deep Web learning is largely inherent, not an additional learning component that vies for space in working memory. Clearly, the specific cognitive load implications of motivation are just beginning to emerge. However, as Pass et al. (2005) noted "meaningful learning can only commence if training experience is coupled with the motivation to achieve well" (p. 26). More specifically, higher levels of learner motivation have the potential to increase the use of mental efforts that are germane to the learning outcomes.

Deep Web learning affords such increased motivation, and it was manifested in surprising ways in our recent study. Several times the subject noted his excitement about a particular path of inquiry, new and promising search phrases based on ideas from the current page, or a significant conceptual breakthrough. In a few cases a sort of learning *momentum* affected his motivations. Why? Although the exact processes are speculative at this point, we offer three ways deep Web learning appears to increase motivation, through attention, choice, and speed.

In Keller's (1987a; 1987b; 1999) Model of Motivation Design, he noted that *attention* and subsequent motivation could be gained through novel, surprising, incongruous, and uncertain events. We argue that novel, surprising, incongruous, and uncertain *ideas* discovered in the course

of deep Web learning have a similarly enhancing effect on learner attention. And, since the Web interactions are not "designed" elements, they do not increase extraneous cognitive load, so that any increase in attention and effort likely serves to optimize germane cognitive load.

In addition, as Brophy has noted, much of what is known about optimal conditions for motivation cannot be easily applied in classrooms (in Gaedke & Shaughnessy, 2003). However, these very same ideas can and often do apply in deep Web learning, such as *learner control*. In typical classrooms, learner choice is minimized; however, considerable choice is afforded to Post-Gutenberg learners. They learn whenever and wherever they want. They choose what search phrases to use. They choose which results to visit. The assemblage of knowledge is personal in every way. The impact of this type of learning on personal attributions, expectations, and self-efficacy needs to be explored in more detail. However, we propose that once learners begin to feel empowered (which does not take long), they begin to *believe* that they can achieve their learning goals.

Finally, *speed* is essential to learner motivation on the Web. Everything happens fast. Resources are available in an instant. However, even more significant, our recent study of deep Web learning demonstrated a *quick transition* from early "fact-finding" to the *advanced stages of meaningful learning* that involved rapid interconnectedness and abstract/problem based thinking (Sheull, 1990). Accordingly, the subject indicated more excitement about these latter stages. The speed with which new information is available also impacts motivation. The learner can read reaction to yesterday's Senate hearings on climate change today, or in some cases can evaluate information in real-time. Access to *information this timely* empowers the learner, and may even make them feel like they know something others do not (including teachers).

Together, the impact of these motivational considerations on cognitive load needs further exploration, particularly for deep Web learning. However, we envision increased motivation, inherent in the learning process itself, providing substantial benefits to the process through increased germane mental efforts.

CONCLUSION

The chapter discusses how deep learning on the Web provides affordances that are well matched to the learning goals and requirements for flexible knowledge construction in ill-structured domains. In so doing, we have outlined a reconceptualization of germane cognitive load that is more appropriate for learning in ill-structured domains than that conceived by traditional Cognitive Load Theory. This new perspective makes it clear that mental efforts that are germane to learning in ill-structured domains are often extraneous in well-structured domains, and vice-versa. We have also discussed how specific aspects of deep Web learning in ill-structured domains help to optimize the ratio of germane cognitive load to extraneous cognitive load, including LICRA searching, serendipitous learning, resource evaluation, blog use, the availability of adjunct cognitive tools, tagging, and learner motivation.

Not everyone is prepared to take advantage of the benefits we have outlined. Nor do all domains of knowledge benefit from unfettered exploration in online multimedia environments. Additionally, cognitive load may be increased at first for novice Web learners. However, for ill-structured domains, deep Web learning holds great promise. The automatization of the basic skills required to successfully learn in depth on the Web happens quickly. The learner's skills improve with practice, and soon these skills are incorporated effortlessly within higher-level aspects of learning (e.g., LICRA searching and integrated resource evaluation), similar to how an advanced driver uses a steering wheel while navigating during rush hour. Expert drivers steer unconsciously while they attend to the landscape around them. So, too, will expert searchers direct themselves around the vast knowledge landscape of the Web without concerted effort. The automaticity of simple search skills leads to decreased extraneous cognitive load, freeing up resources for activities that are germane to flexible knowledge acquisition in ill-structured domains.

We are confident that the learning we describe above can become a large-scale reality. However, while we have concentrated on the potential benefits that deep Web learning will provide, obstacles to its success remain. For instance, the sheer quantity of resources available on the Web imposes a challenge. Learners may, even with the assistance of adjunct cognitive tools, drift away from relevant search results to information that is, in effect, extraneous to their efforts. In order to address these issues, we anticipate the need to develop loose meta-data structures similar to those employed in Cognitive Flexibility Hypertext systems (e.g., see Spiro, Collins & Ramchandran, 2007).

In addition, managing the *personal knowledge landscape* constructed by individuals immersed in deep Web learning may require support beyond what current adjunct online tools provide. Such support may take the form of more integrated tools capable of reducing the associated extraneous cognitive load. One such possibility would be the development of representative dynamic visual displays. We see the need for evolving network mind-maps, developed in an ongoing fashion with input from both the learner and the software in use. The information could be tagged by context so that the visual display highlights different information in different contexts, demonstrates the interconnectedness among ideas, facilitates revisitation, and provides significant meta-cognitive learning benefits. For example, this system could support three-dimensional mind-maps, each node mashed-up with the information from a Clipmarks-like database and relevant Google History details, and include visual representations of the interconnections that have formed.

FUTURE RESEARCH

To conclude, we offer the following: The Web will change the way that we think and learn, and these changes will be dramatic. It is inevitable. The timing of this revolution is fortuitous, since we are faced with increasingly complex and ill-structured educational and societal issues, both local and global in scale. Consider the difficulty we face assuming, as our forefathers did, that we have an "informed constituency" to support democracy. For example, climate change, health care, and globalization are "grand social challenges" that an informed electorate should understand to a much greater extent than is currently the case. These issues and others like them demonstrate ill-structuredness and they therefore require high levels of intrinsic cognitive load to understand. We believe that with concerted research efforts, ways for the Web to make learning about such issues cognitively manageable will result.

As a field, we need to be proactive in thinking about how to ensure that this happens. Our chapter is provided to encourage more researchers to examine this phenomenon in earnest. Myriad research opportunities and lines of inquiry exist and beg examination under both well-controlled and "real-life" conditions to determine the circumstances, knowledge domains, and learner characteristics for which new ways of learning will apply most broadly. What are the best ways to ensure that learners approach deep Web learning with an opening mindset? How will we best use tagging, LICRA searches and blogs to develop flexible knowledge appropriate to the challenges we face? Is the cognitive load for LICRA searching less than that for embedded links? If not, do the benefits outweigh the costs? Do triangulation methods of resource evaluation ensure an acceptable level of credibility? Do learners need to develop a certain level of expertise in the basic skills of deep Web learning in order for the motivational benefits we have offered to emerge? These questions, and many more, require the at-tention of researchers in order to better understand ongoing changes in the way we think and learn about critically important issues.

REFERENCES

Astleitner, H., & Wiesner, C. (2004). An integrated model of multimedia learning and motivation. *Journal of Educational Multimedia and Hypermedia, 13*, 3-21.

Bernstein, M., Bolter, J.D., Joyce, M., & Mylonas, E. (1991) Architectures for volatile hypertext. *Proceedings of Hypertext' 91*, ACM Press, San Antonio, Texas, December, 241-260.

Budiu, R., Pirolli, P., & Hong, L. (2007). Remembrance of things tagged: How tagging affects human information processing. *Palo Alto Research Center.* Retrieved January 17, 2008 from http://asc.parc.googlepages.com/2007-09-12-tagmemory-12-blogged-vers.pdf

DeSchryver, M. & Spiro, R.J. (in preparation). Nonlinear knowledge acquisition in a post-Gutenberg world: An examination of emerging constructs for deep learning on the Web.

DeStefano, D. & LeFevre, J. (2007). Cognitive load in hypertext reading: A review. *Computers in Human Behavior, 23*, 1616-1641.

Ericsson, K. A., & Kintsch, W. (1995). Long-term working memory. *Psychological Review, 102*(2), 211-245.

Feltovich, P.J., Coulson, R.L., & Spiro, R.J. (2001). Learners' understanding of important and difficult concepts: A challenge to smart machines in education. In P.J. Feltovich & K. Forbus (Eds.). *Smart Machines in Education.* Cambridge, MA: MIT Press.

Feltovich, P. J., Spiro, R. J., & Coulson, R. L. (1989). The nature of conceptual understanding in biomedicine: The deep structure of complex ideas and the development of misconceptions. In D. Evans & V. Patel (Eds.), *The Cognitive Sciences in Medicine* (pp. 113-172). Cambridge, MA: M.I.T. Press.

Feltovich, P.J, Spiro, R.J., & Coulson, R.L. (1997). Issues of expert flexibility in contexts characterized by complexity and change. In P.J. Feltovich, K.M. Ford, & R.R. Hoffman (Eds.). *Expertise in context: Human and machine.* Cambridge, MA: MIT Press.

Finding information on the Internet: A tutorial, (2008). Retrieved February 10, 2008 from http://www.lib.berkeley.edu/TeachingLib/Guides/Internet/Evaluate.html

Gaedke, B., & Shaughnessy, M.F. (2003). An interview with Jere Brophy. *Educational Psychology Review, 15*(2), 199-211.

Gerjets, P., & Scheiter, K. (2003). Goals and strategies as moderators between instructional design and cognitive load: Evidence from hypertext-based instruction. *Educational Psychologist, 38*, 33-41.

Graff, M. (2003). Learning from Web-based instructional systems and cognitive style. *British Journal of Educational Technology, 34*(4), 407-418.

Griffiths, J., & Brophy, P. (2005). Student searching behavior and the Web: Use of academic resources and Google," *Library Trends, 53*(4), 539–554.

Head, A.J. (2007). Beyond Google: How do students conducts academic research? *First Monday, 12*(8). Retrieved January 15, 2008 from http://firstmonday.org/issues/issue12_8/head/index.htm

Jones, S. (2002). The Internet goes to college: How students are living in the future with today's technology. *Pew Internet and American Life Project.* Retrieved January 20, 2008 from http://www.pewinternet.org/PPF/r/71/report_display.asp

Keller, J. M. (1987a). Development and use of the ARCS model of motivational design. *Journal of Instructional Development, 10*(3), 2 – 10.

Keller, J. M. (1987b). Strategies for stimulating the motivation to learn. *Performance & Instruction, 26*(8), 1-7.

Keller, J. M. (1999). Motivation in cyber learning environments. *Educational Technology International, 1*(1), 7 – 30.

Kirschner, P. A., Sweller, J., & Clark, R. E. (2006). Why minimal guidance during instruction does not work: An analysis of the failure of constructivist, discovery, problem based, experiential, and inquiry-based teaching. *Educational Psychologist, 41*(2), 75–86.

Kuiper, E., Volman, M., & Terwel, J. (2005). The Web as an information resources in K-12 education: Strategies for supporting students in searching and processing information. *Review of Educational Research, 75* (3), 285-328.

Morville, P. (2005). *Ambient findability: What we find changes who we become.* Cambridge, MA: O'Reilly Media.

Paas, F., Renkl, A., & Sweller, J. (2003). Cognitive load theory and instructional design: Recent developments. *Educational Psychologist, 38*(1), 1-4.

Paas, F., Tuovinen, J.E., van Merriënboer, J.J.G., & Darabi, A. (2005). A motivational perspective on the relation between mental effort and performance: optimizing learners' involvement in instructional conditions. *Educational Technology, Research & Development, 53*, 25–34.

Sheull, T.J. (1990). Toward a unified approach to learning as a multisource phenomenon. *Review of Educational Research, 60*(4), 531-547.

Sinha, R. (2005). A cognitive analysis of tagging (or how the lower cognitive cost of tagging makes it popular). Thoughts About Cognition, Design, and

Technology: Rashmi Sinha's weblog. Retreived December 12, 2007 from http://www.rashmisinha. com/archives/05_09/tagging-cognitive.html

Spiro, R.J. (2006a). The "New Gutenberg Revolution": Radical new learning, thinking, teaching, and training with technology…bringing the future near. *Educational Technology, 46* (1), 3-4.

Spiro, R.J. (2006b). The Post-Gutenberg world of the mind: The shape of the new learning. *Educational Technology, 46* (2), 3-4.

Spiro, R.J. (2006c). Old ways die hard. *Educational Technology, 46* (3), 3-4.

Spiro, R.J. (2006d). Approaching the post-Gutenberg mind: The revolution is in progress. *Educational Technology, 46* (4), 3-4.

Spiro, R.J. (2006e). The "New Gutenberg Revolution": Radical new learning, thinking, teaching, and training with technology…bringing the future near. *Educational Technology, 46*(6), 3-5.

Spiro, R.J., Coulson, R. L., Feltovich, P. J., & Anderson, D. (1988). Cognitive flexibility theory: Advanced knowledge acquisition in ill-structured domains. *Tenth Annual Conference of the Cognitive Science Society*. Hillsdale, NJ: Erlbaum,. [Reprinted in In R. B. Ruddell (Ed.), *Theoretical models and processes of reading* (5th ed.). Newark, DE: International Reading Association, pp. 602-616.]

Spiro, R. J., Collins, B. P., Ramchandran, A. R. (2007). Reflections on a Post-Gutenberg epistemology for video use in ill-structured domains: Things you can do with video to foster complex learning and cognitive flexibility. *Video Research in the Learning Sciences*. Goldman, R., Pea R., Barron B., and Derry, S. (Eds.). Mahwah, NJ: Lawrence Erlbaum Associates.

Spiro, R.J., & DeSchryver, M. (in press). Constructivism: When it's the wrong idea and when it's the only idea. In T. Duffy & S. Tobais (Eds.). Mahwah, NJ: Lawrence Erlbaum.

Spiro, R.J., & DeSchryver, M. (in preparation). The new nonlinear reading comprehension: Deep learning on the Web and the post-Gutenberg mind.

Spiro, R.J., Feltovich, P.J., & Coulson, R.L. (1996). Two epistemic world-views: Prefigurative schemas and learning in complex domains. *Applied Cognitive Psychology, 10*, 52-61.

Spiro, R.J., Feltovich, P. J., Coulson, R. L., & Anderson, D. (1989). Multiple analogies for complex concepts: Antidotes for analogy-induced misconception in advanced knowledge acquisition. In S. Vosniadou & A. Ortony (Eds.), *Similarity and analogical reasoning* (pp. 498-531). Cambridge, MA: Cambridge University Press.

Spiro, R. J., Feltovich, P. J., Jacobson, M. J., & Coulson, R. L. (1991). Knowledge representation, content specification, and the development of skill in situation-specific knowledge assembly: Some constructivist issues as they relate to cognitive flexibility theory and hypertext. *Educational Technology, 31* (9), 22-25.

Spiro, R.J., & Jehng, J. (1990). Cognitive flexibility and hypertext: Theory and technology for the nonlinear and multidimensional traversal of complex subject matter. In D. Nix & R. J. Spiro (Eds.), *Cognition, education, and multimedia* (pp. 163-205). Hillsdale: Lawrence Erlbaum Associates.

Spiro, R. J., Vispoel, W. L., Schmitz, J., Samarapungavan, A., & Boerger, A. (1987). Knowledge acquisition for application: Cognitive flexibility and transfer in complex content domains. In B. C. Britton & S. Glynn (Eds.), *Executive control processes*. Hillsdale, NJ: Lawrence Erlbaum Associates.

Sweller. J. (1988) Cognitive load during problem solving: Effects on learning *Cognitive Science* 12, 157-285.

Sweller, J. (1994) Cognitive load theory, learning difficulty and instructional design *Learning and Instruction* 4, 295-312.

Sweller, J., van Merrienboer, J. J. G., & Paas, F. (1998). Cognitive architecture and instructional design. *Educational Psychology Review 10*(3), 251–296.

Tremayne, M., & Dunwoody, S. (2001). Interactivity, information processing, and learning on the World Wide Web. *Science Communication, 23(2)*, 111-134.

Thompson, C. (2003). Information illiterate or lazy: How college students use the Web for research. *Libraries and the Academy, 3*(2), 259-268.

van Merrienboer, J.J.G. & Sweller, J. (2005). Cognitive load theory and complex learning: Recent developments and future directions. *Educational Psychology Review 17*(2), 147-177.

Van Scoyoc, A.M. (2006). The electronic library: Undergraduate research behavior in a library without books. *Libraries and the Academy, 6*(1), 47-58.

Weinberger, D. (2007). Everything Is Miscellaneous, New York: Henry Holt.

Section II
Multimedia Learning:
Affective Perspectives

Chapter IX
Motivation and Multimedia Learning

Renae Low
University of New South Wales, Australia

Putai Jin
University of New South Wales, Australia

ABSTRACT

In the field of multimedia learning, although research on cognitive effects and their implications for instructional design is rich, research on the effects of motivation in a multimedia learning context is surprisingly scarce. Since one of the major goals of providing multimedia instruction is to motivate students, there is need to examine motivational elements. In this chapter, we focus on 4 major motivation theories–expectancy-value theory, self-efficacy, goal-setting and task motivation, and self-determination theory–and two motivation models–ARCS model and the integrated model of cognitive-motivational processes–that are derived from multimedia research; review the literature on motivation in multimedia learning contexts, suggest that researchers and practitioners take into account a number of essential aspects to ensure that motivation features incorporated in multimedia learning resources optimize learners' experience; and point out future research directions in model building, hypothesis testing, examining individual differences, and carrying out longitudinal studies.

INTRODUCTION

Research in the area of multimedia learning so far has focused on the effectiveness of instructional methods and course design. Various approaches of delivery have been investigated and basic principles in terms of memory and associated cognitive processes identified (e.g., Fletcher & Tobias, 2005; Low & Sweller, 2005; Mayer, 2005). Research in this direction appears to be fruitful, although puzzling, sometimes conflicting results, do occur. As a convention, in an attempt to integrate or develop "mini theories", more theories or models from information processing perspectives are proposed and further tested (e.g., Butcher, 2006). However, as pointed out by a number of researchers (Astleitner & Wiesner, 2004; Bernard et al., 2004; Clark & Feldon, 2005; Keller & Suzuki, 2004; Pass, Tuovinen, van Merriënboer, & Darabi, 2005; Volleyer & Reinberg, 2006), motivational aspects in multimedia learning should be regarded as essential elements and research with sound theoretical bases and methodological rigor is much needed.

In this chapter, we attempt to analyze and discuss motivational determinants in effective multimedia learning from social cognitive perspectives. The main issues covered here are as follows. First, we discuss why researchers and practitioners need to adequately consider motivational issues in multimedia learning. Second, we present well-founded motivation theories that are relevant to learning processes and task performance, and review models that can be specifically applied to multimedia learning, teaching and course material development. Finally, we highlight important factors, topics and directions for future motivational research to guide multimedia teaching and learning.

THE NEED FOR MOTIVATIONAL RESEARCH IN MULTIMEDIA LEARNING

It has been almost axiomatic since ancient times even before Aristotle and Confucius that meaningful learning is associated with motivation. However, despite the efforts of some experts in multimedia learning motivation (e.g., Astleitner & Hufnagl, 2003; Gao & Lehman, 2003; Keller & Suzuki, 2004; Song & Keller, 2001), research in multimedia learning at large has not taken motivational issues into account. Instructors may deem that multimedia material and associated operations are more interesting (e.g., text + pic-

tures + sound) or more accessible (e.g., e-learning at the user's convenient time) than conventional methods. The underlying assumption is that learners who have the opportunity to use multimedia resources should be highly motivated. However, if we scrutinize the literature, we will soon find that multimedia technology together with a certain type of course design may not lead to elevated motivation and superior learning performance. For instance, in a well-controlled study with initial motivational screen and randomization of subject assignment, online evaluation shows that medical students initially with positive attitudes towards computer-based learning (CBL) were not enthusiastic at the end of course, and learning outcomes were significantly affected by students' prior knowledge but not by their CBL use (Hahne, Benndorf, Frey, & Herzig, 2005). The implication is that CBL may hold too much promise in a curriculum scenario, and that hasty implementation of such curriculum-driven CBL program may carry a risk of deteriorating students' positive attitude towards CBL.

In another study which examined the data quality of questionnaire administration, the paper-based group was better than both computer-based and web-based groups, and the affective responses of participants favored the paper-based mode over computer- and web-based modes (Hardré, Crowson, Xie, & Ly, 2007). These results indicate that adopting information technology does not necessarily lead to high motivation. Hoskins and Van Hooff (2005) reported in a study on Web Course Tools (WebCT) that only those students already highly-motivated and academically-able benefited from bulletin board use, suggesting that motivation and academic ability are determinants of achievement in hypermedia learning.

The effect of motivation on multimedia learning was also highlighted by Hwang, Wang and Sharples (2007) in a quasi-experiment. The study found that although the experiment group using VPen (a multimedia annotation tool) appeared to be superior to the control group (learning without a multimedia annotation system) in several learning activities, there was no significant difference between the groups in the final examination. This is a typical example of a Hawthorne effect in multimedia learning, that is, academic outcome is due to motivation to learn and not necessarily owing to the adoption of sophisticated multimedia support.

Previous reviews on the effectiveness of multimedia learning are consistent with the suggestion that motivation plays an important role in multimedia learning. In a comprehensive, strict criterion-based meta-analysis of empirical literature comparing classroom (face-to-face) instruction and distance multimedia instruction, Bernard and colleagues (2004) have identified a bi-modal pattern of multimedia learning effectiveness. They also report that the variability surrounding the mean effect size for achievement is considerably large, indicating that distant multimedia learning works extremely well in some cases and extremely poorly in other cases. According to their explanation, whether the learner is engaged in active learning is an essential issue. They further argue that interest (or satisfaction) may not automatically lead to high achievement, because learners may be just happy to choose a convenient study mode but do not make sufficient effort to study. They suggest that future research should explore student motivational dispositions such as task choice, persistence, effort, self-efficacy, and perceived task value. According to Clark (1983, 1994), the potentially unlimited and inclusive capacity of multimedia instruction does not necessarily facilitate learning. Arguably, the capacity of multimedia instruction to include learner's participation can give rise to motivation to be engaged in multimedia courses learning. However, studies have revealed that such interest does not incontrovertibly translate into achievement (Clark, 2005).

There is research evidence to suggest that instructional support in the form of animations may distract and interfere with learning rather than facilitate it (see Clark, 2005), and one common problem in the use of hypermedia environments is the phenomenon of getting lost in the environment thus losing track of learning (Svinicki, 1999). In addition, meta-analytic evidence suggests that learning tends to decrease in multimedia courses as interest (and thus enrolment) in such courses increases, because learners may believe that such courses require less work (Bernard et al., 2004). Furthermore, in a recent review, Tallent-Runnels et al. (2006) concluded that learning outcomes of web-based courses are the same as traditional ones and suggested that the understanding of learner's goals, needs, and motivations in taking a course is essential for the instructional design of multimedia learning. It is necessary to scrutinize motivational factors in multimedia learning processes.

ACHIEVEMENT MOTIVATION: THEORIES AND APPLICATIONS TO MULTIMEDIA LEARNING

Many achievement motivation theories have been developed in psychological research to explain people's choice of achievement tasks, persistence on those tasks, and resulting performance (Wigfield & Eccles, 2000). Although there have been attempts to integrate these theories, the theories retain their distinctive features (Naylor, Pritchard, & Ilgen, 1980). In this chapter, we focus on expectancy-value theory, self-efficacy, goal-setting theory, self-determination theory, and specific models that have been applied to various multimedia learning processes.

Expectancy-Value Theory

According to Vroom (1964), valence, instrumentality, and expectancy (VIE) are the three major motivational determinants. Valence refers to the anticipated desirability (i.e. importance) of an outcome; instrumentality is the belief that performance will lead to a desired outcome; and expectancy refers to the subjective probability of effort leading to a specific outcome. For example, in choosing a multimedia course, the ultimate outcome for an individual may be a good grade for the selected course. Therefore, valence in this case is the desirability of a good grade in the chosen course. Instrumentality is operationalized as the degree to which the student believes that doing well in the final exam (performance) will lead to a qualification or promotion, and expectancy is the student's belief that his or her effort will lead to a good grade. In the VIE theory, volitional and calculative processes play a critical role in human decision-making. Influence by Lewin's (1939) psychological field theory, Vroom (1964) use the term "force" as a metaphor for the integration of motivational components.

Despite its long history and the considerable amount of empirical support for the expectancy-valence theory, the underlying assumptions of the theory have been questioned. According to Vroom (1964), the choices individuals made are determined by their affective reactions to certain outcomes (valences), their beliefs about the likelihood of the actions leading to those desired outcomes (expectancies), and their perception of the relationship between primary and secondary outcomes (instrumentality). One comment of this type of model is that in making a decision, an individual will have to consider a wide variety of options, outcomes, instrumentalities, and probabilities before taking actions. This will require many mental computations and huge processing capacity (Lord, Hanges, & Godfrey, 2003). However, the human cognitive architecture often does not permit simultaneous processing of all available information. Such processing of information will involve an inordinate amount of working memory. In an attempt to sort out the discrepancy between Vroom's postulation and the limits of the working memory capacity, Lord, Hanges and Godfrey (2003) have presented simulation data to show that Vroom's motivation model holds if computations to reach a decision are performed

by neural networks instead of serial processing. It should be noted that the use of neural networks is possible only when there is extensive experience with a problem situation and with the knowledge structures organized in the form of schemas for automatic processing.

Moreover, in practice, individuals are not always privy to information that is needed. According to Simon (1945), individuals usually only consider a limited amount of information and stop searching alternatives once they believe that they have reached satisfactory (though not necessarily optimal) solutions. Consider the case in a multimedia on-line course, once learners know they have attained a satisfactory level of achievement, it is possible that some learners would stop engaging in the learning activities provided in the on-line course even though their valence, instrumentality and expectancy are high.

Another comment of Vroom's theory is at the operational level. The motivation score can be obtained as either a multiplicative or additive result of the three components, namely, valence, instrumentality, and expectancy. Originally, Vroom proposed a multiplicative model. Consequently, a number of researchers have used this method. However, in a meta-analysis, Van Earde and Thierry (1996) found that the additive model yielded higher effect size in relation to attitudinal criterion variables (e.g., intention and preference) than did the multiplicative model, and therefore argued for the use of the former over the latter. Using the additive model, Sanchez, Truxillo & Bauer (2000) reported that expectancy was positively related to test performance.

In the context of multimedia learning, Rheinberg, Vollmeyer and Rollet (2000) have posited a model of self-regulated learning which includes three types of expectancies: action-outcome-expectancies (the probability of success), outcome-consequence-expectancies (instrumentality), and situation-outcome-expectancies. The situation-outcome-expectancies (SOE) represents "the assumption that the just given situation will lead to the desired outcome on its own without the need to take any action" (Rheinberg et al., 2000, p.510). SOE is regarded as a relatively stable, trait-like factor. Using the SOE model, Astleitner & Hufnagl (2003) investigated the effect of motivation on the learning outcomes of web-lectures consisting of both audio and visual presentations. The findings are: 1) high SOE learners tended to rate the statement "I do not need any activity for critical thinking because I understand everything at once" totally true or true; and 2) low SOE learners tended to rate the same statement not true or not at all true (p.369). Astleitner and Hufnagl (2003) argued that students with low SOE were motivated to be engaged in active learning and sought support to reach a given goal, whereas students with high SOE were not sufficiently motivated to learn because they were not convinced that engagement in learning would change learning outcomes in any significant way.

Self-Efficacy

While the traditional expectancy-value models have focused on outcome expectancies, Bandura (1977, 1993, 1997) has argued that efficacy expectations should also be considered as they are more predictive of performance and choice than outcome expectations. Self-efficacy and outcome expectations do not have the same meaning. Outcome expectations involve beliefs about the anticipated outcomes of those actions. For instance, a student may believe that a positive outcome will result from certain actions but also believe that they lack the competence to produce those actions. The concept of self-efficacy, developed from social learning theory, refers to perceptions of one's capabilities to engage in courses of action that will lead to desired outcomes (Bandura, 1977, 1993, 1997).

There are two important features in Bandura's construct of self-efficacy. First, self-efficacy operates within a specific context (e.g., incorporating internet resources to prepare a PowerPoint presen-

tation on global warming). The second element of the construct refers to judgments of the behavior one is capable of performing independently of the value one attached to the given actions. For example, an individual may have a high self-efficacy for doing a presentation but draws little self-worth if the task is perceived to lack value.

Research shows that self-efficacy can influence behavior in achievement settings (Bandura, 1993; Pajares, 1996, 1997; Schunk, 1989, 1991). Students with low efficacy for learning may avoid attempting tasks; those with high efficacy would participate more eagerly by expending greater effort and persist longer in the face of difficulties. In a study estimating the unique contribution of self-efficacy to work-related performance controlling for personality, general ability, and job or task experience, Judge, Jackson, Shaw, Scott and Rich (2007) found that self-efficacy predicted performance in low complexity task but not in medium or high complexity tasks. Based on Bandura's (1986) guidelines of assessing self-efficacy for specific tasks, scales for computer self-efficacy were developed and validated (e.g., Murphy, Coover, & Owen, 1989; Zweig & Webster, 2004). In our study of students undertaking a teaching qualification, we look at the motivational factors involved in a compulsory computer skills course that consists of face-to-face instruction and self-paced web-based learning. We found a moderate correlation between self-efficacy and test results (Jin & Low, 2007).

Goal-Setting Theory and Task Motivation

As early as 1950s, Atkinson (1958) reported that task difficulty, as indicated by the probability of task success, was related to performance in a curvilinear, inverse function. However, in a meta-analytic investigation, Locke & Latham (1990) found a positive, linear function in that the highest goal produced the highest levels of effort and performance. They also discovered that specific, difficult goals tended to result in higher performance than urging people to do their best. The explanation given to this finding is that do-your-best goals have no external framework of reference, whereas goal specificity can reduce ambiguity regarding what is to be attained. They suggest that goals with specific standards of performance increase motivation and raise self-efficacy because goal progress is easy to judge, and that challenging but attainable goals raise motivation and self-efficacy better than easy or hard goals. According to Locke and Latham (2002), for goals to be effective, feedback is a necessary component; if people do not have information about how they are doing, it is difficult for them to adjust their effort or strategies to match what the goal requires. In addition, individuals who participated in setting goals tended to set higher goals and performed better than those whose goals were assigned.

Based on findings from the empirical research on goal-setting, Locke and Latham (2002) proposed an expanded model of motivation relating assigned goals, self-set goals, self-efficacy, and performance. According to the model, assigned goal affects both self-efficacy and personal goal; self-efficacy influences personal goal; and both self-efficacy and personal goal are predictive of performance. Thus, the goal-setting theory appears to be compatible with Bandura's conceptual framework of self-efficacy in the wider context of social cognitive perspectives.

Goal-setting theory seems to be incongruent with Vroom's theory in that, whereas expectancy is linearly and positively related to performance, expectancy of goal success could be negatively related to performance under difficult goal conditions where goals are hard to attain. This apparent incompatibility is resolved, according to Locke and Latham (2002), when a distinction is made between expectancy within a certain goal level and expectancy between goal conditions. Locke, Motowidlo, and Bobko (1986) found that when goal level is constant (a situation assumed

by valence-instrumentality-expectancy theory), higher expectancies lead to a higher levels of performance. Across goal levels, lower expectancies, associated with high goal levels, are associated with higher performance. More recently, Louro, Pieters, and Zeelenberg (2007) suggest that in multiple goal environments, in addition to goal expectancies for success and goal proximity, positive and negative goal-related emotions contribute to goal-related behavior.

In the learning context, achievement goals or goal orientations refer to the motivational basis of learning (Karabenick & Collins-Baglin, 1997). Research shows that there are four types of goal orientations: learning (mastery) orientation, learning avoidance orientation, performance orientation, and performance avoidance (learned-helplessness) orientation (DeShon & Gillespie, 2005; Elliot & McGregor, 2001; Lee, Sheldon, & Turban, 2003; Midgley, Kaplan, & Middleton, 2001; Zweig & Webster, 2004). Researchers have conducted a number of studies on learning and performance orientations (cf. DeShon & Gillespie, 2005). Learning orientation is characterized by a desire to increase one's competence by mastering new skills while performance orientation reflects a desire to demonstrate one's competence (Bruning, Schraw, Norby, & Ronning, 2004). In the face of failure, individuals with learning orientation tend to adopt an adaptive response pattern while those with performance orientation are associated with a maladaptive response pattern. A typical adaptive response pattern is related to persistence, spending more time on-task, adopting more complex strategies, and seeking appropriate help in the face of difficult tasks. In contrast, a maladaptive response pattern is characterized by a tendency to quit in the face of difficult tasks, and a tendency to seek less challenging materials and tasks on which success is a likely outcome.

Although research on goal orientations and motivation is aplenty, in multimedia learning research, the contribution of goal orientations receives scant attention while the relation between instructional design and cognitive load (see Mayer, 2005) has been a major focus. According to a series of studies on the effects hypertext-based instruction on learning outcomes conducted by Gerjets & Scheiter (2003), configurations of teacher goals, learner goals, as well as learners' processing strategies, may be important mediating variables. Researchers (Gerjets & Scheiter, 2003; Goldman, 1991) suggest that the cognitive load theory, which emphasizes the relationship between instructional design and learning outcomes (Sweller, 1994; Sweller, van Merriënboer, & Pass, 1998; Yeung, Jin, & Sweller, 1998), can be further expanded by inspecting the suitability of instructional procedures for attaining specific goals. For instance, in Gerjets & Scheiter's (2003) experiment using a hypertext environment that contained work-out examples, when the goal of instructor was just to encourage participants to learn very fast to solve problems in a way as shown in the instructional examples, the structure-emphasizing condition elicited more demanding cognitive processes and thus imposed additional cognitive load than did the surface-emphasizing condition. Consequently, participants spent longer time learning and had poorer performance under the structure-emphasizing condition than those under the surface-emphasizing condition. They suggest that different types of goals and learning strategies should be incorporated into the cognitive load theory.

Self-Determination Theory

According to self-determination theory (Deci & Ryan, 1985), one of two types of motivation, extrinsic or intrinsic, gives rise to an action. Intrinsic motivation refers to doing something because it is inherently interesting, and extrinsic motivation refers to doing something because it leads to a separable outcome (usually some kind of reward). Intrinsic motivation is viewed as an innate human need for competence and self-determination (Deci & Ryan, 1985; Deci,

Vallerand, Pelletier & Ryan, 1991) and is therefore influenced by environmental and interpersonal variables that affect experiences of competence and self-determination (Reeve, Nix, & Hamm, 2003). In self-determination theory, motivation is conceptualized as a continuum with intrinsic motivation at one end and extrinsic motivation at the other. In between are behaviors that were extrinsically motivated initially but have become internalized and self-determined. More recently, Ryan and Deci (2000) have added another construct, amotivation, to the theory. Amotivation refers to the state of having no intention to act and it resides next to extrinsic motivation.

Intuitively, intrinsic motivation is an important construct in educational contexts. Consider the situation where students enrolled in a compulsory multimedia computer skills course may want to avoid some difficult web-based activities but work on them to avoid failure (i.e., the students are extrinsically motivated). As they become more competent, they perceive a sense of control and self-determination over the multimedia learning (i.e., they become intrinsically motivated). The activities become more intrinsically motivating and positive social factors (feedback) assist the learning process. However, as some researchers (e.g., Pintrich & Schunk, 2002; Reeve, Nix, & Hamm, 2003) have pointed out, relatively little attention has been paid to educational implications of self-determination theory. Ryan and Deci (2000) have suggested that the basis for maintaining intrinsic motivation and becoming more self-determined lies in the social contextual conditions that support feelings of competence, autonomy, and relatedness. Therefore, in learning contexts, it is important to create instructional conditions that satisfy the innate needs to feel connected and effective as one acquires knowledge and skills. Recently researchers (e.g., Deimann & Keller, 2006; Kuhl, 2000) have reintroduced and validated a relevant construct "volition" (originally raised by James, 1902) to educational research. According to Deimann & Keller (2006), volition (or willpower) is "one's capability of maintaining attention and effort toward goals in spite of possible distractions due to waning motivation or competing goals" (p. 139). They point out that, since multimedia learning design and processes are likely to encounter problems such as learner's uncertainty, distractions, "seductive" details, and cognitive overload, research and teaching programs in the direction of volition enhancement are much needed.

The Attention, Relevance, Confidence, and Satisfaction (ARCS) Model

The ARCS model is an approach to instructional design using multimedia technology based on a synthesis of motivational concepts. Keller and his colleagues (Keller, 1987; Keller & Suzuki, 2004; Song & Keller, 2001) have identified four conditions that are essential for the learner's motivation in e-learning contexts. The first condition is that a lesson must attract and sustain the learner's *attention* (A). This requirement is based on research on curiosity, arousal, and boredom. The second condition for motivation is to build *relevance* (R). This requirement is based on research on intrinsic motivation and competence as highlighted in self-determination theory. The third condition for motivating learners is *confidence* (C). This requirement is based on research on self-efficacy and attribution. The fourth condition is *satisfaction* (S). This requirement is based on reinforcement theory and equity theory that have been commonly used in other areas such as I/O Psychology.

The ARCS model is a systematic ten-step design process for developing motivational elements in instructional settings: obtaining course information, obtaining audience information, analyzing audience, analyzing existing materials, listing objectives and assessments, listing potential tactics, selecting and designing tactics, integrating with instruction, selecting and developing

materials, and evaluating and revising (see Keller & Suzuki, 2004). The model and its simplified versions have been validated in various learning contexts (cf. Astleitner & Hufnagl, 2003; Gao & Lehman, 2003; Keller & Suzuki, 2004; Means, Jonassen & Dwyer, 1997; Small & Gluck, 1994; Song & Keller, 2001; Visser & Keller, 1990). For instance, Song and Keller (2001) conducted a motivational analysis of attention, relevance, and confidence in biology classes to examine the effects of a prototype of motivationally adaptive computer-assisted instruction (CAI). They found that the motivationally adaptive CAI resulted in higher effectiveness, motivation and attention than did the motivationally saturated CAI and the motivationally minimized CAI. In this experiment, the ARCS model was used to construct motivation measures, guide motivational design processes, and provide detailed motivational strategies. In the ARCS model, there are two types of motivational strategies: (1) motivation sustaining (e.g., "keep instructional segments relatively short with progressive disclosure", p. 11), and (2) motivation enhancing (e.g., "use inverse and flash in text and patterns in pictures as attention getters", p. 12). According to Song and Keller (2001), the motivationally adaptive CAI was effective because it was based on the ARCS model to provide optimal motivational stimulations to learners who were bored and to eliminate excessive motivational features that might be annoying or distracting for learners who were already motivated. In general, findings from research on the ARCS model demonstrate that a systematic analysis of learner motivation is an important aspect in the design and implementation of multimedia courses.

An Integrated Model of Cognitive-Motivational Processes

Astleitner and Wiesner (2004) have proposed an expansion of the multimedia learning theory summarized by Mayer (2001) and Hede (2002). The current multimedia learning theory is based mainly on evaluating research on cognitive processing of sensory (visual and audio) inputs (e.g. Low & Sweller, 2005; Mousavi, Low & Sweller, 1995; Yeung et al., 1998). Such research is concerned basically with working memory limitation, an essential element of the cognitive load theory. Astleitner and Wiesner (2004) argue that, because motivation influences learning, and motivational processes need memory resources and therefore affect cognitive load, motivational aspects such as goal-setting and action control should be incorporated in a theory of multimedia learning.

Astleitner & Wiesner (2004) have suggested several avenues for motivational research to facilitate multimedia learning: a) the motivational quality of multimedia elements such as the relation between the utility of content and goal-setting, and the relation between variability in audio and visual effects and attention; b) the effects of learners' characteristics such as success- or failure-oriented learners and action- or state-oriented learners; and 3) motivational features that affect cognitive load in multimedia learning environments such as distraction, disruption, diversion, and saturation. Obviously, these research questions need to be systematically investigated with sound methodology.

ESSENTIAL ASPECTS OF MOTIVATIONAL RESEARCH IN MULTIMEDIA LEARNING

Theoretical Development

For multimedia teaching and learning to be effective, it is necessary to conduct appropriate motivational analyses before and during the implementation of courses. Such analyses should be derived from evidence-based motivational theories. Hence, it is important to develop relevant theoretical perspectives. According to Maddux (1999), major theories of the social-cognitive perspective of motivation share a limited number of important principles, processes and variables. Common basic conceptual elements include behavior-outcome expectancies, stimulus-outcome expectancies, self-efficacy expectancies, outcome value, goal-setting, and competencies. Such similarities suggest that they are not different models of motivation but different versions of some basic elements. As such, it is sensible for the development of an integrated theoretical framework to guide research so as to determine the optimal conditions for best practices in multimedia learning contexts.

Recent research shows some promising developments. For instance, as mentioned earlier, in Astleitner and Hufnagl's (2003) study consistent with the ARCS model, situation-outcome-expectancies (a construct neglected in previous educational psychology research), in addition to action-outcome-expectancies and outcome-consequences-expectancies, was found to play an important role in multimedia learning. They reported that students who did not have strong assumption of "one can fulfil the tasks automatically in a given situation" tended to benefit from the ARCS strategies.

In another study implementing the ARCS strategies in WebCT learning environments, Gao and Lehman (2003) show that feedback plays a significant role: students in both reactive and proactive conditions performed better in achievement tests than those in a controlled condition; and students in the reactive interaction condition demonstrated higher motivational perceptions toward the instructional material than those in the control condition. The control condition was one where the website only incorporated typical, static hyperlinks; the reactive condition was one where the website incorporated an immediate feedback strategy which provided responses during learning; and the proactive condition was where the website incorporated a generative activity strategy which asked learners to generate a new situation after a learning section.

Future research in those aspects covered by Astleitner and Hufnagl (2003) and Gao & Lehman (2003) appears to be warranted. Other explorations to integrate motivational approaches in multimedia learning should be encouraged. For instance, because self-efficacy is task specific and multimedia learning programs have many variations in the design of tasks and procedures, there is room for the expansion of self-efficacy research in this aspect.

Motivational Features and the Design of Multimedia Instruction

In a series of studies to develop and validate a taxonomy of reasons that gives rise to academic amotivation in high school students, Legault, Green-Demers and Pelletier (2006) have found that task characteristics affect task engagement, and unappealing characteristics of an academic task may lead to academic disengagement. This finding has instructional implications for multimedia teaching and learning. Ally (2004), Reed (2006) and Svinicki (1999) have suggested that designs that keep learners active doing meaningful tasks, and allow learners to construct their own knowledge, to control the learning process, and to evaluate their own learning (meta-cognition) are some features that can engage learners.

Learner Characteristics

Learner characteristics are another important aspect to consider in multimedia learning and teaching (Bernard et al., 2004; Tallent-Runnels et al., 2006). For instance, Mayer and Massa (2003) found that some individuals are visual learners while others are verbal. These two types of learners are distinguishable by three facets: cognitive ability, cognitive style, and learning preference. Multimedia learning resources should provide appropriate avenues and options for different types of learners. In a recent study, when learning style differences were considered in designing an interactive multimedia courseware of Mathematics, the program produced high learning motivation and positive learning experiences (Shiong, Aris, Ahmad, Ali, Harun, & Zaidatun, 2008).

Judge et al. (2007), in a meta-analysis, have found that personality (the Big-Five traits), as well as self-efficacy, affect work-related performance. The Big-Five traits are Neuroticism (the tendency to show poor emotional adjustment in the form of stress, anxiety, and depression), Extraversion (the tendency to be sociable, dominant, and positive), Openness to Experience (likely to be creative, flexible curious, and unconventional), Agreeableness (tendency to be kind, gentle, trusting and trustworthy, and warm), and Conscientiousness (likely to be achievement-oriented and dependable). In another meta-analytic review of research on relation between the five-factor model of personality and performance motivation, Judge and Illies (2002) found that the Big-Five traits are an important source of performance motivation. Among them, Neuroticism and Conscientiousness were the strongest and most consistent correlates of performance motivation. Effects of the other three personality traits on achievement motivation need to be investigated in future research.

Other learner characteristics that warrant consideration are goal orientation (Locke & Latham, 2002; Midgley et al., 2001; Lee et al., 2003), technological acceptance (Palaigeorgiou, Siozos, Konstantakis & Tsoukalas, 2005; Saadé, Nebebe & Tan, 2007), adaptive learning environments including learner involvement (Song & Keller, 2001; Paas et al., 2005), procrastination in self-paced learning (Steel, 2007), and disappointment and motivation loss (Miceli & Castelfranchi, 2000). In an era of mass education and student-centered learning, especially in multimedia technology-rich settings, learner characteristics should be scrutinized and accommodated in the entire learning process.

Self-Regulated Learning Strategies and Motivation Training

Research in interactive learning environments, participatory multimedia learning, and learner control in hypermedia environment have recently gained momentum (see Järvelä, & Volet, 2004; Kiili, 2005; Renkl & Atkinson, 2007; Scheiter & Gerjets, 2007). Narciss, Proske and Koerndle (2007) have argued for the promotion of self-regulated multimedia learning which can be applied to WebCT. Self-regulated learning (in the form of problem-based learning, blended learning, project-based learning, etc.) is a specific form of learning distinguishable from learning that is externally regulated in that self-regulated learners use cognitive strategies, metacognition, volition, and motivation to monitor their own learning process (Vollmeyer & Reinberg, 2006). Self-regulated learning involves many strategies of which time planning (involving time management, scheduling, and planning study time) and self-monitoring (involving goal-setting, attention focusing, and monitoring study activities) are important skills to be possessed (Boekaerts & Cascallar, 2006; Van Den Hurk, 2006). The assumptions underlying self-regulated learning are: 1) students construct their own meaning, goals and strategies based on the availability of internal or external information; and 2) students are capable of monitoring and managing aspects of their own cognition, motivation, behavior and learning environment (Pintrich, 2000).

Attractive multimedia platforms contain interesting but sometimes irrelevant information. Competent self-regulated learners need not only to use appropriate cognitive and meta-cognitive skills to determine relevant information for the tasks selected and effort invested in undertaking such tasks, but also are required to properly regulate motivation and attention (Narciss et al., 2007). In self-regulated learning, initial motivation affects learning outcome. According to Vollmeyer and Reinberg (2006), initial motivation

is determined by probability of success, anxiety (or fear of failure), interest in the learning material, and challenge (to succeed in an important task). They also suggest that the influence of initial motivation on performance may be mediated by duration and frequency of the learning activity, systematic learning strategies employed, motivational state during learning, and state of concentration/engagement during learning. Apart from incorporating motivational elements in multimedia learning and teaching, we may also consider motivation training, although evaluation of motivational programs is not an easy exercise (Schober & Zieger, 2002).

Evaluating Quality of Motivational Features in Multimedia Learning Resources

As highlighted by Keller and Suzuki (2004), motivational analysis should be an on-going process to ensure that multimedia resources are compatible with transient motivational factors as the learning progresses. The ARCS model (Keller & Suzuki, 2004; Song & Keller, 2001) has provided a number of specific measures to examine relevant motivational features in multimedia learning. In addition, Leacock and Nesbit (2007) have presented a framework for evaluating the quality of multimedia learning resources named LORI (Learning Object Review Instrument). LORI contains some items that can be used to assess the quality of motivation features incorporated in multimedia learning. These items are learning goal alignment, feedback and adaptation, motivating power (that is, the ability to motivate and interest learners), interaction usability, and accessibility. Items are rated on a 5-point scale. For example, for the aspect of motivating power, if a learning task (or activity or material) is irrelevant to a learner's goal, is too easy or too difficult for a learner, or draws attention at a superficial level, the task would receive a score of 1. In contrast, if a task is perceived as relevant, is able to gain and hold learners' attention, and offers the learner difficulty levels for learners to gain confidence and satisfaction from the learning activities, it would receive a rating of 5. To optimize learners' experiences, multimedia course developers and instructors are encouraged to use tools such as LORI and ARCS to assess motivational qualities of programs.

CONCLUSION

In the field of multimedia learning, research on cognitive effects and their implications for instructional design is rich. Given the importance of motivation in learning and the extensive use of multimedia learning in educational contexts, research on the effects of motivation in a multimedia learning context is surprisingly sparse. One of the major goals of providing multimedia instruction is to motivate students. Abrahamson (1998) sums up this objective very well when he states that "a primary function of the use of television, computers, and telecommunications in distance learning is to motivate students rather than just to provide information to them" (p. 34). However, evidence for motivation in multimedia learning contexts is not solid. In this chapter, we identify four major motivation theories (expectancy-value theory, self-efficacy, goal-setting and task motivation, and self-determination theory) and two motivation models that are derived from multimedia research (the ARCS model, the integrated model of cognitive-motivational processes), review the literature on motivation in multimedia learning contexts, and suggest that researchers and practitioners take into account five aspects to ensure that motivation features incorporated in multimedia learning resources optimize learners' experience. These aspects are: 1) theoretical development; 2) motivational features and the design of multimedia instruction; 3) learner characteristics; 4) self-regulated learning strategies and motivational training; and

5) evaluating quality of motivational features in multimedia learning resources. It is hoped that researchers and teaching professionals will devote more attention to the motivational issues in multimedia learning and teaching.

FUTURE RESEARCH DIRECTIONS

Future research should be theoretically driven and evidence-based. There are at least four lines of motivational research that is important in multimedia learning and teaching. First, the ARCS model has been used by researchers interested in motivational aspects of 'multimedia learning and has generated some promising results. One line of research can continue to validate the ARCS model in various subject domains (e.g., second/foreign language learning, engineering, anatomy, etc.) and cultural contexts.

Second, there have been attempts to combine motivational factors with cognitive elements in an integrated model of multimedia learning. In practice, when engaging in learning, the individual usually does not separate cognitive processing from emotional involvement. Hence this integrated model resembles the natural learning process more than conventional models which tend to treat cognitive and affective aspects separately. Following this line of research, Astleitner and Weisner (2004) propose a comprehensive model from which a number of predictions can be derived. These predictions, including general predictions (e.g., the variability in audio and visual presentations will have differentiated effects on learners' attention; excessive, irrelevant motivational stimuli will impose extraneous cognitive load; limiting links by embedding information will require less working memory thereby reducing negative motivations), and specific predictions (e.g., seductive details will disrupt the learning process; adaptive motivational strategies will improve learning outcomes) should be tested in future research with appropriate methodology.

The third line of research which appears to be fruitful is to examine individual differences in multimedia learning. On the one hand, researchers can identify dispositions and attitudes that are compatible with the nature of multimedia learning, such as self-efficacy, effective goal-setting strategies (setting small, relatively difficult but achievable goals), and volition. On the other hand, researchers can investigate personal factors associated with attrition in multimedia learning, in particular, the nature and mechanisms of the loss of motivation (learned-helplessness tendencies). Previous research has, in general, neglects "students-at-risk." Arguably, both success and failure in multimedia learning should have important educational implications. In addition, sometimes multimedia learning is undertaken collectively (e.g., group project). Group dynamics associated with this particular learning mode and its effect on individual motivation can be investigated.

Fourth, most previous studies conducted in the area of multimedia learning have thus far focused on achievement and task completion in the short term. There is evidence to show that conventional and "innovative" multimedia instruction may result in similar academic outcomes after a longer period of learning. Well-designed longitudinal studies are very much needed to assess the mediating effect of motivation on program effectiveness.

More and more researchers have realized that motivation is an indispensable aspect in multimedia learning and teaching. Despite the urging and suggestions of various researchers in this area, research is surprising limited. It is time to conduct systematic investigations in this potentially rich area.

REFERENCES

Abrahamson, C. E. (1998). Issues in interactive communication in distance education. *College Student Journal, 32*(1), 33-42.

Ally, M. (2004). Foundations of educational theory for online learning. In T. Anderson & F. Elloumi (Eds.), *Theory and practice of Online Learning* (pp. 3-31). Athabasca: Athabasca University.

Astleitner, H., & Hufnagl, M. (2003). The effects of situation-outcome-expectancies and of ARCS-strategies on self-regulated learning with Web-lectures. *Journal of Educational Multimedia and Hypermedia, 12*(4), 361-376.

Astleitner, H., & Wiesner, C. (2004). An integrated model of multimedia learning and motivation. *Journal of Educational Multimedia and Hypermedia, 13*(1), 3-21.

Atkinson, J. W. (Ed.) (1958). *Motives in fantasy, action and society.* Princeton, NJ: Van Nostrand.

Bandura, A. (1977). Self-efficacy: Toward a unifying theory of behavioural change. *Psychological Review, 84*, 191-215.

Bandura, A. (1986). *Social foundations of thought and action: A social cognitive theory.* Englewood Cliffs, NJ: Prentice Hall.

Bandura, A. (1993). Perceived self-efficacy in cognitive development and functioning. *Educational Psychologist, 28*, 117-148.

Bandura, A. (1997). *Self-efficacy: The exercise of control.* New York: Plenum.

Bernard, R. M., Abrami, C., Lou, Y., Borokhovski, E., Wade, A., Wozney, L., Wallet, P. A., Fiset, M., & Huang, B. (2004). How does distance education compare with classroom instruction? A meta-analysis of the empirical literature. *Review of Educational Research, 74*(3), 379-439.

Boekaerts, M., & Cascallar, E. (2006). How far have we moved toward the integration of theory and practice in self-regulation? *Educational Psychology Review, 18*, 199-210.

Bruning, R. H., Schraw, G. J., Norby, M. M., & Ronning, R. R. (2004). *Cognitive Psychology and Instruction.* (4th ed.). Upper Saddle River, NJ: Merrill.

Butcher, K. L. (2006). Learning from text with diagrams: Promoting mental models development and inference generation. *Journal of Educational Psychology, 98,* 182-197.

Clark, R. E. (1983). Reconsidering research on learning from media. *Review of Educational Research, 53*(4), 445-459.

Clark, R. E. (1994). Media and method. *Educational Technology, Research and Development, 42,* 7-10.

Clark, R. E., & Feldon, D. F. (2005). Five common but questionable principles of multimedia learning. In R. E. Mayer (Ed.), *The Cambridge Handbook of Multimedia Learning* (pp. 97-115). New York: Cambridge University Press.

Deci, E. L., & Ryan, R. M. (1985). *Intrinsic motivation and self-determination in human behaviour.* New York: Plenum.

Deci, E. L., Vallerand, R. J., Pelletier, L. C., & Ryan, R. M. (1991). Motivation and education: The self-determination perspective. *Educational Psychologist, 26,* 325-346.

Deimann, M., & Keller, J. M. (2006). Volitional aspects of multimedia learning. *Journal of Educational Multimedia and Hypermedia, 15*(2), 137-158.

DeShon, R. P., & Gillespie, J. Z. (2005). A motivated action theory account of goal orientation. *Journal of Applied Psychology, 90*(6), 1096-1127.

Elliot, A. J., & McGregor, H. (2001). A 2 x 2 achievement goal framework. *Journal of Personality and Social Psychology, 80,* 501-519.

Fletcher, J. D., & Tobias, S. (2005). The multimedia principle. In R.E. Mayer (Ed.), *The Cambridge Handbook of Multimedia Learning* (pp. 117-133). New York: Cambridge University Press.

Gao, T., & Lehman, J. D. (2003). The effects of different levels of interaction on the achievement and motivation perceptions of college students in a Web-based learning environment. *Journal of Interactive Learning Research, 14*(4), 367-386.

Gerjets, P., & Scheiter, K. (2003). Goal configurations and processing strategies as moderators between instructional design and cognitive load: Evidence from hypertext-based instruction. *Educational Psychologist, 38*(1), 33-41.

Goldman, S. R. (1991). On the derivation of instructional applications from cognitive theories: Commentary on Chandler and Sweller. *Cognition and Instruction, 8,* 333-342.

Hahne, A. K., Benndorf, R., Frey, P., & Herzig, S. (2005). Attitude towards computer-based learning: Determinants as revealed by a controlled interventional study. *Medical Education, 39,* 935-943.

Hardré, P. L., Crowson, M., Xie, K., & Ly, C. (2007). Testing differential effects of computer-based Web-based and paper-based administration of questionnaire research instruments. *British Journal of Educational Technology, 38*(1), 5-22.

Hede, A. (2002). An integrated model of multimedia effects on learning. *Journal of Educational Multimedia and Hypermedia, 11,* 177-191.

Hoskins, S. L., & Van Hooff, J. C. (2005). Motivation and ability: Which students use online learning and what influence does it have on their achievement? *British Journal of Educational Technology, 36*(2), 171-192.

Hwang, W., Wang, C., & Sharples, C. (2007). A study of multimedia annotation of Web-based materials. *Computers & Education, 48,* 680-692.

James, W. (1902). *The Principle of Psychology.* New York: Holt.

Järvelä, S., & Volet, S. (2004). Motivation in real-life, dynamic, and interactive learning environments: Stretching constructs and methodologies. *European Psychologist, 9*(4), 193-197.

Jin, P., & Low, R. (2007). Learning motivation and E-learning performance. *Unpublished manuscript,* School of Education, University of New South Wales, Sydney, Australia.

Judge, T. A., & Ilies, R. (2002). Relationship of personality to performance motivation: A meta-analytic review. *Journal of Applied Psychology, 87*(4), 797-807.

Judge, T. A., Jackson, C. L., Shaw, J. C., Scott, B. A., & Rich, B. L. (2007). Self-efficacy and work-related performance: The integral role of individual differences. *Journal of Applied Psychology, 92*(1), 107-127.

Karabenick, S. A., & Collins-Baglin, J. (1997). Relation of perceived instructional goals and incentives to college students' use of learning strategies. *Journal of Experimental Education, 65*, 331-341.

Keller, J. M. (1987). Motivational design and multimedia: Beyond the novelty effect. *Strategic Human Resource Development Review, 1*(1), 188-203.

Keller. J. M., & Suzuki, K. (2004). Learner motivation and E-learning design: A multinationally validated process. *Journal of Educational Media, 29*(3), 229-239.

Kiili, K. (2005). Participatory multimedia learning: Engaging learners, Australasian *Journal of Educational Technology, 21*(3), 303-322.

Kuhl, J. (2000). The volitional basis of personality systems interaction theory: Applications in learning and treatment contexts. *International Journal of Educational Research, 33*(7-8), 665-703.

Leacock, T., & Nesbit, J. C. (2007). A framework for evaluating the quality of multimedia learning resources. *Educational Technology and Society, 10*(2), 44-59.

Lee, F. K., Sheldon, K. M., & Turban, D. B. (2003). Personality and the goal-striving process: The influence of achievement foal patterns, goal level, and mental focus on performance and enjoyment. *Journal of Applied Psychology, 88*(2), 256-265.

Legault, L., Green-Demers, I., & Pelletier, L. (2006). Why do high school students lack motivation in the classroom? Toward an understanding of academic motivation and the role of social support. *Journal of Educational Psychology, 98*(3), 567-582.

Lewin, K. (1939). Field theory and experiment in social psychology: Concepts and methods. *The American Journal of Sociology, 44*(6), 868-896.

Locke, E. A., & Latham, G. P. (2002). Building a practically useful theory of goal setting and task motivation: A 35-year odyssey. *American Psychologist, 57*(9), 705-717.

Locke, E. A., Motowildo, S., & Bobko, P. (1986). Using self-efficacy theory to resolve the conflict between theory and expectancy theory in organization behavior and industrial/organizational psychology. *Journal of Social and Clinical Psychology, 4*, 328-338.

Lord, R. G., Hanges, P. J., & Godfrey, E. G. (2003). Integrating neural networks into decision-making and motivational theory: Rethinking VIE theory. *Canadian Psychology, 44*(1), 21-38.

Louro, M. J., Pieters, R., & Zeelenberg, M. (2007). Dynamics of multiple-goal pursuit. *Journal of Personality and Social Psychology, 93*(2), 174-193.

Low, R., & Sweller, J. (2005). The modality principle in multimedia learning. In R. E.

Mayer (Ed.), *The Cambridge Handbook of Multimedia Learning* (pp. 147-158). New York: Cambridge University Press.

Maddux, J. E. (1999). Expectancies and the social-cognitive perspective: Basic principles, processes, and variables. In I. Kirsch (Ed.), *How expectancies shape experience* (pp. 17-39). Washington, D. C.: American Psychological Association.

Mayer, R. E. (2001). *Multimedia Learning.* Cambridge, UK: Cambridge University Press.

Mayer, R. E. (2005). Cognitive theory of multimedia learning. In R. E. Mayer (Ed.), *The Cambridge Handbook of Multimedia Learning* (pp. 31-48). New York: Cambridge University Press.

Mayer, R. E., & Massa, L. J. (2003). Three facets of visual and verbal learners: Cognitive ability, cognitive style, and learning preference. *Journal of Educational Psychology, 95*(4), 833-846.

Means, T. B., Jonassen, D. H., & Dwyer, R. M. (1997). Enhancing relevance: Embedded ARCS strategies vs. purpose. *Educational Technology Research and Development, 45*(1), 5-18.

Miceli, M., & Castelfranchi, C. (2000). Nature and mechanisms of loss of motivation. *Review of General Psychology, 4*(3), 238-263.

Midgley, C., Kaplan, A., & Middleton, M. (2001). Performance-approach goals: Good for what, for whom, under what circumstances, and at what cost? *Journal of Educational Psychology, 93*(1), 77-86.

Mousavi, S., Low, R., & Sweller, S. (1995). Reducing cognitive load by mixing auditory and visual presentation modes. *Journal of Educational Psychology, 87,* 319-334.

Murphy, C. A., Coover, D., & Owen, S. V. (1989). Development and validation of the computer self-efficacy scale. *Educational and Psychological Measurement, 49,* 893-899.

Narciss, S., Proske, A., & Koerndle, H. (2007). Promoting self-regulated learning in Web-based learning environments. *Computers in Human Behavior, 23,* 1126-1144.

Naylor, J. C., Pritchard, R. D., & Ilgen, D. R. (1980). *A theory of behavior in organizations.* New York: Academic Press.

Paas, F., Tuovinen, J. E., Van Merriënboer, J., & Darabi, A. A. (2005). A motivational perspective on the relation between mental effort and performance: Optimizing learner involvement in instruction. *Educational Technology, Research and Development, 53*(3), 25-34.

Pajares, F. (1996). Self-efficacy beliefs in achievement settings. *Review of Educational Research, 66,* 543-578.

Pajares, F. (1997). Current directions in self-efficacy research. In M. Maehr & P. R. Pintrich (Eds.), *Advances in motivation and achievement* (Vol. 10, pp. 1-49). Greenwich, C. T.: JAI Press.

Palaigeorgiou, G. E., Siozos, P. D., Konstantakis, N. I., & Tsoukalas, I. A. (2005). A computer attitude scale for computer science freshmen and its educational implications. *Journal of Computer Assisted Learning, 21,* 330-342.

Pintrich, P. (2000). The role of goal orientation in self-regulated learning. In M.Boekaerts, P.R. Pintrich & M. Zeidner (Eds.), *Handbook of self-regulation* (pp. 451-502). Mawah, NJ: Lawrence Erlbaum.

Pintrich, P. R., & Schunk, D. H. (2002). Motivation in education: Theory, research and applications *(2ⁿᵈ Ed.).* Upper Saddle River, NJ: Merrill/Prentice Hall.

Reed, S. K. (2006). Cognitive architectures for multimedia learning. *Educational Psychologist, 41*(2), 87-98.

Reeve, J., Nix, G., & Hamm, D. (2003). Testing models of the experience of self-determination in intrinsic motivation and the conundrum of choice. *Journal of Educational Psychology, 95*(2), 375-392.

Renkl, A., & Atkinson, R. K. (2007). Interactive learning environments: Contemporary issues and trends. *Educational Psychology Review, 19,* 235-238.

Rheinberg, F., Vollmeyer, R., & Rollet, W. (2000) Motivation and action in self-regulated learning.

In M. Boekaerts, P. R. Pintrich & M. Zeidner (Eds.), *Handbook of Self-regulation* (pp. 503-529). San Diego, CA: Academic Press.

Ryan, R. M., & Deci, E. L. (2000). Intrinsic and extrinsic motivations: Classic definitions and new directions. *Contemporary Educational Psychology, 25*, 54-67.

Saadé, R. G., Nebebe, F., & Tan, W. (2007). Viability of the "Technology Acceptance Model" in multimedia learning environments: A comparative study. *Interdisciplinary Journal of Knowledge and Learning Objects, 3*, 175-183.

Sanchez, R. J., Truxillo, D. M., & Bauer, T. N. (2000). Development and examination of an expectancy-based measure of test-taking motivation. *Journal of Applied Psychology, 85*(5), 739-750.

Scheiter, K., & Gerjets, P. (2007). Learner control in hypermedia environments. *Educational Psychology Review, 19*, 285-307.

Schober, B., & Ziegler, A. (2002). Theoretical levels in the evaluation of motivational trainings. *European Journal of Psychological Assessment, 18*(3), 204-213.

Schunk, D. H. (1989). Self-efficacy and cognitive skill learning. In C. Ames & R. Ames (Eds.), *Research in motivation in education. Vol. 3: Goals and cognitions* (pp. 13-44). San Diego: Academic Press.

Schunk, D. H. (1991). Self-efficacy and academic motivation. *Educational Psychologist, 26*, 207-231.

Shiong, K. B., Aris, B., Ahmad, M. H., Ali, M. B., Harun, J., & Zaidatun, T. (2008). Learning "Goal Programming" using an interactive multimedia courseware: Design factors and students' preferences. *Journal of Educational Multimedia and Hypermedia, 17*(1), 59-79.

Simon, H. A. (1945). *Administrative behavior: A study of decision-making process in administrative organization.* New York: Free Press.

Small, R. V., & Gluck, M. (1994). The relationship of motivational conditions to effective instructional attributes: A magnitude scaling approach. *Educational Technology, 34*(8), 33-40.

Song, S. H., & Keller, J. M. (2001), Effectiveness of motivationally adaptive computer-assisted instruction on the dynamic aspects of motivation. *Educational Technology, Research & Development, 49*(2), 5-22.

Steel, P. (2007). The nature of procrastination: A meta-analytic and theoretical review of quintessential self-regulatory failure. *Psychological Bulletin, 133*(1), 65-94.

Svinicki, M. (1999). New directions in learning and motivation. *New Directions for Teaching and Learning, 80*, 5-27. San Franciso: Jossey-Bass.

Sweller, J. (1994). Cognitive load theory, learning difficulty, and instructional design. *Learning and Instruction, 4*, 295-312.

Sweller, J., van Merriënboer, J. J. G., & Pass, F. G. W. C. (1998). Cognitive architecture and instructional design. *Educational Psychology Review, 10*, 251-296.

Tallent-Runnels, M. K., Thomas, J. A., Lan, W. Y., Cooper, S., Ahern, T. C., Shaw, S. M., & Liu, X. (2006). Teaching courses online: A review of the research. *Review of Educational Research, 76*(1), 93-135.

Van Den Hurk, M. (2006). The relation between self-regulated strategies and individual study time, prepared participation and achievement in a problem-based curriculum. *Active Learning in Higher Education, 7*(2), 155-169.

Van Earde, W., & Thierry, H. (1996). Vroom's expectancy models and work-related criteria: A meta-analysis. *Journal of Applied Psychology, 81*, 575-586.

Visser, J. & Keller, J. M. (1990). The clinical use of motivational messages: An inquiry into the validity of the Arcs model of motivational design. *Instructional Science, 19*(6), 467-500.

Vollmeyer, R., & Reinberg, F. (2006). Motivational effects on self-regulated learning with different tasks. *Educational Psychology Review, 18,* 239-253.

Vroom, V. H. (1964). Work and motivation. New York: Wiley.

Wigfield, A., & Eccles, J. S. (2000). Expectancy-value theory of achievement motivation, *Contemporary Educational Psychology, 25,* 68-81.

Yeung, A. S., Jin, P., & Sweller, J. (1998). Cognitive load and learner expertise: Split-attention and redundancy effects in reading with explanatory notes. *Contemporary Educational Psychology, 23,* 1-21.

Zweig, D., & Webster, J. (2004). Validation of multidimensional measure of goal orientation. *Canadian Journal of Behavioral Science, 36*(3), 232-243.

ADDITIONAL READING

Ackerman, D. S., & Gross, B. L. (2005). My instructor made me do it, Task characteristics of procrastination. *Journal of Marketing Education, 27,* 5-13.

Aleven, V., McLaren, B. M., & Koedinger, K. R. (2006). Toward computer-based tutoring of help-seeking skills. In S. A. Karabenick (Ed.), *Help seeking in academic setting: Goals, groups, and contexts* (pp. 259-296). Mahwah, NJ: Lawrence Erlbaum.

Allen, M., Bourhis, J., Burrell, N., & Mabry, E. (2002). Comparing student satisfaction with distance education to traditional classrooms in higher education: A meta-analysis. *American Journal of Distance Education, 16*(2), 83-97.

Anglin, G., & Morrison, G. (2000). An analysis of distance research: Implications for the instructional technologist. *Quarterly Review of Distance Education, 1,* 180-194.

Ainley, M., Hidi, S., & Berndoff, D. (2002). Interest, learning, and the psychological psychological processes that mediate their relationship. *Journal of Educational Psychology, 94,* 545-561.

Astleiner, H. & Keller, J. M. (1995). A model for motivationally adaptive computer-assisted instruction. *Journal of Research on Computing in Education, 27,* 270-280.

Astleiner, H. & Leutner, D. (2000). Designing instructional technology from an emotional perspective. *Journal of Research on Computing in Education, 32,* 497-510.

Baker, S. R. (2004). Intrinsic, extrinsic, and motivational orientations: Their role in university adjustment, stress, well-being, and subsequent academic performance. *Current Psychology: Developmental, Learning, Personality, Social, 23,* 189-202.

Bell, B. S., & Kozlowzi, W. J. (2002). Goal orientation and ability: Interactive effects on self-efficacy, performance, and knowledge. *Journal of Applied Psychology, 87,* 497-505.

Bisciglia, M. G., & Monk-Turner, E. (2002). Differences in attitudes between on-site and distance-site students in group teleconference courses. *American Journal of Distance Education, 16*(2), 37-52.

Brown, B. W., & Liedholm, C. E. (2002). Can Web courses replace the classroom in principles of microeconomics? *American Economic Review, 92,* 444-448.

Brown, K.G. (2001). Using computers to deliver training: Which employees learn and why? *Personnel Psychology, 54,* 271-296.

Church, M.A., Elliot, A. J., & Gable, S. L. (2001). Perceptions of classroom environment, achievement goals, and achievement outcomes. *Journal of Educational Psychology, 93,* 43-54.

Clarebout, G., & Elen, J. (2006). Tool use in computer-based learning environments towards a research framework. *Computers in Human Behavior, 22,* 389-411.

Covington, M. V. (2000), Goal theory, motivation, and school achievement: An integrated review. *Annual Review of Psychology, 5,* 171-200.

Dillon, A., & Gabbard, R. (1998). Hypermedia as an educational technology: A review of quantitative research literature on learner comprehension, control, and style. *Review of Educational Research, 68,* 322-349.

Elliot, A. J., & Thrash, T. M. (2002). Approach-avoidance motivation in personality: Approach-avoidance temperaments and goals. *Journal of Personality and Social Psychology, 82,* 804-818.

Frankola, K. (2001). Why online learners drop out. *Workforce, 80,* 53-60.

Fritz, S., Bek, T. J., & Hall, D. L. (2001). Comparison of campus and distance undergraduate leadership students' attitudes. *Journal of Behavioral and Applied Management, 3,* 3-12.

Jonassen, D. H. & Land, S. M. (Eds.) (2000). *Theoretical foundations of learning environments.* Mahwah, NJ: Lawrence Erlbaum.

Kashihara, A., Kinshuk, Operrmann, R., Rashev, R., & Simm, H. (2000). A cognitive load reduction approach to exploratory learning and its application to an interactive simulation-based learning system. *Journal of Educational Multimedia and Hypermedia, 9,* 253-276.

Kester, L., & Paas, F. (2005). Instructional interventions to enhance collaboration in powerful learning environments. *Computers in Human Behavior, 21,* 689-696.

Maki, R. H., & Maki, W. S. (2003). Prediction of learning and satisfaction in web-based and lecture courses. *Journal of Educational Computing Research, 28,* 197-219.

Van Merriënboer, J. J. G., Kirschner, P.A., & Kester, L. (2003). Taking the load off a learner's mind: Instructional design for complex learning. *Educational Psychologist, 38,* 5-13.

Watson, D. C. (2001). Procrastination and the five-factor model: A facet level analysis. *Personality and Individual Differences, 30,* 149-158.

Wolters, C. A. (2003). Understanding procrastination from a self-regulated learning perspective. *Journal of Educational Psychology, 95,* 179-187.

Zimmerman, B. (2001). Theories of self-regulated learning and academic achievement: An overview and analysis. In B. J. Zimmerman & D. H. Schunk (Eds.), *Self-regulated learning and academic achievement: Theoretical perspectives* (2nd Ed.) (pp. 1-37), Mahwah, NJ: Lawrence Erlbaum.

Chapter X
What Factors Make a Multimedia Learning Environment Engaging:
A Case Study

Min Liu
University of Texas at Austin, USA

Paul Toprac
Southern Methodist University, USA

Timothy T. Yuen
University of Texas at Austin, USA

ABSTRACT

The purpose of this study is to investigate students' engagement with a multimedia enhanced problem-based learning (PBL) environment, Alien Rescue, and to find out in what ways students consider Alien Rescue motivating. Alien Rescue is a PBL environment for students to learn science. Fifty-seven sixth-grade students were interviewed. Analysis of the interviews using the constant comparative method showed that students were intrinsically motivated and that there were 11 key elements of the PBL environment that helped evoke students' motivation: authenticity, challenge, cognitive engagement, competence, choice, fantasy, identity, interactivity, novelty, sensory engagement, and social relations. These elements can be grouped into 5 perspectives of the sources of intrinsic motivation for students using Alien Rescue: problem solving, playing, socializing, information processing, and voluntary acting, with problem solving and playing contributing the highest level of intrinsic motivation. The findings are discussed with respect to designing multimedia learning environments.

INTRODUCTION

In order for technology to positively impact classroom learning, students must be motivated to use the technology in addition to learning the content presented with that technology. Literature on motivation and classroom learning has shown that motivation plays an important role in influencing learning and achievement (Ames, 1990). If motivated, students tend to approach challenging tasks more eagerly, persist in difficult situations, and take pleasure in their achievement (Stipek, 1993). Studies have indicated strong positive correlations between intrinsic motivation and academic achievement (Cordova & Lepper, 1996; Gottfried, 1985; Hidi & Harackiewicz, 2000; Lepper, Iyengar, & Corpus, 2005). This suggests that motivational problems or lack of effort is often a primary explanation for unsatisfactory academic performance (Hidi & Harackiewicz, 2000).

Students' lack of interest in mathematics and science has been cited as one of the primary reasons contributing to U.S. students lagging far behind other high-performing countries in math and science, especially at the middle-school level (National Science Board, 1999). According to Osborne, Simon, and Collins (2003), research has indicated a decline in attitudes toward science from age 11 onward. Other researchers have also found that as children become older, their intrinsic motivation to learn science tends to decline (Eccles & Wigfield, 2002; Gottfried, 1985; Lepper, Iyengar, & Corpus, 2005). Therefore, in order to help students succeed in learning math and science, instructional technologists must create technology enhanced learning environments that can motivate students and facilitate learning.

In an effort to meet this goal, we have designed and developed a multimedia enhanced problem-based learning (PBL) environment for six-grade science, *Alien Rescue* (Liu, Williams, & Pedersen, 2002). This program has been used by thousands of middle school students in multiple states. Our previous research examining the impact of this multimedia PBL environment has primarily focused on its cognitive effects such as its use on acquiring science knowledge and problem-solving skills (Liu, 2004; Liu & Bera, 2005; Li & Liu, 2008), cognitive tools and cognitive processes (Liu, Bera, Corliss, Svinicki, & Beth, 2004), and its effect on reducing cognitive load (Li & Liu, 2007). Studies on *Alien Rescue* have shown it to be an effective learning environment for science knowledge and problem-solving (Liu, 2004, 2005; Liu & Bera, 2005).

As we continued to work with students and teachers in different classrooms, it became apparent that students often considered their experience with *Alien Rescue* "fun" and enjoyed using it. The following quote from a teacher captured the essence of this observation:

Kids are talking about science outside of the classroom. They talk about *Alien Rescue* in the halls and they talk about *Alien Rescue* after school. All of the sixth graders are doing this, and so some of them have friends in different class periods that are working with *Alien Rescue*. They will say, "what did you find out today or have you found where this alien can go?" I think that the most exciting thing is that they are talking science outside of the classroom; I think that is the most impressive thing.

This sentiment led us to ask questions regarding the affective effects of *Alien Rescue*. Why did students like using *Alien Rescue*? What did they find interesting? How did it compare to other school activities they usually do in the classroom? The purpose of this study is to investigate sixth-graders' affective experiences, specifically motivation, as they were using *Alien Rescue* and to find out in what ways *Alien Rescue* was motivating to these students. Our guiding research question was:

*How does a multimedia enhanced problem-based learning (PBL) environment, **Alien Rescue**, motivate students to learn science?*

BACKGROUND

Using Multimedia to Enhance the Delivery of Problem-Based Learning

Problem-based learning emphasizes solving complex problems in rich contexts and aims at developing higher order thinking skills (Savery & Duffy, 1995). According to Savery and Duffy, PBL environments have three primary underlying constructivist propositions: (1) understanding is in our interactions with the environment, (2) cognitive conflict is the stimulus for learning and determines the organization and nature of what is learned, and (3) knowledge evolves through social negotiation and by the evaluation of the viability of one's understanding (Savery & Duffy, 1995). In PBL environments, the focus of learning is not only the knowledge outcome, but also the process by which students become self-reliant and independent.

The benefits of PBL, such as the activation of prior learning, self-directed learning, and motivation, have been documented in medical education and with college and gifted students (Albanese, & Mitchell, 1993; Gallagher, Stepien, & Rosenthal, 1992; Hmelo & Ferrari, 1997; Norman & Schmidt, 1992; Stepien, Gallagher, & Workman, 1993). However, literature has also indicated that implementing complex and ill-structured learning environments such as PBL in K-12 classrooms has been challenging (Airasian & Walsh, 1997).

Multimedia-enhanced PBL environments provide a new and different means that can assist students to develop problem-solving skills, to reflect on their own learning, and to develop a deep understanding of the content domain (Cognition and Technology Group at Vanderbilt, 1997), and if designed well, can also be more motivating to students than text-based delivery methods. Multimedia technology can enhance the PBL delivery through its video, audio, graphics, and animation capabilities as well as its interactive affordances to allow students to access information according to their own learning needs and present multiple related problems in one cohesive environment (Hoffman & Richie, 1997).

Motivation as an Important Factor for Learning

For preschool children, learning is fun. There are no motivational problems for learning in these years (Cordova & Lepper, 1996). Their motivation is manifested by their choice of behavior, latency of behavior, intensity of behavior, and persistence of behavior, and is accompanied with cognitive (e.g. goal setting) and emotional reactions (Graham & Weiner, 1996). Motivation is often considered to be a necessary antecedent for learning (Gottfried, 1985; Lepper, Iyengar, & Corpus, 2005) and is a function of expectancy of attaining a goal that is valued (Klinger, 1977; Pintrich & Schunk, 2002; Weiner, 1991). When students are intrinsically motivated to learn something, they may spend more time and effort learning, feel better about what they learn, and use it more in the future (Malone, 1981; Okan, 2003). An activity is said to be intrinsically motivating if people engage in it 'for its own sake' and if they do not engage in it for extrinsic reasons or motivators (Malone, 1981). Extrinsic motivators, such as external rewards and punishments, can destroy the continuing motivation of students to learn more about subjects outside of class (Greeno, Collins, & Resnick, 1996; Maehr, 1976).

Unfortunately, in later years, instruction in school, rather than being fun, is often boring and dull to students, and students' motivational problems to learn quickly appear: "In a variety of settings and using a variety of measures, investigators have found children's reported intrinsic motivation in school to decrease steadily from at least third grade through high school" (Cordova & Lepper, 1996, p. 715). The problem of motivating students is particularly acute when the subject matter is science (Tuan, Chin, & Shieh, 2005), from the point of entry to secondary school

(Osborne at al., 2003) — when their intrinsic motivation to learn science, interest in science, and attitudes toward science decline (Eccles & Wigfield, 2002; Gottfried, 1985; Lepper, Iyengar, & Corpus, 2005; Stake & Mares, 2001). Thus, promoting intrinsic motivation is critical to help students learn science.

Sources of Intrinsic Motivation for Learning Environments

There are many different perspectives of the sources of intrinsic motivation since it may vary over time, circumstances, and how people view what they are doing (Pintrich & Schunk, 2002). Lepper and Malone (1987) summarized past views of the sources of intrinsic motivation and their characteristics (p. 258):

- Humans as problem solvers: challenge, competence, efficacy or mastery
- Humans as information processors: curiosity, incongruity, or discrepancy
- Humans as players: fantasy involvement using graphics, story, and sound
- Humans as voluntary actors: control and self-determination

These four perspectives on the sources of intrinsic motivation are commonly expressed as challenge, curiosity, fantasy, and control, respectfully (Pintrich & Schunk, 2002). Though listed as separate categories, these perspectives overlap each other. For example, people become curious (i.e. humans as information processors) because of an incongruity in information. This often leads people to want to solve the problem or challenge (i.e. humans as problem solvers) presented by the discrepancy. Each perspective separately cannot sufficiently explain the phenomenon of intrinsic motivation. However, in total, they provide a comprehensive understanding of how learners can be motivated by a learning environment and its implementation in the classroom, which may

reduce the need for the teacher as the source of motivation.

Purpose of the Study and Methodology

To address our research question, we used interviews as our primary data source and the constant comparative method as our analysis technique. We also include descriptive statistics to illustrate specific aspects of the multimedia PBL environment that affect motivation and learning.

A Multimedia PBL Environment: *Alien Rescue*

Alien Rescue is a multimedia enhanced PBL environment for 6th grade science and is designed in accordance with the National Science Education Standards and the Texas Essential Knowledge and Skills (TEKS) guidelines (Liu, Williams, & Pedersen, 2002). The learning objectives include increasing knowledge of our solar system and improving problem-solving skills. It typically takes fifteen 45-minute class periods to complete. *Alien Rescue* presents a complex problem for scientific investigation and decision-making by students. The story of *Alien Rescue* has a science fiction premise that allows students to take on the role of a scientist in charge of finding habitats (e.g., the planets and moons) in our solar system for six endangered aliens by using a rich set of technology enriched cognitive tools. *Alien Rescue*'s cognitive tools include information databases with various media, simulation tools, expert modeling, and charts and a notebook tool.

Participants and Research Setting

One hundred and ten sixth graders from a middle school in a mid-sized southwestern city used *Alien Rescue* as part of their science curriculum for three weeks. The demographics of these sixth graders were approximately 71% White, 15 %

Hispanic, 10% Asian/Pacific Islander, and 4% African American. About 50.8% were female students and 49.2% were male students.

We observed students' interaction with *Alien Rescue* for the entire duration, and interviewed roughly 50% of the students (n=57). Both individual and focus group interviews were conducted during and after using the program. Focus groups of two to five students were randomly formed as time and seating arrangement permitted. We made an effort to talk to as many students as the time and situation allowed. Altogether, sixty interviews occurred, including ones performed during and after the completion of the program. The time for each interview ranged from 5 to 20 minutes.

Interviews and Analysis

All interviews were audiotaped and transcribed. The interview questions sought to capture students' cognitive and affective experiences during and after using *Alien Rescue*. As recommended by Suchman (1990), these semi-structured interviews occurred as informal conversations that were open-ended but guided by students' activities. Sample interview questions included the following:

- What are you working on now?
- Have you found a planet for the alien species? Which one? Why do you think it is a good home for species X? How did you reach that conclusion?
- Why did you need to launch probes? What did you find out? Do you understand the data? If you find something you do not know, what do you do?
- Which parts did you like or dislike most about *Alien Rescue*? Why?

Interviews after the completion of the program were also semi-structured and conversational, focusing on students' overall experience and impression of the program. The following were eight core questions used as the interview guides:

- What did you think of *Alien Rescue* (AR)? On a scale of 1 to 5 (highest number meaning the best), how do you like AR?
- Which part did you like the most/least about *Alien Rescue*? Why?
- Did you find the problem challenging? Did you like to solve it? Why?
- What have you learned? Did you think that you learned any science content by using *Alien Rescue*? What scientific topics, concepts, or skills have you learned by using *Alien Rescue*? How did you learn?
- How different is working with *Alien Rescue* from working on other school activities? Did you like researching and how was it different from researching in other classes or subjects?
- Did you choose your own team member? How did you work together?
- Did you talk with your peers about *Alien Rescue* outside of class? If so, what did you talk about?
- Would you want to work on programs like *Alien Rescue* in the future? Why?

Transcribed interviews were analyzed using the constant comparative method (Lincoln & Guba, 1985). Relevant information from the students' utterances or incidents was extracted through a systematic set of methodological procedures that inductively generated and connected raw data to codes, codes to categories, and categories to themes (Creswell, 2005). First, the data was examined for evidence or indicators of motivation and/or affect, since these two psychological concepts are considered to be highly linked (Eccles & Wigfield, 2002). The relevant incidents in the transcripts were coded to describe what the students said about motivation and emotion, a process referred to as "focused coding" (Charmaz, 2006, p. 57). At the next level, the codes were compared with each other and categories emerged at a higher level of abstraction that subsumed these codes. The analyses continued until an "emergence of regularities" (Lincoln & Guba, 1985, p. 350) was reached. The emerged themes were compared with and against conventional intrinsic motivational theory perspectives with the purpose of framing our categories as well as informing existing knowledge.

RESULTS AND DISCUSSION

Findings

Of the approximately 500 paragraphs of text recording the students' spoken words in the transcript, there were 145 incidents where students spoke of their motivation and affect. A paragraph consisted of as little as one word to as much as several sentences. Some paragraphs contained more than one incident. Of the 145 incidents, 142 incidents expressed positive motivation and affect. Table 1 summarized students' expression of motivation and affect. Beyond these 145 incidents of motivation and affect, there were 288 incidents describing the reasons driving their motivation and affect, such as "I liked researching on the aliens and stuff like finding stuff out."

After analyzing 288 incidents of students' motivational drives, eleven themes emerged that influenced the students' positive motivation and affect while using *Alien Rescue*. The themes for motivation and affect were: authenticity, challenge, cognitive engagement, competence, choice,

fantasy, identity, interactivity, novelty, sensory engagement, and social relations. These themes and categories are shown in Table 2, along with the number of incidents and percentages.

Authenticity

Students found situated authentic learning to be motivating and valuable. There were three sub-categories for authenticity: authentic activity, scientific practices, and scientific roles. When asked how different was working with *Alien Rescue* from other school activities, some students responded that the activity was different because it was authentic in nature: "It [*Alien Rescue*] was just like doing something that a real scientist would do."

In addition, students were motivated by taking on the role of a scientist and performing what they described as scientific practices. Students were able to role-play as a scientist and work within a space station while using the tools afforded by the environment. When asked questions on what they liked about *Alien Rescue*, students' answers included statements such as: "I liked *Alien Rescue* because how else were you going to learn if you want to be a real scientist because it has a lot of the things you have to do and have to learn how to do" and "I like the program it was neat and... I think it was a good experience if you were going to be scientist some day—it just made you ready for that stuff."

Table 1. Students' expressions of motivation and affect

Categories	No. of Incidents	Percentage of Total
Concentration	3	2%
Fun	50	35%
Interesting	9	6%
Like	67	46%
Persistence	6	4%
Self-esteem	7	5%
Frustration (negative)	3	2%
Total	145	100%

Table 2. Students' sources of motivation while using Alien Rescue

Themes	Categories	No. of Incidents
Authenticity (19 incidents, 7% of total)	Authentic Activity	5
	Scientific Practices	8
	Scientific Roles	6
Challenge (28 incidents, 10% of total)	—	28
Choice (34 incidents, 12% of total)	Confiscation	12
	Control	7
	Freedom	15
Cognitive Engagement (54 incidents, 18% of total)	Learning	18
	Problem solving	10
	Researching	21
	Thinking	5
Competence/Confidence (12 incidents, 4% of total)	—	12
Fantasy (39 incidents, 14% of total)	Empathy	10
	Fiction	29
Identity (11 incidents, 4% of total)	Attainment Value	11
Interactivity (25 incidents, 9% of total)	Activeness	4
	Computer-based	7
	Feedback	4
	Playing	2
	Miscellaneous	8
Novelty (15 incidents, 5% of total)	Novelty	13
	Variety	2
Sensory Engagement (21 incidents, 7% of total)	Multimedia	8
	Probes	13
Social Relations (30 incidents, 10% of total)	Debate	6
	Group Work	10
	Peer Interaction	14

Challenge

In general, students liked the challenge of using *Alien Rescue* and found it motivating: "I thought it was hard, but it was fun at the same time because it was a challenge and I personally like challenges." For some students, *Alien Rescue* was "more of challenge, so you can't give up," which shows a desire to attempt solving the problem. Other responses to whether *Alien Rescue* was challenging or difficult included "I think it's fun and it's kind of hard" and "*Alien Rescue* gave me a good challenge because it made me exercise my brain more than I would normally if it was an easier game." However, there were a few instances of students expressing frustration that *Alien Rescue* was too challenging or that there was not enough time to complete it. A student said, "I just think that the reason that it [*Alien Rescue*] could probably be better is because it could have been easier."

Choice

Students' feeling of control and choice were important with both positive and negative affective valences. When asked what was liked about *Alien Rescue*, a student replied, "They [probes] were fun because you got to create them and tell them what to do." Students thought it was fun to explore the program, choose what to do, create probes, and launch them to targeted planets and moons. On the flip side, students did not like losing control, such as when using the expert tool for guidance. The expert tool is a set of video clips in which an expert explains how they would address aspects of the problem and share their problem-solving strategies. Students did not like this and were able to explain exactly why:

Student: well the thing I hate about it [*Alien Rescue*] is the expert.

Group: OH! [agreement from the group]

Student (cont.): He would immediately take control of everything. You can't get rid of him, he would just stand there and start talking and he would just take control for some reason…

Cognitive Engagement

The students interviewed liked the cognitive engagement that *Alien Rescue* afforded. In fact, this was the most mentioned reason why they thought *Alien Rescue* was fun. The four main sub-categories expressed by students were learning, problem solving, researching, and thinking. For instance, a student articulated, "…I like the program. It was neat and I learned a lot of terms, a lot of scientific names that I didn't know before…" When asked why they liked researching on *Alien Rescue*, one student summed it up by saying, "I think that it was fun, doing the research on the planets because you got to figure out different things about the planets and you get to send probes and get information that you don't know and then you have to research all the aliens and figure out what they need and then try to match them up." A student appreciated that *Alien Rescue* is "like a puzzle that's kind of hard to solve but kind of easy at the same time, not easy I should say but difficult. Yeah, and it's fun and good." Another student said, "It was neat converting things from Kelvin to Celsius and how you could like figure out their temperatures and stuff."

Competence/Confidence/ Self-Efficacy

Some students felt competent or confident of his or her knowledge of *Alien Rescue* and his or her recommendations of habitats for the aliens. This may also be considered self-efficacy, which according to Eccles and Wigfield (2002), is a person's self-evaluation of his or her ability and beliefs about the probability of success in tasks. During engagement with *Alien Rescue*, students attained the feeling of competence and self-efficacy. After completing *Alien Rescue*, this feeling manifested itself as confidence regarding the selection of habitats for the aliens. One student expressed his or her confidence as, "I'm very confident because I really researched, I'm pretty sure that it was right." Another student said, "I'm pretty confident, well, we are because we think that we researched it a lot and we think that we got it right."

However, not all the students felt confident about their recommendations. For example, a student who was not expressing confidence because of computer problems said "I was sort of confident on some because the computers we had kept messing up and it erased my notes but we did the best we could and I think that's all that matters."

Fantasy

Fantasy was the second major reason, after cognitive engagement, for why students liked and were motivated to use *Alien Rescue*. Fantasy was expressed in terms of empathy for the aliens and space exploration. With regards to aliens, students were motivated by the fictional narrative of saving the aliens' lives and as students said, "you've got to do it to help save the aliens" and "if you miss something the alien will die for that" and "[I like *Alien Rescue*] because [of the] aliens, 'cause it's also fun to imagine having them and being friends with them." Others expressed positive affect for *Alien Rescue* because it was fictional, such as "I thought *Alien Rescue* was pretty cool because you got to actually have some fiction fun in it."

The science fiction aspect of *Alien Rescue* made one student remark, that in "most other experiments, you don't have this much fun because you have to do it in real life, this is like science fiction or something."

Identity/Attainment Value

According to Eccles and Wigfield (2002), the attainment value is the individual's determination about whether the task confirms or disconfirms the core aspects of the person's beliefs and self-concepts about his or her self. That is, the task confirms or disconfirms an individual's self-identity, which is informed by the communities that the student wishes to participate in, whether in school or beyond.

For some of the students, *Alien Rescue* affirmed their identity. These students were motivated to learn science in order to fulfill their desire to be-come a scientist or space explorer, or both. *Alien Rescue*'s science fiction narrative brought special personal meanings to the activities for some students. For instance, a student said, "I want to one day go out of space and find a new planet plus the ones already discovered and study asteroids and comets because I really like space 'cause its very interesting". Another student stated, "And considering the fact that I have been wanting to be an astronaut since I was like three or four years old, this was just like the best program for me…" Another student wanted to "know what it would be like standing on the moon or going to other places" and wanted to eventually "go out of space and find a new planet plus the ones already discovered and study asteroids and comets" because of an individual interest in space.

Interactivity

Students were highly engaged with *Alien Rescue* because of its interactive features. Students' comments on interactivity can be broken down to activeness, computer-based, feedback, playing, and miscellaneous. Of these, activeness and being computer-based were the most important for these students. When asked, "How different is working with *Alien Rescue* from working on other school activities?," a student summed up his peers' comments by saying, "It [*Alien Rescue*] was better because instead of being stuck on the desk, you got to play around with the computer and kind of do whatever you wanted." Another student who liked "hands-on projects a lot more than reading out of a book" reiterated this point. One student summed up how interactivity evoked positive affect and motivation, saying"…it's funner because you are not just looking through textbooks you get to actually play around and it's funner than just sitting there in class."

However, a few students did not think there was adequate feedback from the program. One student commented on the lack of feedback, "… I think it should tell you if you got it right and show how if they like where they live." In other words, *Alien Rescue* did not present the outcomes of the students' recommendations for the habitats of the aliens, and some students desired this feedback.

Novelty

Students liked to have new and different experiences. This was reflected by their preference for the novelty of *Alien Rescue*, especially since it is computer based, and how it varied from regular classroom instruction. For instance, when asked "On a scale of one to five, one being not very much and five being very much, how much do you like *Alien Rescue*?," a student replied, "I would give it a five because I like doing things that are irregular."

Sensory Engagement

Not only did students find cognitive engagement motivating, but also the engagement of their visual and audio senses. Students enjoyed the multimedia presentation in general (e.g. video scenario of the problem at the beginning of the program, graphics), but the aliens (including 3D alien videos) and probe simulations, in particular. For instance, when students were asked, "Did you like researching and how was it different from researching in other classes or subjects?" one student answered, "[I like *Alien Rescue*] because you have fun and you get to look at the aliens, you get to look at the graphs, you get to look at the pictures and then just kind of go from there" and another student answered, "I like this one part about watching probes."

Social Relations

Interaction with fellow classmates and peers was an important feature of *Alien Rescue*. These interactions took the form of debating within groups on where an alien should go, "one of the things

that I liked about the research was working in a group because I think it would have been a lot less fun working by ourselves because I think its fun to talk and, it's actually fun to argue because you are actually getting all that information out and its fun all around."

Not only did the debate occur within groups but also between friends from other groups and peers outside of class:

"Well, I talked about it with my friends, because one of my friends was, 'Oh my gosh I'm totally clueless about this one alien. Do you know where they go?' And I said, 'Well I think they go over there' and she said, 'No, that's wrong they need to go here.' And we would have messed up if it weren't for my friends, because my friend stopped me in the hall and she said, 'guess what we finished Alien Rescue today' and I said, 'That's [habitat] what I chose and she said, 'No, it isn't [right]. Then, I figured it out and so my friend ended up being a little bit wrong and then I had to call Lynn. And then they had a big argument with me because they thought I was wrong and my friends were wrong. I said, 'No I'm right' and then I had to do more research."

Students also found that group interaction afforded them the teamwork needed to solve the problem. As a student pointed out, "when you work in groups, you don't have to do all the research" and the different tasks can be distributed to the appropriate people. As an example, the same student cited the conversion of Celsius to Kelvin problem as being a topic one student may know, but another student may not know. The sense of camaraderie is enhanced by the fact that students within the same group can help each other since "your partner tells you information that you don't know." Unfortunately, not all the members of groups were helpful, as a student stated, "I sort of did work by myself because my partner never helped me."

GENERAL DISCUSSION

The purpose of this study was to explore the characteristics of a multimedia enhanced problem-based learning environment that intends to provide a rich context for learning science and afford students a motivating experience. The coding and categorizing procedures found eleven key elements that middle-school students considered motivating and/or evoked affect: authenticity, challenge, cognitive engagement, competence, choice, fantasy, identity, interactivity, novelty, sensory engagement, and social relations.

These elements were in congruence with the four sources of intrinsic motivation as discussed in the literature. A new source of intrinsic motivation was revealed through the analysis: humans as socializers - interpersonal relationships, identity, and group membership. Thus, our study was able to expand upon the existing theory on sources of intrinsic motivation with the addition of "humans as socializers" as a fifth source.

Humans as Problem Solvers

Activities are intrinsically motivating when the problems or challenges are personally meaningful. To best promote this motivation, the task should be optimally challenging (Csikszentmihalyi, 1990), and if possible, adaptable to the learner's ability.

Figure 1. Summarizes the motivating characteristics as exhibited in Alien Rescue with their corresponding theoretical motivational perspectives

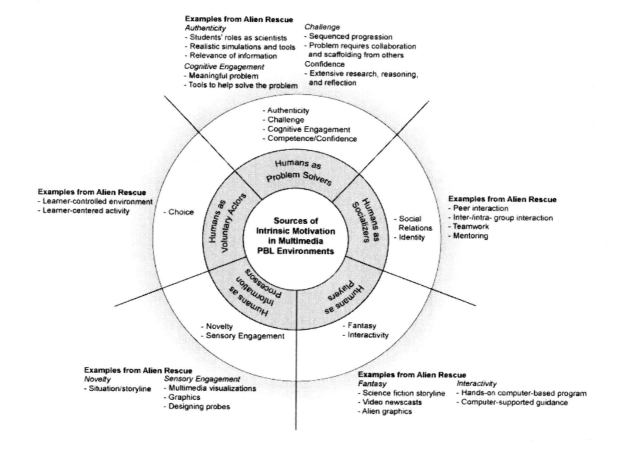

As the individual masters challenges in an activity, s/he also attains a feeling of competence, mastery, and self-efficacy for accomplishing that activity. Challenges that are too easy bring on boredom and challenges that are too difficult evoke feelings of frustration or helplessness.

The results showed that *Alien Rescue* was able to evoke the humans-as-problem-solvers motivation within students. This was the single largest source of intrinsic motivation. This is not surprising since problem-based learning environments often have been found to be intrinsically motivating (Gallagher, Stepien, & Rosenthal, 1992; Hmelo & Ferrari, 1997; Savery & Duffy, 1995), and the core task of a PBL environment is problem solving.

The sources of motivation in *Alien Rescue* that comprised this perspective were: authenticity, challenge, cognitive engagement, and competence. As has been found by other researchers, challenge was a key source of motivation among students (Lepper & Malone, 1987; Malone & Lepper, 1987; Ryan & Deci, 2000). Cognitive engagement was the single most discussed theme by the students in this study. The students were intrinsically motivated in using *Alien Rescue* because it cognitively engaged them to research and learn new concepts and facts, and to think and solve the complex problem presented. Thus, *Alien Rescue* does not only present a challenge but provides an environment in which students valued the learning and thinking processes required to meet the challenge. The rich set of technology-based tools within *Alien Rescue* (Liu & Bera, 2005) supported the learning and thinking processes as well as encouraged interactivity.

In addition, many students knew that they were engaged in authentic activities and understood that solving the problem in *Alien Rescue* required skills that were authentic to the practices and roles of being a scientist. Results suggested that this authenticity was a source of intrinsic motivation, perhaps because it brought more meaning to the problem-solving exercise. Some students found

personal meaning because they valued space exploration and science (i.e. identity/attainment value). However, a learning environment cannot accommodate for all the different, sometimes idiosyncratic, attainment values of students. Instead, the best way to accomplish the inclusion of meaningful activities is to present them in a way that convinces students that the processes employed are authentic in nature.

Finally, some students believed that they found the correct habitats for the endangered species and were confident about their decision. This perceived competence may be viewed as a source of intrinsic motivation and/or the result of intrinsic motivation. *Alien Rescue* scaffolds and reciprocally builds a student's perceived competence as the students proceed to complete the program. This is an important design consideration: students should develop the feeling of self-efficacy as they progress through the learning environment in order to promote intrinsic motivation.

Humans as Players

People play because it is fun. Fantasy involvement using graphics, characters, story, and sound can promote the feeling of play. Fantasy, heightened by using sophisticated multimedia techniques, removes students from everyday (non-play) life, which in turn promotes the feeling that the activity at hand is playing. A playful activity affords the learner to focus on the activity, which drives engagement (Csikszentmihalyi, 1990). However, if the activity is too playful, then the learner may focus on the playing aspects and less on the learning objectives.

Fantasy and interactivity combined, i.e. human as a player, were strong sources of intrinsic motivation for students to use *Alien Rescue*. Fantasy was the second biggest contributor to intrinsic motivation for the students. Fantasy involvement was promoted by using a science fiction narrative that was expressed through multimedia and interactivity. Interactivity is closely aligned with the concept of playing, and in particular, students liked playing on the computer. Results suggested that the activeness (see Vinter & Perruchet, 2000) and feedback that *Alien Rescue* afforded via computer-based activities evoked positive affect for students. Finally, an indication that the students were experiencing play was that many of them called *Alien Rescue* a computer game and compared it to other games they played.

Humans as Information Processors

We take pleasure in resolving the mystery or disequilibrium and prefer activities that are neither very familiar nor very different (Pintrich & Schunk, 2002). Like challenges, to best promote this motivation is to provide optimal, intermediate levels of surprise and incongruence. Interestingly, curiosity was not explicitly mentioned by students using *Alien Rescue*. Instead, students described being motivated by novelty. That is, they were attracted to novel and different experiences as presented by *Alien Rescue*.

Piaget (1977) theorized that organisms (humans) not only desire experiences that are close to their existing schema, but also radically new experiences that require new cognitive structures or schemata to be accommodated. "Piaget explains how, at times, this process results in a 'reach beyond the grasp' in the search for new knowledge" (Fosnot, 1996, p. 13). Here, it seems that there is some overlap of the metaphor of humans as problem solvers and humans as information processors. Students were not only interested in meaningful challenges but their interest was piqued if the experience was novel to them. This novelty was especially enhanced by the multimedia delivery of *Alien Rescue*. Such use of multimedia effects promotes sensory curiosity (Malone & Lepper, 1987).

Yet, it is interesting that "human as information processors" was not as strong as a source of intrinsic motivation for students using *Alien Rescue* as expected. This could have been be-

cause the interpretation and categorization by the researchers may have unintentionally marginalized this source. For instance, perhaps when students expressed their fondness for designing and using probes to find information about specific planetoids, this was an indication of their need to resolve their curiosity instead of preference for fantasy involvement using graphics. Or maybe it was both.

Humans as Voluntary Actors

The sources of intrinsic motivation from the perspective of 'humans as voluntary actors', as stated by Malone and Lepper (1987), are: control and self-determination. People are fond of the feeling that they are in control of their environment. Environments that provide choices and self-direction support the feeling of autonomy, which enhances intrinsic motivation. This motivation is best promoted when the activity provides "a sense of personal control over meaningful outcomes" (Lepper & Malone, 1987, p. 258). Yet, too much control over the outcomes can reduce the meaningfulness of the activity.

The open-ended nature of *Alien Rescue* affords a significant amount of choices. Therefore, it was expected that students would have mentioned choices and control more often than was found. Yet, as an indication of their desire for control, students had a strong negative reaction to the expert-modeling tool, which they felt had confiscated their control.

Humans as Socializers

The theme of social relations was an essential motivating factor of *Alien Rescue* users. Most students found the socializing aspect of working with their peers motivating. Debating and arguing their perspectives about the problem and possible solutions were engaging and fun. Such lively discourse occurred both inside and outside the classroom. Collaboration is an important aspect of PBL environments. Unfortunately, the difficulty in logistics of performing group assessment in K-12 classrooms often discourages curricula incorporating group work. The results of this study pointed to the need to consider peer collaboration as part of the implementation of learning environments.

Developing and maintaining social relations or socializing is not explicitly stated as a source of motivation in most classical descriptions of intrinsic motivation because it appears to be extrinsic in nature. However, Lepper and Malone implicitly incorporated socializing by including self-determination (Deci and Ryan 1992; Ryan & Deci, 2000) as part of the humans as voluntary actors perspective. Self-determination theory of intrinsic motivation posits that people are innately motivated to seek out optimal stimulation and challenges that meet the needs of autonomy, competence, and relatedness. In self-determination theory, the competence need is the desire to feel capable of acting appropriately in an environment, which overlaps directly with the concept of humans as problem solvers. The autonomy need is the need of humans to feel that they are in control of their environment, as discussed in the metaphor of humans as voluntary actors. Thus, a more accurate portrayal of humans as voluntary actors is that it is about control and autonomy, rather than self-determination.

However, self-determination theory also includes relatedness as a source of intrinsic motivation. Relatedness is the need to feel secure and connected to others in the learning environment. The need for security and connectedness is closely aligned with Maslow's (1955) theory of hierarchy of human needs of safety and belongingness. In Maslow's theory, safety needs can be seen in individual's preference for familiar (e.g. social) surroundings, and belongingness needs involve the need for affectionate relationships and the feeling of being part of a group (Petri, 1981).

In support of the existence of the need to be connected to others and interpersonal relations as a motivator, there have been numerous studies demonstrating that cooperative learning and group activities, such as those provided in problem-based learning environments, have a positive effect on students' interest, engagement, and motivation (Shernoff, Csikszentmihalyi, Schneider, & Shernoff, 2003). And although not mentioned in the above intrinsic motivation metaphors, Lepper and Malone's (1987, p. 248) taxonomy of intrinsic motivations includes interpersonal motivations, which are promoted by organizing activities with cooperation, competition, and recognition. A fundamental design element of PBL environments is organizing the activity so that learners cooperate to solve a problem, which affords the opportunity to enhance interpersonal relations and motivation.

The innate desire of individuals to establish, strengthen, and maintain interpersonal relations—the sense of belonging to and participating in a social group or community—is aligned with the social constructivist view of motivation (Greeno, Collins, & Resnick, 1996; Wentzel, 1999), which is an underlying theory behind problem-based learning environments. In the classroom, this social group comprises of friends and classmates. The super-motive is the reciprocal process of valuing the social group and the development of one's identity within that social group. Individuals have the innate need to belong to a social group or community where they can develop their self-esteem and attain esteem (via social recognition) from others through participation in that social group or community (Bandura, 1986; Hickey, 2003; Maslow, 1955; Ryan & Deci, 2000). Motivation is the process of negotiation of one's identity and participation in a community in order to attain esteem (Lave & Wenger, 1991).

The Significance of Using Technology in PBL Delivery

Within the context of PBL, the eleven elements that the students found to be motivating about

Alien Rescue were, to a large extent, delivered and enhanced with the assistance of technology. Situating the central problem within a science fiction premise, using video newscasts to announce the arrival of the aliens, placing students in the role of a scientist, providing a space station environment for the student to explore, and providing numerous databases of rich information make the learning environment more compelling and engaging for these sixth-graders.

Students' research and problem solving in *Alien Rescue* are assisted with the set of cognitive tools, each with a specific function. These cognitive tools are an important part of enhancing intrinsic motivation. This includes providing tools that students consider are authentic and used in the "adult world" such as the notebook, probe designing, and informational databases about NASA missions, and our solar system. These tools are interactive, supporting fantasy and sensory engagement. They provide necessary cognitive scaffolding during students' problem solving. As students develop more expertise during the process, they feel more confident with their work, which ultimately leads to enhancing students' self-efficacy. The cognitive tools provide students both cognitive scaffolding in assisting them to solve a complex problem, and also motivational scaffolding in making them feel less overwhelmed or helpless. Together with the incorporation of teamwork, students are in control of their own learning, relying less on the teachers, and are encouraged to be self-reliant and independent. The cognitive tools, however, should not be considered to have a one-to-one correspondence to the sources of motivation. Instead, the relationship between the tools and sources of motivations are one-to-many. That is, every tool can afford different sources of intrinsic motivation. For instance, the probe-designing tool supports the fantasy narrative, provides control for the students to test hypotheses and multimedia sensory curiosity while affording the students to continue the process of problem solving. When designing cognitive tools within a learning en-

vironment, designers should consider how tools, individually and collectively, support the sources of intrinsic motivation (See Figure 1).

CONCLUSION

Intrinsic motivation is shown to be highly correlated with the academic success of students, and is thought to be the antecedent to learning. Thus, it would behoove designers of multimedia learning environments to consider incorporating elements that promote the five sources of intrinsic motivation: problem solving, playing, information processing, voluntary acting, and socializing.

The findings of this study showed that students using *Alien Rescue* repeatedly described their experience as fun, interesting, and enjoyable, which are the characteristics of being intrinsically motivated. The two strongest sources of intrinsic motivation for students using *Alien Rescue* are their participation in problem solving and playing. The students expressed pleasure in engaging cognitive challenges while problem solving and the environment afforded these middle school students the feeling of playing while problem solving. Thus, removing them from everyday life and immersing them in a fantasy appeared to motivate the students to engage in solving a difficult task. The importance of incorporating these sources of intrinsic motivation into designing multimedia learning environments for this age group is obvious.

Other sources of intrinsic motivation such as social relations, curiosity, and choice—though less mentioned in comparison, also merit attention in designing multimedia learning environments. A learning environment that promotes social relations is important because it is not only a source of intrinsic motivation, but peer collaboration is also a way to scaffold student learning through the zone of proximal development (Vygotsky, 2006). In addition, students are motivated by the novelty of the computer program, as well as with the sensory curiosity afforded by the rich multimedia design. Finally, choice is an essential source of intrinsic motivation and becomes salient to the students who, as shown in this study, had strong negative reactions when it was insufficient or taken away.

Taken together, the eleven elements (authenticity, challenge, cognitive engagement, competence, choice, fantasy, identity, interactivity, novelty, sensory engagement, and social relations) as exhibited in *Alien Rescue* have shown what makes a learning environment engaging to the sixth-graders, and reflect the five sources of intrinsic motivation. Thus, these motivational factors are important for designers to consider in designing learning environments.

FUTURE RESEARCH DIRECTIONS

This study provided some empirical based insights into how a multimedia learning environment can motivate students to learn academic subject matter. One possible future direction of research relates to how to optimize the sources of intrinsic motivation using multimedia. Is it possible to find an optimal level of motivation for a target group of students or is it better to try to develop an adaptable system to accommodate idiosyncratic motivational levels of each student? If the adaptable system approach is taken, how does one measure the student's motivation without interrupting working/playing and confiscating control?

Another possible future research direction is to determine how to enhance the sources of intrinsic motivation of PBL environments, such as *Alien Rescue*. Socializing, evoking curiosity, and choice-making were appreciably less mentioned by students in this study as compared to other sources such as problem solving and playing. How can these secondary sources be enhanced? Also, will all the sources of intrinsic motivation be enhanced when focusing on improving one or more of the sources' efficacy?

Finally, it is possible to use the five sources of intrinsic motivation as a rubric for evaluating future research on motivational characteristics of multimedia learning environments. Quantitative instruments can be developed to evaluate a wide range of multimedia learning environments to determine which sources were the major contributors for each genre. For instance, how do the results of this study compare to other multimedia enhanced problem-based learning environments? The results from studying each genre of multimedia learning environments can also be compared and contrasted to gain greater understanding of how to motivate students. From this research, we would not only understand how to enhance motivation through multimedia, but we could also be able to add new insights and dimensions to motivational theories as well.

REFERENCES

Airasian, P. W., & Walsh, M.E. (1997). Constructivist cautions. *Phi Delta Kappan*, *78*(6), 444-449.

Albanese, M.A., & Mitchell, S. (1993). Problem-based learning: A review of literature on its outcomes and implementation issues, *Academic Medicine*, *68*(1), 52-81.

Ames, C. A. (1990). Motivation: What teachers need to know. *Teacher College Record*, *90*(3), 409-421.

Bandura, A. (1986). Social foundations of thought and action: A social cognitive theory. Englewood Cliffs, NJ: Prentice-Hall, Inc.

Charmaz, K. (2006). Constructing grounded theory: A practical guide through qualitative analysis. Thousand Oaks, NJ: Sage Publications.

Cognition and Technology Group at Vanderbilt. (1997). The jasper project: Lessons in curriculum, instruction, assessment, and professional development. Mahwah, NJ: Erlbaum.

Cordova, D. I., & Lepper, M. R. (1996). Intrinsic motivation and the process of learning: Beneficial effects of contextualization, personalization, and choice. *Journal of Educational Psychology, 88*(4), 715-730.

Creswell, J. (2005). Educational Research: planning, conducting, and evaluating quantitative and qualitative research (2nd Ed.). New Jersey: Merrill.

Csikszentmihalyi, M. (1990). Flow: The psychology of optimal experience. New York, NY: HarperCollins Publishing.

Deci, E. L., & Ryan, R. M. (1992). The initiation and regulation of intrinsically motivated learning and achievement. In A. K. Boggiano & T. S. Pittman (Eds.), *Achievement and motivation: A social-developmental perspective* (pp. 9-36). New York, NY: Cambridge University Press.

Eccles, J. S., & Wigfield, A. (2002). Motivational beliefs, values, and goals. *Annual Review of Psychology, 53*(1), 109-132.

Fosnot, C. T. (1996). Constructivism: A psychological theory of learning. In C. T. Fosnot (Ed.), *Constructivism: Theory, perspectives, and practice* (pp. 9-33). New York: Teachers College Press.

Gallagher, S. A., Stepien, W. J., & Rosenthal, H. (1992). The effects of problem-based learning on problem solving. *Gifted Child Quarterly, 36*, 195-200.

Gottfried, A. E. (1985). Academic intrinsic motivation in elementary and junior high school students. *Journal of Educational Psychology, 77*(6), 631-645.

Graham, S., & Weiner, B. (1996). Theories and principles of motivation. In D. Berliner & R. Calfee (Eds.), *Handbook of educational psychology* (pp. 63-84). New York: Simon & Schuster Macmillan.

Greeno, J. G., Collins, A. M., & Resnick, L. B. (1996). Cognition and learning. In D. Berliner & R. Calfee (Eds.), *Handbook of educational psychology* (pp. 15-46). New York, NY: Simon & Schuster Macmillan.

Hickey, D. T. (2003). Engaged participation versus marginal nonparticipation: A stridently sociocultural approach to achievement motivation. *Elementary School Journal, 103*(4), 401-429.

Hidi, S., & Harackiewicz, J. M. (2000). Motivating the academically unmotivated: A critical issue for the 21st Century. *Review of Educational Research, 70*(2), 151-179.

Hmelo, C. E., & Ferrari, M. (1997). The problem-based learning tutorial: Cultivating higher order thinking skills. *Journal for the Education of the Gifted, 20*(4), 401-422.

Hoffman, B., & Richie, D. (1997). Using multimedia to overcome the problems with problem-based learning. *Instructional Science, 25*, 97-115.

Klinger, E. (1977). Meaning & void: Iinner experience and the incentives in people's lives. Minneapolis: University of Minnesota Press.

Lave, J., & Wenger, E. (1991). Situated learning: Legitimate peripheral participation. New York, NY: Cambridge University Press.

Lepper, M. R., Iyengar, S. S., & Corpus, J. H. (2005). Intrinsic and extrinsic motivational orientations in the classroom: Age differences and scademic correlates. *Journal of Educational Psychology, 97*(2), 184-196.

Lepper, M. R., & Malone, T. W. (1987). Intrinsic motivation and instructional effectiveness in computer-based education. In R. E. Snow & M. J. Farr (Eds.), *Aptitude, Llearning andIinstruction: Cognitive and Affective Process Analysis* (Vol. 3, pp. 255-287): Hillsdale, NJ: Lawrence Erlbaum Associates.

Li, R., & Liu, M. (2007). Understanding the effects of databases as cognitive tools in a problem-based multimedia learning environment. *Journal of Interactive Learning Research, 18*(3), 345-363.

Li, R., & Liu, M. (2008). The effects of using a computer database tool on middle school students' cognitive skill acquisition in a multimedia learning environment. In R. Kobayashi, (Ed.) *New Educational Technology*. Hauppauge, NY: Nova Science Publishers, Inc.

Lincoln, Y. S., & Guba, E. D. (1985). *Naturalistic Inquiry*. Thousand Oaks, CA Sage Publications, Inc.

Liu, M. (2004). Examining the performance and attitudes of sixth graders during their use of a problem-based hypermedia learning environment. *Computers in Human Behavior, 20*(3), 357-379.

Liu, M. (2005). The effect of a hypermedia learning environment on middle school students' motivation, attitude, and science knowledge. *Computers in the Schools, 22*(3/4), 159-171.

Liu, M, & Bera, S. (2005). An analysis of cognitive tool use patterns in a hypermedia learning environment. *Educational Technology Research and Development, 53*(1), 5-21.

Liu, M., Bera, S., Corliss, S., Svinicki, M., & Beth, A. (2004). Understanding the connection between cognitive tool use and cognitive processes as used by sixth graders in a problem-based hypermedia learning environment. *Journal of Educational Computing Research. 31*(3), 309-334.

Liu, M., Williams, D., & Pedersen, S. (2002). Alien Rescue: A problem-based hypermedia learning environment for middle school science. *Journal of Educational Technology Systems, 30*, 255-270.

Maehr, M. L. (1976). Continuing motivation: An analysis of a seldom considered educational outcome. *Review of Educational Research, 46*(3), 443-462.

Malone, T. W. (1981). Toward a theory of intrinsically motivating instruction. *Cognitive Science, 4*, 333-369.

Malone, T. W., & Lepper, M. R. (1987). Making learning fun: A taxonomy of intrinsic motivations for learning. In R. E. Snow & M. J. Farr (Eds.), *Aptitude, Learning andIinstruction: Cognitive and Affective Process Analysis 3*, 223-253. Hillsdale, NJ: Lawrence Erlbaum Associates.

Maslow, A. H. (1955). *Deficiency Motivation and Growth Motivation*. Paper presented at the Nebraska Symposium on Motivation.

National Science Board (1999). Preparing our children: Math and science education in the national interest. Retrieved November 10, 1999, http://www.nsf.gov/pubs/1999/nsb9931/start.htm

Norman, G. R., & Schmidt, H. G. (1992). The psychological basis of problem-based learning: A review of the evidence. *Academic Medicine, 67*(9), 557-565.

Okan, Z. (2003). Edutainment: Is learning at risk? *British Journal of Educational Technology, 34*(3), 255-264.

Osborne, J., Simon, S., & Collins, S. (2003). Attitudes towards science: A review of the literature and its implication. *International Journal of Science Education, 25*(9), 1049-1079.

Petri, H. L. (1981). Motivation: theory and research. Belmont, CA: Wadsworth Publishing Company.

Piaget, J. (1977). Equilibration of cognitive structures. New York: Viking.

Pintrich, P., & Schunk, D. H. (2002). Motivation in education: Theory, research, and applications (2nd Ed.). Upper Saddle River, NJ: Prentice Hall.

Ryan, R. M., & Deci, E. L. (2000). Self-determination theory and the facilitation of intrinsic motivation, social development, and well-being. *American Psychologist, 55*(1), 68-78.

Savery, J. R., & Duffy, T. M. (1995). Problem-based learning: An instructional model and its constructivist framework. In B. Wilson (Ed.), *Constructivist Learning Environments: Case Studies in Instructional Design, 35,* 31-38. Englewood Cliffs, NJ: Educational Technology Publications.

Shernoff, D. J., Csikszentmihalyi, M., Schneider, B., & Shernoff, E. S. (2003). Student engagement in high school classrooms from the perspective of flow theory. *School Psychology Quarterly, 18*(2), 158-176.

Stake, J. E., & Mares, K. R. (2001). Science enrichment programs for gifted high school girls and boys: Predictors of program impact on science confidence and motivation. *Journal of Research in Science Teaching, 38*(10), 1065-1088.

Stepien, W. J., Gallagher, S. A., & Workman, D. (1993). Problem-based learning for traditional and interdisciplinary classrooms. *Journal for the Education of the Gifted, 16*(4), 338-357.

Stipek. D. (1993). *Motivation to learn: From theory to practice.* Needham Heights, MA: Allyn & Bacon.

Suchman, L., & Jordan, B. (1990). Interactional troubles in face-to-face survey interviews. *Journal of the American Statistical Association, 85*(409), 232-241.

Tuan, H. L., Chin, C. C., & Shieh, S. H. (2005). The development of a questionnaire to measure students' motivation towards science learning. Research Report. *International Journal of Science Education, 27*(6), 639-654.

Vinter, A., & Perruchet, P. (2000). Implicit learning in children is not related to age: Evidence from drawing behavior. *Child Development, 71*(5), 1223-1240.

Vygotsky, L. S. (2006). *Mind in Society: Development of Higher Psychological Processes.* Cambridge, Massachusetts: Harvard University Press.

Wentzel, K. R. (1999). Social-motivational processes and interpersonal relationships: Implications for understanding. *Journal of Educational Psychology, 91*(1), 76-97.

ADDITIONAL READINGS

Alsop, S., & Watts, M. (2003). Science education and affect. *International Journal of Science Education, 25*(9), 1043-1047.

Ames, C. (1992). Achievement Goals and the Classroom Motivational Climate. In D. H. Shunk & J. L. Meece (Eds.), *Student Perceptions in the Classroom* (pp. 327-348). Hillsdale: Lawrence Erlbaum Associates.

Anderman, E. M., & Maehr, M. L. (1994). Motivation and Schooling in the Middle Grades. *Review of Educational Research, 64*(2), 287-309.

Barab, S., Thomas, M., Dodge, T., Carteaux, R., & Tuzun, H. (2005). Making Learning Fun: Quest Atlantis, A Game Without Guns. *Educational Technology Research and Development, 53*(1), 86-107.

Dweck, C. S., & Leggett, E. L. (1988). A Social-Cognitive Approach to Motivation and Personality. *Psychological Review, 95*(2), 256-273.

Garris, R., & Ahlers, R. (2002). Games, motivation, and learning: A research and practice model. *Simulation & Gaming, 33*(4), 441-467.

Gee, J. P. (2003). *What Video Games Have to Teach Us About Learning and Literacy.* New York, NY: Palgrave Macmillan.

Guay, F., Boggiano, A. K., & Vallerand, R. J. (2001). Autonomy support, intrinsic motivation, and perceived competence: Conceptual and empirical linkages. *Personality and Social Psychology Bulletin, 27*(6), 643-650.

Rieber, L. P., & Matzko, M. J. (2001). Serious Design for Serious Play in Physics. *Educational Technology, 41*(1), 14-24.

Schiefele, U. (1991). Interest, Learning, and Motivation. *Educational Psychologist, 26*(3-4), 299-323.

Simpkins, S. D., Davis-Kean, P. E., & Eccles, J. S. (2006). Math and Science Motivation: A Longitudinal Examination of the Links Between Choices and Beliefs. *Developmental Psychology, 42*(1), 70-83.

Weiner, B. (2000). Intrapersonal and Interpersonal Theories of Motivation from an Attributional Perspective. *Educational Psychology Review. 12*(1), 1-14.

Section III
Teaching and Learning with Multimedia

Chapter XI
The Cognitive Demands of Student–Centered, Web–Based Multimedia:
Current and Emerging Perspectives

Michael J. Hannafin
University of Georgia, USA

Richard E. West
University of Georgia, USA

Craig E. Shepherd
University of Wyoming, USA

ABSTRACT

This chapter examines the cognitive demands of student-centered learning from, and with, Web-based multimedia. In contrast to externally-structured directed learning, during the student-centered learning, the individual assumes responsibility for determining learning goals, monitoring progress toward meeting goals, adjusting or adapting approaches as warranted, and determining when individual goals have been adequately addressed. These tasks can be particularly challenging in learning from the World Wide Web, where billions of resources address a variety of needs. The individual, in effect, must identify which tools and resources are available and appropriate, how to assemble them, and how to manage the process to support unique learning goals. We briefly analyze the applicability of current cognitive principles to learning from Web-based multimedia, review and critically analyze research and practice specific to student-centered learning from Web-based multimedia, and describe implications for research.

INTRODUCTION

Several time-tested cognitive principles are applicable to both face-to-face and print-based learning environments. Indeed, the research summarized throughout this text supports several principles and constructs relevant to multimedia. However, much of this research is rooted in objectivist epistemology, where the individual selects, organizes, and integrates knowledge in an effort to acquire and demonstrate externally prescribed, canonical meaning. While the effectiveness of didactic, directed methods have been demonstrated using multimedia (see, for example, Azevedo, Moss, Greene, Winters, & Cromley, 2008; Gerjets, Scheiter, & Schuh, 2008), significant growth has been evident in user-centered, Web-based multimedia applications that are individually rather than externally directed and managed.

This chapter focuses on student-centered learning in Web-based multimedia environments wherein the individual assumes primacy in determining goals, selecting or devising approaches to address these goals, and responsibility for interpreting and constructing unique meaning. We examine the applicability of research related to Web-based multimedia and address both similarities and differences in cognitive demands between ill-structured and externally-structured multimedia learning environments. The purposes of the chapter are to briefly review selected principles of human cognition that are applicable to Web-based multimedia, to review cognitive perspectives, research, and practice specific to student-centered learning from Web-based multimedia, and to describe implications for research, theory, and practice.

BACKGROUND

Cognitive Roots of Technology-Enhanced Learning

During the past two decades, researchers have studied technology-enhanced learning from several perspectives. Initially, for example, we examined the applicability of cognitive theories to computer-based instruction (Hannafin & Rieber, 1989; Hooper & Hannafin, 1991). It became apparent that while many research-based learning and cognition principles were readily applicable, epistemological shifts and advances in technologies raised important questions about the nature of computer-assisted learning. Constructivists suggested basic shifts in both beliefs as to the locus of knowledge and educational practices (Jonassen, 1991). Concurrently, technologies emerged that extended, augmented, and/or supplanted individual cognitive processes, reflecting a shift from delivery to tools that supported and enhanced thinking (Iiyoshi, Hannafin, & Wang, 2005). Thus, the focus on technology and constructivist, student-centered approaches has become increasingly evident in the efforts of cognition and multimedia theorists, researchers, and practitioners.

Hannafin, Land and Oliver (1999) described student-centered activity during "open learning" where the locus of activity and control shifts from external to individual responsibility for establishing learning goals and/or determining learning means. As a result, the cognitive demands shift from selecting and processing externally-provided stimuli to anticipating and seeking based on individual needs and learning goals. In many cases, the associated cognitive shifts have proven problematic. Researchers have noted that students failed to develop theories or explanations and retained initial misconceptions (de Jong & Van

Joolingen, 1998; Gyllenhaal & Perry, 1998; Land & Hannafin, 1997; Nicaise & Crane, 1999), to reflect or enact metacognitive processes (Atkins & Blissett, 1992; Hill & Hannafin, 1997; Wallace & Kupperman, 1997), and to develop coherent, evidence-based explanations (Land & Greene, 2000; Nicaise & Crane, 1999). Land (2000, pp 75-76) concluded that without effective support,

misperceptions, misinterpretations, or ineffective strategy use ... can lead to significant misunderstandings that are difficult to detect or repair. When learners have little prior knowledge ... metacognitive and prior knowledge are needed to ask good questions and to make sense out of the data and events being modeled.

The continued emergence of the World Wide Web has both extended and, to some extent, redefined user interactions involving multimedia. Hill and Hannafin (2001) described transformations where heretofore intact traditional media have been increasingly granularized, noting that while "Predigital educational resources conveyed meaning consistent with and supportive of established goals and standards" (p. 38), a digital resource's "meaning is influenced more by the diversity than the singularity of the perspectives taken...resources are accessed and interpreted for meaning, evaluated for veracity and utility, compared with competing perspectives, and acted upon" (p. 40). In effect, the increased potential for granularity alters the cognitive demands associated with resource access and use. Similarly, individual self-regulation, metacognitive, and navigation capabilities vary considerably across a vast and ill-structured array of Web resources (Land & Hannafin, 2000).

Thus, student-centered, Web-based learning may reflect fundamental shifts in cognitive load requirements as well as the foundations and assumptions underlying their design and use (Hannafin & Land, 1997). While several principles and constructs may well provide a reasonable basis for

extrapolation, the demands of student-centered, Web-based learning often vary as a function of available resources and the learner's intent. In the following sections, we briefly highlight selective research on cognition and multimedia, examine similarities and differences attributed to student-centered learning, and identify implications for future study.

Externally Mediated Multimedia Learning: A Primer

Perception, Selection, and Encoding

According to information processing theory, learners must first perceive information in order to encode it. This perception is mediated by prior knowledge and mental models. Learners selectively attend to particular aspects of an instructional message, which influences what is processed and encoded (Lieberman, 2000; Schacter, 1990). Multimedia researchers report that the format or design of the message can influence the perception and selection processes. Seels, Berry, Fullerton, and Horn (1996) grouped this research according to visual complexity (i.e., how much information is presented) and perceptual salience (i.e., how that information may be more or less perceptible due to differences in intensity, contrast, change, and novelty).

Recent perspectives on multimedia encoding, reflected in Mayer's (2005) Cognitive Theory of Multimedia Learning (CTML), were influenced by three perspectives: cognitive load theory, dual-coding theory, and constructivist learning theory. Cognitive load theory suggests that cognitive resources are limited in the amount of information that can be processed at a given time. Whereas dual-coding theory (Clark & Paivio, 1991) describes independent verbal and visual processing systems during acquisition, constructivists suggest that students learn by generating uniquely individual representations. CTML, therefore, emphasizes the use of both verbal and visual representations to foster constructivist thinking and deep learning. According to CTML, most students attend to key words in a narration and hold them simultaneously in verbal working memory; they also hold key aspects of the multimedia presentation in visual working memory. The learner then builds mental connections between the two types of information, stimulating cause-and-effect chains that are linked with and through prior knowledge (Mayer & Moreno, 2005, 1998).

In support of this theory, Mayer and his colleagues reported that students learn more effectively through narration and animation than by either method alone (Mayer & Anderson, 1991), and that visual and verbal components are best when occurring simultaneously rather than successively. In effect, the visual and verbal information is processed concurrently in working memory, enabling connections between the two to be readily established (Mayer & Anderson, 1992). Mayer and Moreno (2005) further suggested that multimedia may help students to transfer knowledge to problem solving situations when verbal/visual components are presented simultaneously, extraneous material is reduced or eliminated, presentations include narration and animation (rather than animation and on-screen text), and presentations provide narration and animations only (versus redundant transcriptions, on-screen text, and animations depicting verbal concepts).

Processing and Retrieving

According to information processing theory, information is processed by activating schemata related to new knowledge: The greater schemata are activated, the richer the processing and the deeper the learning. John Anderson (1996) noted that the number of concepts activated at a given point in time constitutes the capacity of working memory. Anderson theorized that encoding, storage, retrieval, matching, and execution processes influence temporal, spatial, or abstract content in working memory. As information is encoded and temporarily stored in working (then declarative) memory, relevant connected concepts are retrieved and matched to new information, thereby becoming synthesized to make a new idea. Mayer extended these notions, and hypothesized that the depth and meaningfulness of processing is influenced by selection of relevant stimuli, organization of information in memory, and integration of new knowledge with prior mental schemas.

Several researchers have documented the influence of depth of processing. In one study, Evans and Gibbons (2007) divided 33 undergraduates into groups that used either an interactive or non-interactive computer-based multimedia lesson about how to operate a bicycle pump. The interactive system allowed users to control the pace of instruction, provided interactive simulations, and contained self-assessment questions. The interactive group performed significantly better and needed less time to perform on both memorization and problem-solving assessments. Other researchers reported that multimedia deepened processing while encouraging self-explanation (Roy, Chi, & Mayer, 2005).

According to social agency theorists, multimedia can also improve the meaningfulness of learning when the environments closely approximate human interaction. Atkinson, Mayer, and Merrill (2005) explored the influence of narration on near and far transfer. In experiments with high school students and beginning-level college students, the researchers gave participants worked-out examples of mathematical word problems accompanied by either a human-sounding voice narration or a machine-synthesized voice. They then assessed performance on near and far transfer posttest items as well as perceptions of the narrations. With both groups, transfer improved when the pedagogical agent narration was provided via a human-sounding voice; students also preferred "human" over "machine" narration.

In related studies, Mayer, Sobko, and Mautone (2003) gave 68 college students a narrated animation about how lightning forms; half received a narration with a native English accent while the others received English narration with a Russian accent. In a second study, 40 college students received either native narration or a computer-synthesized narration. Again, in both cases, students reported a significant "voice" effect: Transfer was most effective with native narration and students again preferred the native voice. Mayer, Fennell, Farmer, and Campbell (2004) also reported that personalizing narrated animations by changing instances of "the" to "your" significantly improved transfer. In a series of experiments, they divided college students into personalized ("your") or non-personalized ("the") groups and asked them to complete a retention and transfer posttest following the lesson. In each experiment, students receiving the personalized multimedia presentation performed significantly better on transfer tests.

These studies demonstrate the potential for multimedia instruction to positively impact the ability of students to process, and later retrieve information. This processing and learning can be deepened by using multimedia to stimulate interactivity or aspects of a student's experience, such as their native dialect. Presumably, according to information processing theory, students actively engage information and activate multiple schemas to assimilate as they associate new with prior knowledge.

Cognitive Styles and Strategies

According to information processing theory, the ability to encode, structure, and retrieve information is mediated by individual learning styles, levels of motivation, and self-regulatory tendencies. Multimedia has been hailed for its potential to customize learning to individual needs (M. Hannafin, K. Hannafin, Hooper, Rieber, & Kini, 1996). Indeed, Smith and Woody (2000)

divided 80 college students into groups receiving the same material either through multimedia or nonvisual lectures. By determining the students' learning style through a visual/verbal orientation assessment, the researchers reported that visual learners in the multimedia environment performed most effectively.

However, cognitive style and learning style differences may not be apparent in many contexts. Indeed, researchers have been unable to generate convincing evidence for differentiating multimedia instruction based on presumed verbal or visual learner styles. Massa and Mayer (2006) used help screens with text, illustrations, both, or neither (no help given) to assess participants' visual or verbal preferences and assigned them to various combinations based on their learning preferences. Across three experiments, verbal and visual learners perform comparably on a learning test, thus providing no evidence for hypothesized interactions between their learning style and mode of presentation.

Self-Regulation

Azevedo conducted several studies examining the relationship between self-regulatory processes and scaffolding in multimedia contexts (see, for example, Azevedo & Cromley, 2004; Azevedo, Cromley, Winters, Moss, & Greene, 2005; Azevedo, Guthrie, & Seibert, 2004; Azevedo, et al., 2008; Azevedo, Winters, & Moos, 2004; Greene & Azevedo, 2007; Moos & Azevedo, 2006). This series of studies examined the influence of adaptive scaffolding, fixed scaffolding, and no scaffolding on student comprehension of complex science ideas, learning of declarative knowledge, and self-regulation of learning. Azevedo (2005) concluded that the learning of complex science topics is best achieved through externally guided or adaptive human scaffolding designed to augment both the subject material and support self-regulation processes.

Cognition and Web-Based Learning

Substantial research has been published related to the Web's impact on motivation, cognitive demands, and metacognition. While multimedia has played an important role in learning, student-centered learning via Web's ill-structured resources and tools can differ markedly from learning via designer-centered instruction featuring structured Web resources.

Motivation

Motivation has been characterized as the process of encouraging desirable behavior to accomplish particular goals (Driscoll, 2000; Schunk, 1990). Classically, motivation is derived from events of incentives external to the learner (extrinsic) or from values and goals internal to the learner (intrinsic). Web-based learning has improved student motivation in situations involving the use of newer, particularly innovative, technology. For example, Hee Jun and Johnson (2005) studied participant learning and motivation during an online masters degree program using video-based and text-based instruction. The researchers found positive differences in students' motivation and perceived learning favoring video-based instruction. Multimedia motivation may also be influenced by gender and learning styles. Hsinyi, Chin-Chung, and Ying-Tien (2006) reported that male undergraduates were more motivated to learn online than females, and that those who perceive the Web to be a leisure tool rather than a functional tool reported higher communicative self-efficacy and more positive attitudes.

Astleitner and Wiesner (2004) argued that motivational processes have been largely ignored in multimedia learning theory. While technology generally (and the Web specifically) have been lauded for increasing student motivation to learn, the scant available research evidence reveals contradictory results. Whipp and Chiarelli (2004) analyzed interview transcripts, course documents, and student journals for six students who were using Lotus Notes/Learning Space for their online module. The researchers reported that student motivation varied based upon how well they managed the technical and social aspects of the course. Other researchers (West, Waddoups, & Graham, 2007; West, Waddoups, Kennedy, & Graham, 2007) examined the adoption and use of a course management system by 120 instructors and 160 students across 13 colleges and concluded that technical challenges involved with learning the system influenced negatively both instructors' and students' satisfaction with and motivation to use it.

Finally, Schrum, Burbank, Engle, Chambers, and Glassett (2005) studied the motivation of 22 higher education faculty from 8 colleges and universities enrolled in an online professional development course. Faculty members reported that difficulties in sustaining the learning community and learning new technologies reduced their motivation to participate. Thus, contrary to popular and intuitive beliefs about the motivational nature of Web-based learning, some research indicates that both learner and teacher motivation may decline rather than improve when Web-based technologies are difficult to learn or perform unreliably.

Cognitive Demands

Information processing, encoding, and retrieving requirements demand the simultaneous management of multiple cognitive resources; multimedia attributes may enhance or detract from learning. Intrinsic cognitive load reflects the complexity inherent in the information to be learned; germane cognitive load is the effort needed to create relevant, new schemas and mental models to aid in future learning; and extraneous cognitive load is a function of non-relevant cognitive requirements associated with the instructional materials, method, and environment (Gerjets & Scheiter, 2003; van Merrionboer & Ayres, 2005; Renkl & Atkinson, 2003).

Many researchers have concluded that hyperlinked learning materials can significantly increase extraneous cognitive load (Niederhauser, Reynolds, Salmen, & Skolmoski, 2000). Eveland and Dunwoody (2001), for example, compared the performance of 219 students assigned to groups browsing a Website with different hyperlinking and navigation structures with a paper-based format. The paper-based control group outperformed two of the three online groups, indicating that using hyperlinked materials likely increased extraneous cognitive load.

Others researchers have reported that familiarity with learning technologies influences cognitive load. In one study, Clarke, Ayres, and Sweller (2005) assigned 24 Australian 9th graders into groups based on their experience using spreadsheets and their mathematics abilities, and compared learning when instruction on spreadsheet software was given prior to or concurrent with math instruction. They reported that student performance improved when they taught the technology to the students before the content. Presumably, learning both the computer applications and the mathematics simultaneously increased extraneous cognitive load associated with learning domain-related concepts. Given the unusual demands associated with student-centered, Web-based, multimedia learning, the ability to meter or manage cognitive load may prove essential for online students (Hill, Domizi, Kim, Kim, & Hannafin, 2007; Hill, Hannafin & Domizi, 2005).

Nonlinear Websites may increase germane cognitive load for particular types of learning, but increase extraneous cognitive load for text-based learning (Eveland, et al., 2001). In an online learning study, Eveland, Cortese, Park and Dunwoody (2004) observed two groups (college students and nonstudents) as they explored Websites using either linear or nonlinear navigation structures to learn about a health topic. By comparing evidence of factual knowledge with understanding of relationships between concepts

(knowledge structure density), they concluded that students learned factual information best from linear Websites, but understood the relationships between the concepts better with the nonlinear Websites. In effect, Web-based multimedia learning can also increase germane cognitive load and learning efficiency.

Metacognition

Some researchers have suggested that hyperlinked multimedia learning environments may improve students' abilities to monitor their learning. In self-paced computer-based education, learning often occurs sequentially, is presented in multiple modes, and allows students to review their progress periodically. This may improve metacognitive abilities by "prompting learners to reflect on their learning progress and allowing them to repeat material at critical junctures if needed" (Workman, 2004, p. 520). Kaufman (2004) studied 119 undergraduate students either taking freeform notes or strategic notes with the aid of a matrix. While taking notes, some students received prompts to reflect on their learning and notetaking. The combination of matrix-structured notes and metacognitive scaffolding yielded the greatest improvement in achievement. This benefit was realized with only three prompts per hour of notetaking. Similarly, when Bannert (2003) asked 40 university students to study psychology online for 35 minutes, those that received only three prompts performed significantly better on posttests.

Zion, Michalsky, and Mevarech (2005) divided 407 Israeli 10th-grade microbiology students according to their mode of instruction [asynchronous learning network (ALN) or face-to-face]; one group in each mode of instruction was provided metacognitive scaffolding. Zion, et al. reported that the ALN group receiving scaffolding performed significantly better than the face-to-face group without, but no differences were found between the ALN group without scaffolding and the face-to-face group without scaffolding. These findings suggest that online learning may be most conducive to and effective for learning when metacognitive scaffolding is provided.

Students who have, or develop, metacognitive strategies tend to perform more successfully than those who do not. Smidt and Heigelheimer (2004) interviewed 9 adult Web-based learners identified as high, middle, or low-performing regarding their learning strategies, and subsequently categorized strategies as cognitive or metacognitive. Only advanced learners used strategies (as well as cognitive ones). Intermediate and lower-level students mainly relied on cognitive strategies only, suggesting that advanced metacognitive abilities may be associated with effective online learning.

Land and Greene (2000) found metacognitive knowledge can compensate for limited subject matter understanding. They studied four undergraduate preservice teachers working alone, in pairs, or in groups during an online instructional technology course. Through in-depth case study analysis, Land and Greene reported that two participants demonstrated metacognitive knowledge based on their domain knowledge, but the two with low domain knowledge did not.

Student-Centered Learning

Although some researchers have demonstrated multimedia effects on learning, most emphasized direct instruction (Jonassen, 1991). With the re-emergence of constructivism, researchers have shifted attention from objectivist models that emphasize external mediation and meaning to uniquely individual perspectives (Hannafin & Land, 1997; Land & Hannafin, 1996). Building from Piaget (1976) and Vygotsky (1978), constructivists assert that meaning is derived from and interpreted through individual beliefs, experiences, and social contexts. Thus, individual meaning is constructed through personal interactions with the world rather than assimilations (Phillips, 1995).

The American Psychological Association's learner-centered psychological principles (APA Work Group of the Board of Educational Affairs, 1997) delineated criteria for effective student-centered learning design and implementation (Alexander & Murphy, 1998). Recently, researchers have identified several assumptions that differentiate constructivist from externally-based perspectives. We focus on assumptions regarding the locus and nature of knowledge, role of context, and prior experiences.

Locus and Nature of Knowledge

Constructivists assert that learners construct meaning uniquely based on personal interactions with society, individuals, and objects. Multimedia environments often provide resources for learners to manage their own learning through exploration, hypothesis formation, and student-relevant feedback (Hannafin & Land, 1997; Orrill, 2001). Papert (1980, 1993), for example, advocated open-ended multimedia tools to promote problem solving activities among children. By writing directions for a turtle, Papert reported that explorations of angles, vectors, and geometry principles fostered deeper student understanding than directed classroom activity. Similarly, Uribe, Klein, and Sullivan (2003) found that when students collaborated as dyads on ill-defined problems in an online course, they outperformed individuals working alone and spent more time investigating problems. Using online supports and group collaboration, learners were able to explore ill-defined problems, consider and test hypotheses each might have otherwise overlooked, and gain a better understanding of problem-solving processes.

McCombs and Whisler (1997) described learner-centered environments as places where learners engage in complex and relevant activities, collaborate with their peers, and employ resources such as technology to collect, analyze, and represent information. However, evidence of their use in schools is limited (McCombs, 2001,

2003). Although student-centered learning environments are believed to foster exploration and hypothesis formation, implementation has proven problematic. Remillard's (2005) synthesis of research indicated that teachers' content knowledge, pedagogical content knowledge, beliefs, and their interpretation of the curriculum influenced how learner-centered activities are enacted in classrooms. Researchers have documented instances where teachers undermined learner-centered activities by supplying rote algorithms for students (Cognition and Technology Group at Vanderbilt: CTGV, 1992; Doyle, 1988; Greeno, 1983).

It has also proven difficult to establish relationships between multimedia technology and student learning (e.g., Roschelle, Pea, Hoadley, Gordin, & Means, 2001). Some researchers have documented positive effects when using technology to facilitate problem solving, conceptual development, and critical thinking (CTGV, 1992; Ringstaff & Kelley, 2002; Sandholtz, Ringstaff, & Dwyer, 1997). Wenglinsky (1998) reported that where teachers used technology in conjunction with learner-centered pedagogies, classes scored significantly higher on the mathematics portion of the National Assessment of Educational Progress (NAEP) than classes that did not. According to the 2000 NAEP mathematics assessment, 8th graders who used multimedia for mathematics drill and practice scored significantly lower than peers who used no technology (NCES, 2000). Clearly, both the nature of the learning task and the extent to which learner-centered activity is evident influence student learning.

Although some research suggests that multimedia and Web-based tools can promote deeper learning when intended strategies are followed, these strategies are often not utilized. In an effort to deepen understanding of mathematics through investigation, teachers have engaged open-ended environments during professional development. Orrill (2006) created an extensive Website including open-ended investigations, a mathematics dictionary, discussion board, and electronic portfolios. Teachers explored available resources, selected problems, and identified their own instructional paths (combined with attendance in face-to-face workshops). Whereas improvements in mathematics skills and depth of knowledge were expected, teachers typically focused on technology skills and perceptions of student knowledge and did not refine their own mathematics understandings and skills.

Context

According to Norman (2002), objects contain symbols that orient individuals to their use; well-designed symbols identify how the object should be used. Societal norms also affect how we interact differently in different contexts. Individuals may behave differently when eating at a restaurant with friends or family than when eating at the same restaurant with business associates. Events are linked through food consumption, similar tools are used, and the location is identical, but individual goals and methods for achieving those goals alters how people interact. Context is considered integral to, rather than simply a stimulus for, learning (Brown, Collins, & Duguid, 1989).

Given the importance of context, student-centered learning environments often rely on authentic experiences or realistic stories to facilitate interaction and learning. In the Jasper Woodbury Series (CTGV, 1991, 1992), students watched a short video to provide context and orient learning before solving mathematics problems situated in realistic settings (e.g., determining how much gas is needed and what route to take to navigate a boat to desired locations). Thus, contexts may help students to identify learning goals, form and test hypotheses, and situate learning in authentic experiences (Land & Hannafin, 1997).

Prior Experience

Prior experiences, considered critical across virtually all approaches, are posited to influence how individuals interact with and acquire meaning during student-centered learning (e.g., Schuh, 2003). Schön (1983) described how experienced professionals could attend to work-related stimuli, process information, and make immediate decisions because of their deep understanding of the involved processes. Although professionals receive similar preparation prior to entering their fields, field experiences enable practitioners to attend to and interact with their environment in ways unavailable to novices. According to Schön, prior experiences help seasoned professions attend to, interact with, and construct meaning from present situations more rapidly than those without prior experiences.

In their review, Kalyuga, Ayers, Chandler, and Sweller (2003) identified how scaffolds intended to structure experiences can guide novices through novel situations but yield negative consequences among experts who need no guidance. The researchers suggested that experts who receive too much support experience a redundancy effect that hinders learning and performance. We may underestimate how prior experience and expertise, their presence as well as limitations, affect on learning and using Web-based tools to support student-centered inquiry among novices compared with experts.

Distinctions between Externally-Directed and Student-Centered Web-Based Multimedia

Although Web-enhanced multimedia has facilitated several aspects of student-centered learning, we examine the role of technology system knowledge, orientation, misconceptions, knowledge utility, and motivation.

System Knowledge

Recent research suggests that familiarity with multimedia and Web-based tools may play a significant role in individual success or failure.

Song, Singleton, Hill, and Koh (2004) administered a survey to assess perceived supports and challenges to online learning environments to 74 university students. They found that students who preferred online learning reported greater previous knowledge of online tools and managed their time more efficiently than students preferring traditional instruction. Hill and Hannafin (1997) asked 15 pre- and inservice teachers to locate Internet content and grade-appropriate materials on a subject of their choosing. They reported that those with previous experience with the Internet were more successful and reported greater confidence in the task—regardless of their prior teaching experiences. In both studies, researchers noted that prior tool expertise facilitated learning more than prior domain knowledge or experience. Thus, in some contexts, familiarity with specific Web-based tools may better predict success than prior domain knowledge and experience.

Disorientation

Because student-centered learning environments support individual goals and trajectories, Web-based tools often provide hyperlinks to a multitude of varied resources and materials. Yet, researchers have found that hypertext links can confuse and overtax learners. Niederhauser, et al. (2000) reviewed documents read by 39 students using a presentation shell without related multimedia (e.g., graphics, video, audio), controlling for reading ability and background knowledge. Students were given complete control regarding navigation and were provided with a topic map for guidance purposes. Researchers found that even the topic guidance map had minimal effects on student learning, perhaps because students chose to use the maps only at the beginning or the end of their learning session rather than continuously. Students who disregarded the hypertext links and read all materials sequentially performed better than those who compared and contrasted text using hyperlinks, suggesting that the external sequence was more effective in conveying intended knowledge than user-selected, hypertext-based links. Similar findings were reported by Eveland and Dunwoody (2001) when examining instruction from printed and Web-based text. Given the volume and ill-structured nature of available resources, becoming "lost in hyperspace"—initially described for hypertext navigation (e.g., Conklin, 1987; Edwards & Hardman, 1999), has become increasingly problematic during Web-based, student-centered learning (e.g., Baylor, 2001; Chen, Lee, & Chen, 2005; Chiu & Wang, 2000).

Given the rapidly growing but ill-structured nature of the Web, learners need to identify, select, and evaluate available resources based on their unique tasks and goals. Traditionally, Web resources provided physical locations and narrative descriptors to convey their contents. More recently, metadata have emerged to better catalogue and describe functionality (Friesen & Anderson, 2004; Maule, 2001). Different metadata mechanisms and standards (e.g., Dublin Core, SCORM) have emerged. While beneficial in cataloguing Web-based materials based on designer-intended goals and objectives, current metadata methods may be insufficient to support student-generated goals. Cataloguing systems often rely on content creators to generate metadata tags for online materials (Gaide, 2004; Jones, 2003; Maule, 2001). Intelligent tutoring systems have used prior assessment results, individually selected learning goals (limited to those embedded within the system), and learning traits to personalize instruction (Papanikolaou, Grigoriadou, Magoulas, & Kornilakis, 2002). While potentially effective, adaptive tools are rarely available via Web-based learning. Thus, current metadata technology may provide generic, cursory references and prove insufficient to support unique learner goals.

Misconceptions

Typically, constructivist learning environments emphasize personal investigation and hypothesis formation and testing. Without explicit support, learners may fail to detect inaccurate information or reject erroneous hypotheses in the face of contradictory evidence. Land and Zembal-Saul (2003), for example, developed student-centered labs and computer-based inquiries into the nature of light. Participants obtained evidence during experiments, stored it in portfolios with their findings, and generated hypotheses to orient future inquiries. While some groups benefited from computer-assisted inquiry, others relied on faulty results from prior experiments and subsequently misdirected future inquiries. Additionally, they retained erroneous results even when later studies contradicted them. Land and Zembal-Saul suggested that student-centered inquiry functioned as anticipated when students had sufficient background knowledge, self-evaluated their knowledge limitations, engaged in critical questioning and clarification, and received feedback to challenge faulty explanations. This "situated learning paradox" (Land & Hannafin, 2000, p. 18) suggests that prior knowledge, while important for orienting learners and helping them make sense of environmental phenomena, is often based on incomplete and inaccurate misconceptions. Without appropriate support, misinformation and disinformation may go undetected. Fundamental misunderstandings may become reified rather than reconciled.

Knowledge Utility

Nearly a century ago, Whitehead (1929) distinguished between transferable knowledge (knowledge as a tool) versus non-transferable knowledge (inert knowledge). Inert knowledge is relevant to well-defined, specific tasks such as individual lesson or test preparation, but may have limited productive value beyond the immediate context. Rote memorization of mathematical algorithms, for example, may enable a child to mimic timestables but prove of little use in actually solving everyday arithmetic problems.

Tool-based knowledge, valued in student-centered learning, is presumed to facilitate goal acquisition and transfer to differing contexts. When students grasp the underlying reasoning behind the algorithms and their application to authentic problems, their knowledge becomes a tool that facilitates learning and problem solving in other contexts. Yet, researchers suggest that tools touted to support student-centered learning are often used inappropriately and foster inert knowledge (CTGV, 1992; Doyle, 1988). Because learners select individual goals, resources and activities, existing metadata may fail to support student-centered Web-based learning and the resulting knowledge may or may not prove transferable.

Scaffolding

Several frameworks have been proposed to account for similarities and differences between "human" and technology-enhanced scaffolds (see, for example, Ge & Er, 2005; Hogan & Pressley, 1997; Lepper, Drake, & O'Donnell-Johnson, 1997; Jacobson, 2008; Masterman & Rogers, 2002; Puntambekar & Hubscher, 2005). Traditionally, scaffolding supported the learning of externally-defined concepts. With the shift to individually mediated learning, scaffolding has become increasingly process oriented. In their multimedia research, Saye and Brush (2007) distinguished between "hard" and "soft" scaffolds: Hard scaffolds are fixed, and primarily technology-mediated while soft scaffolds are usually provided by humans and thus are customizable and negotiable. According to Sharma and Hannafin (2007), hard scaffolds are presumed to support common learning needs across students, freeing the instructor to provide adaptable, on-demand, contextually sensitive support based on emergent, individual needs. Kim, Hannafin, and Bryan (2007) proposed a scaffolding framework to optimize the interplay between and among technology, teachers and students in everyday

rather than theoretically ideal learning contexts. However, they note that despite the wealth of available research for externally defined learning goals, little progress has been made in scaffolding the individual's unique learning efforts in open, largely ill-structured learning environments.

Attitudes, Beliefs and Practices

According to Zimmerman and Bandura (1994), self-efficacy involves one's beliefs about the ability to influence events: Those with high self-efficacy tend to view difficult tasks as a challenge while those with low self-efficacy often avoid difficult tasks. Self-efficacy may be influenced, positively or negatively, by past experiences (Song et al., 2004), modeling (Zimmerman & Bandura, 1994), and feedback (Land & Zembal-Saul, 2003). In student-centered environments, the individual assumes responsibility for goal attainment and resource selection, thereby increasing the cognitive demands associated with learning.

Similarly, engagement is influenced by individual prior beliefs, goals, and expectations, which affect how learners approach and interact with learning activities (King & Kitchener, 2004; Schommer, 1993). According to Song, Hannafin and Hill (2007), conflicts arise when learners engage resources that are inconsistent or incompatible with their individual goals and beliefs—especially when they are unable to identify and reconcile the differences. Thus, while designers and instructors of Web-based multimedia may assume that extending the array of resources will enhance learning, the individual's familiarity, beliefs, motivations, and practices may influence the extent to which available resources complement or confound student-centered learning.

CONCLUSION

We began this chapter by noting that cognitive psychology research and theory has made significant contributions to learning from multimedia and highlighting the applicability of several constructs. With the shift to student-centered learning underscores important, however, often-fundamental differences become apparent in underlying epistemology, foundations, and assumptions about the nature and locus of learning activity. These shifts require that we reconsider the applicability of several theories and constructs, determine where we need to modify or develop alternative perspectives and approaches, and develop appropriate methodologies to pursue these issues and evolve our knowledge base accordingly.

FUTURE DIRECTIONS

We highlight five questions related to student-centered learning from and with Web-based multimedia, and provide our perspectives on research needed for each.

To what extent can student-centered, Web-based learning be scaffolded? While research has yielded useful guidelines for supporting externally-specified learning, research on scaffolding student-centered learning has only begun to emerge. Since individual prior knowledge, goals, and intents are not known in advance, and they can vary dramatically across learners using the same Web-based multimedia, scaffolding often focuses on cognitive processes. Research is needed to examine where and when to provide process scaffolding, the types of scaffolding needed, and the extent to which individual goals and intents are addressed effectively (Azevedo & Jacobson, 2008).

How will individuals assess the legitimacy, veracity, and accuracy of Web-based multimedia resources? While the Web has democratized the publication of and access to information, its resources are largely unregulated. Resource quality varies widely in terms of accuracy, authority, and completeness. Web resources have been criticized for containing naïve and ill-informed

information, but also for propagating deliberate misinformation, disinformation, and propaganda. Since students must assess veracity and relevance while attempting to address their individual learning needs and monitoring their understanding, research is needed to examine how students' evaluate and adapt based on perceptions of a resource's integrity. *To what extend can/will the cognitive complexity associated with student-centered Web-based learning be addressed via hard versus soft technologies?* While the potential to intelligently adapt to individual differences holds promise, existing research suggests that soft scaffolding technologies have the potential to address the varied needs of individual student-centered learners. Unlike embedded domain supports, soft scaffolding provided by teachers, peers and other "human" resources is thought to accommodate real-time, dynamic changes in learner needs and cognitive demands. Given that research on learning strategies has provided little evidence of transfer, this claim needs to be validated.

How will individuals negotiate differences between available resources and their individual needs? Web-based multimedia resources have been developed for a broad array of needs and purposes. Some intact resources may address student-centered learning needs effectively, but most will not. Often, understanding is derived by accessing and examining individual resources that provide partial, potentially contradictory information. Their meaning for student-centered learning, in effect, must be interpreted and derived based on the individual's ongoing metacognitive efforts and supporting processes. Research is needed to examine how negotiation occurs, meaning is assembled differentially based on unique needs and goals, and the extent to which individual needs are addressed. *Will metadata standards enable students to identify relevant Web-based multimedia resources?* Some have suggested that while metadata standards have been in place for several years, they emphasize physical and audience attributes. Despite geometric increases in availability and improved accessibility, metadata standards offer only limited pedagogical utility for open and resource-based learning. Thus, the fundamental student-centered learning task of identifying candidate resources appropriate to an individual's need is complicated by the raw number of false "hits" generated by a typical search. Research is needed to develop and refine alternative metadata standards that support student-centered learning and to refine and customize search engine technology capable of identifying user-relevant resources.

REFERENCES

Alexander, P. A., & Murphy, P. K. (1998). The research base for APA's learner-centered psychological principles. In N. M. Lambert & B. L. McCombs (Eds.), *Issues in school reform: A sampler of psychological perspectives on learner-centered schools* (pp. 33-60). Washington, DC: American Psychological Association.

Anderson, J. R. (1996). *The architecture of cognition.* Mahwah, NJ: Lawrence Erlbaum Associates.

APA Work Group of the Board of Educational Affairs. (1997). *Learner-centered psychological principles: A framework for school reform and redesign.* Washington, DC: Author.

Astleitner, H., & Wiesner, C. (2004). An integrated model of multimedia learning and motivation. *Journal of Educational Multimedia and Hypermedia, 13*(1), 3.

Atkins, M., & Blissett, G. (1992). Interactive video and cognitive problem-solving skills. *Educational Technology, 32*(1), 44-50.

Atkinson, R. K., Mayer, R. E., & Merrill, M. M. (2005). Fostering social gency in multimedia learning: Examining the impact of an animated agent's voice. *Contemporary Educational Psychology, 30*(1), 117.

Azevedo, R. (2005). Using hypermedia as a meta-cognitive tool for enhancing student learning? The role of self-regulated learning. *Educational Psychologist, 40*(4), 199.

Azevedo, R., & Cromley, J. G. (2004). Does training on self-regulated learning facilitate students' learning with hypermedia? *Journal of Educational Psychology, 96*(3), 523.

Azevedo, R., Cromley, J. G., Winters, F. I., Moos, D. C., & Greene, J. A. (2005). Adaptive human scaffolding facilitates adolescents' self-regulated learning with hypermedia. *Instructional Science, 33*(5-6), 381.

Azevedo, R., Guthrie, J. T., & Seibert, D. (2004). The role of self-regulated learning in fostering students' conceptual understanding of complex systems with hypermedia. *Journal of Educational Computing Research, 30*(1-2), 87.

Azevedo, R., & Jacobson, M. (2008). Advances in scaffolding learning with hypertext and hypermedia: A summary and critical analysis. *Educational Technology Research and Development, 56*(1), 93-100.

Azevedo, R., Moos, D., Greene, J., Winters, F., & Cromley, J. (2008). Why is externally facilitated regulated learning more effective than self-regulated learning with hypermedia? *Educational Technology Research and Development, 56*(1), 45-72.

Azevedo, R., Winters, F. I., & Moos, D. C. (2004). Can students collaboratively use hypermedia to learn science? The dynamics of self-and other-regulatory processes in an ecology classroom. *Journal of Educational Computing Research, 31*(3), 215.

Bannert, M. (2003). Effekete metakognitiver Lernhilfen auf den Wissenserwerb in vernetzten Lernumgebungen. *German Journal of Educational Psychology, 17*(1), 13-25.

Baylor, A. L. (2001). Perceived disorientation and incidental learning in a Web-based environment: Internal and external factors. *Journal of Educational Multimedia and Hypermedia, 10,* 227-251.

Brown, J. S., Collins, A., & Duguid, P. (1989). Situated cognition and the culture of learning. *Educational Researcher, 18*(1), 32-41.

Chen, C., Lee, H., & Chen, Y. (2005). Personalized E-learning systems using item response theory. *Computers in Education, 44,* 237-255.

Chiu, C., & Wang, F. (2000). The influence of navigation map scope on disorientation of elementary students in learning a Web-based hypermedia course. *Journal of Educational Computing Research, 22,* 135-144.

Clark, J. M., & Paivio, A. (1991). Dual coding theory and education. *Educational Psychology Review, 3*(3), 149-170.

Clarke, T., Ayres, P., & Sweller, J. (2005). The impact of sequencing and prior knowledge on learning mathematics through spreadsheet applications. *Educational Technology Research & Development, 53*(3), 15-24.

Cognition and Technology Group at Vanderbilt. (1991). Technology and the design of generative learning environments. *Educational Technology, 31*(5), 34-40.

Cognition and Technology Group at Vanderbilt. (1992). The Jasper experiment: An exploration of issues in learning and instructional design. *Educational Technology Research and Development, 40*(1), 65-80.

Conklin, J. (1987). New technology and the curriculum. *Thrust, 16,* 18-20.

deJong, T., & van Joolingen, W. (1998). Scientific discovery learning with computer simulations of conceptual domains. *Review of Educational Research, 68*(2), 179-201.

Doyle, W. (1988). Work in mathematics classes: The context of students' thinking during instruction. *Educational Psychologist, 23*(2), 167-180.

Driscoll, M. P. (2000). *Psychology of learning for instruction* (2nd ed.). Needham Heights, MA: Allyn & Bacon.

Edwards, D. M., & Hardman, L. (1999). 'Lost in hyperspace': Cognitive mapping and navigation in a hypertext environment. In R. McAleese (Ed.), *Hypertext: Theory into practice,* (2nd ed., pp. 90-105). Oxford: Intellect Books.

Evans, C., & Gibbons, N. J. (2007). The interactivity effect in multimedia learning. *Computers & Education, 49*(4), 1147-1160.

Eveland, W. P., Cortese, J., Park, H., & Dunwoody, S. (2004). How Web site organization influences free recall, factual knowledge, and knowledge structure density. *Human Communication Research, 30*(2), 208-233.

Eveland, W. P., & Dunwoody, S. (2001). User control and structural isomorphism or disorientation and cognitive load? *Communication Research, 28*(1), 48.

Friesen, N., & Anderson, T. (2004). Interaction for lifelong learning. *British Journal of Educational Technology, 35,* 679-687.

Gaide, S. (2004). Reusing learning objects: Improving instructional design, reducing costs at Athabasca U. *Distance Education Report, 8*(13), 8.

Ge, X., & Er, N. (2005). An online support system to scaffold real-world problem solving. *Interactive Learning Environments, 13*(3), 139 – 157.

Gerjets, P., & Scheiter, K. (2003). Goal configurations and processing strategies as moderators between instructional design and cognitive load: Evidence from hypertext-based instruction. *Educational Psychologist, 38*(1), 33-41.

Gerjets, P, Scheiter, K, & Schuh, J. (2008). Information comparisons in example-based hypermedia environments: Supporting learners with processing prompts and an interactive comparison tool. *Educational Technology Research and Development, 56*(1), 73-92.

Greene, J. A., & Azevedo, R. (2007). Adolescents' use of self-regulatory processes and their relation to qualitative mental model shifts while using hypermedia. *Journal of Educational Computing Research, 36*(2), 125.

Greeno, J. G. (1983, April). *Skills for representing problems.* Paper presented at the annual meeting of the American Educational Research Association, Montreal.

Gyllenhaal, E., & Perry, D. (1998, May). *Doing something about the weather: Summative evaluation of Science Museum of Minnesota's atmospheric explorations computer interactives.* Paper presented at the Annual Meeting of the American Association of Museums, Los Angeles, CA.

Hannafin, M. J., Hannafin, K. M., Hooper, S. R., Rieber, L. P., & Kini, A. (1996). Research on and research with emerging technologies. In D. Jonassen (Ed.), *Handbook of research in educational communication and technology* (pp. 378-402). New York: Macmillan.

Hannafin, M. J., & Land, S. (1997). The foundations and assumptions of technology-enhanced, student-centered learning environments. *Instructional Science, 25,* 167-202.

Hannafin, M. J., Hill, J., & Land, S. (1997). Student-centered learning and interactive multimedia: Status, issues, and implications. *Contemporary Education, 68*(2), 94-99.

Hannafin, M. J., & Rieber, L. P. (1989). Psychological foundations of instructional design for emerging computer-based instructional technologies: Part I. *Educational Technology Research and Development, 37,* 91-101.

Hannafin, M. J., Land, S., & Oliver, K. (1999). Open learning environments: Foundations and models. In C. Reigeluth (Ed.), *Instructional design theories and models: A new paradigm of instructional theory* (pp. 115-140). Mahwah, NJ: Erlbaum.

Hee Jun, C., & Johnson, S. D. (2005). The effect of context-based video instruction on learning and motivation in online courses. *American Journal of Distance Education, 19*(4), 215-227.

Hill, J., Domizi, D., Kim, M., Kim, H., & Hannafin, M. J. (2007). Teaching and learning in negotiated and informal environments. In M. Moore (Ed.), *Handbook of distance education* (2nd ed.) 271-284. Mahwah, NJ: Erlbaum.

Hill, J., & Hannafin, M. J. (1997). Cognitive strategies and learning from the World Wide Web. *Educational Technology Research and Development, 45*(4), 37-64.

Hill, J., & Hannafin, M. J. (2001). Teaching and learning in digital environments: The resurgence of resource-based learning. *Educational Technology Research and Development, 49*(3), 37-52.

Hill, J., Hannafin, M. J., & Domizi, D. (2005). Resource-based learning and informal learning environments: Prospects and challenges. In R. Subramaniam (Ed.), *E-Learning and virtual science centers* (pp. 110-125). Hershey, PA: Idea Group, Inc.

Hogan, K., & Pressley, M. (1997). Scaffolding scientific competencies within classroom communities of inquiry. In K. Hogan & M. Pressley (Eds.), *Scaffolding Student Learning: Instructional Approaches and Issues* (pp. 74 – 107). Cambridge, MA: Brookline Books.

Hooper, S., & Hannafin, M. J. (1991). Psychological perspectives on emerging instructional technologies: A critical analysis. *Educational Psychologist, 26,* 69-95.

Hsinyi, P., Chin-Chung, T., & Ying-Tien, W. (2006). University students' self-efficacy and their attitudes toward the Internet: The role of students' perceptions of the Internet. *Educational Studies, 32*(1), 73-86.

Iiyoshi, T., Hannafin, M.J., & Wang, F. (2005). Cognitive tools and student-centered learning: Rethinking tools, functions, and applications. *Educational Media International, 42*(4), 281-296.

Jacobson, M. (2008). A design framework for educational hypermedia systems: Theory, research and learning emerging scientific conceptual perspectives. *Educational Technology Research and Development, 56*(1), 5-28.

Jonassen, D. (1991). Objectivism versus constructivism: Do we need a new philosophical paradigm? *Educational Technology Research and Development, 39*(3), 5-14.

Jones, D. L. (2003). An overview of the sharable content object reference model. *Media Review, 10*(1), 27-36.

Kalyuga, S., Ayers, P., Chandler, P., & Sweller, J. (2003). The expertise reversal effect. *Educational Psychologist, 38*(1), 23-31.

Kaufman, D. F. (2004). Self-regulated learning in Web-based environments: Instructional tools designed to facilitate cognitive strategy use, meta-cognitive processing, and motivational beliefs. *Journal of Educational Computing Research. 30*, 139-161.

Kim, M., Hannafin, M. J., & Bryan, L. (2007) Technology-enhanced inquiry tools in science education: An emerging pedagogical framework for classroom practice. *Science Education, 96*(6), 1010-1030.

King, P. M., & Kitchener, K. S. (2004). Reflective judgment: Theory and research on the development of epistemic assumptions through adulthood. *Educational Psychologist, 39*(1), 5-18.

Land, S. (2000). Cognitive requirements for learning with open-ended learning environments. *Educational Technology Research and Development, 48*(3), 61-78.

Land, S. M., & Greene, B. A. (2000). Project-based learning with the World Wide Web: A qualitative study of resource integration. *Educational Technology Research and Development, 48*(1), 45-67.

Land, S., & Hannafin, M. J. (1997). Patterns of understanding with open-ended learning environments: A qualitative study. *Educational Technology Research and Development, 45*(2), 47-73.

Land, S., & Hannafin, M. J. (1996). A conceptual framework for the development of theories-in-action with open learning environments. *Educational Technology Research and Development, 44*(3), 37-53.

Land, S., & Hannafin, M. J. (2000). Student-centered learning environments. In D.H. Jonassen, & S. M. Land (Eds.), *Theoretical Foundations of Learning Environments* (pp. 1-23). Mahwah, NJ: Erlbaum.

Land, S. M., & Zembal-Saul, C. (2003). Scaffolding reflection and articulation of scientific explanations in a data-rich, project-based learning environment: An investigation of Progress Portfolio. *Educational Technology Research and Development, 51*(4), 65-84.

Lepper, M. R., Drake, M. F., & O'Donnell-Johnson, T. (1997). Scaffolding techniques human tutors. In K. Hogan & M. Pressley (Eds.), *Scaffolding Student Learning: Approaches and Issues* (pp. 108–144). Cambridge, MA: Brookline Books.

Lieberman, D. A. (2000). *Learning: Behavior and cognition. Belmont*, BA: Wadsworth/Thomson Learning.

Massa, L. J., & Mayer, R. E. (2006). Testing the ATI hypothesis: Should multimedia instruction accommodate verbalizer-visualizer cognitive style? *Learning and Individual Differences, 16*(4), 321.

Masterman, E., & Rogers, Y. (2002). A framework for designing interactive multimedia to scaffold young children's understanding of historical chronology. *Instructional Science, 30*(3), 221–241.

Maule, R. W. (2001). Framework for metacognitive mapping to design metadata for intelligent hypermedia presentations. *Journal of Educational Multimedia and Hypermedia, 10*(1), 27-45.

Mayer, R. E. (2005). Cognitive theory of multimedia learning. In R. E. Mayer (Ed.), *The Cambridge Handbook of Multimedia Learning* (pp. 31-48). Cambridge: Cambridge University Press.

Mayer, R. E., & Anderson, R. B. (1991). Animations need narrations: An experimental test of a dual-coding hypothesis. *Journal of Educational Psychology, 83*(4), 484-490.

Mayer, R. E., & Anderson, R. B. (1992). The instructive animation: Helping students build connections between words and pictures in multimedia learning. *Journal of Educational Psychology, 84*(4), 444-452.

Mayer, R. E., Fennell, S., Farmer, L., & Campbell, J. (2004). A personalization effect in multimedia learning: Students learn better when words are in conversational style rather than formal style. *Journal of Educational Psychology, 96*(2), 389.

Mayer, R. E., & Moreno, R. (1998). A split-attention effect in multimedia learning: Evidence for dual processing systems in working memory. *Journal of Educational Psychology, 90*(2), 312.

Mayer, R. E., Sobko, K., & Mautone, P. D. (2003). Social cues in multimedia learning: Role of speaker's voice. *Journal of Educational Psychology, 95*(2), 419.

McCombs, B. L. (2001). What do we know about learners and learning? The learner-centered framework: Bringing the educational system into balance. *Educational Horizons, 79*(4), 182-193.

McCombs, B. L. (2003). A framework for the redesign of K-12 education in the context of current educational reform. *Theory into Practice, 42*(2), 163-167.

McCombs, B. L., & Whisler, J. S. (1997). *The learner-centered classroom and school: Strategies for increasing student motivation and achievement.* San Francisco: Jossey-Bass.

Moos, D. C., & Azevedo, R. (2006). The role of goal structure in undergraduates' use of self-regulatory processes in two hypermedia learning tasks. *Journal of Educational Multimedia and Hypermedia, 15*(1), 49-86.

Nicaise, M., & Crane, M. (1999). Knowledge constructing through hypermedia authoring. *Educational Technology Research and Development, 47*(1), 29-50.

Niederhauser, D. S., Reynolds, R. E., Salmen, D. J., & Skolmoski, P. (2000). The influence of cognitive load on learning from hypertext. *Journal of Educational Computing Research, 23*(3), 237-255.

Norman, D. A. (2002). *The design of everyday things.* New York: Basic Books.

Orrill, C. H. (2006). What learner-centered professional development looks like: The pilot studies of the InterMath professional development project. *The Mathematics Educator, 16*(1), 4-13.

Orrill, C. H. (2001). Building technology-based, learner-centered classrooms: The evolution of a professional development framework. *Educational Technology Research and Development, 49*(1), 15-34.

Papanikolaou, K. A., Grigoriadou, M., Magoulas, G. D., & Kornilakis, H. (2002). Towards new forms of knowledge communication: The adaptive dimension of a Web-based learning environment. *Computers in Education, 39*, 333-360.

Papert, S. (1993). *The children's machine: Rethinking school in the age of the computer.* New York: Basic Books.

Papert, S. (1980). *Mindstorms: Children, computers, and powerful ideas.* New York: Basic Books.

Puntambekar, S., & Hubscher, R. (2005). Tools for scaffolding students in a complex learning environment: What have we gained and what have we missed? *Educational Psychologist, 40*(1), 1–12.

Piaget, J. (1976). *The grasp of consciousness.* Cambridge, MA: Harvard University Press.

Phillips, D. C. (1995). The good, the bad, and the ugly: The many faces of constructivism. *Educational Researcher, 24*(7), 5-12.

Remillard, J. T. (2005). Examining key concepts in research on teachers' use of mathematics curricula. *Review of Educational Research, 75,* 211-246.

Renkl, A., & Atkinson, R. K. (2003). Structuring the transition from example study to problem solving in cognitive skill acquisition: A cognitive load perspective. *Educational Psychologist, 38*(1), 15-22.

Ringstaff, C., & Kelley, L. (2002). *The learning return on our educational technology investment.* San Francisco: WestEd.

Roschelle, J., Pea, R., Hoadley, C., Gordin, D., & Means, B. (2001). Changing how and what children learn in schools with computer-based technologies. *The Future of Children, 10*(2), 76-101.

Roy, M., Chi, M. T. H., & Mayer, R. E. (2005). *The self-explanation principle in multimedia learning.* New York, NY, US: Cambridge University Press.

Sandholtz, J. H., Ringstaff, C., & Dwyer, D. C. (1997). *Teaching with technology: Creating student-centered classrooms.* New York: Teachers College Press.

Saye, J. W., & Brush, T. (2007). Using technology-enhanced learning environments to support problem-based historical inquiry in secondary school classrooms. *Theory and Research in Social Education, 35,* 196-230.

Schacter, D. L. (1990). Memory. In M. I. Posner (Ed.), *Foundations of cognitive science* (pp. 683-725). Cambridge: MIT Press.

Schommer, M. (1993). Epistemological development and academic performance among secondary students. *Journal of Educational Psychology, 85,* 406-411.

Schön, D. D. (1983). *The reflective practitioner: How professionals think in action.* New York: Basic Books.

Schrum, L., Burbank, M. D., Engle, J., Chambers, J. A., & Glassett, K. F. (2005). Post-secondary educators' professional development: Investigation of an online approach to enhancing teaching and learning. *Internet & Higher Education, 8*(4), 279-289.

Schuh, K. L. (2003). Knowledge construction in the learner-centered classroom. *Journal of Educational Psychology, 95,* 426-442.

Schunk, D. H. (1990). Goal setting and self-efficacy during self-regulated learning. *Educational Psychologist, 25,* 71-86.

Seels, B., Berry, L. H., Fullerton, K., & Horn, L. J. (1996). Research on learning from television. In D. H. Jonassen (Ed.), *Handbook of research for educational communications and technology* (pp. 299-377). New York: Simon & Schuster Macmillan.

Sharma, P., & Hannafin, M. J. (2007). Scaffolding in technology-enhanced learning environments. *Interactive Learning Environments, 15*(1), 27-46.

Smidt, E., & Hegelheimer, V. (2004). Effects of online academic lectures on ESL listening comprehension, incidental vocabulary acquisition, and strategy use. *Computer Assisted Language Learning, 17*(5), 517-556.

Smith, S. M., & Woody, P. C. (2000). Interactive effect of multimedia instruction and learning styles. *Teaching of Psychology, 27*(3), 220-223.

Song, L, Hannafin, M.J., & Hill, J. (2007). Reconciling beliefs and practices in teaching and learning. *Educational Technology Research and Development, 55*(1), 27-50.

Song, L., Singleton, E. S., Hill, J. R., & Koh, M. H. (2004). Improving online learning: Student perceptions of useful and challenging characteristics. *Internet and Higher Education, 7*(1), 59-70.

Uribe, D., Klein, J. D., & Sullivan, H. (2003). The effect of computer-mediated collaborative learning on ill-defined problems. *Educational Technology Research & Development, 51*(1), 5-19.

van Merrionboer, J. J. G., & Ayres, P. (2005). Research on cognitive load theory and its design implications for E-learning. *Educational Technology Research & Development, 53*(3), 5-13.

Vygotsky, L. (1978). *Mind in society: The development of higher psychological processes.* Cambridge, MA: Harvard University Press.

Wallace, R., & Kupperman, J. (1997, April). *Online search in the science classroom: Benefits and possibilities.* Paper presented at the annual meeting of the American Educational Research Association, Chicago, IL.

Wenglinsky, H. (1998). *Does it compute? The relationship between educational technology and student achievement in mathematics.* Retrieved November 5, 2007 from http://searcheric.org/ericdc/ED425191.htm

West, R. E., Waddoups, G., & Graham, C. R. (2007). Understanding the experiences of instructors as they adopt a course management system. *Educational Technology Research and Development, 55*(1), 1-26.

West, R. E., Waddoups, G., Kennedy, M., & Graham, C. R. (2007). Evaluating the impact on users from implementing a course management system. *International Journal of Technology and Distance Learning, 4*(2). Retrieved November 5, 2007 from http://itdl.org/Journal/Feb_07/article01.htm.

Whipp, J. L., & Chiarelli, S. (2004). Self-regulation in a Web-based course: A case study. *Educational Technology Research & Development, 52*(4), 5-22.

Whitehead, A. N. (1929). *The aims of education.* New York: Macmillan.

Workman, M. (2004). Performance and perceived effectiveness in computer-based and computer-aided education: Do cognitive styles make a difference? *Computers in Human Behavior, 20*(4), 517.

Zimmerman, B. J., & Bandura, A. (1994). Impact of self-regulatory influences on writing course attainment. *American Educational Research Journal, 31*, 845-862.

Zion, M., Michalsky, T., & Mevarech, Z. (2005). The effects of metacognitive instruction embedded within an asynchronous learning network on scientific inquiry skills. *International Journal of Science Education, 27*(8), 957-983.

ADDITIONAL READING

Astleitner, H. (1997). Effects of external learning aids on learning with ill-structured hypertext. *Journal of Educational Computing Research, 17*(1), 1.

Astleitner, H., & Leutner, D. (1995). Learning strategies for unstructured hypermedia--a framework for theory, research, and practice. *Journal of Educational Computing Research, 13*(4), 387.

Atkinson, R. K., Mayer, R. E., & Merrill, M. M. (2005). Fostering social agency in multimedia learning: Examining the impact of an animated agent's voice. *Contemporary Educational Psychology, 30*(1), 117.

Azevedo, R., & Cromley, J. G. (2004). Does training on self-regulated learning facilitate students' learning with hypermedia? *Journal of Educational Psychology, 96*(3), 523.

Azevedo, R., Cromley, J. G., & Seibert, D. (2004). Does adaptive scaffolding facilitate students' ability to regulate their learning with hypermedia? *Contemporary Educational Psychology, 29*(3), 344.

Brophy, D. R. (1996). *The initial testing of a 'tri-level matching theory' of creative problem solving.* ProQuest Information & Learning, US.

Byrnes, J. P. (1996). *Cognitive development and learning in instructional contexts.* Boston: Allyn and Bacon.

Cognition and Technology Group at Vanderbilt. (1991). Technology and the design of generative learning environments. *Educational Technology, 31*(5), 34-40.

deJong, T., & van Joolingen, W. (1998). Scientific discovery learning with computer simulations of conceptual domains. *Review of Educational Research, 68*(2), 179-201.

Dutke, S., & Rinck, M. (2006). Multimedia Learning: Working Memory and the Learning of Word and Picture Diagrams. *Learning and Instruction, 16*(6), 526.

Eveland, W. P., Cortese, J., Park, H., & Dunwoody, S. (2004). How Web site organization influences free recall, factual knowledge, and knowledge structure density. *Human Communication Research, 30*(2), 208-233.

Gerlic, I., & Jausovec, N. (2001). Differences in EEG power and coherence measures related to the type of presentation: Text versus multimedia. *Journal of Educational Computing Research, 25*(2), 177.

Goncalo, J. A. (2004). Past success and convergent thinking in groups: The role of group-focused attributions. *European Journal of Social Psychology, 34*(4), 385-395.

Hannafin, M. J., Hannafin, K. M., Land, S., & Oliver, K. (1997). Grounded practice and the design of constructivist learning environments. *Educational Technology Research and Development, 45*(3), 101-117.

Hannafin, M. J., & Hill, J. (2007). Epistemology and the design of learning environments. In R. Reiser, & J. Dempsey (Eds.), *Trends and issues in instructional design and technology* (2nd Ed., pp. 53-61). Upper Saddle River, NJ: Merrill/Prentice-Hall.

Hannafin, M. J., Hill, J., & Glazer, E. (in press). Designing grounded learning environments: Linking epistemology, pedagogy, and design practice. In G. Anglin (Ed.), *Instructional technology: Past, present, and future* (3rd Ed.). Englewood Cliffs, NJ: Libraries Unlimited.

Hannafin, M. J., Hill, J., Oliver, K., Glazer, E., & Sharma, P. (2003). Cognitive and learning strategies in Web-based distance learning environments. In M. Moore & W. Anderson (Eds.), *Handbook of distance education* (pp. 245-260). Mahwah, NJ: Erlbaum.

Hannafin, M. J., Hill, J., Song, L., & West, R. (2007). Cognitive perspectives on technology-enhanced distance learning environments. In M. Moore (Ed.), *Handbook of distance education* (2nd ed., pp. 123-136). Mahwah, NJ: Erlbaum.

Hannafin, M. J., Kim, M., & Kim, J. (2004). Reconciling research, theory and practice in Web-based teaching and learning. *Journal of Computing in Higher Education, 15*(2), 3-20.

Hannafin, M. J., & Land, S. M. (2000). Technology and student-centered learning in higher education: Issues and practices. *Journal of Computing in Higher Education, 12*(1), 3-30.

Hannafin, M. J., Hill, J., & Land, S. (1997). Student-centered learning and interactive multimedia: Status, issues, and implications. *Contemporary Education, 68*(2), 94-99.

Hannafin, M. J., & Rieber, L. P. (1989). Psychological foundations of instructional design for emerging computer-based instructional technologies: Part II. *Educational Technology Research and Development, 37*, 102-114.

Hill, J., Domizi, D., Kim, M., Kim, H., & Hannafin, M. J. (2007). Teaching and learning in negotiated and informal environments. In M. Moore (Ed.), *Handbook of distance education* (2nd ed., pp. 271-284). Mahwah, NJ: Erlbaum.

Hill, J., Hannafin, M. J., & Domizi, D. (2005). Resource-based learning and informal learning environments: Prospects and challenges. In R. Subramaniam (Ed.), *E-Learning and virtual science centers* (pp. 110-125). Hershey, PA: Idea Group, Inc.

Jaques, P. A., & Vicari, R. M. (2007). A BDI approach to infer student's in an intelligent learning environment. *Computers & Education, 49*, 360-384.

Kaner, M., & Karni, R. (2007). Engineering design of a service system: An empirical study. *Information Knowledge Systems Management, 6*(3), 235-263.

Kim, M., & Hannafin, M. J. (2004). Designing on-line learning environments to support scientific inquiry. *Quarterly Review of Distance Education, 5*(1), 1-10.

Larey, T. S. (1995). *Convergent and divergent thinking, group composition, and creativity in brainstorming groups.* ProQuest Information & Learning, US.

Lawless, K. A., & Brown, S. W. (1997). Multimedia learning environments: Issues of learner control and navigation. *Instructional Science, 25*(2), 117.

Lieberman, D. A. (2000). *Learning: Behavior and cognition.* Belmont, BA: Wadsworth/Thomson Learning.

Mayer, R. E. (1999). Multimedia aids to problem-solving transfer. *International Journal of Educational Research, 31*(7), 611.

Mayer, R. E., & Chandler, P. (2001). When learning is just a click away: Does simple user interaction foster deeper understanding of multimedia messages? *Journal of Educational Psychology, 93*(2), 390.

Mayer, R. E., Heiser, J., & Lonn, S. (2001). Cognitive constraints on multimedia learning: When presenting more material results in less understanding. *Journal of Educational Psychology, 93*(1), 187.

Mayer, R. E., & Moreno, R. (2003). Nine ways to reduce cognitive load in multimedia learning. *Educational Psychologist, 38*(1), 43-52.

McGlynn, R. P., McGurk, D., Effland, V. S., Johll, N. L., & Harding, D. J. (2004). Brainstorming and task performance in groups constrained by evidence. *Organizational Behavior and Human Decision Processes, 93*(1), 75-87.

Means, B. (1994). *Technology and education reform.* San Francisco: Jossey-Bass.

Mei-Mei, C. (2005). Applying self-regulated learning strategies in a Web-based instruction: An investigation of motivation perception. *Computer Assisted Language Learning, 18*(3), 217-230.

Meskill, C. (1996). Listening skills development through multimedia. *Journal of Educational Multimedia and Hypermedia, 5*(2), 179.

Moreno, R. (2004). Decreasing cognitive load for novice students: Effects of explanatory versus corrective feedback in discovery-based multimedia. *Instructional Science: An International Journal of Learning and Cognition, 32*(1-2), 99.

Moreno, R., & Duran, R. (2004). Do multiple representations need explanations? The role of verbal guidance and individual differences in multimedia mathematics learning. *Journal of Educational Psychology, 96*(3), 492.

Moreno, R., & Mayer, R. E. (2000). Engaging students in active learning: The case for personalized multimedia messages. *Journal of Educational Psychology, 92*(4), 724.

Moreno, R., & Mayer, R. E. (2002). Learning science in virtual reality multimedia environments: Role of methods and media. *Journal of Educational Psychology, 94*(3), 598.

Moreno, R., & Valdez, A. (2005). Cognitive load and learning effects of having students organize pictures and words in multimedia environments: The role of student interactivity and feedback. *Educational Technology Research and Development, 53*(3), 35.

Nemeth, C. J. (1986). Differential contributions of majority and minority influence. *Psychological Review, 93*(1), 23-32.

Nicaise, M., & Crane, M. (1999). Knowledge constructing through hypermedia authoring. *Educational Technology Research and Development, 47*(1), 29-50.

Oliver, K., & Hannafin, M. J. (2001). Developing and refining mental models in open-ended learning environments: A case study. *Educational Technology Research and Development, 49*(4), 5-33.

Ollerenshaw, A., Aidman, E., & Kidd, G. (1997). Is an illustration always worth ten thousand words? Effects of prior knowledge, learning style and multimedia illustrations on text comprehension. *International Journal of Instructional Media, 24*(3), 227.

Pea, R. D. (2004). The social and technological dimensions of scaffolding and related theoretical concepts for learning, education, and human activity. *Journal of the Learning Sciences, 13*(3), 423–451.

Quintana, C., Reiser, B. J., Davis, E. A., Krajcik, J., Fretz, E., Duncan, R. G., et al. (2004). A scaffolding design framework for software to support science inquiry. *Journal of the Learning Sciences, 13*(3), 337 – 386.

Sharma, P., Oliver, K., & Hannafin, M. J. (2007). Teaching and learning in directed environments. In M. Moore (Ed.), *Handbook of distance education* (2nd ed., pp. 259-270). Mahwah, NJ: Erlbaum.

Tabak, I. (2004). Synergy: A complement to emerging patterns of distributed scaffolding. *Journal of the Learning Sciences, 13*(3), 305 – 335.

Van Den Berg, E., Jansen, L., & Blijleven, P. (2004). Learning with multimedia cases: An evaluation study. *Journal of Technology and Teacher Education, 12*(4), 491.

Winn, W. (1996). Cognitive perspectives in psychology. In D. H. Jonassen (Ed.), *Handbook of research for educational communications and technology*. New York: Simon & Schuster Macmillan.

Winters, F. I., & Azevedo, R. (2005). High-school students' regulation of learning during computer-based science inquiry. *Journal of Educational Computing Research, 33*(2), 189-217.

Chapter XII
Supporting Discovery–Based Learning within Simulations

Lloyd P. Rieber
The University of Georgia, USA

ABSTRACT

This chapter presents a review of research on the use and role of interactive simulations for learning. Contemporary theories of learning, instruction, and media, suggest that learning involves a complex relationship and dependency between a learner's prior knowledge, a learner's motivation, the context, the task, and the resources (e.g., simulations) provided to, and used by the learner to support or enable the task. Given this perspective, and data from an evolving research program, simulations are best used to help learners construct knowledge and make meaning by giving them control over phenomena modeled by the simulation. Several theoretical frameworks have guided this research program: dual coding theory, mental models, and constructivist learning theory. An overall result of this research is that learning should be based on experience, such as that derived from interacting with a simulation, and supported with explanations. This is counter to traditional educational wisdom where explanations rule instructional strategies.

INTRODUCTION

Since the late 1980s, I have studied children and adults using educational simulations based on various pedagogical (e.g. inductive and deductive learning) and philosophical approaches (i.e. constructivist and objectivist). My goal in this chapter is to summarize some of this research and also provide some of the background that frames my research questions. As an instructional technologist, I have been influenced by the use of instruction to shape learning, but as someone who accepts a constructivist orientation to learning, I know that instruction is but one path to learning. When given little or no instructional support, I am interested in the strategies that people use to learn given the opportunities of an interactive simulation. Even more important, I am interested in those times when they run into problems and need help. My goal is not to withhold instruction from them, but to gain a better understanding of when instructional support is unnecessary or, conversely, most needed.

The general conclusions I have drawn from this research and experience are not neat and tidy. I am unable to say that simulations are "better" than other learning approaches. One of the most important conclusions is simply that learning with simulations is heavily context-bound (Kluge, 2007). The influence or role of a simulation on learning is interrelated to the other elements of the instructional system. This is a useful reminder that human cognition and motivation are among the most complex phenomenon we can study. As a researcher, this generates curiosity in me leading to more research. Yet, as an educator, I admit that I grow restless at times when design principles prove elusive.

This chapter is presented in three sections. First, I discuss important background on visualization principles needed in the design of highly visual educational simulations. This background section in presented in two parts: 1) a brief overview of visualization in education; and 2) theories relevant to the simulation research considered afterwards. The two theories I emphasize are dual coding theory, a well-established and studied theory that offers much guidance in deciding when and how to design visualization for educational materials, and mental models, a theory that attempts to model and explain human understanding of complex phenomena. In the second section, I present the main thrust of the chapter by considering what is meant by interactive multimedia, basing most of my discussion on the use of simulations. However, I also consider how attributes of microworlds and gaming can influence simulation design. I then turn attention to some recommendations and implications for design. I use the relatively new literature on universal design for learning

(UDL) as an additional lens for understanding the implications. Although UDL focuses on people with disabilities, one might argue that we all have challenges to learning depending on the context we find ourselves in, the materials and resources given to us, and expectations placed on us. The label "disability" is often attached to people facing such challenges in arbitrary and unfortunate ways. Finally, I offer some conclusions and consider future research directions.

BACKGROUND

Visualization in Education: A Primer

The decision to incorporate visuals as part of instruction or training is often made without a well-articulated justification or rationale. The lack of a firm set of design criteria can lead to unexpected results. Research has demonstrated conditions under which visuals – static and dynamic —are generally effective, as well as those where graphics serve no purpose or, worse, do harm (Levin, Anglin, & Carney, 1987; Mayer, 2001, 2005; Rieber, 1994). For example, consider the cultural symbolism of the owl. Many American teachers like to adorn their classrooms with fanciful images of a friendly wise owl to symbolize an educated person. Yet, an owl often represents an evil omen for many Native Americans, leading some students to be alienated by such graphics. All designers should carefully consider the impact of such innocent graphics in their materials.

The use of graphics in education can generally be classified three ways (Alesandrini, 1984; Rieber, 1994): Representational, analogical, and arbitrary. Representational graphics physically resemble the object they are designed to represent. For example, an instructional text describing a Venus fly trap plant probably would be accompanied by a picture of this plant. This seems simple enough, but what kind of picture should be used? Representational visuals range somewhere between highly realistic (photographs) and abstract (simple line drawings). Should a photograph or artistic rendering be used? Should the picture show the rather dramatic scene of a fly caught in its trap or with the trap open and waiting for a fly to land on it? Should a static or animated graphic be used to portray the predatory behavior of the plant? Each choice will likely convey as well as hide some critical information. Some choices may even trigger an emotional reaction leading to increased or decreased motivation.

Presenting students with an accurate representation of something may not always be the best learning approach. One such example is when students have little or no prior knowledge of the concept being portrayed by the picture. In these instances, analogies or metaphors may be effective instructional strategies (Glynn, 1995; Glynn, Duit, & Thiele, 1995). For example, if students do not understand the idea of a Venus fly trap, then comparing the plant to a carnivorous animal, such as a lion, may be useful. A better analogy would be comparing it to a frog because a frog tends to sit in one place and often catches and eats flies. Of course, a Venus fly trap is a plant, not an animal. Learners must understand that the analogy is being used only to represent similarities between the target object and the analogous example. If students do not recognize the differences between the target object and the analogy, or understand other limits of the analogy, then misconceptions may result.

Unlike representational and analogical graphics, arbitrary graphics do not share any physical resemblances to the target object. Instead, arbitrary graphics provide other visual or spatial characteristics or cues that convey meaning. Among the most common examples of arbitrary graphics are flowcharts, bar charts, and line graphs.

So, the instructional designer is faced with many choices with how to represent information, concepts, and principles in educational material. Consider, too, all of the other representations available beyond graphics — text, voice, music, sound

effects, etc. This is further complicated by the options that technology provides us. Of particular interest to me have been the computer's animation and interaction capabilities. Graphics can be animated, thus allowing a dynamic process to be represented visually over time. Animation can also be produced based on a person's responses to the software, such as a flight simulation program in which a virtual plane dives to the ground when the mouse is pushed forward.

Finally, all of these representations can be produced with highly differing degrees of quality. Just as the written word is expressed differently by a tabloid newspaper writers and acclaimed authors such as John Steinbeck, so too can instructional materials using graphics, text, and sounds, be produced with different quality assurances. All of these differences surely matter in how a person will eventually use the materials for learning.

There is a large body of research demonstrating that the way information is represented matters greatly in the learning process. Two theories that are relevant to research on highly visual interactive simulations are dual coding theory and mental models.

Theoretical Support for Visualization in Learning: Dual Coding Theory

In general, research indicates that pictures are superior to words for remembering concrete concepts. Paivio's dual coding theory is the most established and most empirically validated theory to account for this (Paivio, 1990, 1991; Sadoski & Paivio, 1994, 2001). This theory suggests a model of human cognition divided into two dominant processing systems — one verbal and one nonverbal. The verbal system specializes in linguistic or "language-like" processing. The nonverbal system concerns the processing of all nonverbal phenomena, including emotional reactions. However, since we are mostly concerned with visual information here, I will refer to this system hereafter simply as the visual system.

Dual coding theory predicts three distinctive levels of processing within and between the verbal and visual systems: representational, associative, and referential. Representational processing describes the link between incoming stimuli from the environment and either the verbal or visual system. Associative processing refers to the activation of stored information *within* either the verbal or visual systems. In contrast, referential processing refers to connections *between* the verbal and visual systems. A few simple examples will help to explain these types of processing.

Consider students in a high school social studies class learning about Spanish explorers in North America. The teacher explains that Ponce de Leon was searching for the fountain of youth in present-day Florida. If the teacher says and writes "Ponce de Leon" and "Fountain of Youth" on the board, the student is exposed to only verbal stimuli. Hence, at least initially, there is only representational processing occurring within the verbal system. However, if the teacher also points out that "leon" is the Spanish word for lion and encourages students to draw a picture of a lion in their notebooks beside a picture of a fountain, the students are also receiving and generating visual stimuli. If students actively think about the connection between the pictures of the lion and fountain and the verbal information (i.e. Ponce de Leon was searching for the fountain of youth), referential processing is occurring— the verbal and visual codes are being related together then stored in their minds. Some days later, on a text-only test, when the students are trying to remember what Ponce de Leon was searching for, many may not remember the answer as they first use only the verbal stimuli provided in the test (i.e. representational processing). However, those that recall that leon means lion and then "see" in their mind's eye a lion beside a fountain are likely to trigger referential processing between the verbal and visual systems which greatly increases the likelihood they will remember the answer.

At the simplest level, dual coding theory predicts that words and pictures provided by instruction will activate these coding systems in different ways. On the basis of two important assumptions, dual coding theory explains why pictures have repeatedly been found to be superior to words for increasing a person's ability on memory tasks. First, it is believed that the verbal and visual codes produce additive effects. That is, if information is coded *both* verbally and visually, the chances of retrieval are doubled. In other words, two codes are better than one, at least when you are trying to remember something. The second assumption is that words and pictures activate mental processing in different ways. Pictures are believed to be far more likely to be coded both visually and verbally, whereas words are believed to be far less likely to be coded visually.

The main application and study of dual coding theory to education has been in reading education. Although adaptations of dual coding theory exist (e.g. Mayer, 2001), it remains a robust theory for explaining learning and guiding efforts in designing multimedia for learning. Producing more referential connections should be expected when a user has the opportunity to interact with information in meaningful ways, especially given a variety of multiple representations. Simulations seem very well suited for such learning opportunities.

When designing instruction, we should be interested in how to dually code information because of the clear advantages for memory retrieval. But the learning goal of most interactive software is not mere recall of factual information. Instead, the learning goal when using a simulation is typically on identifying and using relationships being modeled in the simulation. Dual coding theory would predict that the verbal system is more apt to store explanatory forms of conceptual relationships, whereas the visual system would be more apt to store experiential forms, especially in a non-sequential order. Well-designed simulations provide students with the opportunity to build strong referential connections between both explanatory and experiential representations of the concepts and principles being modeled in the simulation. For example, schools are often successful at having students learn equations in verbal ways, such as "force equals mass times acceleration." The goal is to have students make strong connections between such verbal information and their experiences of controlling how a ball speeds up and slows down during a simulation. In order for students to make these relationships, they need time and guidance for reflection.

Theoretical Support for the Design of Interactions: Mental Models

A mental model is best thought of as a person's personal theory of some domain or environment (Gentner & Stevens, 1983; Johnson-Laird, Girotto, & Legrenzi, 2004; Jonassen, Strobel, & Gottdenker, 2005). People develop and use mental models as a way to explain and predict their interactions in a complex environment. Mental models help people to understand and solve problems in virtually all domains including school subjects such as chemistry and biology as well as everyday domains, such as using cell phones, microwaves, or ordering merchandise online. Mental models do not become "fixed" inside a person's head, but instead are always changing and "updated" by people as they interact with the environment and encounter new challenges. Applying mental model theory to education requires consideration of three things: the target system (i.e. using a cell phone), the person's mental model of the target system, and the building of a conceptual model by someone else (such as an engineer or a teacher) to help the user understand the target system (Norman, 2002).

The target system is the actual system that a user is trying to understand. Let's explore the everyday example of summoning an elevator in a very tall building. A person who holds the theory that pushing the elevator button repeatedly while standing in the lobby will send an elevator more quickly believes that the control system is keeping track of the number of times the button has been pressed. If pressing the button instead simply activates a switch to send an elevator to that floor and nothing else, repeated pressing of the button will not increase the response time. As a result, the person may become frustrated because their action, based on their mental model of the system, does not match how the system really works. A solution is to design the interface between the user and the target system in such as way as to better communicate the target system to the user, perhaps with messages that only display if the button is pressed multiple times. Such a design is called a *conceptual model*.

Conceptual models are often metaphorical, thus corresponding nicely to the use of analogical graphics described earlier. When ordering merchandise online, companies typically use the metaphor of a shopping cart. This helps customers to understand the exact moment when items they've chosen are actually purchased and their credit cards are charged. One of the most well known conceptual models is the metaphor that likens a computer to a desktop. Of course, the computer is not really a desktop, but this metaphor has proven to help people operate a computer even though there are not really tiny folders with files inside of them being moved from place to place inside the computer. Older operating systems, such as MS-DOS, were more difficult to understand by ordinary people, which is part of the reason why Apple and Microsoft chose to adopt the desktop metaphor. Is a desktop the *best* metaphor for a computer? Interestingly, experienced computer users usually have a hard time thinking of a computer in any other way, even though metaphors based on a library, bulletin board, or even a grocery store could have been used. Of course, conceptual models, like metaphors, can lead to clarification or confusion. If a person has no experience with the metaphor, they will not benefit from it or they might even develop misconceptions. (As an amusing example, a television commercial on American television likens information technology to a basketball game with information being the ball. If you have never played basketball before, it unlikely this metaphor will help you understand the meaning of the commercial).

INTERACTIVE MULTIMEDIA: ISSUES, CONTROVERSIES, PROBLEMS

There are many forms of interactive multimedia, so the focus here will only be on the use of simulations. There are two main ways to use simulations in education: Model-using and model-building (Penner, 2000/2001). Model-using is when you learn from a simulation designed by someone else. This is common of *instructional* approaches where simulations are used as an interactive strategy or event, such as practice. Learning from using a simulated model of a system is different from learning from building working models in that the student does not have access to the programming of the simulation. The student is limited to manipulating only the parameters or variables that the designer of the simulation embedded into the simulation's interface. For example, in a simulation on Newtonian motion the user may only have the ability to change the mass of an object in certain increments, but not have the ability to change the initial starting positions of the objects or even how many objects will interact when the simulation is run. In contrast, model-building is where the learner has a direct role in the construction of the simulation. This approach is closely related to the work with microworlds. The concept of a microworld had its start with the Logo programming language developed out of the Massachusetts Institute of Technology in the 1960s and gained huge popularity with the advent of the personal computer in the early 1980s

(Papert, 1980a, 1980b). Research and development of microworlds has come far since then, producing wonderfully creative products and approaches. A sampling includes StarLogo (Resnick, 1994), Boxer (diSessa & Abelson, 1986; diSessa, Abelson, & Ploger, 1991), ThinkerTools (White, 1993; White & Horowitz, 1987), SimCalc (Roschelle, Kaput, & Stroup, 2000), Geometer's Sketchpad (Olive, 1998), and GenScope (Horwitz, 1999). Related to microworlds are modeling tools, such as StageCast, Geometer's Sketchpad (Olive, 1998), Interactive Physics, and SimQuest (Van Joolingen, King, & de Jong, 1997).

A review of microworlds is outside the scope of this short paper (see Rieber, 2003 for a thorough review). Suffice it to say that the distinction between microworlds, modeling tools, and simulations can be very fuzzy. A simple delineation is in how the tool is used. I believe that a microworld possesses three main characteristics: 1) it provides an immediate doorway to a learner's inquiry in a domain by matching the learner's cognitive readiness to explore the domain; 2) it is intrinsically interesting to the user such that the user *wants* to explore the domain once seeing how the microworld works; and 3) the software allows the user to adapt (i.e. program) the software to explore new and interesting questions. Not surprisingly, the most celebrated microworlds, like Logo, are programming languages designed explicitly for the learning process. However, other software tools that have non-scripting interfaces, like Geometer's Sketchpad or Interactive Physics, can be considered either a modeling tool or microworld depending on their use in a classroom. It is very important to note that successful learning with a microworld assumes a conducive classroom environment with a very able teacher serving a dual role: teacher-as-facilitator and teacher-as-learner. The teacher's role is critical by supporting and challenging student learning while at the same time modeling the learning process with the microworld.

The question of when a microworld is or is not a simulation often troubles people. While Thinker-Tools or Interactive Physics display trajectories of simulated falling balls, the underlying mathematical model makes the resulting representation much more "real" that a paper/pencil model. And although the ability to stop a ball in mid-flight has no analog in the real world, including features such as this in a simulation make understanding the real world more likely. What is important is that the mathematical models of these environments represent the phenomenon or concept in question accurately followed by exploiting the representation for educational purposes. However, a tool like Geometer's Sketchpad is clearly *not* a simulation — its geometry is as real as it gets.

The model-using approach to simulations has had a long history in instructional technology, particularly in corporate and military settings. However, simulations have become very popular designs in the education market. There are three major design components to an educational simulation: The underlying model, the simulation's scenario, and the simulation's instructional overlay. The underlying model refers to the mathematical relationships of the phenomenon being simulated. The scenario provides a context for the simulation, such as space travel or sports. The instructional overlay includes any features, options, or information presented before, during, or after the simulation to help the user explicitly identify and learn the relationships being modeled in the simulation. The structure and scope of the instructional overlay is, of course, an interesting design question and one that has shaped my research. Mental model theory offers much guidance to the design of an effective scenario and instructional overlay, such as thinking of them as an interactive conceptual model. This supports the idea of using metaphors to help people interact with the simulation.

My research with highly visual and interactive simulations has taken two paths. First, I have studied the use of different representations — graphical and textual/numerical — to convey the continual stream of feedback to students within science simulations. The difference is similar to the analogy of flying an airplane by looking out the window versus flying by the instruments. For example, when designing a simulation on Newtonian mechanics, one can represent feedback from the simulation in qualitative (pictures of moving balls) and quantitative (displays of the mathematics, such as the coordinates of the speed, direction, and position of an object), as shown in Figure 1. Second, I have investigated the relationship between how different scenario designs and varying levels of instruction support learning within a simulation. For example, I have studied how people make meaning from a simulation when it is designed with metaphors and model cases. I have also studied the strategy of breaking down the respective parts of a complex simulation so as to allow the user to focus on one aspect of the process at a time.

A common goal for both research paths is my interest in understanding the relationship between presentation and interaction. So much of education is based on a teacher presenting information to students, followed by practice. I have long wondered if such an emphasis on up-front presentation is really necessary, especially when it is so divorced from the everyday experiences of the students. Using the rallying cry of "experience first, explanation later," I have investigated ways in which simulations can be designed to see if students are able to "discover" for themselves the rules underlying the simulation. If they are not, then what types of instructional inventions are necessary and when? Consequently, I have taken a minimalist approach to the use of instructional interventions in simulations.

De Jong and van Joolingen (1998) present one of the most thorough reviews of scientific discovery learning within computer-based simulations (of the model-using type). The goal of this type of research is to present a simulation to students and ask them to infer the underlying model on

Figure 1. An example of a physics simulation in which feedback is presented solely in a numeric format

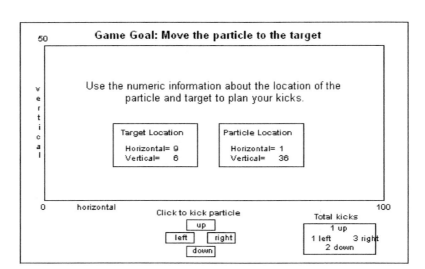

which the simulation is based. Scientific discovery learning is based on a cycle corresponding to the steps of scientific reasoning: defining a problem, stating a hypothesis about the problem, designing an experiment to test the hypothesis, collecting and analyzing data from the experiment, making predictions based on the results, and making conclusions and possible revisions about the robustness of the original hypotheses.

The research de Jong and van Joolingen (1998) reviewed shows that students find it difficult to learn from simulations using discovery methods and need much support to do so successfully. Research shows that students have difficulty throughout the discovery learning process. For example, students find it difficult to state or construct hypotheses that lead to good experiments. Furthermore, students do not easily adapt hypotheses on the basis of the data collected. That is, they often retain a hypothesis even when the data they collect disconfirm the hypothesis. Students do not design appropriate experiments to give them pertinent data to evaluate their hypotheses. Students are prone to *confirmation bias*, that is, they often design experiments that will lead to support their hypotheses. Students also find inter-

preting data in light of their hypotheses to be very challenging. In light of these difficulties de Jong and van Joolingen (1998) also reviewed research that studied ways to mitigate these difficulties. One conclusion they draw is that information or instructional support needs to come *while* students are involved in the simulation, as compared to providing instruction prior to working with the simulation, a conclusion supported by current research (Hulshof & de Jong, 2006; Manlove, Lazonder, & de Jong, 2006). That is, students are likely to benefit from such instructional interventions at the time they are confronted with the task or challenge. This often flies in the face of conventional wisdom that students should be prepared thoroughly before being given access to the simulation. The research also shows that embedding guided activities within the simulation, such as exercises, questions, or even games, help students to learn from the simulation. When designing experiments, students can benefit from experimentation hints, such as the recommendation to only change one variable at a time.

De Jong and van Joolingen (1998) also conclude that the technique of *model progression* can be an effective design strategy. Instead of presenting the entire simulation to students from the onset, students are given a simplified version, followed by having variables added as their understanding unfolds. For example, a Newtonian simulation could be presented first with only one-dimensional motion represented, followed by two-dimensional motion.

Finally, de Jong and van Joolingen (1998) also point out the importance of understanding how learning was measured in a particular study. There is a belief that learning from simulations leads to "deeper" cognitive processing than learning from expository methods (such as presentations). However, many studies did not test for application and transfer, so it is an open question whether a student who only successfully learns how to manipulate the simulation can apply this knowledge to other contexts. A student who successfully manipulates the simulation may not have acquired the general conceptual knowledge to succeed at other tasks. This review by de Jong and van Joolingen shows that there is still much researchers need to learn about the role of simulations in discovery learning and also how to design supports and structure to help students use the affordances of simulations most effectively. There are also many styles and strategies beyond scientific discovery learning. For example, an experiential or inductive approach would have students explore a simulation first, followed by providing organized instruction on the concepts or principles modeled by the simulation. With this approach, the simulation provides an experiential context for anchoring later instruction.

Results of our research closely match that found by de Jong and van Joolingen. Our research shows that adults are largely unable to learn from simulations without some form of guidance or structure (Rieber & Parmley, 1995). Adults also find the task of discovery learning very uncomfortable — they expect and want guidance. But, we also have found that it is also *not* necessary to design full-fledged instruction to support learning. For example, we have found just providing people

with very short statements of the physical laws as a type of content "hint" *while* they are interacting with the simulation is enough to produce learning mastery (Rieber, Tzeng, & Tribble, 2004). Also, we have found that the model progression technique, where a complex simulation is broken down systematically into smaller elements, then given to adults in an organized sequence, is as effective as a full-blown tutorial (Rieber & Parmley, 1995). Interestingly, there are also ramifications to a person's perceived self-efficacy when not using direct instruction to support learning in a simulation. For example, these same participants who learned as much given a simulation based on the model progression technique as participants given a tutorial had less confidence in how they were performing on a test of their physics understanding as compared to those participants who were given the tutorial (Rieber & Parmley, 1995).

Our qualitative research shows that not everyone approaches a discovery oriented activity in a strategic fashion (Rieber et al., 1996). Although most prefer an experiential approach at first with graphical feedback, many are unable to break through to engage in strategic thinking. Put another way, many simply cannot get out of "twitch mode" to engage the simulation in a reflective, strategic way. As a consequence, they cannot form any articulate hypotheses to guide their experimentation in the simulation. But, those who engaged in strategizing early on show interesting patterns of preference with the way the task is represented in a simulation. For example, while most prefer a graphical representation at the start, as they gain expertise, they often prefer to switch to a textual representation. Numerical data gives them opportunities to build strategies.

In our research on the role of different forms of feedback (e.g. graphical vs. textual/numeric) in a simulation we have learned that different representations lead to different learning outcomes, but the type of representation that is best for learning shifts over time (Rieber, 1996). People are also not easily able to switch between different representations, even though it may be in their best interest to do so. For example, although many tasks can be made easier at first using a highly visual interface, there may be limits to how much understanding can be achieved without switching to a verbal or textual interface. But, switching from a graphical to a non-graphical interface prematurely may lead to excessive confusion and frustration. So, it is not simply a matter of having multiple representations available to learners that matters, but how to guide them to the most appropriate representation given their expertise and goals with the content. Other research on using multiple representations support the notion that simply giving users more than one representation does not lead to learning. For example, Ainsworth (1999; Ainsworth, Bibby, & Wood, 2002) has theorized that the conflicting research on multiple representations can be interpreted as caused by a lack of consistency in the use and purpose of multiple representations. Ainsworth has proposed three functions of multiple representations, each calling for different levels of *translation* between the various representations. Translation refers to the ability of a learner to see the relation between two representations. The first function is to use representations to complement one another. That is, the same information is presented in multiple ways. The second function is to have one representation constrain interpretations of a second representation. The third function is to use multiple representations to construct a deeper understanding of a learning task. Different students will have different needs, depending on their learning goals and expertise in the domain. A student should not be expected to intuitively know how best to use multiple representations, so the simulation must be designed carefully to cue the student to use which representation when, and also to scaffold the student's learning.

Another group of research we have conducted has varied the design of the simulation's scenario with radically different model cases (Rieber, Noah, & Nolan, 1998). Each can highlight certain physical attributes differently — none is perfect, so exploring each provides a unique lens for capturing a little more understanding of the physics. For example, we have tried to teach about the relationship between acceleration and velocity by presenting the following four models to people: 1) a pure Newtonian model without any context; 2) a ball rolling on a table top that one can tilt up and down; 3) a spaceship floating in outer space; and 4) an unorthodox model consisting of a refrigerator coasting on a frictionless floor. Two of these — the ball on the table top model and "rogue" refrigerator model — are shown in Figure 2.

Of these two models, the ball on the table top model has some very distinct advantages from the physicist's point of view. For example, consider the non-intuitive situation of an object moving one direction (velocity) while its acceleration is in the other direction. The object would slow down gradually, eventually coming to a stop, and then slowly gain speed in the other direction for as long as the force producing the acceleration is applied. Students who are presented with this example without any context (i.e. pure Newtonian model) become very confused and confounded by this example. Many give up. However, the rolling ball on the tilting table model, as shown at the top in Figure 2, makes these motion relationships much clearer. As Figure 3 further illustrates, the acceleration force is generated by the earth's gravitation and can be changed from left to right or from right to left just by tilting the table in either direction. Once the ball gains speed in one direction, tilting the table in the *other* direction would make the ball slow down *while it continues moving in the same direction* for a short distance, followed by the ball coming to a stop, then reversing direction with the ball slowly gaining speed.

However, the "rogue refrigerator" example (shown in the bottom of Figure 2), while an accurate representation, fails to capture well the importance of the acceleration force being con-

Figure 2. Two very different ways to represent a simulation about acceleration and velocity: a ball rolling on a table top that can be tilted (top) and a refrigerator moving on a frictionless floor (bottom)

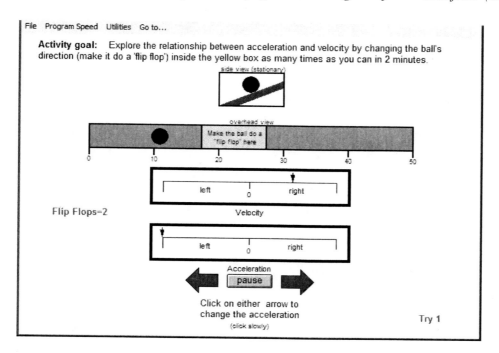

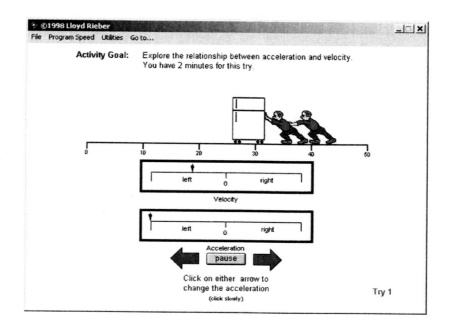

stant. One must imagine that the fellows pushing the refrigerator are doing so with a constant force throughout the refrigerator's movement. These fellows also magically appear on either side of the refrigerator instantaneously as the user clicks either acceleration arrow. Interestingly, in our research, people strongly prefer interacting with the refrigerator model. We think this is so simply because it is such an amusing example.

Finally, we have also studied the use of gaming within a simulation to help student focus their attention on developing strategic thinking (Rieber & Noah, 1997). Interestingly, in the research we have done, the use of a game generally interferes with explicit learning (ability to answer test questions), but improves participants' tacit learning (ability to perform on other tasks embedded in the simulation). Participants' level of enjoyment is also higher when given the game. Rather than improve their strategic thinking, participants tend to default into "video game mode" or "twitch mode" — they became so preoccupied with the game that this inhibits their ability to reflect on what they are doing and what they are learning. This antagonism between learning and enjoyment caused by the use of a game is most interesting. It is similar to the distinction that Norman (1993) makes between experiential cognition and reflective cognition. Experiential cognition is "a state in which we perceive and react to the events around us, efficiently and effortlessly" (Norman, 1993, p. 16). Reflective cognition, on the other hand requires deliberate thought and reasoning over time. One is not superior to the other. We rely on both. However, our research suggests that an over-enthusiastic view of gaming may inadvertently lead to learning environments that promote experience over reflection.

SOLUTIONS AND RECOMMENDATIONS: IMPLICATIONS FOR DESIGN

The study of educational uses of simulations is finally beginning to mature. I assert this because enough serious research has been done to point to both strengths and weaknesses of using simulations in education. We are beyond the tendency of making hypish and overly enthusiastic promises about how simulations can impact learning. This is a sign that we are making progress. What are the implications of the research so far on design? I will offer two fundamental principles that I believe can be derived from existing research. I then offer a completely different design model for conceptualizing the use of simulations in educational practice using the evolving design approach called Universal Design (Estes, 2004).

Experience and explanations are important in learning from a simulation, but explanations should be used to support experience, not visa

Figure 3. Imagine that the ball is moving down to the right. What would the ball's motion be if the person tilts the table the other way (i.e. change the acceleration, due to the earth's gravity, from "left to right" to "right to left")? The ball would continue moving to the right a short distance, stop, then starting moving the other way.

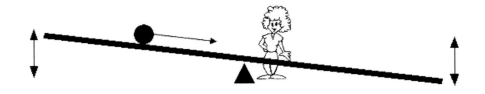

versa. As instructional strategies, explanations and activities have long been partners or allies. The longstanding tradition in education is to base instruction on well-crafted explanations followed by practice. However, this point of view is derived from educational practice based on old technologies, mainly those of teacher talk, textbooks, and simple educational media such as chalkboards and overheads. The technology of interactive multimedia, such as simulations, has progressed to the point where it is fair to question this hierarchy. Conversely, there is enough research now to indicate that experience without explanations (i.e. discovery learning) is problematic for most learners. So, this research also offers affirmation about the importance of explanations. The profound difference is to now to give experience the dominant role (Taylor & Chi, 2006). The question of how much explanation to give and when remains elusive, so this is a fruitful area for more research. Perhaps a good place to start is to observe master teachers expertly using interactive multimedia to see how and when they offer explanations and debriefings that capitalize on a student's meaningful and engaging experience with a simulation.

To be effective aids to learning, simulations must promote reflection. This principle is strongly related to the previous one. The whole point of education is to induce and promote reflection by students. The highly interactive nature of simulations, especially when coupled with game-like features, is a powerful way to engage students in meaningful tasks. However, the research shows that students do not spontaneously reflect on or about what they are doing in the simulation. But, one must have something to reflect *about*, so the highly interactive experiences made possible in a simulation become the all-important "grist" for the reflection "mill." One strategy to promote reflection in a discovery-based simulation is to give students the task of designing assignments for other students (Vreman-de Olde & de Jong, 2004).

I end this section by offering a very different way of understanding the design and role of simulations on educational practice. Most of the simulations I have created and studied have been in the area of physics, namely Newtonian mechanics. In all the research I've done, I have been fascinated by those times when people who previously thought of themselves as simply unable to learn physics were now able to "get it" when they used my simulation. What struck me most is their emotional reaction to their learning. Although they signed up to participate in the research, with the promise of receiving some extra course credit and absolute assurance that their performance would be held in strictest confident, most seemed convinced that they would not learn anything about physics simply because they never could before. In a real sense, these people thought of themselves as "physics disabled." Their past school experiences made them believe they were simply not born with some necessary intellectual attribute that would make the learning of physics possible. Learning physics from the simulation offered them an approach that either stepped around or overcame their "disability." Of course, the simulation was not designed for people who thought of themselves this way. In fact, many people who saw no such disability in themselves also perceived the simulation as effective and useful. Somehow, the simulation was flexible enough in its design to accommodate such a wide range of learners.

The phenomena of one design being flexible enough to be beneficial to people with and without a disability is known as Universal Design (UD), a term first coined by Ron Mace of the Center for Universal Design at North Carolina State University. He defined UD as "…the design of products and environments to be usable by all people, to the greatest extent possible, without the need for adaptation or specialized design" (The Center for Universal Design, 2004). The principles of UD originate from the barrier-free movement associated with the passing in the United States of the

Rehabilitation Act of 1973 and American with Disabilities Act of 1990. Most of the examples of UD are in architecture and engineering, such as curb cuts for people in wheelchairs and closed captioning for the hearing impaired. But, curb cuts are equally beneficial to someone pulling a heavy suitcase or pushing a baby stroller. Closed captioning is an even better example of UD because it shows how the decision to implement UD can lead to cheap and practical improvements for all people. Before the decision was made to include the special closed captioning computer chip in all televisions, it was extremely expensive to retrofit a television for closed captioning. Including the closed captioning chip in all televisions costs almost nothing, about one US dollar per television. The almost ubiquitous availability of closed captioning has led to unexpected users of this technology. For example, one of the largest groups using closed captioning are not people with hearing impairments, but couples who like to watch TV in bed but tend to fall asleep at different times. Here are the core principles of UD (The Center for Universal Design, 2004):

1. Equitable use
2. Flexibility in use
3. Simple and intuitive to use
4. Perceptible information
5. Tolerance for error
6. Low physical effort
7. Size and space for approach and use

Universal Design for Learning is based on using inclusive instructional strategies that benefit a broad range of learners (McGuire, Scott, & Shaw, 2006; Rose & Meyer, 2000, 2002). Although intended primarily to serve students with disabilities, the concepts apply to all learners if one accepts that all people have their own unique differences, some of which are well aligned with mainstream educational practice and some that are not. While UD is embraced by special educators and others who work with people with disabilities,

its principles and tenets apply well to all students. Many concepts of UD rely on the affordances of digital media. A simple example is the flexible way in which digital text can be accessed and manipulated by people (e.g. magnification, screen reader software). But I have come to view the interactive affordances of interactive multimedia — especially those designed by blending the attributes of simulations, microworlds, and games — as a perfect example of universal design for learning. Well-designed simulations meet all of the principles of UD. The field of human-computer interaction and its applications, such as interface design, has been a prominent influence on UD. As a field, instructional technology is well known for its integration of research, theory, and practice. Instructional Technology has long embraced very different theoretical and research perspectives, and the affordances of technology, in the search to better understand how learning occurs with the help of technology. Similarly, Universal Design seeks to use all existing understanding of learning and instruction, coupled with the advantages/affordances of digital media, to design instruction that is accessible to all people.

CONCLUSION

In this chapter, I have outlined several broad themes related to learning within computer-based simulations. The field of instructional technology has wrestled with the implications of designing learning environments based on very different philosophical orientations. A key question is when to defer to instruction as an intervention. Presenting too much instruction with a simulation too soon may inhibit a student from the advantages of discovery learning — using the scientific method to think like a scientist. Instead, students may just continue to see science as an accumulation of facts and principles needing to be memorized. However, research clearly shows that most students are ill-equipped to handle the full discovery learning process without some level of support. Instruction is surely a viable means to provide some of this support. But other means for support deserve continued attention, such as providing hints and suggestions during the simulation, model progression techniques, carefully chosen model cases and metaphors, and appropriate use of multiple representations. Perhaps the most important support is a teacher who knows how to capitalize on the simulation's affordances for learning. Interestingly, emphasizing the importance of the teacher again relates simulations to microworlds.

I believe that representations matter a great deal in the design of simulations. Effective representations must do three things (Norman, 1993):

1. Appropriately show important, critical features of a domain while ignoring the irrelevant;
2. Be appropriate for the person; and
3. Be appropriate for the task.

Decisions on the representation of a simulation's feedback are likely to depend on a complex interrelationship between many variables, such as the domain or content being modeled, learning outcomes, levels of cognitive processing, levels of instructional support, and the user's preferred style of learning.

FUTURE RESEARCH DIRECTIONS

One of the most important directions for future research is understanding the educational role and potential of massively multi-player online role-playing games, or MMORPGs. In these environments, a large number of players, sometimes in the thousands, interact with one another online in a "virtual world." Examples currently popular (this is sure to change) include World of Warcraft and Rise of Nations. Not only is the technology of these highly visual, 3D, persistent virtual worlds

constantly improving at a "Moore's law-like" rate, but the rate at which people (children, teens, and adults) are joining and participating in MMORPGs is likewise growing at a phenomenal pace. Serious research into these virtual worlds has just begun (Dickey, 2005, 2006; Squire, 2006). Very few MMORPGs are designed specifically for education (a notable exception is Quest Atlantis; see Barab, Dodge, Thomas, Jackson, & Tuzun, 2007; Barab, Thomas, Dodge, Carteaux, & Tuzun, 2005). A problem that must be overcome is how to bridge the serious research that already taken place on the topics of simulation and modeling tools to evolving research on MMORPGs. Many of the simulations and games designed for educational research have resulted from relatively small groups with limited funds. Indeed, even those projects funded by large NSF grants are dwarfed in comparison to the investment required to design high-end MMORPGs and other persistent virtual worlds, such as Second Life (Childress & Braswell, 2006). There is a need to also link the MMORPG design community with the educational research community. Without doing so, the data of educational research will be limited to small scale ethnographies of MMORPG player behavior, with much of this limited to self-report data.

The educational research community also needs to reconcile (or mature) in the way it views or considers constructivist interpretations of learning with simulations and other forms of interactive multimedia. Recent articles, highly critical of discovery-based or constructivist learning, such as Kirschner, Sweller and Clark (2006) and Mayer (2004) inappropriately confuse constructivist learning with "sink or swim" learning approaches where students are seemingly left to discover a content's concepts and principles solely on their own. Guided forms of learning, whether these strategies are called "instruction" or not, are not antithetical to constructivist perspectives. Research with simulations within discovery-based contexts is designed to understand the boundaries of learners' capabilities to uncover the relationships of a simulation's underlying model. As students succeed and struggle with their interactions the simulation, researchers learn where any number of forms of structure, guidance, scaffolding, etc. can then be added to mitigate obstacles to learning while hopefully not subverting or thwarting those times when learners are successful (e.g. Sins, Savelsbergh, & van Joolingen, 2005). Much of the added structure can be in the form of variations to the simulation's interface, help strategies, and the like. Much of the effort, similar to our own research investigating the role of explanations (Rieber et al., 2004), is aimed to support student learning while involved in the simulation. Understanding where instruction is not necessary, or most needed, remains a core research and design objective.

REFERENCES

Ainsworth, S. (1999). The functions of multiple representations. *Computers and Education, 33*, 131-152.

Ainsworth, S., Bibby, P., & Wood, D. (2002). Examining the effects of different multiple representational systems in learning primary mathematics. *Journal of the Learning Sciences, 11*(1), 25-61.

Alesandrini, K. (1984). Pictures and adult learning. *Instructional Science, 13*, 63-77.

Barab, S., Dodge, T., Thomas, M. K., Jackson, C., & Tuzun, H. (2007). Our designs and the social agendas they carry. *Journal of the Learning Sciences, 16*(2), 263.

Barab, S., Thomas, M., Dodge, T., Carteaux, R., & Tuzun, H. (2005). Making learning fun: Quest atlantis, A game without guns. *Educational Technology Research and Development, 53*(1), 86.

Childress, M. D., & Braswell, R. (2006). Using massively multiplayer online role-playing games for online learning. *Distance Education, 27*(2), 187-196.

de Jong, T., & van Joolingen, W. R. (1998). Scientific discovery learning with computer simulations of conceptual domains. *Review of Educational Research, 68*(2), 179-201.

Dickey, M. D. (2005). Engaging by design: How engagement strategies in popular computer and video games can inform instructional design. *Educational Technology Research & Development, 53*(2), 67-83.

Dickey, M. D. (2006). Game design narrative for learning: Appropriating adventure game design narrative and techniques for the design of interactive learning environments. *Educational Technology Research & Development, 54*(3), 245-263.

diSessa, A., & Abelson, H. (1986). Boxer: A reconstructible computational medium. *Communications of the ACM, 29*(9), 859-868.

diSessa, A., Abelson, H., & Ploger, D. (1991). An overview of Boxer. *Journal of Mathematical Behavior, 10*, 3-15.

Estes, M. (2004). Universal design. In M. Orey, M. A. Fitzgerald & R. M. Branch (Eds.), *Educational Media and Technology Yearbook 2004, 29*, 86-92. Westport, CT: Libraries Unlimited.

Gentner, D., & Stevens, A. (Eds.). (1983). *Mental models*. Hillsdale, NJ: Lawrence Erlbaum Associates.

Glynn, S. M. (1995). Conceptual bridges: Using analogies to explain scientific concepts. *The Science Teacher, 62*(9), 25-27.

Glynn, S. M., Duit, R., & Thiele, R. B. (1995). Teaching science with analogies: A strategy for constructing knowledge. In S. Glynn & R. Duit (Eds.), *Learning science in the schools: Research reforming practice* (pp. 247-273). Mahwah, NJ: Lawrence Erlbaum Associates.

Horwitz, P. (1999). Designing computer models that teach. In W. Feurzeig & N. Roberts (Eds.), *Modeling and Simulation in Science and Mathematics Education* (pp. 179-196). New York: Springer-Verlag.

Hulshof, C. D., & de Jong, T. (2006). Using Just-in-Time Information to Support Scientific Discovery Learning in a Computer-Based Simulation. *Interactive Learning Environments, 14*(1), 79.

Johnson-Laird, P. N., Girotto, V., & Legrenzi, P. (2004). Reasoning from inconsistency to consistency. *Psychological Review, 111*(3), 640.

Jonassen, D., Strobel, J., & Gottdenker, J. (2005). Model building for conceptual change. *Interactive Learning Environments, 13*(1-2), 15-37.

Kirschner, P. A., Sweller, J., & Clark, R. E. (2006). Why minimal guidance during instruction does not work: An analysis of the failure of constructivist, discovery, problem-based, experiential, and inquiry-based teaching. *Educational Psychologist, 41*(2), 75-86.

Kluge, A. (2007). Experiential learning methods, simulation complexity and their effects on different target groups. *Journal of Educational Computing Research, 36*(3), 323.

Levin, J. R., Anglin, G. J., & Carney, R. N. (1987). On empirically validating functions of pictures in prose. In D. M. Willows & H. A. Houghton (Eds.), *The psychology of illustration, volume 1: Basic research* (pp. 51-85). New York: Springer-Verlag.

Manlove, S., Lazonder, A. W., & de Jong, T. (2006). Regulative support for collaborative scientific inquiry learning. *Journal of Computer Assisted Learning, 22*(2), 87.

Mayer, R. E. (2001). *Multimedia learning*. Cambridge, UK: Cambridge University Press.

Mayer, R. E. (2004). Should there be a three-strikes rule against pure discovery learning? The case for guided methods of instruction? *American Psychologist, 59*, 14-19.

Mayer, R. E. (Ed.). (2005). *Handbook of multimedia learning*. New York: Cambridge University Press.

McGuire, J. M., Scott, S. S., & Shaw, S. F. (2006). Universal design and its applications in educational environments. *Remedial and Special Education, 27*(3), 166.

Norman, D. A. (1993). *Things that make us smart: Defending human attributes in the age of the machine*. Reading, MA: Addison-Wesley Publishing Co.

Norman, D. A. (2002). *The design of everyday things*. New York: BasicBooks.

Olive, J. (1998). Opportunities to explore and integrate mathematics with "The Geometer's Sketchpad" in designing learning environments for developing understanding of geometry and space. In R. Lehrer & D. Chazan (Eds.), *Designing learning environments for developing understanding of geometry and space* (pp. 395-418). Mahwah, NJ: Lawrence Erlbaum Associates.

Paivio, A. (1990). *Mental representations: A dual coding approach* (2nd ed.). New York: Oxford University Press.

Paivio, A. (1991). Dual coding theory: Retrospect and current status. *Canadian Journal of Psychology, 45*, 255-287.

Papert, S. (1980a). Computer-based microworlds as incubators for powerful ideas. In R. Taylor (Ed.), *The computer in the school: Tutor, tool, tutee* (pp. 203-210). New York: Teacher's College Press.

Papert, S. (1980b). *Mindstorms: Children, computers, and powerful ideas*. New York: BasicBooks.

Penner, D. E. (2000/2001). Cognition, computers, and synthetic science: Building knowledge and meaning through modeling. *Review of Research in Education, 25*, 1-35.

Resnick, M. (1994). *Turtles, termites, and traffic jams.* Cambridge, MA: MIT Press.

Rieber, L. P. (1994). *Computers, graphics, and learning.* Madison, WI: Brown & Benchmark.

Rieber, L. P. (1996). Animation as feedback in a computer-based simulation: Representation matters. *Educational Technology Research & Development, 44*(1), 5-22.

Rieber, L. P. (2003). Microworlds. In D. Jonassen (Ed.), *Handbook of research for educational communications and technology* (2nd ed., pp. 583-603). Mahwah, NJ: Lawrence Erlbaum Associates.

Rieber, L. P., & Noah, D. (1997). *Effect of gaming and graphical metaphors on reflective cognition within computer-based simulations.* Paper presented at the annual meeting of the American Educational Research Association, Chicago.

Rieber, L. P., Noah, D., & Nolan, M. (1998). *Metaphors as graphical representations within open-ended computer-based simulations*: Paper presented at the annual meeting of the American Educational Research Association, San Diego.

Rieber, L. P., & Parmley, M. W. (1995). To teach or not to teach? Comparing the use of computer-based simulations in deductive versus inductive approaches to learning with adults in science. *Journal of Educational Computing Research, 13*(4), 359-374.

Rieber, L. P., Smith, M., Al-Ghafry, S., Strickland, W., Chu, G., & Spahi, F. (1996). The role of meaning in interpreting graphical and textual feedback during a computer-based simulation. *Computers and Education, 27*(1), 45-58.

Rieber, L. P., Tzeng, S., & Tribble, K. (2004). Discovery learning, representation, and explanation within a computer-based simulation: Finding the right mix. *Learning and Instruction, 14,* 307-323.

Roschelle, J., Kaput, J., & Stroup, W. (2000). SimCalc: Accelerating student engagement with the mathematics of change. In M. J. Jacobson & R. B. Kozma (Eds.), *Learning the sciences of the 21st Century: Research, design, and implementing advanced technology learning environments* (pp. 47-75). Hillsdale, NJ: Lawrence Erlbaum Associates.

Rose, D., & Meyer, A. (2000). Universal design for learning. *Journal of Special Education Technology, 15*(1), 67-70.

Rose, D., & Meyer, A. (2002). *Teaching every student in the digital age: Universal design for learning.* Alexandria, VA: Association for Supervision and Curriculum Development.

Sadoski, M., & Paivio, A. (1994). A dual coding view of imagery and verbal processes in reading comprehension. In R. B. Ruddell, M. R. Ruddell & H. Singer (Eds.), *Theoretical models and processes of reading* (4th ed., pp. 582-601). Newark, DE: International Reading Association.

Sadoski, M., & Paivio, A. (2001). *Imagery and text: A dual coding theory of reading and writing.* Mahwah, NJ: Lawrence Erlbaum Associates.

Sins, P. H. M., Savelsbergh, E. R., & van Joolingen, W. R. (2005). The Difficult Process of Scientific Modelling: An Analysis Of Novices' Reasoning During Computer-Based Modelling. *International Journal of Science Education, 27*(14ov), 1695-1721.

Squire, K. (2006). From content to context: Videogames as designed experience. *Educational Researcher, 35*(8), 19-29.

Taylor, R. S., & Chi, M. T. H. (2006). Simulation versus text: Acquisition of implicit and explicit information. *Journal of Educational Computing Research, 35*(3), 289.

The Center for Universal Design. (2004). What is universal design? Retrieved November 1, 2004, from http://www.design.ncsu.edu/cud/univ_design/ud.htm

Van Joolingen, W. R., King, S., & de Jong, T. (1997). The SimQuest authoring system for simulation-base discovery environments. In B. du Boulay & R. Mizoguchi (Eds.), *Knowledge and media in learning systems* (pp. 79-87). Amsterdam: IOS.

Vreman-de Olde, C., & de Jong, T. (2004). Student-Generated Assignments about Electrical Circuits in a Computer Simulation. *International Journal of Science Education, 26*(7), 859.

White, B. Y. (1993). ThinkerTools: Causal models, conceptual change, and science education. *Cognition and Instruction, 10*(1), 1-100.

White, B. Y., & Horowitz, P. (1987). *ThinkerTools: Enabling children to understand physical laws* (No. 6470): Bolt, Beranek, and Newman, Inc.

ADDITIONAL READING

Bransford, J. B., Brown, A. L., & Cocking, R. R. (Eds.). (1999). *How people learn: Brain, mind, experience, and school.* Washington, DC: National Academy Press.

Csikszentmihalyi, M. (1990). *Flow: The psychology of optimal experience.* New York: Harper & Row.

Dickey, M. D. (2005). Brave New (Interactive) Worlds: A Review of the Design Affordances and Constraints of Two 3D Virtual Worlds as Interactive Learning Environments. *Interactive Learning Environments, 13*(1-2), 121.

Dickey, M. D. (2005). Three-Dimensional Virtual Worlds and Distance Learning: Two Case Studies of Active Worlds as a Medium for Distance Education. *British Journal of Educational Technology, 36*(3), 439.

Dickey, M. D. (2006). Girl gamers: The controversy of girl games and the relevance of female-oriented game design for instructional design. *British Journal of Educational Technology, 37*(5), 785-793.

diSessa, A. (2000). *Changing minds: Computers, learning, and literacy.* Cambridge, MA: The MIT Press.

Elkind, D. (2007). *The power of play: How spontaneous, imaginative activities lead to happier, healthier children.* Cambridge, MA: Da Capo Lifelong.

Gee, J. P. (2003). *What video games have to teach us about learning and literacy.* New York: Palgrave MacMillan.

Greene, J. A., & Azevedo, R. (2007). A Theoretical Review of Winne and Hadwin's Model of Self-Regulated Learning: New Perspectives and Directions. *Review of Educational Research, 77*(3), 334.

Kafai, Y. (1995). *Minds in play: Computer game design as a context for children's learning.* Hillsdale, NJ: Lawrence Erlbaum Associates.

Lowe, R., & Schnotz, W. (Eds.). (2008). *Learning with animation: Research implications for design.* Cambridge, UK: Cambridge University Press.

Mayer, R. E. (1997). Multimedia learning: Are we asking the right questions? *Educational Psychologist, 32*(1), 1-19.

Norman, D. A. (2002). *The design of everyday things.* New York: BasicBooks.

Norman, D. A. (2004). *Emotional design: Why we love (or hate) everyday things.* New York: Basic Books.

Pinker, S. (1999). *How the mind works.* New York: Norton.

Prensky, M. (2001). *Digital game-based learning.* New York: McGraw-Hill.

Prensky, M. (2006). *Don't bother me, Mom, I'm learning! : How computer and video games are preparing your kids for 21st century success and how you can help!* St. Paul, MN: Paragon House.

Quinn, C. N. (2005). *Engaging learning: Designing e-learning simulation games.* San Francisco, CA: Pfeiffer.

Reed, S. K. (2006). Cognitive Architectures for Multimedia Learning. *Educational Psychologist, 41*(2), 87.

Resnick, M. (1998). Technologies for lifelong kindergarten. *Educational Technology Research & Development, 46*(4), 43-55.

Rieber, L. P. (1995). A historical review of visualization in human cognition. *Educational Technology Research & Development, 43*(1), 45-56.

Rieber, L. P. (1996). Seriously considering play: Designing interactive learning environments based on the blending of microworlds, simulations, and games. *Educational Technology Research & Development, 44*(2), 43-58.

Rieber, L. P., Davis, J. M., Matzko, M. J., & Grant, M. M. (in press). Children as critics of educational computer games designed by other children. In R. E. Ferdig (Ed.), *Handbook of research on effective electronic gaming in education.* Hershey, PA: Information Science Reference.

Schnotz, W., & Rasch, T. (2005). Enabling, Facilitating, and Inhibiting Effects of Animations in Multimedia Learning: Why Reduction of Cognitive Load Can Have Negative Results on Learning. *Educational Technology Research and Development, 53*(3), 47.

Sefton-Green, J. (2006). Youth, technology, and media cultures. *Review of Research in Education, 30*, 279-306.

Squire, K. (2002). Cultural framing of computer/video games. *The International Journal of Computer Game Research, 2*(1), Available online: http://www.gamestudies.org/0102/squire/.

Sutton-Smith, B. (1997). *The ambiguity of play.* Cambridge, Mass: Harvard University Press.

Tufte, E. R. (1983). *The visual display of quantitative information.* Cheshire, Connecticut: Graphics Press.

Tufte, E. R. (1990). *Envisioning information.* Cheshire, Connecticut: Graphics Press.

Tufte, E. R. (1997). *Visual explanations: Images and quantities, evidence and narrative.* Cheshire, Connecticut: Graphics Press.

Vadeboncoeur, J. A. (2006). Engaging Young People: Learning in Informal Contexts. *Review of Research in Education, 30*(1), 239.

Veletsianos, G. (2007). Cognitive and Affective Benefits of an Animated Pedagogical Agent: Considering Contextual Relevance and Aesthetics. *Journal of Educational Computing Research, 36*(4), 373.

Chapter XIII
Fostering Transfer in Multimedia Instructional Environments

Gina J. Mariano
Virginia Tech, USA

Peter E. Doolittle
Virginia Tech, USA

David Hicks
Virginia Tech, USA

ABSTRACT

The role and promotion of transfer in multimedia instructional environments is an oft-neglected concept in instructional multimedia research. However, while most instructional multimedia research does not focus specifically on transfer, the majority of basic multimedia research conducted uses retention and transfer as dependent measures. The purposes of this chapter are to (a) provide a review of the current state of the transfer literature, (b) provide a synthesis of the existing literature on the evidence for transfer in multimedia instructional environments, and (c) provide a series of strategies for constructing and using multimedia for the purpose of fostering transfer. The significance of proactively creating multimedia instructional environments that fosters transfer lies in the benefits of creating knowledge that may be generalized and applied in the "real world." Specifically, knowledge that may be generalized, applied, or transferred broadly facilitates the learner's ability to solve problems of all types. In addition and unfortunately, even under the best of conditions, fostering transfer is challenging; thus, a proactive stance in fostering transfer is necessary to increase the likelihood of generating knowledge transfer.

INTRODUCTION

Multimedia instructional environments have become an integral part of modern education. Through the use of simulations, tutorials, games and animations, multimedia has become a bona fide instructional strategy. As multimedia is used with greater frequency in educational contexts, however, questions arise as to the efficacy of multimedia instruction in fostering cognitive change. Current research addressing the efficacy of multimedia instruction has found mostly positive, though some negative, results on cognitive performance as measured by recall and transfer of multimedia instructional episodes. In several cases, variation in performance is evident by significant transfer effects in the presence of non-significant recall effects (e.g., Mautone & Mayer, 2001). This variation across recall and transfer is not entirely surprising as there is evidence that transfer may be a more sensitive measure of learning than basic recall (Bransford & Schwartz, 1999). Therefore, as instruction ventures into the realm of multimedia instructional environments it is imperative that transfer become a central pillar in multimedia research. The objectives of this chapter are to (a) provide a review of the current state of the transfer literature, (b) provide a synthesis of the existing literature on the evidence for transfer in multimedia instructional environments, and (c) provide a series of strategies for constructing and using multimedia for the purpose of fostering transfer.

BACKGROUND

Multimedia learning involves learning from instruction that involves more than one type of media (e.g., computer, speakers), modality (e.g., visual, auditory), and/or representation (e.g., animation, narration) (Reed, 2006; Schnotz & Bannert, 2003). For example, Mayer and Anderson (1991) found that students learned more from a multimedia tutorial addressing "how a tire pump works" that included both an animation *and* a narration as opposed to an animation or narration only. Research into multimedia learning has determined that, in general, multiple forms of media, modalities, and representations facilitate learning (e.g., Eilam & Poyas, in press; Mayer, 2005). This research into multimedia learning tends to focus on knowledge recall and transfer as dependent measures. The current chapter focuses on the dependent measure of knowledge transfer.

An examination of knowledge transfer in multimedia learning needs to begin with an understanding of transfer, in general. Knowledge transfer can be described as the ability to use or apply knowledge learned from one problem, situation or context to different problems, situations or contexts (Salomon & Perkins, 1989). In education, the goal is that knowledge learned in the classroom will be transferred to problems and situations outside of the classroom. Unfortunately, this goal is not always achieved and students are often unable to transfer information to contexts other then the one in which the knowledge was first learned (see Detterman & Sternberg, 1993). Detterman and Sternberg, in a review of the transfer literature, state: "First, most studies fail to find transfer. Second, those studies claiming transfer can only be said to have found transfer by the most generous of criteria" (p. 15). That said, transfer *is* evident in the literature on learning (see Fuchs et al., 2003; Georghiades, 2000; Singley & Anderson, 1989) and must be addressed in a comprehensive theory or approach to multimedia learning.

Researchers in the area of learning have studied the concept of transfer in academic settings for decades. Edward Thorndike, in the early 1900s, developed the "identical elements" theory of transfer that posited that the amount of transfer between familiar and unfamiliar situations is determined by the number of elements the different situations have in common (Thorndike, 1903; Thorndike & Woodworth, 1901). He argued that this was the reason school curricula should emphasize skills that will be important outside of the school setting. That is, the more of a connection there is between the information being taught and how it can be applied, the better the chances of students being able to transfer this information in the future. Similarly, Charles Osgood (1949), building on Thorndike's concept of identical elements and the theory of behaviorism, developed a theory of transfer stating that when stimulus-response pairs are similar in two situations, positive transfer will occur; when stimuli are different but responses are the same in two situations, some degree of positive transfer will occur; and, finally, when stimuli are the same but response are different in two situations, no transfer will occur. Finally, building on Thorndike's concept of identical elements and Osgood's concept of similarity, as well as current models of information processing, John Anderson (see Singley & Anderson, 1989) stated that transfer was the product of overlapping or shared cognitive elements or abstract knowledge structures between a learned task and a new task. This focus on the role of cognition in transfer currently dominates the transfer literature; however, before addressing the findings of this cognition and transfer literature, a brief expansion of the concept of transfer is necessary.

Types of Transfer

Throughout the investigation of transfer, there have been several distinctions made between different types of transfer: positive versus negative transfer, vertical versus lateral transfer, and near versus far transfer (see Haskell, 2000). When learning in one situation or environment facilitates learning or performance in another situation or environment, *positive transfer* is said to have occurred. For example, students who engaged in a narrated multimedia tutorial addressing the fundamentals of the lift force on airplanes demonstrated increased problem solving transfer when the narration included aural attentional cues,

that is, key words and phrases spoken in a slower, deeper intonation (Mautone & Mayer, 2001). On the other hand, if knowledge that was learned in one situation or environment impedes a person's ability to learn or perform in another situation or environment, *negative transfer* has occurred. For example, Mayer, Sobko, and Mautone (2003) found that native-English speaking students' problem solving transfer decreased after engaging in a narrated multimedia tutorial addressing lightning formation where the narration was in a foreign accent (i.e., a Russian accent for English speakers) as compared to a narrated multimedia tutorial where the narration was in a standard-English accent.

Expanding on positive and negative transfer, *lateral transfer* implies that the original learning situation and the subsequent learning or performance situation are approximately of the same level of complexity. For example, Lee, Plass, and Homer (2006) determined that students demonstrated significant transfer between a low complexity multimedia simulation of the ideal gas law and a low complexity problem solving transfer task, answering questions such as "Why does a toy balloon burst when it rises in the air?" *Vertical transfer*, however, occurs when the learning of less complex knowledge or skills affects the learning of more complex knowledge or skills, especially when the less and more complex knowledge and skills are hierarchically related. For example, Keiler (2007) found that high school students' learning of advanced science and mathematics – graphing skills, data analysis skills and interpretation skills – were based on the learning of component or subordinate science and mathematics skills in elementary and middle school. Thus, learning less complex science and mathematics skills in elementary and middle school facilitated the learning of more complex science and mathematics skill in high school.

Finally, *near transfer* occurs when the original learning situation, environment or problem is very similar to the subsequent learning or performance situation, environment or problem. For example, Doolittle and Mariano (in press) engaged students in a multimedia tutorial designed to address historical inquiry through the analysis of historical letters and then asked the students to solve highly related (near) problems, such as "How might you go about analyzing a picture taken during the Great Depression?" In contrast, *far transfer* occurs when the original and subsequent learning or performance situations, environments, or problems are very different. While far transfer would seem to be present in the use of language or mathematics in everyday life – language or math learned in elementary or secondary school being used in everyday adult situations – empirically and methodologically, far transfer is difficult to demonstrate. However, Adey and Shayer (1993) provided students with cognitive conflict and metacognition training embedded within bi-weekly science lessons for two years. Adey and Shayer determined that this training led to both immediate improvements in students' science learning (near transfer), but also subsequent improvement in mathematics and

English (far transfer). Thus, while far transfer is difficult to demonstrate, it is not impossible.

This difficulty in demonstrating far transfer makes visible the concept that these types of transfer – positive/negative transfer, lateral/vertical transfer, and near/far transfer – are continua, not discrete, dichotomous categories. These three continua may be represented as a "transfer space" (see Figure 1), allowing the representation of a transfer situation across all three continua simultaneously. For example, the previous case from Lee, Plass, and Homer (2006), where students transferred between a low complexity multimedia simulation of the ideal gas law and a low complexity problem solving task, demonstrates a positive, lateral, and near transfer situation and is represented in Figure 1. This three-dimensional transfer space provides a heuristic for the graphic comparison of various types of transfer.

Fostering Transfer

Transfer is an essential concept in human learning, education and training. If we, as human beings,

Figure 1. A three-dimensional transfer space representing the positive/negative, lateral/vertical, and near/far transfer continua

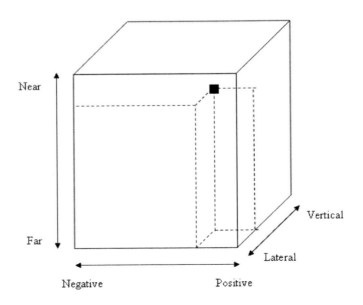

simply learn specific solutions to specific prob- lems, then the nature of education and training must change significantly and what it means to be human must be re-examined. The bad news is that transfer is often not found in research addressing human cognition: "The question for which we do have some empirical answers has to do with how generalizable cognitive training is from one subject area to another. As for now, the answer is not very much" (Schooler, 1989, p. 11). The good news is that,

A large body of empirical research on transfer in psychology...demonstrates that there can be either large amounts of transfer, a modest amount of transfer, no transfer all, or even negative transfer. How much there is and whether transfer is posi- tive depends in reliable ways on the experimental situation and the relation of the material originally learned to the transfer material. (Anderson, Reder, & Simon, 1996).

Thus, given the existing literature on transfer and the importance of transfer in cognitive and behavioral functioning: How can teachers, train- ers and instructional designers proactively foster transfer? What follows are a few instructional strategies – a non-exhaustive, but essential, list – designed to foster transfer.

1. *Provide students with an opportunity to learn information deeply and meaningfully.* Perhaps the most salient finding related to the fostering of transfer is that transfer is enhanced when knowledge and skills are learned deeply and thoroughly. Deep learning, learning with understanding, or conceptual learning, has been demonstrated to result in more significant transfer than superficial, mimetic, or rote learning (Brown & Kane, 1988; Fuchs et al., 2003; Reed & Saavedra, 1986). Students who learn infor- mation thoroughly will be better able to build on this foundation and apply it to other tasks

(Katayama, 2005; Prawat, 1989; Salomon & Perkins, 1989). Barnett and Cici (2002), in discussing the work of Brown (1989) and Brown and Kane (1988), conclude:

Children transferred most successfully when they understood events at a causal level rather than merely learned to replicate par- ticular behaviors. That is, they transferred when they developed a deep, rather than surface, understanding. (p. 616)

This essential principle encapsulates all of the guidelines that follow. It should also be noted, however, that in some cases, engaging in these guidelines may impede the initial acquisition of knowledge. That is, while initial learning may be fostered by instruc- tional environments that involve discrete and concrete content experienced in a limited and well-defined context (see Anderson, 2005), learning for transfer is fostered by instructional environments that emphasize learning of principles over discrete facts and practicing knowledge and skills in varied contexts (Bjork & Richardson-Klahaven, 1989; Gick & Holyoak, 1980, 1983). This principle, that transfer benefits from deep learning, also helps to frame many cases of transfer failure; that is, a failure to transfer is often linked to a failure to learn deeply, originally (e.g., see Klahr & Carver, 1988; Lee, 1998; Lee & Pennington, 1993).

2. *Provide students with an opportunity to develop a metacognitive understanding.* Extending the first guideline of fostering transfer through the development of deep cognitive understanding, the development of metacognitive understanding – aware- ness, planning, monitoring, reflecting and improving of cognitive processes for com- prehension and performance – has also been demonstrated to lead to increased transfer (Bransford & Schwartz, 1999; Butterfield

& Nelson, 1991). Specifically, several types of metacognitive interventions have been demonstrated to improve transfer, including teaching students to value and become self-aware of transfer, teaching students to self-identify their learning goals, teaching students to employ and monitor cognitive strategies, and teaching students to reflect, elaborate, self-question and explain their understandings (Adey & Shayer, 1993; Fuchs et al., 2003; Georghiades, 2000; Montague, & Boss, 1986; Palinscar & Brown, 1984; Pirolli & Recker, 1994; Scardamalia, Bereiter, & Steinbach, 1984). For example, Fuchs et al. (2003) sought to foster problem-solving transfer by explicitly teaching students to group or categorize problems that have a common solution and to actively search new or novel problems for the existence of these problem categories. These two processes of categorizing and searching are metacognitive strategies that focus on the control of cognition, "the treatment encourages students to engage in metacognitive processes by familiarizing them with the notion of transfer, alerting them to the need to transfer skills across situations, and cautioning them to search novel-looking problems to recognize familiar problem structures" (p. 302). Fuchs et al. found that students who employed the categorize and search strategies were better able to solve familiar problems (near transfer) as well as novel problems (far transfer). These findings demonstrate that not only should students employ cognitive processes to learn deeply, but that having students aware and in control of their cognitive processes (metacognition) is also important to transfer.

3. *Provide students with an opportunity to learn abstract principles, not simply discrete facts.* Relative to transfer, while it is important that students develop and use their cognitive and metacognitive skills

to foster deep learning, the nature of *what* is learned is also important. Specifically, it has been demonstrated that transfer is increased when students learn abstract and underlying principles and rules, rather than discrete facts (Anderson, Reder, & Simon, 1996; Barnett & Ceci, 2002; Brown, 1989; Gick & Holyoak, 1987, Perkins & Saloman, 1987; Singley & Anderson, 1989). For example, Novick (1988) examined the ability of novices and experts to transfer an underlying mathematical principle from a source problem to a target problem; the underlying principle was least common multiples. Novick found that without any pre-exposure to a similar problem only 6.3% of novices and experts employed the LCM in solving the target problem. However, following pre-exposure to a problem whose solution involved the use of LCM, still only 6.3% of novice solved the target problem using LCM, while 56.3% of experts now solved the target problem using LCM. This drastic increase for experts indicates their ability to better transfer abstract principles than novices. These findings demonstrate the benefits from learning to transfer abstract principles and rules, and not simply specific information or solutions to specific requests or problems.

4. *Provide students with the opportunity to learn from multiple and varied examples.* Developing a deep learning, that includes principles and rules, is facilitated by learning from multiple and varied examples, which then also facilitates transfer (see Bransford & Schwartz, 1999). When teaching concepts and procedures, providing practice with diverse examples increases the use of the concepts and procedures in a variety of situations (Engle, 2006; Gick & Holyoak, 1987; Schmidt & Bjork, 1992; Wagner, 2006;). For example, Gentner, Loewenstein and Thompson (2003) compared students

who were given multiple cases (examples) involving negotiating strategies to students who received no such examples. Gentner et al. determined that (a) students who received multiple cases of the negotiating strategies, and were taught a strategy to compare the cases, transferred the strategies more frequently to new cases than students who received neither multiple cases nor comparison training; (b) students who were simply asked to compare multiple cases of the negotiating strategies (i.e., no strategy instruction) transferred the strategies more frequently to new cases than students who were not asked to compare the multiple cases; and (c) students who were asked or trained to compare the multiple cases used the strategies more often in face-to-face negotiations than students who were not asked or trained to compare the multiple cases and students who did not receive the multiple cases. These findings provide evidence that learning from multiple and varied examples leads to more transfer.

5. *Provide students with the opportunity to learn new knowledge and skills in multiple contexts.* From Thorndike to the present, the issue of contextualization and transfer has been central. Is knowledge bound to the context in which it is learned to such an extent that it cannot be transferred to new situations? There are classic examples of context-bound knowledge including caretakers who could make sophisticated mathematical calculations in a supermarket, but had difficulty making similar calculations involving paper-and-pencil school-based tasks (Lave 1988) and similarly, children who could make sophisticated mathematical calculations when selling candy on the streets of Brazil, but performed less well on similar calculations in a school setting (Saxe, 1988). Anderson et al. (1996), however, argue against such a strong view of contextualiza-

tion: "There are many demonstrations of learning that transfer across contexts and of failures to find any context specificity in the learning (e.g., Fernandez & Glenberg, 1985; Saufley, Otaka, & Bavaresco, 1985) – a fact that has often frustrated researchers who were looking for context sensitivity" (p. 6). One avenue to reduce contextualization is to teach students to develop knowledge across multiple contexts. For example, Wagner (2006) examined the growth of transferability of statistical concepts and statistical understanding of one student, Maria, in an 8-week course. Wagner framed his investigation of Maria's growth of transferability as the acquisition and eventual transfer of "pieces" of knowledge or skill, what Wagner calls "knowledge resources," from one context to another. This approach differs from the traditional view of transfer as occurring in wholes, that is, concept A is transferred in whole from situation X to situation Y. Wagner noted that Maria's ability to transfer pieces of statistical knowledge and skill improved only as she was able to experience the knowledge and skill in multiple contexts, and even then, only after considerable effort. "Maria took different ideas initially applicable only in isolated contexts…and associated them within a single knowledge frame. In doing so, the isolated contexts to which they applied individually grew incrementally into a larger family of situations perceived by Maria to be alike" (p. 63). These findings provide evidence that knowledge, while context related, is transferable across contexts "through the incremental refinement of knowledge resources that account for – rather than overlook – contextual variation" (Wagner, 2006, p. 1).

Ultimately, transfer has a checkered past, existing somewhat ephemerally. That said, transfer does exist and any comprehensive theory of learning should account for it. As the domain of multimedia learning and instruction continues to develop, it is necessary that transfer be examined within the boundaries of learning in multimedia environments.

TRANSFER IN MULTIMEDIA INSTRUCTIONAL ENVIRONMENTS

Over the past two decades, research addressing the role of transfer in multimedia instructional environments has included both basic research, which is designed to expand the current knowledge base regarding learning in multimedia environments, and applied research, which is designed to operationalize basic research findings to solve problems, produce new results or products, or fulfill a need. Both this basic and applied research, however, are based on models of multimedia learning founded upon information processing models of human cognition. These multimedia learning models (see Hede, 2002; Mayer, 2001; Reed, 2006; Schnotz & Bannert, 2003) all focus on the selection, organization and integration of visual and auditory stimuli for the purpose of developing representations and mental models. Each of these models has spawned research that continues to inform the general conversation regarding the process and product of multimedia learning and instruction. The following discussion focuses solely on basic multimedia research that serves as the foundation of subsequent applied research.

The *basic research* focused on transfer in multimedia instructional environments arises primarily from the work of Mayer and colleagues (see Mayer, 2001), but is also informed by the work of others (see Hede, 2002; Mayer, 2001; Reed, 2006; Schnotz & Bannert, 2003). Through this work, Mayer developed the *cognitive theory of multimedia learning* as a theoretical foundation for the investigation of learning in multimedia

environments. While this theory does not focus specifically on transfer, the majority of empirical research conducted to establish and expand the theory uses retention and transfer as dependent measures. Thus, in developing the cognitive theory of multimedia learning, Mayer and colleagues have provided a foundation of basic research principles addressing transfer in multimedia environments. The following discussion of basic research addressing transfer and multimedia learning and instruction is based on a series of principles derived from, but not limited to, Mayer's work (see Mayer, 2005; see Table 2 for a summary).

The first of these multimedia transfer principles, the *multimedia principle*, provides a basis for the rest. Specifically, the multimedia principle states that students transfer more basic scientific knowledge – what causes lightning, how does a car brake work, how do plants survive – to new, yet similar problems (near, lateral, and positive transfer) when the instructional media involves animation *and* narration (e.g., a visual animation demonstrating how lightning forms with concurrent audio narration), as opposed to animation *or* narration alone (Mayer & Anderson, 1991). Providing a multimedia learning environment with concurrent animation and narration allows students to construct a more integrated mental model when compared to an animation or narration only instructional environment (Fletcher & Tobias, 2005). In addition, Gemino, Parker and Kutzschan (2006) found that adding context relevant graphics to a technology-mediated collaborate environment also improved students' transfer of the concepts discussed. This basic finding that multimedia instruction (e.g., animation + narration, pictures + text) provides for better transfer than single-media instruction serves as a foundation for transfer in multimedia environments.

In refining the multimedia principle, it has been determined that students will transfer basic knowledge better if the multimedia learning environment includes animations/diagrams with concurrent narration rather than animations/diagrams with concurrent on-screen text, the *modality principle* (Harskamp, Mayer, & Suhre, 2007; Mayer & Moreno, 1998; Moreno & Mayer, 1999), or animations/diagrams with both concurrent narration and on-screen text, the *redundancy principle* (Jamet & Le Bohec, 2007; Leahy, Chandler, Sweller, 2003). For example, Kalyuga, Chandler and Sweller (1999) provided participants with a physical science diagram accompanied by either an auditory narration, on-screen text narration, or both auditory and on-screen text narration. The results indicated that participants in the diagram + auditory narration condition recalled and transferred more information than either the diagram + on-screen text narration condition (modality principle) or the diagram + auditory narration + on-screen text narration condition (redundancy principle). In the case of both the modality and redundancy principles, the presence of a visual animation or diagram and a visual on-screen text description leads to a split-attention effect where learners are forced to divide their attention between the two stimuli occurring in the same modality (e.g., visual), reducing learners ability to experience and integrate the sources of knowledge. These two principles, modality and redundancy, indicate that multimedia instructional environments should be constructed to distribute the information to be presented across both visual and auditory cognitive processing channels (Baddeley, 2007; Baddeley & Hitch, 1974). Thus, a teacher could convert textbook pictures and text into narrated slide shows or movies.

While the aforementioned principles provide support for multimedia instructional environments that are constructed using animation and narration, additional research has indicated that transfer of learning is enhanced when these animation/narration messages are divided into short segments which the learner can control (Mayer & Chandler, 2001; Mayer, Dow, & Mayer, 2003), the *segmenting principle*. For example, Doolittle,

Lusk, Bryd and Mariano (in press) assessed students for recall and transfer who engaged in a comprehensive (150 minutes) multimedia tutorial addressing historical inquiry that was either segmented or non-segmented. In the segmented version, the tutorial stopped every 45-60 seconds and the students had the ability to stop and think about the tutorial or press a "Continue" button and proceed with the tutorial. In the non-segmented version, the tutorial played from beginning to end without stopping. The results indicated that students who engaged in a segmented multimedia tutorial recalled and transferred more information that students that engaged in a non-segmented tutorial. The segmentation principle specifies that students should be given some control over the pacing of multimedia tutorial (Aly, Elen, & Willems, 2005; Dalton, 1990; Milheim, 1990). Thus, a teacher could construct a movie of short Vietnam Veteran interviews that allow students to stop after each interview to think about the interview before beginning the next interview.

In addition to segmentation, another attribute of multimedia instructional tutorials that has been demonstrated to have a positive effect on transfer is the *signaling principle*. Signaling occurs when important or essential concepts within the message are signaled, cued, or emphasized through the use of previously stated learning objectives (Harp & Mayer, 1998); section headers, preview summary paragraphs, and keywords (Mautone & Mayer, 2001, Exp 1); altering the intonation of keywords and headers in the narration (Mautone & Mayer, 2001, Exp 2); or using colored arrows to point out key elements of a narration (Mautone & Mayer, 2001, Exp 3). The signaling principle indicates that providing students with scaffolds designed to direct their attention or guide their cognitive processing of information can benefit knowledge transfer. Thus, a teacher could create multimedia tutorial addressing Roman architecture that includes photos with arrows that point to particular architectural features in the photo as the narrator describes them.

While segmentation and signaling focus primarily on the visual aspect of the media, two multimedia principles, the personalized message principle and the voice principle, focus on the auditory aspect of the media. Specifically, transfer has been enhanced when the multimedia narration is in first or second person, rather than third person (Mayer, Fennell, Farmer & Campbell, 2004; Moreno & Mayer, 2000, 2004), the *personalized message principle*, and in a "standard" American accent, for American college students (Atkinson, Mayer, & Merrill, 2005; Mayer, Sobko, & Mautone 2003), the *voice principle*. For example, Mayer, Fennell, Farmer, and Campbell (2004) determined that changing 12 occurrences of the word "the" to the word "your" in a 60-second tutorial addressing human respiration led to significant gains in problem solving transfer (personalization principle), while Mayer, Sobko, and Mautone (2003) concluded that students transferred more information when the narration of a multimedia tutorial uses a human voice rather than a computer generated voice (voice principle). The personalization and voice principles demonstrate that it is important to attend to the form, focus and tonality of the narration. Thus, a teacher could produce narrated slideshows of historical events where the narration is in the second person rather than the third person.

A mediating principle of all of the preceding principles is the *coherence principle*. The *coherence principle* states that transfer is inhibited when extraneous words, sounds, pictures, or music are included in a multimedia tutorial (Mayer, Heiser, & Lonn, 2001; Mayer & Jackson, 2005; Moreno & Mayer, 2000). Thus, in implementing the modality, redundancy, segmenting, signaling, personalization, and voice principles, it is important not to distract attention away from the tutorial's central message or overload students' cognitive resources with extraneous media. For example, Gemino, Parker, and Kutzschan (2006) had students interpret an event planning diagram in a graphical chat room that included both the event planning diagram and either a relevant graphic (a data flow diagram related to the event), an irrelevant graphic (a series of rooms to represent the available chat rooms), or no graphic. The results of Gemino et al.'s study indicate no effect on recall by a significant increase in transfer when the event planning diagram was accompanied by the relevant data flow diagram. The coherence principle is similar to the redundancy principle in that both principles indicate "more is not better" and instructional multimedia must be created so as not to distract attention or overload cognition. Thus, a teacher could refine web pages addressing cellular division by removing gratuitous pictures and video, including on the web page only those instructional elements that are necessary.

Finally, there is evidence that all of the stated principles are subject to individual differences. Previous research has identified spatial ability (Moreno & Mayer, 1999), prior knowledge (Cooper, Tindall-Ford, Chandler, & Sweller, 2001; Mayer & Sims, 1994) and working memory capacity (Doolittle, McCloud, Byrd, & Mariano, 2008) as individual difference variables that affect multimedia learning performance. For example, Doolittle et al. found that students with high working memory capacity, a measure of attentional control, who engaged in a multimedia tutorial addressing the cause of lightning recalled and transferred more information than students with low working memory capacity. The *individual difference principle* makes clear that while "on average" the preceding principles positively affect transfer; the individual learner must be taken into account when any of these principles are utilized. Thus, a teacher could make sure that students are taught all prerequisite skills before engaging in a multimedia tutorial addressing modern art.

Types of Transfer in Multimedia Learning Research

The previous discussion of transfer in multimedia learning research provides significant evidence

Table 1. Types of transfer present in multimedia research

Reference		Principle	Duration	Learning Effects			Types of Transfer		
				Significant Recall	Significant Transfer	Timing	Positive/ Negative	Lateral/ Vertical	Near/ Far
Atkinson et al. (2005)	Exp 1	Voice	40 m	Yes	Yes	Immediate	Positive	Lateral	Near
	Exp 1	Voice	40 m	na	Yes	Immediate	Positive	Lateral	Far
	Exp 2	Voice	40 m	Yes	Yes	Immediate	Positive	Lateral	Near
	Exp 2	Voice	40 m	na	Yes	Immediate	Positive	Lateral	Far
Doolittle & Mariano (press)	Exp 1	Prior Knowledge	3-4 m	Yes	Yes	Immediate	Positive	Lateral	Near
Doolittle et al. (2008)	Exp 1	Prior Knowledge	< 1 m	Yes	Yes	Immediate	Positive	Lateral	Near
	Exp 1	Modality	< 1 m	No	No	Immediate	Positive	Lateral	Near
	Exp 1	Redundancy	< 1 m	No	No	Immediate	Positive	Lateral	Near
	Exp 2	Prior Knowledge	2-3 m	Yes	Yes	Immediate	Positive	Lateral	Near
	Exp 2	Coherence	2-3 m	No	No	Immediate	Positive	Lateral	Near
	Exp 3	Prior Knowledge	1-2 m	Yes	Yes	Immediate	Positive	Lateral	Near
	Exp 3	Signaling	1-2 m	No	No	Immediate	Positive	Lateral	Near
	Exp 4	Prior Knowledge	na	Yes	na	na	na	na	na
Cooper et al. (2001)	Exp 1	Coherence	15 m	No	Yes	Immediate	Positive	Lateral	Near
Gemino et al. (2005)	Exp 1	Coherence	15 m	No	Yes	Immediate	Positive	Lateral	Near
	Exp 1	Multimedia	15 m	No	Yes	Immediate	Positive	Lateral	Near
Harp & Mayer (1998)	Exp 1	Signaling	6 m	No	No	Immediate	Zero	Lateral	Near
	Exp 1	Coherence	6 m	Yes*	Yes	Immediate	Negative	Lateral	Near
	Exp 2	Signaling	6 m	Yes	Yes	Immediate	Positive	Lateral	Near
	Exp 2	Coherence	6 m	Yes*	Yes	Immediate	Negative	Lateral	Near
	Exp 3	Signaling	6 m	No	No	Immediate	Zero	Lateral	Near
	Exp 3	Coherence	6 m	Yes*	Yes	Immediate	Negative	Lateral	Near
	Exp 4	Coherence	6 m	Yes	Yes	Immediate	Negative	Lateral	Near
Harskamp et al. (2007)	Exp 1	Modality	11 m	No	Yes	Immediate	Positive	Lateral	Near
	Exp 2	Modality	11 m	No	Yes	Immediate	Positive	Lateral	Near

continued on following page

Table 1. continued

Jamet & Le Bohec (2007)	Exp 1	Redundancy	11 m	Yes	Yes	Immediate	Positive	Lateral	Near
Kalyuga et al., (1999)	Exp 1	Modality	40 m	Yes	Yes	Immediate	Positive	Lateral	Near
	Exp 1	Redundancy	40 m	Yes	Yes	Immediate	Positive	Lateral	Near
	Exp 2	Signaling	2-3 m	Yes	No	Immediate	Zero	Lateral	Near
Leahy et al. (2003)	Exp 1	Modality	3 m	Yes	na	na	na	na	na
	Exp 2	Redundancy	1-2 m	Yes	na	na	na	na	na
Mautone & Mayer (2001)	Exp 1	Signaling	3-4 m	No	Yes	Immediate	Positive	Lateral	Near
	Exp 2	Signaling	3-4 m	Yes	Yes	Immediate	Positive	Lateral	Near
	Exp 3	Signaling	3-4 m	No	Yes	Immediate	Positive	Lateral	Near
Mayer & Anderson (1991)	Exp 1	Multimedia	<1 m	na	Yes	Immediate	Positive	Lateral	Near
	Exp 2a	Multimedia	<1 m	No	Yes	Immediate	Positive	Lateral	Near
	Exp 2b	Multimedia	<1 m	No	Yes	Immediate	Positive	Lateral	Near
Mayer & Chandler (2001)	Exp 1	Segmentation	2-3 m	No	Yes	Immediate	Positive	Lateral	Near
	Exp 2	Segmentation	2-3 m	No	Yes	Immediate	Positive	Lateral	Near
Mayer & Jackson (2005)	Exp 1a	Coherence	7 m	na	Yes	Immediate	Positive	Lateral	Near
	Exp 1b	Coherence	7-10 m	na	Yes	Immediate	Positive	Lateral	Near
	Exp 2	Coherence	7-10 m	na	Yes	Immediate	Positive	Lateral	Near
Mayer & Morenao (1998)	Exp 1	Modality	2-3 m	Yes	Yes	Immediate	Positive	Lateral	Near
	Exp 2	Modality	1-2 m	Yes	Yes	Immediate	Positive	Lateral	Near
Mayer & Simms (1994)	Exp 1	Spatial Ability	2-3 m	na	Yes	Immediate	Positive	Lateral	Near
	Exp 2	Spatial Ability	2-3 m	na	Yes	Immediate	Positive	Lateral	Near
Mayer, Dow et al. (2003)	Exp 1	Modality	2-3 m	na	Yes	Immediate	Positive	Lateral	Near
	Exp 2a	Segmentation	3-4 m	na	Yes	Immediate	Positive	Lateral	Near
	Exp 2b	Segmentation	3-4 m	na	Yes	Delayed	Positive	Lateral	Near
	Exp 3	Self-Explanation	20 m	na	Yes	Immediate	Positive	Lateral	Near
	Exp 4	Coherence	20 m	na	No	Immediate	Zero	Lateral	Near
Mayer et al. (2001)	Exp 1	Redundancy	20 m	Yes	Yes	Immediate	Positive	Lateral	Near

continued on following page

Table 1. continued

Study	Exp	Principle	Distance			Time	Effect		
	Exp 1	Coherence	20 m	Yes*	Yes	Immediate	Negative	Lateral	Near
	Exp 2	Redundancy	20 m	Yes	Yes	Immediate	Positive	Lateral	Near
	Exp 3	Coherence	2-3 m	No	Yes	Immediate	Negative	Lateral	Near
	Exp 4	Coherence	2-3 m	No	Yes	Immediate	Negative	Lateral	Near
Mayer et al. (2004)	Exp 1	Personalization	1 m	No	Yes	Immediate	Positive	Lateral	Near
	Exp 2	Personalization	1 m	No	Yes	Immediate	Positive	Lateral	Near
	Exp 3	Personalization	1 m	No	Yes	Immediate	Positive	Lateral	Near
Mayer, Sobko et al. (2003)	Exp 1	Voice	<1 m	No	Yes	Immediate	Positive	Lateral	Near
	Exp 2	Voice	1 m	Yes	Yes	Immediate	Positive	Lateral	Near
Moreno & Mayer (1999)	Exp 1	Modality	3 m	Yes	Yes	Immediate	Positive	Lateral	Near
	Exp 2	Modality	5 m	Yes	Yes	Immediate	Positive	Lateral	Near
Moreno & Mayer (2000)	Exp 1	Personalization	2-3 m	No	Yes	Immediate	Positive	Lateral	Near
	Exp 2	Personalization	2-3 m	No	Yes	Immediate	Positive	Lateral	Near
	Exp 3	Personalization	24-28 m	Yes	Yes	Immediate	Positive	Lateral	Near
	Exp 4	Personalization	24-28 m	Yes	Yes	Immediate	Positive	Lateral	Near
	Exp 5	Personalization	24-28 m	Yes	Yes	Immediate	Positive	Lateral	Near
Moreno & Mayer (2004)	Exp 1	Personalization	24-28 m	Yes	Yes	Immediate	Positive	Lateral	Near
	Exp 1	Personalization	24-28 m	Yes	Yes	Immediate	Negative	Lateral	Near
Westelinck et al. (2005)	Exp 1	Multimedia	na	No	No	Immediate	Positive	Lateral	Near
	Exp 2	Spatial Contiguity	na	No	No	Immediate	Positive	Lateral	Near
	Exp 3	Modality	na	No	No	Immediate	Positive	Lateral	Near
	Exp 4	Redundancy	na	No	No	Immediate	Positive	Lateral	Near

that transfer does occurs as a result of students engaging in multimedia learning environments. What is missing, however, from the multimedia learning research is an indication of what types of transfer are being assessed and produced. In an attempt to determine the types of transfer that are being assessed and produced, each research study addressed in the previous section has been parsed in order to determine what types of transfer are present (see Table 1). This analysis is meant as a gross measure of the types of transfer in the multimedia research literature, not an exhaustive measure.

As is evident from Table 1, the vast majority of multimedia learning experiments address positive, lateral, and near transfer involving transfer tasks that occur immediately following the instructional episode. Specifically, of 74 analyses, 59 involved positive transfer, 8 involved negative transfer and four involved zero transfer, while 71 also involved lateral transfer and none involved vertical transfer, and finally, 70 analyses involved near transfer and only 2 analyses involved far transfer. In addition, 59 of the 74 analyses found transfer of some type, while 12 did not find any transfer. These descriptive results indicate that multimedia learning research tends to focus on the types of transfer that are easier to find (Anderson, Reder, & Simon, 1996; Bransford & Schwartz, 1999). An exception to this is the presence of negative transfer when investigating the coherence principle. In the case of the coherence principle, negative transfer is hypothesized as the coherence principle states that learning and performance will be degraded when the initial multimedia learning episode includes extraneous (irrelevant) material.

Beyond the indication that multimedia learning research tends to focus on positive, lateral and near transfer, there is evidence that as a dependent measure, transfer is more sensitive to learning differences than recall. As Bransford and Schwartz (1999) state, "different kinds of learning experiences can look equivalent given

tests of memory yet look quite different on tests of transfer" (p. 62). This differential in cognitive performance assessment is evident in Figure 1; that is, while only 57% of the *recall* analyses yielded significant differences, 88% of the *transfer* analyses yielded significant differences. Thus, "transfer is a better measure than retention when the goal is to evaluate how well learners understand a multimedia explanation" (Mayer & Chandler, 2001, p. 396).

FOSTERING TRANSFER IN MULTIMEDIA INSTRUCTIONAL ENVIRONMENTS

The previous sections have delineated the nature of transfer, the fostering of transfer (in general), the role of transfer in multimedia research, and the presence of transfer in multimedia research. The previous discussion of fostering transfer delineated five general guidelines for the development of transfer.

1. Provide students with an opportunity to learn information deeply and meaningfully.
2. Provide students with an opportunity to develop a metacognitive understanding.
3. Provide students with an opportunity to learn abstract principles, not simply discrete facts.
4. Provide students with the opportunity to learn from multiple and varied examples.
5. Provide students with the opportunity to learn new knowledge and skills in multiple contexts.

These five general guidelines are appropriate for fostering transfer in multimedia instructional environments as well. Thus, to foster transfer in multimedia instructional environment the multimedia instruction should promote deep learning of abstract principles and discrete facts from multiple and varied examples within multiple and varied

Table 2. Summary of several multimedia principles and their applications

Principle	Definition	Application
Multimedia Principle	Individuals learn, retain, and transfer information better when the instructional environment involves words and pictures, rather than word or pictures alone.	• A geometry teacher could include animations to go along with text-based descriptions of two column proofs. • A management professor could add narrations to the content slides.
Modality Principle	Individuals learn, retain, and transfer information better when the instructional environment involves auditory narration and animation, rather than on-screen text and animation.	• An art teacher could create narrated slide shows of modern art with descriptions rather than slides with text. • A calculus professor could use narration with worked-out examples, rather than on-screen text descriptions.
Redundancy Principle*	Individuals learn, retain, and transfer information better when the instructional environment involves narration and animation, rather than on-screen text, narration, and animation.	• A social studies teacher could create an historical photo slide show with narration, but not include texts. • An engineering professor could convert static drawings into an animation, but included a narrative description of the animation rather than a text description.
Segmenting Principle	Individuals learn and transfer information better in an instructional environment where individuals experience concurrent narration and animation in short, user-controlled segments, rather than as a longer continuous presentation	• An English teacher could create a movie depicting the story of Out of the Dust (Hesse, 1999) and provide students with the ability to start and stop the movie as needed. • A philosophy professor could construct a movie of John Dewey's life and provide students with the ability to start and stop the movie as needed.
Signaling Principle	Individuals learn and transfer information better when the instructional environment involves cues that guide an individual's attention and processing during a multimedia presentation.	• A computer teacher could create an animated tour of computer hardware that included arrows point to components of interest and a narration that emphasizes these components by a change in tone. • A psychology professor could use a movie that depicts brain physiology that highlights brain structures as they are discussed.
Personalization Principle	Individuals learn better when words and narrations are in a less formal (i.e., first or second person), rather than more formal (i.e., third person), tone.	• A Spanish teacher could create an animated and narrated story in the first person rather than the third person. • An apparel professor could construct a fashion review in the first person, rather than the third person.
Coherence Principle	Individuals learn, retain, and transfer information better when the instructional environment is free of extraneous words, pictures, or sounds.	• A music teacher could use a tutorial of master composers that does not conflate the content knowledge with musical overlays. • A human development professor could simplify web pages by removing non-relevant graphics that were added only for interest purposes.
Individual Differences	Learning in multimedia environments is mediated by personal or individual differences; thus, individuals may learn differently in multimedia environments based their levels of prior knowledge, spatial ability or working memory capacity.	• A literacy teacher could have students watch a video that critiques Shakespeare's Hamlet only after the students have read the play. • A chemistry professor could have students use a tutorial addressing chemical interactions only after they have engaged in instruction on chemical compositions.

* *The decision to eliminating text from multimedia presentations must be made with accessibility standards in mind. Most often text should not be completely removed for a multimedia presentation, but rather maintained as an option.*

contexts. In addition, to foster transfer multimedia instruction should cultivate metacognitive awareness and control of knowledge, skills, and strategies. As mentioned previously, however, the extant multimedia learning research focuses on transfer as a dependent variable for measuring learning, not as an independent variable to be manipulated. Thus, there is no corpus of multimedia learning research that focuses on the generation of transfer as a primary concern. That said, given the transfer evidence in Table 1, does the existing multimedia learning research already foster the deep learning of principles and facts from multiple and varied examples and context?

Mayer (2005) emphasizes the goal of developing deep, meaningful learning through the cognitive processing of multimedia tutorials, "my goal for multimedia is to help people develop an understanding of important aspects of the presented material.... Understanding is the ability to construct a coherent mental representation from the presented material. It is reflected in the ability to use the presented material in novel situations, and is assessed by transfer tests" (p. 13). A concern, however, in the development of deep, meaningful learning within the existing multimedia learning research is the short duration of most multimedia instructional treatments. Based on Table 1, the average multimedia instructional treatment duration is 10 minutes, however, the median duration is only 3 minutes. Can deep, meaningful learning occur in a 3-10 minute timeframe? One approach to testing the depth of learning resulting from multimedia instructional treatments would be to use a delayed transfer assessment and/or to assess for far transfer instead of near transfer. As evident in Table 1, however, only one of the 22 studies involved delayed transfer (see Mayer, Dow et al., 2003) and only one of the studies involved far transfer (see Atkinson et al., 2005). There is an evident need for new studies to be conducted that better address delayed and far transfer in order to better assess the depth of learning that is occurring within multimedia learning environments.

In addition to the short multimedia instructional duration times, only one of the 22 studies described in Table 1 focuses on the development of a metacognitive skill, an historical inquiry strategy (Doolittle & Mariano, in press), and none of the studies involves the learning of underlying principles, but rather, focus on the development of factual or causal knowledge. Relative to the provision of multiple and varied examples, two of

the studies use multiple worked examples (three to four) during the course of their respective multimedia instructional episodes (Atkinson et al., 2005; Cooper et al., 2001). Finally, none of the studies in Table 1 provides students with a multimedia instructional episode that involves multiple and varied contexts. These results reinforce the idea that while current multimedia learning research uses transfer as a dependent measure, transfer is not currently being investigated as a multimedia learning independent measure.

The findings extracted from Table 1 provide a divided picture. While transfer is often found in the multimedia learning research, transfer has yet to become a variable of interest. In order to fully understand the nature and role of transfer in multimedia learning and multimedia instructional environments, transfer needs to become the focus of multimedia research.

CONCLUSION

Transfer represents the ability to use and apply knowledge and skills learned in one situation or environment to another situation or environment. Historically, transfer has been a challenge to investigate, although there has been ample evidence of transfer across the past century of research. Previous research on transfer has identified several types of transfer – positive/negative, lateral/vertical, and near/far – and several mechanisms for fostering transfer of learning, including learning information deeply, learning to be aware and in control of cognition, learning the principles that underlie knowledge as well as discrete facts, learning from multiple and varied examples, and learning from multiple and varied contexts. These types and mechanisms of transfer are well represented in the transfer literature, but less well represented in the multimedia learning literature.

Multimedia learning research over the past several decades has investigated and constructed several principles of multimedia design that have been demonstrated to foster learning and transfer. This research has demonstrated that students will transfer information more readily when the instruction involves animations/diagrams with complementary and concurrent narration. Relative to the animations/diagrams themselves, transfer is promoted when the animations/diagrams are provided in segments and the learner is provided control over the progress of those segments. Student transfer is further advanced when the important and relevant knowledge within the animations/diagrams is brought to the attention of the student through the use of signals or cues. Relative to the narration, transfer is promoted when the narration is in first or second person, rather than third person, and when the narrators voice is in a familiar dialect, not a machine generated voice. Finally, all adjustments and features of multimedia must be in moderation – less is more.

The importance of transfer in learning and performance necessitates that instructors engage in the proactive development of multimedia instructional environments that are designed to foster transfer. The attributes of instruction that lead to transfer are well known; thus, fostering transfer in multimedia instructional environments should be completed with forethought. Unfortunately, there is a paucity of research examining the fostering of transfer in multimedia instructional environment; however, that should not prevent instructors from pursuing transfer in their own multimedia instructional environments.

FUTURE RESEARCH DIRECTIONS

Transfer has a long history in the learning research, but a fairly short and narrow history within the multimedia learning research. As indicated previously, the typical role of transfer within the current multimedia learning research is as a measurement of learning. What is missing from this research is a coherent set of studies designed to explore the use of multimedia to proactively foster transfer. How is metacognition developed within a multimedia environment? How can knowledge of underlying principles best be learned within a multimedia environment? How can multimedia be used to bring multiple and varied contexts to the desktop or palmtop of learners in order to encourage transfer?

In addition, it is time to extend the concept of transfer within multimedia environments beyond near and lateral transfer to far and vertical transfer, including the use of delayed transfer instead of immediate transfer. As a measure of learning, near-vertical-immediate transfer does not adequately assess deeper learning; yet, most of the transfer measured in current studies uses only near-vertical-immediate transfer. Therefore, it is unknown if the modality, segmenting, signaling, personalized, and voice principles have a lasting impact on student knowledge. Our current understanding of multimedia learning is incomplete until we have a better understanding of the role of transfer in multimedia learning.

REFERENCES

Adey, P., & Shayer, M. (1993). An exploration of long-term far-transfer effects following an extended intervention program in the high school science curriculum. *Cognition and Instruction, 11*(1), 1-29.

Aly, M., Elen, J., & Willems, G. (2005). Learner-control vs. program-control instructional multimedia: A comparison of two interaction when teaching principles of orthodontic appliances. *European Journal of Dental Education, 9*, 157-163.

Anderson, J. R. (2005). *Cognitive psychology and its Implications.* New York: Worth.

Anderson, J. R., Reder, L. M., & Simon, H. A. (1996). Situated learning and education. *Educational Researcher, 25*(4), 5-11.

Atkinson, R., Mayer, R., & Merrill, M. (2005). Fostering social agency in multimedia learning: Examining the impact of an animated agent's voice. *Contemporary Education Psychology, 30*, 117-139.

Baddeley, A. (2007). *Working memory, thought, and action.* Oxford: Oxford University Press.

Baddeley, A. & Hitch, G. (1974). Working memory. In G. A. Bower (Ed.), *Recent advances in learning and motivation* (vol. 8, pp. 47-89). New York: Academic Press.

Barnett, S. M., & Ceci, S. J. (2002). When and where do we apply what we learn? A taxonomy for far transfer. *Psychological Bulletin, 128*(4), 612-637.

Bjork, R. A., & Richardson-Klavehn, A. (1989). On the puzzling relationship between environment context and a human memory. In C. Izawa (Ed.), *Current issues in cognitive process: The Tulane Flowerree Symposium on Cognition.* Hillsdale, NJ: Erlbaum.

Bransford, J. D., & Schwartz, D. L. (1999). Rethinking transfer: A simple proposal with multiple implications. In A. Iran-Nejad & P. D. Pearson (Eds.), *Review of research in education, 24,* 61-100. Washington, D.C.: American Educational Research Association.

Brown, A. L. (1989). Analogical learning and transfer: What develops? In S. Vosniadou & A. Ortony (Eds.), *Similarity and analogical reasoning* (pp. 369-412). New York: Cambridge University Press.

Brown, A. L., & Kane, M. J. (1988). Preschool children can learn to transfer: Learning to learn and learning from example. *Cognitive Psychology, 20,* 493-523.

Butterfield, E. C., & Nelson, G. D. (1991). Promoting positive transfer of different types. *Cognition and Instruction, 8*(1), 69-102.

Cooper, G., Tindall-ford, S., Chandler, P., & Sweller, J. (2001). Learning by imagining. *Journal of Experimental Psychology: Applied, 7*(1), 68-82.

Dalton, D. W. (1990). The effects of cooperative learning strategies on achievement and attitudes during interactive video. *Journal of Computer-Based Instruction, 17*(1), 8-16.

Detterman, D.K., & Sternberg, R.J. (1993). *Transfer on trial: Intelligence, cognition, & instruction.* Norwood, NJ: Ablex.

Doolittle, P. E., & Mariano, G. J. (in press). Working memory capacity and mobile multimedia learning environments: Is mobile learning from portable digital media players for everyone? *Journal of Educational Multimedia and Hypermedia.*

Doolittle, P. E., Lusk, D. A., Byrd, C. N., & Mariano, G. J. (in press). Mobile multimedia learning environments: iPods as an educational platform. In H. Ryu & D. Parsons (Eds.), *Innovative mobile learning.* Hershey, PA: Idea Group.

Doolittle, P. E., McCloud, J., Byrd, C. N., & Mariano, G. J. (2008). *Working memory capacity, attentional control and multimedia learning.* Paper presented at the annual conference of the Eastern Educational Research Association, Hilton Head, SC.

Eilam, B., & Poyas, Y. (in press). Learning with multiple representations: Extending multimedia learning beyond the lab. *Learning and Instruction.*

Engle, R. A. (2006). Framing interactions to foster generative learning: A situative explanation of transfer in a community of learners classroom. *The Journal of the Learning Sciences, 15*(4), 451-498.

Fernandez, A., & Glenberg, A. M. (1985). Changing environmental context does not reliably affect memory. *Memory & Cognition, 13*, 333-345.

Fletcher, J. D., & Tobias, S. (2005). The multimedia principle. In R. Mayer (Ed.) *Cambridge handbook of multimedia learning* (pp. 117-133). New York, NY: Cambridge University Press.

Fuchs, L. S., Fuchs, D., Prentice, K., Burch, M., Hamlett, C. L., Owen, R., Hosp, M., & Jancek, D. (2003). Explicitly teaching for transfer: Effects on third-grade students' mathematical problem solving. *Journal of Educational Psychology, 95*, 293-305.

Gemino, A., Parker, D., & Kutzschan, A. O. (2006). Investigating coherence and multimedia effects of a technology-mediated collaborative environment. *Journal of management Information Systems, 22*(3), 97-121.

Gentner, D., Loewenstein, J., & Thompson, L., (2003). Learning and transfer: A general role for analogical encoding. *Journal of Educational Psychology, 95*(2), 393-408.

Georghiades, P. (Summer 2000). Beyond conceptual change learning in science education: Focusing on transfer, durability and metacognition, *Educational Research. 42*(2), 119-139.

Gick, M. L., & Holyoak, K. J. (1980). Analogical problem solving. *Cognitive Psychology, 12*, 306-355.

Gick, M. L., & Holyoak, K. J. (1983). Schema induction and analogical transfer. *Cognitive Psychology, 15*, 1-38.

Gick, M. L., & Holyoak, K. J. (1987). The cognitive basis of knowledge transfer. In S. M. Cormier & J. D. Hagman (Eds.). *Transfer of learning: Contemporary research and application* (pp. 9-46). San Diego, CA: Academic Press.

Harp, S. F., & Mayer, R. E. (1998). How seductive details do their damage. A theory of cognitive interest in science learning. *Journal of Educational Psychology, 90*, 414-434.

Harskamp, E. G., Mayer, R. E., & Suhre, C. (2007). Does the modality principle for multimedia learning apply to science classrooms? *Learning and Instruction, 17*, 465-477.

Haskell, R. E. (2000). *Transfer of learning: Cognition, instruction and reasoning.* New York: Academic Press.

Hede, A. (2002). An integrated model of multimedia effects on learning. *Journal of Educational Multimedia and Hypermedia, 11*, 177-191.

Jamet, E., & Le Bohec, O. (2007). The effect of redundant text in multimedia instruction. *Contemporary Education Psychology, 32*, 588-598.

Kalyuga, S., Chandler, P., & Sweller, J. (1999). Managing split-attention and redundancy in multimedia instruction. *Applied Cognitive Psychology, 13*, 351-371.

Katayama, A. D. (2005). Promoting knowledge transfer with electronic note taking. *Teaching of Psychology, 32*(2), 129-131.

Keiler, L. (2007). Students' explanations of their data handling: Implications for transfer of learning. *International Journal of Science Education, 29*(2), 151-172.

Klahr, D., & Carver, S. M. (1988). Cognitive objectives in a LOGO debugging curriculum: Instruction, learning, and transfer. *Cognitive Psychology, 20*, 362-404.

Lave, J. (1988). Cognition in practice: Mind, mathematics, and culture in everyday life. Cambridge, England: Cambridge University Press.

Leahy, W., Chandler, P., & Sweller, J. (2003). When auditory presentations should and should not be a component of multimedia instruction. *Applied Cognitive Psychology, 17*, 401-418.

Lee, A. Y. (1998). Transfer as a measure of intellectual functioning. In S. Soraci & W. J. McIlvane (Eds.), *Perspectives on fundamental processes in intellectual functioning: A survey of research approaches, 1* 351-366. Stamford, CT: Ablex.

Lee, A. Y., & Pennington, N. (1993). Learning computer programming: A route to general reasoning skills? In C.R. Cook, J.C. Scholtz, & J.C. Spohrer (Eds.), *Empirical studies of programmers: Fifth workshop* (pp. 113-136). Norwood, NJ: Ablex.

Lee, H., Plass, J. L., & Homer, B. D. (2006). Optimizing cognitive load for learning form computer-based science simulations. *Journal of Education psychology, 98*(4), 902-913.

Mautone, P. D., & Mayer, R. E. (2001). Signaling as a cognitive guide in multimedia learning. *Journal of Educational Psychology, 93*(2), 377-389.

Mayer, R. E. (2001). *Multimedia learning.* Cambridge, UK: Cambridge University Press.

Mayer, R. E. (Ed.) (2005). *The Cambridge Handbook of Multimedia Learning.* Cambridge: Cambridge Press.

Mayer, R. E., & Anderson, R. B. (1991). Animations need narrations: An experimental test of a dual-coding hypothesis. *Journal of Educational Psychology, 83*(4), 484-490.

Mayer, R. E., & Chandler, P. (2001). When learning is just a click away: Does simple user interaction foster deeper understanding of multimedia messages? *Journal of Educational Psychology, 93*(2), 390-397.

Mayer, R. E., & Sims, V. (1994). For whom is a picture worth a thousand words? Extensions of a dual-coding theory of multimedia learning. *Journal of Educational Psychology, 86,* 389-401.

Mayer, R., Dow, G., & Mayer, S. (2003). Multimedia learning in an interactive self-explaining environment: What works in the design of agent-based microworlds? *Journal of Educational Psychology, 95*(4), 806-813.

Mayer, R., Fennell, S., Farmer, L., & Campbell, J. (2004). A personalization effect in multimedia learning: Students learn better when words are in conversational style rather than formal style. *Journal of Educational Psychology, 96*(2), 389-395.

Mayer, R. E., Heiser, J., & Lonn, S. (2001). Cognitive constraints on multimedia learning: When presenting more material results in less understanding. *Journal of Educational Psychology, 93*(1), 187-198.

Mayer, R., & Jackson, J. (2005). The case for coherence in scientific explanations: Quantitative details can hurt qualitative understanding. *Journal of Experimental Psychology: Applied, 11*(1), 13-18.

Mayer, R. E., & Moreno, R. (1998). A split-attention effect in multimedia learning: Evidence for dual processing systems in working memory. *Journal of Educational Psychology, 90*(2), 312-320.

Mayer, R., Sobko, K., & Mautone, P. (2003). Social dues in multimedia learning: Role of speaker's voice. *Journal of Educational Psychology, 95,* 419-425.

Milheim, W. D. (1990). The effects of pacing and sequence control in an interactive video lesson. *Educational & Training Technology International, 27*(1), 7-19.

Montague, M., & Boss, C. S. (1986). The effect of cognitive strategy training on verbal math problem solving performance of learning disabled adolescents. *Journal of Learning Disabilities, 19*(1), 26-33.

Moreno, R., & Mayer, R. E. (1999). Cognitive principles of multimedia learning: The role of modality and contiguity. *Journal of Educational Psychology, 91*(2), 358-368.

Moreno, R., & Mayer, R. E. (2000). A coherence effect in multimedia learning: The case for minimizing irrelevant sounds in the design of multimedia instructional messages. *Journal of Educational Psychology, 92*(1), 117-125.

Moreno, R., & Mayer, R. E. (2004). Personalized messages that promote science learning in virtual environments. *Journal of Educational Psychology, 96*(1), 165-173.

Novick, L. R. (1988). Analogical transfer, problem similarity, and expertise. *Journal of Experimental Psychology: Learning, Memory, and Cognition, 14*(3), 510-520.

Osgood, C. E. (1949). The similarity paradox in human learning: A resolution. *Psychological Review, 56*, 132-143.

Palinscar, A. S., & Brown, A. L. (1984). Reciprocal teaching of comprehension monitoring activities. *Cognition and Instruction, 1*, 117-175.

Perkins, D. N., Salomon, G. (1987). Transfer and teaching thinking. In D. N. Perkins, J. Lochhead, & J. Bishop (Eds.), *Thinking: The Second International Conference* (pp. 285-303). Hillsdale, NJ: Erlbaum.

Pirolli, P., & Recker, M. (1994). Learning strategies and transfer in the domain of programming. *Cognition and Instruction, 12*(3), 235-275.

Prawat, R. S. (1989). Promoting access to knowledge, strategy, and disposition in students: A research synthesis. *Review of Educational Research, 59*, 1-41.

Reed, S. K. (2006). Cognitive architectures for multimedia learning. *Educational Psychologist, 41*(2), 87-98.

Reed, S. K., & Saavedra, N. C. (1986). A comparison of computation, discovery, and graph procedures for improving students' conception of average speed. *Cognition and Instruction, 3*, 31-62.

Saufley, W. H., Otaka, S. R., & Bavaresco, J. L. (1985). Context effects: Classroom tests and context independence. *Memory and Cognition, 13*, 522-528.

Saxe, G. B. (1988). Candy selling and math learning. *Educational Researcher, 17*(6), 14-21.

Scardamalia, M. C., Bereiter, M. C. & Steinbach, R. (1984). Teachability of reflective processes in written composition. *Cognitive Science. 8*, 173-190.

Schnotz, W., & Bannert, M. (2003). Construction and interference in learning from multiple representation, *Learning and Instruction, 13*, 141–156.

Schooler, C. (1989). Social structural effects and experimental situations. In K. W. Schaie & C. Schooler (Eds.), *Social structure and aging: Psychological processes* (pp. 1-21). Hillsdale, NJ: Erlabaum.

Schmidt, R. A., & Bjork, R. A. (1992). New conceptualizations of practice: Common principles in three paradigms suggest new concepts for training. *Psychological Sciences, 3*, 207-217.

Singley, M. K., & Anderson, J. R. (1989). *The transfer of cognitive skill.* Cambridge, MA: Harvard University Press.

Salomon, G., and Perkins, D.N. (1989). Rocky roads to transfer: Rethinking mechanisms of a neglected phenomenon. *Educational Psychologist, 24*(2), 113-142.

Thorndike, E. L. (1903). *Educational psychology.* New York: Lemcke & Buechner.

Thorndike, E.L., & Woolworth, R.S. (1901). The influence of improvement in one mental function upon the efficiency of their functions. *Psychological Review, 8*, 247-261.

Wagner, J. F. (2006). Transfer in pieces. *Cognition and Instruction, 24*(1), 1-71.

ADDITIONAL READINGS

Alexander, P. A., &Murphy, P. K. (1999). Nurturing the seeds of transfer: A domain-specific perspective. *International Journal of Educational Research, 31*, 561–576.

Bassok, M. (1997). Two types of reliance on correlations between content and structure in reasoning about word problems. In L. D. English (Ed.), *Mathematical reasoning: Analogies, metaphors, and images* (pp. 221-246). Mahwah, NJ: Erlbaum.

Bereby-Meyer, Y., Moran, S., & Unger-Aviram, E. (2004). When performance goals deter performance: Transfer of skills in integrative negotiations. *Organizational Behavior and Human Decision Processes, 93*, 142–154.

Besnard, D., and Cacitti, L. (2005). Interface changes causing accidents. An empirical study of negative transfer. *International Journal of Human-Computer Studies, 62.* 105-125.

Blanton,W. E.,Moorman, G. B., Hayes, B. A., &Warner,M. L. (1997). Effects of participation in The Fifth Dimension on far transfer. *Journal of Educational Computing Research, 16*, 371–396.

Dimitrov, D., McGee, S., & Howard, B. (2002). Changes in students' science ability produced by multimedia learning environments: Application f the linear logistic model for change. *School Science and Mathematics, 102*(1), 15-25.

Ford, J. K.,Weissbein, D. A., Smith, E.M., Gully, S.M., & Salas, E. (1998). Relationship of goal orientation, metacognitive activity, and practice strategies with learning outcomes and transfer. *Journal of Applied Psychology, 83*, 218–233.

Ginns, P. (2005). Meta-analysis of the modality effect. *Learning and Instruction, 15*, 313-331.

Herrington, J., Herrington, A., & Sparrow, L. (2000). Learning to assess school mathematics:

Context, multimedia and transfer. *Mathematics Teacher Education and Development, 2*, 75-92.

Hesketh, B. (1997). Dilemmas for training transfer and retention. *Applied Psychology: An International Review, 46*, 317-386.

Holladay, C. L., & Quiñones, M. A. (2003). Practice variability and transfer of training: The role of self-efficacy generality. *Journal of Applied Psychology, 88*, 1094–103.

Hummel, K., Paas, F., & Koper, E., (2004a). Cuing for transfer in multimedia programmes: Process worksheets vs. worked-out examples. *Journal of Computer Assisted Learning, 20*, 387-397.

Hutchins, E. (1995). *Cognition in the wild.* Cambridge, MA: Holt.

Jacobson, M. J., & Spiro, R. J. (1995). Hypertext learning environments, cognitive flexibility, and the transfer of complex knowledge: An empirical investigation. *Journal of Educational Computing Research, 12*, 301–333.

Klahr, D., & Li, J. (June 2005). Cognitive research and elementary science instruction: From the laboratory, to the classroom, and back. *Journal of Science Education and Technology, 14*(2), 217-238.

Kolodner, J. L., Gray, J. T., & Fasse, B. B. (2003). Promoting transfer through case-based reasoning: Rituals and practices in Learning by Design ™ classrooms. *Cognitive Science Quarterly, 3*, 183–232.

Lemire, D (2002). Commentary: Math Problem Solving and Mental Discipline – the Myth of Transferability, *Journal of College Reading and Learning, 32*(2), 229-238.

Luchins, A. S. and Luchins, E. H. (1970). *Wertheimer's seminar revisited: Problem solving and thinking* (Vol. 1). Albany, NY: State University of New York.

Maclellan, E. (June 2005). Conceptual Learning: The Priority of Higher Education. *British Journal of Educational Studies, 53*(2), 129-147.

Mayer, R. E., & Anderson, R. B. (1992). The instructive animation: Helping students build connections between words and pictures in multimedia learning. *Journal of Educational Psychology, 84*(4), 444-452.

Ollerenshaw, A., Aidman, E., & Kidd, G. (1997). Is an illustration always worth ten thousand words? Effects of prior knowledge, learning style, and multimedia illustrations on text comprehension. *International Journal of Instructional Media, 24*, 227-238.

Pea, R. D. (1987). Socializing the knowledge transfer problem. *International Journal of Educational Research, 11*, 639–664.

Perry, M. (1991). Learning and transfer: Instructional conditions and conceptual change. *Cognitive Development, 6*, 449–468.

Sanchez, C. A., & Wiley, J. (2006). An examination of the seductive details effect in terms of working memory capacity. *Memory & Cognition, 34*(2), 344-355.

Schmidt, R. A. & Young, D. E. (1987). Transfer of movement control in motor skill learning. In S. M. Cormier & J. D. Hagman (Eds.), *Transfer of learning: Contemporary research and applications*. San Diego: Academic Press.

van den Berg, E., Jansen, L., & Blijleven, P. (2004). Learning with multimedia cases: An evaluation study. *Journal of Technology and Teacher Education, 12*(4), 491-509.

Chapter XIV
Conceptual Customization for Learning with Multimedia:
Developing Individual Instructional Experiences to Support Science Understanding

Kirsten R. Butcher
University of Utah, USA

Sebastian de la Chica
University of Colorado at Boulder, USA

Faisal Ahmad
University of Colorado at Boulder, USA

Qianyi Gu
University of Colorado at Boulder, USA

Tamara Sumner
University of Colorado at Boulder, USA

James H. Martin
University of Colorado at Boulder, USA

ABSTRACT

This chapter discusses an emerging theme in supporting effective multimedia learning: developing scalable, cognitively-grounded tools that customize learning interactions for individual students. We discuss the theoretical foundation for expected benefits of customization and current approaches in educational technology that leverage a learner's prior knowledge. We then describe the development of a customized tool for science learning, called CLICK, that uses automatic techniques to create knowledge models that can be fed into cognitively-informed pedagogical tools. CLICK leverages existing multimedia resources in educational digital libraries for two purposes: (a) to generate rich representations of domain content relevant for learner modeling that are easily scaled to new domains and disciplines, and (b) to serve as a repository of instructional resources that support customized pedagogical interactions. The potential of the CLICK system is discussed, along with initial comparisons of knowledge models created by CLICK and human experts. Finally, the chapter discusses the remaining challenges and relevant future extensions for effective customization tools in educational technology.

INTRODUCTION

Increasingly, classrooms are comprised of diverse learners who are experienced with technology and expect it to play an increasingly significant role in their educational experiences (Hanson & Carlson, 2005). The challenge for researchers and multimedia designers is to identify how educational technology can support useful learning processes and improve outcomes for a broad array of students. However, developing effective educational technology that is robust for a wide variety of learners in a range of educational contexts has been an elusive goal.

We take a learner-centered approach to improving the impact of multimedia materials. We use automatic techniques to develop rich representations of domain knowledge and student understanding that allow us to customize learning interactions based on the conceptual needs of individual learners. Our work targets the large-scale development of individually-targeted materials for educational technology, and can be contrasted with a long history of design-centered efforts to improve the general quality of learning materials that are used by all students regardless of their individual learning needs or existing knowledge. Early efforts to improve the design of learning materials included attempts to supplement traditional learning materials with visual representations, effectively creating simple forms of multimedia by the addition of diagrams (Dwyer, 1967, 1968, 1969) and pictures (see Levie & Lentz, 1982, for a review) to text resources. As multimedia resources with varied content such as

text, audio, diagrams, and animations have become more common, researchers have had some success in identifying general design principles to support student learning (e.g., Mayer, 2001). However, these design-centered principles have been targeted toward broad categories of learners (e.g., students with existing high or low prior knowledge). There is little evidence that design-centered approaches can successfully remediate specific student knowledge deficits, especially for learners who have existing knowledge in a domain.

Adaptive technologies that respond to individual student knowledge and interactions do exist—for example, intelligent tutors (Anderson, Corbett, Koedinger, & Pelletier, 1995; Koedinger, Anderson, Hadley, & Mark, 1997) and animated conversational agents (Graesser et al., 2004)—but these technologies typically are difficult and impractical to implement for a wide variety of topics. As a general rule, the more detailed the conceptual feedback offered by technology, the less able the technology has been to scale quickly to new tasks, domains, and disciplines. However, as the prevalence and availability of educational multimedia increases, so does the opportunity to leverage existing computational techniques and digital resources to achieve the next generation of educational technology: tools that perform conceptually-rich student assessment, that scale to new topics and domains using automated processes, and that support customized pedagogical interactions for individual students with a range of prior domain knowledge.

We take an interdisciplinary approach to educational technology design and assessment that builds on existing multimedia resources in digital libraries. Our goal is to assess whether customized interactions with multimedia can increase students' conceptual science understanding. Our approach uses cognitive theories of multimedia and comprehension, learner discourse, and techniques in computer science (especially natural language processing) to push the multimedia envelope toward successful implementation of fully automated but conceptually customized learning environments.

We are developing a "customized learning service for concept knowledge" (hereafter referred to as CLICK) that uses an automated diagnosis of students' incorrect and missing conceptual knowledge to inform the selection and presentation of multimedia resources from educational digital libraries. CLICK uses natural language processing techniques to construct a detailed conceptual learner model that gauges student understanding in a domain. This conceptual learner model incorporates three key components: a domain competency model that represents what students should know about a domain, a student knowledge model that represents what learners currently know, and a knowledge trace that identifies mismatches between domain knowledge and student understanding—this knowledge trace feeds into instructional interventions that are customized according to individual student needs. This chapter describes the theoretical underpinnings of our work and summarizes the technological methods that we employ. We discuss initial results evaluating CLICK's success in developing accurate knowledge models and in identifying conceptual knowledge issues in essays written by 23 novice students. In both cases, we compare artifacts created by CLICK to those generated by human experts in domain content and curriculum design. Finally, we discuss challenges facing the design and implementation of cognitively-informed instructional interventions that use the output of CLICK's automatic knowledge modeling.

BACKGROUND

We are developing CLICK as an educational technology to support effective learning strategies based on students' unique knowledge needs. An individualized approach to multimedia learning has strong potential to promote meaningful learning gains, especially when compared to a "one size fits all" approach to multimedia development. Researchers have long recognized that an individual's existing knowledge in a domain influences learning outcomes. Studies in text comprehension, for example, repeatedly have demonstrated that learners with higher prior domain knowledge are better able to remember the content of a text and to summarize it after reading (e.g., McKeown, Beck, Sinatra, & Loxterman, 1992; Means & Voss, 1985; Moravcsik & Kintsch, 1993; Spilich, Vesonder, Chiesi, & Voss, 1979). These findings provide a strong theoretical foundation to suggest that the forms of support provided by educational technology should take students' existing knowledge into account. Before describing CLICK in detail, we review relevant research on background knowledge effects in multimedia learning and previous efforts to customize educational technology for individual students.

Designing Resources for Broad Levels of Prior Knowledge

Consistent with findings from text comprehension, research in multimedia learning also has demonstrated that individual background knowledge is an important factor in predicting student learning outcomes. For instance, Mayer and his colleagues (Mayer & Gallini, 1990; Mayer, Steinhoff, Bowers, & Mars, 1995) have found that their instructional multimedia presentations show significant learning benefits only for low-knowledge learners. In Mayer's studies, higher-knowledge learners show little additional benefit from diagrams or animations over text alone. However, other researchers have found that low prior knowledge can compromise learning from multimedia, especially when visual representations contain non-critical features that can be distracting to novices (Lowe, 1996, 1999) or when the interpretation of external representations relies upon abstract conventions that must be learned in a domain (Petre, 1995; Petre & Green, 1993). These findings suggest that supporting optimal learning outcomes requires careful attention to interactions between learner background knowledge and the characteristics of multimedia materials.

Indeed, existing research evidence shows that background knowledge and material format can interact to predict outcomes during multimedia learning. Kalyuga, Chandler, and Sweller (2000) have proposed the *expertise reversal effect* to explain their findings that higher- and lower-knowledge learners learn optimally from inverse forms of multimedia materials. Kalyuga et al. found that a visual-only format was optimal for high-knowledge learners whereas lower-knowledge learners learned most from visual information that included ample, integrated text and learned least from the visual-only format. This finding complements earlier results from text comprehension research showing that lower-knowledge learners need more clear and explicit materials, while higher-knowledge learners benefit more from materials that require them to use their knowledge to make relevant inferences (McNamara, Kintsch, Songer, & Kintsch, 1996; McNamara & Kintsch, 1996; Voss & Silfies, 1996). Research findings showing an interaction between learner background knowledge and learning materials often have prompted a resource-optimization approach to customizing materials, where researchers or designers vary targeted aspects of learning resources to support knowledge development in students with varied levels of prior knowledge.

In principle, giving appropriate materials to different learners seems straightforward; in practice, it can be difficult to decide what characteristics of the learning materials are critical for optimization. Moreover, with a few exceptions (e.g., Wolfe et al., 1998), customization of materials has been achieved via human analysis and revision. For example, researchers successfully improved learning in lower-knowledge students by analyzing the inferences required to understand a text, then rewriting the text to include more clear and explicit explanations that required fewer inferences (Britton & Gulgoz, 1991). In many science domains, complex materials and changing scientific knowledge makes hand-revision of resources a daunting prospect for large-scale learning interventions.

A complicating factor that makes hand-customization of materials difficult is emerging evidence that fine-grained student interactions with multimedia can influence learning outcomes. In a study on mastery learning of a procedural skill – knot tying – from video presentations, Schwan and Riempp (2004) found that domain novices were more efficient learners when given the opportunity to interact with videos by controlling the pace and progression of the presentation. Moreover, the pattern of effective interactions varied by learner and reflected students' unique knowledge needs at a given point during learning. In a separate study using hyperlinked video systems, student learning was not influenced by the overall design of the system – this was true even for interactive features that had been designed to comply with existing multimedia principles. However, students' active implementation of individual strategies for using the hypermedia did improve learning outcomes regardless of the overall hypermedia design (Zahn, Barquero, & Schwan, 2004). These findings are consistent with evidence that support for relevant cognitive processes is a critical factor in promoting successful learning with multimedia (Butcher, 2006; Narayanan & Hegarty, 2002). Further, these findings suggest that subtle differences in individual knowledge may play an important role in predicting optimal multimedia resources and learning interactions for students.

Learning Modeling: Customization for Individual Student Knowledge

Recent advances in our theoretical understanding of conceptual change (Chi, in press) suggest that differences in the nature of learners' misunderstandings in a domain, rather than their global level of topic knowledge, may influence the potential for deep learning and knowledge revision. Chi argues that more sensitive categorization of incorrect knowledge and misconceived or conflicting knowledge should be considered in order to effectively target student learning. However, assessing the background knowledge and existing conceptions of individual learners can be difficult and time-consuming, especially in a classroom environment where teachers are working with numerous students and may themselves have varied levels of content and pedagogical expertise (NRC, 2000). Even domain-knowledgeable tutors in a one-on-one tutoring task perform quite poorly when diagnosing students' alternative understandings and often fail to detect and remediate deficits in student knowledge (Chi, Siler, & Jeong, 2004). The development of personalized instruction plans based on learners' existing knowledge and understanding remains a daunting task for teachers in most classrooms. Research has repeatedly found that educators need support in customizing educational content and activities for students (Hanson & Carlson, 2005; Jonassen & Grabowski, 1993).

Given the difficulty of assessing detailed knowledge levels of individual learners, it is not surprising that researchers have shown great interest in using computer tutors to model and remediate fine-grained student understanding (Anderson et al., 1995; Conati, Gertner, & Vanlehn, 2002; Graesser et al., 2004; Koedinger et al.,

1997; VanLehn et al., 2005; Wade-Stein & Kintsch, 2004). Intelligent tutoring systems (ITSs) are designed to engage and support individual learners in knowledge articulation and the development and practice of correct skills or concepts. ITSs have been implemented successfully to support student learning in algebra, geometry (Koedinger et al., 1997), quantitative physics (Conati et al., 2002; VanLehn et al., 2005), qualitative physics (Graesser et al., 2004), and summary writing (Wade-Stein & Kintsch, 2004). These systems share a common approach to supporting student learning: based upon interactions with the student, each tutor generates a representation of student understanding and compares it to a knowledge model that provides an ideal representation of what students ought to know about a domain.

Cognitive Tutors (Anderson et al., 1995), for example, use an ACT-R (Anderson, 1993) production-rule model of human problem-solving to characterize student actions in the tutor as either on-path or off-path. The tutor automatically selects problems for the student to complete, based on the current assessment of student understanding, and provides immediate feedback on a student's problem-solving attempts during learning. AutoTutor (Graesser et al., 2004) also uses a detailed model of optimal knowledge in a domain, represented as curriculum scripts created by subject matter experts. Curriculum scripts include the important concepts, questions, and problems to be covered in a particular lesson. AutoTutor uses an animated pedagogical agent to engage students in conversation that simulates the dialog moves of human tutors (Person, Graesser, Kreuz, Pomeroy, & the Tutoring Research Group, 2001). Although both tutors have been shown to successfully improve student learning outcomes, they also highlight the major disadvantage of detailed knowledge modeling: there is significant initial cost and human-intensive effort required to develop appropriate domain models. The estimated number of development hours required to produce one hour of intelligent tutoring instruction has ranged from 100-1000, with Cognitive Tutor estimates at about 200 development hours per instructional hour (Koedinger, Aleven, Heffernan, McLaren, & Hockenberry, 2004). Not surprisingly, the developers of both Cognitive Tutors and AutoTutors have been working to build authoring tools to ease the burden involved in expanding to new topics, domains, and skills (Koedinger et al., 2004; Susarla, Adcock, Van Eck, Moreno, & Graesser, 2003). To date, these authoring tools automate some of the processes used by human developers rather than removing or reducing the need for human developers by automating the development process itself. Recent work with the Cognitive Tutor also has been exploring the use of educational data mining—using log files of student interactions with existing tutors—to improve the efficiency of student learning during intelligent tutoring by prioritizing skills that need more practice and deemphasizing skills that are quickly learned (Cen, Koedinger, & Junker, 2007). This work leverages the significant work invested in a Cognitive Tutor by using student interactions to feed into more detailed cognitive models of student learning in the tutored domain.

There are cases in which automated tools have been used to facilitate student knowledge assessment in domains without detailed domain modeling, but additional automation has typically come at the price of less detailed knowledge modeling and, consequently, less detailed student feedback. Latent Semantic Analysis (LSA) provides a method for automatically assessing the content of text, using singular value decomposition to represent the meaning of collections of words as vectors in a high-dimensional semantic space derived from a large corpus of text materials. The similarity between vectors is represented as a cosine that indicates the semantic relationship of the represented texts (Landauer, 1998; Landauer & Dumais, 1997). For accurate results, the corpus from which the semantic space is derived must include a sufficient number of documents relevant to the target domain. Summary Street is a tutoring

application for summary writing that uses LSA to provide students with feedback on summary content and topic coverage (Wade-Stein & Kintsch, 2004). Summary Street has been successful in improving the quality of student summary writing in classroom environments, but its feedback is more general than that offered by intelligent tutoring systems. Summary Street does not address the nature of students' existing knowledge deficits or confusions, concentrating instead on supporting students' articulation of correct and complete information. Intelligent tutors and Summary Street highlight the pedagogical trade-offs that have been heretofore associated with detailed feedback and automatic knowledge modeling, even in successful educational technology.

Our work attempts to take a significant step forward in the development of automatic knowledge models that include conceptually-rich and detailed information on student understanding that can be fed into cognitively-motivated instructional interventions. We have extended natural language processing techniques to automatically generate knowledge maps of domain information and student knowledge. We then use computational methods to align and compare these knowledge map representations in order to create a detailed understanding of students' knowledge needs in a domain. Knowledge maps are a type of node-link diagram—similar to concept maps—in which key ideas are expressed as text in the nodes, and links between the nodes depict relationships between relevant ideas (O'Donnell, Dansereau, & Hall, 2002). Research on knowledge maps as educational tools have found that students are better able to learn main ideas from a knowledge map representation (O'Donnell et al., 2002) and general training on knowledge map representations results in improved learning from an expository text (Chmielewski & Dansereau, 1998). In our work, automatically generated knowledge maps serve both computational and educational purposes.

Our automatic generation of knowledge map representations leverages the existence of large, well-developed educational digital libraries that contain a variety of multimedia resources. Two prominent educational digital libraries are the National Science Digital Library (www.nsdl. org) and the Digital Library for Earth System Education (www.dlese.org). The National Science Digital Library (NSDL) is funded by the National Science Foundation, with the mission to provide a national digital library that provides access to exemplary educational resources for science, technology, engineering, and mathematics (STEM) disciplines. The Digital Library for Earth Systems Education (DLESE) is guided by a similar mission, but with a more concentrated focus on specific earth systems science materials. Both NSDL and DLESE include a large selection of multimedia resources; for example, DLESE includes resources with text, imagery, illustrations and video as well as hands-on activities and data simulations. The wide variety of resources cataloged by these libraries provide a collection of good quality, educationally-focused multimedia that can be used to create a detailed model of key information in a domain and also can serve as a bank of high-quality multimedia resources to be utilized in customized instructional interventions.

In the remainder of this chapter, we describe our efforts to develop a conceptually-advanced, automatic tool to assess student understanding: CLICK.

THE CUSTOMIZED LEARNING SERVICE FOR CONCEPT KNOWLEDGE (CLICK)

In order to support adaptive pedagogical interactions for students that identify and address deficits and errors in students' scientific domain knowledge, the CLICK service includes two main components that are generated computationally: 1) a *domain competency model*—automatically derived from collections of educational multimedia resources—that provides the knowledge

model of ideal student understanding, and 2) a *student knowledge model*—automatically generated from common student learning artifacts (e.g., essays)—that represents current student understanding. CLICK performs a detailed analysis of the completeness and correctness of student knowledge by extending natural language processing techniques to align the student knowledge model to the domain competency model. CLICK's output is a rich set of data on student conceptual gaps and errors that is used in an *instructional intervention* component. The instructional intervention component creates a pedagogical framework for remediation of the knowledge problems identified by the CLICK system, providing cognitively-motivated support for learning via customized system responses and multimedia selection based on a learner's identified conceptual needs.

Our work targets three major challenges facing automatically implemented tools for conceptual learning with multimedia:

1. Developing domain knowledge models with sufficient accuracy and breadth to perform detailed assessment of student knowledge
2. Developing accurate and useful representations of students' existing conceptual knowledge that can be successfully compared to domain knowledge models
3. Identifying cognitively-informed strategies for the customized remediation of student knowledge problems using existing educational multimedia

Identifying What Students Should Know: Generating a Domain Competency Model

The first step to achieving conceptually-informed and customized pedagogical interactions is to identify the target knowledge of instruction. The knowledge model includes key domain ideas and conceptual connections between those ideas. One approach to generating these conceptual knowledge models is a cognitive task analysis approach.

Researchers perform detailed analysis of expert processes (Graesser, Person, Harter, & the Tutoring Research Group, 2001; Koedinger & Anderson, 1990; VanLehn, 2006) and implement these models in the design of instructional technology practice and assessment. We are exploring a more automated approach to the generation of conceptual knowledge models—we use existing, digital multimedia to extract relevant domain content and to represent meaningful conceptual relationships that are represented in these resources.

Automated domain modeling from digital library collections. The automatic generation of domain competency models from digital library collections is a highly scalable method for extending educational technology. Automated domain modeling facilitates the development of instructional interventions in numerous domains and results in a knowledge model that can be easily updated as new scientific materials are added to the digital library. In this way, the automatic generation of domain competency models facilitates not only customized learning interactions using multimedia instruction, but also a sustainable development process. Although there are obvious advantages to automating the development of knowledge models in terms of implementation time and expansion to new topics, it is critical to determine whether the resulting knowledge model is sufficiently accurate and conceptually rich enough to serve as the foundation for detailed student knowledge assessment.

Given enormous range in the quality and purpose of information on the World Wide Web, concerns regarding the accuracy and coherence of automatically-generated knowledge models using existing multimedia resources are well founded. To ensure that only high-quality educational resources are used in knowledge modeling, our solution has been to build upon resources in large-scale educational digital libraries. The two educational digital libraries that we have targeted—NSDL and DLESE—have policies that govern the quality of multimedia resources that

are selected for inclusion in the library. DLESE, for example, evaluates resource quality on seven principles that include scientific accuracy and educational utility (http://www.dlese.org/Metadata/collections/resource-quality.htm).

Using educational digital libraries circumvents the challenge to accuracy that would result from broad inclusion of unvetted web content. Further, the educational focus of these digital libraries promotes coherence and contextualized background information that may not be present in resources designed for other purposes. The breadth of digital library resources may not be sufficient for specialized topics in which multimedia resources are more rarely produced or where rapid changes in the field make existing resources quickly obsolete, but the majority of educational topics have a significant number of catalogued resources. For example, at the time this chapter was written, DLESE alone held over 810 resources related to *plate tectonics*.

Although the use of digital library materials ensures a baseline level of quality for input materials, it does not ensure accuracy and sufficient breadth in the knowledge model that is generated by automatic methods. In the development of CLICK, we used qualitative expert processes observed during our research to inform the multi-document summarization techniques used to develop the automatic knowledge model. We evaluate the automatic domain model by comparing the CLICK-generated domain competency model against the hand-generated model developed by human experts, and by assessing its usefulness for accurately detecting student knowledge needs in the represented domain.

Using expert domain models to inform automatic computational techniques. CLICK's approach to the automatic construction of domain competency models has been informed by an in-depth study of expert processes in selection and integration of domain concepts from existing digital library resources (Ahmad, de la Chica, Butcher, Sumner, & Martin, 2007). As part of this study, two geology experts and two instructional design experts created a domain competency model by selecting, organizing, and linking the important scientific and pedagogical concepts contained in DLESE resources on earthquakes and plate tectonics. Experts developed their domain competency model through a series of iterative individual and collaborative activities, as described in Ahmad et al. (2007). The resulting domain competency model is represented as an expert-generated knowledge map (see Figure 1) with key domain ideas in nodes that are linked according to conceptual relationships.

Because the expert domain competency model was generated using digital library resources, it was necessary to determine if the resources resulted in sufficient breadth to serve as an appropriate knowledge model for the chosen topic. We assessed the sufficiency of topic coverage in the expert domain competency model using an independent domain expert to evaluate the model based on a collection of nationally-recognized learning goals published by the American Associa-

tion for the Advancement of Science (AAAS) in *Benchmarks for Scientific Literacy* (AAAS, 1993). These AAAS benchmarks provide a standardized representation of ideal student knowledge of content and processes in common science topics at key checkpoints during a student's educational progression (grades 2, 5, 8, and 12). The domain expert found that the expert-generated model covered all four AAAS benchmarks related to earthquakes and plate tectonics (using Likert-style assessment questions), and indicated direct alignment of 82 (15%) of the nodes in the expert knowledge map to the benchmarks (Ahmad et al., 2007). The fact that such a small number of nodes could account for the AAAS benchmarks reflects the exhaustive nature of the expert knowledge model; experts included a large number of nodes that broke down core concepts into more detailed and elaborated representations. Almost 30% of the total nodes in the expert domain competency model were elaboration and examples of concepts.

Figure 1. Excerpt from the expert-generated domain competency model on earthquakes and plate tectonics for high-school learners

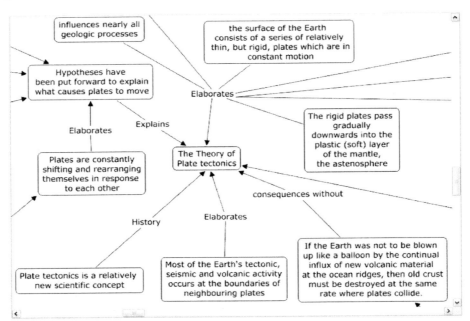

A key finding from the expert knowledge model generation activities was that experts found the digital library materials sufficient for representing the content of the domain. Experts first created individual knowledge maps, and then merged these maps into a domain knowledge map through collaborative work and discussion (Ahmad et al., 2007). Experts were given a great deal of freedom during these activities—they were free to choose whatever content they wished to represent at whatever grain size (e.g., words to entire paragraphs) they desired. Experts also were encouraged to use their own knowledge to express the relationships between nodes; experts were provided with an initial set of 24 link labels but were explicitly encouraged to generate new relationship terms to best capture scientific ideas and information. Despite the potential for expert inferences and revision of digital library materials during knowledge map construction, analyses of the final expert knowledge map (de la Chica, Ahmad, Sumner, Martin, & Butcher, in press) demonstrate that its content is strikingly consistent with the content of the digital library resources themselves. A full 95% of the concepts in the domain competency model knowledge map were closely related to the content of the digital library resources, with 58% of the concepts drawn directly from the resources and 37% paraphrased. The remaining 5% of the expert concepts were inferences that did not directly correspond to the resources. This finding validates our assumption that digital library resources should provide adequate domain coverage for automatic generation of knowledge models. Moreover, it directly informs our choice of automatic computational techniques. Because experts construct a domain knowledge model that is very closely tied to the contents of the digital library resources, our automatic generation of domain competency models builds directly upon a widely-used and publicly available platform for multi-lingual multi-document summarization and evaluation: MEAD (Radev et al., 2004).

We extended the MEAD platform to identify educationally relevant sentences, thereby improving the conceptual adequacy of sentences extracted from digital library resources. A detailed discussion of our technical extensions to the MEAD platform is found elsewhere (de la Chica et al., in press). However, it is important to note that the CLICK extensions are based on general, educationally-relevant processes that experts used when generating the domain knowledge model. As discussed earlier, human experts use a great number of examples in the domain knowledge map, many of which reference specific locations (e.g., "The port zone of Kobe, Japan, was also damaged severely by liquefaction during the 1995 earthquake.") Thus, CLICK uses a *gazetteer* feature to find sentences that include references to named geographical locations in the Alexandria Digital Library (ADL) Gazetteer service (Hill, 2000). Our qualitative analyses show that human experts also use national educational standards to prioritize their concept selection from the digital library resources. Thus, CLICK uses an *educational standards* feature to weight sentences in digital library resources according to their similarity to AAAS benchmarks (AAAS, 1993) and the National Science Educational Standards (NRC, 1996).

Representing What Students Know Now: The Student Knowledge Model

Because both the domain competency model and the student knowledge model are represented as knowledge maps, we can perform a computational concept alignment that categorizes differences between the student knowledge map and the domain competency model in order to identify inaccuracies and gaps in student knowledge. This concept alignment is informed by research on algorithms for concept map comparisons (e.g., Conlon, 2006; Gouli, Gogoulou, Papanikalaou, & Grigoriadou, 2004). We recognize that knowledge map production is an unfamiliar task for many students, so CLICK automatically generates knowledge maps from student essays. Our choice of student essays as a learning task is motivated by the desire to use common educational artifacts (e.g., artifacts that require no up-front training for students) as input into the CLICK system.

CLICK supports the comparison of student knowledge by automatically analyzing student essays to generate a knowledge map that represents student understanding in the domain. CLICK maximizes its fidelity to the student essays by keeping all sentences from the student work, and performing minimal transformations on that text. In order to create links between concepts (sentences) in the automatically generated student knowledge map, CLICK uses lexical chains (Morris & Hirst, 1991) to analyze the semantic relatedness of words. Lexical

chains utilize semantic text relationships—such as synonymy, hypernymy, and hyponymy—to sequence individual words with similar meaning. These sequences of words are used to generate links between sentences in a student knowledge map. CLICK takes a conservative approach to link generation, using essay organization to weight the likelihood of links. CLICK generates one link per noun in a lexical chain and connects the link to the closest preceding sentence that contains a noun from the same lexical chain. Sentences without nouns in identified lexical chains are linked by their relative position in the essay—links are generated to preceding and following sentences as necessary. Figure 2 shows an excerpt of text and its CLICK-generated knowledge map. A lexical chain containing *plates* connects sentences 9 and 11. Sentence 10 is not connected to the other

Figure 2. Excerpt from a student essay and its CLICK-generated knowledge map representation

Student Essay Excerpt: Sentences 9-11
Pangaea, the original super continent, has been rearranged by the moving plates to now form the modern contents. This is shown through, glacier remains, fossil discoveries, and erosion patterns. As these plates shift around and collide, as it takes thousands of years for them to move, we experience the collisions as a sliding of the plates.

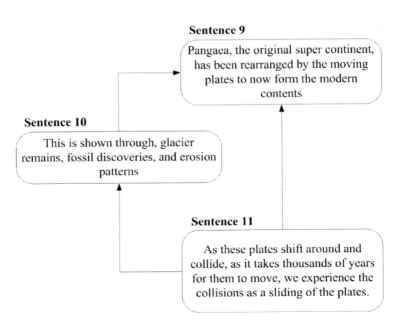

sentences by a lexical chain, so it is integrated into the map using its position in the essay.

Do automatic knowledge maps successfully represent student knowledge? To determine the success of the CLICK-generated student knowledge maps, we compared the automatically generated student knowledge maps to those generated by the four experts who participated in the domain competency model development. For this initial evaluation, 23 undergraduate students with low knowledge about our topic—earthquakes and plate tectonics—generated essays after a short exploration of suggested web resources. Experts generated knowledge maps of these essays by hand, with the instructions to faithfully represent the conceptual knowledge of the student as much as possible. Two experts analyzed each essay. Experts differ somewhat in their approach to organizing and representing these knowledge maps—experts do not represent all of a student's sentences, and some experts choose to focus on different grain sizes for representation (e.g., words vs. multiple sentences). To account for these differences, we use the union of the two expert maps for each essay as a gold standard to which CLICK can aspire since both representations reflect expert knowledge.

We evaluated whether CLICK agreed with at least one expert on the sentences that were selected for representation as nodes in the knowledge map and on the links between sentence nodes. We compared the agreement between CLICK and an expert with the agreement between the two experts for each knowledge map (see Table 1).

Agreement between the human experts is computed using "prevalence-adjusted bias-adjusted" kappa, or PABA-kappa (Byrt, Bishop, & Carlin, 1993). The PABA-kappa measure adjusts the interrater agreement to account for the prevalence of judgments in this task (each node is either connected or not) and conflicting biases among the experts in binary labeling tasks (Byrt et al., 1993; Di Eugenio & Glass, 2004; Viera & Garrett, 2005). Experts show strong agreement in the concepts that they select from student essays for representation in the student knowledge map (PABA-kappa = .71), as well as in the way that they make connections between these concepts (PABA-kappa = .81).

CLICK's knowledge map generation performs very well in selecting relevant concepts from student maps (PABA-kappa = .92). In the more rigorous test of concept connectivity, CLICK also shows substantial agreement with human experts in the connectivity that it creates or rejects between selected concepts (PABA-kappa = .66).

Although these results show clear promise in CLICK's generation of student knowledge maps, the most stringent test of these knowledge maps is their usefulness in identifying conceptual knowledge issues for remediation. That is, are the CLICK-generated maps similar enough to human maps to support effective analysis of student conceptual knowledge as compared to the domain competency model? Moreover, can these CLICK comparisons support the development of effective instructional interventions?

Table 1. PABA-kappa results for evaluation of student knowledge maps

	Expert-Expert Agreement	CLICK-Expert Agreement
Concept Selection	0.71	0.92
Concept Connectivity	0.81	0.66

Moving from Representations to Intervention: Conceptual Knowledge Remediation

We addressed the usefulness of the automatically-generated domain competency model and student knowledge maps by having both CLICK and human experts analyze the conceptual content of the 23 essays generated by low-knowledge learners (the same essays that were used for development of student knowledge map generation techniques).

CLICK successfully targets student knowledge issues. We developed a set of qualitative and quantitative data to serve as the baseline for evaluation of the CLICK-identified student knowledge issues by having our experts assess students' knowledge and identify useful remediation strategies. Using the knowledge maps that they had generated by hand for each of the student essays, experts assessed the conceptual content of the maps to detect errors, ambiguities, and isolated knowledge that should be targeted for remediation. Experts also developed an instructional plan for each student, in which they categorized the conceptual problems they had identified and described an instructional approach that they thought was relevant for revising the knowledge. For each suggested revision, the experts identified digital library resources to support remediation. Expert identification of student knowledge issues served as the gold standard to assess the success of the CLICK conceptual analysis.

CLICK analyzes the content of student essays by using concept map comparison techniques (Conlon, 2006; Gouli et al., 2004) to align the knowledge map that it generates from a student essay to the domain competency model that it has generated from digital library resources. One important challenge for the identification of incorrect domain knowledge is bridging potential gaps in the terminology used by students and that represented in the domain competency model. To account for potential mismatches in terminology, CLICK expands the terms associated with each concept being compared. That is, CLICK extracts terms from the concept being aligned as well as its neighboring concepts and also uses WordNet (Fellbaum, 1998) to augment the terms with relevant synonyms. CLICK's computational processes for knowledge map alignment are discussed in detail elsewhere (de la Chica et al., in press)

We examined whether the same knowledge was selected for remediation by two human experts, or CLICK and a human expert. Note that this *recall* statistic does not necessarily indicate whether the same knowledge was consistently identified as the same knowledge issue. This more fine-grained agreement is reflected in the *precision* statistic (see Table 2). These results show that CLICK performs very well in detecting student conceptual knowledge that may need remediation, but it is more difficult to diagnose these knowledge issues. Our algorithm identified 78% of the statements identified by humans that were targeted for instructional remediation, and 37% of the time CLICK found this knowledge to be lacking in the same manner as did human experts. It should be noted that these numbers reflect CLICK performance when using CLICK-generated representations for both the domain competency model and the student essays. CLICK agreement with experts on the type of knowledge

Table 2. Agreement in student knowledge selected for remediation by experts and CLICK

	Precision	Recall
Expert-Expert Agreement	69%	69%
CLICK-Expert Agreement	37%	78%

deficit that students demonstrate is considerably higher (57%) when using the concept maps of student essays that experts created, likely because experts choose to ignore a number of knowledge problems for representation and remediation but CLICK considers all sentences and all identified problems for analysis.

CLICK's reliable detection of erroneous student knowledge shows promising results for strength of its conceptual analysis. By linking errors in student knowledge models to the digital library resources associated with relevant concepts from the domain competency model, CLICK can support conceptually-informed, customized instructional interventions. Table 3 shows example of CLICK-identified student knowledge issue related to *incomplete understanding*. Note that some issues are relatively straightforward, such as the *knowledge gap* for behaviors of tectonic plates. However, other CLICK-identified knowledge issues are more subtle, as the *shallow terminology* example shows. Although the student correctly states that oceanic crust dives under continental crust, this statement demonstrates a lack of knowledge regarding the scientific rationale for this process.

The output of the CLICK system provides a rich set of learner-specific data on conceptual understanding that could be used in a variety of multimedia tools, but the richness and detail of its knowledge representations makes it particularly well-suited to cognitively-informed intervention strategies. Our approach to learning interactions using CLICK is instantiated in an *instructional intervention* component. As we discuss in the next section, the instructional intervention component draws upon cognitive theory in interactive learner discourse and effective human tutoring.

Instructional Intervention: Using Click Data for Cognitively-Targeted Support

CLICK organizes the erroneous knowledge identified during comparison of student knowledge maps to the domain competency model into three categories of knowledge issues that can be targeted for remediation:

- **Knowledge integration problems:** Student knowledge in this category is connected to inappropriate concepts, or is not connected to relevant concepts.
- **Incomplete understanding:** Student knowledge in this category reflects gaps in existing knowledge, or evidence that this knowledge may be conceptually shallow rather than deep.
- **Incorrect statements:** Student knowledge in this category reflects explicitly incorrect content, such as erroneous definitions

Table 3. Sample CLICK-identified knowledge issues compared to correct domain information

CLICK Knowledge Issues	CLICK Knowledge Issue Subcategories	Example of CLICK-identified Student Knowledge Issue	Correct Knowledge drawn from the CLICK-generated Domain Competency Model
Incomplete Understanding	Shallow terminology	Oceanic crust dives under continental crust	Usually the *older* oceanic crust is subducted because it is colder and slightly denser. Otherwise, the densities of the two plates are similar
	Knowledge gap	Tectonic plates can only collide	At their boundaries, plates converge (move toward), diverge (away from), slide past each other (transform boundary), or some combination thereof.

of terminology or misunderstandings that reflect problematic extensions or limitations of prior knowledge.

CLICK's high level categories were derived from the expert assessment of novice essays in our research. It is interesting to note that our derived categories correspond roughly to the three conditions of complex learning with prior knowledge that have been described by Chi (in press). Chi argues that prior knowledge can have three relationships to correct, desired knowledge. Prior knowledge can be missing (corresponds to CLICK incomplete understanding), can be incomplete (corresponds to CLICK knowledge integration problems), or can be in conflict with correct knowledge (corresponds to CLICK incorrect statements, particularly with a subset of incorrect statements called "false beliefs"). Although our research is not specifically targeted to facilitate the difficult processes of conceptual change that Chi targets, the correspondence of our data to cognitive theory about conceptual learning bodes well for the potential of CLICK data to support the implementation of cognitively-informed multimedia and instructional technology that builds upon theory in learner discourse, tutoring, and deep learning processes.

Key challenges facing the development of CLICK's instructional components are 1) to promote student interactions that support effective learning, 2) to prompt learners to use effective cognitive processes while engaging with CLICK, and 3) to use CLICK-generated data on knowledge issues to provide students with custom-selected multimedia materials that support their conceptual learning activities.

Promoting Effective Instructional Interactions through Learner Discourse

CLICK's instructional support is modeled on learner discourse theory and research on effective human tutoring. Approaches to learning based on learner discourse have a long history. An early, and still relevant, approach is that of conversational learning theory (Pask, 1975; Scott, 2001). Conversational learning theory includes *discursive, adaptive, interactive,* and *reflective* interactions (Laurillard, 1993) during an instructional situation. Discursive interactions make thinking visible through external representations of learner and instructor knowledge, while adaptive interactions customize the content and activities in a learning episode through the assessment of existing student knowledge. Interactive phases use mixed-initiative turns to drive relevant student activities that support knowledge extension and revision, and reflective interactions are more metacognitive in nature. Reflective interactions help the learner form connections between their knowledge, instructor feedback, and the learning task.

Conversational learning theory has clear connections to research on human tutoring activities and effectiveness. Effective tutoring has been identified as following a 5-step dialog frame (Graesser & Person, 1994). The first three steps are driven by the tutor: the tutor asks a question, the student answers that question, and the tutor gives a short form of immediate feedback. In effective tutoring situations, the three initial steps are followed by a collaborative fourth step—in which the tutor and the tutee work together to improve the quality of the student response—and a fifth step in which the tutor assesses the student's understanding. Person et al. (2001) hypothesize that the fourth and fifth steps are responsible for the significant advantage of tutors over classrooms in promoting student learning.

Conversational learning theory and tutoring research identify at least two critical activities for customized instructional support based on learner discourse: Leaner knowledge should be articulated and assessed, and iterative mixed-initiative support should be used to build student understanding. CLICK is being developed to include multimedia support that targets these general processes, using methods that are informed by previous cognitive learning research. Figure 3 demonstrates how the CLICK conceptual framework aligns with key interactions in conversational learning theory.

The CLICK computational components discussed so far facilitate the first two levels of interaction in conversational learning theory. CLICK's *discursive* interactions make thinking visible by externalizing learner and domain conceptualizations using the knowledge maps that it generates automatically. Unlike student-tutor approaches to interactive learner discourse, CLICK's instructor representations reflect knowledge that is distributed across numerous instructional materials—and presumably instructors—in a domain. CLICK's *adaptive* interactions—guiding instructor-learner dialogue based on the instructor's assessment of the learner's current conceptual understanding—is grounded in CLICK's knowledge map comparison. This comparison between the domain competency model and the student

knowledge map forms the foundation for future interactions, by categorizing the type of erroneous knowledge that has been identified.

CLICK's discursive and adaptive interactions are largely behind-the-scenes computational processes that produce conceptual representations and data that CLICK can reuse in the implementation of effective learning interactions. The instructional intervention component of CLICK makes use of the automatically-generated knowledge maps and conceptual knowledge analysis to support two types of activities: 1) iterative conceptual knowledge building, and 2) conceptually-informed multimedia selection.

Iterative Conceptual Knowledge Building

CLICK's final discursive move sets the stage for student interaction. CLICK selects conceptual issues to remediate based on its current model

Figure 3. The CLICK Conceptual Framework

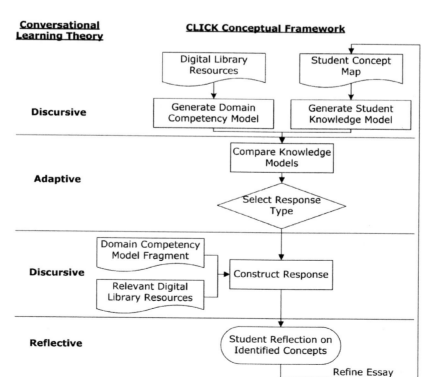

of learner knowledge. CLICK extracts relevant portions of the knowledge maps and chooses prompts that are appropriate for the identified conceptual issue. As the student updates his or her essay, CLICK regenerates its knowledge map representation of student understanding and selects a new response based on an updated conceptual alignment between the student knowledge map and the domain competency model. This repeated cycling through student knowledge articulation and interactive instructional support is one aspect of CLICK's iterative support for student knowledge building. CLICK also includes support for student knowledge building within a single learning cycle. This support is provided by encouraging comparison and contrast of the student and domain knowledge representations and by using prompts to increase deep processing of multimedia materials. From a conversational learning theory standpoint, these activities represent CLICK's support for *interactive* episodes, in which students have the opportunity to build knowledge by actively engaging with CLICK feedback. These activities also enable *reflective* interactions that enable the learner to establish meaningful connections between current understanding, CLICK feedback, and the learning task.

Comparing and contrasting knowledge map representations. CLICK-generated knowledge map representations of student understanding and domain knowledge serve a unique dual-role; they function both as a basis for computational processes that drive CLICK's pedagogical responses and as an instructional representation to facilitate comparison and contrast. CLICK shows the learner selected portions of his or her knowledge map that have been identified as problematic—missing information or containing erroneous information—in juxtaposition to relevant portions of the domain competency model.

The visually-organized representation of articulated knowledge allows students to identify and analyze conflicts between their internal knowledge representations and a correct domain representation. This process of comparison between an individual's knowledge and optimal understanding has strong basis in cognitive learning research; identification and articulation of one's own knowledge deficits has been advocated as an explanation for the robust learning effects achieved through self-explanation during text learning and problem solving (Chi, de Leeuw, Chiu, & LaVancher, 1994). Further, comparison strategies between knowledge representations can improve students' readiness to learn from expository materials (Schwartz & Bransford, 1998). When students are given examples that highlight key differences in domain features, Schwartz and Bransford found that students are better prepared to learn deeply from materials provided later. In CLICK, articulation of differences in the maps sets the stage for deeper processing of the multimedia resources that will be encountered during learning.

Given the importance of matching multimedia resources to student background knowledge, one might question whether low-knowledge learners are capable of using knowledge maps for articulation and reflection. Knowledge map representations provided to students by CLICK are consistent with novice-friendly multimedia tools. Although the knowledge map representations are visually organized, they include ample text that can be used by learners to make sense of the content—as would be warranted by expertise reversal findings (Kalyuga, Ayres, Chandler, & Sweller, 2003). Indeed, previous research has shown that low knowledge students can use and benefit from knowledge map representations (O'Donnell et al., 2002). Our own previous research has shown that knowledge map representations can promote effective learning processes. Students who used knowledge maps to search an educational digital library were more likely to engage with and analyze domain content and relationships compared to students who used a typical keyword search interface (Butcher, Bhushan, & Sumner, 2006). These findings suggest that knowledge maps are an appropriate type of visual-verbal representation for low-knowledge learners. However, it remains to be determined if this representation is the optimal format for supporting articulation and reflection during student learning.

Prompting knowledge building. CLICK's strategic use of knowledge map representations for student processing is only effective if students actively engage with the representations. From a conversational theory perspective, it is critical that learners iterate through reflection and interaction. Students must have appropriate guidance to engage in knowledge building and then must use this knowledge in meaningful ways. In human tutoring contexts, tutors typically guide the learner's discourse contributions by using prompts to elicit student knowledge (Chi, Siler, Jeong, Yamauchi, & Hausmann, 2001; Graesser & Person, 1994). In CLICK's case, system responses are used to guide students' analysis and revision of knowledge.

CLICK's selection of remediation strategies is a significant challenge as we develop instructional interventions. In our research with experts, the remediation strategies that they select for individual student knowledge issues are quite variable. This variability is consistent with other research in instructional technology (VanLehn et al., 2005). For specific knowledge gaps and errors, we found little direct correspondence in the chosen remediation strategies of two experts. However, expert strategies can be categorized into two general types: remediation heuristics and resource selection strategies.

Remediation heuristics describe the type of approach that experts identified as appropriate for a given misunderstanding, error, or knowledge gap. Common remediation heuristics include:

- Add new knowledge
- Integrate relevant knowledge
- Connect to educational standards
- Focus the student on core concepts

Resources selection strategies describe the type of digital library resources that experts selected to support their chosen remediation approaches. Common resource selection strategies include providing a link to:

- An interactive resource
- A resource with a picture
- A resource that includes interactive activities
- A resources that includes complete coverage of the relevant topic

As seen in Table 4, experts do demonstrate some agreement on basic strategies that are relevant for a particular student. Our initial examination of expert agreement examined 35 knowledge issues from three student essays, where each essay was assessed by two experts. Overall, for a given essay, experts tended to approach student remediation in similar ways. If we assume expert remediation approaches to be a gold standard for CLICK, then CLICK prompting during remediation should target relatively high-level strategies. As

Table 4. Agreement in expert remediation approaches for a sample of 35 knowledge issues from 3 student essays

	Expert A	Expert B	Expert C
% (Mean) of Remediation Heuristics Shared with a Second Expert	67%	42%	75%
% (Mean) of Resource Selection Strategies Shared with a Second Expert	50%	45%	75%

we continue to evaluate student essays and expert remediation plans, it will be important to identify if some strategies and heuristics enjoy stronger agreement than others. The identification of a small number of remediation approaches could serve as starting points for CLICK interactions.

Our approach to instantiating successful high-level prompting in CLICK is informed by research on supporting student knowledge building in tutoring contexts. Chi et al. (2001) found that, in human tutoring, knowledge-targeted prompts—those that ask students to generate content-specific answers—were not any more effective than general content-free prompts that were used in contextualized ways. Indeed, when students were prompted with the content-free prompts they were more generative. Thus, asking students "Anything else?" when they mention two types of faults may be as effective as asking them "What is a third type of fault?" when CLICK detects this incomplete knowledge. We have selected a subset of prompts used by Chi et al. (2001) that are appropriate for student reflection in each of CLICK's knowledge-issue categories. For example, CLICK detection of incorrect knowledge triggers content-free prompts that prompt additional explanation while fragmented knowledge triggers prompts that encourage generation of new content. We suspect that any prompting will be more effective than no prompting, but that selection of prompts that encourage processes relevant to the CLICK categories of conceptual learning situations will lead to greater amounts of student generation and deeper processing of the multimedia resources that CLICK recommends.

Conceptually-Informed Selection of Multimedia

CLICK also provides instructional support through the customized selection of existing multimedia resources based on an individual student's identified conceptual knowledge needs. When CLICK selects its response to identified issues in the student knowledge map, it provides learners with links to targeted digital library materials. Students can read relevant portions of digital library resources, investigate phenomena by manipulating simulations, interact with complex visualizations, and use exemplary resources that support inquiry-oriented learning.

We are implementing CLICK's instructional intervention component to utilize two factors in selecting appropriate multimedia. First, the digital library multimedia must include relevant conceptual content that is appropriate to the portion of the domain competency map that CLICK has selected for presentation to the student. Because CLICK generates its domain competency model from existing collections of digital library resources, links between nodes in the domain competency model's knowledge map and individual multimedia resources already exist by the time CLICK forms its instructional response. For very common knowledge gaps or errors, a large number of digital library resources may have relevant links to the snippet of the domain competency model that is being used for remediation. A bigger challenge is prioritizing the type of student interaction needed and helping learners focus on relevant portions of large sets of digital materials.

Prioritizing resources can be informed by current findings in multimedia learning. Novice learners might be identified by simple errors in their knowledge maps, leading CLICK to choose multimedia resources that have been shown to be effective with lower knowledge students, such as resources that include relevant pictures and diagrams (e.g., Butcher, 2006; Mayer, 2001) in addition to text. According to expertise reversal theory (Kalyuga et al., 2003), as CLICK detects fewer problems and greater complexity in student knowledge, digital library resources should be prioritized to emphasize visual resources, simulations, and activities that are relevant to the student's knowledge needs.

Pedagogical Considerations in Designing Instructional Interventions

In a current learning study, we are designing a prototype of the CLICK essay tool to support analysis and revision using the CLICK components. This tool is designed to embody the cognitive support that CLICK provides. However, the instantiation of this support in a working prototype requires numerous design decisions. Because CLICK is intended to be a useful educational technology for classrooms, the design of the CLICK essay tool was informed by a participatory design workshop with teachers. The workshop highlighted a number of principles that need to be considered in the development of conceptually-informed learning interactions for classroom use. Teachers seek *flexible guidance* that adapts to changing learner expertise and to different student learning processes; *salient feedback* that is easy for students to identify and understand; and *prioritized revision* to present the most critical errors or issues for revision first.

The amount of desired learner control in CLICK varied according to whether teachers were designing for a student with low or high prior knowledge. For struggling students, teachers sought to implement a more strictly-controlled instructional tool where students' knowledge maps served as the source for revision activities. For these students, teachers wanted to require knowledge map revision before the student could return to the essay in order to support deeper consideration of domain issues.

For more knowledgeable students, teachers noted that mixed-initiative interactions were important. Teachers felt that students should be able to show some independence in their work and in their requests for evaluation, but also felt that CLICK should step in when it was clear that the student was struggling or failing to prioritize important revisions. This desire for smart-interactions based on student processes (in addition to articulated knowledge) creates a significant dilemma that is familiar to those in intelligent tutoring: when should the system provide the student with information and support, and when should it prompt the student to generate this information on his or her own? Koedinger and Aleven (2007) refer to this as the assistance dilemma—and emphasize the need for further research that might illuminate the conditions under which optimal learner support can be identified and implemented.

Remaining Questions

The assistance dilemma is just one of the remaining questions facing CLICK during its continued development. Given CLICK's unique approach to customization, using knowledge maps both as computational input and as an instructional representation, a critical challenge is deciding upon the right level of granularity. Where are the boundaries of student knowledge issues identified in knowledge maps, especially for novice students who may have significant knowledge gaps as well as misunderstandings?

A related question is how CLICK should prioritize knowledge issues when there are many choices for remediation. We have seen that our experts routinely ignore some knowledge problems when deciding on remediation—for example, experts often accept vague statements or ignore extraneous additions in student essays. We do not know how wise these choices are in all cases. However, it also seems clear that a lack of flexibility in this regard will overwhelm students. Multimedia developers have long been cautioned to avoid extraneous cognitive load that draws student attention away from relevant learning activities; at the same time, developers should maximize intrinsic cognitive load that forces students to spend the majority of their cognitive resources on conceptually-relevant tasks (Chandler & Sweller, 1991; Kalyuga, Chandler, & Sweller, 1999)

Other challenges include targeted retrieval of relevant portions of digital library resources—these resources often can include many associated web pages, hyperlinks, and activities. Too little constraint during retrieval likely will lead to learner frustration as they struggle to see the relevance between the multimedia content and their individual learning situations. Too much constraint limits the opportunities for knowledge building and creates new challenges for fine-grained retrieval within digital library resources. These issues reflect the need for instructional design that provides appropriate student guidance in a learning environment that is flexible enough to accommodate different student learning processes and changing student knowledge.

For CLICK to perform optimally, we will need to leverage student interest and motivation by providing clear and frequent feedback that highlights student progress and by making increasingly sensitive matches between learners and available learning materials. We also will need to optimize the type of multimedia resources that are selected for remediation. Selection of resources with relevant multimedia content may be more engaging for students and may lead to greater persistence in a given educational task.

CONCLUSION

Our development of the CLICK service so far suggests that there is great promise in using existing multimedia resources as the foundation for a conceptually-advanced educational tool that provides customized interactions for individual learners. The existence of mature digital libraries that contain large collections of educational multimedia provides a key resource to leverage in representing domain content. Moreover, these educational digital libraries provide a large bank of relevant multimedia resources that can be used in the service of customized learning interactions.

In order to take advantage of the resources provided in these educational digital libraries, our work has extended natural language processing techniques to automatically generate useful representations of optimal domain content and of existing student knowledge. Our findings show that CLICK generates domain competency models—in the form of knowledge maps—that faithfully represent the content and relationships that experts select when representing domain content from digital library resources. CLICK's generation of student knowledge maps from essays is similarly successful. Most importantly, CLICK techniques that align the domain competency models and the student knowledge maps correctly identify a large number of knowledge issues in a domain.

The representations and conceptual knowledge data produced by CLICK are designed to provide strong support for cognitively-motivated instructional interactions. Cognitive approaches to student learning have served as the foundation for the design of CLICK's instructional interactions, drawing upon theories of learner discourse (Pask, 1975; Scott, 2001), research on effective human tutoring (Chi et al., 2001; Graesser & Person, 1994), and multimedia interactions with learner prior knowledge (Kalyuga et al., 2003; Kalyuga et al., 2000).

A number of challenges remain before CLICK is fully realized as a customized multimedia technology in classrooms. We must develop methods for CLICK to prioritize student errors and knowledge deficits, deciding what students should fix first and when they should stop. We must deal with issues of granularity in directing students to useful multimedia resources. We, like the rest of the intelligent tutoring community (Koedinger & Aleven, 2007), must decide when to let students struggle for their own good, and when to give them additional support to ensure their success.

Regardless of these challenges, CLICK represents an important step forward in developing multimedia tools that are customized but scalable to new domains and disciplines. CLICK's automatic generation of knowledge models and its potential to use these models in effective, cognitively-based instructional practices demonstrates an effective integration of interdisciplinary methodologies to support deep student learning.

FUTURE RESEARCH DIRECTIONS

The work presented in this chapter focuses on multimedia support for student learners in science, evaluating the potential of creating customized learning interactions based on individual needs and existing multimedia resources. Customized learning interactions have broad potential use that can extent beyond students—especially when considering the needs of their teachers. Although teachers frequently turn to the World Wide Web to help them find interactive and engaging resources for their classrooms, many teachers express frustration with the time it takes to locate useful resources and report difficulties assessing the scientific quality of resources and their alignment with state standards (Hanson & Carlson, 2005). Teachers also may need help in identifying the unique knowledge needs of individual learners in a large classroom. CLICK's existing capabilities for modeling student understanding provide a useful potential method for teachers to track the changing knowledge of their individual students. CLICK also may support teachers in identifying conceptually-relevant multimedia resources for students with common misunderstandings or knowledge gaps.

Extending CLICK's knowledge modeling techniques might also provide more direct support to teachers. Teachers could write essays that describe their desired content coverage, using CLICK to automatic analyze and align these essays to a domain competency model. Teachers could then select topics for multimedia support, receiving both CLICK's knowledge map representation of their topic coverage and the related portions of the domain competency map. Beginning teachers or those teaching out of area may find that these representations help them identify and articulate

new areas for their own learning. They also could use the CLICK connections to multimedia materials as an efficient method to build multimedia content into their curricula. CLICK's potential support for richly assessing student knowledge and providing conceptually-relevant multimedia curriculum enhancement suggests that CLICK may be uniquely well-suited to improving teachers' pedagogical content knowledge—domain-specific teaching skills that include understanding of common student difficulties and beliefs, and methods to move students past these barriers.

As we develop increasingly customized interactions with multimedia, we also need to consider ways that we can further increase student engagement with multimedia resources. There is much room for research on effective methods to improve student processing of multimedia materials—these might include the use of deep questions (Graesser & Person, 1994), self-explanation prompts (Chi et al., 1994), or embedded tools for collaborative learning. One method for improving learner engagement that deserves special consideration is the customization of visual representations that can be used to communicate knowledge. Researchers should consider the potential impact of customizing visual *representations* of important domain content in addition to customizing the selection of content and the interactions that surround it. Truly effective and robust multimedia may need to be customized on multiple levels in order to support unique student needs effectively during learning.

REFERENCES

AAAS. (1993). *Benchmarks for Science Literacy.* New York: Project 2061, American Association for the Advancement of Science, Oxford University Press.

Ahmad, F., de la Chica, S., Butcher, K. R., Sumner, T., & Martin, J. H. (2007). Towards Automatic

Conceptual Personalization Tools. In *Proceedings of the 5th ACM/IEEE-CS Joint Conference on Digital Libraries*, Vancouver, BC (pp. 452-461). New York, NY: ACM Press.

Anderson, J. R. (1993). *Rules of the mind*. Hillsdale, NJ: Lawrence Erlbaum.

Anderson, J. R., Corbett, A. T., Koedinger, K. R., & Pelletier, R. (1995). Cognitive tutors: Lessons learned. *Journal of the Learning Sciences, 4*(2), 167-207.

Britton, B. K., & Gulgoz, S. (1991). Using Kintsch's computational model to improve instructional text: Effects of repairing inference calls on recall and cognitive structures. *Journal of Educational Psychology 83*, 329-345.

Butcher, K. R., Bhushan, S., & Sumner, T. (2006). Multimedia displays for conceptual search processes: Information seeking with strand maps. *ACM Multimedia Systems Journal, 11*(3), 236-248.

Butcher, K. R. (2006). Learning from text with diagrams: Promoting mental model development and inference generation. *Journal of Educational Psychology, 98*(1), 182-197.

Byrt, T., Bishop, J., & Carlin, J. B. (1993). Bias, prevalence, and kappa. *Journal of Clinical Epidemiology, 46*(5), 423-429.

Cen, H., Koedinger, K. R., & Junker, B. (2007). Is over practice necessary? Improving learning efficiency with the cognitive tutor through educational data mining. In R. Lunkin, K. R. Koedinger & J. Greer (Eds.), *Proceedings of the 13th International Conference on Artificial Intelligence in Education* (pp. 511-518). Marina Del Ray, CA: IOS Press.

Chandler, P., & Sweller, J. (1991). Cognitive load theory and the format of instruction. *Cognition and Instruction, 8*, 293-332.

Chi, M. T., de Leeuw, N., Chiu, M.-H., & LaVancher, C. (1994). Eliciting self-explanations improves understanding. *Cognitive Science, 18*(3), 439-477.

Chi, M. T., Siler, S. A., & Jeong, H. (2004). Can tutors monitor students' understanding accurately? *Cognition and Instruction, 22*(3), 363-387.

Chi, M. T. H. (in press). Three types of conceptual change: Belief revision, mental model transformation, and categorical shift. In S. Vosniadou (Ed.), *Handbook of research on conceptual change*. Hillsdale, NJ: Erlbaum.

Chi, M. T. H., Siler, S. A., Jeong, H., Yamauchi, T., & Hausmann, R. G. (2001). Learning from human tutoring. *Cognitive Science, 25*(4), 471-533.

Chmielewski, T. L., & Dansereau, D. F. (1998). Enhancing the recall of text: Knowledge mapping training promotes implicit transfer. *Journal of Educational Psychology, 90*(3), 407-413.

Conati, C., Gertner, A., & Vanlehn, K. (2002). Using bayesian networks to manage uncertainty in student modeling. *User Modeling and User-Adapted Interaction, 12*(4), 371-417.

Conlon, T. (2006). *But is our concept map any good? Classroom experiences with the Reasonable Fallible Analyser*. Paper presented at the Second International Conference on Concept Mapping, San José, Costa Rica.

de la Chica, S., Ahmad, F., Sumner, T., Martin, J. H., & Butcher, K. (in press). Computational foundations for personalizing instruction with digital libraries. *International Journal on Digital Libraries*.

Di Eugenio, B., & Glass, M. (2004). The kappa statistic: A second look. *Computational Linguistics, 30*(1), 95-101.

Dwyer, F. M. (1967). The relative effectiveness of varied visual illustrations in complementing programmed instruction. *Journal of Experimental Education, 36*, 34-42.

Dwyer, F. M. (1968). The effectiveness of visual illustrations used to complement programmed instruction. *Journal of Psychology, 70*, 157-162.

Dwyer, F. M. (1969). The effect of varying the amount of realistic detail in visual illustrations designed to complement programmed instruction. *Programmed Learning and Educational Technology, 6*, 147-153.

Fellbaum, C. (1998). *WordNet: An electronic lexical database*. Cambridge, MA: MIT Press.

Gouli, E., Gogoulou, A., Papanikalaou, K., & Grigoriadou, M. (2004, September). *Compass: An adaptive web-based concept map assessment tool*. Paper presented at the First International Conference on Concept Mapping, Pamplona, Spain.

Graesser, A. C., Lu, S., Jackson, G. T., Mitchell, H. H., Ventura, M., Olney, A., & Louwerse, M. M. (2004). AutoTutor: A tutor with dialogue in natural language. *Behavior Research Methods, Instruments, & Computers, 36*(2), 180-192.

Graesser, A. C., & Person, N. K. (1994). Question asking during tutoring. *American Educational Research Journal, 31*(1), 104-137.

Graesser, A. C., Person, N. K., Harter, D., & the Tutoring Research Group. (2001). Teaching tactics and dialogue in AutoTutor. *International Journal of Artificial Intelligence and Education, 12*, 257-279.

Hanson, K., & Carlson, B. (2005). Effective access: Teachers' use of digital resources in STEM teaching. Retrieved November 15, 2007, from http://www2.edc.org/gdi/publications_SR/EffectiveAccessReport.pdf

Hill, L. L. (2000). Core elements of digital gazetteers: Placenames, categories, and footprints. In J. Borbinha & T. Baker (Eds.), *Proceedings of the 4th European Conference on Digital Librar-*

ies, Lisbon, Portugal (pp. 380-390). Heidelberg: Springer-Verlag.

Jonassen, D. H., & Grabowski, B. L. (1993). *Handbook of individual differences, learning and instruction*. Hillsdale, NJ: Lawrence Erlbaum.

Kalyuga, S., Ayres, P., Chandler, P., & Sweller, J. (2003). The expertise reversal effect. *Educational Psychologist, 38*(1), 23-31.

Kalyuga, S., Chandler, P., & Sweller, J. (1999). Managing split-attention and redundancy in multimedia instruction. *Applied Cognitive Psychology, 13*(4), 351-371.

Kalyuga, S., Chandler, P., & Sweller, J. (2000). Incorporating learner experience into the design of multimedia instruction. *Journal of Educational Psychology, 92*(1), 126-136.

Koedinger, K. R., & Aleven, V. (2007). Exploring the assistance dilemma in experiments with cognitive tutors. *Educational Psychology Review, 19*, 239-264.

Koedinger, K. R., Aleven, V., Heffernan, N., McLaren, B. M., & Hockenberry, M. (2004). Opening the door to non-programmers: Authoring intelligent tutor behavior by demonstration. In J. C. Lester, R. M. Vicari & F. Paraguaçu (Eds.), *Proceedings of the 7th annual Intelligent Tutoring Systems Conference* (pp. 162-174). Berlin: Springer-Verlag.

Koedinger, K. R., & Anderson, J. R. (1990). Abstract planning and perceptual chunks: Elements of expertise in geometry. *Cognitive Science, 14*(4), 511-550.

Koedinger, K. R., Anderson, J. R., Hadley, W. H., & Mark, M. A. (1997). Intelligent tutoring goes to school in the big city. *International Journal of Artificial Intelligence in Education, 8*, 30-43.

Landauer, T. K. (1998). Learning and representing verbal meaning: The latent semantic analysis theory. *Current Directions in Psychological Science, 7*, 161-164.

Landauer, T. K., & Dumais, S. T. (1997). A solution to Plato's problem: The latent semantic analysis theory of acquisition, induction and representation of knowledge. *Psychological Review, 104,* 211-240.

Laurillard, D. (1993). *Rethinking university teaching: A framework for the effective use of educational technology.* New York: Routledge.

Levie, W., & Lentz, R. (1982). Effects of text illustrations: A review of research. *Educational Communication & Technology Journal, 30*(4), 195-232.

Lowe, R. K. (1996). Background knowledge and the construction of a situtational representation from a diagram. *European Journal of Psychology of Education, XI*(4), 377-397.

Lowe, R. K. (1999). Extracting information from an animation during complex visual learning. *European Journal of Psychology of Education, 14*(2), 225-244.

Mayer, R. E. (2001). *Multimedia Learning.* Cambridge: Cambridge University Press.

Mayer, R. E., & Gallini, J. (1990). When is an illustration worth ten thousand words? *Journal of Educational Psychology, 82,* 715-726.

Mayer, R. E., Steinhoff, K., Bowers, G., & Mars, R. (1995). A generative theory of textbook design: Using annotated illustrations to foster meaningful learning of science text. *Educational Technology Research and Development, 43*(1), 31-43.

McKeown, M. G., Beck, I. L., Sinatra, G. M., & Loxterman, J. A. (1992). The contribution of prior knowledge and coherent text to comprehension. *Reading Research Quarterly, 27,* 79-93.

McNamara, D. S., Kintsch, E., Songer, N. B., & Kintsch, W. (1996). Are good texts always better? Interactions of text coherence, background knowledge, and levels of understanding in learning from text. *Cognition & Instruction, 14*(1), 1-43.

McNamara, D. S., & Kintsch, W. (1996). Learning from text: Effect of prior knowledge and text coherence. *Discourse Processes, 22,* 247-288.

Means, M., & Voss, J. F. (1985). Star wars: A developmental study of expert and novice knowledge structures. *Memory and Language, 24,* 746-757.

Moravcsik, J. E., & Kintsch, W. (1993). Writing quality, reading skills, and domain knowledge as factors in text comprehension. *Canadian Journal of Experimental Psychology, 47,* 360-374.

Morris, J., & Hirst, G. (1991). Lexical cohesion computed by thesaural relations as an indicator of the structure of text. *Computational Linguistics, 17*(1), 21-48.

Narayanan, N. H., & Hegarty, M. (2002). Multimedia design for communication of dynamic information. *International Journal of Human-Computer Studies, 57*(4), 279-315.

NRC. (1996). *National Science Education Standards.* Washington, DC: National Research Council (NRC), National Academy Press.

NRC. (2000). *How people learn: brain, mind, experience, and school: Expanded edition.* Washington, DC: National Research Council: Commission on Behavioral and Social Sciences and Education, National Academy Press.

O'Donnell, A. M., Dansereau, D. F., & Hall, R. H. (2002). Knowledge maps as scaffolds for cognitive processing. *Educational Psychology Review, 14*(1), 71-86.

Pask, G. (1975). *Conversation, cognition, and learning: A cybernetic theory and methodology.* Amsterdam, Netherlands: Elsevier.

Person, N. K., Graesser, A. C., Kreuz, R. J., Pomeroy, V., & the Tutoring Research Group. (2001). Simulating human tutor dialog moves in AutoTutor. *International Journal of Artificial Intelligence in Education, 12,* 23-39.

Petre, M. (1995). Why looking isn't always seeing: Readership skills and graphical programming. *Communications of the ACM, 38*(6), 33-44.

Petre, M., & Green, T. R. (1993). Learning to read graphics: Some evidence that "seeing" an information display is an acquired skill. *Journal of Visual Languages and Computing, 4*, 55-70.

Radev, D., Allison, T., Blair-Goldensohn, S., Blitzer, J., Celebi, A., Dimitrov, S., et al. (2004, May). *MEAD - A platform for multidocument multilingual text summarization.* Paper presented at the 4th International Conference on Language Resources and Evaluation, Lisbon, Portugal.

Schwan, S., & Riempp, R. (2004). The cognitive benefits of interactive videos: Learning to tie nautical knots. *Learning and Instruction, 14*(3), 293-305.

Schwartz, D. L., & Bransford, J. D. (1998). A time for telling. *Cognition and Instruction, 16*(4), 475-522.

Scott, B. (2001). Conversation theory: A constructivist, dialogical approach to educational technology. *Cybernetics & Human Knowing, 8*(4), 25-46.

Spilich, G. J., Vesonder, G. T., Chiesi, H. L., & Voss, J. F. (1979). Text processing of domain related information for individuals with high and low domain knowledge. *Journal of Verbal Learning and Verbal Behavior, 18*, 275-290.

Susarla, S. C., Adcock, A., Van Eck, R., Moreno, K., & Graesser, A. (2003). *Development and evaluation of a lesson authoring tool for AutoTutor.* In V. Aleven, U. Hoppe, J. Kay, R. Mizoguchi, H. Pain, F. Verdejo, & K. Yacef (Eds.), *Proceedings of the 11th International Conference on Artificial Intelligence in Education*, Sydney, Australia (pp. 378-387). Amsterdam: IOS Press.

VanLehn, K. (2006). The behavior of tutoring systems. *International Journal of Artificial Intelligence and Education, 16*, 227-265.

VanLehn, K., Lynch, C., Schulze, K., Shapiro, J. A., Shelby, R., Taylor, L., et al. (2005). The Andes physics tutoring system: Lessons learned. *International Journal of Artificial Intelligence and Education, 15*, 147-204.

Viera, A. J., & Garrett, J. M. (2005). Understanding interobserver agreement: The kappa statistic. *Family Medicine, 37*(5), 360-363.

Voss, J. F., & Silfies, L. N. (1996). Learning from history text: The interaction of knowlede and comprehension skill with text structure. *Cognition and Instruction, 14*(1), 45-68.

Wade-Stein, D., & Kintsch, E. (2004). Summary Street: Interactive computer support for writing. *Cognition and Instruction, 22*(3), 333-362.

Wolfe, M. B. W., Schreiner, M. E., Rehder, B., Laham, D., Foltz, P. W., Kintsch, W., et al. (1998). Learning from text: Matching readers and texts by latent semantic analysis. *Discourse Processes, 25*(2-3), 309-336.

Zahn, C., Barquero, B., & Schwan, S. (2004). Learning with hyperlinked videos--design criteria and efficient strategies for using audiovisual hypermedia. *Learning and Instruction, 14*(3), 275-291.

ADDITIONAL READING

Computational Techniques

Anderson, J. R., & Pelletier, R. (1991). A development system for model-tracing tutors. In L. Birnbaum (Ed.), In *Proceedings of the International Conference of the Learning Sciences*, (pp 1-8). Charlotesville, VA: AACE.

Barzilay, R., & Elhadad, M. (1997, August). *Using lexical chains for text summarization.* Paper presented at the Association for Computational Linguistics Intelligent Scalable Text Summarization Workshop, Madrid, Spain.

Brusilovsky, P., Farzan, R., & Ahn, J. (2005). Comprehensive personalized information access in an educational digital library. In *Proceedings of the 5th ACM/IEEE-CS Joint Conference on Digital Libraries, Denver, Colorado* (pp. 9-18). New York, NY: ACM Press.

Budzik, J., & Hammond, K. J. (2000). User interactions with everyday applications as context for just-in-time information access. In *Proceedings of the 5th International Conference on Intelligent User Interfaces, New Orleans, Louisiana* (pp. 44-51). New York, NY: ACM Press.

Burstein, J., Marcu, D., & Knight, K. (2003). Finding the WRITE stuff: Automatic identification of discourse structure in student essays. *IEEE Intelligent Systems, 18*(1), 32-39.

Corbett, A. T., McLaughlin, M., & Scarpinatto, K. C. (2000). Modeling student knowledge: Cognitive tutors in high school and college. *User Modeling and User-Adapted Interaction, 10*(2-3), 81-108.

Fischer, G. (2001). User modeling in human-computer interaction. *User Modeling and User-Adapted Interaction, 11*(1&2), 65-86.

Gouli, E., Gogoulou, A., & Grigoriadou, M. (2003). A coherent and integrated framework using concept maps for various educational assessment functions. *Journal of Information Technology Education, 2*, 215-240.

Hwang, G.-J. (2003). A conceptual map model for developing intelligent tutoring systems. *Computers and Education, 40*(3), 217-235.

Jurafsky, D., & Martin, J. H. (2000). *Speech and Language Processing: An Introduction to Natural Language Processing, Computational Linguistics, and Speech Recognition*. Upper Saddle River, New Jersey: Prentice Hall.

Lin, C. Y. (2004, July). *ROUGE: A package for automatic evaluation of summaries*. Paper presented at the Workshop on Text Summarization Branches Out, Barcelona, Spain.

Mani, I. (2001). *Automatic Summarization*. Amsterdam, The Netherlands: John Benjamins B.V.

Marcu, D., & Echihabi, A. (2002). An unsupervised approach to recognizing discourse relations. In *Proceedings of the 40th Annual Meeting of the Association for Computational Linguistics, Philadelphia, Pennsylvania* (pp. 368-375). East Stroudsburg, PA: Association for Computational Linguistics.

McCalla, G. I. (1992). The search for adaptability, flexibility, and individualization: Approaches to curriculum in intelligent tutoring systems. In M. Jones & P. H. Winne (Eds.), *Adaptive Learning Environments: Foundations and Frontiers* (pp. 91-121). Berlin Heidelberg: Springer-Verlag.

McKeown, K. R., Klavans, J. L., Hatzivassiloglou, V., Barzilay, R., & Eskin, E. (1999). Towards multidocument summarization by reformulation: Progress and prospects. In *Proceedings of the 16th National Conference on Artificial Intelligence and 11th Innovative Applications of Artificial Intelligence Conference, Orlando, Florida* (pp. 453-460). Menlo Park, CA: American Association for Artificial Intelligence.

Rye, J. A., & Rubba, P. A. (2002). Scoring concept maps: An expert map-based scheme weighted for relationships. *School Science and Mathematics, 102*(1), 33-44.

Sumner, T., Ahmad, F., Bhushan, S., Gu, Q., Molina, F., Willard, S., et al. (2005). Linking learning goals and educational resources through interactive concept map visualizations. *International Journal on Digital Libraries, 5*(1), Special Issue on Information Visualization Interfaces for Retrieval and Analysis), 18-24.

Willms, S. (2003). Visualizing a user model for educational adaptive information retrieval. *User Modeling 2003, Proceedings, 2702*, 432-434.

Zhang, Z., Otterbacher, J., & Radev, D. (2003). Learning cross-document structural relationships using boosting. In *Proceedings of the 12th International Conference on Information and Knowledge Management, New Orleans, Louisiana* (pp. 124-130). New York, NY: ACM Press.

Learning Strategies/Learning with Multimedia

Aleven, V., & Koedinger, K. R. (2002). An effective metacognitive strategy: Learning by doing and explaining with a computer-based Cognitive Tutor. *Cognitive Science, 26*(2), 147-179.

Butcher, K. R., & Kintsch, W. (2003). Text comprehension and discourse processing. In A. F. Healy & R. W. Proctor (Eds.), *Experimental psychology* (Vol. 4, pp. 575-595). New York: Wiley.

Chi, M. T., Bassok, M., Lewis, M. W., Reimann, P., & et al. (1989). Self-explanations: How students study and use examples in learning to solve problems. *Cognitive Science, 13*(2), 145-182.

Chi, M. T. H. (2000). Self-explaining expository texts: The dual process of generating inferences and repairing mental models. In R. Glaser (Ed.), *Advances in Instructional Psychology* (pp. 161-238). Mahwah, NJ: Erlbaum.

Cox, R. (1999). Representation construction, externalised cognition and individual differences. *Learning and Instruction, 9*(4), 343-363.

Cuevas, H. M., Fiore, S. M., & Oser, R. L. (2002). Scaffolding cognitive and metacognitive processes in low verbal ability learners: Use of diagrams in computer-based training environments. *Instructional Science, 30*(6), 433-464.

Hall, R. H., Hall, M. A., & Saling, C. B. (1999). The effects of graphical postorganization strategies on learning from knowledge maps. *Journal of Experimental Education, 67*(2), 101-112.

Hall, R. H., & O'Donnell, A. M. (1996). Cognitive and affective outcomes of learning from knowledge maps. *Contemporary Educational Psychology, 21*(1), 94-101.

Hausmann, R. G., & Chi, M. T. (2002). Can a computer interface support self-explaining? *Cognitive Technology, 7*(1), 4-14.

Hegarty, M. (2004). Dynamic visualizations and learning: getting to the difficult questions. *Learning & Instruction, 14*(3), 343-351.

Kozma, R. (2003). The material features of multiple representations and their cognitive and social affordances for science understanding. *Learning and Instruction, 13*, 205-226.

Lowe, R. K. (1996). Background knowledge and the construction of a situtational representation from a diagram. *European Journal of Psychology of Education, XI*(4), 377-397.

Mannes, S. M., & Kintsch, W. (1987). Knowledge organization and text organization. *Cognition & Instruction, 4*(2), 91-115.

Marchionini, G. (1995). *Information seeking in electronic environments.* Cambridge: Cambridge University Press.

Mautone, P. D., & Mayer, R. E. (2001). Signaling as a cognitive guide in multimedia learning. *Journal of Educational Psychology, 93*(2), 377-389.

Reiser, B. J. (2004). Scaffolding Complex Learning: The Mechanisms of Structuring and Problematizing Student Work. *Journal of the Learning Sciences, 13*(3), 273-304.

Schnotz, W., & Bannert, M. (2003). Construction and interference in learning from multiple representation. *Learning & Instruction, 13*(2), 141-156.

Schnotz, W., Picard, E., & Hron, A. (1993). How do successful and unsuccessful learners use texts and graphics? *Learning and Instruction, 3*(3), 181-199.

Chapter XV
Designing Multimedia to Trace Goal Setting in Studying

Mingming Zhou
Simon Fraser University, Canada

Philip H. Winne
Simon Fraser University, Canada

ABSTRACT

We suggest that multimedia environments can benefit from learning as well as offer significant capacity to serve as research purposes. Because motivational processes can support or inhibit complex learning, we first review current hypermedia learning models by specifically focusing on how they integrate motivational elements into their frameworks. Following our observation of a gap in the way motivational constructs (e.g., achievement goal orientation) are operationally defined, we suggest alternative methods, called traces, which make these latent constructs visible and measurable. The goal-tracing methodology we describe draws on achievement goal theory and extensive empirical studies in various settings. Using it, we treat learners' use of cognitive tools as traces that express their goal orientations. By applying data mining techniques to these data, we show how it is possible to identify goal patterns together with study tactic patterns. We propose that future research can benefit substantially by merging trace methodologies with other methods for gathering data about motivation and learning.

INTRODUCTION

Technological advances have stimulated educational researchers and educators to expand designs for learning environments as well as conceptions of multimedia learning. Along with descriptions of the latest features of new learning systems have come newer theoretical accounts about how those features scaffold learning and teaching.

Validating learning theories in this context has proven challenging. Research in the last decade has demonstrated that multiple and contingent factors affect learning in highly complex knowledge systems; examples include the layout of multimedia information, learning dynamics, and multiple forms of cognitive processing (Astleitner & Wiesner, 2004). As well, additional attention has begun to be paid to motivation in software-supported multimedia learning. Motivation is one of the most important factors that affects learning in any educational environment (Maehr, 1984), accounting for approximately 20% of the variance in achievement and about 29% of the variance in transfer of knowledge (Colquitt, LePine, & Noe, 2000). We agree with Hidi and Harackiewicz (2000) that motivating learning, particularly the academically unmotivated student, represents a critical issue in establishing a viable platform for life-long learning that increasingly involves multimedia-based content.

In this wider view that includes motivational factors in modeling learning from multimedia, the main targets have been to: (a) investigate how motivation moderates achievement when learning multimedia content, (b) explain discordant empirical evidence about achievement by augmenting models that omitted motivational variables; and (c) improve designs for multimedia systems to improve learning. But merely observing a gain in achievement as a function of adding motivational scaffolds is insufficient for constructing a valid account about how knowledge is constructed through motivated goal seeking activities (Borsboom, Mellenbergh, & van Heerden, 2004; Winne, 2006a). Gaining knowledge of processes learners engage in *as* they study multimedia content is essential to advancing theory and informing designs for learning environments.

Measures of motivational factors that play a role in goal-directed learning have typically been narrowly operationalized as learners' responses to questions posed on paper and answered outside the envelope of time when learners actually study. Such data, as we discuss later, may not be sufficient to capture motivation fully, accurately, and its effects on learning "on the fly." We describe how

this gap affects research on the roles of motivation in multimedia learning, and we propose alternative ways to track motivational constructs, such as achievement goal orientation, *during* learners' engagement with content.

Our presentation has four parts. The next section overviews major multimedia learning theories from a motivational perspective. The second section discusses issues in empirical investigations of motivational factors during multimedia learning processes when motivational constructs are operationally defined in traditional forms, i.e., self-reports gathered outside the learning episode. The following section examines how motivation can be operationally defined as traces that are logged within a multimedia system as learners learn. We make a case for the value of using tracing methodology to investigate motivation during learning. The last section considers implications of trace methodology for motivational research.

BACKGROUND

New technologies are rapidly being introduced into schools and other learning settings, and multimedia is an increasingly common format for learning. This offers new possibilities to structure, represent, adapt and integrate various learning content and materials as multimedia learning environments implement the latest technological features. Rarely, however, have these implementations been grounded in research-based principles (Kozma, 1991; Moore, Burton, & Myers, 1996). Further, a great opportunity has gone unfulfilled because too little attention has been paid to significant and almost cost-free capabilities to log extensive, detailed data about learning processes without much intrusion into learners' activities (Winne, 2006a). However, before capitalizing on this opportunity, it is first necessary to know what data should be gathered to describe learning as a process. Guidance on this front comes from models and theories.

We lack space to provide a comprehensive review of relevant literature, but an overview will suffice for our purposes. The vast bulk of research on multimedia learning has focused on the consequences of interacting with multimedia content that is presented in various formats. Much of this work has been guided by Mayer's cognitive theory (Mayer, 2001). In Mayer's theory, working memory is partitioned into independent auditory and visual working capabilities that separately represent verbal and nonverbal information. Each working memory system has a limited capacity. Meaningful learning occurs when a learner selects relevant information in each store, organizes it to construct a coherent representation, and assembles connections between corresponding representations in each store. Mayer's theory has stimulated a considerable volume of empirical research but findings have sometimes been surprising. For example, individuals have better short-term recall of auditory than of visual information (Penney, 1989) but will read a document on screen while ignoring a narrated summary (Grimes, 1990). In the area of audio-video redundancy, Lang (1995) observed that half the studies demonstrated that redundant audio and video channels improve retention of information whereas half showed redundancy impedes retention.

A possible gap in using Mayer's (2001) theory as the only account of multimedia learning may arise because it does not consider various non-cognitive aspects of learning. For example, learners are known to set goals for learning (e.g, Urdan & Mestas, 2006; Weinstein, 2004; Winne & Marx, 1982). When they do, motivational factors may play an equally important, if not greater, role in knowledge construction processes because: (a) motivation significantly influences learning; (b) motivational processes require memory resources and thus can increase or decrease cognitive load; and, (c) there is typically strong associations among cognitive and motivational variables (Astleitner & Wiesner, 2004). On these grounds, we suggest it is desirable to develop a theoreti-

cal account of multimedia learning that couples relevant motivational concepts and theories with already productive cognitively-based models.

One often cited model of motivation in the context of multimedia learning is Keller's ARCS model (1997, 1999). The acronym ARCS refers to four motivational factors: attention, relevance, confidence, and satisfaction. Keller's model, based on an integration of motivational concepts and theories according to their shared and discriminative attributes, forecasts how instructional materials can be designed to promote learning (Astleitner & Koller, 2006; Keller & Suzuki, 1988). To boost the learner's attention, elevate perceptual arousal and inquiry, and introduce variability. To promote perceptions of relevance, take advantage of familiarity or particular goal orientations. To build confidence, learners can be afforded: expectancy for success, appreciation of challenge, and attributions to controllable features of learning that invite further engagement. To enhance satisfaction, provide natural and positive consequences as a basis for perceptions about incentives. A modest criticism of the ARCS model is that, outside the bounds of the category of attention, it does not give explicit consideration to multimedia elements, e.g., audio-visual components of instructional materials (Astleitner & Wiesner, 2004).

Theoretically, learners monitor and control learning activities throughout study (Butler & Winne, 1995; Zimmerman, 1994). When self-directed monitoring and control is challenged, scaffolds are recommended to help over the short run and provide grounds for improving self-regulation. Promoting self-regulated multimedia learning is challenging because learners must cope efficiently with a large number of demands, including selecting learning activities which match learning objectives, carrying out and monitoring learning activities, as well as searching for feedback on their progress and making adaptations to improve both learning and achievement (Winne, 2001). This requires not only task and content-related cognitive strategies but also metacognitive strategies, such as the selection and activation of appropriate strategies. Throughout this demanding work, motivation is necessary to sustain effective cognitive and metacognitive engagement. Therefore, a model paying heed to both cognitive and motivational parameters holds promise as a better reflection of the scope of variables that matter in multimedia learning.

Only a few models are dedicated to this task. Hede's (2002) model integrates motivational factors, inputs to learning processes, information processing based on attention and working memory, aptitude, long-term storage, reflection and learning multimedia content. A criticism of this model was that it lacked an innovative integration of concepts but merely added together variables arising from multiple theoretical backgrounds (Astleitner & Wiesner, 2004). Astleitner and Wiesner (2004) proposed a model that blends cognitive and motivational aspects of memory use and learning. Their model recognizes that learners must manage mental resources, such as focusing attention, integrating representations of information and metacognitively monitoring progress. Resources are managed as a function of motivational parameters whose values are set when learners set goals. When learners re-evaluate and modify goals, outcome expectations and incentives are reframed, and action control must be judiciously exercised to pursue goals in the face of competing demands. This account shares much with Winne and Marx's (1989) model of motivation as information processing. Astleitner and Wiesner present their model as an integrated and comprehensive model of multimedia learning and motivation. They believe it can stimulate multimedia research in a variety of areas, such as the motivational qualities of multimedia environments, personality characteristics, and aptitude-treatment-interaction research. Despite these improvements, a basic question remains: "What do we know about learners' motivation in multimedia learning environments?"

Answering this question presents several challenges. For example, which motivational constructs should be examined? How should these variables be operationally defined and measured? How can these data contribute to investigating the dynamic self-regulated learning process in multimedia learning? In this chapter, we focus on achievement goal orientation as an instance to demonstrate how multimedia environments can be utilized as research tools to address these critical issues.

ISSUES

Goal orientation theories, which evolved from research on achievement motivation, were developed primarily to account for learning and performance on academic tasks (Pintrich & Schunk, 1996). According to these theories, goals manifest as different ways of approaching, engaging, and responding in achievement-related activities (Ames, 1992; Dweck & Leggett, 1988). Research in this tradition is prevalent and quite consistently shows that achievement beliefs and goals predict widely different student outcomes (Weinstein, 2004).

Various researchers contrast apparently different types of achievement goals in studies examining goals per se and their relations to cognitive, affective and behavioral outcomes. Results are mixed. (For reviews, see Ames, 1992; Urdan, 1997.) One possible reason for inconsistencies in this literature is lack of clarity about the psychological nature of this construct. DeShon and Gillespie (2005) claim there is no common definition of goal orientation, so it is possible that researchers refer to very different processes by the same term. Smith, Duda, Allen and Hall (2002) conducted a study to determine whether different goal orientation measures assessed the same construct by attending to Marsh's (1994) warning about the "jingle" (scales with the same label assess similar constructs) and "jangle" (scales with different labels assess different constructs) fallacies that often befall questionnaires in this field. The results of two separate confirmatory factor analyses by Smith and colleagues highlighted that, although a degree of convergence emerged among subscales labeled as tapping the same constructs across the instruments (mono-trait, multi-method convergence), very few were statistically strong. The variance accounted for ranged from 1% to 36%. These researchers claimed this might be due to "differences in the operational definition proffered by the author of each measure, and the subsequent item content of the subscales" (p. 185).

One example of this issue is the debate concerning whether goal orientation is a trait-like or state-like disposition. According to the former school of thought, goal orientation is a personality variable that contributes to individual differences in behavior and is relatively invariant over time and across contexts (e.g., Bell & Kozlowski, 2002; Colquitt & Simmering, 1998). From the latter perspective, it is proposed that an individual develops different states of goal orientation in response to the particular and immediately present characteristics of the performance environment (e.g., Button, Mathieu, & Zajac, 1996; Elliot & Church, 1997; Mangos & Steele-Johnson, 2001; VandeWalle, Cron, & Slocum, 2001). These conceptual differences may partially account for some inconsistent empirical results regarding associations among goal orientation and achievement outcomes (e.g., Elliot & Thrash, 2005; Grant & Dweck, 2003). In turn, such discrepancies about what goal orientation is and how it should be measured weaken the foundation for fruitful scientific research involving goal orientation and its role as an antecedent, moderating, and outcome variable. In this light, a first task appears to be seeking a valid and more widely adopted definition of this construct with which learning models can be built and empirical studies can be conducted.

CHALLENGES OF CONVENTIONAL OPERATIONAL DEFINITIONS

A path toward addressing this problem has been presented under the heading of the method of "operational definition" (Blumer, 1940, p. 710; see also Borsboom, Mellenbergh, & van Heerden, 2002). Operational definitions bind the meaning of a concept to actions that generate occurrences or instantiations of that concept. This method, obviously, would confine the meaning of a concept to quantitative (at least nominal) and measurable data upon which subsequent theoretical and empirical work can be grounded. It has the benefit of generating precise content amenable to exacting empirical tests (Borsboom et al., 2002).

Initial attempts to operationalize goal orientation took the form of learners' responses to questionnaire items, probes in an interview, or content revealed in think aloud protocols (Kelley, 1992). Several significant factors threaten the reliability of such self-reported information. Most surveys or interviews ask people questions about what happened in a relatively non-specific prior context (e.g., "In this course, ..." or "During this semester, ..."). One potential drawback affecting responses generated by this operational definition is invalidity. The content of thoughts that learners report in self-report protocols on goal orientation describes what they perceive about themselves in the context of remembered task conditions. But, because memory is subject to loss (forgetting), distortion (biased sampling of memories), and reconstruction, variance in responses may reflect these factors more so than goal orientation (Winne, 2004). This is not to deny that a correlation is observed between sets of these responses and other variables. What is at risk is determining *what* is correlating with those other variables.

Asking students to respond to survey items also may produce a "now-that-you-mention-it effect whereby students agree they want to do better than others when asked about it, but if they were not asked about it, they would rarely think in such terms" (Urdan & Mestas, 2006, p. 355). Some research suggests that when students are not directly asked about mastery and performance goals, they tend to mention other concerns more often, such as avoiding trouble, avoiding work, and going to college (Lemos, 1996; Urdan, Kneisel, & Mason, 1999). Because surveys obviously must provide wording for items, when students attempt to fit their own perceptions to that wording, they may be led to report factors that otherwise would not be thought of and, therefore, would not affect the process of setting goals (Urdan & Mestas, 2006).

What are goals? Intuitively, goals are cognitive representations of what a student wants to achieve (Ford & Nichols, 1991) by applying strategies and tactics for learning (Pintrich & Garcia, 1991). It is important to acknowledge the interdependence of the cognitive and motivational aspects of learning (Ainley, 1993). Maehr and Pintrich (1991) characterized goal and strategy as the "how" and "why" of achievement behavior while emphasizing their "inherent unity" and complementary nature. In a similar vein, Ford and Nichols (1991) emphasized the essential interdependence of goals and self-regulatory processes in their analysis of motivational patterns in learning. They represented "behavior episodes" as nested hierarchies within which layers of increasingly context-specific goals can be identified. This interdependence between goals and cognitive events that construct learning poses serious challenges for modeling learning processes based on self-reports. Whereas these two variables are simultaneously operative during learning, self-reports of goal orientation typically ignore tactics and strategies, and cannot address how each may influence the other as learning unfolds.

Consider this example: A student set a goal to achieve a better mark on the next quiz and then began to study the chapter assigned this week. As he read deeper in the chapter, he found the topic quite interesting. This temporarily aroused his eagerness to explore. He suspended his usual memorization and note-taking tactics, methods that were chosen to meet the goal of raising quiz marks, and replaced these with more metacognitive activities, such as investigating Wikipedia and making annotations that linked his prior knowledge to what he was reading. After satisfying his curiosity, he returned to "normal" studying procedures which he believed were better for elevating his marks.

Shifts like these, we believe, are common. Self-regulated learners are generally characterized as active learners who adapt not only methods for learning but also goals for learning. They draw on a set of cognitive and metacognitive strategies and, when they judge it necessary, modify these in response to shifting task demands (Butler & Winne, 1995; Pintrich & Garcia, 1991; Zimmerman, 1989). This self-regulated learning (SRL) process is dynamic and cyclic such that goals drive strategies just as much as the outcomes of strategic engagement may lead to changing prior goals. As Wolters (1998) pointed out, learners regulate and monitor cognitive and motivational aspects during learning processes. This implies that both study tactics – cognitive tools of learning, and achievement goals – motivational reasons for learning are mutually interacting and jointly responsive to the unfolding learning situation.

No survey instruments we have examined capture perceptions about these features. Nor can such instruments reflect actual occurrences of those shifts *as* students study (Zimmerman, 1994) or *as* they engage in different tasks. For example, Hadwin and her colleagues' study (Hadwin, et al., 2001) demonstrated that responses to self-report items about study tactics, goal selection, and use of external resources vary when study context varies. If responses to survey instruments don't capture such variation in goals and simultaneously instruct learners to generalize across contexts in responding to items, it is no wonder that correlations between goal orientation and achievement are attenuated and sometimes inconsistent. From this perspective, traditional means of operationalizing goal orientation unequivocally represent students' interpretations about type(s) of goal(s) they believe they hold or may adopt in the near-term. But such data are inadequate indicators of the goals students orient to as they study and self-regulate studying in response to unfolding circumstances. We seek new technology-based methods that can compensate for these limitations of traditional methods in capturing motivational variation on the fly, and relating this variance to studying tactics that are the engines of knowledge construction. Tracking can collect valuable information such as onset and offset of events, duration, and decision-making expressed by key presses, mouse clicks, and menu choices (Harvey & Nelson, 1995; Winne et al., 2006). Data collected with such a system can be overwhelming and difficult to analyze (Schwier & Misanchuk, 1990) but the unobtrusiveness of this method enables researchers to track a learning events in a non-linear environment without disrupting the learner's thinking or navigation through content. More importantly, data obtained in real-time allow "virtual" re-creation of learners' actions.

Building on the concept of trace methodologies (Winne, 1982; Winne et al., 2006), we invented a goal-tracing method to minimize conceptual ambiguities and model on-the-fly processes in goal-setting and self-regulated learning. Specifically, we operationalized students' expressions of goal orientation on the fly by their (a) use of a tool for tagging content with categories that reflected goal orientations and (b) following hyperlinks named to instantiate types of goal orientations. We operationalized study tactics as students' choice between these tools. In the next section, we elaborate these methods.

SOLUTIONS

Stage I: Developing Tags and Traces of Goal Orientation

It is mundane to point out that learning is a partial function of the student's use of cognitive tools. In multimedia learning environments, tools may appear to promote deep understanding by helping students actively construct knowledge (Pea, 1985); or reflect on their problem solving processes, as in hypothesis generation (Lajoie, 2005). Other tools may seem to promote surface level learning, such as simply highlighting portions of content or clicking a button to seek correct answers to questions. However, no absolute standard differentiates surface-level from deep-level use of cognitive tools. Any cognitive tool can be used in a way. Whether use of a tool leads to surface or deep learning depends on the agent who defines its function (Winne, 1979). Thus, inferring a link between goals and behavior based solely on a researcher's classification of a tool's function is an incomplete solution. Learner's perceptions and interpretations of tools mediate when they use a tool and which tool they use.

In our research, we used gStudy (see Figure 1), an advanced multimedia learning system that offers nearly 30 tools students can use to operate on structured multimedia content represented in hypertext markup language (HTML) and packaged for study as learning kits (Winne et al., 2006 and Nesbit & Winne, 2007 provide fuller descriptions.). Because gStudy presents documents through a web browser, learning kits may contain any of the media commonly found on the web such as text, video, diagrams, and video clips. As learners study in a learning kit, they use gStudy tools to create information objects and links that connect those information objects. gStudy's tools include: making notes based on a choice of schemas (e.g., question and answer, summary, etc.), tagging selected content to classify

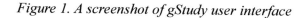

Figure 1. A screenshot of gStudy user interface

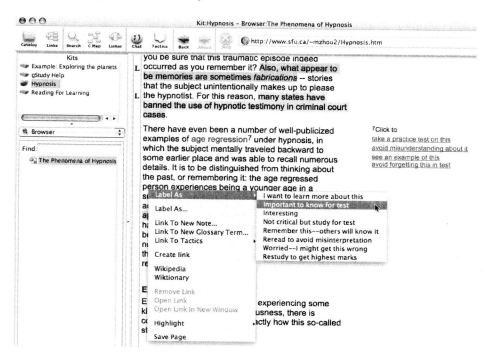

it (e.g., important, review this, don't understand, etc.), hyperlinks that expose new information according to the content developer's model of the domain, constructing new glossary entries, drawing and manipulating concept maps to assemble information within and across elements of the content (e.g., selections in a text; among notes, glossary items, etc.), a powerful multi-faceted search tool, and a chatting tool, to name a few. In short, students have access to a wide variety of cognitive tools that afford them options for exercising and expressing tactics for constructing knowledge and self-regulating learning.

In the work reported here, our theory of types of goals was exposed to students by tags they could use to catalog content. When students choose content and tag it, they manifest goals they hold. For example, tagging a selection with "I want to know about this" identifies a mastery goal whereas tagging it with "Review this to earn higher marks" expresses to a performance goal. Two students who select the same content can express different

goals by tagging it differently. As well, a student can apply multiple tags to one selection. This is trace evidence that the student simultaneously held multiple goals regarding that content. The key to this method is to justify labels for the tags so they (a) represent researchers' theory of goals as accurately as possible and (b) communicate this message clearly to the student.

The tags we offered to students were justified by two means. First, goal theory provides a basis for composing these terms and phrases. We grounded our work within the currently prevalent 2 x 2 goal framework of goal type and approach/avoidance model developed by Elliot and McGregor (2001). According to their model, mastery-approach students tend to focus on learning and their command of the content or task. This orientation is theoretically related to a series of adaptive outcomes, such as higher levels of efficacy, interest, and persistence; using more cognitive and metacognitive strategies; and better performance (Pintrich, 2000). The instrumental nature of a performance-approach goal parallels mastery-approach goals in a common need for achievement but diverges from mastery-approach orientation in emphasizing extrinsic achievement outcomes (Elliot, 1997). Performance-avoidance goals, on the other hand, are posited to link to anxiety and task distraction that produce a helpless pattern of engagement (Elliot & Church, 1997) and evoke a host of negative processes, such as distraction, anxiety, and self-protective divestment. These undermine performance in most achievement settings (Elliott, Shell, & Henry, 2005) owing to a focus on avoiding negative or undesirable events (Linnenbrink & Pintrich, 2000). Mastery-avoidance goals are most likely to be pursued when individuals discover, or become concerned, that their skills or abilities are in a state of deterioration (Elliot, 1999). Therefore, these indifferent individuals may experience neither the benefits nor the costs associated with the other achievement goals (Elliot & McGregor, 2001).

Second, to validate that our interpretation of tags was shared by students, we conducted a pilot study. University students (N=21) responded to the 12-item Achievement Goal Questionnaire (Elliot & McGregor, 2001) with minor revisions to accommodate our context. Afterwards, they read a 300-word article at their own pace and were instructed to choose 5 of 16 labels (tags) to annotate the article. We designed these tags to represent the four types of goal orientations in Elliot and McGregor's framework. Their choices were analyzed to investigate the correspondence between responses to the questionnaire and traces of their goal-directed learning behavior expressed in their choices of tags.

Results demonstrated nearly zero support for the correspondence between self-reported goals and actual studying behavior reflected by tags chosen. This parallels studies in the achievement domain where students were positively biased (overestimated) their use of study tactics (Jamieson-Noel & Winne, 2003; Winne & Jamieson-Noel, 2002). In those studies, a plausible reason

for this finding is that students report strategy use because they know or believe some strategies are effective, not because they actually use those strategies to any great extent (Samuelstuen & Bråten, 2007). Another possible reason is that students might have difficulties interpreting the meaning of the items in self-reports and matching their behavior to the descriptions, under the assumption that current learning theories hold true. Our pilot data do not afford grounded speculations about poor calibration between self-reported goal orientation and traces of goal orientation operationalized as tags they chose to describe studying. However, that students chose tags indicates they held goal orientations. After consulting colleagues with extensive knowledge of goal orientations, we reconstructed tags for labels and finalized the hyperlink names to be presented to participants in the main study.

We also hypothesize that choices between cognitive tools in gStudy, aside from the meanings their names convey, may reflect goals. For example, compared to labeling, hyperlink clicking is an effort-minimizing behavior. A student need do nothing more than click to express goal orientation versus a 3-step labeling procedure (select content, right- or control-click the selection, and choose tag from a contextual popup menu). While this difference in effort required to use a tool may appear small, it nonetheless may further distinguish a mastery goal student from a performance goal student. Hence, two sets of behavioral measures can be combined to trace goal setting operationally: choices of tags and choices between labels and hyperlinks.

Stage II: Analyzing Trace Data to Link Motivated Actions to Goals Orientations

Many researchers adopt qualitative methods to analyze log data (e.g., MacGregor, 1999; Schroeder & Grabowski, 1995). Others generate frequency counts of actions that learners perform (e.g.,

Lawless & Kulikowich, 1996; Barab, Bowdish, Young, & Owen, 1996; Nesbit, et al, 2007). These approaches to analysis fail to capture either patterns of individual's study tactics or navigation in hypermedia environments (Barab, Fajen, Kulikowich, & Young, 1996). We aim to identify which goals students establish and how they pursue goals as reflected by choices they make for using cognitive tools as they engage in goal-directed achievement-oriented activities. To do this, it is necessary to go beyond counting actions and correlating those counts with other variables. Several special analytical tools have been developed to meet these needs, such as PathFinder (Schvaneveldt, 1990) and Webminer (Cooley, Mobasher, & Srivastava, 1997). We describe shortly a new method based on data mining to identify patterns of studying activities that can be interpreted to reflect motivation.

Regardless of analytic approach, studies of motivation's role in learning within multimedia environments are rare. One exception is Barab, Bowdish, Young, and Owen's (1996) study. Traces they collected about students' viewing time were interpreted as showing students in a problem-based condition were more goal directed because they required less time per screen to determine whether the information was relevant to the prob-

lem posed. We seek to go further by identifying what learners' intentions are for choices they make among cognitive tools for learning.

Trace data logged in gStudy are elaborate in the sense that they record the context in which study actions occur as well as each action taken at its time point over the course of study, logged to the millisecond and written to an XML file. In effect, the log file allows researchers to reconstruct what students do as they study. We aggregate these very fine-grained data by defining sets of sequential traces that make up a studying "action." For example, consider creating a template-guided note (e.g., a critique note in which several labeled fields are instantiated). As a learner uses this tool, gStudy records: which content was selected to which the note is linked, when the selection was made, how the learner directed gStudy to open a note window (e.g., a choice from the menu bar or a selection from a contextual popup menu), which note template (type of note) the learner chose among options available (critique, in this example), which fields of the note the learner filled in, what information was entered in each field, and when the learner closed the note window. Together, these trace data constitute the action of making a critique note. Figure 2 shows a fragment of gStudy log file.

Figure 2. A snapshot of gStudy log files

action="created" target="link" timeStamp="2007-01-12T14:44:44.793-08:00" user="sub004">
xt kitID="14258195208learningkitsfuca56d8951910ff151b41e7fad" kitName="Hypnosis"
81101G5localece3610a29a0541a7fc6">
hor="sub004" dateCreated="2007-01-12T14:44:44.776-08:00" dateModified="2007-01-12T14:44:44.776-08:00"
7145bbywiredgen1907authentsfuca4fb5185f1101879546f7fd3" modifiedBy="sub004" templateRef="">
: QTmedia="false" endpointX="471" endpointY="598" image="false" rangeEnd="1776" rangeStart="1643" selection="It w
ought that the releas...s possibility now seems less likely" startpointX="458" startpointY="548" useRange="true"
:"http://www.sfu.ca/~mzhou2/Hypnosis.htm" moClass="htmlDoc"
kitID="14258195208learningkitsfuca56d8951910ff151b41e7fad"/>

10>
intry author="brianshi@nowhere.com" dateCreated="2006-03-23T16:47:36.664-08:00"
ified="2007-01-12T14:44:44.776-08:00" id="1921681101G5localece3610a29a0541a7fc6" modifiedBy="sub004"
iteresting" templateRef="">
nks>
link author="sub004" dateCreated="2007-01-12T14:43:42.522-08:00" dateModified="2007-01-12T14:43:42.523-08:00"
1425867145bbywiredgen1907authentsfuca4fb5185f1101879546f7fd5" modifiedBy="sub004" templateRef="">
n:destination>
  <ln:doc QTmedia="false" endpointX="172" endpointY="335" image="false" rangeEnd="823" rangeStart="762" selection=
general no one method is necessarily better than any other" startpointX="223" startpointY="311" useRange="true"
target="http://www.sfu.ca/~mzhou2/Hypnosis.htm" moClass="htmlDoc"
targetKitID="14258195208learningkitsfuca56d8951910ff151b41e7fad"/>
ln:destination>

To investigate learners' sequences of actions, i.e., traces of studying strategies that reflect inherent individual differences or treatment-induced group differences, we developed Log Validator (Xu, Nesbit, Zhou, & Winne, 2007). Log Validator uses data mining algorithms to identify sequences of actions. In principle, this is a matter of discovering sequences of actions that are common to a group of learners. (See Winne, Gupta, & Nesbit, 1994. for another method based on graph theory).

Mathematically, a *sequence* is an ordered set. In our case, members of the set are various study actions and the ordering rule is time. A *subsequence* is extracted from the full sequence or timeline of actions by leaving out some actions while preserving the relative positions of remaining actions that are focal. To constrain the potential for combinatorial explosion, a subsequence is deemed a *pattern* only if it occurs more often than a threshold specified in terms of a proportion of the subsequences (Agrawal & Srikant, 1995). A pattern represents one particular sequence of learning actions that describe students in a group (e.g., an experimental group or a classroom). The algorithm is illustrated in Figure 3 where letters

Figure 3. A sequential pattern exemplification

Given two sequences X and Y
X = < A, C, B, D, E, G, C, E, D, B, G >
Y = < B, E, G, C, F, E, F, B, A >,
the longest common subsequence of X and Y is
< B, E, G, C, E, B>.

A to G represent study actions and X and Y stand for two sequences for two learners, respectively. To find the best indicator of the common pattern embedded in multiple sequences, we adopt the *longest common subsequence* criterion (see http://en.wikipedia.org/wiki/Longest_common_subsequence_problem).

Analyzing log data with Log Validator unfolds in two steps: parsing and mining. To prepare for parsing a log file, we create an action library that specifies how each multi-event action is defined in terms of fine-grained traces recorded in the log. For example, the action of making a note within a concept map in gStudy contains such events included in the action library as: opening a concept map, selecting "making a new note"

Figure 4. A screenshot of Action Library user interface

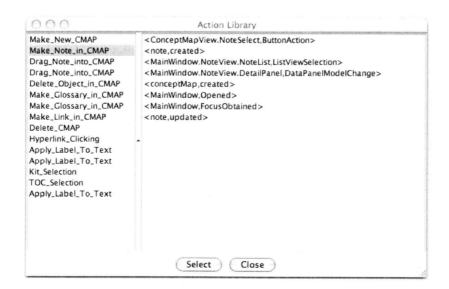

from the map menu, posting of a new note pop-up window, selecting a particular template (type of note), inputting information in the fields to instantiate the note, and closing the note window (see Figure 4). Some actions can be constituted in terms of varying events, e.g., a window can be opened using any one of several different methods in gStudy's interface.

Once actions are listed in an action library, we use Log Validator to parse (identify) actions in each student's detailed log file (or a set of files, e.g., if the student studied over multiple sessions). The output of this parsing analysis is a time-sequenced list of actions that represents the students' studying (see Figure 5). Basic statistics describing the actions are available in this step such as: the description of each action, frequency counts of occurrences of an action, and the times spent on completing each action (see Figure 6). We can modulate this analysis by specifying several parameters such as the time span for a set of actions that make up a learning strategy, the content selected and so on.

An important feature of the action library is flexible control of grain size, i.e., the level of detail at which researchers decide *a priori* to address research questions in learning science. The issue of granularity arises not because of the operational definitions of the examined constructs, but because researchers intend to model how an individual learns (Winne, 2006b). In the action library, researchers can aggregate finer-grained learning events into bigger chunks. They can also divide coarser-grained events into smaller units to increase granularity. We believe this flexibility for exploring grain size is critical to new investigations of learning in multimedia environments.

Once action sequences have been identified, we apply a data mining technique to locate patterns in the sequence of parsed actions. Our algorithm uses a bottom-up parsing strategy known as shift-reduce parsing (see http://en.wikipedia.org/wiki/Shift-reduce_parsing#Shift-reduce_parsers). Basically, this method first attempts to identify the shortest tactics, where a tactic is defined as two or more sequential actions. Then, it infers higher-order structures (strategies) from lower ones (tactics). In real data files, noise and extraneous events would normally halt the shift-reduce

Figure 5. A snapshot of the parsing output — action list

	Action List	Parse Result	Statistics	Patterns	

Action Name	Template	Start Time	Duration(s)
Log_Start		2007.01.16*T*09.40.53.653	0.0
mastery-approach label	Doc_Panel.Interesting	2007.01.16*T*09.43.59.019	16.903
Hyperlink	http://www.sfu.ca/%7Emzhou2/Link1-map....	2007.01.16*T*09.44.25.551	48.376
mastery-avoidance label	Doc_Panel.Worried--I might get this wrong	2007.01.16*T*09.46.32.033	12.583
Hyperlink	http://www.sfu.ca/%7Emzhou2/Link1-pap-...	2007.01.16*T*09.47.22.539	11.564
Hyperlink	http://www.sfu.ca/%7Emzhou2/Link1-pap....	2007.01.16*T*09.46.46.855	58.918
performance-approach label	Doc_Panel.Important to know for test	2007.01.16*T*09.48.37.495	11.06
Hyperlink	http://www.sfu.ca/%7Emzhou2/Link2-mav....	2007.01.16*T*09.49.03.926	14.592
mastery-approach label	Doc_Panel.Interesting	2007.01.16*T*09.50.24.257	9.282
mastery-avoidance label	Doc_Panel.Reread to avoid misinterpretation	2007.01.16*T*09.51.21.778	11.995
Hyperlink	http://www.sfu.ca/%7Emzhou2/Link5-pap-...	2007.01.16*T*09.53.01.867	26.387
Hyperlink	http://www.sfu.ca/%7Emzhou2/Link5-pap-...	2007.01.16*T*09.53.00.395	35.114
Hyperlink	http://www.sfu.ca/%7Emzhou2/Link5-pap....	2007.01.16*T*09.52.53.602	55.315
Hyperlink	http://www.sfu.ca/%7Emzhou2/Link5-pap....	2007.01.16*T*09.52.25.281	0.0
performance-approach label	Doc_Panel.Important to know for test	2007.01.16*T*09.56.13.150	6.959
mastery-approach label	Doc_Panel.I want to learn more about this	2007.01.16*T*09.57.50.747	7.605
Hyperlink	http://www.sfu.ca/%7Emzhou2/Link7-pap-...	2007.01.16*T*09.58.27.867	10.702
Hyperlink	http://www.sfu.ca/%7Emzhou2/Link7-pap....	2007.01.16*T*09.58.05.425	40.304
mastery-approach label	Doc_Panel.I want to learn more about this	2007.01.16*T*09.59.41.156	11.169
Hyperlink	http://www.sfu.ca/%7Emzhou2/Link8-map....	2007.01.16*T*10.00.01.851	43.424
mastery-avoidance label	Doc_Panel.Worried--I might get this wrong	2007.01.16*T*10.03.12.404	10.121
Hyperlink	http://www.sfu.ca/%7Emzhou2/Link10-pav...	2007.01.16*T*10.04.08.439	32.331
Hyperlink	http://www.sfu.ca/%7Emzhou2/Link9-pap-...	2007.01.16*T*10.06.33.232	11.389
Hyperlink	http://www.sfu.ca/%7Emzhou2/Link9-pap....	2007.01.16*T*10.06.14.094	39.931
Log_End		2007.01.16*T*10.07.58.073	0.0

Figure 6. A snapshot of the parsing output — action statistics

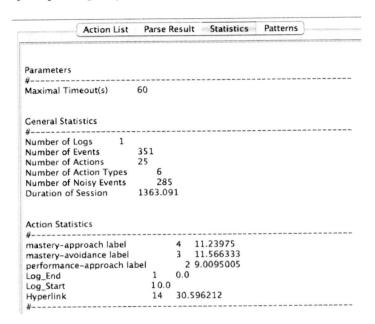

parsing process because traditional compilers fail if an error is detected in the input (e.g., an intruding action). To address this challenge, we designed an adapted shift-reduce parser that allows parsing to continue in the presence of noise. It works by keeping track of all possible sequences that might involve a certain action. An example of the output is presented in Figure 7.

Here is an example of the process. Consider a list of time-sequenced actions traced about student X within one studying session:

1. Open a learning kit to access new material.
2. Scroll to continue reading.
3. Label the first heading with "Important!"
4. Scroll to continue reading.
5. Make a note about the conclusion of one argument.
6. Switch between the main window presenting the material and the note window while editing the note.
7. Label the note he just made as "Review for midterm."
8. Scroll to continue reading to the end.

The events such as kit opening, scrolling, and switching windows are extraneous for some research questions (but not all). If this is the case, we "tell" the parser to leave out these "noisy events" and focus on parsing the "signal" actions, say, "labeling, note-making, and labeling." After the sequences of all the students in student X's group are identified, the *pattern-miner* within Log Validator detects the longest common subsequence in this group.

In a large data set, it is usual for sequence modeling to return several hundred common patterns. Most have no relevance to the researchers' goals. Therefore, in the next step, the researcher searches and filters patterns to identify relevant ones (Nesbit, Zhou, Xu, & Winne, 2007). In this phase, the software searches for the patterns and counts the frequency of patterns for each learner (or other unit of observation). These patterns of sequenced actions are then aggregated to infer higher-order structures, such as a surface learning approach versus a deep learning approach; or, performance-

Figure 7. The adapted shift-reduce parser output screenshot

	Action List	Parse Result	Statistics	**Patterns**		
Minimum Frequency: 0			Minimum Length: 3		Action Contained:	

ID	Pattern	Length	Frequency
24	performance-avoidance label->mastery-approach label->performance-avoidance label->performance-approach label->...	7	6
25	performance-avoidance label->mastery-approach label->performance-approach label	3	7
26	performance-avoidance label->mastery-approach label->performance-approach label->performance-approach label	4	7
27	performance-avoidance label->mastery-approach label->performance-approach label->performance-approach label->p...	5	6
28	performance-avoidance label->mastery-approach label->performance-approach label->performance-approach label->p...	6	6
29	performance-avoidance label->mastery-approach label->mastery-approach label	3	6
30	performance-avoidance label->mastery-approach label->mastery-approach label->mastery-approach label	4	6
31	performance-avoidance label->mastery-approach label->Hyperlink	3	6
32	performance-avoidance label->mastery-approach label->Hyperlink->Hyperlink	4	6
34	performance-avoidance label->Hyperlink->mastery-approach label	3	6
35	performance-avoidance label->Hyperlink->Hyperlink	3	7
36	performance-avoidance label->Hyperlink->Hyperlink->mastery-approach label	4	6
37	performance-avoidance label->Hyperlink->Hyperlink->Hyperlink	4	7
38	performance-avoidance label->Hyperlink->Hyperlink->Hyperlink->Hyperlink	5	7
39	performance-avoidance label->Hyperlink->Hyperlink->Hyperlink->Hyperlink->Hyperlink	6	6
40	performance-avoidance label->Hyperlink->Hyperlink->Hyperlink->Hyperlink->Hyperlink->Hyperlink	7	6
43	performance-approach label->performance-avoidance label->performance-avoidance label	3	6
44	performance-approach label->performance-avoidance label->performance-avoidance label->performance-approach label	4	6
45	performance-approach label->performance-avoidance label->performance-avoidance label->performance-approach lab...	5	6
46	performance-approach label->performance-avoidance label->performance-avoidance label->performance-approach lab...	6	6
47	performance-approach label->performance-avoidance label->performance-avoidance label->performance-approach lab...	7	6
48	performance-approach label->performance-avoidance label->performance-approach label	3	7
49	performance-approach label->performance-avoidance label->performance-approach label->performance-approach label	4	7
50	performance-approach label->performance-avoidance label->performance-approach label->performance-approach labe...	5	6
51	performance-approach label->performance-avoidance label->performance-approach label->performance-approach labe...	6	6
52	performance-approach label->performance-avoidance label->performance-approach label->performance-approach labe...	5	6
53	performance-approach label->performance-avoidance label->performance-approach label->mastery-approach label	4	6
54	performance-approach label->performance-avoidance label->performance-approach label->mastery-approach label->p...	5	6
55	performance-approach label->performance-avoidance label->performance-approach label->Hyperlink	4	6
56	performance-approach label->performance-avoidance label->mastery-approach label	3	7
57	performance-approach label->performance-avoidance label->mastery-approach label->performance-avoidance label	4	6

oriented learning tactics versus mastery-oriented learning tactics. This method allows building up even larger "learning strategies" of how students' behavior expresses motivation. The data from this phase can be exported to conventional statistical software for further analysis.

Laboratory Research Report

Rather than stipulating which particular goal a student holds *a priori*, we explored goal types using traces of students' actions logged while they studied in our multimedia learning environment. The process of analyzing these traces has two phases analogous to the exploratory and confirmatory phases in factor analysis. In the exploratory phase the methodology uses one data set to discover action patterns that correspond to sequences where students adopt goals. After patterns are found in the exploratory phase, the analysis proceeds to a confirmatory phase of pattern-matching. In the confirmatory phase, the objective is to show that the discovered action patterns are evident in other data sets generated in similar studying contexts,

such as other studying sessions involving the same students or a new sample of students. We adopted a split sample cross-validation technique. Once patterns have been identified they can be counted and statistically analyzed like other data.

Our ongoing research in the first stage has yielded surprising findings relative to the current literature on goal orientations. Here, we note the most important of these. First, students hold multiple goal orientations simultaneously. This stands in sharp contrast to the common practice of classifying a student as holding only one dominant goal orientation identified by the subscale on a self-report inventory with the highest mean item score. Second, we have observed near zero correspondence (calibration) between self-reported responses about goal orientations on paper-and-pencil surveys and traces of goals logged while students studied. While this might seem to undermine the use of self-report inventories, we interpret this discrepancy to imply that students are guided by different perceptions in different situations. Perceptions about goals when they generate self-report data do not correspond to perceptions of goals on the fly that are reflected by trace data. What these differences imply for theorizing about students' motivations merits further investigation.

In an empirical study we conducted (Zhou & Winne, 2008), 103 undergraduates (mean age, 23.1 years; 73.8% female) used gStudy to study content about hypnosis by reading, assigning tags to selected text, or clicking hyperlinks leading to brief passages providing further information. The tags and hyperlinks were created in the way we described earlier to represent the four types of goal orientations. A posttest was administered at the end of studying.

Trace data of learning activities were overall moderately positively associated with test performance whereas self-report data about goal orientation collected prior to the task had no statistically detectable relationships with achievement scores. When considering only students' on-the-fly use of labels and hyperlinks, results indicated that a pattern of LLL...LLHH...H ("L" represents a labeling action and "H" represents a hyperlink clicking action) occurred much more frequently than a pattern of HH...HLLL...L. Undergraduates in our sample were more likely to label content before navigating to additional content by clicking the hyperlinks.

Various interpretations might fit these action patterns. We speculate about one that illustrates the potential value of pattern-based analyses of trace data. Recall our conjecture about effort required to label (higher effort) versus click a hyperlink (lower effort). First, our data indicate that students changed effort expenditure – more shifted from high to low effort than the opposite. Relative to clicking a hyperlink, which traces an intention to view additional information, labeling could be considered a relatively demanding activity (but not very demanding in an absolute sense) in that the learner must metacognitively monitor content to identify parts of it that correspond to one of the supplied labels and deem it worth the effort to label it. Clicking a hyperlink,

on the other hand, requires minimal decision making at the time of the click but perhaps quite different cognitive effort to comprehend the content that is presented at the destination of the link. Students in our study more often shifted from (a) metacognitively-triggered labeling to (b) viewing additional information explicitly labeled for them by the words in the hyperlink than vice versa. A picture that can be sketched is that participants in our study were more willing to shift effort to using a tool that didn't require them to metacognitively monitor the content they were studying at the time they selected a tool – clicking a hyperlink that was explicitly labeled for them what kind of information they would find at the link's destination. Speculatively, this shift in patterns of studying actions suggests more students became more performance oriented as they worked through the passage we asked them to study. They preferred not to engage in deeper metacognitive processing of the content on their own but choose to rely on the content to do this metacognitive monitoring for them presented in the form of explicit descriptions about information that would be found at the destination of the hyperlink.

Approaching inferences like this is not new to the research on learning in hypermedia environments. Other researchers have identified various navigation profiles and, although labels vary, the existence of distinct navigation patterns is supported (e.g., Anderson-Inman, Horney, Chen, & Lewin, 1994; Barab, Bowdish, & Lawless, 1997; Hill & Hannafin, 1997). Some researchers use motivational constructs when interpreting such patterns, such as need for cognition or self-efficacy (e.g., MacGregor, 1999). We suggest that pattern-based analyses of traces can add to these efforts.

Pattern-based analyses of trace data also can broaden views about motivational processes that relate to learning. To explore this, we clustered participants on the basis of posttest achievement scores into high- versus low-achieving groups.

Consistent with previous theoretical descriptions, high achievers were more actively engaged in the reading task – they engaged in more actions in working with content. Our analysis of action patterns revealed several other differences between students with high versus low achievement on the posttest. High achievers typically evidenced longer patterns (less variation) of actions than low achievers. They also tended to oscillate more frequently between patterns representing mastery-approach and performance-approach goals, as determined by the semantics of hyperlinks they clicked and the labels they applied while studying. In contrast, low achievers maintained a single shorter pattern throughout the study period. That pattern represented either performance-approach goals or mastery-approach goals alone. If low achievers did mix mastery-approach and performance-approach goals, there was just one shift from one orientation to another.

Our results also conflict with current theories in terms of the stability or ubiquity of goal orientation. Specifically, a stable pattern of studying behaviors that expresses mastery-approach goals does not ensure higher achievement. This echoes Senko and Miles' (in press) recent observation that mastery goal learners are more likely to dwell on tangential versus central information to suit his/her own interest. This personal preference does not necessarily accord to teachers' or test designers' agendas, which might not lead to better test performance. Instead, a studying pattern marked by shifting between mastery-approach and performance-approach goals yielded more positive achievement. Also, differences in the length of goal patterns across high versus low achievers these groups study differently. High achievers might be more engaged in building larger structures of information, as reflected by the longer patterns, whereas low achievers develop more but less integrated structures of information.

CONCLUSION

Green (1992) criticized methodologies used in studying learning. "What is required is a more sophisticated approach to conceptual analysis in general. Phenomena such as learning, memory, reasoning, perception and emotion can be neither adequately defined in terms of, nor reduced to, a small set of measurement operations" (p. 315). Recent advances in technology have broadened opportunities for measuring processes involved in learning and data mining algorithms have provided us the power to interpret these process data. Goal-tracing methodology of the sort we outlined here is one of them. It helps gain insights into students' implicit goals. As well, trace methodology can allay concerns about the reliability and validity of data about the dynamics of learning on the fly that researchers gather point samples in concurrent think-aloud protocols, free descriptions, or self-report questionnaires (Winne, 2006a; Winne, Jamieson-Noel, & Muis, 2002). Thus, analyses of traces in log files and the patterns they represent has potential to elaborate the picture of learning processes by better describing what is "going on" during learning.

Winne (2006a) called for software tools to genuinely support students as well as researchers in their respective tasks of researching how to make learning effective. Multimedia learning tools like gStudy offer promise to meet this call when coupled with the sort of analysis of traces we illustrated. Our goal-tracing method provides a bridge to join students' perceptions about goals with traces that reveal how they seek goals. Such data also afford descriptions of patterns of actions that implement motivational features of learning. Identifying how motivation is enacted on the fly has heretofore been elusive. The union of self-report data with trace data creates new opportunities to sharpen theories about learning and motivation in multimedia learning environments.

FUTURE RESEARCH DIRECTIONS

The potential for computer-based tools to boost learning remains high, although the current contribution of technology to research innovation is exasperatingly difficult to demonstrate. Although we are beginning to understand how learners go about learning and how their motivation fluctuates over the course of studying sessions, sufficient attention has not been paid to strengths and weaknesses of different operational definitions for psychological constructs. Self-report is essential because these are the kind of data learners have "in mind" when they engage in self-regulated learning. However, to provide a fuller account of how learning and motivational processes entwine and vary over the course of learning, we need to augment those data gathering methods with techniques that are sensitive to dynamic manifestations of psychological engagement in the course of engaging complex learning activities. Tracing methodology takes promising steps toward this goal of capturing such dynamic learning process and advancing educational research.

An obvious next step in developing this methodology involves mapping a variety of motivational factors onto patterns of actions over the course of learning. If a correspondence emerges between motivation patterns and patterns of actions, then predictions may be made about motivation based on actions collected on-the-fly. This brings theorizing closer to the phenomena at hand. Due to inevitable conceptual ambiguities in some motivational constructs (such as goal orientation), the mapping between motivation patterns and patterns of actions should have an empirical as well as a rational or logical basis. Future work should collect more empirical data to validate this methodology, as we attempted to do.

Traces of goals are not confined to the methods we reported here. Other behavioral indicators of achievement goals should be developed. One illustration of this call is the well-regarded trace of intrinsic motivation represented by persistence with an unsatisfying experimental activity when enticing external contingencies are withdrawn (for a review, see Cameron & Pierce, 1994.) We urge researchers to continue to explore for other behavioral records or traces and test the justification of each to bridge the gap between theory and empirical observation. In order to track learners' conceptual and motivational development as accurately as possible, the trace data need to be triangulated with other sources of data. We believe this kind of "thick description" can provide multiple levels of integrated information about learners' attitudes, beliefs, and interactions with the content.

ACKNOWLEDGMENT

Support for this research was provided by grants to Philip H. Winne from the Social Sciences and Humanities Research Council of Canada (410-2002-1787 and 512-2003-1012), the Canada Research Chair Program and Simon Fraser University.

REFERENCES

Agrawal, R., & Srikant, R. (1995). Mining sequential patterns. In P. S. Yu & A. L. P. Chen (Eds.), *Proceedings of the 11th International Conference on Data Engineering* (pp. 3-14). Taipei, Taiwan: IEEE Computer Society.

Ainley, M. D. (1993). Styles of engagement with learning: Multidimensional assessment of their relationship with strategy use and school achievement. *Journal of Educational Psychology, 85,* 395-405.

Ames, C. (1992). Classrooms: Goals, structures, and student motivation. *Journal of Educational Psychology, 84,* 261-271.

Anderson-Inman, L., Horney, M., Chen, D-T, & Lewin, L. (1994). Hypertext literacy: Observations from the ElectroText project. *Language Arts, 71,* 279-287.

Astleitner, H., & Koller, M. (2006). An aptitude-treatment-interaction-approach on motivation and student's self-regulated multimedia-based learning. *Interactive Educational Multimedia, 13,* 11-23.

Astleitner, H., & Wiesner, C. (2004). An integrated model of multimedia learning and motivation. *Journal of Educational Multimedia and Hypermedia, 13,* 3-21.

Barab, S. A., Bowdish, B. E., & Lawless, K. A. (1997). Hypermedia navigation: Profiles of hypermedia users. *Educational Technology Research and Development, 45,* 23–41.

Barab, S. A., Bowdish, M. F., Young, M., & Owen, S. V. (1996). Understanding kiosk navigation: Using log files to capture hypermedia searches. *Instructional Science, 24,* 377-395.

Barab, S. A., Fajen, B. R., Kulikowich, J. M., & Young, M. (1996). Assessing hypermedia navigation through pathfinder: Prospects and limitations. *Journal of Educational Computing Research, 15,* 185-205.

Bell, B. S., & Kozlowski, W. J. (2002). Goal orientation and ability: Interactive effects on self-efficacy, performance, and knowledge. *Journal of Applied Psychology, 87,* 497-505.

Blumer, H. (1940). The problem of the concept in social psychology. *American Journal of Sociology, 45,* 707-719.

Borsboom, D., Mellenbergh, G. J., & van Heerden, J. (2002). Different kinds of DIF: A distinction between absolute and relative forms of measurement invariance and bias. *Applied Psychological Measurement, 26,* 433-450.

Borsboom, D., Mellenbergh, G. J., & van Heerden, J. (2004). The concept of validity. *Psychological Review, 111,* 1061–1071.

Butler, D., & Winne, P. (1995). Feedback and self-regulated learning: A theoretical synthesis. *Review of Educational Research, 65,* 245–281.

Button, S. B., Mathieu, J. E. & Zajac, D. M. (1996). Goal orientation in organizational research: A conceptual and empirical foundation. *Organizational Behaviour & Human Decision Processes, 67,* 26-48.

Cameron, J., & Pierce, W. D. (1994). Reinforcement, reward, and intrinsic motivation: A meta-analysis. *Review of Educational Research, 64,* 363-423.

Colquitt, J. A., & Simmering, M. J. (1998). Conscientiousness, goal orientation, and motivation to learn during the learning process: A longitudinal study. *Journal of Applied Psychology, 83,* 654-665.

Colquitt, J. A., LePine, J. A., & Noe, R. A. (2000). Toward an integrative theory of training motivation: A meta-analytic path analysis of 20 years of research. *Journal of Applied Psychology, 85,* 678-707.

Cooley, R., Mobasher, B., & Srivastava, J. (1997). Web mining: Information and pattern discovery on the World Wide Web. In *Proceedings of the 9th IEEE International Conference on Tools with Artificial Intelligence* (pp. 0558). Newport Beach, CA.

DeShon, R. P., & Gillespie, J. Z. (2005). A motivated action theory account of goal orientation. *Journal of Applied Psychology, 90,* 1096-1127.

Dweck, C., & Leggett, E. (1988). A social-cognitive approach to motivation and personality. *Psychological Review, 95,* 256-273.

Elliot, A. J. (1997). Integrating the "classic" and "contemporary" approaches to achievement motivation: A hierarchical model of approach and avoidance achievement motivation. In M. L. Maehr & P. R. Pintrich (Eds.), *Advances in motivation and achievement* (Vol. 10, pp. 143-179). Greenwich, CT: JAI Press.

Elliot, A. J. (1999). Approach and avoidance motivation and achievement goals. *Educational Psychologist, 34*(3), 169-189.

Elliot, A. J., & Church, M. A. (1997). A hierarchical model of approach and avoidance achievement motivation. *Journal of Personality and Social Psychology, 72*, 218-232.

Elliot, A. J., & McGregor, H. A. (2001). A 2 x 2 achievement goal framework. *Journal of Personality and Social Psychology, 80*, 501-519.

Elliot, A. J., & Thrash, T. M. (2001). Achievement goals and the hierarchical model of achievement motivation. *Educational Psychology Review, 13*, 139-156.

Elliott, A. J., Shell, M. M., & Henry, K. B. (2005). Achievement goals, performance contingencies, and performance attainment: An experimental test. *Journal of Educational Psychology, 97*, 630-640.

Ford, M. E., & Nichols, C. W. (1991). Using goal assessments to identify motivational patterns and facilitate behavioral regulation and achievement. In M. L. Maehr & P. R. Pintrich (Eds.), *Advances in motivation and achievement, 7*, 51-84. Greenwich, CT: JAI Press.

Grant, H., & Dweck, C. S. (2003). Clarifying achievement goals and their impact. *Journal of Personality and Social Psychology, 85*, 541-553.

Green, C. D. (1992). Of immortal mythological beasts: Operationism in psychology. *Theory & Psychology, 2*, 291-320.

Grimes, T. (1990). Audio-video correspondence and its role in attention and memory. *Educational Technology Research and Development, 38*, 15-25.

Hadwin, A. F., Winne, P. H., Stockley, D. B., Nesbit, J. C., & Wosczyna, C. (2001). Context moderates students' self-reports about how they study. *Journal of Educational Psychology, 93*, 477-487.

Harvey, F. A., & Nelson, A. (1995). A hybrid investigation of hypermedia training. *Proceedings of the Association for Educational Communications and Technology, USA.*

Hede, A. (2002). An integrated model of multimedia effects on learning. *Journal of Educational Multimedia and Hypermedia, 11*, 177-191.

Hidi, S., & Harackiewicz, J. M. (2000). Motivating the academically unmotivated: A critical issue for the 21st Century. *Review of Educational Research, 70*, 151-179.

Hill, J., & Hannafin, M. (1997). Cognitive strategies and learning from the World Wide Web. *Educational Technology Research & Development, 45*, 37-64.

Jamieson-Noel, D., & Winne, P. H. (2003). Comparing self-reports to traces of studying behaviour as representations of student' studying and achievement. *German Journal of Educational Psychology, 17*, 159-171.

Keller, J. M. (1997). Motivational design and multimedia. Beyond the novelty effect. *Strategic Human Resource Development Review, 1*, 188-203.

Keller, J. M. (1999). Motivation in cyber learning environments. *International Journal of Educational Technology, 1*, 7-30.

Keller, J. M., & Suzuki, K. (1988). Application of the ARCS model to courseware design. In D. Jonassen (Ed.), *Instructional designs for microcomputer courseware design* (pp. 401-434). New York: Erlbaum.

Kelley, H. H. (1992). Common sense psychology and scientific psychology. *Annual Review of Psychology, 43*, 1-24.

Kozma, R. B. (1991). Learning with media. *Review of Educational Research, 61*, 179-211.

Lajoie, S. P. (2005). Extending the Scaffolding Metaphor. *Instructional Science, 33*, 541-557.

Lang, A. (1995). Defining audio/video redundancy from a limited-capacity information processing perspective. *Communication Research, 22*, 86-115.

Lawless, K. A., & Kulikowich, J. M. (1996). Understanding hypertext navigation through cluster analysis. *Journal of Educational Computing Research, 14*, 385-399.

Lemos, M. S. (1996). Students' and teachers' goals in the classroom. *Learning and Instruction, 6*, 151-171.

Linnenbrink, E. A., & Pintrich, P. R. (2000). Multiple pathways to learning and achievement: The role of goal orientation in fostering adaptive motivation, affect, and cognition. In C. Sansone & J. M. Harackiewicz (Eds.), *Intrinsic and extrinsic motivation: The search for optimal motivation and performance* (pp. 195-227). San Diego, CA: Academic Press.

MacGregor, S. K. (1999). Hypermedia navigation profiles: Cognitive characteristics and information processing strategies. *Journal of Educational Computing Research, 20*, 189-206.

Maehr, M. L. (1984). Meaning and motivation: Toward a theory of personal investment. In R. Ames & C. Ames (Eds.), *Research on motivation in education, 1*, 115-144. New York: Academic Press.

Maehr, M. L., & Pintrich, P. R. (1991). [Preface]. In: *Advances in motivation and achievement, 7*, ix-xiii. Greenwich, CT: JAI Press.

Mangos, P. M. & Steele-Johnson, D. (2001). The role of subjective task complexity in goal orientation, self-efficacy, and performance relations. *Human Performance, 14*, 169-186.

Marsh, H. W. (1994). Sport motivation orientations: Beware of jingle-jangle fallacies. *Journal of Sport and Exercise Psychology, 16*, 365–380.

Mayer, R. E. (2001). *Multimedia learning.* Cambridge, UK: Cambridge University Press.

Moore, D. M., Burton, J. K., & Myers, R. J. (1996). Multiple-channel communication: The theoretical and research foundations of multimedia. In D. H. Jonassen (Ed.), *Handbook of research for educational communication and technology* (pp. 851–875). New York: Macmillan.

Nesbit, J. C., & Winne, P. H. (2007). Tools for learning in an information society. In T. Willoughby & E. Wood (Eds.), *Children's learning in a digital world.* Oxford, UK: Blackwell.

Nesbit, J. C., Winne, P. H., Jamieson-Noel, D., Code, J., Zhou, M., MacAllister, K., Bratt, S., Wang, W., & Hadwin, A. F. (2007). Using cognitive tools in gStudy to investigate how study activities covary with achievement goals. *Journal of Educational Computing Research, 35*, 339-358.

Nesbit, J. C., Zhou, M., Xu, Y., & Winne, P. H. (2007, August). *Advancing log analysis of student interactions with cognitive tools.* Paper presented at the European Association for Research on Learning and Instruction (EARLI) 2007 Conference, Budapest, Hungary.

Pea, R. D. (1985). Beyond amplification: Using the computer to reorganize mental functioning. *Educational Psychologist, 20*, 167–182.

Penney, C. G. (1989). Modality effects and the structure of short-term memory. *Memory & Cognition, 17*, 398-422.

Pintrich, P. R. (2000). Multiple goals, multiple pathways: The role of goal orientation in learning and achievement. *Journal of Educational Psychology, 92*, 544-555.

Pintrich, P. R., & Garcia, T. (1991). Student goal orientation and self-regulation in the college classroom. In M. L. Maehr & P. R. Pintrich (Eds.), *Advances in motivation and achievement* (Vol. 7, pp. 371-402). Greenwich, CT: JAI Press.

Pintrich, P. R., & Schunk, D. H. (1996). *Motivation in education: Theory, research, and applications.* Englewood Cliffs, NJ: Merrill.

Samuelstuen, M. S., & Bråten, I. (2007). Examining the validity of self-reports on scales measuring students' strategic processing. *British Journal of Educational Psychology, 77*, 351-378.

Schroeder, E. E., & Grabowski, B. L. (1995). Patterns of exploration and learning with hypermedia. *Journal of Computing Research, 13*, 313-335.

Schvaneveldt, R.W. (1990). *Pathfinder associative networks.* Norwood, NJ: Ablex.

Schwier, R., & Misanchuk, E. R. (1990). *Analytical tools and research issues for interactive media.* (Report No. IR014519). Saskatchewan, Canada.

Senko, C., & Miles, K. M. (in press). Pursuing their own learning agenda: How mastery-oriented students jeopardize their class performance. *Contemporary Educational Psychology.*

Smith, M., Duda, J., Allen, J. & Hall, H. (2002). Contemporary measures of approach and avoidance goal orientations: Similarities and differences. *British Journal of Educational Psychology, 72*, 155-190.

Urdan, T. (1997). Achievement goal theory: Past results, future directions. In M. Maehr & P. Pintrich (Eds.), *Advances in motivation and achievement* (pp. 99-141). Greenwich, CT: JAI.

Urdan, T., & Mestas, M. (2006). The goals behind performance goals. *Journal of Educational Psychology, 98*, 354-365.

VandeWalle, D., Cron, W. L., & Slocum, J. W. (2001). The role of goal orientation following performance feedback. *Journal of Applied Psychology, 86*, 629–640.

Weinstein, R. (2004). Performance goals guide current educational reform: Are we on the best path? *PsycCRITIQUES, 49*, 32-35.

Winne, P. H. (1979). Experiments relating teachers' use of higher cognitive questions to student achievement. *Review of Educational Research, 49*, 13-49.

Winne, P. H. (1982). Minimizing the black box problem to enhance the validity of theories about instructional effects. *Instructional Science, 11*, 13–28.

Winne, P. H. (2001). Self-regulated learning viewed from models of information processing. In B. J. Zimmerman & D. H. Schunk (Eds.), *Self-regulated learning and academic achievement: Theoretical perspectives* (2nd ed., pp. 153–189). Mahwah, NJ: Lawrence Erlbaum Associates.

Winne, P. H. (2004). Comments on motivation in real-Life, dynamic, and interactive learning environments: Theoretical and methodological challenges when researching motivation in context. *European Psychologist, 9*, 257-263.

Winne, P. H. (2006a). How software technologies can improve research on learning and bolster school reform. *Educational Psychologist, 41*, 5–17.

Winne, P. H. (2006b). Meeting challenges to researching learning from instruction by increasing the complexity of research. In J. Elen & R. E. Clark (Eds.), *Handling complexity in learning environments: Theory and research* (pp. 221-236). Amsterdam, Netherlands: Elsevier.

Winne, P. H., & Jamieson-Noel, D. L. (2002). Exploring students' calibration of self-reports about study tactics and achievement. *Contemporary Educational Psychology, 27*, 551-572.

Winne, P. H., Gupta, L., & Nesbit, J. C. (1994). Exploring individual differences in studying strategies using graph theoretic statistics. *Alberta Journal of Educational Research, 40*, 177-193.

Winne, P. H., Jamieson-Noel, D. L., & Muis, K. (2002). Methodological issues and advances in researching tactics, strategies, and self-regulated learning. In P. R. Pintrich & M. L. Maehr (Eds.), *Advances in motivation and achievement: New directions in measures and methods* (Vol. 12, pp. 121-155). Greenwich, CT: JAI Press.

Winne, P. H., & Marx, R. W. (1989). A cognitive processing analysis of motivation within classroom tasks. In C. Ames and R. Ames (Eds.), *Research on motivation in education 3*, 223-257. Orlando, FL: Academic Press.

Winne, P. H., Nesbit, J. C., Kumar, V., Hadwin, A. F., Lajoie, S. P., Azevedo, R. A., & Perry, N. E. (2006). Supporting self-regulated learning with gStudy software: The Learning Kit Project. *Technology, Instruction, Cognition and Learning, 3*, 105-113.

Wolters, C. A. (1998). Self-regulated learning and college students' regulation of motivation. *Journal of Educational Psychology, 90*, 224-235.

Xu, Y., Nesbit, J. C., Zhou, M., & Winne, P. H. (2007). *LogValidator: A tool for identifying and mining patters in gStudy log data.* [computer program]. Simon Fraser University, Burnaby, BC.

Zhou, M., & Winne, P. H. (2008, April). *Differences in achievement goal-setting among high-achievers and low-achievers.* Paper to be presented at the American Educational Research Association 2008 Annual Meeting, New York.

Zimmerman, B. (1989). Models of self-regulated learning and academic achievement. In B. Zimmerman & D. Schunk (Eds.), *Self-regulated learning and academic achievement: Theory, research, and practice* (pp. 1-25). New York: Springer-Verlag.

Zimmerman, B. J. (1994). Dimensions of academic self-regulation: A conceptual framework for education. In D. H. Schunk & B. J. Zimmerman (Eds.), *Self-regulation of learning and performance: Issues and educational applications* (pp. 3-21). Hillsdale, NJ: Erlbaum.

ADDITIONAL READINGS

Ablard, K. E., & Lipschultz, R. E. (1998). Self-regulated learning in high-achievement students: relations to advanced reasoning, achievement goals and gender. *Journal of Educational Psychology, 90*, 94-101.

Altun, A. (2000). Patterns in cognitive processes and strategies in hypertext reading: A case study of two experienced computer users. *Journal of Educational Multimedia and Hypermedia, 9*, 35-55.

Bråten, I., & Samuelstuen M. S. (2007). Measuring strategic processing: Comparing task-specific self-reports to traces. *Metacognition Learning, 2*, 1-20.

Castelli, C., Colazzo, L., & Molinari, A. (1998). Cognitive variables and patterns of hypertext performances: lessons learned for educational hypermedia construction. *Journal of Educational Multimedia and Hypermedia, 7*, 177-206.

Clark, R. E. (1999). Yin and yang cognitive motivational processes operating in multimedia learning environments. In J. J. G. van Merrienböer (Ed.) *Cognition and multimedia design* (pp. 73-107). Herleen, Netherlands: Open University Press.

d'Ydewalle, G. (1987). Is it still worthwhile to investigate the impact of motivation on learning? In E. de Corte, H. Lodewijks, R. Parmentier, & P. Span (Eds.), *Learning and instruction* (Vol.1, pp. 191-200). Oxford, England: Pergamon.

Dillon, A., & Gabbard, R. (1998). Hypermedia as an educational technology: A review of the quantitative research literature on learner comprehension, control, and style. *Review of Educational Research, 68*, 322-349.

Elliot, A. J. (2005). A conceptual history of the achievement goal construct. In A. J. Elliot & C. S. Dweck, (Eds.), *Handbook of competence and motivation* (pp. 52–72). NY: Guilford.

Hadwin, A. F., Winne, P. H., & Nesbit, J. C. (2005). Roles for software technologies in advancing research and theory in educational psychology. *British Journal of Educational Psychology, 75*, 1-24.

Järvelä, S., Salonen, P., & Lepola, J. (2001). Dynamic assessment as a key to understanding student motivation in a classroom context. In P. Pintrich & M. Maehr (Eds.), *Advances in motivation and achievement* (Vol. 12, pp. 207-240). Amsterdam: JAI Press.

Nesbit, J. C., & Hadwin, A. F. (2005). Methodological issues in educational psychology. In P. A. Alexander & P. H. Winne (Eds.). *Handbook of educational psychology* (2nd ed., pp. 825-848). Mahwah NJ: Erlbaum.

Patrick, J., & James, N. (2004). Process tracing of complex cognitive work tasks. *Journal of Occupational and Organizational Psychology, 77*, 259-280.

Perrin, D. (2003). Progression analysis (PA): Investigating writing strategies at the workplace. *Journal of Pragmatics, 35*, 907-921.

Richardson, J. T. E. (2004). Methodological issues in questionnaire-based research on student learning in higher education. *Educational psychology Review, 16*, 347-358.

Rouet, J., & Levonen, J. (1996). Studying and learning with hypertext: Empirical studies and their implications. In J. Rouet, J. Levonen, A. Dillon, & R. J. Spiro (Eds.), *Hypertext and cognition* (pp. 9-24). Mahwah, NJ: Lawrence Erlbaum.

Rowe, A. L., Cooke, N. J., Hall, E. P., & Halgren, T. L. (1996). Toward an on-line knowledge assessment methodology: Building on the relationship between knowing and doing. *Journal of Experimental Psychology, 2*, 31-47.

Schott, F., Hillebrandt, D., Al Diban, S., Schubert, T., Heyne, N., & Herrmann, U. (2002). *Complex learning in multimedia environments – Which kind of learning and how to do research on it?* Paper presented at the EARLI SIG 6 Biannual Workshop, Erfurt, Germany.

Schroeder, E. E., & Grabowski, B. L. (1995). Patterns of exploration and learning with hypermedia. *Journal of Educational Computing Research, 13*, 313-335.

Shapiro, A. & Niederhauser, D. (2004). Learning from hypertext: Research issues and findings. In D. H. Jonassen (Ed.) *Handbook of research on education communications and technology* (2nd ed., pp. 605-620). Mahwah, NJ: Lawrence Erlbaum.

Stanovich, K. E. (1998). Twenty-five years of research on the reading process: The grand synthesis and what it means for our field. In T. Shanahan & F. Rodriguez-Brown (Eds.), *Forty-seventh yearbook of the national reading conference* (pp. 44-58). Chicago: NRC.

Underwood, G., Everatt, J. (1992). The role of eye movements in reading: Some limitations of the eye-mind assumption. In E. Chekaluk & K. R. Llewellyn (Eds.), *The role of eye movements in perceptual processes* (pp. 111-169). Oxford, England: North-Holland.

Winne, P. H. (1995). Inherent details in self-regulated learning. *Journal of Educational Psychology, 87*, 397-410.

Winne, P. H. (2005). Key issues in modeling and applying research on self-regulated learning. *Applied Psychology: An International Review, 54*, 232–238.

Winne, P. H., & Hadwin, A. F. (1998). Studying as self-regulated learning. In D. J. Hacker, J. Dunlosky, & A. C. Graesser (Eds.), *Metacognition in educational theory and practice* (pp. 277–304). Mahwah, NJ: Lawrence Erlbaum.

Winne, P. H., & Perry, N. E. (2000). Measuring self-regulated learning. In M. Boekaerts, P. Pintrich, & M. Zeidner (Eds.), *Handbook of self-regulation* (pp. 531–566). Orlando, FL: Academic Press.

Chapter XVI
Using Narrative and Game–Schema Acquisition Techniques to Support Learning from Educational Games

Alan D. Koenig
University of California–Los Angeles, USA

Robert K. Atkinson
Arizona State University, USA

ABSTRACT

The first part of this chapter explores how narrative can be used as a cognitive aid in educational video games. It discusses how narrative is currently used in games, and how that modality of presentation, when combined with instruction, is complimentary to the way we comprehend, store, and retrieve information. The second part of the chapter reviews the cognitive prerequisites needed in the minds of players to adequately attend to and leverage the instructional aspects of games. To this end, it offers suggestions for how to instill a functional game-schema in the minds of novice players so that they can be productive in the game environment. The focus on the interplay of narrative and game schema construction in this chapter is also meant to serve as a model for a holistic approach to games research in which a game's cognitive prerequisites are explicitly studied alongside the more traditional pedagogical measures.

INTRODUCTION

As of the close of 2006, game usage in the United States continued to soar, not only among the traditional gamer demographic (i.e. teenage boys), but among all age groups from infants to senior citizens. According to The Nielson Company's Fourth Quarter 2004 Video Game Console Usage Report (The Nielson Company, 2004), almost 94 million Americans played a console video game for one minute or longer between Sept. 18th and Dec. 31st 2006. Furthermore, during any given minute of that 3 1/2 month time period, approximately 1.6 million Americans aged 2 and older were actively engaged with playing a console video game. And from a total usage standpoint, the Neilson report suggests that approximately 52 million males and 42 million females across all age ranges used a video game console at least once during the 4th quarter of 2006.

With such widespread adoption in our society, video games are beginning to change the nature of entertainment – from that of individuals being passive consumers of media to people becoming more active participants in the shaping of their amusement. Among kids in particular, this societal transformation arguably raises the bar of student expectations and capabilities when it comes to interacting with information presented in the classroom. As educators, we must not only acknowledge the existence of such changes, but must make concerted efforts to leverage potential learning opportunities afforded by the use of breakthrough game engine technology.

However game engine technology is becoming increasingly complex, and the notion of game-play and engagement can vary widely across different genres of games. Indeed the very notion of a video game nowadays has become a vague generalization, evoking images of 1st person style shoot-em' up gore in the minds of some, while for others the term evokes images of solitaire or 3-D Tetris.

When exploring the potential benefits video games offer to learning and instruction, the gaming literature is surprisingly vague in distinguishing one type of game genre from another. Unsuspecting readers may easily be led to believe, for example, that findings concerning motivation and engagement from the use of a 2-D puzzle game to help students practice their multiplication times tables would be applicable in predicting motivation and engagement for students playing a 3-D role-playing game that endeavors to teach global economic commerce among warring nations. Despite the fact that these two environments are regarded as video games, their relation to one another is practically non-existent. At best, any similarities found between the two could arguably be regarded as mere coincidence.

When discussing the educational nuances of games, we need to break the tendency of speaking in generalities concerning video games, and instead focus our discussions on the myriad sub-genres of video games that exist so that we can more accurately make "apples-to-apples" comparisons. Indeed, the cognitive aspects associated with playing a 2-D puzzle game are arguably very different from those associated with a 3-D role playing game.

With that said each sub-genre of the video game family offers its own potential benefits to learning and instruction, as each involves subtle differences in the way players interact in the game-playing experience. As educators, we ought to begin to examine the nuances of interaction associated with each genre of game-play and identify how those interactions can be married to sound instructional design in order to develop innovative, next-generation learning experiences.

Although research specific to how interactivity in *games* relates to learning is scarce, there is evidence to suggest that providing students with the ability to physically interact and/or manipulate objects in an instructional realm may help improve their recall of the experience. Engelkamp (1998) described this phenomenon as the "enactment effect". His research has shown that when asked to recall certain action phrases (such as "bend the wire" or "close the umbrella"), participants exhibited a greater ability to recall the phrases if they actually performed the tasks compared to when these phrases were merely heard. One explanation for this effect is that in order to carry out the action, one must first semantically process the command, resulting in greater attentiveness to the phrase. This may bode well for gaming environments that endeavor to teach – especially ones that leverage movement, interaction, and the manipulation of objects in the process.

However, as Clements (1999) suggests, truly effective manipulatives in educational settings cannot be random, but instead must be meaningful to the learner, and provide assistance in making cognitive connections to the content being learned. Furthermore, most instructional environments (including educational games) involve greater degrees of organization and integration than merely engaging in the free recall of unrelated phrases (Reed, 2006). For these reasons, we must be cautious in our assumptions about how interactivity in games can assist learning until more extensive research has been conducted.

A starting point in this process, though, might be to examine two key issues. The first is how the nature of the interactivity for a given game genre can be leveraged to facilitate learning within the confines of our cognitive architecture, and the second is how to manage the potential cognitive load arising in the minds of players who are unfamiliar with the chosen game genre modality.

The intent of this book chapter is to exemplify this mode of thinking by first exploring one of the nuances of 3-D role-playing games (namely narrative) to see how it can be used to enhance learning within a gaming context, and then investigate the cognitive prerequisites (or game schema) a player must have to adequately succeed in such a gaming environment. It is our hope in writing this chapter that readers will not only come away with a heightened sense of curiosity for the use of narrative in pedagogical gaming environments, but also garner an appreciation for the complexity associated with modern gaming systems and the corresponding game schemas needed on the part of players to adequately engage with them.

BACKGROUND

Games as Narrative-Centric Learning Environments

As academic researchers are beginning to realize, the value of playing video games can extend far beyond the pleasures of entertainment. Pedagogical video game environments have the potential to be immersive instruments through which students can develop critical thinking skills and interact with content in greater depth and sophistication than typically afforded by classroom instruction. Such environments are often 3-dimensional in nature and include vibrant graphical depictions of characters, objects, and settings, thus imbuing the player with a sense of authenticity and realism. As a result, many of these gaming environments offer players the ability to explore complex worlds, ponder physical, social, and ethical dilemmas, and witness the implications of their actions play out in real time, and often in unpredictable ways. As such, these settings have the potential to be ideal platforms for helping students creatively apply abstract concepts learned in the classroom to simulated real-world scenarios.

A key feature of pedagogical gaming environments is the means through which they communicate to the player the context of the situation at hand or the scenario being simulated. Indeed, such games must provide the player with a sense of where they are, what challenges await them and why, and what resources (human or otherwise) are available to overcome those challenges. Unlike with real-world settings that naturally have unique contextual characteristics, virtual environments must artificially create this illusion of context. This is often done using narrative. For example, the Cognition and Technology Group at Vanderbilt (1990) used narrative in their *Jasper Series* – a videodisc-based situated learning environment – to contextualize the actions and problems of the main character, Jasper Woodbury. In that environment, the problem encountered, its context, and the data needed to solve it were all embedded within the story of Jasper Woodbury's adventure.

In a similar vein, video games often employ back-stories to inform the player of the dramatic, historical events that led up to the player's current situation, or use cut-scenes to further the story during game-play after significant events occur. Sometimes the 3-D game environment itself is used a vehicle for narrative. Such *environmental* narratives make use of semiotics, lighting, sound, etc. to infuse story elements into the physical space through which the player moves (Carson, 2000). These can be thought of as "narrative spaces" in which various events are enacted, the results of which give rise to player immersion in the game world (Jenkins, 2004).

When games exhibit these types of embodied narratives, players often use them to derive situational meaning of the events and challenges faced in the game (Gee, 2003). In this way, game narratives help promote learning through a model of situated cognition in which knowledge arises from the perceptual meanings formed by the player as a result of his agency in the game environment (Young, 1993). Hence, narrative in educational video games can serve as a potential cognitive aid that players use to tie the events and character interactions of the game (both temporally and spatially) to specific, educational constructs presented in the game (Ryan, 2003).

The use of narrative in this way may help facilitate the student's understanding of the instructional content (Dickey, 2006). When people encounter something new, they attempt to comprehend it in terms of existing scripts (or schemas) they already posses about similar entities (Schank, 1999; Ratcliff and McKoon, 1988; Wattenmaker, 1992). These scripts are recalled and understood not based on factual content alone, but on the

storied context that integrates these facts with particular experiences (Ferguson et al., 1992). By contextualizing educational constructs into comprehensible narratives, we can increase the likelihood that students will find related scripts (or schemas) from their own experiences to help with encoding and retrieval of these constructs into and out of long-term memory.

For example, Graesser et al. (1980) compared the ease of recall of information presented in expository, encyclopedia-style texts, versus that presented in narrative-based, storied contexts. They found that independent of the participant's familiarity with the content, information presented in narrative form was recalled twice as much compared to information that was presented in the non-storied, expository format.

Many video games (particularly role-playing games) make extensive use of narrative in order to orient the player to the game's goals, rules, challenges, and consequences. As such, they provide numerous opportunities for students to relate their own scripts and experiences to new situations and constructs they encounter while inside the gaming environment.

ISSUES, CONTROVERSIES, PROBLEMS

Game Narrative Types

The means through which narrative is incorporated into games is a hotly debated topic among game scholars (Aarseth, 2001; Eskelinen, 2001; Frasca, 1999; Juul, 1998). At issue is whether the video game as a medium is synergistic with storytelling, or whether video games and storytelling are separate, distinct entities that cannot be coerced together. The issues raised in this debate have implications in the design of video games – particularly *educational* video games that use narrative as a means to facilitate instruction.

On one side of the debate, *narratologists* tend to prescribe to the notion that game designers can and should embed narrative elements into video games to influence and enhance the game playing experience. This so-called *embedded* narrative can serve to guide the overall plot of the game while still giving the player agency to control individual actions and choices. The intent is to bring about greater significance to the player's actions by having them exist against a thematic story context, which in turn can increase the player's motivation and involvement with the game (Salen & Zimmerman, 2004).

Hence, in games that employ embedded narratives, typically a detailed back-story is present to both influence and contextualize the player's actions. In such games, a pre-scripted, overarching story is usually experienced by the player as progression through the game occurs. The player's character will generally have a specific role in the story and would likely be responsible for moving it through to completion by overcoming specific game challenges (i.e. progressing through the levels of the game). Although the player's actions and decisions cannot *alter* the underlying story, they can impact the pace with which it proceeds.

Narratologists tend to regard embedded narrative in video games as synergistic with the overall game-playing experience. For example, Murray (2004) contends that narrative and game-play are overlapping and not easily distinguished from one another. As such, players who assume protagonist roles in storied contexts necessarily embody the narrative of the game as they make decisions and carry out actions *as* that character within the rules and framework of the environment.

Other proponents of embedded narrative see it as a way to bring about greater emotional involvement among the player. For example, Adams (2001) suggests that by embedding a linear story into a game, the player has the opportunity to not only experience the events of the narrative, but also to become emotionally involved in the telling. This, in turn, he argues, can give rise to game re-playability, which is often an important consideration among game designers.

In contrast, *ludologists* tend to oppose the embedding of narrative into games as a means of telling stories. They argue that narrative in video games, if present at all, should be *emergent* in nature, arising out of the action of game-play rather than coming from a pre-scripted story. In essence, such an emergent narrative should be generated only by the characters, their psychologies, their background histories, and the general context of the user experience (Louchart & Aylett, 2004). Ludologists see games and stories as being inherently different structures (Aarseth, 2004). For example, Juul (2001) asserts that, in essence, game narration and player interactivity cannot exist simultaneously because the elements of game time vs. narrative time are necessarily different.

Games that employ emergent narrative typically contain an *initial* background story to set up the overall game context and to provide information about who the player's character is, and how and why they've arrived in their current situation. However, once game-play begins, the narrative that emerges is entirely dependent on the actions of the player. In such games, there is not necessarily a single correct or incorrect path to success. Rather, the player is faced with a variety of choices regarding such things as which characters to interact with, which resources to utilize (and how), whether to form cooperative alliances or assume a more self-serving posture, etc. Therefore the narrative that emerges unfolds gradually as the game progresses, and is therefore completely unscripted. In such cases, a post-game reflection on the overall narrative experienced by the player would likely be different each time the game is played.

Although this debate between narratologists and ludologists is highly theoretical and subjective, it has highlighted some fundamental design issues that bear consideration when designing pedagogical video games – namely, how and to what extent should narrative be used? Ultimately, this question cannot be answered through ongoing conjecture and debate, but rather requires empirical research.

Unfortunately, despite the wide-spread use of educational games in both classroom settings (such as chemistry and physics labs) and professional domains such as aviation, urban planning, farming, disaster management, medicine, health care, marketing, and finance (Wainess, 2006), relatively little empirical research has been conducted on the efficacy of educational video games on learning outcomes. In fact, in a literature review of educational games spanning a 15 year period (from 1990 to 2005), O'Neil, Wainess, & Baker (2005) found only 19 (out of several thousand) articles published on educational games to be based on empirical research.

The scope of research narrows even more when refined to exploring how *narrative* impacts learning in games. Although the use of narrative in classroom and in more traditional multimedia-based instructional contexts has been shown to improve comprehension (Laurillard, 1998; Mandler & DeForest, 1979), research into the use of narrative in pedagogical games is virtually non-existent.

From an instructional design standpoint, it might be tempting to favor embedded narratives in games to ensure greater control over the experiences a player has – and hence increase the likelihood that he/she will engage with the instructional content as intended. However doing so may prove to undermine the gaming experience and serve to distract or disengage the player. Further research into which type of narrative is more beneficial to education is needed, and remains the focus of future research we plan to conduct at the Learning Sciences Research Lab at Arizona State University.

Game Schemas

Before adequately being able to assess the benefits that narrative offers to learning in games, designers of educational video games face another

daunting challenge that is not widely discussed in the literature – that of game-schema awareness.

In recent years, many academic researchers have increasingly alluded to the potential benefits video games can have on learning and instruction (Dickey, 2005; Gee, 2004; Simpson, 2005; Squire, 2003; Squire & Jenkins, 2003). Often mentioned are the power of games to bring about greater emotional engagement, increased motivation, enhanced interactions with educational content and concepts, etc. All of this, though, is predicated on the notion that the student, while playing the game, is attentive to all of its salient features and not distracted by the complexity of the environment.

Indeed, 3-D gaming environments with all of their sophistication can be imposing to novice gamers, and lead to high levels of cognitive load. In essence, inexperienced gamers face many unfamiliar challenges that are entirely separate and distinct from the game itself when engaged in such 3-D environments. These challenges include purely physical things such as grasping how to control a moving camera view, how to coordinate the movement of an avatar (i.e. walking, running, strafing, etc.), and how to pick and place objects. All of these physical challenges pose high element interactivity in the mind of the novice gamer, which in turn strains working memory.

As Sweller (1999) describes, element interactivity occurs when several related and unfamiliar concepts must be considered together in order for comprehensive (rather than rote) learning to occur, and this is often the genesis of intrinsic cognitive load. For a novice gamer, learning each of the individual elements responsible for directing the movement and coordination of actions in a 3-D gaming environment is impractical to do in isolation from one another. Instead, these actions must occur as a coordinated effort simultaneously. Hence, players with little or no prior experience interacting in these settings tend to experience relatively high levels of intrinsic cognitive load.

If this occurs, much of the benefits of utilizing a gaming modality for instruction can be lost. For example, novice gamers may become so preoccupied with the challenges of basic movement and interaction in the environment that they may not selectively attend to the narrative back-story of the game, or may not model the behavior of character role models that they encounter, or may completely ignore the instructional content presented. In essence, this intrinsic cognitive load occurs at the expense of intended germane load, which involves the directing and/or redirecting of the player's attention toward those resources and experiences in the game that are relevant to the instructional content.

At its core, this issue centers on the differences between experts and novices. Experts and novices differ not only in their general abilities and types of strategies utilized for a given situation, but also in what they notice and how they organize, represent, and interpret information from their environment (Bransford, Brown, & Cocking, 2000). Experienced gamers, over time, develop schemas for handling the basic mechanics of movement and interaction in 3-D environments, and hence are more likely to attend to the unique features of the game.

Moreover, having this game schema will also provide them with a sense of how to *behave* in these environments as well. Unlike more traditional learning environments, or even many computer-based learning environments in which students are relatively passive as information is presented to them, many games are exploratory by nature. Without having a pre-defined schema for how to behave and be productive in these settings, novice gamers can become confused as to what is expected of them, and face difficulty in acquiring and utilizing information and resources. Hence both their in-game productivity and post-game learning outcomes can suffer.

SOLUTIONS AND RECOMMENDATIONS

This is precisely what Koenig (2007) found when contrasting the performance of novice gamers (vs. experts) who played a 3-D role-playing video game that teaches about electricity and energy conversion. As part of the experiment, various in-game metrics were recorded to capture the participant's comprehension and utilization of the educational constructs presented in the game. In addition, participants were tasked with demonstrating their knowledge of these same constructs on a posttest. Results showed that more experienced gamers took significantly less time to overcome the in-game challenges, and performed better on the posttest compared to their less experienced counterparts. This effect had seemingly little to do with the participant's prior knowledge of the content, as there were no significant differences between gaming novices and experts in their pre-test scores. All of this furthers the argument that when designing educational video games, particularly those that leverage 3-D game engine technology, scaffolding for novice users must be considered.

Within video gaming environments (particularly those of a 3-D genre), such scaffolding traditionally exists in one of two formats. The first format is based on the idea of task classes (van Merrienboer & Paas, 2003). Task classes can be thought of as individual component tasks which collectively comprise a single, more complex task. In this scenario, scaffolding is provided to learners by having them first work through relatively simple representations of more complex tasks that they'll eventually encounter downstream in the learning environment (van Merrienboer & Paas, 2003). This is typically carried out in games by having new players complete an obstacle course of sorts, in which the player is given the opportunity to learn and practice the mechanics of avatar movement, view control, object interaction, etc.

The obstacle course typically looks and feels just like the real game environment, but does not place any demands on the player to attend to anything other than learning the mechanics of the game. In this way, movement and interaction tasks can be mastered before the player is called upon to utilize these skills while having to also attend to the goals of the game. The intent of this approach is to reduce in-game cognitive load through pre-game training. An example video game that utilizes this type of scaffolding is Half Life.

A second scaffolding approach commonly employed in video games is to provide in-game assistance for new, unfamiliar tasks that the player encounters. The modality of this assistance can exist in a variety of formats including on-screen text, static images or diagrams, narrated voice-overs, video demonstrations, or interactive tutorials (Paras, 2003). The instruction for this type of scaffolding is typically succinct and provides specific procedures for how to perform the act, such as "To jump, press the space bar." Players typically would have the ability to request this scaffolding as needed while playing the game. Games such as Tomb Raider employ this approach to scaffolding to quickly empower the player to be productive in the environment.

The benefit of both of theses types of scaffolding is that they provide novice learners with a path to schema acquisition for how to function in 3-D gaming environments – specifically that which pertains to the game at hand. However, the potential danger of providing this scaffolding – especially that which is mandatory and which occurs *in* the game – is that more experienced players who don't require this assistance may become distracted by it and not attend to the pertinent features of the game. As a result, experienced gamers run the risk of degradation in their performance. Kalyuga et al. (2003) describe this phenomenon as the expertise reversal effect, in which instructional interventions that are beneficial to novice learners lose their effect and may actually become detrimental to more experienced learners.

The consequences of the expertise reversal effect in educational video games can be significant, potentially nullifying the pedagogical benefits such environments offer. The challenge, therefore, is to design instructional gaming environments that adequately scaffold the acquisition of functional game schemas in order to reduce cognitive load, while at the same time not stunting learning opportunities for more experienced players.

CONCLUSION

To date, most of the literature surrounding games in education is speculative, highlighting the salient features of games and how they can potentially benefit learning and instruction. However, as gaming environments continue to increase in sophistication, and their use in society becomes more ubiquitous, the need for empirical research into the effective design and use of games in pedagogical settings is paramount.

Of particular importance is researching the interplay between the cognitive prerequisites players need in order to be productive in gaming environments, and the modalities of content presentation & interaction that games afford players from an engagement and learning standpoint. This chapter has focused on the use of narrative in 3-D role-playing games as a tool for both the presentation of educational constructs, as well as a means through which player engagement and motivation is maintained. As such, the degree to which a corresponding game schema is developed in the mind of the player pertaining to avatar movement and interaction would likely impact the efficacy of the narrative on learning. Educational research surrounding this genre of game, therefore, should not be conducted in a vacuum in which only narrative is researched, but rather should be looked at more holistically by also considering the specific cognitive prerequisites needed to properly engage with the game.

However, for other types of games that operationalize player interactions differently, different cognitive prerequisites will likely be present. It is therefore vital that researchers distinguish games based on their genre and modality of interaction, as the educational implications drawn from one type of game may not carry over to another type.

For example, so-called 'god games' such as Civilization require players to think and act very differently than a 1st-person shooter style of game, and present the player with a very different type of interface through which they engage the game. The cognitive prerequisites associated with a 'god game' might include learning the nuances of managing resources, or comprehending the symbolic representations of the game, for example. Therefore research surrounding the pedagogical benefits of this type of game arguably should focus on the interplay of different characteristics than those appropriate to 1st-person shooter style games.

Identifying the cognitive prerequisites of a particular game – or genre of game – can be a daunting task, however. In many cases, it requires extensive player observation along with an analysis of in-game player performance. We took this approach at the Learning Sciences Research Lab at Arizona State University to determine what cognitive prerequisites were necessary for adequate interaction with a custom-designed 3-D role-playing game. The genesis of our research began with teasing out potential gender differences that exist in role-playing games regarding player avatar preferences, efficiency of play, and success with game-based educational tasks. Findings from a prior study focusing on the use of narrative in 3-D role-playing games (Koenig, 2007) indicated that female participants took significantly longer to complete the game than did males, and did not perform as well on the posttest. It was hypothesized that since a male avatar was used uniformly to represent the player in the game, perhaps female students did not resonate as well as the males with the character,

and therefore did not experience the same degree of immersion in the game.

As a follow-up, Koenig, Atkinson, and Harrison (2008) devised a new study that explicitly explored the relationship between participant gender and avatar gender on learning, in-game performance, and player preferences. Once again, male players were observed to outperform females on in-game tasks and on overall player efficiency. In fact, in an independent samples t-test, statistically significant differences were found between the males and females on these measures, suggesting that gender differences in gaming relating to cognitive performance genuinely do exist.

However, logically, this seemed counter-intuitive. After all, the males did not perform significantly better on the pre-test measure, and we had no evidence to suggest that the males in our study were any more intelligent than the females. After mining our demographic data that we collected from the participants, we quickly realized that for this genre of game-play, the males had significantly more gaming experience, and therefore had more fully developed game schemas for interacting and strategizing in this type of setting. It was obvious that we were dealing with a division in our participant pool between experts and novices that happened to fall almost exclusively along gender lines.

Although not officially part of the study, we went back and interviewed some of the female participants who exhibited a low level of game-playing efficiency. Almost without exception, these players described being confused and uncoordinated for the first 30 to 45 minutes of game-play as they tried to comprehend the nuances of how to move and interact in the environment. During this phase, their attention was almost exclusively focused on achieving these basic tasks, and therefore little attention was paid to other facets of the game or on the educational constructs that were presented. As a result, their productivity in the game was hampered until they acquired enough practice interacting in the environment such that it became cognitively less demanding.

With that said, we do not deny the fact that genuine gender differences conceivably do exist with regard to gaming. For example Kafai (1996) found distinct feature differences in the games that young girls endeavor to design compared to features fancied by young boys. And Inkpen et al. (1994) found that girls tend to favor storylines and character personas in games over such things as competition and notions of winning. Agosto (2004) suggests that perhaps at an early age during childhood these differences begin to emerge, resulting in a 'gaming gender rift' between males and females.

However the point we are stressing here is that some apparent gaming differences observed between males and females may not actually be gender-based, but rather experience-based. Clearly in our society, boys and girls gravitate toward different types of play, and consequently different types of video games (if played at all). As educational researchers, we must be careful not to be too quick to attribute these differences to gender alone, but instead take the time to investigate what the deeper underlying issues might be.

It is our hope in writing this chapter that educational researchers will be inspired to not only explore the salient features of games (such as narrative) that have the potential to make games valuable platforms for learning and instruction, but to also consider the cognitive price tag these features come with in terms of their imposing complexity to novice players. Research of games as an educational medium is in its infancy, and no doubt there are numerous aspects of gaming pedagogy that has yet to be researched. Our focus on the interplay of narrative and game schema construction in this chapter is but one facet of gaming, and is not meant to be exhaustive or conclusive in any way. Instead our hope is that it will serve as an example of a more holistic approach to games research in which a game's cognitive prerequisites are explicitly studied alongside the more traditional pedagogical measures.

FUTURE RESEARCH DIRECTIONS

With video gaming technology advancing at an astonishing rate, and with ever-decreasing costs, the degree of sophistication of modern gaming systems is astounding. Individual developers can now create their own highly immersive 3-D games using the latest physics engines, lighting, shading and texturing technology for little or no cost – other than their time to program it. Resources such as DevMaster.net (http://www.devmaster. net) are devoted to assisting individual developers by providing extensive information on literally hundreds of game engines and related technology – most of which is freely available.

As barriers to game production continue to decrease, educators can and should consider using these powerful technologies as valuable tools for research. Not only can they be used to explore the intrinsic characteristics that video games potentially offer to learning (as described throughout this chapter), but gaming technology can also be used to study the external modes of engagement that players exhibit while immersed in a game-playing experience. Studying such experiences can be extremely valuable because they involve high levels of interactivity, which ultimately blends action with decision-making, often in contrived situations that can explicitly be designed to evaluate transference of knowledge from the classroom to an applied setting.

For example, computer and console gaming systems can be synced with non-invasive eye-tracking equipment to study where, in what order, and for how long players look at various elements on the game screen. This type of information can be crucial in elaborating on the ways in which students use information and resources in multimedia environments. Although the computer can be programmed to record *when* a resource is displayed on the screen, only through syncing that information with eye-tracking technology would a researcher be able to know the extent to which the student attended to that information. This, in turn, could provide insight into such things as identifying extraneous cognitive load, player metacognition, and engagement with content.

At the Learning Sciences Research Lab at Arizona State University, this is precisely the type of research that is under way. One of our primary goals is to gain a deeper understanding of our cognitive architecture by studying how people dynamically interact in both instructional and non-instructional 3-D virtual environments.

Similarly, other external bio-feedback measuring devices could be used in concert with gaming systems to better understand affect and emotion. One of the salient features of games – particularly character-based role-playing games – is that players, over time, often develop an emotional 'rooting interest' for the non-player characters they encounter. This emotional investment could arguably be both an asset and distraction to learning, depending on the situation. By measuring such things as posture, pupil dilation, and heart rate as players interact with role-playing games, valuable insight could potentially be added to the body of knowledge concerning the link between emotion and learning.

These are merely a few of the many possibilities modern game platforms afford researchers to help better understand the nuances of learning. By not only embracing game technology in its own right as a valuable research tool, but also by thinking creatively in how it can be combined with other new or existing technologies, educational researchers have potentially boundless opportunities for exploring learning and developing innovative instructional interventions.

REFERENCES

Aarseth, E. (2001). Computer game studies, Year one. *Game Studies: The International Journal of Computer Game Research, 1*(1), Retrieved May 20, 2006, from http://www.gamestudies. org/0101/editorial.html

Aarseth, E. (2004). Genre trouble: Narrativism and the art of simulation. In P. Harrigan & N. Wardrip-Fruin (Ed.), *First person: New media as story, performance, and game* (pp. 45-55). Cambridge: MIT Press.

Adams, E. (2001). Replayability, Part One: Narrative. *Gamasutra*, 05.21.01. [Online] Available http://www.gamasutra.com/features/20010521/ adams_01.htm.

Agosto, D. (2004). Girls and gaming: A summary of the research with implications for practice. *Teacher Librarian, 31*(3), 8-14.

Bransford, J., Brown, A. L., & Cocking, R. R. (Eds.). (2000). *How people learn: Brain, mind, experience, and school (Expanded Edition)*. Washington, DC: National Academy Press.

Carson, D. (2000). Environmental storytelling: Creating immersive 3-D worlds using lessons learned from the theme park industry. Gamasutra. Retrieved October 3, 2006, from http://www.gamasutra.com/features/20000301/carson_pfv.htm

Clements, D. H. (1999). "Concrete" manipulatives, concrete ideas. *Contemporary Issues in Early Childhood, 1*, 45–60.

Cognition and Technology Group at Vanderbilt. (1990). Anchored instruction and its relationship to situated cognition. *Educational Researcher, 19*(6), 2-10.

Dickey, M. D. (2005). Engaging by design: How engagement strategies in popular computer and video games can inform instructional design. *Educational Technology Research & Development, 53*(2), 67-83.

Dickey, M. D. (2006). Game design narrative for learning: Appropriating adventure game design narrative devices and techniques for the design of interactive learning environments. *Educational Technology Research & Development, 54*(3), 245-263.

Engelkamp, J. (1998). *Memory for actions.* Hove, UK: Psychology Press.

Eskelinen, M. (2001). Computer game studies, Year one. *Game Studies: The International Journal of Computer Game Research, 1*(1), Retrieved September 20, 2006, from http://www.gamestudies.org/0101/eskelinen/

Ferguson, W. (1992). ASK systems: An approach to the realization of story-based teachers. *The Journal of the Learning Sciences, 2*(1), 95-134.

Frasca, G. (1999). Ludology meets narratology: Similitude and differences between (video) games and narrative. *Ludology.org Game Theory.* Retrieved October 1, 2006, from http://www.ludology.org/articles/ludology.htm

Gee, J. P., (2003). *What video games have to teach us about learning and literacy.* New York: Palgrave Macmillan.

Gee, J. P., (2004). Learning by design: Games as learning machines. *Interactive Educational Multimedia, 8,* 15-23.

Graesser, A. C., Hauft-Smith, K., Cohen, A. D., & Pyles, L. D. (1980). Advanced outlines, familiarity, text genre, and retention of prose. *Journal of Experimental Education, 48,* 209-220.

Inkpen, K., Klawe, M., Lawry, J., Sedighian, K., Leroux, S. & a Hsu, D. (1994). "We have never-forgetful flowers in our garden": Girls' responses to electronic games. *Journal of Computers in Mathematics and Science Teaching, 13,* 383-403.

Jenkins, H. (2004). Game design as narrative architecture. In P. Harrigan & N. Wardrip-Fruin (Ed.), *First person: New media as story, performance, and game* (pp. 118-130). Cambridge: MIT Press.

Juul, J. (1998). *A Clash between game and narrative.* Paper presented at the *Digital Arts and Culture* conference, Bergen, Norway. Retrieved October 1, 2006, from http://www.jesperjuul.net/text/clash_between_game_and_narrative.html

Juul, J. (2001). Games telling stories? – A brief note on games and narratives. *Game Studies: The International Journal of Computer Game Research, 1*(1). Retrieved October 16, 2006, from http://www.gamestudies.org/0101/juul-gts/

Kafai, Y. (1996). Gender differences in children's constructions of video games. In P. Greenfield a R. Cocking (Eds.), *Interacting with video* (pp. 39-66). Norwood, NJ.

Kalyuga, S., Ayres, P., Chandler, P., & Sweller, J. (2003). The expertise reversal effect. *Educational Psychologist, 38*(1), 23-31.

Koenig, A. (2007). *Exploring narrative as a cognitive aid in educational video games.* Paper presented at the 13th International Conference on Artificial Intelligence in Education (AIED), Marina Del Ray, CA.

Koenig, A., Atkinson, R.K., & Harrison, C.J. (2008). *The embodiment of gender-specific characters in educational video games: Does it affect learning and in-game performance?* Paper at the Annual Conference of the American Educational Research Association, New York, NY.

Laurillard, D. (1998). Multimedia and the learner's experience of narrative. *Computers & Education, 31,* 229-242.

Louchart, S., & Aylett, R. (2004). Narrative theory and emergent interactive narrative. *Int. J. Continuing Engineering Education and Lifelong Learning, 14*(6), 506-518.

Mandler, J. M., & DeForest, M. (1979). Is there more than one way to recall a story. *Child Development, 50,* 886-889.

Murray, J. (2004). From game-story to cyberdrama. In P. Harrigan & N. Wardrip-Fruin (Ed.), *First person: New media as story, performance, and game* (pp. 2-11). Cambridge: MIT Press.

O'Neil, H. F., Wainess, R., & Baker, E. L. (2005). Classification of learning outcomes: Evidence from the computer games literature. *The Curriculum Journal, 16*(4), 455-474.

Paras, B. S. (2003). *Learning to play: The design of in-game training to enhance video game experience.* Un-published master's thesis, Simon Fraser University, Surrey, British Columbia, Canada.

Ratcliff, R., & McKoon, G. (1988). A retrieval theory of priming in memory. *Psychological Review, 95*(3), 385-408.

Reed, S.K. (2006). Cognitive architectures for multimedia learning. *Educational Psychologist, 41*(2), 87-98.

Ryan, M. L. (2003). Cognitive maps and the construction of narrative space, in *Narrative Theory and the Cognitive Sciences* (D. Herman). Stanford: CSLI Publications.

Salen, K., & Zimmerman, E. (2004). *Rules of play: Game design fundamentals*, Cambridge: MIT Press.

Schank, R. C. (1999). *Dynamic Memory Revisited.* New York: Cambridge University Press.

Simpson, E. S. (2005). Evolution in the classroom: What teachers need to know about the video game generation. *Tech Trends, 49*(5), 17-22.

Squire, K. (2003). Video games in education. *International Journal of Simulations and Gaming, 2*(1).

Squire, K., & Jenkins, H. (2003). *Harnessing the power of games in education. Insight, 3, 5.* [Online journal]. Retrieved May 1, 2007, from the World Wide Web: http://website.education.wisc.edu/kdsquire/manuscripts/insight.pdf

Sweller, J. (1999). *Instructional design in technical areas.* Camberwell: Acer Press.

The Nielson Company (2004). *The state of the console: Video game console usage report* (4th Quarter). New York, NY.

Van Merrienboer, J.J.G., & Paas, F. (2003). Powerful learning and the many faces of instructional design: Toward a framework for the design of powerful learning environments. In E. De Corte, L. Verschaffel, N. Entwistle, & J. van Merrienboer (Eds), *Powerful Learning Environments: Unraveling Basic Components and Dimensions* (pp. 3-22). Elsevier Science Ltd.

Wainess, R. A. (2006) *The effect of navigation maps on problem solving tasks instantiated in a computer-based video game.* Ph.D. dissertation, University of Southern California, United States -- California. Retrieved February 11, 2008, from ProQuest Digital Dissertations database. (Publication No. AAT 3237181).

Wattenmaker, W.D. (1992). Relational properties and memory-based category construction. *Journal of Experimental Psychology, 18*(5), 1125-1138.

Young, M. F. (1993). Instructional design for situated learning. *Educational Technology Research & Development, 41*(1), 43-58.

ADDITIONAL READINGS

Apperley, T. H. (2006). Genre and game studies: Toward a critical approach to video game genres. *Simulation & Gaming, 37*(6), 6-23.

Calleja, G. (2007). Digital game involvement. A conceptual model. *Games and Culture, 2*(3), 236-260.

Dickey, M.D. (2006). Game design narrative for learning: Appropriating adventure game design narrative devices and techniques for the design of interactive learning environments. *Educational Technology Research & Development, 54*(3),245-263.

Jonassen, D.H. (2002). Case-based reasoning and instructional design: Using stories to support problem solving. *Educational Technology Research & Development*, 50(2),65-77.

Kalyuga, S., Ayres, P., Chandler, P., & Sweller, J. (2003). The expertise reversal effect. *Educational Psychologist*, 38(1), 23-31.

Murray, J. (1998). *Hamlet on the Holodeck*, Cambridge: MIT Press.

Robinson, J.A. & Hawpe, L. (1986). Narrative thinking as a heuristic process. In *Narrative Psychology: The Storied Nature of Human Conduct*, Sarbin, T.R. (Ed.). Westport, CT: Praeger Publishers.

Salen, K., & Zimmerman, E. (2004). *Rules of play: Game design fundamentals*, Cambridge: MIT Press.

Schank, R. C., & Abelson, R. P. (1995). Knowledge and Memory: The Real Story. In Wyer, R. S. (Ed.), *Knowledge and Memory: The Real Story*, (pp. 1-82). Hillsdale, NJ: Lawrence Erlbaum Associates.

Paas, F., Tuovinen, J. E., Tabbers, H., & van Gerven, P. W. (2003). Cognitive load measurement as a means to advance cognitive load theory. *Educational Psychologist, 38*(1), 63-71.

Sweller, J., van Merrienboer, J. J., & Paas, F. (1998). Cognitive architecture and instructional design. *Educational Psychology Review, 10*(3), 251-296.

Sweller, J. (1999). *Instructional design in technical areas.* Camberwell: Acer Press.

Waldrip-Fruin, N. & Harrigan, P. (2004). *First Person: New Media as Story, Performance, and Game*, Cambridge: MIT Press.

Chapter XVII
How Literacy Emerges from Living Books in the Digital Era:
New Chances for Young Linguistically Disadvantaged Children

Marian J.A.J. Verhallen
Leiden University, The Netherlands

Adriana G. Bus
Leiden University, The Netherlands

ABSTRACT

Advanced digital storybooks offer, in addition to an oral rendition of text, the possibility of enhancing story content through the use of video. In three experiments, effects of added video with accompanying music and sound on language comprehension and language acquisition were tested in a group of second language learners from low educated families. Three questions were posed. Do video additions positively influence young children's story understanding over and above still images when listening to a storybook? How does video add to language acquisition; through added information or through the appraisal of helpfulness of the added information? Do these extra information sources benefit all young children to the same extent or especially children with insufficient prior knowledge?

INTRODUCTION

The rapid growth of new digital technology over the last few decades has enabled the use of multimedia for an ever-increasing number of people. In the Netherlands 90% of all households have a computer at their disposal and 83% have access to Internet at home (CBS, 2007). In many other Western countries the situation will not be very different. Personal computers, digital cameras, digital music carriers, cellular phones and the Internet allow cultural exchange and virtually instant global communication at the stroke of a key. The singular purpose of technical devices have become more fluid as new technologies have made integration of separate symbol systems like spoken and written language, music, pictures, film and sound possible. For instance, personal computers may combine text with pictures or film as well as music and sound. Most of the new media are screen media, and as larger screens with higher resolution and clearer audio become available the quality and impact of the experience may increase (Detenber & Reeves, 1996). Young children today will have spent most of their lives surrounded by these digital technologies (Prensky, 2001) and the changing technological environment will influence home practices like storybook reading (Close, 2004).

Reading picture storybooks to young children is a powerful way to enhance emergent literacy skills as it creates ample opportunities for contact with language typical of written texts (e.g., Bus, 2001; Bus, van IJzendoorn, & Pellegrini, 1995; Frijters, Barron, & Brunello, 2000; Sénéchal, LeFevre, Thomas, & Daley, 1998). Even texts for the youngest contain complex vocabulary and phrases that rarely occur in other language situations. Storybook reading therefore, has been a treasured activity between parents and young children in the majority of Western countries for a long time (Blok, 1999; Fitzgerald, Spiegel & Cunningham, 1991) and the effects of storybook reading on literacy are well researched: frequent shared reading fosters the development of language, which in turn facilitates the acquisition of literacy skills. Children, who have regularly been read to from an early age, have larger vocabularies (Sénéchal & Lefevre, 2002), become more proficient decoders, and have better reading comprehension skills (Bus, van IJzendoorn, & Pellegrini, 1995).

Technological advances change the ways in which young children experience picture storybooks; in addition to print versions, a growing number of picture storybooks have become avail-

able in digitized format on CD-ROM, DVD or video. In contrast to print versions children can access these digitized storybooks independent of adults as digitized storybooks include an oral rendition of text in addition to all the qualities of the print version such as pictures (Reinking, Labbo, & McKenna, 1997). For instance, the pages of the digitized picture storybook "Winnie the Witch" (Thomas & Gorky, 1996) resemble pages in the print version. They show a full screen picture with text. Unlike the print version the digitized version allows children to hear an oral rendition of the story text without adult mediation as often as they wish. Children can access the oral text by clicking on the mini picture of a witches' cauldron at the beginning of the printed text. In order to virtually turn the page they only need to click the corner of the screen.

Apart from spoken text, more elaborate digitized picture storybooks offer additional multimedia features like motion, music and sound effects allowing for precise coordination of visual and oral information (Calvert, Huston, Watkins, & Wright, 1982; de Jong & Bus, 2004; Neuman, 1997). The Winnie Witch CD-ROM includes two versions: a static version and a video version. The static version offers an oral rendition of text as a multimedia feature in addition to the pictures, comparable to a print version. In the video version of Winnie the Witch the pictures are similar to those in the print version but turned into a video by animating the characters and using zooms, pans and cuts. Instead of a picture of Winnie lying on the floor and looking angry, the video version shows how the witch stumbles over Wilbur, her cat, and lands on the floor while the text explains that she feels uncomfortable because she often falls over her black cat. Despite of the video additions, living storybooks on the one hand and films and cartoons on the other are not one and the same. In living storybooks text is the main source of information, unlike films and cartoons where a story is told by using visualization and dialogue. However, the video additions may be more instructive than the static pictures in print books, thus supporting learning from book encounters.

The video, music and sound effects in living storybooks may supply children with additional sources of information that act as mediators between child and story text (e.g., Calvert, Huston, Watkins, & Wright, 1982; Neuman, 1997) and enable the learner to fill gaps in (oral) text comprehension (Mayer & Moreno, 1998). These additions may be especially beneficial for children at the lower end of the language proficiency scale. As the language in storybooks is complex and not readily understood, young children with a limited vocabulary will experience many gaps in understanding the story text and may be unable to distract meaning from storybook reading without additional tools or mediators. In particular children from low-educated families and minorities enter school with far fewer language skills than their more affluent peers (Juel, 2006) probably because they lack stimulating linguistic experiences like book reading from an early age (Brooks-Gunn, Han, & Waldfogel, 2002).

Digitized storybooks that offer additional features like video, music and sound effects congruent with the story text may present information in unique ways and provide linguistically disadvantaged children with extra sources of information through which they can profit from book reading in a more enriched manner than simply the information provided by storybooks with static pictures (cf. Sharp et al., 1995). These additional features may be especially indispensable as intermediaries between child and story text when children come from low-educated ethnic minority families. These children have a formidable task of mastering a second language and experience large gaps in their understanding of the school language.

Video as Scaffold

Video in living storybooks may support story comprehension and language acquisition in a number of ways: they may help children to select relevant visual information, or may provide additional content or elicit more extensive processing. It is feasible that video, music and sound may provide children with an additional set of processing tools to understand the story and make inferences about story events. As illustrations offer numerous irrelevant details, filmic codes like zoom shots and other visual and auditory effects may draw attention to important visual information related to the story text. These features may thus act as a guide in selecting important content of images that relate to the narration thus limiting the overload of information (Calvert, Huston, Watkins, & Wright, 1982; Gibbons, Anderson, Smith, Field, & Fischer, 1986; Greenfield et al., 1996; James, 1999; Kamil, Intrator, & Kim, 2000). Being guided in this manner to attend to important story content, young children's comprehension of stories may go beyond a simple recounting of salient actions as young children are inclined to do (Gibbons et al., 1986). Their retellings may also include aspects that create coherence between story elements.

Multimedia additions like video, music and sound may help children to do what readers with good comprehension skills do spontaneously, namely visualizing the events described in a narration. For instance in the video version of Winnie the Witch when Winnie trips over Wilbur yet again, you see Winnie coming into the garden tripping over Wilbur, flying through the air and landing in a rosebush accompanied by upbeat music and matching sound effects. In the static version only the end result is visible, namely Winnie upside down in a rosebush with a bewildered Wilbur next to her. It is left to the reader to derive from the narration what happened prior to the scene depicted by the illustration.

The dual-coding model explains how video accompanying the narration can support extensive processing of the story language. Paivio (1986) proposed that information sources are coded in separate memory systems, one specializing in language and the other for spatial information and mental imagery. The model assumes that memorizing information encoded one way does not interfere with memorizing information encoded the other way and that the two memory systems can support each other. Information in one of the memory systems can activate information in the other and as visual information is more likely to be dual-coded than language, the abundance of visual information in video compared to static images may have an additive effect on recall of story language. Following this model, Dubois and Vial (2000) predicted that information processing is facilitated by multimodal presentations when the information given in the various modes is complementary. As living books allow a more precise coordination of visual and audio information than static books, a deeper processing of story content and story language is expected, resulting in improved story comprehension and language gains.

Video as Distracter

On the other hand, it is conceivable that film-like additions to a storybook may exert a negative influence on story understanding and language acquisition. Formal features like edits, cuts and zooms, typical of the medium of film, represent information in ways not readily understood and which children must learn to interpret (Salomon, 1979). Nevertheless, most young children today will have had ample experience with television and film and are likely to have learned to construe meaningful information from these codes (Robinson & Mackey, 2003).

A more consequential argument is that video may divert young children's attention from the narration. The rapidly changing images may be so mesmerizing that (spoken) text is ignored. Young children may have a tendency to look and not listen when they interact with living books. A visual superiority effect would imply retention of visual information of the story but not retention

of story language (Hayes & Birnbaum, 1980; Hayes, Chemelski, & Birnbaum, 1981). Gibbons, Anderson, Smith, Field, and Fischer (1986) found no evidence that visual input inhibited young children's processing of auditory information; they did however find an action effect. As actions are vividly depicted in pictures and especially in video, children may be more inclined to pay attention to these salient story events and less to information that is only presented orally: like reasons for actions.

EXPERIMENTS AT INNER-CITY SCHOOLS IN THE HAGUE

In order to explore effects of multimedia additions on storybooks for young linguistically disadvantaged children we performed a series of three experiments at inner-city schools in The Hague that were for 80%-90% populated by children from low-educated minority families. We tested effects of exposure to picture storybooks with video additions in a group of five year olds (N=165) from Moroccan and Turkish low-educated parents (Verhallen, Bus, & de Jong, 2006; Verhallen & Bus, 2008) who are at risk for developing reading problems due to a linguistic lag (Verhoeven, 2000). All children were lagging behind in linguistic development scoring at the lower end on a standardized Dutch language test. Children in the intervention groups heard the story with either static pictures or video. Children in the control groups either played with an interactive nonverbal computer game on four occasions or received no intervention.

Our aim was to study the effect of living books, when well designed and produced, on these young children's narrative comprehension and linguistic skills (Verhallen, Bus, & de Jong, 2006; Verhallen & Bus, 2008). We contrasted the outcomes of two versions of the same multimedia storybook; one version included static images and the other included a video-like presentation created with cinematic techniques such as zooms, pans, cuts, music, and sound effects. We used the CD-ROM Heksenspul [Winnie the Witch] as it allowed a comparison between a static digitized version with a video version of the same picture storybook, while the story text is identical in both versions. Winnie the Witch - a developmentally appropriate storybook - appeared to have a relatively high proportion of unknown words for our target group thereby making it less probable that the context of the spoken text could be used to derive the meaning of unfamiliar words (Swanborn & de Glopper, 1999).

A second reason for the experiments was to test effects of repeated encounters with the same story. To figure out the meaning of the unfamiliar vocabulary and grammatical structures in the story text and to memorize those, repetition may be indispensable (e.g., Sulzby, 1985). However, repetition may not always produce learning. Without sufficient information sources, children may no longer be inclined to invest mental effort in understanding the story text when the story is repeated again and again. In other words, we tested the hypothesis that repetition is not by definition profitable to young children, but could be only so long as that children continue to invest mental effort.

Following the argumentation that additional information sources make up for gaps in understanding the narration we expected living storybooks to have added value in groups of children scoring at the lower end of a standardized language test but not in more proficient groups. The third purpose of this series of studies was therefore to test outcomes of repeated encounters with living storybooks in groups that differ in language proficiency. We contrasted immigrant kindergarten children scoring below the 25th percentile of a standardized language test with children scoring about average.

Effects of Video on Children's Comprehension of Digitized Storybooks

We found no evidence that visual input inhibited young children's processing of language. Even children at the lower end of language proficiency, who are likely to experience serious gaps in understanding the narrative, did not ignore the story text. These results are comparable to findings reported by Gibbons et al. (1986).

Our results (Verhallen et al., 2006) and those of other research groups (Shamir, & Korat, in press) were quite the contrary. Adding extra information, like video, to an oral reading increased the story understanding of young linguistically disadvantaged children, more so than hearing the story accompanied by static pictures. Combining the spoken text with video, sound effects and music in the living storybook was an effective way to increase story understanding. These findings are in line with Paivio (1986) and Dubois and Vial (2000): adding video with music and sound effects to spoken text in a living storybook provides precise coordination of visual and audio information and allows deeper processing of story content, than the addition of static pictures to a story text.

When actions are highly salient and vividly visualized by video, they appear to be more memorable than when information must be inferred. Preceding the intervention all children recalled more action story elements than story elements that refer to causal and enabling relations between events. Their retellings did not include reasons for actions, like goals or states of minds of characters. After the intervention with only static pictures available to support the story text, children's retellings mainly consisted of a series of actions mostly leaving implied elements out of their retelling. Adding video, music and sound effects to the spoken text was exceptionally effective. After four repetitions children were more aware of the state of minds of characters as reasons for actions when they had heard the story with video additions; they not only mentioned in their retelling that Winnie stumbled over Wilbur for the umpteenth time, but also that she got upset and decided to do something about it (see Figure 1). As young children are better able to notice implied elements that create coherence in a story, their understanding of the story improves. These findings suggest that nonverbal symbols may assist children in forming a mental image of the story text, comparable to what good readers spontaneously do when they read a text (Glenberg & Langston, 1992).

Effects of Living Storybooks on Language Acquisition

Repeating a story, normally a successful way to enhance language learning, does not guarantee language acquisition in a group of young linguistically disadvantaged children. Children's language skills improved after repeated encounters with the video version but not after repeated encounters with the static version. This outcome suggests that children who heard the story repeatedly with added video, music and sound effects were better equipped to use contextual cues to derive the meaning of unknown words (Jenkins, Stein, & Wysocki, 1984; Nagy, Anderson, & Herman, 1987). Normally, when children encounter unknown words, the adult reading the book to the child will help by explaining the meaning of these words or by pointing at the illustrations. Reading a digitized storybook with video seemed to substitute for adult scaffolding. Likewise, children's knowledge of grammatical structures also improved as a result of repeated encounters with the living version of the digitized storybook; hearing the story several times with static pictures did not contribute significantly to learning new phrases from the story text.

Amount of Invested Mental Effort during Repeated Readings of Living Storybooks

Normally, in shared readings of print books, an adult monitors and if necessary scaffolds the child's emerging comprehension by drawing attention to important story content and explaining crucial language elements, or connecting novel information with the familiar. In collaboration with an adult, the child learns to identify the mean-

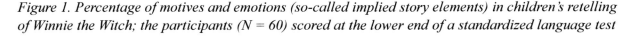

Figure 1. Percentage of motives and emotions (so-called implied story elements) in children's retelling of Winnie the Witch; the participants (N = 60) scored at the lower end of a standardized language test

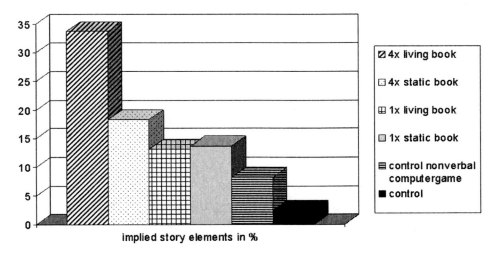

Figure 2. Mean Z-scores on vocabulary growth in experiment 1 (N = 60) and 2 (N = 46)

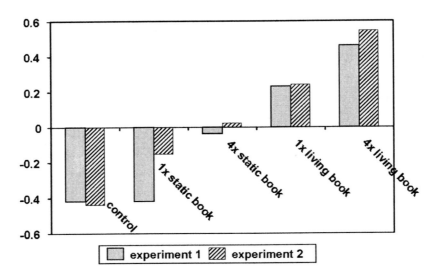

ing of the text and transforms the information in the text into a meaningful and coherent mental representation. Interaction with adults may raise children's willingness to continue their attempts to negotiate meaning from the story text. Encounters with living storybooks occur mostly without an adult present to keep children interested. As television and computers are mainly used at home and are associated with leisure activities, children may perceive both media as "easy" and invest little effort when they "read" a living storybook (Salomon, 1984).

However, in line with the findings that living books support learning, children may not respond to the medium per se but more to the perceived helpfulness of additional information sources when attempting to comprehend the story. When interacting with a living book, children may find the additional information sources supportive of their story understanding and invest mental effort in processing the story, even without an adult. If digitized storybooks include an oral rendition of text as the only addition in the digitized version, children may judge the task as too demanding and become unengaged and intellectually passive. Findings with televised stories support these hypotheses: When the story is comprehensible

for children, they stay attentive and process the story content; if, on the other hand, the story is too difficult or too easy, children cease to pay visual attention and their understanding does not improve (Anderson & Lorch, 1983; Huston & Wright, 1983).

In line with this argumentation, we expect that the amount of mental effort that children are willing to invest in independent encounters with stories is a function of qualities of the digitized storybook. Additional information provided by living books may sustain mental effort, because children gain a deeper understanding of the story line with every repetition of the story (Phillips & McNaughton, 1990). Missing support in understanding the story, children may no longer be inclined to invest mental effort to understand the story text when the story is repeated. When "reading" the story with only static pictures, linguistically disadvantaged children may be willing to invest mental effort during the first session, but with every repetition the amount of invested effort may decrease as too little support is experienced. In other words, we expected that repetition is profitable in a group of linguistically disadvantaged children provided the redundancy of information is high.

Figure 3. Number of skin conductance responses: An indicator of the amount of invested mental effort during repeated storybook readings

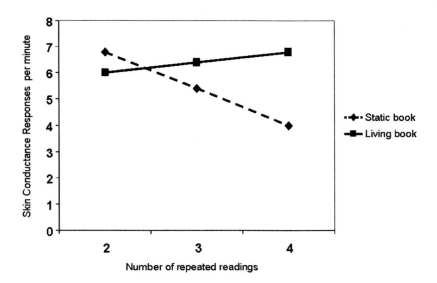

The invested mental effort was found to vary systematically over sessions as a result of the qualities of the digitized picture storybook (Verhallen & Bus, 2008). In this study, skin conductance responses were assessed as an indicator of mental effort invested in story comprehension (Reinking, 1994). The number of skin conductance responses may be one of the best indicators for mental effort without interfering with the natural viewing process (e.g., Dawson, Schell & Filion, 1990; Sundar & Kalyanaraman, 2004; Pecchinenda & Smith, 1996). For instance, previous studies have shown that solving mental arithmetic problems or anagrams increases the number of skin conductance responses (Dawson, Schell, & Filion, 2000; Jennings, 1986; Pecchinenda & Smith, 1996) indicating that during exacting work an effortful allocation of mental resources takes place (Jennings, 1986).

All children invested mental effort in processing a digitized storybook. Compared to the number of skin conductance responses at rest, skin conductance responses increased substantially when children were involved in listening to a storybook on the computer by themselves. However, children responded differently to repeated encounters with living books with video additions compared with digitized storybooks with static pictures. The number of skin conductance responses remained stable over sessions when children "read" the living book with video, music and sound effects, contrary to the children who were assigned to the condition with the static digitized story with static pictures and an oral rendition of text as the only addition. In the latter group, the rate of skin conductance responses statistically significantly declined over sessions, indicating that low appraisals of coping potential resulted in selective disengagement from the task as appeared from reduced skin conductance activity. In sum, kindergarten children invested more mental effort in processing the living book with video additions than in processing the static version of the same book. Apparently learning from storybook encounters is conditional upon the amount of effort that children are willing to invest in processing materials during repeated exposures (Salomon & Leigh, 1984).

The Role of Prior Knowledge

The extent to which children are able to profit from encounters with living books may be influenced by differences in language proficiency. Prior knowledge of words and phrases can provide children with an additional context to derive the meaning of new story language. Robbins and Ehri (1994) found that 6-year-old children with larger initial vocabularies gained more new word meanings while listening to an adult reading a storybook than children with small initial vocabularies. Differences in growth after interventions due to initial language ability of young children were also found by Penno, Wilkinson, and Moore (2002), who demonstrated that all children gained from the intervention but higher language ability children made greater vocabulary gains than lower ability children.

These findings may mean that when children interact with digitized storybooks and no adult is present to make the story and the text comprehensible during reading, initial differences in vocabulary knowledge of words and phrases may affect learning from storybook reading. As the experiments presented above suggest, living books provide linguistically disadvantaged children with extra tools and mediators that support story understanding and memory of linguistic information (de Jong & Bus, 2004; Shamir, & Korat, 2008; Sharp, Bransford, Goldman, Risko, Kinzer, & Vye, 1995, Verhallen et al., 2006). It seems reasonable to hypothesize that the beneficial effects of video additions are less pronounced as young children are more linguistically advanced. More advanced children may not need an additional set of processing tools as their background knowledge enables them to construct mental models of the story events without additional information sources (Glenberg, & Langston, 1992; Sharp et al., 1995). However, when children are linguistically disadvantaged, additional information sources and tools may be essential and without those, children are not likely

to profit from encounters with digitized storybooks. Since the language in storybooks is rather complex they may experience many gaps in their understanding of the story language and lack the necessary background knowledge to benefit from story encounters. On the other hand, the synergy of information sources in living books may help children to understand the story line and derive the meaning of unknown words by effectively using contextual cues (Neuman, 1997).

To test whether or not benefiting from additional video does indeed depend on children's prior knowledge, we replicated the Winnie the Witch experiment in a linguistically more advanced sample. The children came from families similar to those of the children in the previous experiments (low-educated minorities) but were more proficient in Dutch than the children in our first experiments. In contrast to the above-mentioned samples that scored below the 25th percentile on a standardized language test, this new sample scored about average (Verhallen & Bus, 2008). The outcomes support the theory that not all children need a synergy of information sources to benefit from independent encounters with a digitized picture storybook. Similar to the previous samples, the children in this new sample needed repeated encounters to learn new language. But unlike the linguistically disadvantaged samples, this more advanced sample of kindergarten children profited about equally from independent encounters with static and living picture storybooks on the computer. Children who had heard the story four times with static pictures learned about as many words as children who heard the story enriched with additional information sources. Pretest scores confirm that this linguistically more advanced group encountered a substantial number of unfamiliar words and grammatical structures in the Winnie the Witch story. In spite of this, they were able to figure out the meaning of unknown vocabulary and grammatical structures without the extra information in living books. Apparently static illustrations and text were sufficient to make

Figure 4. *Differential effects of language proficiency on vocabulary growth according to Posttest Scores (N = 135); review of outcomes for all children participating in the intervention conditions of the three experiments*

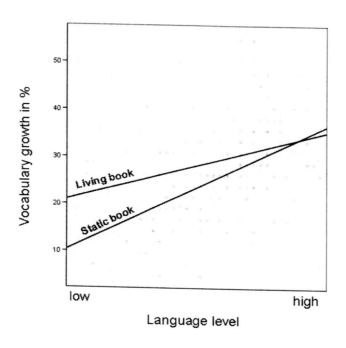

CONCLUSION

Digitized storybooks provide educators with new ways of encouraging young children to "read" storybooks and get in touch with the complex language in written texts. The additional options like video with accompanying sound effects and music provide extra sources of information that may act as mediators between child and story text.

We found that "reading" a living book was especially beneficial for children at the lower end of the language proficiency scale. After hearing the story with added video, music and sound effects, young immigrant children, learning a second language, could retell more of the story than children hearing the story accompanied by static pictures. After encounters with the living storybook, children not only retold highly salient actions, but they were more aware of the state of minds of characters as reasons for actions. The added information sources in the living books provided children with a context from which to derive the meaning of unknown words and phrases: children's language skills improved after repeated encounters with the living storybook but not significantly after repeated encounters with the static version of the same story.

Reading the same book repeatedly, a common practice in shared readings of print storybooks (Sénéchal, LeFevre, Hudson, & Lawson, 1996), allows children to gain a more complete understanding of the story and the meaning of unfamiliar words. However, when no adult is present to keep children interested and focused on the story, as happens with digitized storybooks, children may

good guesses at the meaning of unknown words and phrases. They did not need extra information to compensate for gaps in understanding the narration.

soon cease to invest effort to understand the story when they encounter numerous unknown words and phrases. "Reading" a story independently, young children were more inclined to continue investing mental effort in processing the living book than in the static version of the same picture storybook. They may experience the extra information sources in living books as scaffolds in their attempt to understand the story.

For young linguistically disadvantaged children, the additional information and tools in digitized storybooks were essential as the language in storybooks is complex. More advanced children profited about equally from encounters with digitized static and living storybooks. Repeating a story was essential even in this more advanced group but children who had heard the story four times while looking at static pictures learned as many words as children who were exposed to the living storybook enriched with additional information sources.

Taking into account our findings so far, we have high hopes for digitized libraries with a broad range of living storybooks for the very young. As children can access digitized storybooks independently without the help of an adult, more frequent exposure to storybooks is made possible than can ever be realized through adult-child book sharing. We observed that in Dutch preschool and kindergarten classrooms it is more common to utilize static than living onscreen versions of picture storybooks. Our studies showed the need for living books with additional features to achieve an optimum effect of independent encounters with onscreen storybooks especially for the linguistically "poor." For a group with a linguistic lag it is especially important that onscreen storybooks have additional qualities beyond those of print books and include additional information sources like video, music and sound. The information provided by living books, more so than information provided by static storybooks, makes linguistically disadvantaged children feel capable of improving their understanding of the story including the story text.

FUTURE RESEARCH DIRECTIONS

We assume that the exact co-ordination of story text and visual information in the living storybook makes a story more comprehensible which in turn influences children's appraisal of coping options and thereby the amount of invested mental effort in processing the story. Future research, using eye fixations as a measure, would allow a test of this assumption.

REFERENCES

Anderson, D. R., & Lorch, E. P. (1983). Looking at television action or reaction? In J. Bryant & D. R. Anderson (Eds.), *Children's understanding of television: Research on attention and comprehension* (pp. 1-33). New York: Academic Press.

Blok, H. (1999). Reading to young children in educational settings: A meta-analysis of recent research. *Language Learning, 49*, 343-371.

Brooks-Gunn, J., Han, W.-J., & Waldfogel, J. (2002). Maternal employment and child cognitive outcomes in the first three years of life: The NICHD study of early child care. *Child Development, 73*, 1052-1072.

Bus, A.G. (2001). Early book reading in the family: A route to literacy. In: S. Neuman & D. Dickinson (Eds.), *Handbook on Research in Early Literacy* (pp.179-191). New York: Guilford Publications.

Bus, A.G., Van IJzendoorn, M.H., & Pellegrini, A.D. (1995). Storybook reading makes for success in learning to read. A meta-analysis on intergenerational transmission of literacy. *Review of Educational Research, 65*, 1-21.

Calvert, S. L., Huston, A. C., Watkins, B. A., & Wright, J. C. (1982). The relation between selective attention to television forms and children's comprehension of content. *Child Development, 53*, 601-610.

CBS, Centraal Bureau voor de Statistiek [Statistics Netherlands] (2007).Retrieved November 2007 from http://www.cbs.nl/nl-NL/default.htm

Close, R. (2004). *Television and language development in the early years: A review of the literature.* London: National Literacy Trust.

Dawson, M. D., Schell, A. M., & Filion, D. L. (1990). In J. T. Cacioppo & L. G. Tassinary (Eds.), *Principles of psychophysiology: Physical, social and inferential elements* (pp. 295-324). New York: Cambridge University Press.

Dawson, M. D., Schell, A. M., & Filion, D. L. (2000). The electrodermal system. In J.T. Cacioppo, L. G. Tassinary, & G. G. Berntson (Eds.), *Handbook of Psychophysiology* (pp. 200-223). Cambridge: Cambridge University Press.

De Jong, M. T., & Bus, A. G. (2004). The efficacy of electronic books in fostering kindergarten children's emergent story understanding. *Reading Research Quarterly, 39*, 378-393.

Detenber, B.H. and Reeves, B. (1996). A bio-informational theory of emotion: Motion and image size effects on viewers. *Journal of Communication, 46*, 66-84.

Dubois, M., & Vial, I. (2000). Multimedia design: The effects of relating multimodal information. *Journal of Computer Assisted Learning, 16*, 157-165.

Fitzgerald, J., Spiegel, D., & Cunningham, J. (1991). The relationship between parental literacy level and perceptions of emergent literacy. *Journal of Reading Behavior, 23*, 191–214.

Frijters, J. C., Barron, R. W., & Brunello, M. (2000). Direct or mediated influences of home literacy and literacy interest on prereaders' oral vocabulary and early written language skill. *Journal of Educational Psychology, 92*, 466-477.

Gibbons, J., Anderson, D. R., Smith, R., Field, D. E., & Fischer, C. (1986). Young children's recall and reconstruction of audio and audiovisual narratives. *Child Development, 57*, 1014-1023.

Glenberg, A. M., & Langston, W. E. (1992). Comprehension of illustrated text: Pictures help to build mental models. *Journal of Memory and Language, 31*, 129-151.

Greenfield, P. M., Camaioni, L., Ercolani, P., Weiss, L., Lauber, B. A., & Perucchini, P. (1996). Cognitive socialization by computer games in two cultures: Inductive discovery or mastery of an iconic code? In I. E. Sigel (Series Ed.), P. M. Greenfield, & R. R. Cocking (Vol. Eds.), *Advances, in applied developmental psychology: Vol.11. Interacting with video* (pp. 141-167). Norwood, NJ: Ablex.

Hayes, D. S., & Birnbaum, D. W. (1980). Preschoolers' retention of televised events: Is a picture worth a thousand words? *Developmental Psychology, 16*, 410-416.

Hayes, D. S., Chemelski, B. E., & Birnbaum, D. W. (1981). Young children's incidental and intentional retention of televised events. *Developmental Psychology, 17*, 230-232.

Huston, A., & Wright, J. (1983). Children's processing of television: The informative functions of formal features. In J. Bryant & D. R. Anderson (Eds.), *Children's understanding of television: Research on attention and comprehension* (pp. 35-68). New York: Academic Press.

James, R. (1999). Navigating CD-ROMs: An exploration of children reading interactive narratives. *Children's Literature in Education, 30*, 47-63.

Jenkins, J. R., Stein, M. L., & Wysocki, K. (1984). Learning vocabulary through reading. *American Educational Research Journal, 21*, 767–787.

Jennings, J. R. (1986). Bodily changes during attending. In M. G. H. Coles, E. Donchin, & S. W. Porges (Eds.), *Psychophysiology: Systems, processes, and applications*, pp. 268-89. New York: Guilford.

Juel, C. (2006). The impact of early school experiences on initial reading. In: D.K. Dickinson & S.B. Neuman (Eds.), *Handbook of Early Literacy Research, 2*, 410-426. New York: The Guilford Press.

Kamil, M. L., Intrator, S. M., & Kim, H. S. (2000). The effects of other technologies on literacy and literacy learning. In M. L. Kamil, P. B. Mosenthal, P. D. Pearson, & R. Barr (Eds.), *Handbook of Reading Research, 3*, 771-788. Mahwah, NJ: Lawrence Erlbaum.

Mayer, R.E., & Moreno, R. (1998). A split-attention effect in multimedia learning: Evidence for dual processing systems in working memory. *Journal of Educational Psychology, 90*, 312-320.

Nagy, W., Anderson, R. and Herman, P. (1987). Learning Word Meanings from Context during Normal Reading', *American Educational Research Journal, 24*, 237-70.

Neuman, S. B. (1997). Television as a learning environment: A theory of synergy. In J. Flood, S. Brice Heath & D. Lapp (Eds.), *Handbook of research on teaching literacy through the communicative and visual arts* (pp.15-30). New York: Simon & Schuster.

Paivio, A. (1986). *Mental representations: A dual coding approach*. Oxford: Oxford University Press.

Pecchinenda, A., Smith, C.A., (1996). The affective significance of skin conductance activity during a difficult problem-solving task. *Cognition and Emotion, 10*, 481–503.

Penno J. F., Wilkinson I. A. G., Moore D. W. (2002). Vocabulary acquisition from teacher explanation and repeated listening to stories: Do they overcome the Matthew effect? *Journal of Educational Psychology, 94*, 23–33.

Phillips, G., & McNaughton, S. (1990). The practice of storybook reading to preschool children in mainstream New Zealand families. *Reading Research Quarterly, 25*, 196-212.

Prensky, M. (2001). Digital Natives, Digital Immigrants. *On the Horizon. 9*(5), 1-15.

Reinking, D. (1994). *Electronic literacy.* Perspectives in Reading Research (4) Athens, GA: National Reading Research Center.

Reinking, D., Labbo, L., & McKenna, M. (1997). Navigating the changing landscape of literacy: Current theory and research in computer-based reading and writing. In J. Flood, S.B. Heath, & D. Lapp (Eds.), *Handbook of research on teaching literacy through the communicative and visual arts* (pp. 77-92). New York: Macmillan Library Reference.

Robbins, C., & Ehri, L. (1994). Reading storybooks to kindergartners helps them learn new vocabulary words. *Journal of Educational Psychology, 86*(1), 54-64.

Robinson, M., & Mackey, M. (2003). Film and television. In N. Hall, J. Larson & J. Marsh (Eds.), *Handbook of early childhood literacy* (pp. 126-141). London: Sage.

Salomon, G. (1979). *Interaction of media, cognition and learning*. San Francisco: Jossey-Bass.

Salomon, G. (1984). Television is "easy" and print is "tough": The differential investment of mental effort as a function of perceptions and attributions. *Journal of Educational Psychology, 76*, 647–658.

Salomon, G., & Leigh, T. (1984). Predispositions about learning from print and television. *Journal of Communication, 34*, 119–135.

Sénéchal, M., & LeFevre, J. (2002). Parental involvement in the development of children's reading skill: A five-year longitudinal study. *Child Development, 73*, 445–460.

Sénéchal, M., LeFevre, J., Hudson, E., & Lawson, E.P. (1996). Knowledge of storybooks as a predictor of young children's vocabulary. *Journal of Educational Psychology, 88*, 520-536.

Sénéchal, M., LeFevre, J., Thomas, E. M., & Daley, K. E. (1998). Differential effects of home literacy experiences on the development of oral and written language. *Reading Research Quarterly, 33*, 96-116.

Shamir, A., & Korat, O. (in press). The educational electronic book as a tool for supporting children's emergent literacy. In Adriana G. Bus & Susan B. Neuman (Eds.), *Multimedia and literacy development: Improving achievement for young learners*. London: Routledge.

Sharp, D. L. M., Bransford, J. D., Goldman, S. R., Risko, V. J., Kinzer, C. K., & Vye, N. J. (1995). Dynamic visual support for story comprehension and mental model building by young, at-risk children. *Educational Technology Research and Development, 43*, 25-40.

Sulzby, E. (1985). Children's emergent reading of favorite storybooks: A developmental study. *Reading Research Quarterly, 20*, 458-481.

Sundar, S. S., & Kalyanaraman, S. (2004). Arousal, memory, and impression-formation effects of animation speed in Web advertising. *Journal of Advertising, 33*(1), 7-17.

Swanborn, M. S. L., & de Glopper, K. (1999). Incidental word learning while reading: A meta-analysis. *Review of Educational Research, 69*, 261-285.

Thomas, V., & Gorky, P. (1996). *Heksenspul met Hennie de Heks en de Kat Helmer* [Winnie Witch] [CD-ROM]. Nieuwegein, The Netherlands: Bombilla.

Verhallen, M.J.A.J., & Bus, A.G. (2008). Exploring the relationship between repeated readings of a storybook, attentional arousal, and vocabulary learning in young children at-risk. Manuscript submitted for publication.

Verhallen, M.J.A.J., Bus, A.G., & de Jong, M.T. (2006). The promise of multimedia stories for kindergarten children at risk. *Journal of Educational Psychology, 98*, 410-419.

Verhoeven, L. (2000). Components in early second language reading and spelling. *Scientific Studies of Reading, 4*(4), 313–330.

ADDITIONAL READINGS

Bus, A., de Jong, M., & Verhallen, M. (2006). CD-ROM talking books: A way to enhance early literacy? In M. C. McKenna, L. D. Labbo, R. D. Kieffer, & D. Reinking (Eds.), *International handbook of literacy and technology* (Vol. 2, pp. 129-139). Mahwah, New Jersey: Lawrence Erlbaum Associates.

Bus, A., de Jong, M., & Verhallen, M. (in press). How multimedia representations contribute to a literate mind for second language learners. In A. G. Bus & S. B. Neuman (Eds.), *Multimedia and literacy development: Improving achievement for young learners*. London: Routledge.

de Jong, M.T., & Bus, A.G. (2002). Quality of book-reading matters for emergent readers: An experiment with the same book in a regular or electronic format. *Journal of Educational Psychology, 94*, 145-155.

de Jong, M.T., & Bus, A.G. (2003). How well suited are electronic books to supporting literacy? *Journal of Early Childhood Literacy, 3*, 147-164.

Mol, S. E., Bus, A. G., De Jong, M. T., & Smeets, D. J. H. (2008). Added value of dialogic parent-child book readings: A Meta-Analysis. *Early Education and Development, 19*, 7-26.

Chapter XVIII
Emergence of Analogies in Collaboratively Conducted Computer Simulations

Wolff-Michael Roth
University of Victoria, Canada

ABSTRACT

To learn by means of analogies, students have to see surface and deep structures in both source and target domains. Educators generally assume that students, presented with images, texts, video, or demonstrations, see what the curriculum designer intends them to see, that is, pick out and integrate information into their existing understanding. However, there is evidence that students do not see what they are supposed to see, which precisely inhibits them to learn what they are supposed to learn. In this extended case study, which exemplifies a successful multimedia application, 3 classroom episodes are used (a) to show how students in an advanced physics course do not see relevant information on the computer monitor; (b) to exemplify teaching strategies designed to allow relevant structures to become salient in students' perception, allowing them to generate analogies and thereby learn; and (c) to exemplify how a teacher might assist students in bridging from the multimedia context to the real world.

INTRODUCTION

Multimedia have shown to increase learning opportunities, both in face-to-face and distant, asynchronous collaborative settings (e.g., Hwang, Wang, & Sharples, 2007; Shih, Wang, Chang, Kao, & Hamilton, 2007). However, few researchers in educational multimedia research ask themselves whether students actually perceive what designers intend them to see. Although it was an innovation in the 1960s (Hanson, 1965), it now is a platitude to state that all observation is theory laden. Yet most educators still have not drawn the radical consequences that derive from this statement.

Thus, although many science educators (especially those with a constructivist penchant), for example, will claim that they take into account students' current views and understandings, they nevertheless use demonstrations and modeling software with the assumption that students will see science concepts in actions. Taking the theory-laden nature of observation seriously means that we expect students to observe phenomena that are very different from what scientists observe, so that precisely that which is scientific in some demonstration is *not* available to students who bring their everyday, common sense, frequently Aristotelian understanding to bear on observational tasks. Yet we also know that (at least some) students can and do eventually see certain events (demonstrations, laboratory experiments) in scientific ways. A key question for instructional designers must be what the roles of teachers and computing technology may be in mediating students' access to phenomena such that their everyday ways of seeing them change to making scientific observations. In other words, because seeing and perceiving are central to any form of cognition, because these processes provide the materials that cognitive agents work with, I am interested in understanding the role teachers and computing technology might be in the transformation of everyday to scientific ways of seeing, and, simultaneously, in the transformation of everyday into scientific ways of understanding certain phenomena. The purpose of this chapter is to show how through the use of multimedia, students can be stimulated into seeing the crucial aspects of some phenomenon that allows them to learn by means of analogies: this involves as a crucial element the fact that students need to identify deep structures in their common sense ways of seeing and understanding that also are valid in the scientific ways of seeing and understanding. The learning context that I use to exemplify my point is a collaborative setting where students and teacher use computer-based simulations of physical phenomena. Of special interest to this research are student–teacher transactions and

how these mediate student perception, teacher assessment, and teacher intervention.

BACKGROUND

In this study, I report and analyze ongoing class-room conversations that occur over and about computer simulations, teacher-student transactions, and the emergence of productive analogies from teacher-student-computer transactions. Although the students begin with seeing physical phenomena (produced by a simulation on a computer monitor) in non-scientific ways, they eventually come to see them, as a result of the particular configuration, to see them in scientific ways. They do so by producing analogies that constitute bridges to scientific ways of seeing and understanding. Analogies, however, constitute double-edged swords, as they require and are based on the identification of common structures in some source (base) domain and the target (scientific) domain. But the second domain precisely is unknown to students. In this section, I briefly

Analogical Learning

Analogies have shown to be powerful tools for learning in science (Duit, 1991) or to provide cognitive support for learning in mathematics classrooms (Richland, Zur, & Holyoak, 2007). An analogy requires aspects of a source domain to be transferred (and likened) to a target domain (Gentner, 1989). Learning occurs as students become aware of the similarities in the two domains; this awareness can be used productively in the mutual elaboration of both source and target domains. For this to occur, however, students need to recognize deep structures; researchers have come to understand that the failure to learn through analogies lies in the fact that students do not perceive the deep structures in the two domains (Duit, Roth, Komorek, & Wilbers, 2001). That is, as these authors point out, analogical learning presents a situation "between Scylla and Charybdis," that is, a situation between two dangers often denoted in the phrase "between a rock and a hard place." From teacher and student perspectives, the contexts of particular analogies differ, leading different participants to see differently and to evolve different observation sentences. Because analogical relations are build on the basis of the similarity of observations and observation sentences in two domains, which here are those of common sense and science, and because the number of observation sentences for any given phenomenon is infinite, the evolution of specific analogical relations has to be seen as an accomplishment rather than an unproblematic matter of course. There is an assumption that students tend to get lost in the outward appearances of the phenomena they look at and therefore fail to establish the analogical link that requires bridging of the deep structures. But there is more to seeing: evidence shows that without the theory that they are supposed to learn, students do not even perceive the surface aspects crucial to learning (Roth, 2006). The visibility of science in worldly phenomenon therefore is a form of ideology, which philosophers have articulated as the view in which the mind *mirrors* the natural world *as it really is*.

The Ideology of Seeing

"*Now* I see!" and "I see your point" are familiar English expressions that not only indicate to the listener that the speaker sees something, here unspecified, but also that the speaker understands. Seeing not only is an analogy in everyday discourse for knowing and understanding but also has been the fundamental way in which scientists have understood how the mind and philosophy work (Rorty, 1979). If this view were true, science teaching would be much easier than it turns out to be: students of all ages would simply look at the world and see it in scientific ways. The fact that there is a cultural-historical evolution of scientific

ways of seeing the world already should suggest to us seeing the world consistent with today's science is based not on a mirror effect but on a long and arduous cultural-historical achievement, which individuals in their ontogenetic development have to reproduce.

Educators all too often assume that students are presented with *information* when texts, images, artifacts, life demonstrations, or videos are made available to them. Thus, science professors use demonstrations and teachers ask their students to use the Internet to get this or that information. But is it warranted to assume that such exposure presents students with the desired information? Information theorists have shown that the sender and receiver have to be tuned in the same way, coding and decoding signs in the same ways, for information to get from one place to another (Shannon & Weaver, 1949). Are students and teachers tuned in the same way? There are theoretical and empirical grounds based on which we ought to take a cautionary stance responding to this question: everyday and scientific ways of knowing are different. Students, who do not know, who do not have a theory, and who employ (naïve) alternative theories, see something different than the very thing that educators need them to see in support of the new (correct) theory they are to learn (e.g., Roth, 2006). Students are caught in a quandary where they are asked to see something that they cannot see, because it requires them to know the very theory that the lesson is designed to teach them.

Second, a number of empirical studies have shown that students do not see what they are expected and need to see in a demonstration to learn the theory subsequently exposed and articulated by the teacher (Roth, McRobbie, Lucas, & Boutonné, 1997). More so, even experienced scientists confronted with unfamiliar graphs culled from undergraduate textbooks in their own discipline frequently do not see what they need to see to provide a correct interpretation, that is, one that the course instructors of first-year courses would expect them to (Roth, 2003). Such findings show that educators need to be more cautious with their assumption that students have received information and they have to begin to ask how to ascertain the nature of what students actually rather than supposedly see and the information they get, for example, from the displays on computer monitors. But there are possibilities that arise for teaching from the fact that students themselves see things differently; and computer tools provide possibilities for teachers to vary the displays in ways that provoke individual students to change what they see and to do so in ways that differ between students. Collaborative learning in computer supported learning environments offer particular opportunities for instructional designers and teachers.

Collaborative Learning

When people collaborate groups, they often articulate seeing different things—not unlike the frequently observed wide gaps that exist between the testimonies provided by different court witnesses. This possibility of different perceptions is actively exploited in collaborative learning environments (such a CSCL), as the students come to face different ways of seeing within and between groups, which allows them to grabble with the nature and source of the differences. The relevant discussions allow them working toward understanding, which sociocultural and cultural-historical theories of learning articulated first to occur at the interpsychological (social) level and subsequently at the intrapsychological (personal) level (Vygotsky, 1986). But for a variety of reasons, including the operation of mirror neurons in perception (Rizzolatti, Fadiga, Fogassi, & Gallese, 1997) and social cognition (Gallese, 2003), we now need to understand the interpsychological and intrapsychological dimensions to occur and emerge simultaneously. This provides an explication for the fact that in computer clubs, youths developed knowledge that far exceeded what any

individual initially knew, even in the absence of a teacher (Collins, Brown, & Newman, 1989). Although such potential exists when students in their school science classes work in collaborative groups, we would be over-extending the findings of these researchers if we were to assume that students learn the *specific content* that the curriculum prescribes. Here, therefore, teachers play an important role as an additional mediational component of the learning environment, who, while not determine, can facilitate the emergence of specific subject matter knowledge.

In this section of the paper, I describe the naturalistic **case study** designed to investigate knowing and learning in a real classroom setting where students, among many other forms of engagement, also used a computer simulation tool—Interactive Physics—to learn about Newtonian motion. I begin by articulating the research design before reporting some central findings, which are illustrated with exemplary materials: (a) the experiential and interpretive flexibility of phenomena in multimedia environments which leads to the fact that students *do not see* what the multimedia environment was designed to show them; (b) the teacher-mediated processes by means of which students actually come to see what the multimedia environment was design for letting them see; and (c) the teacher-mediated processes by means of which students come to link the multimedia content to their understanding of the real world.

Research Design

In three sections of an advanced physics course for twelfth graders, groups of students were videotaped while completing a series of tasks during a four-week period that began with explorations of forces on the motion of objects and ended with the design of games for younger students. (This task design was based on research in learning with computers that had shown significant motivational and learning effects when students *designed for* same-age and younger peers to teach them something, Kafai, 1994.) The methods used here are those standard in cognitive anthropology (e.g., Hutchins, 1995) and applied linguistics (Goodwin, 2000).

Setting and participants. The study was conducted in a private, British-style college-preparatory, co-educational school in Canada. The students generally were from well-to-do families, though students from lower income families attended, too, having received general or sports scholarships. Though predominantly white, students came from a range of countries (Hong Kong, Korea, Germany, Caribbean) and cultures (Asian, Hispanic, African [American]). The achievement levels were comparable to the local public schools. The students ($N = 47$) were enrolled in an advance-level physics course focusing on qualitative understandings of concepts. The course was designed following principles of social constructivism, focusing primarily on the development and evolution of physics as a form of special purpose language. For the purposes of this chapter, I exemplify the findings from the study with the transactions involving one of the three groups of students, including two males (Glen, Ryan) and one female (Elizabeth) and their teacher. This group was chosen for exemplifying the general findings, because the three students in this group were typical of the school population in that they all aspired to go—and since have gone—to college, though not into the sciences, opting instead for more lucrative careers in business and law.

Task environment. Interactive Physics is a computer-based Newtonian microworld that allows users to conduct motion-related experiments; its interface layers worldly objects (such as a circle [ball]) and physical representations (vectors) (Figure 1a). Observables such as force, velocity or acceleration can be made visible as vectors or represented via instruments such as strip chart recorders and digital and analog meters; a range of tools was arranged on the left-hand side of the screen (Figure 1a).

All student activities, especially those in the early parts of the curriculum included, at a minimum, one circular object. A force (full arrow [Figure 1b]) could be attached to this object by highlighting and moving it with the mouse. The object's velocity (students could modify its initial value by highlighting the object, "grabbing" the tip of the vector, and manipulating its magnitude and direction) was always displayed as a vector (line arrow [Figure 1b]). Students were asked to find out more about the microworld, especially the meaning of the arrows. The denotations "«force»" and "«velocity»" are used here as convenient way to denote force and velocity vectors whatever the students' current way of calling them (across the three classes and even within individual groups, there were up to 15 names used for the same arrows).

Figure 1a. Interface of Interactive Physics and typical task configuration. b. Magnified image of the situation, including circular (worldly) object and physics representations of force (upward, full arrow) and velocity (narrow arrow pointing toward 5 o'clock).

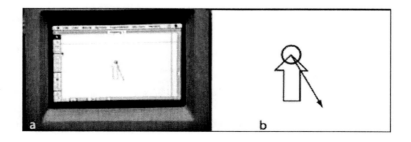

Cognitive task analysis. Physicists articulate the relationship between the net force $\underline{F}$ acting on an object and its velocity $\underline{v}$ in the form of

$$\underline{v}(t) = \frac{F}{m}t + \underline{v}(t = 0) \qquad (1)$$

where m is the mass of the object, *t* the amount of time that the force has acted upon the object, and $\underline{v}(t=0)$ the velocity at the moment that the force has begun to act. The underbar denotes the vector nature of velocity and force, meaning that these quantities have both magnitude and direction. Thus, in considering the effect of the force on the present velocity, the relative directions of the two has to be taken into account. If, for example, the direction of force is opposite to the direction of velocity, the speed (i.e., magnitude of velocity) of the object decreases; if the two vectors point into the same direction, the speed of the object (i.e., magnitude of velocity) increases. In Interactive Physics, the vector nature of velocity and force is implemented by means of arrows, which both have magnitude and direction. In the situation depicted in Figure 1, the object would begin moving in the direction of 5 o'clock but, accelerated by the upward pointing force, change its direction and eventually increase its speed in upward direction until, in the limit, it moves in the same direction as the force, that is, straight upward (12 o'clock).

For students to learn the relationship between the two variables, and therefore, to learn the canonical form of physics, they need to perceive both changes in direction *and* magnitude of the velocity vector (arrow). To aid students in seeing these changes, Interactive Physics was designed to display the position and velocity vector at equal time intervals such as if flash photography were used. Despite this fact, the experience in this and other studies using similar software to mediate cognitive communication (e.g., Roschelle, 1996) shows that students frequently precisely do *not* see what they need to see to produce observation sentences consistent with standard physics.

Data and analyses. Conversations of three randomly selected student groups over and about the Interactive Physics tasks were recorded during four one-hour periods separated

Figure 2. In this reproduction of the display PRAAT provides to the user, we can see the sound wave for the left and right audio channels (top), the speech intensity in decibels (continuous line from left to the right), and pitch in Hertz (interrupted line). Below the display, I placed the transcription of what can heard as being said including the pauses.

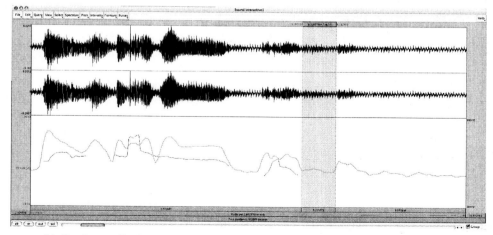

H O : L :: B A : B E E : (0.17) y e s : (0.22) object

by two-week intervals yielding a total of 12 hours of videotapes. Although the students had self-selected into groups, all groups were mixed in terms of achievement levels. The video was digitized and completely transcribed, including pauses, overlaps, and images of relevant screen displays. The freely downloadable, multi-platform software package PRAAT (www.praat.org) was used in the transcriptions to measure pauses to one-hundreds of a second and to identify special features of the soundtrack noted in the transcript, such as the movement of pitch toward the end of utterances (which allows listeners to hear an utterance as statement, question, interjection etc.), (relative) speech volume and intensity (allowing participants and analysts to hear an utterance as emphasized, self-talk, or to be shared production), and speech rate (allowing listeners to hear something as not precisely pertaining to the topic but mediating it). Figure 2 shows a typical display of PRAAT, featuring the sound wave for the left and right channel of the audio track (top), the speech intensity (continuous line from left to right), and the pitch (line is interrupted because the software could not extract consistent estimates for pitch from the sound track). Below the display, I placed the first turn of the transcript in Episode 1 and the beginning of turn 2. I highlighted in grey (drawing on a feature of the software) the pause between the two speakers involved—the length of the pause is displayed, unreadable because of the scales involved.

Figure 2. In this reproduction of the display PRAAT provides to the user, we can see the sound wave for the left and right audio channels (top), the speech intensity in decibels (continuous line from left to the right), and pitch in Hertz (interrupted line). Below the display, I placed the transcription of what can heard as being said including the pauses.

My analytic method is based on cognitive and linguistic anthropological and microsociological research on everyday work practices and human-machine interactions and conversational analysis,

which assumes that participants in social situations articulate for one another precisely those things that they struggle with but leave unarticulated those things that "go without saying" (Suchman, 1987). The nature of the tasks required students and teacher to talk about the screen displays, which thereby produced natural protocols of sense-in-the-making. I do not really interpret what a person says but describe how the next speaker(s) act on and react to what has been said previously; it is therefore the listeners' interpretations that come to the fore. I used the conventions of conversation analysis to transcribe the events recorded. (Note 1) Furthermore, I do not make assumptions about what participants see but follow their descriptions of the display and aspects of situation that they orient to, and how they otherwise make available to one another what it is that they are attuned to (e.g., by means of hand gestures [pointing, iconic], body orientations, etc.). (An extensive description of this method, as it applies to the interests of cognitive psychology, can be found in Roth & Pozzer-Ardenghi, 2006.)

Experiential and Interpretive Flexibility of Phenomena

Students' learning could be described as an adaptive change in their talk about the objects and events in the computer-based microworld. Possibilities for change arose from the ontological ambiguity (multiple meanings) of these objects and events that allowed for their *interpretive flexibility*. This flexibility turns out to be both a hindrance to learning, when students see and understand aspects of the display in different ways without being aware of it, and an opportunity for learning, when students recognize that they see and understand aspects of the display differently and use this situation to reflect on the problem at hand. In the transactions, participants take the computer display as a shared feature of the material world, which provides the opportunity and condition for shared observations and understanding to emerge. I use the following episode to illustrate the *perceptual* and *interpretive flexibility* of the microworld, its objects, feedbacks, and events, and the observational expressions used to describe this microworld and its content. Here, interpretive flexibility means that students see and talk about phenomena that appear on the monitor in ways that are inconsistent with what designers and physicists intend. This has consequences for the content of student learn at the moment, and potentially in the long run.

The episode begins immediately after the three students have set up an experiment in the microworld where they attached «force» directed slightly south of east to a circular object that has a line arrow («velocity») as its characteristic pointing to the right (east) (video off-print a). At this point, students do not see or talk about «force» as force or about «velocity» as velocity but simply manipulate the arrows. The "run" the configuration by hitting the run button (little black area on the top left of their screen) and the object rapidly accelerates and disappears off the screen (video offprint b). Glen, in a voice much louder than normal, calls out "holy baby, yes" (turn 01). A feedback box appears (video offprint c), which Ryan reads barely audible articulating the words (see the "piano," <<p>>, in the transcript): "object velocities are high for this simulation. Reduce time step for greater accuracy" (turn 02). From the perspective of the software designer, the feedback pertains to the fact that the simulation becomes inaccurate when the velocities and displacements are large (here due to the large force [video offprint a shows that it is large]), requiring smaller time steps for calculating the velocities at neighboring points. The students, however, read the feedback in a different way, asking one another which of the arrows is time (turns 03, 05, 07, 10). Their talk is interspersed by pauses and describing actions aloud, such as when Glen, who operates the mouse, resets the configuration so that the display is precisely the same as at the beginning of the episode.

Given that they have described "the big arrow" as time, Elisabeth then proposes the "little arrow" to be direction (turn 13). After a pause that nears the standard maximum silence of approximately 1 second in conversation (Jefferson, 1989), Glen appears to first agree with her ("yea") but then proposes the "big arrow" to be direction, and then, after flagging with a rapidly uttered "no I mean" (see <<all> [turn 15]) that he is making a change, proposes that the "big arrow is velocity" (turn 15). Right after he utters "big," Elizabeth, overlapping Glen's production of "arrow," says "little" (turn 16) and continues, 0.27 seconds after Glen has finished, adds "is time" (turn 18). Ryan begins the next turn by announcing a difference ("no"), and, in talking much louder than normal, doing so with insistence; but he then confirms what Elizabeth has said ("it's time") only to add that "it also directs" (turn 20) leaving open what the associated arrow directs. After a conversationally long pause (turn 21), Elizabeth begins to speak, but, despite three starts ("then the little," "no the little," and "isn't the little arrow" [turn 22]), never utters a full statement or question. Ryan responds by saying that they do not know yet, and then comments on something else that he was doing ("what did I do?" [turn 24]). I end the episode with Glen's statement of an observation categorical, "the little arrow always stays straight whatever we do" (turn 26).

Just prior to this episode, Glen had changed the size and direction of «force», which led to a very different trajectory of the object and, importantly, to the feedback from the software. This feedback mediated what students were inquiring and talking about in the course of this episode, ending with an observation categorical. There are repeated changes in student descriptions and denotations of the "small arrow" and "big arrow," which, as Ryan's commentary in turn 24 makes evident, they do not yet know what they mean. Some readers, especially those unfamiliar with observations and recordings of real-time conversations in everyday settings, may think of this episode as pathological.

Figure 3. Episode 1

Episode 1

```
01  G: ↑HO:L:: BA:BEE:. (0.17) ↑yes: (0.22)
02  R: ((reads feedback) <<p>object velocities are hhh high for this
        simulation. reduce time step for greater accuracy.>
03  E: <<p>which ones the ti[me?]
04  G:                         [kay] reset.
05  R: its that big arrow
06          (0.56)
07  G: OH YEA the big arrow=s time; (0.90) <<p>kay>
08      (1.49)
09      <<p>[big kind of are]os time.>
10  R: <<p>[why that big?  ]>
11          (1.04)
12          <<pp>yea we can try>
13  E: so the little arrow is d direction.
14          (0.94)
15  G: YEA (0.16) big arrow is direction. <<all>no I mean the>
    big [arrow=s] velocity
16  E: [little  ]
17          (0.27)
18  E: s=time
19          (0.24)
20  R: NO it=s ti::me but it also directs.
21          (1.58)
22  E: yea (0.35) and then the little; (0.19) no the little, <<p>isnt the
    little arrow?>
23          (1.28)
24  R: <<p>we dont know yet.> (0.68) <<pp>what did i do?>
25          (1.28)
26  G: <<all>so=the=little> (0.19) the little arrow; (0.31) AY YAI ahhhh
    the little arrow (0.82) always stays straight (0.40) whatever we do.
```

But, in my 20-year experience of viewing tapes with everyday conversations in many different situations in and out of schools and across different geographical regions (Australia, Canada, US) and languages (English, German, French immersion), this episode is rather typical (e.g., Roth, 2005a). Here, then, students talk about something (the two arrows) even though they, self-avowedly, do not yet know what it is; this something becomes part of their discourse in and through this very conversation. But at this moment, the talk makes evident that the students do not see and talk about the entities and phenomena on the monitor in the way a physicist or the designer of Interactive Physics would.

Readers should closely note of the transcript, which shows the form real classroom conversations take, which, according to my research experience in scientific laboratories and other science-related workplaces, is the form real-time conversation takes generally. It is evident that the students' talk resembles very little the textual forms of writing, which one would expect if they had some mental model that was output, and therefore made public, in and through talk. A better and more productive way of theorizing this talk is to consider it as a phenomenon sui generis, precisely because this talk is all that the conversation participants make available for one another as resource for others (e.g., the next speaker) to act and respond. This talk is full of stumbles ("is direction no I mean" [turn 15]), mumbles ("ay yai ahhh" [turn 26]), malapropisms (e.g., "areos" [turn 09], "area" instead of "arrow"), pauses (throughout the transcript), stupidities and contradictions ("the big arrow is direction . . . is velocity" [turn 15]), solecisms ("and then the little, no the little, isn't the little arrow?" [turn 22]), and other productions that lessen—from a perspective of written text production—the clarity of an utterance. We do hear and understand, even though the sound stream is not parsed in the same way as a written text. Thus, participants and analysts of the tape can hear "stime" (turn

18) as "is time," even though the "s" and "time" are fused (the display of the PRAAT program shows one peak rather than the two peaks that two clearly distinguished words would lead to). But rather than viewing these features in a deficit way, as a pathological phenomenon, I see them as one of the conditions for variations in existing talk that lead to the evolution of new forms of talk, including scientifically correct forms.

Because the two forms of talking—mundane and theoretically correct—the forms of talk between the two stages *necessarily* consisted of hybrid, heterogeneous language, which was neither the pre-lesson vernacular nor the specialized physics discourse. Linguistic anthropologists are familiar with such hybridized discourses, which tend to emerge in the confrontation of cultures, and go under the names of Creole, pidgin, or Sabir (Roth, 2005b). These are contact languages, which, in the case of Sabir—an admixture of Portuguese, French, Italian, Arabic, Greek, and other less dominant languages—allowed merchants to trade anywhere in the Mediterranean Basin (e.g., Roth, 2008). Exemplified in this episode, the changes in students' talk were achieved collaboratively and evolved cumulatively through minute evolutions of their observation descriptions and *observation categoricals* (e.g., "the little arrow always stays straight whatever we do" [turn 26]). Such observation categoricals, which take the form "when X then Y," as in "When the sun rises, [then] birds sing" (Quine, 1995, p. 25), are first articulations of scientific laws and emergent theories. Much of their collaborative work was expended in stabilizing the emerging discourses. The computing technology (i.e., the microworld) facilitated students' sense-making activities in that it offered (a) a taken-as-stable backdrop against which they could develop shared ways of talking and (b) an immediately available referent for grounding any arguments and difference so it functioned as an anchor for achieving topical cohesion their talk. Over time, therefore, students' talk *converged* so that they shared a descriptive language in their groups; in some instances this talk converged with the normative ways of talking about the Newtonian microworld without further teacher mediation. That is, the students evolved appropriate observations, observation descriptions, and theory talk from their initial everyday ways of seeing and mundane ways of talking.

In many cases, however, the teacher—who saw his role as "teaching" rather than as letting students "discover" and perhaps err forever—mediated this evolution. The teacher was crucial here in the sense he sometimes set up experiments in the microworld with special conditions that allowed students to *see* what they were not seeing, but which was crucial for making observations and evolving observation descriptions and associated observation categoricals consistent with standard physics. In many instances, the teacher mediated students' talk in ways that allowed students to bridge what they observed and described to their real world experiences by means of analogies. The two aspects, learning to see in standard ways and bridging the microworld to the real world by means of analogies constitutes the content of the next two sections.

Learning to See

This study investigates how students come to see phenomena that they have not perceived before although opportunities have existed for this to occur. It is in the course of episodes such as the ones discussed below that students, from their perspective come to perceive new phenomena or to perceive phenomena in new ways, which sets them up to learn about and theorize what they see in the way that the standard sciences do. Thus, as exemplified in the previous section, in the context of their tasks doing simulations in the Interactive Physics environment and similar software used in other studies, it turns out that many students initially do not provide observation descriptions of events suitable for understanding the theory that the events are said to provide evidence off. In the

present study, the teacher played an important role in (a) getting students to articulate what they have found up to the respective encounters, (b) identifying aspects of perception and understanding, and (c) engaging in interventions that mediated what students perceived and how they articulated their perceptions in observation sentences. The following episodes exemplify the kinds of interactions recorded across the different course sections and participating students. Prior to the next episode, the teacher had approached the group and asked what they had done and learned.

Beginning the intervention. Up to the point of the following episode in the transcript, what has happened follows the spirit of the opening query, "What have you found out so far?" The session then takes a turn. From the conversation, the teacher—as his next discursive move exhibits—evidently has not gotten the sense that students have found out what the task had asked them to. (The students' talk was as hybridized and full of features as discussed in the previous section.) The teacher now set up a configuration of «velocity» and «force» such that the former points straight up and the latter straight down. Inherently, there is no difference to any other configuration where the two arrows are set in opposite direction; however, this particular configuration, because it embodies the "up–down schema" grounded in the everyday experience of living in the gravitational field of the earth (Johnson, 1987), provides the possibility of an analogy with throwing an object (such as a ball) into the air, which is then pulled to the earth by the gravitational force. Such analogies are foundational for relating new experiences to an already familiar world shot through with meaning. That is, new words, objects, and perceptual experiences accrue to meaning, allowing students to further articulate how the world works.

The teacher then engages students in an interaction in the course of which they come to describe the motion in a way consistent with the Newtonian theory that they are to learn as part

Episode 2

50 T: see (2.48) WHAT if you had that point up? (2.93) <<p>and this one would
point like this?> ((The teacher moves first «velocity» then «force» into configuration shown, velocity straight up, force straight down.))

Figure 4. Episode 2a

51 G: it would go straight down.
52 R: yea [it would go] downward.
53 T: <<p>[okay:]>
54   (1.04) ((Teacher runs the simulation, which results in the screen
   display depicted to the right.))

Figure 5. Episode 2b

55 E: and [a se[E] it <u>went</u> b<u>ackw</u>ards °] first tho][ugh].
56 T: [this [a]
57 R: <<p>[i think it went upwards]>
58 T: [th-] <u>but</u>? (0.40) fi[<u>rst</u>?]
59 R: [the]
   initial velocity <<p>would go the way the little arrow is.>
60 E: didnit go backwards firs[t? an]d-
61 R: [yea].

```
62 E: then get both arrows?
63 R: i think so.
64 E: yea.
```

of the tasks that they currently complete. The episode begins by shifting his position so that he can reach and manipulate the mouse, and with it, the objects that appear in the microworld. As he rotates «force» to point downward and «velocity» in the opposite direction, he asks students a question of the type "What happens if . . .?" (turn 50), which, as previous research has shown, is a productive question that invites students to think and spend extended amounts of time investigating (Harlen, 1985). For a physicist or any other person knowing about the physics of motion, it is clear that the teacher reduced the complexity of the situation because students now only consider linear rather than curved motion. More so, the specific orientation chosen is up–down. What happen when this configuration is "run" does not depend on the up–down orientation—any orientation will do. But the up–down configuration sets up the possibility of drawing a real-world analogy with throwing an object straight up into the air.

Glen immediately suggests that the circular object will go straight down, and Ryan nods and expresses agreement (turns 52, 53). This apparently reifies what may have incited the teacher to begin this demonstration in the first place, as, from a physicist's perspective, the answer is not correct; because of the initial velocity pointing upward, the object should move into that direction prior to the reversal of the velocity due to the force (see task analysis). Because the students have been working with this particular simulation for nearly 15 minutes, it is possible and perhaps even likely that these experiences have mediated what they learned so far.

Running the simulation. The teacher's "okay" (turn 53), may confirm having heard students' hypotheses about how the object would move, but, uttered at low speech intensity, he may have

been talking to himself as if confirming his hypothesis about students' current understanding. In the pause that follows, the teacher "runs" the simulation he has prepared (turn 54), yielding an event in the microworld as shown in the offprints (turn 54).

Central to a cognitive anthropological approach is that it studies the resources people actually make available to one another rather than cognitive frameworks that are inaccessible to the participants in the situation. We do not know what is in the teacher's head and therefore what drives his moves, that is, why he does what he does. But the students do not know this either. All they can go by is what the teacher makes available to them. We therefore need to theorize these public resources the participants have and make available *for* one another. However, because the teacher moves the object, there is the possibility to see significance in his action for whatever (hidden) reason. The very fact that he does engage with them may be a resource for constructing that what they have said as inappropriate. But then, the episode is unfolding so quickly that nobody really has the time to stop and think; rather, the teacher has set up this intervention within seconds and then engages students in a question–answer sequence that does not contain the frequently observed evaluation component typical in what researchers have come to denote as the initiation–response–evaluation (IRE) pattern (Lemke, 1990).

An alternate observation description. With the traces of the object positions over time displayed on the monitor—this feature of Interactive Physics works like time-laps photography—three individuals speak at the same time (turns 55–57). This is not unusual for conversations especially when there has been a pause, which is a feature that goes away only when someone speaks. The longer the pause, the more there is a social obligation (at least in Western societies) to speak—the standard maximum being of the order of one second (Jefferson, 1989). Elizabeth notes for everyone to hear that the object has first moved upward before engaging the downward motion that Glen and Ryan previously predicted. The teacher begins but immediately stops again at about the same time that Ryan—simultaneously with Elizabeth—describes the motion as having been "upwards."

We can almost hear (and certainly in the transcript see) Elizabeth's surprise and change in orientation. She begins her utterance and in the middle of the word "see," her speech volume increases, thereby hearably drawing the attention of others to something that she has seen and that therefore can be seen generally. She stresses both the words "went" and "back," and then adds the temporal adverb "first" and the conjunctive "though." I now unpack this part of the interaction. The particle "though" is both conjunctive and an adversative particle that expresses a relation between two opposed facts or circumstances in which one of the facts is inadequate but both do occur. The utterance of "though" thereby renders the earlier descriptions (the object as moving down) as matters of fact—rather than as hypotheses in the way they have been proffered before the simulation. That is, although Ryan and Glen have made their statements prior to the simulation, their utterances now have become observation sentences. But Elizabeth's contribution constrains the applicability of the two earlier utterances, which now have become observation sentences. How? In her turn, Elizabeth provides an improved observation, "it went backwards first." That is, because "though" has conjunctive function, the current state of affairs is this: *First* it [object] went backwards and *then* it goes downward/straight down. This state of affairs is actually stabilized by events that have occurred simultaneously—Ryan also proffers an observation description, "it went upwards" (turn 57).

Confirmatory power of uncertainty. Although uncertainty in conversations generally creates further uncertainty, it can also be a resource for confirmation (Roth & Middleton, 2006). Here, Ryan prefaces his observation description by the modifier of uncertainty, "I think." It is a statement typically found very early in scientific discoveries, constituting a rhetorical move that allows for the possibility to be incorrect because of this or that contingency (Latour & Woolgar, 1986). That is, the "I think" modifies an observation as a possibility without requiring the speaker's commitment so that he or she can easily renegue. Modifiers are used in the first stage in the social construction of scientific facts. In the present episode, the confirmation and stabilization actually occur simultaneously and for everyone to hear—it comes from Elizabeth's utterance, which articulates a compatible observation sentence precisely then when "backwards" and "upwards" are heard as denoting identical states of affairs.

My analysis appears to indicate that the issue has been settled. However—certainly because of the rate at which real time events unfold and the time it takes for human being to become aware of what has happened—the issue about the correct observation description remains open as the subsequent turns at talk show.

Overlapping the very end of Elizabeth's talk, the teacher utters several, even unfinished but seemingly disconnected words (turn 58). The first sound "th-" terminates in a sudden stop; the second is heard as "but" with a rising inflection generally attributed to questions; then there is a pause, followed by a repetition of the "first" that Elizabeth has finished uttering precisely 1.09 seconds before—though, again, with rising inflection. The particle "but" is a conjunctive marking that some statement is to be delimited, a fact has not been considered, or an exception. Here it is uttered with rising inflection as in a question that asks students to consider something the nature of which is not evident from the talk so far. There is a 0.40-second pause, and then the teacher repeats the temporal adverb "first?" with rising inflection (turn 58). These rising inflections allow the words to be heard as elliptic forms of the question, "But what has happened first?" That is, in this case the teacher asks the question to which Elizabeth and Ryan have already provided the answer. This raises two issues.

First, the appearance of this question at precisely this point is not surprising when we consider that even experienced Tetris players would require more than 1.2 seconds to become conscious of an object on the screen and to reflect on the next move (Kirsh & Maglio, 1994). Here, the teacher's utterance comes about faster than it would take for simple objects to be processed in mind. This speed has to be considered in the light of the fact that Tetris players are familiar with the objects that may appear, whereas the teacher is in an entirely novel, never exactly repeating practical situation. Second, the fact that the teacher raises an admittedly indeterminate question can be interpreted by other participants that something requires further talk, that is, that the answer provided so far still is insufficient to answer the larger question about what has happened in this simulation.

Ryan immediately responds suggesting that the initial velocity "would" go in the direction of the little arrow. It is not certain which arrow he signifies, because, as my analyses show, these students use the same term for both arrows and without apparently being aware of the fact that in any one situation, two speakers may use the same signifier to signify different arrows. In the present case, «force» is the shorter arrow whereas «velocity» is skinnier but longer. It therefore comes as no surprise that Elizabeth raises the question opposition, "didn't it go backwards first?" Whatever Ryan has wanted to say, Elizabeth has heard it as an observation description that opposes her own. That is, whereas she has earlier described the object as moving "backwards," her present statement exhibits that she understands Ryan to have reconfirmed his initial description according to which the object "goes downward."

Closing uncertainty. Before Elizabeth has ended, Ryan already articulates agreement with her (turn 61). They finish this episode with elliptical utterances but in apparent agreement. Following her conjunctive "and," Elizabeth queries—as indicated by the rising pitch toward the end—whether they would "then get both arrows." With the compound sentence produced by the conjunctive "and," Elizabeth raises the question whether the object "goes backwards first and then get both arrows." A possible hearing is that after the having moved "backward first," both arrows would point in the same direction because the object moves in the direction Ryan has indicated (i.e., downward). Ryan confirms, though with the qualifier "I think so," and Elizabeth concludes with an affirmative "yea."

Looking back over the episode, we note that initially observation sentence—the legitimacy of which may have been grounded in students' prior experiences with the software—come to be questioned after the teacher has run a particular simulation. Elizabeth and Ryan—in contrast to what he has just said—raise the possibility that the object has moved upward prior to moving in the way the two male students said it would happen before the simulation was run. In the course of several utterances that raise an alternative observation description as a possibility, at least two of the three students eventually make affirmative statements, which turn out to terminate the episode.

Bridging Simulation and the World

A central problem in the teaching of mathematics and science is the isolation of subject matters treated in schools and the experiences students have in their everyday lives outside schools. Frequently there exists little if any relationship between levels of schooling and years of mathematics courses to the competencies people of all walks of life exhibit in everyday settings such as supermarkets, street markets, street-corner book-making shops, and so on (Lave, 1988). It is not surprising then that some scholars use the expression of "knowledge in pieces" (diSessa, 1988). An important aspect of teaching therefore lies in the provision of resources that students can utilize to make connections between the entities and phenomena relevant to school and those that they encounter in their everyday life outside of schools.

The conversation reproduced in this section shows that the teacher accepts what the students have formulated, which is evidenced in his didactic move to allow students to link the micro-world phenomenon to something in the real world. That is, although one can possibly read this transcript as not having settled the issues, the teacher, in going on, also declares it as settled, and therefore, as having satisfactorily answered his question.

Making the analogy emerge. Throughout the episode, the students have treated the simulation as an object in its own right. They have not used everyday situations as resources for making sense of what was happening. They have not even noticed, as I show in the previous section, an important element of the motion: the circular object moves upward before moving downward. In the present instance, the teacher raises the crucial question. The context for this question already has been set with the foregoing simulation, which the teacher had set up such that it featured a structural equivalence with a ball thrown straight up into the air in a gravitational field. The episode begins immediately after students had seen, collaboratively and for a first time, the crucially important initial part of the trajectory.

In response to the teacher's question, Glen articulates spinning a hula-hoop (turn 73); Elizabeth interrupts him, apparently familiar with the situation, suggesting that the toy needs to be spun toward the person (turn 74). The teacher appears to struggle with this answer; perhaps he is expecting students to make the throwing of a ball the source of a bridging analogy? Glen then elaborates the structure that allows bridging

between his hula-hoop example and the computer simulation: it moves away and then returns. From the conceptual perspective of physics, however, the deep structures are not identical, though on the surface, the phenomena are as Glen described them.

Elizabeth offers a second situation as a candidate for bridging the simulation to real-world events: a yo-yo (turn 83); again, the conceptual underpinnings—i.e., the deep structures—are not those that physicists would make thematic. However, the situation unfolds relentlessly and before anyone has time to reflect on the yo-yo example, Ryan suggests the analogy that the teacher apparently wants them to arrive at. Ryan begins by giving the explanation: they are looking at gravity (turn 84) and, after a brief pause, he describes a phenomenon (turn 86). Glen then frames the phenomenon in a popular adage, "What goes up must come down" (turns 87, 89). Elizabeth adds an implication: one of the arrows on the monitor "is the force– (1.00) isn't it?" (turn 90). It is at this point that the students have arrived at a description of the two surface phenomena in terms of a common language—upward and downward movement—and in terms of a common theoretical structure: force (gravity).

Collaboration, mediation, emergence. In this situation, the three students, mediated by the teacher, arrive at a description of surface and deep structure in a collaborative manner. As the situation unfolds, students contribute bits and pieces of theoretical and observational discourse even before they know how all of this connects. Here, the teacher's contributions *mediate* the development without however *determining* it. The indeterminate nature of his contributions can be taken from the fact that there are multiple contributions, some of which do not contribute to establishing a suitable source domain required to establish the analogy. Here, even comments that may appear to be value free—such as "but here?" (turn 76)—constitute resources for establishing doubts about the appropriateness of

Episode 3

```
71 T: [is there some]thing in real life?
72        (0.38)
73 G: yea, when you spin: a hulahoop. (1.48) and its=
74 E: =towards you
     [yea] [that like [run]
75 G: [yea] [towards    [you].
76 T:                   [yea]
     [but here?]
77 G: [it goes  ]((Hand moves forward and away from him)) that way and it
   comes back to you. ((Hand returns.))
78 E: hhh
79        (0.56)
80 R: no:: [s:.]
81 E:      [hhh].h ((cackle))
82        (2.73)
83 E: it reminds me of a yo[yo    ].
84 R:                      <<p>[thats] thats gravity, thats like gravity>.
85        (2.10)
86        cause when you throw it [up ];
87 G:                            [yea]
     what must goes [up]
88 T:             [uh] [hu]
89 G:             [it] must come down.
90 E: and then one of them is the force- (1.00) isnt it?
```

what has been said. Although such comments do not and cannot in themselves tell students what it means to know the phenomenon and the analogy, they constitute resources. As a study of analogical learning in the context of chaos theory showed, if completely unconstrained by teacher input, students may construct analogies that in fact lead them away from understanding the relevant phenomena in a scientific way (Roth & Duit, 2003). A good descriptor for the nature of learning therefore is emergence, which allows the process to be constrained—e.g., by teacher-produced discursive and material resources (on-screen events)—without leading us to theorize teaching as a deterministic event.

Contradictions. Some readers may think that it may suffice just telling students what there is to see. Whereas this might have assisted students in the present situation, we cannot be certain about whether they would actually see what is required for evolving fruitful analogies. More so,

telling leads to a form of passive learning that is insufficient to lead to the production and reproduction of scientific knowledge: For knowledge to remain alive, it has to be actively produced; only after having been actively produced at least once before can it be remembered and reproduced (Merleau-Ponty, 2002). Active production and reproduction, however, requires the *intention*; and intention requires an object. But because students do not yet know what they are to learn, they find themselves in a quandary. To intend the knowledge that the curriculum prescribes, they need to know beforehand what is supposed to be the result and outcome of the curriculum. More so, without access to the knowledge to be learned, they have no way of assessing how far they are away from the instructional target while they are on their learning trajectory.

In the context of these contradictions—which are part of "the learning paradox" (Bereiter, 1985)—the usefulness of student–student collaboration and (teacher, computer) mediation in the emergence of knowledge becomes evident. All three forms of transactions constitute constraints on the evolution of the instructional conversation in which observational and explanatory descriptions are evolved. Precisely because students do not know, they can only proceed in a tentative manner, attempting to evolve descriptions that allow them to perceive and understand new aspects, and these constitute new resources for revising the descriptions.

CONCLUSION

This extended analysis exemplifies how even in the simplest of displays—two arrows changing as an object moves—students may not perceive those features and relations that are essential for understanding introductory physics. In this study, the participating students attended an elite school where 99 percent subsequently go to college and university. As a whole, this episode exemplifies my general observation in this and other databases that students do not "extract information" from whatever is available on the computer monitor, in hands-on experiments of their own design, or in teacher demonstrations (Roth, 2006). That is, although the three students in this episode have run such simulations before, it is at precisely *this* moment that they first articulate the observation description that is required by and consistent with the Newtonian perspective that their physics course is designed to teach them. This description also is required for making the analogy with events in the surrounding world. Initially the observation description is inconsistent with standard physics and with what the teacher can see and knows to be there. This and other studies therefore seriously question assumptions that education can *determine* learning outcomes.

The data presented here also exemplify how a teacher can be an essential element in overcoming the chicken-and-egg situation whereby students have to know the theory in order to see, but what they are asked to see is supposed to help them learn the theory. Ultimately, teacher talk would not be so much different than other forms of presenting students with text if it were not for the adaptability of human beings to the contingencies of the setting in which they are constitutive participants. So while the difficulty inherent in any form of communication is not overcome in and by the teacher presence, the latter provides opportunities for adaptive assessment and intervention. Because such assessment and intervention emerge on the spot, based on the teacher's sense of the game, the processes are themselves error prone, though both become increasingly reliable with the experience of the teacher.

In the end, the students in this and other groups arrive at evolving analogies between the micro-world and real-world phenomena and, in the process, come to understand the relationship between the force on an object and its velocity as expressed in equation (1).

This study somewhat undermines claims some researchers make about the usefulness of group work. Even if students work collaboratively, there is no guarantee that their different perceptions—if any—will allow them to isolate the one necessary to learn. In the example presented, two students at least apparently had extracted the same conclusion from their previous experiences with the microworld events—the ball would immediately drop rather than rise before falling, despite the fact that there was an initial upward velocity vector (arrow). More so, in this situation as elsewhere in this group as well as in other groups, the students use the same words to signify different things without becoming aware of these differences, leading to an unnoticed breakdown in their sense-making processes. Again, the collaborative work and mediations constrain but are no guarantee for making sense in a prescribed way.

FUTURE RESEARCH DIRECTIONS

Studies of learning by means of analogies frequently note whether students use analogies rather than how analogies emerge from classroom transactions during student–student and student–teacher conversations. More research is required to study *how* analogies can be promoted in the context of multi-media learning especially given the fact that to work, students need to generate deep structures both in the source *and* target domains, which provides a contradiction as students are supposed to *learn* this target domain. More so, multi-media environment have definitive advantages over other learning environments in that they easily can provide layered information, such that the conceptual and experiential worlds come to co-appear in the same plane as in the present study. However, careful investigations need to be designed to see whether students can transfer what they learn in multi-media environments to other environments that they experience in their everyday lives. Such studies of transfer are especially needed considering the fact that it may occur by means of analogies. Whether the production of analogies between the two domains is possible, how teachers and multi-media environments can support the production of analogies to facilitate the transfer, and what field looks like by actual learning trajectories all are subject to further empirical research.

Past research on the use of analogies has shown that students attend to surface rather than deep structures of the domains to be analogically related. Given that students do not know (much about) the target domain, this failure is not surprising. More micro-analytic studies similar to the present one need to be conducted to investigate how students go from the initial recognition of surficial features to the unknown and to-be-learned deep structures. What kinds of multi–media- and teacher-mediated support mechanisms will facilitate (impede with) the production of deep structures from surface structures and any available sources for analogies?

The present study also highlights the expertise required on the part of the teacher in guiding students to produce analogies in multi-media contexts. There is some evidence that many adults, including university science students and science preservice teachers have misconceptions about physical concepts such as those studied here (e.g., Kikas, 2003); and there is evidence that teachers induce misconceptions, including through the use of analogies. Empirical micro-analytic studies are required to show how the different forms of teacher and student knowledge transact in the process of conversations over and about multimedia resources. How do the different forms of knowledge—those presented in the multi-media format and those of students and teacher—transact in computer-supported collaborative learning environments?

REFERENCES

Bereiter, C. (1985). Towards a solution to the learning paradox. *Review of Educational Research, 55*, 201–226.

Collins, A., Brown, J. S., & Newman, S. (1989). Cognitive apprenticeship: Teaching the crafts of reading, writing, and mathematics. In L. Resnick (Ed.), *Knowing, learning and instruction: Essays in honor of Robert Glaser* (pp. 453–494). Hillsdale, NJ: Lawrence Erlbaum Associates.

diSessa, A. (1988). Knowledge in pieces. In G. Forman & P. B. Burall (Eds.), *Constructivism in the computer age* (pp. 49–70). Hillsdale, NJ: Lawrence Erlbaum Associates.

Duit, R. (1991). The role of analogies and metaphors in learning science. *Science Education, 75*, 649–672.

Duit, R., Roth, W.-M., Komorek, M., & Wilbers, J. (2001). Fostering conceptual change by analogies: Between Scylla and Charybdis. *Learning and Instruction, 11*, 283–303.

Gallese, V. (2003). The roots of empathy: The shared manifold hypothesis and the neural basis of intersubjectivity. *Psychopathology, 36*, 171–180.

Gentner, D. (1989). The mechanisms of analogical learning. In S. Vosniadou & A. Ortony (Eds.), *Similarity and analogical reasoning* (pp. 119–241). Cambridge, UK: Cambridge University Press.

Goodwin, C. (2000). Action and embodiment within situated human interaction. *Journal of Pragmatics, 32*, 1489–1522.

Hanson, N. R. (1965). *Patterns of discovery: An inquiry into the conceptual foundations of science.* Cambridge, UK: Cambridge University Press.

Harlen, W. (1985). *Primary science: Taking the plunge.* London, UK: Heineman.

Hutchins, E. (1995). *Cognition in the wild.* Cambridge, MA: MIT Press.

Hwang, W., Wang, C., & Sharples, M. (2007). A study of multimedia annotation of Web-based materials. *Computers & Education, 48*, 680–699.

Jefferson, G. (1989). Preliminary notes on a possible metric which provides for a "standard maximum" silence of approximately one second in conversation. In D. Roger & P. Bull (Eds.), *Conversation: An interdisciplinary perspective* (pp. 166–196). Clevedon: Multilingual Matters.

Johnson, M. (1987). *The body in the mind: The bodily basis of imagination, reason, and meaning.* Chicago: Chicago University Press.

Kafai, Y. B. (1994). *Minds in play: Computer game design as a context for children's learning.* Hillsdale, NJ: Lawrence Erlbaum Associates.

Kikas, E. (2003). University students' conceptions of different physical phenomena. *Journal of Adult Development, 10*, 139–150.

Kirsh, D., & Maglio, P. (1994). On distinguishing epistemic from pragmatic action. *Cognitive Science, 18*, 513–549.

Latour, B., & Woolgar, S. (1986). *Laboratory life: The social construction of scientific facts.* Princeton, NJ: Princeton University Press.

Lave, J. (1988). *Cognition in practice: Mind, mathematics and culture in everyday life.* Cambridge, UK: Cambridge University Press.

Lemke, J. L. (1990). *Talking science: Language, learning and values.* Norwood, NJ: Ablex.

Merleau-Ponty, M. (2002). *Husserl at the limits of phenomenology.* Evanston, IL: Northwestern University Press.

Quine, W. V. (1995). *From stimulus to science.* Cambridge, MA: Harvard University Press.

Richland, L. E., Zur, O., & Holyoak, K. J. (2007). Cognitive supports for analogies in the mathematics classroom. *Science, 316*, 1128–1129.

Rizzolatti, G., Fadiga, L., Fogassi, L., & Gallese, V. (1997). The space around us. *Science, 277*, 190–191.

Rorty, R. (1979). *Philosophy and the mirror of nature.* Princeton, NJ: Princeton University Press.

Roschelle, J. (1996). Designing for cognitive communication: Epistemic fidelity or mediating collaborative inquiry. In D. L. Day & D. K. Kovacs (Eds.), *Computers, communication, and mental models* (pp. 13–25). London: Taylor and Francis.

Roth, W.-M. (2003). *Toward an anthropology of graphing.* Dordrecht, The Netherlands: Kluwer Academic Publishers.

Roth, W.-M. (2005a). *Talking science: Language and learning in science.* Lanham, MD: Rowman & Littlefield.

Roth, W.-M. (2005b). Telling in purposeful activity and the emergence of scientific language. In R. Yerrick & W.-M. Roth (Eds.), *Establishing scientific classroom discourse communities: Multiple voices of research on teaching and learning* (pp. 45–71). Mahwah, NJ: Lawrence Erlbaum Associates.

Roth, W.-M. (2006). *Learning science: A singular plural perspective.* Rotterdam, The Netherlands: SensePublishers.

Roth, W.-M. (2008). Bricolage, métissage, hybridity, heterogeneity, diaspora: Concepts for thinking science education in the 21st Century. *Cultural Studies in Science Education, 3.*

Roth, W.-M., & Duit, R. (2003). Emergence, flexibility, and stabilization of language in a physics classroom. *Journal for Research in Science Teaching, 40,* 869–897.

Roth, W.-M., McRobbie, C., Lucas, K.B., & Boutonné, S. (1997). Why do students fail to learn from demonstrations? A social practice perspective on learning in physics, *Journal of Research in Science Teaching, 34,* 509–533.

Roth, W.-M., & Middleton, D. (2006). The making of asymmetries of knowing, identity, and accountability in the sequential organization of graph interpretation. *Cultural Studies of Science Education, 1,* 11–81.

Roth, W.-M., & Pozzer-Ardenghi, L. (2006). Tracking situated, distributed, and embodied communication in real time. In M. A. Vanchevsky (Ed.), *Focus on cognitive psychology research* (pp. 237–261). Hauppauge, NY: Nova Science.

Selting, M., Auer, P., Barden, B., Bergmann, J., Couper-Kuhlen, E., Günthner, S., Meier, C., Quasthoff, U., Schlobinski, P., & Uhmann, S. (1998).

Gesprächsanalytisches Transkriptionssystem. *Linguistische Berichte, 173,* 91–122.

Shannon, C. E., & Weaver, W. (1949). *The mathematical theory of communication.* Urbana, IL: University of Illinois Press.

Shih, T. K., Wang, T. H., Chang, C.-Y., Kao, T.-C., & Hamilton, D. (2007). Ubiquitous e-learning with multimodal devices. *IEEE Transactions on Multimedia, 9,* 487–499.

Suchman, L.A. (1987). *Plans and situated actions: The problem of human-machine communication.* Cambridge, UK: Cambridge University Press.

Vygotsky, L.S. (1986). *Thought and language.* Cambridge, MA: MIT Press.

ADDITIONAL READINGS

Ardac, D., & Akaygun, S. (2004). Effectiveness of multimedia-based instruction that emphasizes molecular representations on students' understanding of chemical change. *Journal of Research in Science Teaching, 41,* 317–337.

Aubusson, P. J. Harrison, A. G., & Ritchie, S. M. (Eds.). (2006). *Metaphor and analogy in science education.* Dordrecht, The Netherlands: Springer-Verlag.

Burns, B. D. (1996). Meta-analogical transfer: Transfer between episodes of analogical reasoning. *Journal of Experimental Psychology: Learning, Memory and Cognition, 22,* 1032–1048.

Chiu, M.-H., & Lin, J.-W. (2005). Promoting fourth graders' conceptual change of their understanding of electric current via multiple analogies. *Journal of Research in Science Teaching, 42,* 429–464.

Gentner, D., Brem, S., Ferguson, R. W., Markman, A. B., Levidow, B. B., Wolff, P., & Forbus, K. D. (1997). Analogical reasoning and conceptual change: A case study of Johannes Kepler. *Journal of the Learning Sciences, 6,* 3–40.

Gordon, P.C., Moser, S. (2007). Insight into analogies: Evidence from eye movements. *Visual Cognition, 15,* 20–35.

Harpaz-Itay Y, Kaniel S, Ben-Amram E. (2006). Analogy construction versus analogy solution, and their influence on transfer. *Learning and Instruction, 16,* 583–591.

James, M. C., & Scharmann, L. C. (2007). Using analogies to improve the teaching performance of preservice teachers. *Journal of Research in Science Teaching, 44,* 565–585.

Richland, L. E., Holyoak, K. J., & Stigler, J. W. (2004). Analogy use in eighth-grade mathematics classrooms. *Cognition and Instruction, 22,* 37–60.

Tzuriel D, Shamir A (2007). The effects of Peer Mediation with Young Children (PMYC) on children's cognitive modifiability. *British Journal of Educational Psychology, 77,* 143–165.

Yerrick, R., Doster, E., Nugent, J. S., Parke, H. M., & Crawley, F. E. (2003). Social interaction and the use of analogy: An analysis of preservice teachers' talk during physics inquiry lessons. *Journal of Research in Science Teaching, 40,* 443–463.

ENDNOTE

This study was in part supported by a grant from the Social Sciences and Humanities Research Council of Canada.

[1] The transcription does not follow grammatical rules (e.g., capitalization or punctuation marks) but rather, consistent with conversation analysis (e.g., Selting et al., 1998), follows following transcription conventions are used: WHAT – caps indicate louder speech; (0.40) – pauses in seconds; ((moves)) – transcriber's comments; <<p> go> – piano, pianissimo lower than normal volume; , <<pp> go> very low volume, next to inaudible; <<all>no i mean> – allegro, faster than normal; then – underline indicate stressed syllables; [the] – brackets indicate overlapped speech; .,;? – punctuation denotes direction of pitch as in statements, questions, clauses; ya:: – colons for sound lengthening; = – equal sign means latching, no separation between two words or two speakers; ↑HO – jump upward in pitch level.

Compilation of References

AAAS. (1993). *Benchmarks for Science Literacy.* New York: Project 2061, American Association for the Advancement of Science, Oxford University Press.

Aarseth, E. (2001). Computer game studies, Year one. *Game Studies: The International Journal of Computer Game Research, 1*(1), Retrieved May 20, 2006, from http://www.gamestudies.org/0101/editorial.html

Aarseth, E. (2004). Genre trouble: Narrativism and the art of simulation. In P. Harrigan & N. Wardrip-Fruin (Ed.), *First person: New media as story, performance, and game* (pp. 45-55). Cambridge: MIT Press.

Abrahamson, C. E. (1998). Issues in interactive communication in distance education. *College Student Journal, 32*(1), 33-42.

Ackerman, P. L., Beier, M. E., & Boyle, M. O. (2002). Individual differences in working memory within a nomological network of cognitive and perceptual speed abilities. *Journal of Experimental Psychology: General, 131,* 567–589.

Adams, E. (2001). Replayability, Part One: Narrative. *Gamasutra,* 05.21.01. [Online] Available http://www.gamasutra.com/features/20010521/adams_01.htm.

Adey, P., & Shayer, M. (1993). An exploration of long-term far-transfer effects following an extended intervention program in the high school science curriculum. *Cognition and Instruction, 11*(1), 1-29.

Agosto, D. (2004). Girls and gaming: A summary of the research with implications for practice. *Teacher Librarian, 31*(3), 8-14.

Agrawal, R., & Srikant, R. (1995). Mining sequential patterns. In P. S. Yu & A. L. P. Chen (Eds.), *Proceedings of the 11th International Conference on Data Engineering* (pp. 3-14). Taipei, Taiwan: IEEE Computer Society.

Ahern S., & Beatty, J. (1979). Pupillary responses during information processing vary with Scholastic Aptitude Test scores. *Science, 205,* 1289-1292.

Ahmad, F., de la Chica, S., Butcher, K. R., Sumner, T., & Martin, J. H. (2007). Towards Automatic Conceptual Personalization Tools. In *Proceedings of the 5th ACM/IEEE-CS Joint Conference on Digital Libraries,* Vancouver, BC (pp. 452-461). New York, NY: ACM Press.

Ainley, M. D. (1993). Styles of engagement with learning: Multidimensional assessment of their relationship with strategy use and school achievement. *Journal of Educational Psychology, 85,* 395-405.

Ainsworth, S. (1999). A functional taxonomy of multiple representations. *Computers and Education, 33,* 131-152.

Ainsworth, S. (1999). The functions of multiple representations. *Computers and Education, 33,* 131-152.

Ainsworth, S. (2006). DeFT: A conceptual framework for considering learning with multiple representations. *Learning and Instruction, 16,* 183-198.

Ainsworth, S., Bibby, P., & Wood, D. (2002). Examining the effects of different multiple representational systems in learning primary mathematics. *Journal of the Learning Sciences, 11*(1), 25-61.

Airasian, P. W., & Walsh, M.E. (1997). Constructivist cautions. *Phi Delta Kappan, 78*(6), 444-449.

Albanese, M.A., & Mitchell, S. (1993). Problem-based learning: A review of literature on its outcomes and implementation issues, *Academic Medicine, 68*(1), 52-81.

Alesandrini, K. (1984). Pictures and adult learning. *Instructional Science, 13,* 63-77.

Alessandrini, K. L. (1987). Computer graphics in learning and instruction. In D. M. Willows & H. A. Houghton (Eds.), *The psychology of illustration* (Vol. 2, pp. 159-188). New York: Springer.

Alexander, P. A., & Murphy, P. K. (1998). The research base for APA's learner-centered psychological principles. In N. M. Lambert & B. L. McCombs (Eds.), *Issues in school reform: A sampler of psychological perspectives on learner-centered schools* (pp. 33-60). Washington, DC: American Psychological Association.

Allen, W.H. (1967). Media stimulus and types of learning. *Audiovisual Instruction. 12*, 27-31.

Allen, W.H. (1971). Instructional media research: Past, present, and future. *AV Communications Review, 19*, 5-18.

Allport, A. (1989). Visual attention. In M. I. Posner (Ed.), *Foundations of cognitive science* (pp. 631-682). Cambridge, MA: MIT Press.

Ally, M. (2004). Foundations of educational theory for online learning. In T. Anderson & F. Elloumi (Eds.), *Theory and practice of Online Learning* (pp. 3-31). Athabasca: Athabasca University.

Aly, M., Elen, J., & Willems, G. (2005). Learner-control vs. program-control instructional multimedia: A comparison of two interaction when teaching principles of orthodontic appliances. *European Journal of Dental Education, 9*, 157-163.

Ames, C. (1992). Classrooms: Goals, structures, and student motivation. *Journal of Educational Psychology, 84*, 261-271.

Ames, C. A. (1990). Motivation: What teachers need to know. *Teacher College Record, 90*(3), 409-421.

Anderson, D. R., & Lorch, E. P. (1983). Looking at television action or reaction? In J. Bryant & D. R. Anderson (Eds.), *Children's understanding of television: Research on attention and comprehension* (pp. 1-33). New York: Academic Press.

Anderson, J. R. (1993). *Rules of the mind*. Hillsdale, NJ: Lawrence Erlbaum.

Anderson, J. R. (1996). *The architecture of cognition*. Mahwah, NJ: Lawrence Erlbaum Associates.

Anderson, J. R. (2005). *Cognitive psychology and its Implications*. New York: Worth.

Anderson, J. R., Corbett, A. T., Koedinger, K. R., & Pelletier, R. (1995). Cognitive tutors: Lessons learned. *Journal of the Learning Sciences, 4*(2), 167-207.

Anderson, J. R., Reder, L. M., & Simon, H. A. (1996). Situated learning and education. *Educational Researcher, 25*(4), 5-11.

Anderson-Inman, L., Horney, M., Chen, D-T, & Lewin, L. (1994). Hypertext literacy: Observations from the ElectroText project. *Language Arts, 71*, 279-287.

Anglin, G. J., Vaez, H., & Cunningham, K. L. (2004). Visual representations and learning: The role of static and animated graphics. In D. Jonassen (Ed.), *Handbook of research on educational communications and technology* (pp. 865-916). Mahwah, NJ: Erlbaum.

APA Work Group of the Board of Educational Affairs. (1997). *Learner-centered psychological principles: A framework for school reform and redesign*. Washington, DC: Author.

Astleitner, H., & Hufnagl, M. (2003). The effects of situation-outcome-expectancies and of ARCS-strategies on self-regulated learning with Web-lectures. *Journal of Educational Multimedia and Hypermedia, 12*(4), 361-376.

Astleitner, H., & Koller, M. (2006). An aptitude-treatment-interaction-approach on motivation and student's self-regulated multimedia-based learning. *Interactive Educational Multimedia, 13*, 11-23.

Astleitner, H., & Leutner, D. (1996). Applying standard network analysis to hypermedia systems: Implications for learning. *Journal of Educational Computing Research, 14*, 285-303.

Astleitner, H., & Wiesner, C. (2004). An integrated model of multimedia learning and motivation. *Journal of Educational Multimedia and Hypermedia, 13*(1), 3-21.

Atkins, M., & Blissett, G. (1992). Interactive video and cognitive problem-solving skills. *Educational Technology, 32*(1), 44-50.

Atkinson, J. W. (Ed.) (1958). *Motives in fantasy, action and society*. Princeton, NJ: Van Nostrand.

Atkinson, R. C., & Shiffrin, R. M. (1968). Human memory: A proposed system and its control processes. In K. W. Spence & J. T. Spence (Eds.), *The Psychology of Learning and Emotion*. London: Academic Press.

Atkinson, R. K., Mayer, R. E., & Merrill, M. M. (2005). Fostering social gency in multimedia learning: Examining the impact of an animated agent's voice. *Contemporary Educational Psychology, 30*(1), 117.

Auble, P. M., Franks, J. J., & Soraci, S. A., Jr. (1979). Effort toward comprehension: Elaboration or "aha"?. *Memory & Cognition, 7*, 426-434.

Ayres, P. (1993). Why goal-free problems can facilitate learning. *Contemporary Educational Psychology, 18*, 376-381.

Ayres, P. (2006). Impact of reducing intrinsic cognitive load on learning in a mathematical domain. *Applied Cognitive Psychology, 20*, 287-298.

Ayres, P., & Sweller, J. (2005). The split-attention effect in multimedia learning. In R. E. Mayer (Ed.), *The Cambridge Handbook of Multimedia Learning* (pp. 135-146). New York: Cambridge University Press.

Azevedo, R. (2005). Using hypermedia as a metacognitive tool for enhancing student learning? The role of self-regulated learning. *Educational Psychologist, 40*(4), 199.

Azevedo, R., & Cromley, J. G. (2004). Does training on self-regulated learning facilitate students' learning with hypermedia? *Journal of Educational Psychology, 96*(3), 523.

Azevedo, R., & Jacobson, M. (2008). Advances in scaffolding learning with hypertext and hypermedia: A summary and critical analysis. *Educational Technology Research and Development, 56*(1), 93-100.

Azevedo, R., Cromley, J. G., Winters, F. I., Moos, D. C., & Greene, J. A. (2005). Adaptive human scaffolding facilitates adolescents' self-regulated learning with hypermedia. *Instructional Science, 33*(5-6), 381.

Azevedo, R., Guthrie, J. T., & Seibert, D. (2004). The role of self-regulated learning in fostering students' conceptual understanding of complex systems with hypermedia. *Journal of Educational Computing Research, 30*(1-2), 87.

Azevedo, R., Moos, D., Greene, J., Winters, F., & Cromley, J. (2008). Why is externally facilitated regulated learning more effective than self-regulated learning with hypermedia? *Educational Technology Research and Development, 56*(1), 45-72.

Azevedo, R., Winters, F. I., & Moos, D. C. (2004). Can students collaboratively use hypermedia to learn science? The dynamics of self-and other-regulatory processes in an ecology classroom. *Journal of Educational Computing Research, 31*(3), 215.

Baddeley, A. & Hitch, G. (1974). Working memory. In G. A. Bower (Ed.), *Recent advances in learning and motivation* (vol. 8, pp. 47-89). New York: Academic Press.

Baddeley, A. (1986). *Working memory.* Oxford, UK: Clarendon Press.

Baddeley, A. (2007). *Working memory, thought, and action.* Oxford: Oxford University Press.

Baddeley, A. D. (1986). *Working memory.* Oxford, England: Oxford University Press.

Baddeley, A. D. (1996). Exploring the central executive. *Quarterly Journal of Experimental Psychology: Human Experimental Psychology, 49,* 5-28.

Baddeley, A. D. (1999). *Essentials of human memory.* Hove, England : Psychology Press.

Baddeley, A. D. (2002). Is working memory still working? *European Psychologist, 7,* 85-97.

Baddeley, A. D., & Hitch, G. (1974). Working Memory. In G. H. Bower (Ed.), *The psychology of learning and motivation: Advances in research and theory.* New York: Academic Press.

Baddeley, A. D., Emslie, H., Kolodny, J., & Duncan, J. (1998). Random generation and the executive control of working memory. *Quarterly Journal of Experimental Psychology, 51A,* 818-852.

Baddeley, A. D., Lewis, V. J., & Vallar, G. (1984). Exploring the articulatory loop. *Quarterly Journal of Experimental Psychology, 36,* 233–252.

Baddeley, A.D. (1992). Working memory. *Science, 255,* 556-559.

Baddeley, A.D. (1999). *Human memory.* Boston. Allyn & Bacon.

Baddeley, A.D., & Hitch, G.J. (1974). Working memory, In G.A. Bower (Ed.), *The psychology of learning and motivation: advances in research and theory* (Vol. 8, pp. 47-89), New York: Academic Press.

Baggett, P. (1987). Structurally equivalent stories in movie and text and the effect of the medium on recall. *Journal of Verbal Learning & Verbal Behavior, 18,* 333-356.

Baggett, P. (1984). Role of temporal overlap of visual and auditory material in forming dual media associations. *Journal of Educational Psychology, 76,* 408-417.

Banathy, B. (1996). Systems inquiry and its application in education. In D. Jonassen (Ed.), *The Handbook of Research for Educational Communications Technology* (pp. 74-92). New York: Simon & Schuster MacMillan.

Bandura, A. (1977). Self-efficacy: Toward a unifying theory of behavioural change. *Psychological Review, 84,* 191-215.

Bandura, A. (1986). *Social foundations of thought and action: A social cognitive theory.* Englewood Cliffs, NJ: Prentice Hall.

Bandura, A. (1986). Social foundations of thought and action: A social cognitive theory. Englewood Cliffs, NJ: Prentice-Hall, Inc.

Bandura, A. (1993). Perceived self-efficacy in cognitive development and functioning. *Educational Psychologist, 28,* 117-148.

Bandura, A. (1997). *Self-efficacy: The exercise of control.* New York: Plenum.

Bannert, M. (2003). Effekete metakognitiver Lernhilfen auf den Wissenserwerb in vernetzten Lernumgebungen. *German Journal of Educational Psychology, 17*(1), 13-25.

Barab, S. A., Bowdish, B. E., & Lawless, K. A. (1997). Hypermedia navigation: Profiles of hypermedia users. *Educational Technology Research and Development, 45,* 23–41.

Barab, S. A., Bowdish, M. F., Young, M., & Owen, S. V. (1996). Understanding kiosk navigation: Using log files to capture hypermedia searches. *Instructional Science, 24,* 377-395.

Barab, S. A., Fajen, B. R., Kulikowich, J. M., & Young, M. (1996). Assessing hypermedia navigation through pathfinder: Prospects and limitations. *Journal of Educational Computing Research, 15,* 185-205.

Barab, S., Dodge, T., Thomas, M. K., Jackson, C., & Tuzun, H. (2007). Our designs and the social agendas they carry. *Journal of the Learning Sciences, 16*(2), 263.

Barab, S., Thomas, M., Dodge, T., Carteaux, R., & Tuzun, H. (2005). Making learning fun: Quest atlantis, A game without guns. *Educational Technology Research and Development, 53*(1), 86.

Barnett, S. M., & Ceci, S. J. (2002). When and where do we apply what we learn? A taxonomy for far transfer. *Psychological Bulletin, 128*(4), 612-637.

Baroody, A. J., Feil, Y., & Johnson, A. R. (2007). An alternative reconceptualization of procedural and conceptual knowledge. *Journal for Research in Mathematics Education, 38,* 115-131.

Barthes, R. (1964). Rhétorique de l'image. *Communications, 4,* 40–51.

Baylor, A. L. (2001). Perceived disorientation and incidental learning in a Web-based environment: Internal and external factors. *Journal of Educational Multimedia and Hypermedia, 10,* 227-251.

Beatty, J. (1982). Task-evoked pupillary responses, processing load, and the structure of processing resources. *Psychological Bulletin, 91,* 276-292.

Beatty, J., & Lucero-Wagner, B. (2000). The pupillary system. In J. T., Cacioppo, L. G. Tassinary, & G. G. Berntson (Eds.), *Handbook of psychophysiology* (2nd ed., pp. 142-162). Cambridge, UK: Cambridge University Press.

Bell, B. S., & Kozlowski, W. J. (2002). Goal orientation and ability: Interactive effects on self-efficacy, performance, and knowledge. *Journal of Applied Psychology, 87,* 497-505.

Bereiter, C. (1985). Towards a solution to the learning paradox. *Review of Educational Research, 55,* 201–226.

Bernard, R. M., Abrami, C., Lou, Y., Borokhovski, E., Wade, A., Wozney, L., Wallet, P. A., Fiset, M., & Huang, B. (2004). How does distance education compare with classroom instruction? A meta-analysis of the empirical literature. *Review of Educational Research, 74*(3), 379-439.

Bernsen, N. O. (1994). Foundations of multimodal representations: A taxonomy of representational modalities. *Interacting with Computers, 6,* 347-371.

Bernstein, M., Bolter, J.D., Joyce, M., & Mylonas, E. (1991) Architectures for volatile hypertext. *Proceedings of Hypertext' 91,* ACM Press, San Antonio, Texas, December, 241-260.

Bertin, J. (1983). *Semiology of graphics: Diagrams networks maps* (W. J. Berg, Trans.). Madison, WI: University of Wisconsin Press.

Bertoline, G. R., & Wiebe, E. N. (2003). *Technical graphics communications* (3rd ed.). New York, NY: McGraw-Hill.

Biederman, I., & Shiffrar, M. M. (1987). Sexing day-old chicks: A case study and expert systems analysis of a difficult perceptual learning task. *Journal of Experimental Psychology: Learning, Memory, & Cognition, 13,* 640-645.

Bieger, G. R., & Glock, M. D. (1984). The information content of picture-text instructions. *The Journal of Experimental Education, 53,* 68-76.

Bishop, M. J., & Cates, W. M. (2001). Theoretical foundations for sound's use in multimedia instruction to enhance learning. *Educational Technology Research and Development, 49,* 5-22.

Bjork, R. A., & Richardson-Klavehn, A. (1989). On the puzzling relationship between environment context and a human memory. In C. Izawa (Ed.), *Current issues in cognitive process: The Tulane Flowerree Symposium on Cognition.* Hillsdale, NJ: Erlbaum.

Bjork, R. A., & Richardson-Klavehn, A. (1989). On the puzzling relationship between environmental context and human memory. In C. Izawa (ed.), *Current Issues in Cognitive Processes: The Tulane Flowerree Symposium on Cognition* (pp. 313-344. Hillsdale, NJ: Lawrence Erlbaum.

Blok, H. (1999). Reading to young children in educational settings: A meta-analysis of recent research. *Language Learning, 49*, 343-371.

Blumer, H. (1940). The problem of the concept in social psychology. *American Journal of Sociology, 45*, 707-719.

Bobis, J., Sweller, J., & Cooper, M. (1993). Cognitive load effects in a primary school geometry task. *Learning and Instruction, 3*, 1-21.

Boekaerts, M., & Cascallar, E. (2006). How far have we moved toward the integration of theory and practice in self-regulation? *Educational Psychology Review, 18*, 199-210.

Borg, Bratfish, & Dornic (1971). On the problem of perceived difficulty. *Scandinavian Journal of Psychology, 12*, 249-260.

Borsboom, D., Mellenbergh, G. J., & van Heerden, J. (2002). Different kinds of DIF: A distinction between absolute and relative forms of measurement invariance and bias. *Applied Psychological Measurement, 26*, 433-450.

Borsboom, D., Mellenbergh, G. J., & van Heerden, J. (2004). The concept of validity. *Psychological Review, 111*, 1061–1071.

Bowers, J. S., & Doerr, H. M. (2001). An analysis of prospective teachers' dual roles in understanding the mathematics of change: Eliciting growth with technology. *Journal of Mathematics Teacher Education, 4*, 115-137.

Bransford, J. D., & Schwartz, D. L. (1999). Rethinking transfer: A simple proposal with multiple implications. In A. Iran-Nejad & P. D. Pearson (Eds.), *Review of research in education, 24*, 61-100. Washington, D.C.: American Educational Research Association.

Bransford, J. D., Franks, J. J., Vye, N. J., & Sherwood, R. D. (1989). New approaches to instruction. Because wisdom can't be told. In S. Vosniadou & A. Ortony (Eds.), *Similarity and analogical reasoning* (pp. 470-497). Cambridge, UK: Cambridge University Press.

Bransford, J., Brown, A. L., & Cocking, R. R. (Eds.). (2000). *How people learn: Brain, mind, experience, and school (Expanded Edition)*. Washington, DC: National Academy Press.

Bray, J. H., & Howard, G. S. (1980). Methodological considerations in the evaluation of a teacher-training program. *Journal of Educational Psychology, 72*, 62-70.

Britton, B. K., & Gulgoz, S. (1991). Using Kintsch's computational model to improve instructional text: Effects of repairing inference calls on recall and cognitive structures. *Journal of Educational Psychology 83*, 329-345.

Brooks-Gunn, J., Han, W.-J., & Waldfogel, J. (2002). Maternal employment and child cognitive outcomes in the first three years of life: The NICHD study of early child care. *Child Development, 73*, 1052-1072.

Broudy, H. S. (1977). Types of knowledge and purposes of education. In R. Anderson, C. Shapiro, & W. E. Montagne (Eds). *Schooling and the Acquisition of Knowledge* (pp. 1-17). Hillsdale, NJ: Lawrence Erlbaum Associates.

Brown, A. L. (1989). Analogical learning and transfer: What develops? In S. Vosniadou & A. Ortony (Eds.), *Similarity and analogical reasoning* (pp. 369-412). New York: Cambridge University Press.

Brown, A. L., & Kane, M. J. (1988). Preschool children can learn to transfer: Learning to learn and learning from example. *Cognitive Psychology, 20*, 493-523.

Brown, J. S., Collins, A., & Duguid, P. (1989). Situated cognition and the culture of learning. *Educational Researcher, 18*(1), 32-41.

Bruning, R. H., Schraw, G. J., Norby, M. M., & Ronning, R. R. (2004). *Cognitive Psychology and Instruction.* (4th ed.). Upper Saddle River, NJ: Merrill.

Brünken, R., & Leutner, D. (2001). Aufmerksamkeitsverteilung oder Aufmerksamkeitsfokussierung? Empirische Ergebnisse zur "Split-Attention-Hypothese" beim Lernen mit Multimedia. [Split attention or focusing of attention? Empirical results on the split-attention hypothesis in multimedia learning.]. *Unterrichtswissenschaft, 29*, 357-366.

Brünken, R., Plass, J. L., & Leutner, D. (2003). Direct measurement of cognitive load in multimedia learning. *Educational Psychologist, 38*, 53-61.

Brünken, R., Plass, J. L., & Leutner, D. (2004) Assessment of cognitive load in multimedia learning with dual task methodology: Auditory load and modality effects. *Instructional Science, 32*, 115-132.

Brunken, R., Plass, J., & Leutner, D. (2003). Direct measurement of cognitive load in multimedia learning. *Educational Psychologist, 38*(1), 53-61.

Brunken, R., Plass, J., & Leutner, D. (2004). Assessment of cognitive load in multimedia learning with dual-task methodology: Auditory load and modality effects. *Instructional Science, 32*, 115-132.

Brünken, R., Steinbacher, S., Plass, J. L., & Leutner, D. (2002). Assessment of cognitive load in multimedia learning using dual-task methodology. *Experimental Psychology*, *49*, 109-119.

Brunyé, T. T., & Taylor, H. A. (2008). Extended experience benefits spatial mental model development with route but not survey descriptions. *Acta Psychologica, 127*, 340-354.

Brunyé, T. T., & Taylor, H. A. (in press). Working memory in developing and applying mental models from spatial descriptions. *Journal of Memory and Language, doi:10.1016/j.jml.2007.08.003.*

Brunyé, T. T., Rapp, D. N., & Taylor, H. A. (in press). Representational flexibility and specificity following spatial descriptions of real world environments. *Cognition.*

Brunyé, T. T., Taylor, H. A., & Rapp, D. N. (in press). Repetition and dual coding in procedural multimedia learning. *Applied Cognitive Psychology, DOI: 10.1002/acp.1396.*

Brunyé, T. T., Taylor, H. A., & Worboys, M. (2007). Levels of detail in descriptions and depictions of geographic space. *Spatial Cognition and Computation, 7*(3), *227-266.*

Brunyé, T. T., Taylor, H. A., Rapp, D. N., & Spiro, A. B. (2006). Procedural Learning: The Role of Working Memory in Multimedia Learning Experiences. *Applied Cognitive Psychology, 20*, 917-940.

Brunye, T. T., Taylor, H. A., Rapp, D. N., Spiro, A. B. (2006). Learning procedures: The role of working memory in multimedia learning experiences. *Applied Cognitive Psychology, 20*, 917-940.

Budiu, R., Pirolli, P., & Hong, L. (2007). Remembrance of things tagged: How tagging affects human information processing. *Palo Alto Research Center.* Retrieved January 17, 2008 from http://asc.parc.googlepages.com/2007-09-12-tagmemory-12-blogged-vers.pdf

Buehner, M., Krumm, S., & Pick, M. (2005). Reasoning = working memory ≠ attention. *Intelligence, 33*, 251-272.

Bus, A.G. (2001). Early book reading in the family: A route to literacy. In: S. Neuman & D. Dickinson (Eds.), *Handbook on Research in Early Literacy* (pp.179-191). New York: Guilford Publications.

Bus, A.G., Van IJzendoorn, M.H., & Pellegrini, A.D. (1995). Storybook reading makes for success in learning to read. A meta-analysis on intergenerational transmission of literacy. *Review of Educational Research, 65*, 1-21.

Butcher, K. R. (2006). Learning from text with diagrams: Promoting mental model development and inference generation. *Journal of Educational Psychology, 98*(1), 182-197.

Butcher, K. R., Bhushan, S., & Sumner, T. (2006). Multimedia displays for conceptual search processes: Information seeking with strand maps. *ACM Multimedia Systems Journal, 11*(3), 236-248.

Butler, D., & Winne, P. (1995). Feedback and self-regulated learning: A theoretical synthesis. *Review of Educational Research, 65*, 245–281.

Butterfield, E. C., & Nelson, G. D. (1991). Promoting positive transfer of different types. *Cognition and Instruction, 8*(1), 69-102.

Butterworth, G. (1990). On reconceptualising sensori-motor development in dynamic systems terms. In H. Bloch, B. I. Bertenthal (Eds.), *Sensory-motor organizations and development in infancy and early childhood (pp. 57-73).* New York, NY: Kluwer Academic.

Button, S. B., Mathieu, J. E. & Zajac, D. M. (1996). Goal orientation in organizational research: A conceptual and empirical foundation. *Organizational Behaviour & Human Decision Processes, 67*, 26-48.

Byrnes, J. P. (1996). *Cognitive development and learning in instructional contexts.* Boston: Allyn and Bacon.

Byrt, T., Bishop, J., & Carlin, J. B. (1993). Bias, prevalence, and kappa. *Journal of Clinical Epidemiology, 46*(5), 423-429.

Calvert, S. L., Huston, A. C., Watkins, B. A., & Wright, J. C. (1982). The relation between selective attention to television forms and children's comprehension of content. *Child Development, 53*, 601-610.

Cameron, J., & Pierce, W. D. (1994). Reinforcement, reward, and intrinsic motivation: A meta-analysis. *Review of Educational Research, 64*, 363-423.

Campbell, R. L. (Ed.). (2001). *Studies in reflecting abstraction.* Hove, England: Psychology Press.

Cantor, J., & Engle, R. W. (1993). Working-memory capacity as long-term memory activation: An individual-differences approach. *Journal of Experimental Psychology: Learning, Memory, and Cognition, 19*(5), 1101-1114.

Carroll, J. B. (1993). *Human cognitive abilities: A survey of factor-analytic studies.* New York: Cambridge University Press.

Carroll, P. J., Young, R. J., & Guertin, M. S. (1992). Visual analysis of cartoons: A view from the far side. In K. Rayner (Ed.), *Eye movements and visual cognition: Scene perception and reading* (pp. 444-461). New York: Springer.

Carson, D. (2000). Environmental storytelling: Creating immersive 3-D worlds using lessons learned from the theme park industry. Gamasutra. Retrieved October 3, 2006, from http://www.gamasutra.com/features/20000301/carson_pfv.htm

Casali, J. G., & Wierwille, W. W. (1983). A comparison of rating scale, secondary-task, physiological, and primary-task workload estimation techniques in a simulated flight task emphasizing communications load. *Human Factors, 25,* 623-641.

CBS, Centraal Bureau voor de Statistiek [Statistics Netherlands] (2007).Retrieved November 2007 from http://www.cbs.nl/nl-NL/default.htm

Cen, H., Koedinger, K. R., & Junker, B. (2007). Is over practice necessary? Improving learning efficiency with the cognitive tutor through educational data mining. In R. Lunkin, K. R. Koedinger & J. Greer (Eds.), *Proceedings of the 13th International Conference on Artificial Intelligence in Education* (pp. 511-518). Marina Del Ray, CA: IOS Press.

Chandler, P., & Sweller, J. (1991). Cognitive load theory and the format of instruction. *Cognition and Instruction, 8,* 293-332.

Chandler, P., & Sweller, J. (1996). Cognitive load while learning to use a computer program. *Applied Cognitive Psychology, 10,* 151-170.

Chang, L., Satava, R. M., Pelligrini, C. A., & Sinanan, M. N. (2003). Robotic surgery: Identifying the learning curve through objective measurement of skill. *Surgical Endoscopy, 17,* 1744-1748.

Charmaz, K. (2006). Constructing grounded theory: A practical guide through qualitative analysis. Thousand Oaks, NJ: Sage Publications.

Chase, W. G., & Simon, H. A. (1973). Perception in chess. *Cognitive Psychology, 4,* 55-81.

Chen, C., Lee, H., & Chen, Y. (2005). Personalized E-learning systems using item response theory. *Computers in Education, 44,* 237-255.

Chi, M. T. H. (in press). Three types of conceptual change: Belief revision, mental model transformation, and categorical shift. In S. Vosniadou (Ed.), *Handbook of research on conceptual change.* Hillsdale, NJ: Erlbaum.

Chi, M. T. H., De Leeuw, N., Chiu, M., & Lavancher, C. (1994). Eliciting self-explanations improves understanding. *Cognitive Science, 18,* 439-477.

Chi, M. T. H., Feltovich, P. J., & Glaser, P. (1980). Categorization and representation of physics problems by experts and novices. *Cognitive Science, 5,* 121-152.

Chi, M. T. H., Siler, S. A., Jeong, H., Yamauchi, T., & Hausmann, R. G. (2001). Learning from human tutoring. *Cognitive Science, 25*(4), 471-533.

Chi, M. T., de Leeuw, N., Chiu, M.-H., & LaVancher, C. (1994). Eliciting self-explanations improves understanding. *Cognitive Science, 18*(3), 439-477.

Chi, M. T., Siler, S. A., & Jeong, H. (2004). Can tutors monitor students' understanding accurately? *Cognition and Instruction, 22*(3), 363-387.

Childress, M. D., & Braswell, R. (2006). Using massively multiplayer online role-playing games for online learning. *Distance Education, 27*(2), 187-196.

Chiu, C., & Wang, F. (2000). The influence of navigation map scope on disorientation of elementary students in learning a Web-based hypermedia course. *Journal of Educational Computing Research, 22,* 135-144.

Chmielewski, T. L., & Dansereau, D. F. (1998). Enhancing the recall of text: Knowledge mapping training promotes implicit transfer. *Journal of Educational Psychology, 90*(3), 407-413.

Ciernak, G., Scheiter, K., & Gerjets, P. (2007, August). *Eye movements of differently knowledgeable learners during learning with split-source of integrated format.* Paper presented at the bi-annual meeting of the European Association of Research on Learning and Instruction (EARLI). Budapest, Hungary.

Clark, A. (1990). Embodied, situated, and distributed cognition. In W. Betchel, & G. Graham (Eds.), *A companion to cognitive science.* Malden, MA: Blackwell Publishing.

Clark, J. M., & Paivio, A. (1991). Dual coding theory and education. *Educational Psychology Review, 3*(3), 149-170.

Clark, R. E. (1983). Reconsidering research on learning from media. *Review of Educational Research, 53*(4), 445-459.

Clark, R. E. (1994). Media and method. *Educational Technology, Research and Development, 42,* 7-10.

Clark, R. E., & Feldon, D. F. (2005). Five common but questionable principles of multimedia learning. In R. E.

Mayer (Ed.), *The Cambridge Handbook of Multimedia Learning* (pp. 97-115). New York: Cambridge University Press.

Clarke, T., Ayres, P., & Sweller, J. (2005). The impact of sequencing and prior knowledge on learning mathematics through spreadsheet applications. *Educational Technology Research & Development, 53*(3), 15-24.

Clarke, T., Ayres, P., & Sweller, J. (2005). The impact of sequencing and prior knowledge on learning mathematics through spreadsheet application. *Educational Technology, Research and Development, 53*(3), 15-24.

Clements, D. H. (1999). "Concrete" manipulatives, concrete ideas. *Contemporary Issues in Early Childhood, 1*, 45–60.

Clements, D. H., & Sarama, J. (2007). Effects of a preschool mathematics curriculum: Summative research on the Building Blocks project. *Journal for Research in Mathematics Education, 38*, 136-163.

Close, R. (2004). *Television and language development in the early years: A review of the literature*. London: National Literacy Trust.

Cognition and Technology Group at Vanderbilt. (1990). Anchored instruction and its relationship to situated cognition. *Educational Researcher, 19*(6), 2-10.

Cognition and Technology Group at Vanderbilt. (1991). Technology and the design of generative learning environments. *Educational Technology, 31*(5), 34-40.

Cognition and Technology Group at Vanderbilt. (1992). The Jasper experiment: An exploration of issues in learning and instructional design. *Educational Technology Research and Development, 40*(1), 65-80.

Cognition and Technology Group at Vanderbilt. (1997). The jasper project: Lessons in curriculum, instruction, assessment, and professional development. Mahwah, NJ: Erlbaum.

Cohen, R. L. (1989). Memory for enactment events: The power of enactment. *Educational Psychology Review, 1*, 57-80.

Collins, A., Brown, J. S., & Newman, S. (1989). Cognitive apprenticeship: Teaching the crafts of reading, writing, and mathematics. In L. Resnick (Ed.), *Knowing, learning and instruction: Essays in honor of Robert Glaser* (pp. 453–494). Hillsdale, NJ: Lawrence Erlbaum Associates.

Colquitt, J. A., & Simmering, M. J. (1998). Conscientiousness, goal orientation, and motivation to learn during the learning process: A longitudinal study. *Journal of Applied Psychology, 83*, 654-665.

Colquitt, J. A., LePine, J. A., & Noe, R. A. (2000). Toward an integrative theory of training motivation: A meta-analytic path analysis of 20 years of research. *Journal of Applied Psychology, 85*, 678-707.

Conati, C., Gertner, A., & Vanlehn, K. (2002). Using bayesian networks to manage uncertainty in student modeling. *User Modeling and User-Adapted Interaction, 12*(4), 371-417.

Conklin, J. (1987). New technology and the curriculum. *Thrust, 16*, 18-20.

Conlon, T. (2006). *But is our concept map any good? Classroom experiences with the Reasonable Fallible Analyser*. Paper presented at the Second International Conference on Concept Mapping, San José, Costa Rica.

Conway, A. R. A., Cowan, N., & Bunting, M. F. (2001). The cocktail party phenomenon revisited: The importance of working memory capacity. *Psychonomic Bulletin & Review, 8*, 331–335.

Conway, A. R., Cowan, N., Bunting, M. F., Therriault, D. J., & Minkoff, S. R. (2002). A latent variable analysis of working memory capacity, short-term memory capacity, processing speed, and general fluid intelligence. *Intelligence, 30*, 163-183.

Cook, A. E., Hacker, D. J., Webb, A., Osher, D., Kristjansson, K., Woltz, D. J., & Kircher, J. C. (2007). Lyin' Eyes: Oculomotor Measures of Reading Reveal Deception. Manuscript under review.

Cook, D. T., & Campbell, T. D. (1979). *Quasi-experimentation: design & analysis issues for field settings*. Boston, MA: Houghton Mifflin.

Cook, M. P., Carter, G., & Wiebe, E. N. (2008). The interpretation of cellular transport graphics by students with low and high prior knowledge. *International Journal of Science Education 30*, 241-263.

Cooley, R., Mobasher, B., & Srivastava, J. (1997). Web mining: Information and pattern discovery on the World Wide Web. In *Proceedings of the 9th IEEE International Conference on Tools with Artificial Intelligence* (pp. 0558). Newport Beach, CA.

Cooper, G., & Sweller, J. (1987). The effects of schema acquisition and rule automation on mathematical problem-solving transfer. *Journal of Educational Psychology, 79*, 347-362.

Cooper, G., & Sweller, J. (1987). The effects of schema acquisition and rule automation on mathematical problem-solving transfer. *Journal of Educational Psychology, 79,* 347-362.

Cooper, G., Tindall-ford, S., Chandler, P., & Sweller, J. (2001). Learning by imagining. *Journal of Experimental Psychology: Applied, 7*(1), 68-82.

Cooper, G., Tindall-Ford, S., Chandler, P., & Sweller, J. (2001). Learning by imagining. *Journal of Experimental Psychology: Applied, 7,* 68-82.

Cordova, D. I., & Lepper, M. R. (1996). Intrinsic motivation and the process of learning: Beneficial effects of contextualization, personalization, and choice. *Journal of Educational Psychology, 88*(4), 715-730.

Creswell, J. (2005). Educational Research: planning, conducting, and evaluating quantitative and qualitative research (2nd Ed.). New Jersey: Merrill.

Csikszentmihalyi, M. (1990). Flow: The psychology of optimal experience. New York, NY: HarperCollins Publishing.

d'Ydewalle, G., & Gielen, I. (1992). Attention allocation with overlapping sound, image, and text. In K. Rayner (Ed.), *Eye movements and visual cognition: Scene perception and reading.* (pp. 415-427). New York: Springer.

d'Ydewalle, G., Praet, C., Verfaillie, K., & Van Rensbergen, J. (1991). Watching subtitled television: Automatic reading behavior. *Communication Research, 18,* 650-666.

Dalton, D. W. (1990). The effects of cooperative learning strategies on achievement and attitudes during interactive video. *Journal of Computer-Based Instruction, 17*(1), 8-16.

Daneman M., & Green, I. (1986). Individual differences in comprehending and producing words in context. *Journal of Verbal Learning and Verbal Behavior, 19,* 450–466.

Daneman, M, & Tardif, T. (1987). Working memory and reading skill re-examined. In M. E. Coltheart (Ed.), *Attention and performance XII: The psychology of reading* (pp. 491-508). Hove, UK: Lawrence Erlbaum.

Daneman, M., & Carpenter, P. A. (1980). Individual differences in working memory and reading. *Journal of Verbal Learning and Verbal Behavior, 19,* 450-466.

Daneman, M., & Carpenter, P. A. (1983). Individual differences in integrating information between and within sentences. *Journal of Experimental Psychology: Learning, Memory, and Cognition, 9,* 561-584.

Danemann, M., & Carpenter, P. (1980). Individual differences in working memory and reading. *Journal of Verbal Learning and Verbal Behavior, 19,* 450-466.

Dawson, M. D., Schell, A. M., & Filion, D. L. (1990). In J. T. Cacioppo & L. G. Tassinary (Eds.), *Principles of psychophysiology: Physical, social and inferential elements* (pp. 295-324). New York: Cambridge University Press.

Dawson, M. D., Schell, A. M., & Filion, D. L. (2000). The electrodermal system. In J.T. Cacioppo, L. G. Tassinary, & G. G. Berntson (Eds.), *Handbook of Psychophysiology* (pp. 200-223). Cambridge: Cambridge University Press.

De Beni, R., Pazzaglia, F., Gyselinck, V., & Meneghetti, C. (2005). Visuospatial working memory and mental representation of spatial descriptions. *European Journal of Cognitive Psychology, 17,* 77-95.

De Bock, D., Verschaffel, L., & Janssens, D. (2002). The effects of different problem presentations and formulations on the illusion of linearity in secondary school students. *Mathematical Thinking and Learning, 4,* 65-89.

De Groot, A. (1965). *Thought and choice in chess.* The Hague, Netherlands: Mouton. (Original work published 1946).

De Jong, M. T., & Bus, A. G. (2004). The efficacy of electronic books in fostering kindergarten children's emergent story understanding. *Reading Research Quarterly, 39,* 378-393.

de Jong, T., & van Joolingen, W. R. (1998). Scientific discovery learning with computer simulations of conceptual domains. *Review of Educational Research, 68*(2), 179-201.

de la Chica, S., Ahmad, F., Sumner, T., Martin, J. H., & Butcher, K. (in press). Computational foundations for personalizing instruction with digital libraries. *International Journal on Digital Libraries.*

Deci, E. L., & Ryan, R. M. (1985). *Intrinsic motivation and self-determination in human behaviour.* New York: Plenum.

Deci, E. L., & Ryan, R. M. (1992). The initiation and regulation of intrinsically motivated learning and achievement. In A. K. Boggiano & T. S. Pittman (Eds.), *Achievement and motivation: A social-developmental perspective* (pp. 9-36). New York, NY: Cambridge University Press.

Deci, E. L., Vallerand, R. J., Pelletier, L. C., & Ryan, R. M. (1991). Motivation and education: The self-determination perspective. *Educational Psychologist, 26*, 325-346.

Deimann, M., & Keller, J. M. (2006). Volitional aspects of multimedia learning. *Journal of Educational Multimedia and Hypermedia, 15*(2), 137-158.

deJong, T., & van Joolingen, W. (1998). Scientific discovery learning with computer simulations of conceptual domains. *Review of Educational Research, 68*(2), 179-201.

Della Sala, S., Baddeley, A., Papagno, C., Spinnler, H. (1995). Dual-task paradigm: A means to examine the central executive. Annals of the New York Academy of Science, 769, 161-171.

DeLoache, J. S. (1995). Early understanding and use of symbols: The model model. *Current Directions in Psychological Science, 4*, 109-113.

DeLoache, J. S., Pierroutsakos, S. L., & Uttal, D. H. (2003). The origins of pictorial competence. *Current Directions in Psychological Science, 12*, 114-118.

DeSchryver, M. & Spiro, R.J. (in preparation). Nonlinear knowledge acquisition in a post-Gutenberg world: An examination of emerging constructs for deep learning on the Web.

DeShon, R. P., & Gillespie, J. Z. (2005). A motivated action theory account of goal orientation. *Journal of Applied Psychology, 90*, 1096-1127.

DeShon, R. P., & Gillespie, J. Z. (2005). A motivated action theory account of goal orientation. *Journal of Applied Psychology, 90*(6), 1096-1127.

DeStefano, D. & LeFevre, J. (2007). Cognitive load in hypertext reading: A review. *Computers in Human Behavior, 23*, 1616-1641.

Detenber, B.H. and Reeves, B. (1996). A bio-informational theory of emotion: Motion and image size effects on viewers. *Journal of Communication, 46*, 66-84.

Detterman, D.K., & Sternberg, R.J. (1993). *Transfer on trial: Intelligence, cognition, & instruction.* Norwood, NJ: Ablex.

Di Eugenio, B., & Glass, M. (2004). The kappa statistic: A second look. *Computational Linguistics, 30*(1), 95-101.

Diao, Y., & Sweller, J. (2007). Redundancy in foreign language reading comprehension instruction: Concurrent written and spoken presentations. *Learning and Instruction, 17*, 78-88.

Dickey, M. D. (2005). Engaging by design: How engagement strategies in popular computer and video games can inform instructional design. *Educational Technology Research & Development, 53*(2), 67-83.

Dickey, M. D. (2006). Game design narrative for learning: Appropriating adventure game design narrative and techniques for the design of interactive learning environments. *Educational Technology Research & Development, 54*(3), 245-263.

diSessa, A. (1988). Knowledge in pieces. In G. Forman & P. B. Burall (Eds.), *Constructivism in the computer age* (pp. 49–70). Hillsdale, NJ: Lawrence Erlbaum Associates.

diSessa, A., & Abelson, H. (1986). Boxer: A reconstructible computational medium. *Communications of the ACM, 29*(9), 859-868.

diSessa, A., Abelson, H., & Ploger, D. (1991). An overview of Boxer. *Journal of Mathematical Behavior, 10*, 3-15.

Doolittle, P. E., & Mariano, G. J. (in press). Working memory capacity and mobile multimedia learning environments: Is mobile learning from portable digital media players for everyone? *Journal of Educational Multimedia and Hypermedia.*

Doolittle, P. E., Lusk, D. A., Byrd, C. N., & Mariano, G. J. (in press). Mobile multimedia learning environments: iPods as an educational platform. In H. Ryu & D. Parsons (Eds.), *Innovative mobile learning.* Hershey, PA: Idea Group.

Doolittle, P. E., McCloud, J., Byrd, C. N., & Mariano, G. J. (2008). *Working memory capacity, attentional control and multimedia learning.* Paper presented at the annual conference of the Eastern Educational Research Association, Hilton Head, SC.

Doyle, W. (1988). Work in mathematics classes: The context of students' thinking during instruction. *Educational Psychologist, 23*(2), 167-180.

Driscoll, M. P. (2000). *Psychology of learning for instruction* (2nd ed.). Needham Heights, MA: Allyn & Bacon.

Dubois, M., & Vial, I. (2000). Multimedia design: The effects of relating multimodal information. *Journal of Computer Assisted Learning, 16*, 157-165.

Duff, S. C. (2000). What's working in working memory: A role for the central executive. *Scandinavian Journal of Psychology, 41*, 9-16.

Duff, S. C., Logie, R. H. (2001). Processing and storage in working memory span. *The Quarterly Journal of Experimental Psychology, 54,* 31-48.

Duit, R. (1991). The role of analogies and metaphors in learning science. *Science Education, 75,* 649–672.

Duit, R., Roth, W.-M., Komorek, M., & Wilbers, J. (2001). Fostering conceptual change by analogies: Between Scylla and Charybdis. *Learning and Instruction, 11,* 283–303.

Dweck, C., & Leggett, E. (1988). A social-cognitive approach to motivation and personality. *Psychological Review, 95,* 256-273.

Dwyer, F. M. (1967). The relative effectiveness of varied visual illustrations in complementing programmed instruction. *Journal of Experimental Education, 36,* 34-42.

Dwyer, F. M. (1968). The effectiveness of visual illustrations used to complement programmed instruction. *Journal of Psychology, 70,* 157-162.

Dwyer, F. M. (1969). The effect of varying the amount of realistic detail in visual illustrations designed to complement programmed instruction. *Programmed Learning and Educational Technology, 6,* 147-153.

Eccles, J. S., & Wigfield, A. (2002). Motivational beliefs, values, and goals. *Annual Review of Psychology, 53*(1), 109-132.

Eco, U. (1976). *A theory of semiotics.* Bloomington, IN: Indiana University Press.

Edwards, D. M., & Hardman, L. (1999). 'Lost in hyperspace': Cognitive mapping and navigation in a hypertext environment. In R. McAleese (Ed.), *Hypertext: Theory into practice,* (2nd ed., pp. 90-105). Oxford: Intellect Books.

Edwards, L. D. (1991). Children's learning in a computer microworld for transformation geometry. *Journal for Research in Mathematics Education, 22,* 122-137.

Eilam, B., & Poyas, Y. (in press). Learning with multiple representations: Extending multimedia learning beyond the lab. *Learning and Instruction.*

Elliot, A. J. (1997). Integrating the "classic" and "contemporary" approaches to achievement motivation: A hierarchical model of approach and avoidance achievement motivation. In M. L. Maehr & P. R. Pintrich (Eds.), *Advances in motivation and achievement* (Vol. 10, pp. 143-179). Greenwich, CT: JAI Press.

Elliot, A. J. (1999). Approach and avoidance motivation and achievement goals. *Educational Psychologist, 34*(3), 169-189.

Elliot, A. J., & Church, M. A. (1997). A hierarchical model of approach and avoidance achievement motivation. *Journal of Personality and Social Psychology, 72,* 218-232.

Elliot, A. J., & McGregor, H. (2001). A 2 x 2 achievement goal framework. *Journal of Personality and Social Psychology, 80,* 501-519.

Elliot, A. J., & Thrash, T. M. (2001). Achievement goals and the hierarchical model of achievement motivation. *Educational Psychology Review, 13,* 139-156.

Elliott, A. J., Shell, M. M., & Henry, K. B. (2005). Achievement goals, performance contingencies, and performance attainment: An experimental test. *Journal of Educational Psychology, 97,* 630-640.

Engelkamp, J. (1998). *Memory for actions.* Hove, UK: Psychology Press.

Engelkamp, J. (1998). *Memory for actions.* Hove, UK: Psychology Press.

Engelkamp, J., & Seiler, K. H. (2003). Gains and losses in action memory. *The Quarterly Journal of Experimental Psychology, 56A,* 829-848.

Engelkamp, J., & Zimmer, H. D. (1994). *Human memory: A multimodal approach.* Seattle, WA: Hogefe and Huber.

Engelkamp, J., & Zimmer, H. D. (1997). Sensory factors in memory for subject-performed tasks. *Acta Psychologica, 96,* 43-60.

Engelkamp, J., Zimmer, H. D., & Mohr, G. (1994). Memory of self-performed tasks: Self-performing during recognition. *Memory & Cognition, 22,* 34-39.

Engle, R. A. (2006). Framing interactions to foster generative learning: A situative explanation of transfer in a community of learners classroom. *The Journal of the Learning Sciences, 15*(4), 451-498.

Ericsson, K. A., & Kintsch, W. (1995). Long-term working memory. *Psychological Review, 102*(2), 211-245.

Ericsson, K. A., Krampe, R. Th., & Tesch-Roemer, C. (1993). The role of deliberate practice in the acquisition of expert performance. *Psychological Review, 100,* 363-406.

Eskelinen, M. (2001). Computer game studies, Year one. *Game Studies: The International Journal of Computer*

Game Research, 1(1), Retrieved September 20, 2006, from http://www.gamestudies.org/0101/eskelinen/

Estes, M. (2004). Universal design. In M. Orey, M. A. Fitzgerald & R. M. Branch (Eds.), *Educational Media and Technology Yearbook 2004, 29*, 86-92. Westport, CT: Libraries Unlimited.

Evans, C., & Gibbons, N. J. (2007). The interactivity effect in multimedia learning. *Computers & Education, 49*(4), 1147-1160.

Eveland, W. P., & Dunwoody, S. (2001). User control and structural isomorphism or disorientation and cognitive load? *Communication Research, 28*(1), 48.

Eveland, W. P., Cortese, J., Park, H., & Dunwoody, S. (2004). How Web site organization influences free recall, factual knowledge, and knowledge structure density. *Human Communication Research, 30*(2), 208-233.

Faraday, P., & Sutcliffe, A. (1996). An empirical study of attending and comprehending multimedia presentations. In *Proceedings ACM Multimedia, 96*, 265-275. Boston MA.

Farmer, E. W., Berman, J. V., Fletcher, Y. L. (1986). Evidence for a visuo-spatial scratchpad in working memory. *Quarterly Journal of Experimental Psychology, 38*, 675-688.

Fedorenko, E., Gibson, E., & Rohde, D. (2007). The nature of working memory in linguistic, arithmetic and spatial integration processes. *Journal of Memory and Language, 56*, 246-269.

Feldman Barrett, L., Tugade, M. M., & Engle, R. A. (2004). Individual differences in working memory capacity and dual-process theories of the mind. *Psychological Bulletin, 130*(4), 553-573.

Fellbaum, C. (1998). *WordNet: An electronic lexical database*. Cambridge, MA: MIT Press.

Feltovich, P. J., Spiro, R. J., & Coulson, R. L. (1989). The nature of conceptual understanding in biomedicine: The deep structure of complex ideas and the development of misconceptions. In D. Evans & V. Patel (Eds.), *The Cognitive Sciences in Medicine* (pp. 113-172). Cambridge, MA: M.I.T. Press.

Feltovich, P.J, Spiro, R.J., & Coulson, R.L. (1997). Issues of expert flexibility in contexts characterized by complexity and change. In P.J. Feltovich, K.M. Ford, & R.R. Hoffman (Eds.). *Expertise in context: Human and machine.* Cambridge, MA: MIT Press.

Feltovich, P.J., Coulson, R.L., & Spiro, R.J. (2001). Learners' understanding of important and difficult concepts: A challenge to smart machines in education. In P.J. Feltovich & K. Forbus (Eds.). *Smart Machines in Education.* Cambridge, MA: MIT Press.

Ferguson, W. (1992). ASK systems: An approach to the realization of story-based teachers. *The Journal of the Learning Sciences, 2*(1), 95-134.

Fernandez, A., & Glenberg, A. M. (1985). Changing environmental context does not reliably affect memory. *Memory & Cognition, 13*, 333-345.

Finding information on the Internet: A tutorial, (2008). Retrieved February 10, 2008 from http://www.lib.berkeley.edu/TeachingLib/Guides/Internet/Evaluate.html

Fitzgerald, J., Spiegel, D., & Cunningham, J. (1991). The relationship between parental literacy level and perceptions of emergent literacy. *Journal of Reading Behavior, 23*, 191–214.

Fletcher, J. D., & Tobias, S. (2005). The multimedia principle. In R. Mayer (Ed.) *Cambridge handbook of multimedia learning* (pp. 117-133). New York, NY: Cambridge University Press.

Folker, S., Ritter, H., & Sichelschmidt (2005). Processing and integrating multimodal material – the influence of color-coding. In: B. G. Bara, L. Barsalou and M. Bucciarelli (Eds.), *Proceedings of the 27th Annual Conference of the Cognitive Science Society 2005 (p.* 690-695). Mahwah, NJ: Erlbaum.

Ford, M. E., & Nichols, C. W. (1991). Using goal assessments to identify motivational patterns and facilitate behavioral regulation and achievement. In M. L. Maehr & P. R. Pintrich (Eds.), *Advances in motivation and achievement, 7*, 51-84. Greenwich, CT: JAI Press.

Fosnot, C. T. (1996). Constructivism: A psychological theory of learning. In C. T. Fosnot (Ed.), *Constructivism: Theory, perspectives, and practice* (pp. 9-33). New York: Teachers College Press.

Frasca, G. (1999). Ludology meets narratology: Similitude and differences between (video) games and narrative. *Ludology.org Game Theory.* Retrieved October 1, 2006, from http://www.ludology.org/articles/ludology.htm

Friedman, N. P., & Miyake, A. (2000). Differential roles for visuospatial and verbal working memroy in situation model construction. *Journal of Experimental Psychology: General, 129*, 61-83.

Friesen, N., & Anderson, T. (2004). Interaction for lifelong learning. *British Journal of Educational Technology, 35*, 679-687.

Frijters, J. C., Barron, R. W., & Brunello, M. (2000). Direct or mediated influences of home literacy and literacy interest on prereaders' oral vocabulary and early written language skill. *Journal of Educational Psychology, 92*, 466-477.

Fuchs, L. S., Fuchs, D., Prentice, K., Burch, M., Hamlett, C. L., Owen, R., Hosp, M., & Jancek, D. (2003). Explicitly teaching for transfer: Effects on third-grade students' mathematical problem solving. *Journal of Educational Psychology, 95*, 293-305.

Gaedke, B., & Shaughnessy, M.F. (2003). An interview with Jere Brophy. *Educational Psychology Review, 15*(2), 199-211.

Gaide, S. (2004). Reusing learning objects: Improving instructional design, reducing costs at Athabasca U. *Distance Education Report, 8*(13), 8.

Gallagher, S. A., Stepien, W. J., & Rosenthal, H. (1992). The effects of problem-based learning on problem solving. *Gifted Child Quarterly, 36*, 195-200.

Gallese, V. (2003). The roots of empathy: The shared manifold hypothesis and the neural basis of intersubjectivity. *Psychopathology, 36*, 171–180.

Gallese, V., Fadiga, L., Fogassi, L., & Rizzolatti, G. (1996). Action recognition in the premotor cortex. *Brain, 119*, 593-609.

Gao, T., & Lehman, J. D. (2003). The effects of different levels of interaction on the achievement and motivation perceptions of college students in a Web-based learning environment. *Journal of Interactive Learning Research, 14*(4), 367-386.

Garden, S., Cornoldi, C., & Logie, R. H. (2001). Visuo-spatial working memory in navigation. *Applied Cognitive Psychology, 16*, 35-50.

Gaultney, J. F., Kipp, K., & Kirk, G. (2005). Utilization deficiency and working memory capacity in adult memory performance: Not just for children anymore. *Cognitive Development, 20*, 205-213.

Ge, X., & Er, N. (2005). An online support system to scaffold real-world problem solving. *Interactive Learning Environments, 13*(3), 139 – 157.

Geary, D. (2007). Educating the evolved mind: Conceptual foundations for an evolutionary educational psychology. In J. S. Carlson & J. R. Levin (Eds.), *Psychological perspectives on contemporary educational issues* (pp. 1-99). Greenwich, CT: Information Age Publishing.

Gee, J. P., (2003). *What video games have to teach us about learning and literacy.* New York: Palgrave Macmillan.

Gee, J. P., (2004). Learning by design: Games as learning machines. *Interactive Educational Multimedia, 8*, 15-23.

Gemino, A., Parker, D., & Kutzschan, A. O. (2006). Investigating coherence and multimedia effects of a technology-mediated collaborative environment. *Journal of management Information Systems, 22*(3), 97-121.

Gentner, D. (1989). The mechanisms of analogical learning. In S. Vosniadou & A. Ortony (Eds.), *Similarity and analogical reasoning* (pp. 119–241). Cambridge, UK: Cambridge University Press.

Gentner, D., & Stevens, A. (Eds.). (1983). *Mental models.* Hillsdale, NJ: Lawrence Erlbaum Associates.

Gentner, D., Loewenstein, J., & Thompson, L., (2003). Learning and transfer: A general role for analogical encoding. *Journal of Educational Psychology, 95*(2), 393-408.

Georghiades, P. (Summer 2000). Beyond conceptual change learning in science education: Focusing on transfer, durability and metacognition, *Educational Research. 42*(2), 119-139.

Gerjets, P, Scheiter, K, & Schuh, J. (2008). Information comparisons in example-based hypermedia environments: Supporting learners with processing prompts and an interactive comparison tool. *Educational Technology Research and Development, 56*(1), 73-92.

Gerjets, P., & Scheiter, K. (2003). Goal configurations and processing strategies as moderators between instructional design and cognitive load: Evidence from hypertext-based instruction. *Educational Psychologist, 38*(1), 33-41.

Gerjets, P., & Scheiter, K. (2003). Goals and strategies as moderators between instructional design and cognitive load: Evidence from hypertext-based instruction. *Educational Psychologist, 38*, 33-41.

Gernsbacher, M. A. (1990). *Language comprehension as structure building.* Hillsdale, NJ: Erlbaum.

Gernsbacher, M. A., Stevenson, J. L., & Schweigert, E. K. (2007). Mirror neurons in humans? *Presentation at the annual meeting of the Psychonomic Society, Long Beach, CA.*

Gibbons, J., Anderson, D. R., Smith, R., Field, D. E., & Fischer, C. (1986). Young children's recall and reconstruction of audio and audiovisual narratives. *Child Development, 57*, 1014-1023.

Gibson, J. J. (1979). *The ecological approach to visual perception.* Boston, MA: Houghton Mifflin.

Gick, M. L., & Holyoak, K. J. (1980). Analogical problem solving. *Cognitive Psychology, 12,* 306-355.

Gick, M. L., & Holyoak, K. J. (1983). Schema induction and analogical transfer. *Cognitive Psychology, 15,* 1-38.

Gick, M. L., & Holyoak, K. J. (1987). The cognitive basis of knowledge transfer. In S. M. Cormier & J. D. Hagman (Eds.). *Transfer of learning: Contemporary research and application* (pp. 9-46). San Diego, CA: Academic Press.

Gilbert, J. K. (2005). Visualization: A metacognitive skill in science and science education. In J. K. Gilbert (Ed.), *Visualization in Science Education* (pp. 9-27). Amsterdam: Springer.

Ginns, P. (2005). Meta-analysis of the modality effect. *Learning and Instruction, 15,* 313-331.

Ginns, P. (2006). Integrating information: A meta-analysis of the spatial contiguity and temporal contiguity effects. *Learning and Instruction, 16,* 511-525.

Glaser, R. (1984). Education and thinking. The role of knowledge. *American Psychologist, 39,* 93-104.

Glaser, R., & Chi, M. T. H. (1988). Overview. In M. T. H. Chi, R. Glaser, & M. J. Farr (Eds.), *The Nature of Expertise* (pp. Xv-xxviii). Hillsdale, NJ: Erlbaum.

Glenberg, A. M. & Langston, W. E. (1992). Comprehension of illustrated text: Pictures help to build mental models. *Journal of Memory and Language, 31,* 129-151.

Glenberg, A. M., Gutierrez, T., Levin, J. R., Japuntich, S., & Kaschak, M. P. (2004). Activity and imagined activity can enhance young children's reading comprehension. *Journal of Educational Psychology, 96,* 424-436.

Glynn, S. M. (1995). Conceptual bridges: Using analogies to explain scientific concepts. *The Science Teacher, 62*(9), 25-27.

Glynn, S. M., Duit, R., & Thiele, R. B. (1995). Teaching science with analogies: A strategy for constructing knowledge. In S. Glynn & R. Duit (Eds.), *Learning science in the schools: Research reforming practice* (pp. 247-273). Mahwah, NJ: Lawrence Erlbaum Associates.

Goldman, H. B., & Healy, A. F. (1985). Detection errors in a task with articulatory suppression: Phonological recoding and reading. *Memory & Cognition, 13,* 463-468.

Goldman, S. R. (1991). On the derivation of instructional applications from cognitive theories: Commentary on Chandler and Sweller. *Cognition and Instruction, 8,* 333-342.

Goldman, S. R. (2005). Designing for scalable educational improvement. In C. Dede, J. P. Honan & L. C. Peters (Eds.), *Scaling up success: Lessons learned from technology-based educational improvement* (pp. 67-96). San Francisco: Jossey-Bass.

Goldstone, R. L., & Son, J. Y. (2005). The transfer of scientific principles using concrete and idealized simulations. *The Journal of the Learning Sciences, 14,* 69-110.

Gombrich, E. H. (1969). *Art and illusion: A study in the psychology of pictorial representation.* Princeton, NJ: Princeton University Press.

Goodman, N. (1976). *Languages of art: An approach to a theory of symbols* (2nd ed.). Indianapolis, IN: Hackett.

Goodwin, C. (2000). Action and embodiment within situated human interaction. *Journal of Pragmatics, 32,* 1489–1522.

Gottfried, A. E. (1985). Academic intrinsic motivation in elementary and junior high school students. *Journal of Educational Psychology, 77*(6), 631-645.

Gouli, E., Gogoulou, A., Papanikalaou, K., & Grigoriadou, M. (2004, September). *Compass: An adaptive web-based concept map assessment tool.* Paper presented at the First International Conference on Concept Mapping, Pamplona, Spain.

Grady, J. L., Kehrer, R. G., Trusty, C., Entin, E. B., Entin, E. E., & Brunyé, T. T. (in press). Learning nursing procedures: The impact of simulator fidelity and student gender on teaching effectiveness. *Journal of Nursing Education.*

Graesser, A. C., & Britton, B. K. (1996). Five metaphors for text understanding. In B. K. Britton, & A. C. Graesser (Eds.), *Models of understanding text.* (pp. 341-352). Mahwah, NJ: Erlbaum.

Graesser, A. C., & Person, N. K. (1994). Question asking during tutoring. *American Educational Research Journal, 31*(1), 104-137.

Graesser, A. C., Hauft-Smith, K., Cohen, A. D., & Pyles, L. D. (1980). Advanced outlines, familiarity, text genre, and retention of prose. *Journal of Experimental Education, 48,* 209-220.

Graesser, A. C., Hoffman, N. L., & Clark, L. F. (1980). Structural components of reading time. *Journal of Verbal Learning and Verbal Behavior, 19,* 135-151.

Graesser, A. C., Lu, S., Jackson, G. T., Mitchell, H. H., Ventura, M., Olney, A., & Louwerse, M. M. (2004). AutoTutor: A tutor with dialogue in natural language. *Behavior Research Methods, Instruments, & Computers, 36*(2), 180-192.

Graesser, A. C., Person, N. K., Harter, D., & the Tutoring Research Group. (2001). Teaching tactics and dialogue in AutoTutor. *International Journal of Artificial Intelligence and Education, 12*, 257-279.

Graff, M. (2003). Learning from Web-based instructional systems and cognitive style. *British Journal of Educational Technology, 34*(4), 407-418.

Graham, S., & Weiner, B. (1996). Theories and principles of motivation. In D. Berliner & R. Calfee (Eds.), *Handbook of educational psychology* (pp. 63-84). New York: Simon & Schuster Macmillan.

Grant, H., & Dweck, C. S. (2003). Clarifying achievement goals and their impact. *Journal of Personality and Social Psychology, 85*, 541-553.

Gray, J. A., Feldon, J. M., Rawlings, J. N. P., Hemsley, D. R., Snith, A. D. (1991). The neuropsychology of schizophrenia. *Behavioral Brain Sciences, 14*, 1-84.

Green, C. D. (1992). Of immortal mythological beasts: Operationism in psychology. *Theory & Psychology, 2*, 291-320.

Greene, J. A., & Azevedo, R. (2007). Adolescents' use of self-regulatory processes and their relation to qualitative mental model shifts while using hypermedia. *Journal of Educational Computing Research, 36*(2), 125.

Greenfield, P. M., Camaioni, L., Ercolani, P., Weiss, L., Lauber, B. A., & Perucchini, P. (1996). Cognitive socialization by computer games in two cultures: Inductive discovery or mastery of an iconic code? In I. E. Sigel (Series Ed.), P. M. Greenfield, & R. R. Cocking (Vol. Eds.), *Advances, in applied developmental psychology: Vol. 11. Interacting with video* (pp. 141-167). Norwood, NJ: Ablex.

Greeno, J. G. (1983, April). *Skills for representing problems.* Paper presented at the annual meeting of the American Educational Research Association, Montreal.

Greeno, J. G., Collins, A. M., & Resnick, L. B. (1996). Cognition and learning. In D. Berliner & R. Calfee (Eds.), *Handbook of educational psychology* (pp. 15-46). New York, NY: Simon & Schuster Macmillan.

Griffiths, J., & Brophy, P. (2005). Student searching behavior and the Web: Use of academic resources and Google," *Library Trends, 53*(4), 539–554.

Grimes, T. (1990). Audio-video correspondence and its role in attention and memory. *Educational Technology Research and Development, 38*, 15-25.

Gyllenhaal, E., & Perry, D. (1998, May). *Doing something about the weather: Summative evaluation of Science Museum of Minnesota's atmospheric explorations computer interactives.* Paper presented at the Annual Meeting of the American Association of Museums, Los Angeles, CA.

Gyselinck, V., & Tardieu, H. (1999). The role of illustrations in text comprehension: What, when, for whom, and why? In van Oostendorp, H. & Goldman, S.R. (Eds.), *The construction of mental representations during reading (pp. 195-218).* Mahwah, NJ, US: Lawrence Erlbaum Associates.

Gyselinck, V., Cornoldi, C., Dubois, V., De Beni, R., & Ehrlich, M. F. (2002). Visuospatial memory and phonological loop in learning from multimedia. *Applied Cognitive Psychology, 16*, 665-685.

Hadwin, A. F., Winne, P. H., Stockley, D. B., Nesbit, J. C., & Wosczyna, C. (2001). Context moderates students' self-reports about how they study. *Journal of Educational Psychology, 93*, 477-487.

Hahne, A. K., Benndorf, R., Frey, P., & Herzig, S. (2005). Attitude towards computer-based learning: Determinants as revealed by a controlled interventional study. *Medical Education, 39*, 935-943.

Hale, K. S., & Stanney, K. M. (2004). Deriving haptic design guidelines from human physiological, psychophysical, and neurological foundations. *IEEE Computer Graphics and Applications, 24*, 33-39.

Hambrick, D., & Oswald, F. L. (2005). Does domain knowledge moderate involvement of working memory capacity in higher–level cognition? A test of three models. *Journal of Memory and Language, 52*, 377-397.

Handley, S. J., Capon, A., Copp, C., & Harper, C. (2002). Conditional reasoning and the Tower of Hanoi: The role of spatial and verbal working memory. *British Journal of Psychology, 93*, 501–518.

Hannafin, M. J., & Land, S. (1997). The foundations and assumptions of technology-enhanced, student-centered learning environments. *Instructional Science, 25*, 167-202.

Hannafin, M. J., & Rieber, L. P. (1989). Psychological foundations of instructional design for emerging computer-based instructional technologies: Part I. *Educational Technology Research and Development, 37*, 91-101.

Hannafin, M. J., Hannafin, K. M., Hooper, S. R., Rieber, L. P., & Kini, A. (1996). Research on and research with emerging technologies. In D. Jonassen (Ed.), *Handbook of research in educational communication and technology* (pp. 378-402). New York: Macmillan.

Hannafin, M. J., Hill, J., & Land, S. (1997). Student-centered learning and interactive multimedia: Status, issues, and implications. *Contemporary Education, 68*(2), 94-99.

Hannafin, M. J., Land, S., & Oliver, K. (1999). Open learning environments: Foundations and models. In C. Reigeluth (Ed.), *Instructional design theories and models: A new paradigm of instructional theory* (pp. 115-140). Mahwah, NJ: Erlbaum.

Hannus, M., & Hyönä, J. (1999). Utilization of illustrations during learning of science textbook passages among low- and high-ability children. *Contemporary Educational Psychology, 24,* 95-123.

Hanson, K., & Carlson, B. (2005). Effective access: Teachers' use of digital resources in STEM teaching. Retrieved November 15, 2007, from http://www2.edc.org/gdi/publications_SR/EffectiveAccessReport.pdf

Hanson, N. R. (1965). *Patterns of discovery: An inquiry into the conceptual foundations of science.* Cambridge, UK: Cambridge University Press.

Hardré, P. L., Crowson, M., Xie, K., & Ly, C. (2007). Testing differential effects of computer-based Web-based and paper-based administration of questionnaire research instruments. *British Journal of Educational Technology, 38*(1), 5-22.

Harlen, W. (1985). *Primary science: Taking the plunge.* London, UK: Heineman.

Harp, S. F., & Mayer, R. E. (1998). How seductive details do their damage. A theory of cognitive interest in science learning. *Journal of Educational Psychology, 90,* 414-434.

Harskamp, E. G., Mayer, R. E., & Suhre, C. (2007). Does the modality principle for multimedia learning apply to science classrooms? *Learning and Instruction, 17,* 465-477.

Hartley, J. T., Stojack, C. C., Mushaney, T. J., Annon, T. A. K., & Lee, D. W. (1994). Reading speed and prose memory in older and younger adults. *Psychology and Aging, 9,* 216-223.

Harvey, F. A., & Nelson, A. (1995). A hybrid investigation of hypermedia training. *Proceedings of the Association for Educational Communications and Technology, USA.*

Haskell, R. E. (2000). *Transfer of learning: Cognition, instruction and reasoning.* New York: Academic Press.

Hayes, D. S., & Birnbaum, D. W. (1980). Preschoolers' retention of televised events: Is a picture worth a thousand words? *Developmental Psychology, 16,* 410-416.

Hayes, D. S., Chemelski, B. E., & Birnbaum, D. W. (1981). Young children's incidental and intentional retention of televised events. *Developmental Psychology, 17,* 230-232.

Head, A.J. (2007). Beyond Google: How do students conducts academic research? *First Monday, 12*(8). Retrieved January 15, 2008 from http://firstmonday.org/issues/issue12_8/head/index.htm

Hede, A. (2002). An integrated model of multimedia effects on learning. *Journal of Educational Multimedia and Hypermedia, 11,* 177-191.

Hee Jun, C., & Johnson, S. D. (2005). The effect of context-based video instruction on learning and motivation in online courses. *American Journal of Distance Education, 19*(4), 215-227.

Hegarty, M. (1992). Mental animation: Inferring motion from static displays of mechanical systems. *Journal of Experimental Psychology: Learning, Memory, and Cognition, 18,* 1084-1102.

Hegarty, M. (1992). The mechanics of comprehension and comprehension of mechanics. In K. Rayner (Ed.), *Eye movements and visual cognition: Scene perception and reading.* (pp. 428-443). New York: Springer.

Hegarty, M., & Just, M. A. (1993). Constructing mental models of machines from text and diagrams. *Journal of Memory & Language, 32,* 717-742.

Hegarty, M., & Sims, V. K. (1994). Individual differences in mental animation during mechanical reasoning. *Memory & Cognition, 22,* 411-430.

Hegarty, M., & Sims, V. K. (1994). Individual differences in mental animation during mechanical reasoning. *Memory & Cognition, 22,* 411-430.

Hegarty, M., & Waller, D. A. (2005). Individual Differences in Spatial Abilities. In P. Shah & A. Miyake (Eds.), *The Cambridge handbook of visuospatial thinking* (pp. 121-169). Cambridge MA: Cambridge University Press.

Heiser, J., Tversky, B. (2006). Arrows in comprehending and producing mechanical diagrams. *Cognitive Science, 30,* 581-592.

Henderson, J. M. (1992). Visual attention and eye movement control during reading and picture viewing. In: Rayner, K. (Ed.), *Eye movements and visual cognition: Scene perception and reading.* (pp. 260-283). New York: Springer.

Henderson, J. M. (1992). Visual attention and eye movement control during reading and picture viewing. In K. Rayner (Ed.), *Eye movements and visual cognition: Scene perception and reading* (pp. 260-283). New York, NY: Springer-Verlag.

Henderson, J. M. (2007). Regarding scenes. *Current Directions in Psychological Science, 16,* 219-222.

Henderson, J. M., & Hollingworth, A. (1999). High-level scene perception. *Annual Review of Psychology, 50,* 243-271.

Hickey, D. T. (2003). Engaged participation versus marginal nonparticipation: A stridently sociocultural approach to achievement motivation. *Elementary School Journal, 103*(4), 401-429.

Hidi, S., & Harackiewicz, J. M. (2000). Motivating the academically unmotivated: A critical issue for the 21st Century. *Review of Educational Research, 70*(2), 151-179.

Hill, J., & Hannafin, M. J. (1997). Cognitive strategies and learning from the World Wide Web. *Educational Technology Research and Development, 45*(4), 37-64.

Hill, J., & Hannafin, M. J. (2001). Teaching and learning in digital environments: The resurgence of resource-based learning. *Educational Technology Research and Development, 49*(3), 37-52.

Hill, J., Domizi, D., Kim, M., Kim, H., & Hannafin, M. J. (2007). Teaching and learning in negotiated and informal environments. In M. Moore (Ed.), *Handbook of distance education* (2nd ed.) 271-284. Mahwah, NJ: Erlbaum.

Hill, J., Hannafin, M. J., & Domizi, D. (2005). Resource-based learning and informal learning environments: Prospects and challenges. In R. Subramaniam (Ed.), *E-Learning and virtual science centers* (pp. 110-125). Hershey, PA: Idea Group, Inc.

Hill, L. L. (2000). Core elements of digital gazetteers: Placenames, categories, and footprints. In J. Borbinha & T. Baker (Eds.), *Proceedings of the 4th European Conference on Digital Libraries,* Lisbon, Portugal (pp. 380-390). Heidelberg: Springer-Verlag.

Hirai, A (1999). The relationship between listening and reading rates of Japanese EFL learners, *Modern Language Journal, 83,* 367–384.

Hmelo, C. E., & Ferrari, M. (1997). The problem-based learning tutorial: Cultivating higher order thinking skills. *Journal for the Education of the Gifted, 20*(4), 401-422.

Hmelo-Silver, C. E., Duncan, R. V., & Chinn, C. A. (2007). Scaffolding and achievement in problem-based and inquiry learning: A response to Kirschner, Sweller, and Clark (2006). *Educational Psychologist, 42,* 99-107.

Hochberg, J. E. (1978). *Perception* (2nd ed.). Englewood Cliffs, NJ: Prentice-Hall.

Hochberg, J. E., & Brooks, V. (1962). Pictorial recognition as an unlearned ability: A study of one child's performance. *American Journal of Psychology, 75,* 624-628.

Hoffman, B., & Richie, D. (1997). Using multimedia to overcome the problems with problem-based learning. *Instructional Science, 25,* 97-115.

Hogan, K., & Pressley, M. (1997). Scaffolding scientific competencies within classroom communities of inquiry. In K. Hogan & M. Pressley (Eds.), *Scaffolding Student Learning: Instructional Approaches and Issues* (pp. 74 – 107). Cambridge, MA: Brookline Books.

Holmqvist, K., Holsanova, J., & Holmberg, N. (2007, August). *Newspaper reading, eye tracking and multimodality.* Paper presented at the bi-annual meeting of the European Association of Research on Learning and Instruction (EARLI). Budapest, Hungary.

Holsanova, J., Rahm, H., & Holmqvist, K. (2006). Entry points and reading paths on newspaper spreads: Comparing a semiotic analysis with eye-tracking measurements. *Journal of visual communication, 5*(1), 65-93.

Holyoak, K. J. (1984). Analogical thinking and human intelligence. In R. J. Sternberg (Ed.), *Advances in the psychology of human intelligence, 2,* 199-230. Hillsdale, NJ: Lawrence Erlbaum.

Hommel, B., Musseler, J., Aschersleben, G., & Prinz, W. (2001). The theory of event coding (TEC): A framework for perception and action planning. *Behavioral & Brain Sciences, 24,* 849-937.

Hooper, S., & Hannafin, M. J. (1991). Psychological perspectives on emerging instructional technologies: A critical analysis. *Educational Psychologist, 26,* 69-95.

Horwitz, P. (1999). Designing computer models that teach. In W. Feurzeig & N. Roberts (Eds.), *Modeling and Simulation in Science and Mathematics Education* (pp. 179-196). New York: Springer-Verlag.

Hoskins, S. L., & Van Hooff, J. C. (2005). Motivation and ability: Which students use online learning and what influence does it have on their achievement? *British Journal of Educational Technology, 36*(2), 171-192.

Hsinyi, P., Chin-Chung, T., & Ying-Tien, W. (2006). University students' self-efficacy and their attitudes toward the Internet: The role of students' perceptions of the Internet. *Educational Studies, 32*(1), 73-86.

Hulshof, C. D., & de Jong, T. (2006). Using Just-in-Time Information to Support Scientific Discovery Learning in a Computer-Based Simulation. *Interactive Learning Environments, 14*(1), 79.

Hussain, T., Weil, S., Brunyé, T. T., Sidman, J., & Ferguson, W. (2007). Eliciting and evaluating large-scale teamwork within a multiplayer game-based training environment. In H. F. O'Neil, & R. Perez (Eds.), *Computer Games and Team and Individual Learning* (pp. 77-104). Amsterdam: Elsevier Science.

Huston, A., & Wright, J. (1983). Children's processing of television: The informative functions of formal features. In J. Bryant & D. R. Anderson (Eds.), *Children's understanding of television: Research on attention and comprehension* (pp. 35-68). New York: Academic Press.

Hutchins, E. (1995). *Cognition in the wild*. Cambridge, MA: MIT Press.

Hwang, W., Wang, C., & Sharples, C. (2007). A study of multimedia annotation of Web-based materials. *Computers & Education, 48*, 680-692.

Hyönä, J., Lorch, R., and Kaakinen, J. (2002). Individual differences in reading to summarize expository text: Evidence from eye fixation patterns. *Journal of Educational Psychology, 94*(1), 44-55.

Iacoboni, M., Woods, R. P., & Brass, M. (1999). Cortical mechanisms of human imitation. *Science, 286*, 2526-2528.

Iiyoshi, T., Hannafin, M.J., & Wang, F. (2005). Cognitive tools and student-centered learning: Rethinking tools, functions, and applications. *Educational Media International, 42*(4), 281-296.

Inkpen, K., Klawe, M., Lawry, J., Sedighian, K., Leroux, S.& a Hsu, D. (1994). "We havenever-forgetful flowers in our garden": Girls' responses to electronic games. *Journal of Computers in Mathematics and Science Teaching, 13*, 383-403.

Jackson, M. D., & McClelland, J. L. (1975). Sensory and cognitive determinants of reading speed. *Journal of Verbal Learning and Verbal Behavior, 14*, 565-574.

Jackson, M. D., & McClelland, J. L. (1979). Processing determinants of reading speed. *Journal of Experimental Psychology: General, 108*, 151-181.

Jacobson, M. (2008). A design framework for educational hypermedia systems: Theory, research and learning emerging scientific conceptual perspectives. *Educational Technology Research and Development, 56*(1), 5-28.

James, R. (1999). Navigating CD-ROMs: An exploration of children reading interactive narratives. *Children's Literature in Education, 30*, 47-63.

James, W. (1902). *The Principle of Psychology*. New York: Holt.

Jamet, E., & Le Bohec, O. (2007). The effect of redundant text in multimedia instruction. *Contemporary Education Psychology, 32*, 588-598.

Jamieson-Noel, D., & Winne, P. H. (2003). Comparing self-reports to traces of studying behaviour as representations of student' studying and achievement. *German Journal of Educational Psychology, 17*, 159-171.

Järvelä, S., & Volet, S. (2004). Motivation in real-life, dynamic, and interactive learning environments: Stretching constructs and methodologies. *European Psychologist, 9*(4), 193-197.

Jefferson, G. (1989). Preliminary notes on a possible metric which provides for a "standard maximum" silence of approximately one second in conversation. In D. Roger & P. Bull (Eds.), *Conversation: An interdisciplinary perspective* (pp. 166–196). Clevedon: Multilingual Matters.

Jenkins, H. (2004). Game design as narrative architecture. In P. Harrigan & N. Wardrip-Fruin (Ed.), *First person: New media as story, performance, and game* (pp. 118-130). Cambridge: MIT Press.

Jenkins, J. R., Stein, M. L., & Wysocki, K. (1984). Learning vocabulary through reading. *American Educational Research Journal, 21*, 767–787.

Jennings, J. R. (1986). Bodily changes during attending. In M. G. H. Coles, E. Donchin, & S. W. Porges (Eds.), *Psychophysiology: Systems, processes, and applications*, pp. 268-89. New York: Guilford.

Jeung, H., Chandler, P., & Sweller, J. (1997). The role of visual indicators in dual sensory mode instruction, *Educational Psychology, 17*, 329-343.

Jin, P., & Low, R. (2007). Learning motivation and E-learning performance. *Unpublished manuscript*, School of Education, University of New South Wales, Sydney, Australia.

Jitendra, A. K., Griffin, C. C., Haria, P., Leh, J., Adams, A., & Kaduvettoor, A. (2007). A comparison of single and multiple strategy instruction on third-grade students' mathematical problem solving. *Journal for Research in Mathematics Education, 99*(1), 115-127.

Johnson, M. (1987). *The body in the mind: The bodily basis of imagination, reason, and meaning.* Chicago: Chicago University Press.

Johnson-Laird, P. N. (1983). *Mental Models: Towards a Cognitive Science of Language, Inference, and Consciousness.* Cambridge, MA: Harvard University Press.

Johnson-Laird, P. N., Girotto, V., & Legrenzi, P. (2004). Reasoning from inconsistency to consistency. *Psychological Review, 111*(3), 640.

Jonassen, D. (1991). Objectivism versus constructivism: Do we need a new philosophical paradigm? *Educational Technology Research and Development, 39*(3), 5-14.

Jonassen, D. H., & Grabowski, B. L. (1993). *Handbook of individual differences, learning and instruction.* Hillsdale, NJ: Lawrence Erlbaum.

Jonassen, D., Strobel, J., & Gottdenker, J. (2005). Model building for conceptual change. *Interactive Learning Environments, 13*(1-2), 15-37.

Jones, D. L. (2003). An overview of the sharable content object reference model. *Media Review, 10*(1), 27-36.

Jones, S. (2002). The Internet goes to college: How students are living in the future with today's technology. *Pew Internet and American Life Project.* Retrieved January 20, 2008 from http://www.pewinternet.org/PPF/r/71/report_display.asp

Joseph, J. H., & Dwyer, F. M. (1984). The effects of prior knowledge, presentation mode, and visual realism ons tudent achievement. *Journal of Experimental Education, 52,* 110-121.

Judge, T. A., & Ilies, R. (2002). Relationship of personality to performance motivation: A meta-analytic review. *Journal of Applied Psychology, 87*(4), 797-807.

Judge, T. A., Jackson, C. L., Shaw, J. C., Scott, B. A., & Rich, B. L. (2007). Self-efficacy and work-related performance: The integral role of individual differences. *Journal of Applied Psychology, 92*(1), 107-127.

Juel, C. (2006). The impact of early school experiences on initial reading. In: D.K. Dickinson & S.B. Neuman (Eds.), *Handbook of Early Literacy Research, 2,* 410-426. New York: The Guilford Press.

Just, M. A., & Carpenter, P. A. (1980). A theory of reading: From eye fixations to comprehension. *Psychological Review, 87,* 329-354.

Just, M. A., & Carpenter, P. A. (1987). *The Psychology of Reading andLlanguage Comprehension.* Newton: Allyn and Bacon.

Just, M. A., & Carpenter, P. A. (1992). A capacity theory of comprehension: Individual differences in working memory. *Psychological Review, 99,* 122-149.

Just, M. A., & Carpenter, P. A. (1993). The intensity of dimension of thought: Pupillometric indices of sentence processing. *Canadian Journal of Experimental Psychology, 47,* 310-339.

Just, M., & Carpenter, P. A. (1992). A capacity theory of comprehension: Individual differences in working memory. *Psychological Review, 99,* 122-149.

Juul, J. (1998). *A Clash between game and narrative.* Paper presented at the *Digital Arts and Culture* conference, Bergen, Norway. Retrieved October 1, 2006, from http://www.jesperjuul.net/text/clash_between_game_and_narrative.html

Juul, J. (2001). Games telling stories? – A brief note on games and narratives. *Game Studies: The International Journal of Computer Game Research, 1*(1). Retrieved October 16, 2006, from http://www.gamestudies.org/0101/juul-gts/

Kaderavek, J. N., Gillam, R. B., & Ukrainetz, T. A.. (2004). School-age children's self-assessment of oral narrative production. *Communication Disorders Quarterly, 26*(1), 37-48.

Kafai, Y. (1996). Gender differences in children's constructions of video games. In P. Greenfield a R. Cocking (Eds.), *Interacting with video* (pp. 39-66). Norwood, NJ.

Kafai, Y. B. (1994). *Minds in play: Computer game design as a context for children's learning.* Hillsdale, NJ: Lawrence Erlbaum Associates.

Kahneman, D. (1973). *Attention and effort.* Englewood Cliffs, NJ: Prentice-Hall.

Kahneman, D., & Beatty, J. (1966). Pupil diameter and load on memory. *Science, 154,* 1583-1585.

Kalyuga, S., Ayers, P., Chandler, P., & Sweller, J. (2003). The expertise reversal effect. *Educational Psychologist, 38*(1), 23-31.

Kalyuga, S., Chandler, P., & Sweller, J. (1999). Managing split-attention and redundancy in multimedia instruction. *Applied Cognitive Psychology, 13*(4), 351-371.

Kalyuga, S., Chandler, P., & Sweller, J. (2000). Incorporating learner experience into the design of multimedia instruction. *Journal of Educational Psychology, 92,* 126-136.

Kamil, M. L., Intrator, S. M., & Kim, H. S. (2000). The effects of other technologies on literacy and literacy learning. In M. L. Kamil, P. B. Mosenthal, P. D. Pearson, & R. Barr (Eds.), *Handbook of Reading Research, 3,* 771-788. Mahwah, NJ: Lawrence Erlbaum.

Kane, M. J., & Engle, R. W. (2000). Working-memory capacity, proactive interference, and divided attention: Limits on long-term memory retrieval. *Journal of Experimental Psychology: Learning, Memory, and Cognition, 26*(2), 336-358.

Kane, M. J., & Engle, R. W., (2003). Working-memory capacity and the control of attention: The contributions of goal neglect, response competition, and task set to Stroop interference. *Journal of Experimental Psychology: General, 132*(1), 47-70.

Kane, M. J., Bleckley, M. K., Conway, A. R., & Engle, R. W., (2001). A controlled-attention view of working memory capacity. *Journal of Experimental Psychology: General, 130*(2), 169-183.

Kane, M. J., Hambrick, D. Z., Tuhoski, S. W., Wilhelm, O., Payne, T. W., & Engle, R. W. (2004). The generality of working memory capacity: A latent-variable approach to verbal and visuospatial memory span and reasoning, *Journal of Experimental Psychology: General, 133*(2), 189-217.

Kane, M. J., Poole, B. J., Tuholski, S. W., & Engle, R. W. (2006). Working memory capacity and the top-down control of visual search: Exploring the boundaries of "executive attention." *Journal of Experimental Psychology: Learning, Memory, and Cognition, 32,* 749-777.

Kaput, J. J. (1994). The representational roles of technology in connecting mathematics with authentic experience. In R. Bieler, R. W. Scholz, R. Strasser & B. Winkelman (Eds.), *Mathematics didactics as a scientific discipline* (pp. 379-397). Dordecht, The Netherlands: Kluwer.

Karabenick, S. A., & Collins-Baglin, J. (1997). Relation of perceived instructional goals and incentives to college students' use of learning strategies. *Journal of Experimental Education, 65,* 331-341.

Karatekin, C., Couperus, J. W., & Marcus, D. J. (2004). Attention allocation in the dual-task paradigm as measured through behavioral and psychophysiological responses. *Psychophysiology, 41,* 175-185.

Katayama, A. D. (2005). Promoting knowledge transfer with electronic note taking. *Teaching of Psychology, 32*(2), 129-131.

Kaufman, D. F. (2004). Self-regulated learning in Web-based environments: Instructional tools designed to facilitate cognitive strategy use, metacognitive processing, and motivational beliefs. *Journal of Educational Computing Research. 30,* 139-161.

Keiler, L. (2007). Students' explanations of their data handling: Implications for transfer of learning. *International Journal of Science Education, 29*(2), 151-172.

Keller, J. M. (1987). Motivational design and multimedia: Beyond the novelty effect. *Strategic Human Resource Development Review, 1*(1), 188-203.

Keller, J. M. (1987). Development and use of the ARCS model of motivational design. *Journal of Instructional Development, 10*(3), 2 – 10.

Keller, J. M. (1987). Strategies for stimulating the motivation to learn. *Performance & Instruction, 26*(8), 1-7.

Keller, J. M. (1997). Motivational design and multimedia. Beyond the novelty effect. *Strategic Human Resource Development Review, 1,* 188-203.

Keller, J. M. (1999). Motivation in cyber learning environments. *International Journal of Educational Technology, 1,* 7-30.

Keller, J. M. (1999). Motivation in cyber learning environments. *Educational Technology International, 1*(1), 7 – 30.

Keller, J. M., & Suzuki, K. (1988). Application of the ARCS model to courseware design. In D. Jonassen (Ed.), *Instructional designs for microcomputer courseware design* (pp. 401-434). New York: Erlbaum.

Keller. J. M., & Suzuki, K. (2004). Learner motivation and E-learning design: A multinationally validated process. *Journal of Educational Media, 29*(3), 229-239.

Kelley, H. H. (1992). Common sense psychology and scientific psychology. *Annual Review of Psychology, 43,* 1-24.

Kiewra, K. A., & Benton, S. L. (1988). The relationship between information-processing ability and note taking. *Contemporary Educational Psychology, 13,* 33-44.

Kiili, K. (2005). Participatory multimedia learning: Engaging learners, Australasian *Journal of Educational Technology, 21*(3), 303-322.

Kikas, E. (2003). University students' conceptions of different physical phenomena. *Journal of Adult Development, 10*, 139–150.

Kim, M., Hannafin, M. J., & Bryan, L. (2007) Technology-enhanced inquiry tools in science education: An emerging pedagogical framework for classroom practice. *Science Education, 96*(6), 1010-1030.

King, P. M., & Kitchener, K. S. (2004). Reflective judgment: Theory and research on the development of epistemic assumptions through adulthood. *Educational Psychologist, 39*(1), 5-18.

Kirschner, P. A., Sweller, J., & Clark, R. E. (2006). Why minimal guidance during instruction does not work: An analysis of the failure of constructivist, discovery, problem-based, experiential, and inquiry-based teaching. *Educational Psychologist, 41*(2), 75-86.

Kirsh, D., & Maglio, P. (1994). On distinguishing epistemic from pragmatic action. *Cognitive Science, 18*, 513–549.

Klahr, D., & Carver, S. M. (1988). Cognitive objectives in a LOGO debugging curriculum: Instruction, learning, and transfer. *Cognitive Psychology, 20*, 362-404.

Klahr, D., Triona, L. M., & Williams, C. (2007). Hands on what? The relative effectiveness of physical vs. virtual materials in an engineering design project by middle school children. *Journal of Research in Science Teaching, 44*, 183-203.

Klatzky, R. L., Marston, J. R., Giudice, N. A., Golledge, R. G., & Loomis, J. M. (2006). Cognitive load of navigating without vision when guided by virtual sound versus spatial language. *Journal of Experimental Psychology: Applied, 12*, 223-232.

Klausmeier, H. J. (1985). *Educational psychology.* New York, NY: Harper & Row.

Klinger, E. (1977). Meaning & void: Iinner experience and the incentives in people's lives. Minneapolis: University of Minnesota Press.

Kluge, A. (2007). Experiential learning methods, simulation complexity and their effects on different target groups. *Journal of Educational Computing Research, 36*(3), 323.

Knopf, M. (1991). Having shaved a kiwi fruit: Memory of unfamiliar subject-performed actions. *Psychological Research, 53*, 203-211.

Knowlton, J. Q. (1966). On the definition of "picture". *AV Communication Review, 14*, 157-183.

Koedinger, K. R., & Aleven, V. (2007). Exploring the assistance dilemma in experiments with cognitive tutors. *Educational Psychology Review, 19*, 239-264.

Koedinger, K. R., & Anderson, J. R. (1990). Abstract planning and perceptual chunks: Elements of expertise in geometry. *Cognitive Science, 14*(4), 511-550.

Koedinger, K. R., Aleven, V., Heffernan, N., McLaren, B. M., & Hockenberry, M. (2004). Opening the door to non-programmers: Authoring intelligent tutor behavior by demonstration. In J. C. Lester, R. M. Vicari & F. Paraguaçu (Eds.), *Proceedings of the 7th annual Intelligent Tutoring Systems Conference* (pp. 162-174). Berlin: Springer-Verlag.

Koedinger, K. R., Anderson, J. R., Hadley, W. H., & Mark, M. A. (1997). Intelligent tutoring goes to school in the big city. *International Journal of Artificial Intelligence in Education, 8*, 30-43.

Koenig, A. (2007). *Exploring narrative as a cognitive aid in educational video games.* Paper presented at the 13th International Conference on Artificial Intelligence in Education (AIED), Marina Del Ray, CA.

Koenig, A., Atkinson, R. K., & Harrison, C. J. (2008). *The embodiment of gender-specific characters in educational video games: Does it affect learning and in-game performance?* Paper at the Annual Conference of the American Educational Research Association, New York, NY.

Kohli, L., Niwa, M., Noma, H., Susami, K., Yanagida, Y., Lindeman, R. W., Hosaka, K., & Kume, Y. (2006). Towards effective information display using vibrotactile apparent motion. In *14th Symposium on Haptic Interfaces for Virtual Environment and Teleoperator Systems* (445-451).

Koriat, A., & Pearlman-Avnion, S. (2003). Memory organization of action events and its relationship to memory performance. *Journal of Experimental Psychology: General, 132*, 435-454.

Kosslyn, S. M. (1980). *Image and mind.* Cambridge, MA: MIT Press.

Kosslyn, S. M. (1994). *Elements of graph design.* New York, NY: W.H. Freeman.

Kozhevnikov, M., Hegarty, M., & Mayer, R. E. (2002). Revising the visualizer-verbalizer dimension: Evidence for two types of visualizers. *Cognition and Instruction, 20*, 47-77.

Kozhevnikov, M., Kosslyn, S., & Shephard, J. (2005). Spatial versus object visualizers: A new characterization of visual cognitive style. *Memory & Cognition, 33*, 710-726.

Kozhevnikov, M., Kosslyn, S., & Shephard, J. (2005). Spatial versus object visualizers: A new characterization of visual cognitive style. *Memory & Cognition, 33*, 710-726.

Kozma, R. B. (1991). Learning with media. *Review of Educational Research, 61*(2), 179-211.

Kozma, R. B. (1994). Will media influence learning? Reframing the debate. *Educational Technology Research & Development, 42*, 7-19.

Kress, G., & van Leeuwen, T. (1996). *Reading images: The grammar of visual design.* London: Routledge.

Kruley, P., Sciama, S. C., & Glenberg, A. M. (1994). On-line processing of textual illustrations in the visuospatial sketchpad: Evidence from dual-task studies. *Memory & Cognition, 22*, 261-272.

Kuhl, J. (2000). The volitional basis of personality systems interaction theory: Applications in learning and treatment contexts. *International Journal of Educational Research, 33*(7-8), 665-703.

Kuiper, E., Volman, M., & Terwel, J. (2005). The Web as an information resources in K-12 education: Strategies for supporting students in searching and processing information. *Review of Educational Research, 75* (3), 285-328.

Kyllonen, P. C., & Christal, R. E. (1990). Reasoning ability is (little more than) working-memory capacity?! *Intelligence, 14*, 389-433.

La Pointe, L. B., & Engle, R. W. (1990). Simple and complex word spans as measures of working memory capacity. *Journal of Experimental Psychology: Learning, Memory and Cognition, 16*, 1118-1133.

Lai, F., Entin, E. B., Brunye, T., Sidman, J., & Entin, E. E. (2007). Evaluation of a simulation-based program for medic cognitive skills training. *Studies in Health Technology and Informatics, 125*, 259-261.

Lajoie, S. P. (2005). Extending the Scaffolding Metaphor. *Instructional Science, 33*, 541-557.

Land, S. (2000). Cognitive requirements for learning with open-ended learning environments. *Educational Technology Research and Development, 48*(3), 61-78.

Land, S. M., & Greene, B. A. (2000). Project-based learning with the World Wide Web: A qualitative study of resource integration. *Educational Technology Research and Development, 48*(1), 45-67.

Land, S. M., & Zembal-Saul, C. (2003). Scaffolding reflection and articulation of scientific explanations in a data-rich, project-based learning environment: An investigation of Progress Portfolio. *Educational Technology Research and Development, 51*(4), 65-84.

Land, S., & Hannafin, M. J. (1996). A conceptual framework for the development of theories-in-action with open learning environments. *Educational Technology Research and Development, 44*(3), 37-53.

Land, S., & Hannafin, M. J. (1997). Patterns of understanding with open-ended learning environments: A qualitative study. *Educational Technology Research and Development, 45*(2), 47-73.

Land, S., & Hannafin, M. J. (2000). Student-centered learning environments. In D.H. Jonassen, & S. M. Land (Eds.), *Theoretical Foundations of Learning Environments* (pp. 1-23). Mahwah, NJ: Erlbaum.

Landauer, T. K. (1998). Learning and representing verbal meaning: The latent semantic analysis theory. *Current Directions in Psychological Science, 7*, 161-164.

Landauer, T. K., & Dumais, S. T. (1997). A solution to Plato's problem: The latent semantic analysis theory of acquisition, induction and representation of knowledge. *Psychological Review, 104*, 211-240.

Lang, A. (1995). Defining audio/video redundancy from a limited-capacity information processing perspective. *Communication Research, 22*, 86-115.

Larkin, J. H., & Simon, H. A. (1987). Why a diagram is (sometimes) worth ten thousand words. *Cognitive Science, 11*, 65-100.

Larkin, J. H., & Simon, H. A. (1987). Why a diagram is (sometimes) worth ten thousand words. *Cognitive Science, 11*, 65-99.

Latour, B., & Woolgar, S. (1986). *Laboratory life: The social construction of scientific facts.* Princeton, NJ: Princeton University Press.

Laurillard, D. (1993). *Rethinking university teaching: A framework for the effective use of educational technology.* New York: Routledge.

Laurillard, D. (1998). Multimedia and the learner's experience of narrative. *Computers & Education, 31*, 229-242.

Lave, J. (1988). *Cognition in practice: Mind, mathematics and culture in everyday life.* Cambridge, UK: Cambridge University Press.

Lave, J., & Wenger, E. (1991). Situated learning: Legitimate peripheral participation. New York, NY: Cambridge University Press.

Lawless, K. A., & Kulikowich, J. M. (1996). Understanding hypertext navigation through cluster analysis. *Journal of Educational Computing Research, 14*, 385-399.

Leacock, T., & Nesbit, J. C. (2007). A framework for evaluating the quality of multimedia learning resources. *Educational Technology and Society, 10*(2), 44-59.

Leahy, W., Chandler, P., & Sweller, J. (2003). When auditory presentations should and should not be a component of multimedia instruction. *Applied Cognitive Psychology, 17*, 401-418.

Lee, A. Y. (1998). Transfer as a measure of intellectual functioning. In S. Soraci & W. J. McIlvane (Eds.), *Perspectives on fundamental processes in intellectual functioning: A survey of research approaches, 1* 351-366. Stamford, CT: Ablex.

Lee, A. Y., & Pennington, N. (1993). Learning computer programming: A route to general reasoning skills? In C.R. Cook, J.C. Scholtz, & J.C. Spohrer (Eds.), *Empirical studies of programmers: Fifth workshop* (pp. 113-136). Norwood, NJ: Ablex.

Lee, F. K., Sheldon, K. M., & Turban, D. B. (2003). Personality and the goal-striving process: The influence of achievement foal patterns, goal level, and mental focus on performance and enjoyment. *Journal of Applied Psychology, 88*(2), 256-265.

Lee, H., Plass, J. L., & Homer, B. D. (2006). Optimizing cognitive load for learning form computer-based science simulations. *Journal of Education psychology, 98*(4), 902-913.

Lee. H., Plass, J. L., & Homer, B. D. (2006). Optimizing cognitive load for learning from computer-based science simulations. *Journal of Educational Psychology, 98*(4), 902-913.

Legault, L., Green-Demers, I., & Pelletier, L. (2006). Why do high school students lack motivation in the classroom? Toward an understanding of academic motivation and the role of social support. *Journal of Educational Psychology, 98*(3), 567-582.

Lemke, J. L. (1990). *Talking science: Language, learning and values.* Norwood, NJ: Ablex.

Lemos, M. S. (1996). Students' and teachers' goals in the classroom. *Learning and Instruction, 6,* 151-171.

Lepper, M. R., & Malone, T. W. (1987). Intrinsic motivation and instructional effectiveness in computer-based education. In R. E. Snow & M. J. Farr (Eds.), *Aptitude, Llearning and linstruction: Cognitive and Affective Process Analysis* (Vol. 3, pp. 255-287): Hillsdale, NJ: Lawrence Erlbaum Associates.

Lepper, M. R., Drake, M. F., & O'Donnell-Johnson, T. (1997). Scaffolding techniques human tutors. In K. Hogan & M. Pressley (Eds.), *Scaffolding Student Learning: Approaches and Issues* (pp. 108–144). Cambridge, MA: Brookline Books.

Lepper, M. R., Iyengar, S. S., & Corpus, J. H. (2005). Intrinsic and extrinsic motivational orientations in the classroom: Age differences and academic correlates. *Journal of Educational Psychology, 97*(2), 184-196.

Leutner, D., & Plass, J. L. (1998). Measuring learning styles with questionnaires versus direct observation of preferential choice behavior: Development of the Visualizer/Verbalizer Behavior Observation Scale (V V-BOS). *Computers in Human Behavior, 14*, 543-557.

Levelt, W. J. M. (1981). The speaker's linearization problem. *Philosophical Transactions of the Royal Society, Series B, 295*, 305-315.

Levie, W., & Lentz, R. (1982). Effects of text illustrations: A review of research. *Educational Communication & Technology Journal, 30*(4), 195-232.

Levin, J. R., Anglin, G. J., & Carney, R. N. (1987). On empirically validating functions of pictures in prose. In D. M. Willows & H. A. Houghton (Eds.), *The psychology of illustration, volume 1: Basic research* (pp. 51-85). New York: Springer-Verlag.

Levin, J. R., Anglin, G. J., & Carney, R. N. (1987). On empirically validating functions of pictures in prose. In D. M. Willows & H. A. Houghton (Eds.), *The psychology of illustration* (Vol. 1, pp. 51-85). New York: Springer.

Lewin, K. (1939). Field theory and experiment in social psychology: Concepts and methods. *The American Journal of Sociology, 44*(6), 868-896.

Li, R., & Liu, M. (2007). Understanding the effects of databases as cognitive tools in a problem-based multimedia learning environment. *Journal of Interactive Learning Research, 18*(3), 345-363.

Li, R., & Liu, M. (2008). The effects of using a computer database tool on middle school students' cognitive skill acquisition in a multimedia learning environment. In

R. Kobayashi, (Ed.) *New Educational Technology.* Hauppauge, NY: Nova Science Publishers, Inc.

Lieberman, D. A. (2000). *Learning: Behavior and cognition.* Belmont, BA: Wadsworth/Thomson Learning.

Lin, Y., Zhang, W. J., & Watson, L. G. (2003). Using eye movement parameters for evaluating human-machine interface frameworks under normal control operation and fault detection situations. *International Journal of Human-Computer Studies, 59,* 837-873.

Lincoln, Y. S., & Guba, E. D. (1985). *Naturalistic Inquiry.* Thousand Oaks, CA Sage Publications, Inc.

Linnenbrink, E. A., & Pintrich, P. R. (2000). Multiple pathways to learning and achievement: The role of goal orientation in fostering adaptive motivation, affect, and cognition. In C. Sansone & J. M. Harackiewicz (Eds.), *Intrinsic and extrinsic motivation: The search for optimal motivation and performance* (pp. 195-227). San Diego, CA: Academic Press.

Liu, M, & Bera, S. (2005). An analysis of cognitive tool use patterns in a hypermedia learning environment. *Educational Technology Research and Development, 53*(1), 5-21.

Liu, M. (2004). Examining the performance and attitudes of sixth graders during their use of a problem-based hypermedia learning environment. *Computers in Human Behavior, 20*(3), 357-379.

Liu, M. (2005). The effect of a hypermedia learning environment on middle school students' motivation, attitude, and science knowledge. *Computers in the Schools, 22*(3/4), 159-171.

Liu, M., Bera, S., Corliss, S., Svinicki, M., & Beth, A. (2004). Understanding the connection between cognitive tool use and cognitive processes as used by sixth graders in a problem-based hypermedia learning environment. *Journal of Educational Computing Research. 31*(3), 309-334.

Liu, M., Williams, D., & Pedersen, S. (2002). Alien Rescue: A problem-based hypermedia learning environment for middle school science. *Journal of Educational Technology Systems, 30,* 255-270.

Locke, E. A., & Latham, G. P. (2002). Building a practically useful theory of goal setting and task motivation: A 35-year odyssey. *American Psychologist, 57*(9), 705-717.

Locke, E. A., Motowildo, S., & Bobko, P. (1986). Using self-efficacy theory to resolve the conflict between theory and expectancy theory in organization behavior and industrial/organizational psychology. *Journal of Social and Clinical Psychology, 4,* 328-338.

Logie, R. H. (1995). *Visuo-spatial working memory.* Hove, UK: Erlbaum.

Lohse, G. J., Biolsi, K., Walker, N., & Rueter, H. H. (1994). A classification of visual representations. *Communications of the ACM, 37,* 36-49.

Longoni, A. M., Richardson, J. T., & Aiello, A. (1993). Articulating rehearsal and phonological storage in working memory. *Memory and Cognition, 21,* 11-22.

Loomis, J. M., & Klatzky, R. L. (2007). Functional equivalence of spatial representations from vision, touch, and hearing: Relevance for sensory substitution. In J. J. Reiser, D. H. Ashmead, F. F. Ebner, & A. L. Corn (Eds.), *Blindness and brain plasticity in navigation and object perception* (pp. 155-184). New York: Lawrence Erlbaum.

Loomis, J. M., Golledge, R. G., Klatzky, R. L., & Marston, J. R. (2007). Assisting wayfinding in visually impaired travelers. In G. Allen (Ed.), *Applied spatial cognition: From research to cognitive technology* (pp. 179-202). Mahwah, N.J.: Lawrence Erlbaum.

Lord, R. G., Hanges, P. J., & Godfrey, E. G. (2003). Integrating neural networks into decision-making and motivational theory: Rethinking VIE theory. *Canadian Psychology, 44*(1), 21-38.

Louchart, S., & Aylett, R. (2004). Narrative theory and emergent interactive narrative. *Int. J. Continuing Engineering Education and Lifelong Learning, 14*(6), 506-518.

Louro, M. J., Pieters, R., & Zeelenberg, M. (2007). Dynamics of multiple-goal pursuit. *Journal of Personality and Social Psychology, 93*(2), 174-193.

Low, R., & Sweller, J. (2005). The modality principle in multimedia learning. In R. E.

Low, R., & Sweller, J. (2005). The modality principle in multimedia learning. In R. E. Mayer (Ed.), *The Cambridge Handbook of Multimedia Learning* (pp. 147-158). New York: Cambridge University Press.

Lowe, R. K. (1996). Background knowledge and the construction of a situtational representation from a diagram. *European Journal of Psychology of Education, XI*(4), 377-397.

Lowe, R. K. (1999). Extracting information from an animation during complex visual learning. *European Journal of Psychology of Education, 14*(2), 225-244.

Lowe, R. K. (2003). Animation and learning: Selective processing of information in dynamic graphics. *Learning and Instruction, 13,* 157-176.

Lusk, D. L., Evans, A., D. Jeffrey, T. R., Palmer, K. R., Wikstrom, C. S., & Doolittle, P. E. (in press). Multimedia learning and individual differences: Mediating the effects of working memory capacity with segmentation. *British Journal of Educational Technology.*

Lustig, C., May, C. P., & Hasher, L. (2001). Working memory span and the role of proactive interference. *Journal of Experimental Psychology: General, 130*(2), 199-207.

Lutz, J., Brigs, A., & Cain, K. (2003). An examination of the value of the generation effect for learning new material. *The Journal of General Psychology, 130,* 171-188.

MacEachren, A. M. (1995). *How maps work: Representation, visualization, and design.* New York: Guilford Press.

MacEachren, A. M., & Kraak, M.-J. (1997). Exploratory cartographic visualization: Advancing the agenda. *Computers and Geosciences, 23,* 335-343.

MacGregor, S. K. (1999). Hypermedia navigation profiles: Cognitive characteristics and information processing strategies. *Journal of Educational Computing Research, 20,* 189-206.

Maddux, J. E. (1999). Expectancies and the social-cognitive perspective: Basic principles, processes, and variables. In I. Kirsch (Ed.), *How expectancies shape experience* (pp. 17-39). Washington, D. C.: American Psychological Association.

Maehr, M. L. (1976). Continuing motivation: An analysis of a seldom considered educational outcome. *Review of Educational Research, 46*(3), 443-462.

Maehr, M. L. (1984). Meaning and motivation: Toward a theory of personal investment. In R. Ames & C. Ames (Eds.), *Research on motivation in education, 1,* 115-144. New York: Academic Press.

Maehr, M. L., & Pintrich, P. R. (1991). [Preface]. In: *Advances in motivation and achievement, 7,* ix-xiii. Greenwich, CT: JAI Press.

Malone, T. W. (1981). Toward a theory of intrinsically motivating instruction. *Cognitive Science, 4,* 333-369.

Malone, T. W., & Lepper, M. R. (1987). Making learning fun: A taxonomy of intrinsic motivations for learning. In R. E. Snow & M. J. Farr (Eds.), *Aptitude, Learning and Instruction: Cognitive and Affective Process Analysis 3,* 223-253. Hillsdale, NJ: Lawrence Erlbaum Associates.

Mandel, T. (1997). *The elements of user interface design.* New York: Wiley.

Mandler, J. M., & DeForest, M. (1979). Is there more than one way to recall a story. *Child Development, 50,* 886-889.

Mangos, P. M. & Steele-Johnson, D. (2001). The role of subjective task complexity in goal orientation, self-efficacy, and performance relations. *Human Performance, 14,* 169-186.

Mani, K., & Johnson-Laird, P. N. (1982). The mental representation of spatial descriptions. *Memory & Cognition, 10,* 181-187.

Manlove, S., Lazonder, A. W., & de Jong, T. (2006). Regulative support for collaborative scientific inquiry learning. *Journal of Computer Assisted Learning, 22*(2), 87.

Marcus, N., Cooper, M., & Sweller, J. (1996). Understanding instruction. *Journal of Educational Psychology, 88*(1), 49-63.

Mark, M. M. (2000). Realism, validity, and the experimenting society. In L. Bickman (Ed.), *Validity and social experimentation: Donald Campbell's legacy* (Vol. 1, pp. 141-166). Thousand Oaks, CA: Sage.

Marsh, H. W. (1994). Sport motivation orientations: Beware of jingle-jangle fallacies. *Journal of Sport and Exercise Psychology, 16,* 365–380.

Marshall, S. P. (1995). *Schemas in problem solving.* New York: Cambridge University Press.

Marston, J. R., Loomis, J. M., Klatzky, R. L., & Golledge, R. G. (2007). Nonvisual route following with guidance from a simple haptic or auditory display. *Journal of Visual Impairment & Blindness, 101,* 203-211.

Maslow, A. H. (1955). *Deficiency Motivation and Growth Motivation.* Paper presented at the Nebraska Symposium on Motivation.

Massa, L. J., & Mayer, R. E. (2006). Testing the ATI hypothesis: Should multimedia instruction accommodate verbalizer-visualizer cognitive style? *Learning and Individual Differences, 16*(4), 321.

Masterman, E., & Rogers, Y. (2002). A framework for designing interactive multimedia to scaffold young children's understanding of historical chronology. *Instructional Science, 30*(3), 221–241.

Maule, R. W. (2001). Framework for metacognitive mapping to design metadata for intelligent hypermedia presentations. *Journal of Educational Multimedia and Hypermedia, 10*(1), 27-45.

Mautone, P. D., & Mayer, R. E. (2001). Signaling as a cognitive guide in multimedia learning. *Journal of Educational Psychology, 93*(2), 377-389.

Maybury, M. T. (1995). Research in multimedia and multimodal parsing and generation. *Artificial Intelligence Review, 9*, 103-127.

Mayer (Ed.), *The Cambridge Handbook of Multimedia Learning* (pp. 147-158). New York: Cambridge University Press.

Mayer, R. E. (1988). From novice to expert. In M. Helander (Ed.), *Handbook of Human-Computer Interaction* (pp. 569-580). Amsterdam: Elsevier.

Mayer, R. E. (2001). *Multimedia Learning*. New York, NY: Cambridge University Press.

Mayer, R. E. (2004). Should there be a three-strikes rule against pure discovery learning? The case for guided methods of instruction? *American Psychologist, 59*, 14-19.

Mayer, R. E. (2005). Cognitive theory of multimedia learning. In R. E. Mayer (Ed.), *The Cambridge Handbook of Multimedia Learning* (pp. 31-48). Cambridge: Cambridge University Press.

Mayer, R. E. (2005). *The Cambridge handbook of multimedia learning*. New York, NY: Cambridge University Press.

Mayer, R. E., & Anderson, R. (1991). Animations need narrations: An experimental test of a dual-coding hypothesis. *Journal of Educational Psychology, 83*, 484-490.

Mayer, R. E., & Anderson, R. (1992). The instructive animation: Helping students build connections between words and pictures in multimedia learning. *Journal of Educational Psychology, 84*, 444-452.

Mayer, R. E., & Anderson, R. B. (1991). Animations need narrations: An experimental test of a dual-coding hypothesis. *Journal of Educational Psychology, 83*(4), 484-490.

Mayer, R. E., & Anderson, R. B. (1991). Animations need narrations: An experimental test of a dual-coding hypothesis. *Journal of Educational Psychology, 83*, 484-490.

Mayer, R. E., & Anderson, R. B. (1992). The instructive animation: Helping students build connections between words and pictures in multimedia learning. *Journal of Educational Psychology, 84*(4), 444-452.

Mayer, R. E., & Chandler, P. (2001). When learning is just a click away: Does simple user interaction foster deeper understanding of multimedia messages? *Journal of Educational Psychology, 93*(2), 390-397.

Mayer, R. E., & Gallini, J. (1990). When is an illustration worth ten thousand words? *Journal of Educational Psychology, 82*, 715-726.

Mayer, R. E., & Massa, L. J. (2003). Three facets of visual and verbal learners: Cognitive ability, cognitive style, and learning preference. *Journal of Educational Psychology, 95*(4), 833-846.

Mayer, R. E., & Moreno, R. (1998). A split-attention effect in multimedia learning: Evidence for dual processing systems in working memory. *Journal of Educational Psychology, 90*(2), 312-320.

Mayer, R. E., & Moreno, R. (2003). Nine ways to reduce cognitive load in multimedia learning. *Educational Psychologist, 38*(1), 43-52.

Mayer, R. E., & Sims, V. K. (1994). For whom is a picture worth a thousand words? Extensions of a dual-coding theory of multimedia learning. *Journal of Educational Psychology, 86*(3), 389-401.

Mayer, R. E., Fennell, S., Farmer, L., & Campbell, J. (2004). A personalization effect in multimedia learning: Students learn better when words are in conversational style rather than formal style. *Journal of Educational Psychology, 96*(2), 389.

Mayer, R. E., Heiser, J., & Lonn, S. (2001). Cognitive constraints on multimedia learning: When presenting more material results in less understanding. *Journal of Educational Psychology, 93*(1), 187-198.

Mayer, R. E., Mautone, P., & Prothero, W. (2002). Pictorial aids for learning by doing in a multimedia geology simulation game. *Journal of Educational Psychology, 94*, 171-185.

Mayer, R. E., Moreno, R., Boire, M., & Vagge, S. (1999). Maximizing constructivist learning from multimedia communications by minimizing cognitive load. *Journal of Educational Psychology, 86*, 389-401.

Mayer, R. E., Sobko, K., & Mautone, P. D. (2003). Social cues in multimedia learning: Role of speaker's voice. *Journal of Educational Psychology, 95*(2), 419.

Mayer, R. E., Steinhoff, K., Bowers, G., & Mars, R. (1995). A generative theory of textbook design: Using annotated illustrations to foster meaningful learning of science text. *Educational Technology Research and Development, 43*(1), 31-43.

Mayer, R., & Jackson, J. (2005). The case for coherence in scientific explanations: Quantitative details can hurt qualitative understanding. *Journal of Experimental Psychology: Applied, 11*(1), 13-18.

Mayer, R., Dow, G., & Mayer, S. (2003). Multimedia learning in an interactive self-explaining environment: What works in the design of agent-based microworlds? *Journal of Educational Psychology, 95*(4), 806-813.

Mayer, R., Fennell, S., Farmer, L., & Campbell, J. (2004). A personalization effect in multimedia learning: Students learn better when words are in conversational style rather than formal style. *Journal of Educational Psychology, 96*(2), 389-395.

Mayer, R., Sobko, K., & Mautone, P. (2003). Social dues in multimedia learning: Role of speaker's voice. *Journal of Educational Psychology, 95*, 419-425.

Mayer, R.E. (1989). Systematic thinking fostered by illustrations in scientific text. *Journal of Educational Psychology, 81*, 240-246.

Mayer, R.E. (1997). Multimedia learning: Are we asking the right questions? *Educational Psychologist, 32*, 1-19.

Mayer, R.E., & Gallini, J.K. (1990). When is an illustration worth ten thousand words? *Journal of Educational Psychology, 82*, 715-726.

Mayer, R.E., & Moreno, R. (1998). A split-attention effect in multimedia learning: Evidence for dual processing systems in working memory. *Journal of Educational Psychology, 90*, 312-320.

Mayer, R.E., Bove, W., Bryman, A., Mars, R., & Tapangco, L. (1995). A generative theory of textbook design: Using annotated illustrations to foster meaningful learning of scientific text. *Educational Technology Research and Development, 43*(1), 31-44.

McCombs, B. L. (2001). What do we know about learners and learning? The learner-centered framework: Bringing the educational system into balance. *Educational Horizons, 79*(4), 182-193.

McCombs, B. L. (2003). A framework for the redesign of K-12 education in the context of current educational reform. *Theory into Practice, 42*(2), 163-167.

McCombs, B. L., & Whisler, J. S. (1997). *The learner-centered classroom and school: Strategies for increasing student motivation and achievement.* San Francisco: Jossey-Bass.

McGuire, J. M., Scott, S. S., & Shaw, S. F. (2006). Universal design and its applications in educational environments. *Remedial and Special Education, 27*(3), 166.

McKeown, M. G., Beck, I. L., Sinatra, G. M., & Loxterman, J. A. (1992). The contribution of prior knowledge and coherent text to comprehension. *Reading Research Quarterly, 27*, 79-93.

McNamara, D. S., & Kintsch, W. (1996). Learning from text: Effect of prior knowledge and text coherence. *Discourse Processes, 22*, 247-288.

McNamara, D. S., Kintsch, E., Songer, N. B., & Kintsch, W. (1996). Are good texts always better? Interactions of text coherence, background knowledge, and levels of understanding in learning from text. *Cognition & Instruction, 14*(1), 1-43.

Means, M., & Voss, J. F. (1985). Star wars: A developmental study of expert and novice knowledge structures. *Memory and Language, 24*, 746-757.

Means, T. B., Jonassen, D. H., & Dwyer, R. M. (1997). Enhancing relevance: Embedded ARCS strategies vs. purpose. *Educational Technology Research and Development, 45*(1), 5-18.

Melcher, J. M., & Schooler, J. W. (1996). The misremembrance of wines past: Verbal and perceptual expertise differentially mediate verbal overshadowing of taste memory. *Journal of Memory and Language, 35*, 231–245.

Merleau-Ponty, M. (2002). *Husserl at the limits of phenomenology.* Evanston, IL: Northwestern University Press.

Messaris, P. (1994). Four aspects of visual literacy. In P. Messaris (Ed.), *Visual literacy: Image, mind and reality* (pp. 1-40). Boulder: Westview Press.

Mestre, J. P. (1994). Cognitive aspects of learning and teaching science. In S. J. Fitzsimmons & L. C. Kerpelman (Eds.), *Teacher Enhancement for Elementary and Secondary Science and Mathematics: Status, Issues, and Problems* (pp. 3-1 - 3-53). Washington, DC: National Science Foundation (NSF 94-80).

Miceli, M., & Castelfranchi, C. (2000). Nature and mechanisms of loss of motivation. *Review of General Psychology, 4*(3), 238-263.

Michas, I. C., & Berry, D. C. (2000). Learning a procedural task: Effectiveness of multimedia presentations. *Applied Cognitive Psychology, 14,* 555-575.

Midgley, C., Kaplan, A., & Middleton, M. (2001). Performance-approach goals: Good for what, for whom, under what circumstances, and at what cost? *Journal of Educational Psychology, 93*(1), 77-86.

Milheim, W. D. (1990). The effects of pacing and sequence control in an interactive video lesson. *Educational & Training Technology International, 27*(1), 7-19.

Millar, S. (1990). Articulatory coding in prose reading: Evidence from braille on changes with skill. *British Journal of Psychology, 81,* 205-219.

Miller, G. A. (1956). The magical number seven, plus or minus two: Some limits on our capacity for processing information. *Psychological Review, 63,* 81-97.

Miller, W. (1937). The picture clutch in reading. *Elementary English Review, 14,* 263-264.

Miyake, A., & Shah, P. (Eds.) (1999). Models of working memory: Mechanisms of active maintenance and executive control. New York, NY: Cambridge University Press.

Miyaki, A., Friedman, N. P., Rettinger, D. A., Shah, P., & Hegarty, M. (2001). How are visuospatial working memory, executive functioning, and spatial abilities related? A latent-variable analysis. *Journal of Experimental Psychology: General, 130,* 621-640.

Montague, M., & Boss, C. S. (1986). The effect of cognitive strategy training on verbal math problem solving performance of learning disabled adolescents. *Journal of Learning Disabilities, 19*(1), 26-33.

Moore, D. M., Burton, J. K., & Myers, R. J. (1996). Multiple-channel communication: The theoretical and research foundations of multimedia. In D. H. Jonassen (Ed.), *Handbook of research for educational communication and technology* (pp. 851–875). New York: Macmillan.

Moos, D. C., & Azevedo, R. (2006). The role of goal structure in undergraduates' use of self-regulatory processes in two hypermedia learning tasks. *Journal of Educational Multimedia and Hypermedia, 15*(1), 49-86.

Moravcsik, J. E., & Kintsch, W. (1993). Writing quality, reading skills, and domain knowledge as factors in text comprehension. *Canadian Journal of Experimental Psychology, 47,* 360-374.

Moreno, R., & Duran, R. (2004). Do multiple representations need explanations? The role of verbal guidance and individual differences in multimedia mathematics learning. *Journal of Educational Psychology, 96,* 492-503.

Moreno, R., & Mayer, R. E. (1999). Cognitive principles of multimedia learning: The role of modality and contiguity. *Journal of Educational Psychology, 91*(2), 358-368.

Moreno, R., & Mayer, R. E. (2000). A coherence effect in multimedia learning: The case for minimizing irrelevant sounds in the design of multimedia instructional messages. *Journal of Educational Psychology, 92*(1), 117-125.

Moreno, R., & Mayer, R. E. (2000). A coherence effect in multimedia learning: The case for minimizing irrelevant sounds in the design of multimedia instructional messages. *Journal of Educational Psychology, 92*(1), 117-125.

Moreno, R., & Mayer, R. E. (2004). Personalized messages that promote science learning in virtual environments. *Journal of Educational Psychology, 96*(1), 165-173.

Moreno, R., Mayer, R. E., Spires, H. A., & Lester, J.C. (2001). The case for social agency in computer-based multimedia learning: Do students learn more deeply when they interact with animated pedagogical agents? *Cognition and Instruction, 19,* 177-214.

Moroney, W. F., Biers, D. W., Eggemeier, F. T. & Mitchell, J. A. (1992). *A Comparison of two scoring procedures with the NASA TASK LOAD INDEX in a simulated flight task.* Proceedings of the IEEE NAECON 1992 National Aerospace and Electronics Conference, New York, 2, 734-740.

Morrell, R. W., & Park, D. C. (1993). The effects of age, illustrations, and task variables on the performance of procedural assembly tasks. *Psychology and Aging, 8,* 389-399.

Morris, J., & Hirst, G. (1991). Lexical cohesion computed by thesaural relations as an indicator of the structure of text. *Computational Linguistics, 17*(1), 21-48.

Morville, P. (2005). *Ambient findability: What we find changes who we become.* Cambridge, MA: O'Reilly Media.

Mousavi, S., Low, R., & Sweller, J. (1995). Reducing cognitive load by mixing auditory and visual presentation modes. *Journal of Educational Psychology, 87,* 319-334.

Moyer, P. S. (2002). Are we having fun yet? How teachers use manipulatives to teach mathematics. *Educational Studies in Mathematics, 47,* 175-197.

Mullet, K., & Sano, D. (1995). *Designing visual interfaces. Communication oriented technique*s. Englewood Cliffs, NJ: Prentice Hall.

Murphy, C. A., Coover, D., & Owen, S. V. (1989). Development and validation of the computer self-efficacy scale. *Educational and Psychological Measurement, 49,* 893-899.

Murray, J. (2004). From game-story to cyberdrama. In P. Harrigan & N. Wardrip-Fruin (Ed.), *First person: New media as story, performance, and game* (pp. 2-11). Cambridge: MIT Press.

Nagy, W., Anderson, R. and Herman, P. (1987). Learning Word Meanings from Context during Normal Reading', *American Educational Research Journal, 24,* 237-70.

Narayanan, N. H., & Hegarty, M. (2002). Multimedia design for communication of dynamic information. *International Journal of Human-Computer Studies, 57*(4), 279-315.

Narciss, S., Proske, A., & Koerndle, H. (2007). Promoting self-regulated learning in Web-based learning environments. *Computers in Human Behavior, 23,* 1126-1144.

National Science Board (1999). Preparing our children: Math and science education in the national interest. Retrieved November 10, 1999, http://www.nsf.gov/pubs/1999/nsb9931/start.htm

Naylor, J. C., Pritchard, R. D., & Ilgen, D. R. (1980). *A theory of behavior in organizations.* New York: Academic Press.

Neal, L., Entin, E., Lai, F., Sidman, J., Mizrahi, G., & Brunyé, T. (2005). Teamwork skills training for medical practitioners. *Proceedings of the 11ᵗʰ International Conference on Human-Computer Interaction.*

Nesbit, J. C., & Winne, P. H. (2007). Tools for learning in an information society. In T. Willoughby & E. Wood (Eds.), *Children's learning in a digital world.* Oxford, UK: Blackwell.

Nesbit, J. C., Winne, P. H., Jamieson-Noel, D., Code, J., Zhou, M., MacAllister, K., Bratt, S., Wang, W., & Hadwin, A. F. (2007). Using cognitive tools in gStudy to investigate how study activities covary with achievement goals. *Journal of Educational Computing Research, 35,* 339-358.

Nesbit, J. C., Zhou, M., Xu, Y., & Winne, P. H. (2007, August). *Advancing log analysis of student interactions with cognitive tools.* Paper presented at the European Association for Research on Learning and Instruction (EARLI) 2007 Conference, Budapest, Hungary.

Neuman, S. B. (1997). Television as a learning environment: A theory of synergy. In J. Flood, S. Brice Heath & D. Lapp (Eds.), *Handbook of research on teaching literacy through the communicative and visual arts* (pp.15-30). New York: Simon & Schuster.

Nicaise, M., & Crane, M. (1999). Knowledge constructing through hypermedia authoring. *Educational Technology Research and Development, 47*(1), 29-50.

Niederhauser, D. S., Reynolds, R. E., Salmen, D. J., & Skolmoski, P. (2000). The influence of cognitive load on learning from hypertext. *Journal of Educational Computing Research, 23*(3), 237-255.

Nilsson, L.-G., Nyberg, L., T., K., Aberg, C., Persson, J., & Roland, P. E. (2000). Activity in motor areas while remembering action events. *Neuroreport, 11,* 2199-2201.

Norman, D. A. (1993). *Things that make us smart: Defending human attributes in the age of the machine.* Reading, MA: Addison-Wesley Publishing Co.

Norman, D. A. (2002). *The design of everyday things.* New York: Basic Books.

Norman, G. R., & Schmidt, H. G. (1992). The psychological basis of problem-based learning: A review of the evidence. *Academic Medicine, 67*(9), 557-565.

Nöth, W. (2003). Press photos and their captions. In H. Lönnroth (Ed.), *Från Närpesdialekt till EU-svenska* (pp. 169–188). Tampere: Tampere University Press.

Novick, L. R. (1988). Analogical transfer, problem similarity, and expertise. *Journal of Experimental Psychology: Learning, Memory, and Cognition, 14*(3), 510-520.

Novick, L. R., & Holyoak, K. J. (1991). Mathematical problem solving by analogy. *Journal of Experimental Psychology: Learning, Memory, and Cognition, 17,* 398-415.

Novick, L.R., & Morse, D.L. (2000). Folding a fish, making a mushroom: The role of diagrams in executing assembly procedures. *Memory & Cognition, 28*(7), 1242-1256.

NRC. (1996). *National Science Education Standards.* Washington, DC: National Research Council (NRC), National Academy Press.

NRC. (2000). *How people learn: brain, mind, experience, and school: Expanded edition.* Washington, DC: National Research Council: Commission on Behavioral and Social Sciences and Education, National Academy Press.

O'Donnell, A. M., Dansereau, D. F., & Hall, R. H. (2002). Knowledge maps as scaffolds for cognitive processing. *Educational Psychology Review, 14*(1), 71-86.

O'Neil, H. F., Wainess, R., & Baker, E. L. (2005). Classification of learning outcomes: Evidence from the computer games literature. *The Curriculum Journal, 16*(4), 455-474.

Oberauer, K., Süß, H. M., Schulze, R., Wilhelm, O., & Wittmann, W. W. (2000) Working memory capacity – facets of a cognitive ability construct. *Personality and Individual Differences, 29*, 1017-1045.

Okan, Z. (2003). Edutainment: Is learning at risk? *British Journal of Educational Technology, 34*(3), 255-264.

Olive, J. (1998). Opportunities to explore and integrate mathematics with "The Geometer's Sketchpad" in designing learning environments for developing understanding of geometry and space. In R. Lehrer & D. Chazan (Eds.), *Designing learning environments for developing understanding of geometry and space* (pp. 395-418). Mahwah, NJ: Lawrence Erlbaum Associates.

Ollerenshaw, A., Aidman, E., & Kidd, G. (1997). Is an illustration always worth ten thousand words? Effects of prior knowledge, learning style, and multimedia illustrations on text comprehension. *International Journal of Instructional Media, 24*, 227-238.

Orrill, C. H. (2001). Building technology-based, learner-centered classrooms: The evolution of a professional development framework. *Educational Technology Research and Development, 49*(1), 15-34.

Orrill, C. H. (2006). What learner-centered professional development looks like: The pilot studies of the InterMath professional development project. *The Mathematics Educator, 16*(1), 4-13.

Osborne, J., Simon, S., & Collins, S. (2003). Attitudes towards science: A review of the literature and its implication. *International Journal of Science Education, 25*(9), 1049-1079.

Osgood, C. E. (1949). The similarity paradox in human learning: A resolution. *Psychological Review, 56*, 132-143.

Owen, E., & Sweller, J. (1985). What do students learn while solving mathematics problems. *Journal of Educational Psychology, 77*, 272-284.

Paas, F. (1992). Training strategies for attaining transfer of problem solving skill in statistics: A cognitive load approach. *Journal of Educational Psychology, 84*, 429-434.

Paas, F. G., Tuovinen, J. E., Tabbers, H., & Van Gerven, P. W. M. (2003). Cognitive load measurement as a means to advance cognitive load theory. *Educational Psychologist, 38*, 63-71.

Paas, F., & Van Merrienboer, J. (1993). The efficiency of instructional conditions: An approach to combine mental-effort and performance measures. *Human Factors, 35*, 737-743.

Paas, F., & van Merriënboer, J. J. G. (1994). Variability of worked examples and transfer of geometrical problem-solving skills: A cognitive-load approach. *Journal of Educational Psychology, 86*, 122-133.

Paas, F., & van Merriënboer, J. J. G. (1994). Instructional control of cognitive load in the training of complex cognitive tasks. *Educational Psychology Review, 6*, 51-71.

Paas, F., Renkl, A., & Sweller, J. (2003). Cognitive load theory and instructional design: Recent developments. *Educational Psychologist, 38*(1), 1-4.

Paas, F., Tuovinen, J. E., Van Merriënboer, J., & Darabi, A. A. (2005). A motivational perspective on the relation between mental effort and performance: Optimizing learner involvement in instruction. *Educational Technology, Research and Development, 53*(3), 25-34.

Paas, F., Tuovinen, J., Tabbers, H., & Van Gerven, P. W. M. (2003). Cognitive load measurement as a means to advance cognitive load theory. *Educational Psychologist, 38*, 63-71.

Paas, F., Tuovinen, J.E., van Merriënboer, J.J.G., & Darabi, A. (2005). A motivational perspective on the relation between mental effort and performance: optimizing learners' involvement in instructional conditions. *Educational Technology, Research & Development, 53*, 25–34.

Paas, F., van Merriënboer J. J. G., & Adam, J. J. (1994). Measurement of cognitive-load in instructional research. *Perceptual and Motor Skills, 79*, 419-430.

Paivio, A. (1965). Abstractness, imagery, and meaningfulness in paired-associate learning. *Journal of Verbal Learning & Verbal Behavior, 4*, 32-38.

Paivio, A. (1971). Imagery and verbal processes. New York: Holt, Rinehart & Winston.

Paivio, A. (1986). *Mental representations: A dual coding approach.* New York: Oxford University Press.

Paivio, A. (1990). *Mental representations: A dual coding approach* (2nd ed.). New York: Oxford University Press.

Paivio, A. (1991). Dual coding theory: Retrospect and current status. *Canadian Journal of Psychology, 45,* 255-287.

Paivio, A. (1991). Dual coding theory: Retrospect and current status. *Canadian Journal of Psychology, 45,* 255-287.

Paivio, A.(1986). *Mental representations: A dual coding approach.* New York: Oxford University Press.

Pajares, F.(1996). Self-efficacy beliefs in achievement settings. *Review of Educational Research, 66,* 543-578.

Pajares, F. (1997). Current directions in self-efficacy research. In M. Maehr & P. R. Pintrich (Eds.), *Advances in motivation and achievement* (Vol. 10, pp. 1-49). Greenwich, C. T.: JAI Press.

Palaigeorgiou, G. E., Siozos, P. D., Konstantakis, N. I., & Tsoukalas, I. A. (2005). A computer attitude scale for computer science freshmen and its educational implications. *Journal of Computer Assisted Learning, 21,* 330-342.

Palinscar, A. S., & Brown, A. L. (1984). Reciprocal teaching of comprehension monitoring activities. *Cognition and Instruction, 1,* 117-175.

Palmer, S. E. (1978). Fundamental aspects of cognitive representation. In E. Rosch & B. B. Lloyd (Eds.), *Cognition and categorization* (pp. 259-303). Hillsdale, NJ: Erlbaum.

Papanikolaou, K. A., Grigoriadou, M., Magoulas, G. D., & Kornilakis, H. (2002). Towards new forms of knowledge communication: The adaptive dimension of a Web-based learning environment. *Computers in Education, 39,* 333-360.

Papert, S.(1980). *Mindstorms: Children, computers, and powerful ideas.* New York: Basic Books.

Papert, S.(1980). Computer-based microworlds as incubators for powerful ideas. In R. Taylor (Ed.), *The computer in the school: Tutor, tool, tutee* (pp. 203-210). New York: Teacher's College Press.

Papert, S.(1980). *Mindstorms: Children, computers, and powerful ideas.* New York: BasicBooks.

Papert, S. (1993). *The children's machine: Rethinking school in the age of the computer.* New York: Basic Books.

Paras, B. S. (2003). *Learning to play: The design of in-game training to enhance video game experience.* Un-published master's thesis, Simon Fraser University, Surrey, British Columbia, Canada.

Parasuraman, R., & Caggiano, D. (2002). Mental workload. In V. S. Ramachandran (Ed.), *Encyclopedia of the Human Brain.* San Diego, CA: Academic Press.

Pask, G. (1975). *Conversation, cognition, and learning: A cybernetic theory and methodology.* Amsterdam, Netherlands: Elsevier.

Passmore, P. J., Nielsen, C. F., Cosh, W. J., & Darzi, A. (2001). Effects of viewing and orientation on path following in a medical teleoperation environment. *Proceedings of the 2001 IEEE Virtual Reality Conference,* (p. 209).

Patrick, M. D., Carter, G., & Wiebe, E. N. (2006). *Visual representations of DNA: A comparison of salient features for experts and novices.* Paper presented at the NARST Annual Meeting, San Francisco, CA.

Pea, R. D. (1985). Beyond amplification: Using the computer to reorganize mental functioning. *Educational Psychologist, 20,* 167–182.

Pecchinenda, A., Smith, C.A., (1996). The affective significance of skin conductance activity during a difficult problem-solving task. *Cognition and Emotion, 10,* 481–503.

Peeck, J. (1987). The role of illustrations in processing and remembering illustrated text. In D. M. Willows & H. A. Houghton (Eds.), *The psychology of illustration* (Vol. 1, pp. 115-151). New York: Springer.

Peirce, C. S. (1960). *The icons, index, and symbol (1902): Collected papers.* Cambridge, MA: Harvard University Press.

Penner, D. E. (2000/2001). Cognition, computers, and synthetic science: Building knowledge and meaning through modeling. *Review of Research in Education, 25,* 1-35.

Penney, C. G. (1989). Modality effects and the structure of short-term memory. *Memory & Cognition, 17,* 398-422.

Penno J. F., Wilkinson I. A. G., Moore D. W. (2002). Vocabulary acquisition from teacher explanation and repeated listening to stories: Do they overcome the Matthew effect? *Journal of Educational Psychology, 94,* 23–33.

Perkins, D. N., Salomon, G. (1987). Transfer and teaching thinking. In D. N. Perkins, J. Lochhead, & J. Bishop (Eds.), *Thinking: The Second International Conference* (pp. 285-303). Hillsdale, NJ: Erlbaum.

Person, N. K., Graesser, A. C., Kreuz, R. J., Pomeroy, V., & the Tutoring Research Group. (2001). Simulating human tutor dialog moves in AutoTutor. *International Journal of Artificial Intelligence in Education, 12*, 23-39.

Peterson, L., & Peterson, M. J. (1959). Short-term retention of individual verbal items. *Journal of Experimental Psychology, 58*, 193-198.

Petre, M. (1995). Why looking isn't always seeing: Readership skills and graphical programming. *Communications of the ACM, 38*(6), 33-44.

Petre, M., & Green, T. R. (1993). Learning to read graphics: Some evidence that "seeing" an information display is an acquired skill. *Journal of Visual Languages and Computing, 4*, 55-70.

Petri, H. L. (1981). Motivation: theory and research. Belmont, CA: Wadsworth Publishing Company.

Philipp, R. A. (1992). The many uses of algebraic variables. In B. Moses (Ed.), *Algebraic thinking, Grades K-12: Readings from NCTM's School-based journals and other publications* (pp. 157-162). Reston, VA: National Council of Teachers of Mathematics.

Phillips, D. C. (1995). The good, the bad, and the ugly: The many faces of constructivism. *Educational Researcher, 24*(7), 5-12.

Phillips, G., & McNaughton, S. (1990). The practice of storybook reading to preschool children in mainstream New Zealand families. *Reading Research Quarterly, 25*, 196-212.

Phye, G. D. (1997). Learning and remembering: The basis for personal knowledge construction. In G. D. Phye (Ed.), *Handbook of academic learning: Construction of Knowledge.* San Diego: Academic Press.

Piaget, J. (1952). *The origins of intelligence in children* (Margaret Cook, Trans). New York: International Universities Press.

Piaget, J. (1976). *The grasp of consciousness.* Cambridge, MA: Harvard University Press.

Piaget, J. (1977). Equilibration of cognitive structures. New York: Viking.

Piaget, J. (1977). *Recherches sur l'abstraction réfléchissante.* Paris: Presses Universitaires de France.

Piaget, J. (1978). *Success and understanding.* London: Routledge and Kegan Paul.

Pinker, S. (1990). A theory of graph comprehension. In R. Friedle (Ed.), *Artificial intelligence and the future of testing* (pp. 73-126). Norwood, NJ: Ablex.

Pintrich, P. (2000). The role of goal orientation in self-regulated learning. In M.Boekaerts, P.R. Pintrich & M. Zeidner (Eds.), *Handbook of self-regulation* (pp. 451-502). Mawah, NJ: Lawrence Erlbaum.

Pintrich, P. R. (2000). Multiple goals, multiple pathways: The role of goal orientation in learning and achievement. *Journal of Educational Psychology, 92*, 544-555.

Pintrich, P. R., & Garcia, T. (1991). Student goal orientation and self-regulation in the college classroom. In M. L. Maehr & P. R. Pintrich (Eds.), *Advances in motivation and achievement* (Vol. 7, pp. 371-402). Greenwich, CT: JAI Press.

Pintrich, P. R., & Schunk, D. H. (1996). *Motivation in education: Theory, research, and applications.* Englewood Cliffs, NJ: Merrill.

Pintrich, P., & Schunk, D. H. (2002). Motivation in education: Theory, research, and applications (2nd Ed.). Upper Saddle River, NJ: Prentice Hall.

Pirolli, P., & Recker, M. (1994). Learning strategies and transfer in the domain of programming. *Cognition and Instruction, 12*(3), 235-275.

Plass, J. L., Chun, D. M., Mayer, R. E., & Leutner, D. (2003). Cognitive load in reading a foreign language text with multimedia aids and the influence of verbal and spatial abilities. *Computers in Human Behavior, 19*, 221-243.

Plass, J. L., Chun, D., Mayer, R. E., & Leutner, D. (1998). Supporting visualizer and verbalizer learning preferences in a second language multimedia learning environment. *Journal of Educational Psychology, 90*, 25-36.

Plass, J. L., Chun, D., Mayer, R. E., & Leutner, D. (2003). Cognitive load in reading a foreign language text with multimedia aids and the influence of verbal and spatial abilities. *Computers in Human Behavior, 19*, 211-220.

Plumert, J. M., Kearney, J. K., & Cremer, J. F. (2007). Children's road crossing: A window into perceptual-motor development. *Current Directions in Psychological Science, 16*, 255-263.

Pollatsek, A., Fisher, D. L., & Pradhan, A. (2006). Identifying and remedying failures of selective attention in younger drivers. *Current Directions in Psychological Science, 15*, 255-259.

Pollock, E., Chandler, P., & Sweller, J. (2002). Assimilating complex information. *Learning and Instruction, 12*, 61-86.

Posner, M. I., & Peterson, S. E. (1990). The attention system of the human brain. *Annual Review of Neuroscience, 13*, 25-42.

Pozzer, L. L., & Roth, W. M. (2003). Prevalence, function, and structure of photographs in high school biology textbooks. *Journal of Research in Science Teaching, 40*, 1089-1114.

Pratt, M.W., Boyes, C., Robins, S., & Manchester, J. (1989). Telling tales: Aging, working memory, and the narrative cohesion of story retellings. *Developmental Psychology, 25*, 628-63

Prawat, R. S. (1989). Promoting access to knowledge, strategy, and disposition in students: A research synthesis. *Review of Educational Research, 59*, 1-41.

Prensky, M. (2001). Digital Natives, Digital Immigrants. *On the Horizon. 9*(5), 1-15.

Puntambekar, S., & Hubscher, R. (2005). Tools for scaffolding students in a complex learning environment: What have we gained and what have we missed? *Educational Psychologist, 40*(1), 1–12.

Pylyshyn, Z. W. (1981). The imagery debate: Analogue media versus tacit knowledge. *Psychological Review, 87*, 16-45.

Quesada, J., Kintsch, W., & Comez, E. (2005). Complex problem-solving: A field in search of a definition? *Theoretical Issues in Ergonomics Science, 6*(1), 5-33.

Quine, W. V. (1995). *From stimulus to science.* Cambridge, MA: Harvard University Press.

Radev, D., Allison, T., Blair-Goldensohn, S., Blitzer, J., Celebi, A., Dimitrov, S., et al. (2004, May). *MEAD - A platform for multidocument multilingual text summarization.* Paper presented at the 4th International Conference on Language Resources and Evaluation, Lisbon, Portugal.

Rapp, D. N. (2005). Mental models: Theoretical issues for visualizations in science education. In J. K. Gilbert (Ed.), *Visualization in Science Education* (pp. 43-60). The Netherlands: Springer.

Rapp, D. N. (2005). The value of attention aware systems in educational settings. *Computers in Human Behavior, 22*, 603-614.

Rapp, D. N., & Taylor, H. A. (2004). Interactive dimensions in the construction of mental representations for text. *Journal of Experimental Psychology: Learning, Memory, and Cognition, 30*, 988-1001.

Rapp, D. N., & van den Broek, P. (2005). Dynamic text comprehension: An integrative view of reading. *Current Directions in Psychological Science, 14*, 276-279.

Ratcliff, R., & McKoon, G. (1988). A retrieval theory of priming in memory. *Psychological Review, 95*(3), 385-408.

Rayner, K. (1998). Eye movements in reading and information processing: 20 years of research. *Psychological Bulletin, 124*, 372-422.

Rayner, K., Rotello, C. M., Stewart, A. J., Keir, J., & Duffy, S. A. (2001). Integrating text and pictorial information: Eye movements when looking at print advertisements. *Journal of Experimental Psychology: Applied, 7*, 219-226.

Reder, L., & Anderson, J. R. (1980). A comparison of texts and their summaries: Memorial consequences. *Journal of Verbal Learning and Verbal Behaviour, 19*, 121-134.

Reder, L., & Anderson, J. R. (1982). Effects of spacing and embellishment on memory for main points of a text. *Memory and Cognition, 10*, 97-102.

Reed, S. K. (2005). From research to practice and back: The Animation Tutor project. *Educational Psychology Review, 17*, 55-82.

Reed, S. K. (2006). Cognitive architectures for multimedia learning. *Educational Psychologist, 41*(2), 87-98.

Reed, S. K. (in press). *Thinking Visually.* New York: Taylor & Francis.

Reed, S. K., & Hoffman, B. (in press). Animation Tutor (Version 1.0) [computer software]. New York: Taylor & Francis.

Reed, S. K., & Johnsen, J. A. (1977). Memory for problem solutions. In G. H. Bower (Ed.), *The psychology of learning and motivation, 11* 161-201. New York: Academic Press.

Reed, S. K., & Saavedra, N. C. (1986). A comparison of computation, discovery, and graph procedures for improving students' conception of average speed. *Cognition and Instruction, 3*, 31-62.

Reed, S.K. (2006). Cognitive architectures for multimedia learning. *Educational Psychologist, 41*(2), 87-98.

Reeve, J., Nix, G., & Hamm, D. (2003). Testing models of the experience of self-determination in intrinsic motivation and the conundrum of choice. *Journal of Educational Psychology, 95*(2), 375-392.

Reichle, E. D., Pollatsek, A., Fisher, D. L., & Rayner, K. (1998). Toward a model of eye movement control in reading. *Psychological Review, 105,* 125-157.

Reinking, D. (1994). *Electronic literacy.* Perspectives in Reading Research (4) Athens, GA: National Reading Research Center.

Reinking, D., Labbo, L., & McKenna, M. (1997). Navigating the changing landscape of literacy: Current theory and research in computer-based reading and writing. In J. Flood, S.B. Heath, & D. Lapp (Eds.), *Handbook of research on teaching literacy through the communicative and visual arts* (pp. 77-92). New York: Macmillan Library Reference.

Reiser, B. J. (2004). Scaffolding complex learning: The mechanisms of structuring and problematizing student work. *Journal of the Learning Sciences, 13*(3), 273-304.

Remillard, J. T. (2005). Examining key concepts in research on teachers' use of mathematics curricula. *Review of Educational Research, 75,* 211-246.

Renkl, A., & Atkinson, R. K. (2003). Structuring the transition from example study to problem solving in cognitive skill acquisition: A cognitive load perspective. *Educational Psychologist, 38*(1), 15-22.

Renkl, A., & Atkinson, R. K. (2007). Interactive learning environments: Contemporary issues and trends. *Educational Psychology Review, 19,* 235-238.

Renshaw, C. E., & Taylor, H. A. (2000). The educational effectiveness of computer-based instruction. *Computers & Geosciences, 26,* 677-682.

Resnick, L., & Omanson, S. (1987). Learning to understand arithmetic. In R. Glaser (Ed.), *Advances in instructional psychology* (41-95). Mahwah, NJ: LEA.

Resnick, M. (1994). *Turtles, termites, and traffic jams.* Cambridge, MA: MIT Press.

Reynolds, K. J., Renshaw, C. E., & Taylor, H. A. (2004). Improving computer-assisted instruction in teaching higher-order skills. *Computers & Education, 42,* 169-180.

Rheinberg, F., Vollmeyer, R., & Rollet, W. (2000) Motivation and action in self-regulated learning. In M. Boekaerts, P. R. Pintrich & M. Zeidner (Eds.), *Handbook of Self-regulation* (pp. 503-529). San Diego, CA: Academic Press.

Richardson, A. (1977). Verbalizer–visualizer: A cognitive style dimension. *Journal of Mental Imagery, 1,* 109–126.

Richland, L. E., Zur, O., & Holyoak, K. J. (2007). Cognitive supports for analogies in the mathematics classroom. *Science, 316,* 1128–1129.

Rieber, L. P. (1990). Animation in computer-based instruction. *Educational Technology Research & Development, 38,* 77-86.

Rieber, L. P. (1994). *Computers, graphics, and learning.* Madison, WI: Brown & Benchmark.

Rieber, L. P. (1996). Animation as feedback in a computer-based simulation: Representation matters. *Educational Technology Research & Development, 44*(1), 5-22.

Rieber, L. P. (2003). Microworlds. In D. Jonassen (Ed.), *Handbook of research for educational communications and technology* (2nd ed., pp. 583-603). Mahwah, NJ: Lawrence Erlbaum Associates.

Rieber, L. P., & Noah, D. (1997). *Effect of gaming and graphical metaphors on reflective cognition within computer-based simulations.* Paper presented at the annual meeting of the American Educational Research Association, Chicago.

Rieber, L. P., & Parmley, M. W. (1995). To teach or not to teach? Comparing the use of computer-based simulations in deductive versus inductive approaches to learning with adults in science. *Journal of Educational Computing Research, 13*(4), 359-374.

Rieber, L. P., Noah, D., & Nolan, M. (1998). *Metaphors as graphical representations within open-ended computer-based simulations*: Paper presented at the annual meeting of the American Educational Research Association, San Diego.

Rieber, L. P., Smith, M., Al-Ghafry, S., Strickland, W., Chu, G., & Spahi, F. (1996). The role of meaning in interpreting graphical and textual feedback during a computer-based simulation. *Computers and Education, 27*(1), 45-58.

Rieber, L. P., Tzeng, S., & Tribble, K. (2004). Discovery learning, representation, and explanation within a computer-based simulation: Finding the right mix. *Learning and Instruction, 14,* 307-323.

Ringstaff, C., & Kelley, L. (2002). *The learning return on our educational technology investment.* San Francisco: WestEd.

Ritter, S., Anderson, J. R., Koedinger, K. R., & Corbett, A. (2007). Cognitive tutor: Applied research in mathematics education. *Psychonomic Bulletin & Review, 14,* 249-255.

Rizzolatti, G., Fadiga, L., Fogassi, L., & Gallese, V. (1997). The space around us. *Science, 277*, 190–191.

Robbins, C., & Ehri, L. (1994). Reading storybooks to kindergartners helps them learn new vocabulary words. *Journal of Educational Psychology, 86*(1), 54-64.

Roberts, R. J., Hager, L. D., & Heron, C. (1994). Prefrontal cognitive processes: Working memory and inhibition in the antisaccade task. *Journal of Experimental Psychology: General, 123*, 374-393.

Robinson, M., & Mackey, M. (2003). Film and television. In N. Hall, J. Larson & J. Marsh (Eds.), *Handbook of early childhood literacy* (pp. 126-141). London: Sage.

Rock, I., & Palmer, S. E. (1990). The legacy of Gestalt psychology. *Scientific American, 263*(6, Dec.), 84-90.

Rorty, R. (1979). *Philosophy and the mirror of nature.* Princeton, NJ: Princeton University Press.

Roschelle, J. (1996). Designing for cognitive communication: Epistemic fidelity or mediating collaborative inquiry. In D. L. Day & D. K. Kovacs (Eds.), *Computers, communication, and mental models* (pp. 13–25). London: Taylor and Francis.

Roschelle, J., Kaput, J., & Stroup, W. (2000). SimCalc: Accelerating student engagement with the mathematics of change. In M. J. Jacobson & R. B. Kozma (Eds.), *Learning the sciences of the 21st Century: Research, design, and implementing advanced technology learning environments* (pp. 47-75). Hillsdale, NJ: Lawrence Erlbaum Associates.

Roschelle, J., Pea, R., Hoadley, C., Gordin, D., & Means, B. (2001). Changing how and what children learn in schools with computer-based technologies. *The Future of Children, 10*(2), 76-101.

Rose, D., & Meyer, A. (2000). Universal design for learning. *Journal of Special Education Technology, 15*(1), 67-70.

Rose, D., & Meyer, A. (2002). *Teaching every student in the digital age: Universal design for learning.* Alexandria, VA: Association for Supervision and Curriculum Development.

Rosen, V. M., & Engle, R. W. (1997). The role of working memory capacity in retrieval. *Journal of Experimental Psychology: General, 126*(3), 211-227.

Roth, W.-M. (2003). *Toward an anthropology of graphing.* Dordrecht, The Netherlands: Kluwer Academic Publishers.

Roth, W.-M. (2005). *Talking science: Language and learning in science.* Lanham, MD: Rowman & Littlefield.

Roth, W.-M. (2005). Telling in purposeful activity and the emergence of scientific language. In R. Yerrick & W.-M. Roth (Eds.), *Establishing scientific classroom discourse communities: Multiple voices of research on teaching and learning* (pp. 45–71). Mahwah, NJ: Lawrence Erlbaum Associates.

Roth, W.-M. (2006). *Learning science: A singular plural perspective.* Rotterdam, The Netherlands: SensePublishers.

Roth, W.-M. (2008). Bricolage, métissage, hybridity, heterogeneity, diaspora: Concepts for thinking science education in the 21st Century. *Cultural Studies in Science Education, 3.*

Roth, W.-M., & Duit, R. (2003). Emergence, flexibility, and stabilization of language in a physics classroom. *Journal for Research in Science Teaching, 40*, 869–897.

Roth, W.-M., & Middleton, D. (2006). The making of asymmetries of knowing, identity, and accountability in the sequential organization of graph interpretation. *Cultural Studies of Science Education, 1*, 11–81.

Roth, W.-M., & Pozzer-Ardenghi, L. (2006). Tracking situated, distributed, and embodied communication in real time. In M. A. Vanchevsky (Ed.), *Focus on cognitive psychology research* (pp. 237–261). Hauppauge, NY: Nova Science.

Roth, W.-M., McRobbie, C., Lucas, K.B., & Boutonné, S. (1997). Why do students fail to learn from demonstrations? A social practice perspective on learning in physics, *Journal of Research in Science Teaching, 34*, 509–533.

Roth, W.-M., Pozzer-Ardenghi, L., & Han, J. Y. (2005). *Critical graphicacy. Understanding visual representation practices in school science.* New York: Springer.

Roy, M., Chi, M. T. H., & Mayer, R. E. (2005). *The self-explanation principle in multimedia learning.* New York, NY, US: Cambridge University Press.

Rumiati, R. I., & Bekkering, H. (2003). To imitate or not to imitate: How the brain can do it, that is the question. *Brain and Cognition, 53*, 479-482.

Ryan, M. L. (2003). Cognitive maps and the construction of narrative space, in *Narrative Theory and the Cognitive Sciences* (D. Herman). Stanford: CSLI Publications.

Ryan, R. M., & Deci, E. L. (2000). Intrinsic and extrinsic motivations: Classic definitions and new directions. *Contemporary Educational Psychology, 25*, 54-67.

Ryan, R. M., & Deci, E. L. (2000). Self-determination theory and the facilitation of intrinsic motivation, social development, and well-being. *American Psychologist, 55*(1), 68-78.

Saadé, R. G., Nebebe, F., & Tan, W. (2007). Viability of the "Technology Acceptance Model" in multimedia learning environments: A comparative study. *Interdisciplinary Journal of Knowledge and Learning Objects, 3*, 175-183.

Sadoski, M., & Paivio, A. (1994). A dual coding view of imagery and verbal processes in reading comprehension. In R. B. Ruddell, M. R. Ruddell & H. Singer (Eds.), *Theoretical models and processes of reading* (4th ed., pp. 582-601). Newark, DE: International Reading Association.

Sadoski, M., & Paivio, A. (2001). *Imagery and text: A dual coding theory of reading and writing.* Mahwah, NJ: Lawrence Erlbaum Associates.

Salen, K., & Zimmerman, E. (2004). *Rules of play: Game design fundamentals,* Cambridge: MIT Press.

Salomon, G. (1979). *Interaction of media, cognition and learning.* San Francisco: Jossey-Bass.

Salomon, G. (1979). Media and symbol systems as related to cognition and learning. *Journal of Educational Psychology, 71*, 131-148.

Salomon, G. (1984). Television is "easy" and print is "tough": The differential investment of mental effort as a function of perceptions and attributions. *Journal of Educational Psychology, 76*, 647–658.

Salomon, G., & Leigh, T. (1984). Predispositions about learning from print and television. *Journal of Communication, 34*, 119–135.

Salomon, G., and Perkins, D.N. (1989). Rocky roads to transfer: Rethinking mechanisms of a neglected phenomenon. *Educational Psychologist, 24*(2), 113-142.

Salvucci, D. D., & Anderson, J. R. (2001). Automated eye-movement protocol analysis. *Human-Computer Interaction, 16*, 39-86.

Samuelstuen, M. S., & Bråten, I. (2007). Examining the validity of self-reports on scales measuring students' strategic processing. *British Journal of Educational Psychology, 77*, 351-378.

Sanchez, C. A., & Wiley, J. (2006). An examination of the seductive details effect in terms of working memory capacity. *Memory & Cognition, 34*(2), 344-355.

Sanchez, R. J., Truxillo, D. M., & Bauer, T. N. (2000). Development and examination of an expectancy-based measure of test-taking motivation. *Journal of Applied Psychology, 85*(5), 739-750.

Sandholtz, J. H., Ringstaff, C., & Dwyer, D. C. (1997). *Teaching with technology: Creating student-centered classrooms.* New York: Teachers College Press.

Saufley, W. H., Otaka, S. R., & Bavaresco, J. L. (1985). Context effects: Classroom tests and context independence. *Memory and Cognition, 13*, 522-528.

Savery, J. R., & Duffy, T. M. (1995). Problem-based learning: An instructional model and its constructivist framework. In B. Wilson (Ed.), *Constructivist Learning Environments: Case Studies in Instructional Design, 35*, 31-38. Englewood Cliffs, NJ: Educational Technology Publications.

Saxe, G. B. (1988). Candy selling and math learning. *Educational Researcher, 17*(6),14-21.

Saye, J. W., & Brush, T. (2007). Using technology-enhanced learning environments to support problem-based historical inquiry in secondary school classrooms. *Theory and Research in Social Education, 35*, 196-230.

Scaife, M., & Rogers, Y. (1996). External cognition: How do graphical representations work? *International Journal of Human-Computer Studies, 45*, 185-213.

Scardamalia, M. C., Bereiter, M. C. & Steinbach, R. (1984). Teachability of reflective processes in written composition. *Cognitive Science. 8*, 173-190.

Schacter, D. L. (1990). Memory. In M. I. Posner (Ed.), *Foundations of cognitive science* (pp. 683-725). Cambridge: MIT Press.

Schank, R. C. (1999). *Dynamic Memory Revisited.* New York: Cambridge University Press.

Scheiter, K., & Gerjets, P. (2007). Learner control in hypermedia environments. *Educational Psychology Review, 19*, 285-307.

Schmidt, R. A., & Bjork, R. A. (1992). New conceptualizations of practice: Common principles in three paradigms suggest new concepts for training. *Psychological Sciences, 3*, 207-217.

Schmidt-Weigand, F. (2008). The influence of visual and temporal dynamics on split attention: Evidences from eye tracking. In R. Zheng (Ed.), *Cognitive effects of multimedia learning* (Chapter Six). Hershey, PA: IGI Global Publishing.

Schmidt-Weigand, F., Kohnert, A., & Glowalla, U. (2008). *Integrating different sources of information in multimedia learning: An eye tracking study on split attention.* Manuscript submitted for publication.

Schneider, W., & Detweiler, M. (1987). A connectionist/control architecture for working memory. In G.H. Bower (Ed.), *The psychology of learning and motivation.* Vol. 21 (pp53-119). New York: Academic Press.

Schnotz, W., & Bannert, M. (2003). Construction and interference in learning from multiple representation, *Learning and Instruction, 13,* 141–156.

Schnotz, W., & Bannert, M. (2003). Construction and interference in learning from multiple representation. *Learning and Instruction, 13,* 141-156.

Schober, B., & Ziegler, A. (2002). Theoretical levels in the evaluation of motivational trainings. *European Journal of Psychological Assessment, 18*(3), 204-213.

Schommer, M. (1993). Epistemological development and academic performance among secondary students. *Journal of Educational Psychology, 85,* 406-411.

Schön, D. D. (1983). *The reflective practitioner: How professionals think in action.* New York: Basic Books.

Schooler, C. (1989). Social structural effects and experimental situations. In K. W. Schaie & C. Schooler (Eds.), *Social structure and aging: Psychological processes* (pp. 1-21). Hillsdale, NJ: Erlabaum.

Schroeder, E. E., & Grabowski, B. L. (1995). Patterns of exploration and learning with hypermedia. *Journal of Computing Research, 13,* 313-335.

Schrum, L., Burbank, M. D., Engle, J., Chambers, J. A., & Glassett, K. F. (2005). Post-secondary educators' professional development: Investigation of an online approach to enhancing teaching and learning. *Internet & Higher Education, 8*(4), 279-289.

Schuh, K. L. (2003). Knowledge construction in the learner-centered classroom. *Journal of Educational Psychology, 95,* 426-442.

Schunk, D. H. (1989). Self-efficacy and cognitive skill learning. In C. Ames & R. Ames (Eds.), *Research in motivation in education. Vol. 3: Goals and cognitions* (pp. 13-44). San Diego: Academic Press.

Schunk, D. H. (1990). Goal setting and self-efficacy during self-regulated learning. *Educational Psychologist, 25,* 71-86.

Schunk, D. H. (1991). Self-efficacy and academic motivation. *Educational Psychologist, 26,* 207-231.

Schvaneveldt, R.W. (1990). *Pathfinder associative networks.* Norwood, NJ: Ablex.

Schwan, S., & Riempp, R. (2004). The cognitive benefits of interactive videos: Learning to tie nautical knots. *Learning and Instruction, 14*(3), 293-305.

Schwartz, D. L. (1995). Reasoning about the referent of a picture versus reasoning about the picture as a referent: An effect of visual realism. *Memory & Cognition, 23,* 709-722.

Schwartz, D. L., & Black, T. (1999). Inferences through imagined actions: Knowing by simulated doing. *Journal of Experimental Psychology: Learning, Memory and Cognition, 25,* 116-136.

Schwartz, D. L., & Bransford, J. D. (1998). A time for telling. *Cognition and Instruction, 16*(4), 475-522.

Schwartz, D. L., & Heiser, J. (2006). Spatial representations and imagery in learning. In R. K. Sawyer (Ed.). *The Cambridge Handbook of the Learning Sciences.* Cambridge, UK: Cambridge University Press.

Schwartz, D. L., & Martin, T. (2004). Inventing to prepare for learning: The hidden efficiency of original student production in statistics instruction. *Cognition and Instruction, 22,* 129-184.

Schwier, R., & Misanchuk, E. R. (1990). *Analytical tools and research issues for interactive media.* (Report No. IR014519). Saskatchewan, Canada.

Scott, B. (2001). Conversation theory: A constructivist, dialogical approach to educational technology. *Cybernetics & Human Knowing, 8*(4), 25-46.

Seels, B., Berry, L. H., Fullerton, K., & Horn, L. J. (1996). Research on learning from television. In D. H. Jonassen (Ed.), *Handbook of research for educational communications and technology* (pp. 299-377). New York: Simon & Schuster Macmillan.

Selting, M., Auer, P., Barden, B., Bergmann, J., Couper-Kuhlen, E., Günthner, S., Meier, C., Quasthoff, U., Schlobinski, P., & Uhmann, S. (1998). Gesprächsanalytisches Transkriptionssystem. *Linguistische Berichte, 173,* 91–122.

Sénéchal, M., & LeFevre, J. (2002). Parental involvement in the development of children's reading skill: A five-year longitudinal study. *Child Development, 73*, 445–460.

Sénéchal, M., LeFevre, J., Hudson, E., & Lawson, E.P. (1996). Knowledge of storybooks as a predictor of young children's vocabulary. *Journal of Educational Psychology, 88*, 520-536.

Sénéchal, M., LeFevre, J., Thomas, E. M., & Daley, K. E. (1998). Differential effects of home literacy experiences on the development of oral and written language. *Reading Research Quarterly, 33*, 96-116.

Senko, C., & Miles, K. M. (in press). Pursuing their own learning agenda: How mastery-oriented students jeopardize their class performance. *Contemporary Educational Psychology.*

Shadish, W. R., Cook, T. D., & Campbell, D. T. (2001). *Experimental and quasi-experimental designs for generalized causal inference.* Boston, MA: Houghton Mifflin Company.

Shah, P., & Hoeffner, J. (2002). Review of graph comprehension research: Implications for instruction. *Educational Psychology Review, 14*, 47-69.

Shah, P., & Miyake, A. (1996). The separability of working memory resources for spatial thinking and language processing: An individual differences approach. *Journal of Experimental Psychology: General, 125*, 4-27.

Shamir, A., & Korat, O. (in press). The educational electronic book as a tool for supporting children's emergent literacy. In Adriana G. Bus & Susan B. Neuman (Eds.), *Multimedia and literacy development: Improving achievement for young learners.* London: Routledge.

Shannon, C. E., & Weaver, W. (1949). *The mathematical theory of communication.* Urbana, IL: University of Illinois Press.

Shannon, C. E., & Weaver, W. (1969). *The mathematical theory of communication.* Urbana, IL: The University of Illinois Press.

Sharma, P., & Hannafin, M. J. (2007). Scaffolding in technology-enhanced learning environments. *Interactive Learning Environments, 15*(1), 27-46.

Sharp, D. L. M., Bransford, J. D., Goldman, S. R., Risko, V. J., Kinzer, C. K., & Vye, N. J. (1995). Dynamic visual support for story comprehension and mental model building by young, at-risk children. *Educational Technology Research and Development, 43*, 25-40.

Shernoff, D. J., Csikszentmihalyi, M., Schneider, B., & Shernoff, E. S. (2003). Student engagement in high school classrooms from the perspective of flow theory. *School Psychology Quarterly, 18*(2), 158-176.

Sheull, T.J. (1990). Toward a unified approach to learning as a multisource phenomenon. *Review of Educational Research, 60*(4), 531-547.

Shih, T. K., Wang, T. H., Chang, C.-Y., Kao, T.-C., & Hamilton, D. (2007). Ubiquitous e-learning with multimodal devices. *IEEE Transactions on Multimedia, 9*, 487–499.

Shiong, K. B., Aris, B., Ahmad, M. H., Ali, M. B., Harun, J., & Zaidatun, T. (2008). Learning "Goal Programming" using an interactive multimedia courseware: Design factors and students' preferences. *Journal of Educational Multimedia and Hypermedia, 17*(1), 59-79.

Shockley, K., & Turvey, M. T. (2006). Dual-task influences on retrieval from semantic memory and coordination dynamcs. *Psychonomic Bulletin & Review, 13*, 985-990.

Shute, V. J. (1991). Who is likely to acquire programming skills? *Journal of Educational Computing Research, 7*, 1-24.

Siegler, R. S., & Alibali, M. W. (2005). *Children's thinking.* Upper Saddle River: Prentice Hall.

Simon, H. A. (1945). *Administrative behavior: A study of decision-making process in administrative organization.* New York: Free Press.

Simpson, E. S. (2005). Evolution in the classroom: What teachers need to know about the video game generation. *Tech Trends, 49*(5), 17-22.

Singley, M. K., & Anderson, J. R. (1989). *The transfer of cognitive skill.* Cambridge, MA: Harvard University Press.

Singley, M. K., & Anderson, J. R. (1989). *The transfer of cognitive skill.* Cambridge, MA: Harvard University Press.

Sinha, R. (2005). A cognitive analysis of tagging (or how the lower cognitive cost of tagging makes it popular). Thoughts About Cognition, Design, and Technology: Rashmi Sinha's weblog. Retrieved December 12, 2007 from http://www.rashmisinha.com/archives/05_09/tagging-cognitive.html

Sins, P. H. M., Savelsbergh, E. R., & van Joolingen, W. R. (2005). The Difficult Process of Scientific Modelling: An Analysis Of Novices' Reasoning During Computer-Based

Modelling. *International Journal of Science Education, 27*(14ov), 1695-1721.

Slamecka, N.J., & Graf, P. (1978). The generation effect: Delineation of a phenomenon. Journal of Experimental Psychology: Human Learning and Memory, 6, 592-604.

Small, R. V., & Gluck, M. (1994). The relationship of motivational conditions to effective instructional attributes: A magnitude scaling approach. *Educational Technology, 34*(8), 33-40.

Smidt, E., & Hegelheimer, V. (2004). Effects of online academic lectures on ESL listening comprehension, incidental vocabulary acquisition, and strategy use. *Computer Assisted Language Learning, 17*(5), 517-556.

Smith, M., Duda, J., Allen, J. & Hall, H. (2002). Contemporary measures of approach and avoidance goal orientations: Similarities and differences. *British Journal of Educational Psychology, 72*, 155-190.

Smith, S. M., & Woody, P. C. (2000). Interactive effect of multimedia instruction and learning styles. *Teaching of Psychology, 27*(3), 220-223.

Solman, R., Singh, N., & Kehoe, E. J. (1992). Pictures block the learning of sight words. *Educational Psychology, 12*, 143-153.

Song, L, Hannafin, M.J., & Hill, J. (2007). Reconciling beliefs and practices in teaching and learning. *Educational Technology Research and Development, 55*(1), 27-50.

Song, L., Singleton, E. S., Hill, J. R., & Koh, M. H. (2004). Improving online learning: Student perceptions of useful and challenging characteristics. *Internet and Higher Education, 7*(1), 59-70.

Song, S. H., & Keller, J. M. (2001), Effectiveness of motivationally adaptive computer-assisted instruction on the dynamic aspects of motivation. *Educational Technology, Research & Development, 49*(2), 5-22.

Spilich, G. J., Vesonder, G. T., Chiesi, H. L., & Voss, J. F. (1979). Text processing of domain related information for individuals with high and low domain knowledge. *Journal of Verbal Learning and Verbal Behavior, 18*, 275-290.

Spiro, R. J., Collins, B. P., Ramchandran, A. R. (2007). Reflections on a Post-Gutenberg epistemology for video use in ill-structured domains: Things you can do with video to foster complex learning and cognitive flexibility. *Video Research in the Learning Sciences.* Goldman, R.,

Pea R., Barron B., and Derry, S. (Eds.). Mahwah, NJ: Lawrence Erlbaum Associates.

Spiro, R. J., Feltovich, P. J., Jacobson, M. J., & Coulson, R. L. (1991). Knowledge representation, content specification, and the development of skill in situation-specific knowledge assembly: Some constructivist issues as they relate to cognitive flexibility theory and hypertext. *Educational Technology, 31* (9), 22-25.

Spiro, R. J., Vispoel, W. L., Schmitz, J., Samarapungavan, A., & Boerger, A. (1987). Knowledge acquisition for application: Cognitive flexibility and transfer in complex content domains. In B. C. Britton & S. Glynn (Eds.), *Executive control processes.* Hillsdale, NJ: Lawrence Erlbaum Associates.

Spiro, R., Feltovich, P., Jacobson, M., & Coulson, R. (1991). Cognitive flexibility, constructivism, and hypertext: Random access instruction for advanced knowledge acquisition in ill-structured domains. *Educational Technology, 31,* 24-33.

Spiro, R.J. (2006). The "New Gutenberg Revolution": Radical new learning, thinking, teaching, and training with technology…bringing the future near. *Educational Technology, 46* (1), 3-4.

Spiro, R.J. (2006). The Post-Gutenberg world of the mind: The shape of the new learning. *Educational Technology, 46* (2), 3-4.

Spiro, R.J. (2006). Old ways die hard. *Educational Technology, 46* (3), 3-4.

Spiro, R.J. (2006). Approaching the post-Gutenberg mind: The revolution is in progress. *Educational Technology, 46* (4), 3-4.

Spiro, R.J. (2006). The "New Gutenberg Revolution": Radical new learning, thinking, teaching, and training with technology…bringing the future near. *Educational Technology, 46*(6), 3-5.

Spiro, R.J., & DeSchryver, M. (in preparation). The new nonlinear reading comprehension: Deep learning on the Web and the post-Gutenberg mind.

Spiro, R.J., & DeSchryver, M. (in press). Constructivism: When it's the wrong idea and when it's the only idea. In T. Duffy & S. Tobais (Eds.). Mahwah, NJ: Lawrence Erlbaum.

Spiro, R.J., & Jehng, J. (1990). Cognitive flexibility and hypertext: Theory and technology for the nonlinear and multidimensional traversal of complex subject matter. In D. Nix & R. J. Spiro (Eds.), *Cognition, education, and multimedia* (pp. 163-205). Hillsdale: Lawrence Erlbaum Associates.

Spiro, R.J., Coulson, R. L., Feltovich, P. J., & Anderson, D. (1988). Cognitive flexibility theory: Advanced knowledge acquisition in ill-structured domains. *Tenth Annual Conference of the Cognitive Science Society*. Hillsdale, NJ: Erlbaum,. [Reprinted in In R. B. Ruddell (Ed.), *Theoretical models and processes of reading* (5th ed.). Newark, DE: International Reading Association, pp. 602-616.]

Spiro, R.J., Feltovich, P. J., Coulson, R. L., & Anderson, D. (1989). Multiple analogies for complex concepts: Antidotes for analogy-induced misconception in advanced knowledge acquisition. In S. Vosniadou & A. Ortony (Eds.), *Similarity and analogical reasoning* (pp. 498-531). Cambridge, MA: Cambridge University Press.

Spiro, R.J., Feltovich, P.J., & Coulson, R.L. (1996). Two epistemic world-views: Prefigurative schemas and learning in complex domains. *Applied Cognitive Psychology, 10*, 52-61.

Squire, K. (2003). Video games in education. *International Journal of Simulations and Gaming, 2*(1).

Squire, K. (2006). From content to context: Videogames as designed experience. *Educational Researcher, 35*(8), 19-29.

Squire, K., & Jenkins, H. (2003). *Harnessing the power of games in education. Insight, 3, 5.* [Online journal]. Retrieved May 1, 2007, from the World Wide Web: http://website.education.wisc.edu/kdsquire/manuscripts/insight.pdf

Stake, J. E., & Mares, K. R. (2001). Science enrichment programs for gifted high school girls and boys: Predictors of program impact on science confidence and motivation. *Journal of Research in Science Teaching, 38*(10), 1065-1088.

Steel, P. (2007). The nature of procrastination: A meta-analytic and theoretical review of quintessential self-regulatory failure. *Psychological Bulletin, 133*(1), 65-94.

Steffens, M. C. (2007). Memory for goal-directed sequences of actions: Is doing better than seeing? *Psychonomic Bulletin & Review, 14*, 1194-1198.

Stenning, K., & Oberlander, J. (1994). A cognitive theory of graphical and linguistic reasoning: Logic and implementation. *Cognitive Science, 19*, 96-140.

Stepien, W. J., Gallagher, S. A., & Workman, D. (1993). Problem-based learning for traditional and interdisciplinary classrooms. *Journal for the Education of the Gifted, 16*(4), 338-357.

Stipek. D. (1993). *Motivation to learn: From theory to practice.* Needham Heights, MA: Allyn & Bacon.

Stone, D.E., & Glock, M.D. (1981). How do young adults read directions with and without pictures? *Journal of Educational Psychology, 73*, 419-426.

Suchman, L., & Jordan, B. (1990). Interactional troubles in face-to-face survey interviews. *Journal of the American Statistical Association, 85*(409), 232-241.

Suchman, L.A. (1987). *Plans and situated actions: The problem of human-machine communication.* Cambridge, UK: Cambridge University Press.

Sulzby, E. (1985). Children's emergent reading of favorite storybooks: A developmental study. *Reading Research Quarterly, 20*, 458-481.

Sundar, S. S., & Kalyanaraman, S. (2004). Arousal, memory, and impression-formation effects of animation speed in Web advertising. *Journal of Advertising, 33*(1), 7-17.

Susarla, S. C., Adcock, A., Van Eck, R., Moreno, K., & Graesser, A. (2003). *Development and evaluation of a lesson authoring tool for AutoTutor.* In V. Aleven, U. Hoppe, J. Kay, R. Mizoguchi, H. Pain, F. Verdejo, & K. Yacef (Eds.), *Proceedings of the 11th International Conference on Artificial Intelligence in Education*, Sydney, Australia (pp. 378-387). Amsterdam: IOS Press.

Svinicki, M. (1999). New directions in learning and motivation. *New Directions for Teaching and Learning, 80*, 5-27. San Francisco: Jossey-Bass.

Swanborn, M. S. L., & de Glopper, K. (1999). Incidental word learning while reading: A meta-analysis. *Review of Educational Research, 69*, 261-285.

Sweller, J. (1988). Cognitive load during problem solving: Effects on learning. *Cognitive Science, 12*, 257-285.

Sweller, J. (1994). Cognitive load theory, learning difficulty, and instructional design. *Learning and Instruction, 4*, 295-312.

Sweller, J. (1999). *Instructional design in technical areas.* Camberwell, Victoria, Australia: ACER Press.

Sweller, J. (2003). Evolution of human cognitive architecture. In B. Ross (Ed.), *The psychology of learning and motivation* (Vol. 43, pp. 215-266). San Diego: Academic Press.

Sweller, J. (2004). Instructional design consequences of an analogy between evolution by natural selection and human cognitive architecture. *Instructional Science, 32*, 9-31.

Sweller, J. (2005). The redundancy principle. In R. E. Mayer (Ed.), *Cambridge handbook of multimedia learning* (pp. 159-167). New York: Cambridge University Press.

Sweller, J., & Chandler, P. (1991). Evidence for cognitive load theory. *Cognition and Instruction, 8*(4), 351-362.

Sweller, J., & Chandler, P. (1994). Why some material is difficult to learn. *Cognition and Instruction, 12*(3), 185-233.

Sweller, J., & Cooper, G. (1985). The use of worked examples as a substitute for problem solving in learning algebra. *Cognition and Instruction, 2*, 59-89.

Sweller, J., & Sweller, S. (2006). Natural information processing systems. *Evolutionary Psychology, 4*, 434-458.

Sweller, J., Chandler, P., Tierney, P., & Cooper, M. (1990). Cognitive load as a factor in the structuring of technical material. *Journal of Experimental Psychology: General, 119*, 176-192.

Sweller, J., van Merrienboer, J. J. G., & Paas, F. (1998). Cognitive architecture and instructional design. *Educational Psychology Review 10*(3), 251–296.

Sweller, J., van Merrienboer, J. J. G., & Paas, F. G. (1998). Cognitive architecture and instructional design. *Educational Psychology Review, 10*, 251-196.

Sweller. J. (1988) Cognitive load during problem solving: Effects on learning *Cognitive Science* 12, 157-285.

Tabbers, H. K. (2002). *The modality of text in multimedia instructions. Refining the design guidelines.* Unpublished doctoral dissertation, Open University of the Netherlands Heerlen.

Tabbers, H. K., Martens, R. O., & van Merrienboer, J. J. G. (2004). Multimedia instructions and cognitive load theory: Effects of modality an cueing. *British Journal of Educational psychology, 74*, 71-81.

Tallent-Runnels, M. K., Thomas, J. A., Lan, W. Y., Cooper, S., Ahern, T. C., Shaw, S. M., & Liu, X. (2006). Teaching courses online: A review of the research. *Review of Educational Research, 76*(1), 93-135.

Tarmizi, R., & Sweller, J. (1988). Guidance during mathematical problem solving. *Journal of Educational Psychology, 80*, 424-436.

Taylor, H. A., & Tversky, B. (1992). Spatial mental models derived from survey and route descriptions. *Journal of Memory and Language, 31*, 261-292.

Taylor, H. A., Brunyé, T. T., & Taylor, S. (in press). Wayfinding and Navigation: Mental Representation and Implications for Navigational System Design. To appear in Carswell, C.M. (Ed.), *Reviews of Human Factors and Ergonomics, Volume 4.*

Taylor, H.A., & Tversky, B. (1996). Perspective in spatial descriptions. *Journal of Memory and Language, 35*, 371-391.

Taylor, R. S., & Chi, M. T. H. (2006). Simulation versus text: Acquisition of implicit and explicit information. *Journal of Educational Computing Research, 35*(3), 289.

The Center for Universal Design. (2004). What is universal design? Retrieved November 1, 2004, from http://www.design.ncsu.edu/cud/univ_design/ud.htm

The Nielson Company (2004). *The state of the console: Video game console usage report* (4th Quarter). New York, NY.

Thomas, V., & Gorky, P. (1996). *Heksenspul met Hennie de Heks en de Kat Helmer* [Winnie Witch] [CD-ROM]. Nieuwegein, The Netherlands: Bombilla.

Thompson, C. (2003). Information illiterate or lazy: How college students use the Web for research. *Libraries and the Academy, 3*(2), 259-268.

Thompson, P. W. (1992). Notations, conventions, and constraints: Contributions to effective use of concrete materials in elementary mathematics. *Journal for Research in Mathematics Education, 23*, 123-147.

Thompson, P. W. (1994). Concrete materials and teaching for mathematical understanding. *Arithmetic Teacher, 40*, 556-558.

Thorndike, E. (1913). *Educational psychology: The psychology of learning.* New York: Teachers College Press.

Thorndike, E. L. (1903). *Educational psychology.* New York: Lemcke & Buechner.

Thorndike, E.L., & Woolworth, R.S. (1901). The influence of improvement in one mental function upon the efficiency of their functions. *Psychological Review, 8*, 247-261.

Tindall-Ford, S., Chandler, P., & Sweller, J. (1997). When two sensory modes are better than one. *Journal of Experimental Psychology: Applied, 3*, 257-287.

Tindall-Ford, S., Chandler, P., & Sweller, J. (1997). When two sensory modes are better than one. *Journal of Experimental Psychology: Applied, 3*, 257-287.

Treisman, A. M., & Gelade, G. (1980). A feature integration theory of attention. *Cognitive Psychology, 12*, 97-136.

Tremayne, M., & Dunwoody, S. (2001). Interactivity, information processing, and learning on the World Wide Web. *Science Communication, 23(2)*, 111-134.

Triona, L. M., & Klahr, D. (2003). Point and click or grab and heft: Comparing the influence of physical and virtual instructional materials on elementary school students' ability to design experiments. *Cognition and Instruction, 21*, 149-173.

Tuan, H. L., Chin, C. C., & Shieh, S. H. (2005). The development of a questionnaire to measure students' motivation towards science learning. Research Report. *International Journal of Science Education, 27*(6), 639-654.

Tufte, E. R. (2001). *The visual display of quantitative information*. Graphics Press.

Turner, M. L., & Engle, R. W. (1989). Is working memory capacity task dependent? *Journal of Memory and Language, 28*, 127-154.

Tversky, B. (2003). Some ways graphics communicate. In K. Nyiri (Ed.), *Mobile communication: Essays on cognition and community* (pp. 143-156). Wien: Passagen Verlag.

Tversky, B., Morrison, J. B., & Betrancourt, M. (2002). Animation: Does it facilitate? *International Journal of Human-Computer Studies, 57*, 247-262.

Twyman, M. (1985). Using pictorial language: A discussion of the dimensions of the problem. In T. M. Duffy & R. Waller (Eds.) *Designing Usable Texts* (pp. 245–312). Orlando, FL: Academic Press.

Umilta, M. A., Kohler, E., Gallese, V., Fogassi, L., Fadiga, L., Keysers, C., & Rizzolatti, G. (2001). I know what you are doing. A neurophysiological study. *Neuron, 31*, 155-165.

Underwood, G. (Ed.) (2005). *Cognitive Processes in Eye Guidance*. Oxford, UK: Oxford University Press.

Unsworth, N., & Engle, R. W. (2007). The nature of individual difference n working memory capacity: Active maintenance in primary memory and controlled search from secondary memory. *Psychological Review, 114*(1), 104-132.

Unsworth, N., & Schrock, J. C., & Engle, R. W. (2004). Working memory capacity and the antisaccade task: Individual differences in voluntary saccade control. *Journal of Experimental Psychology: Learning, Memory, and Cognition, 30*(6), 1302-1321.

Urdan, T. (1997). Achievement goal theory: Past results, future directions. In M. Maehr & P. Pintrich (Eds.), *Advances in motivation and achievement* (pp. 99-141). Greenwich, CT: JAI.

Urdan, T., & Mestas, M. (2006). The goals behind performance goals. *Journal of Educational Psychology, 98*, 354-365.

Uribe, D., Klein, J. D., & Sullivan, H. (2003). The effect of computer-mediated collaborative learning on ill-defined problems. *Educational Technology Research & Development, 51*(1), 5-19.

Van Den Hurk, M. (2006). The relation between self-regulated strategies and individual study time, prepared participation and achievement in a problem-based curriculum. *Active Learning in Higher Education, 7*(2), 155-169.

van Dijk, T. A., & Kintsch, W. (1983). *Strategies of Discourse Comprehension*. New York: Academic Press.

Van Earde, W., & Thierry, H. (1996). Vroom's expectancy models and work-related criteria: A meta-analysis. *Journal of Applied Psychology, 81*, 575-586.

Van Gerven, P. W. M., Paas, F., van Merrienboer, J. J. G., & Schmidt, H. G. (2002). Memory load and the cognitive pupillary response. *Psychophysiology, 41*, 167-174.

Van Gog, T., Paas, F., & van Merriënboer, J. J. G. (2005). Uncovering expertise-related differences in troubleshooting performance: Combining eye movement and concurrent verbal protocol data. *Applied Cognitive Psychology, 19*, 205-221.

Van Joolingen, W. R., King, S., & de Jong, T. (1997). The SimQuest authoring system for simulation-base discovery environments. In B. du Boulay & R. Mizoguchi (Eds.), *Knowledge and media in learning systems* (pp. 79-87). Amsterdam: IOS.

van Merriënboer, J. J. G., & Krammer, H. P. M. (1987). Instructional strategies and tactics for the design of introductory computer programming courses in high school. *Instructional Science, 16*, 251-285.

van Merriënboer, J. J. G., & Krammer, H. P. M. (1990). The "completion strategy" in programming instruction: Theoretical and empirical support. In S. Dijkstra, B. H. M. van Hout-Wolters, and P. C. van der Sijde (Eds.), *Research on instruction* (pp. 45-61). Englewood Cliffs, NJ: Educational Technology Publications.

van Merriënboer, J. J. G., & Sweller, J. (2005). Cognitive load theory and complex learning: Recent developments and future directions. *Educational Psychology Review, 17*(2), 147-177.

van Merrienboer, J.J.G. & Sweller, J. (2005). Cognitive load theory and complex learning: Recent developments and future directions. *Educational Psychology Review 17*(2), 147-177.

Van Merrienboer, J.J.G., & Paas, F. (2003). Powerful learning and the many faces of instructional design: Toward a framework for the design of powerful learning environments. In E. De Corte, L. Verschaffel, N. Entwistle, & J. van Merrienboer (Eds), *Powerful Learning Environments: Unraveling Basic Components and Dimensions* (pp. 3-22). Elsevier Science Ltd.

van Merrionboer, J. J. G., & Ayres, P. (2005). Research on cognitive load theory and its design implications for E-learning. *Educational Technology Research & Development, 53*(3), 5-13.

Van Scoyoc, A.M. (2006). The electronic library: Undergraduate research behavior in a library without books. *Libraries and the Academy, 6*(1), 47-58.

VandeWalle, D., Cron, W. L., & Slocum, J. W. (2001). The role of goal orientation following performance feedback. *Journal of Applied Psychology, 86*, 629–640.

VanLehn, K. (2006). The behavior of tutoring systems. *International Journal of Artificial Intelligence and Education, 16*, 227-265.

VanLehn, K., Lynch, C., Schulze, K., Shapiro, J. A., Shelby, R., Taylor, L., et al. (2005). The Andes physics tutoring system: Lessons learned. *International Journal of Artificial Intelligence and Education, 15*, 147-204.

Verdi, M. P., Kulhavy, R. W., Stock, W. A., Rittschof, K., & Johnson, J. T. (1996). Text learning using scientific diagrams: Implications for classroom use. *Contemporary Educational Psychology, 21*, 487-499.

Verhallen, M.J.A.J., & Bus, A.G. (2008). Exploring the relationship between repeated readings of a storybook, attentional arousal, and vocabulary learning in young children at-risk. Manuscript submitted for publication.

Verhallen, M.J.A.J., Bus, A.G., & de Jong, M.T. (2006). The promise of multimedia stories for kindergarten children at risk. *Journal of Educational Psychology, 98*, 410-419.

Verhoeven, L. (2000). Components in early second language reading and spelling. *Scientific Studies of Reading, 4*(4), 313–330.

Viera, A. J., & Garrett, J. M. (2005). Understanding interobserver agreement: The kappa statistic. *Family Medicine, 37*(5), 360-363.

Vinter, A., & Perruchet, P. (2000). Implicit learning in children is not related to age: Evidence from drawing behavior. *Child Development, 71*(5), 1223-1240.

Visser, J. & Keller, J. M. (1990). The clinical use of motivational messages: An inquiry into the validity of the Arcs model of motivational design. *Instructional Science, 19*(6), 467-500.

Vollmeyer, R., & Reinberg, F. (2006). Motivational effects on self-regulated learning with different tasks. *Educational Psychology Review, 18*, 239-253.

Voss, J. F., & Silfies, L. N. (1996). Learning from history text: The interaction of knowlede and comprehension skill with text structure. *Cognition and Instruction, 14*(1), 45-68.

Vreman-de Olde, C., & de Jong, T. (2004). Student-Generated Assignments about Electrical Circuits in a Computer Simulation. *International Journal of Science Education, 26*(7), 859.

Vroom, V. H. (1964). Work and motivation. New York: Wiley.

Vygotsky, L. (1978). *Mind in society: The development of higher psychological processes.* Cambridge, MA: Harvard University Press.

Vygotsky, L. S. (2006). *Mind in Society: Development of Higher Psychological Processes.* Cambridge, Massachusetts: Harvard University Press.

Vygotsky, L.S. (1986). *Thought and language.* Cambridge, MA: MIT Press.

Wade-Stein, D., & Kintsch, E. (2004). Summary Street: Interactive computer support for writing. *Cognition and Instruction, 22*(3), 333-362.

Wagner, J. F. (2006). Transfer in pieces. *Cognition and Instruction, 24*(1), 1-71.

Wagner, S. M., Nusbaum, H., & Goldin-Meadow, S. (2004). Probing the mental representation of gesture: Is handwaving spatial? *Journal of Memory and Language, 50*, 395-407.

Wainess, R. A. (2006) *The effect of navigation maps on problem solving tasks instantiated in a computer-based video game.* Ph.D. dissertation, University of Southern California, United States -- California. Retrieved February 11, 2008, from ProQuest Digital Dissertations database. (Publication No. AAT 3237181).

Wallace, R., & Kupperman, J. (1997, April). *On-line search in the science classroom: Benefits and possibili-*

ties. Paper presented at the annual meeting of the American Educational Research Association, Chicago, IL.

Ward, M., & Sweller, J. (1990). Structuring effective worked examples. *Cognition and Instruction, 7,* 1-39.

Watson, J. M., Bunting, M. F., Poole, B. J., & Conway, A. R. (2005). Individual differences in susceptibility to false memory in the Deese–Roediger–McDermott Paradigm, *Journal of Experimental Psychology: Learning, Memory, and Cognition, 31*(1), 76–85.

Wattenmaker, W.D. (1992). Relational properties and memory-based category construction. *Journal of Experimental Psychology, 18*(5), 1125-1138.

Weinberger, D. (2007). Everything Is Miscellaneous, New York: Henry Holt.

Weinstein, R. (2004). Performance goals guide current educational reform: Are we on the best path? *PsycCRITIQUES, 49,* 32-35.

Wenglinsky, H. (1998). *Does it compute? The relationship between educational technology and student achievement in mathematics.* Retrieved November 5, 2007 from http://searcheric.org/ericdc/ED425191.htm

Wentzel, K. R. (1999). Social-motivational processes and interpersonal relationships: Implications for understanding. *Journal of Educational Psychology, 91*(1), 76-97.

West, R. E., Waddoups, G., & Graham, C. R. (2007). Understanding the experiences of instructors as they adopt a course management system. *Educational Technology Research and Development, 55*(1), 1-26.

West, R. E., Waddoups, G., Kennedy, M., & Graham, C. R. (2007). Evaluating the impact on users from implementing a course management system. *International Journal of Technology and Distance Learning, 4*(2). Retrieved November 5, 2007 from http://itdl.org/Journal/Feb_07/article01.htm.

Whipp, J. L., & Chiarelli, S. (2004). Self-regulation in a Web-based course: A case study. *Educational Technology Research & Development, 52*(4), 5-22.

White, B. Y. (1993). ThinkerTools: Causal models, conceptual change, and science education. *Cognition and Instruction, 10*(1), 1-100.

White, B. Y., & Horowitz, P. (1987). *ThinkerTools: Enabling children to understand physical laws* (No. 6470): Bolt, Beranek, and Newman, Inc.

Whitehead, A. N. (1929). *The aims of education.* New York: Macmillan.

Wickens, C. D. (1984). Processing resources in attention. In R. Parasuraman & D. R. Davies (Eds.), *Varieties of attention* (pp. 63-102). London: Academic.

Wickens, C. D. (2002). Multiple resources and performance prediction. *Theoretical Issues in Ergonomics Science, 3,* 159-177.

Wigfield, A., & Eccles, J. S. (2000). Expectancy-value theory of achievement motivation, *Contemporary Educational Psychology, 25,* 68-81.

Williams, J. H. G., Whiten, A., Suddendorf, T., & Perrett, D. I. (2001). Imitation, mirror neurons and autism. *Neuroscience and Biobehavioral Reviews, 25,* 287-295.

Wills, T. W., Soraci, S. A., Chechile, R. A., & Taylor, H. A. (2000). "Aha" effects in the generation of pictures. *Memory & Cognition, 28,* 939-948.

Wilson, J. (2001). Methodological difficulties of assessing metacognition: A new approach. (ERIC Document Reproduction Service No. ED460143).

Wilson, J. R., & Rutherford, A. (1989). Mental models: Theory and application in human factors. *Human Factors, 31,* 617-634.

Windell, D., & Wieber, E. N. (2007). *Measuring cognitive load in multimedia instruction: A comparison of two instruments.* Paper presented at American Educational Research Association Annual Conference. Chicago, IL.

Winn, W. D. (1987). Charts, graphics and diagrams in educational materials. In D. Willows & H. Houghton (Eds.). *Knowledge acquisition from text and pictures* (pp. 125-144). North Holland: Elsevier.

Winne, P. H. (1979). Experiments relating teachers' use of higher cognitive questions to student achievement. *Review of Educational Research, 49,* 13-49.

Winne, P. H. (1982). Minimizing the black box problem to enhance the validity of theories about instructional effects. *Instructional Science, 11,* 13–28.

Winne, P. H. (2001). Self-regulated learning viewed from models of information processing. In B. J. Zimmerman & D. H. Schunk (Eds.), *Self-regulated learning and academic achievement: Theoretical perspectives* (2nd ed., pp. 153–189). Mahwah, NJ: Lawrence Erlbaum Associates.

Winne, P. H. (2004). Comments on motivation in real-Life, dynamic, and interactive learning environments: Theoretical and methodological challenges when researching motivation in context. *European Psychologist, 9,* 257-263.

Winne, P. H. (2006). How software technologies can improve research on learning and bolster school reform. *Educational Psychologist, 41*, 5–17.

Winne, P. H. (2006). Meeting challenges to researching learning from instruction by increasing the complexity of research. In J. Elen & R. E. Clark (Eds.), *Handling complexity in learning environments: Theory and research* (pp. 221-236). Amsterdam, Netherlands: Elsevier.

Winne, P. H., & Jamieson-Noel, D. L. (2002). Exploring students' calibration of self-reports about study tactics and achievement. *Contemporary Educational Psychology, 27*, 551-572.

Winne, P. H., & Marx, R. W. (1989). A cognitive processing analysis of motivation within classroom tasks. In C. Ames and R. Ames (Eds.), *Research on motivation in education 3*, 223-257. Orlando, FL: Academic Press.

Winne, P. H., Gupta, L., & Nesbit, J. C. (1994). Exploring individual differences in studying strategies using graph theoretic statistics. *Alberta Journal of Educational Research, 40*, 177-193.

Winne, P. H., Jamieson-Noel, D. L., & Muis, K. (2002). Methodological issues and advances in researching tactics, strategies, and self-regulated learning. In P. R. Pintrich & M. L. Maehr (Eds.), *Advances in motivation and achievement: New directions in measures and methods* (Vol. 12, pp. 121-155). Greenwich, CT: JAI Press.

Winne, P. H., Nesbit, J. C., Kumar, V., Hadwin, A. F., Lajoie, S. P., Azevedo, R. A., & Perry, N. E. (2006). Supporting self-regulated learning with gStudy software: The Learning Kit Project. *Technology, Instruction, Cognition and Learning, 3*, 105-113.

Wittrock, M. C. (1989). Generative processes of comprehension. *Educational Psychologist, 24*, 345-376.

Wolfe, M. B. W., Schreiner, M. E., Rehder, B., Laham, D., Foltz, P. W., Kintsch, W., et al. (1998). Learning from text: Matching readers and texts by latent semantic analysis. *Discourse Processes, 25*(2-3), 309-336.

Wolters, C. A. (1998). Self-regulated learning and college students' regulation of motivation. *Journal of Educational Psychology, 90*, 224-235.

Workman, M. (2004). Performance and perceived effectiveness in computer-based and computer-aided education: Do cognitive styles make a difference? *Computers in Human Behavior, 20*(4), 517.

Xie, B., & Salvendy, G. (2000). Prediction of mental workload in single and multiple tasks environments. *International Journal of Cognitive Ergonomics, 4*, 213-242.

Xu, Y., Nesbit, J. C., Zhou, M., & Winne, P. H. (2007). *LogValidator: A tool for identifying and mining patters in gStudy log data.* [computer program]. Simon Fraser University, Burnaby, BC.

Yaros, R. A., & Cook, A. E. (2007). The use of eye-tracking hardware to assess effects in health news: Is there more than meets the eye? Unpublished manuscript.

Yeung, A. S., Jin, P., & Sweller, J. (1998). Cognitive load and learner expertise: Split-attention and redundancy effects in reading with explanatory notes. *Contemporary Educational Psychology, 23*, 1-21.

Yeung, A. S., Jin, P., & Sweller, J. (1998). Cognitive load and learner expertise: Split-attention and redundancy effects in reading with explanatory notes. *Contemporary Educational Psychology, 23*, 1-21.

Young, M. F. (1993). Instructional design for situated learning. *Educational Technology Research & Development, 41*(1), 43-58.

Zacks, J. M, & Tversky, B. (2003). Structuring information interfaces for procedural learning. *Journal of Experimental Psychology: Applied, 9*, 88-100.

Zahn, C., Barquero, B., & Schwan, S. (2004). Learning with hyperlinked videos--design criteria and efficient strategies for using audiovisual hypermedia. *Learning and Instruction, 14*(3), 275-291.

Zhang, J. (1997). The nature of external representations in problem solving. *Cognitive Science, 21*, 179-217.

Zheng, R., Cook, A. E., & Blaz, J. W. (2008). *Solving complex problems: A convergent approach to cognitive load measurement.* Unpublished manuscript.

Zheng, R., Miller, S., Snelbecker, G., & Cohen, I. (2006). Use of multimedia for problem-solving tasks. *Journal of Technology, Instruction, Cognition and Learning, 3*(1-2), 135-143.

Zhou, M., & Winne, P. H. (2008, April). *Differences in achievement goal-setting among high-achievers and low-achievers.* Paper to be presented at the American Educational Research Association 2008 Annual Meeting, New York.

Zhu, X., & Simon, H. (1987). Learning mathematics from examples and by doing. *Cognition and Instruction, 4*, 137-166.

Zimmer, H. D., Helstrup, T., & Engelkamp, J. (2000). Pop-out into memory: A retrieval mechanism that is enhanced with the recall of subject-performed tasks. *Journal of Experimental Psychology: Learning, Memory, and Cognition, 26*, 658-670.

Zimmerman, B. (1989). Models of self-regulated learning and academic achievement. In B. Zimmerman & D. Schunk (Eds.), *Self-regulated learning and academic achievement: Theory, research, and practice* (pp. 1-25). New York: Springer-Verlag.

Zimmerman, B. J. (1994). Dimensions of academic self-regulation: A conceptual framework for education. In D. H. Schunk & B. J. Zimmerman (Eds.), *Self-regulation of learning and performance: Issues and educational applications* (pp. 3-21). Hillsdale, NJ: Erlbaum.

Zimmerman, B. J., & Bandura, A. (1994). Impact of self-regulatory influences on writing course attainment. *American Educational Research Journal, 31*, 845-862.

Zion, M., Michalsky, T., & Mevarech, Z. (2005). The effects of metacognitive instruction embedded within an asynchronous learning network on scientific inquiry skills. *International Journal of Science Education, 27*(8), 957-983.

Zwaan, R. A., & Radvansky, G. A. (1998). Situation models in language comprehension and memory. *Psychological Bulletin, 123,* 162-185.

Zwaan, R. A., Langston, M. C., & Graesser, A. C. (1995). The construction of situation models in narrative comprehension: an event-indexing model. *Psychological Science, 6,* 292-297.

Zwaan, R. A., Magliano, J. P., & Graesser, A. C. (1995). Dimensions of situation-model construction in narrative comprehension. *Journal of Experimental Psychology: Learning, Memory, & Cognition, 21,* 386-397.

Zweig, D., & Webster, J. (2004). Validation of multidimensional measure of goal orientation. *Canadian Journal of Behavioral Science, 36*(3), 232-243.

About the Contributors

Robert Z. Zheng is a faculty member in the Department of Educational Psychology, University of Utah, USA. His publications include edited books, book chapters and journal papers covering the topics of online learning, multimedia, cognition, and application of educational technology in K-12 schools. His research agenda includes online learning and pedagogy, multimedia and cognition, and educational technology and assessment. He edited and co-edited several books including *Understanding Online Instructional Modeling: Theories and Practices, Cognitive Effects of Multimedia Learning*, and *Adolescent Online Social Communication and Behavior: Relationship Formation on the Internet*. He is the author of numerous book chapters and peer-reviewed journal papers on the topics of cognitive load, multimedia, Web-based instruction, and problem solving in multimedia learning.

* * *

Faisal Ahmad is a PhD candidate in computer science at University of Colorado at Boulder. He is a member of the Boulder Learning Technologies Groups, working under the leadership of Dr. Tamara Sumner. Mr. Ahmad has served as student chair on the Joint Conference on Digital Libraries 2005. His current work focuses on enhancing digital libraries usage by linking resource discovery and educational standards and modeling and developing knowledge organization services. His other interests include knowledge organization systems, ubiquitous computing and educational technologies.

Robert K. Atkinson is an associate professor of educational technology at Arizona State University. His research explores the intersection of cognitive science, instructional design, and educational technology. He currently has several research foci, including: (a) designing computer-based learning environments that are consistent with human cognitive processes, particularly environments that aid human cognition during problem solving in science and mathematics; (b) designing and evaluating animated pedagogical agents, (c) exploring ways of supporting English Language Learners working with multimedia environments focusing on science content; (d) exploring how learners use worked-out examples to solve problems in semantically-rich domains such as mathematics and physics.

Jason S. Augustyn, PhD is a research psychologist with the U.S. Army Natick Soldier Research, Development, and Engineering Center. His research examines human motor control, attention, visual perception, and affordance perception in both real and virtual environments. He is particularly interested in bridging basic and applied research, applying insights from laboratory studies to the design of better tools and technologies. Jason received a PhD from the Pennsylvania State University and completed a postdoctoral fellowship in spatial perception and virtual reality at the University of Virginia.

Tad T. Brunyé, PhD is a cognitive psychologist with the U.S. Army Natick Soldier Research, Development, and Engineering Center, as well as the department of psychology at Tufts University. He focuses on spatial cognition, working memory, spatial and verbal integration, discourse comprehension, training and educational system design, and human-systems integration. Tad received his PhD from Tufts University in experimental cognitive psychology and B.A. from the State University of New York at Binghamton.

Adriana Bus is professor of Education and Child Studies at Leiden University in The Netherlands. A former reading specialist, she teaches courses in reading, writing and learning problems. She is a leading scholar on the impact of attachment theory on children's emergent literacy development, and on developmental changes in storybook reading among parents and children. Currently she is working with computer experts, instructional designers, and content specialists on building an Internet environment to promote rich literacy experiences for young children. She has won several awards including the International Reading Association's 'Computers in Reading Award'.

Kirsten R. Butcher is a postdoctoral research fellow at the University of Pittsburgh's Learning Research and Development Center, with a joint appointment at the Pittsburgh Science of Learning Center. Dr. Butcher holds a PhD in psychology and cognitive science from the University of Colorado, Boulder. Her research focuses on cognitive processes of learning, particularly the impact of interactive technologies and visual information on high-level processes such as integration, inference, and transfer. Dr. Butcher's current research includes intelligent tutoring research in classroom settings as well as laboratory research on learning with multimedia and visual representations.

Sebastian de la Chica is a PhD candidate in computer science at the University of Colorado at Boulder. Mr. de la Chica holds both a master's degree in computer science and a bachelor's degree in computer engineering, from Auburn University. He has over 15 years of commercial software R&D experience primarily focused on the design and evaluation of user interfaces across multiple domains. His current work focuses on scaffold design issues for digital library-based learning environments, integrating natural language processing and human information interaction approaches to support students writing scientific explanations online.

Anne Cook is an associate professor and cognitive psychologist at the University of Utah, whose research focuses on how readers retrieve information from long-term memory during reading, and the factors that affect this reactivation process. Her recent work has focused on the activation of inferences and general world knowledge during reading, as well as studies on cognitive load in problem solving and cognitive impairments in individuals with autism. Her research primarily uses response time and eye tracking methodologies.

Michael DeSchryver is PhD candidate in the Department of Counseling, Educational Psychology and Special Education at the Michigan State University.

Peter E. Doolittle is currently the director of the Educational Psychology Research Program in the Department of Learning Sciences and Technology at Virginia Tech, Blacksburg, VA. He is also the Executive Editor of the *International Journal of Teaching and Learning in Higher Education* (IJTLHE).

His academic background includes 19 years teaching primary, secondary, undergraduate, and graduate students, in public schools and private schools, using traditional and online formats, across several subject areas including mathematics, computer science, statistics, and educational psychology. His current research focus includes the investigation of learning efficacy in multimedia instructional environments.

Tali Ditman, PhD is a research fellow in cognitive neuroscience at Harvard Medical School, working at Massachusetts General Hospital and Tufts University. She focuses on language comprehension in healthy and psychiatric populations, and uses event-related potentials and functional magnetic resonance imaging to elucidate the brain mechanisms involved in discourse-level comprehension. Tali received her PhD from Tufts University in experimental cognitive neuroscience and MA and BA from the State University of New York at Binghamton.

Qianyi Gu is PhD candidate in computer science at the University of Colorado at Boulder. Mr. Gu holds a master's degree in computer science from State University of New York at Stony Brook and a bachelor's degree in chemistry from Peking University. His previous research has used information retrieval and web mining techniques to improve the quality of on-line library services, and to develop a visualization component of conceptual browsing interfaces for digital libraries. Currently, his research investigates the use of information retrieval, user modeling and information visualization techniques to provide personalization services for on-line educational technology.

Michael J. Hannafin is the Charles H. Wheatley-Georgia Research Alliance Eminent Scholar in Technology-Enhanced Learning, professor of Educational Psychology and Instructional Technology, and director of the Learning and Performance Support Laboratory at the University of Georgia. Previously, he held academic positions at the University of Colorado, Penn State University and Florida State University. His research examines the psychological and pedagogical principles underlying student-centered learning. He earned his doctorate in Educational Technology from Arizona State University in 1981.

David Hicks is currently an associate professor of history and social science education in the Department of Teaching and Learning at Virginia Tech, Blacksburg, VA. His current research interests include the teaching of history in England and the U.S., the use of technology as a partner to support the teaching of history, the impact of standards on student learning, the history of education, and special education and parental advocacy.

Jana Holsanova is an associate professor at the Cognitive Science Department at Lund University, Sweden. Important topics in her research include the relationship between visual perception, spoken language production and cognition; interactive aspects of communication, multimodal discourse, the interplay between linguistic, pictorial and graphic representations and users' interaction with new media. Her recent book *Discourse, Vision and Cognition* has been published at Benjamins (Amsterdam/Philadelphia). Jana Holsanova is currently working as a visiting research fellow at the Hansa Institute for Advanced Study in Delmenhorst, Germany with her project "Multiple Windows on the Mind and Action".

Putai Jin, (PhD), has published his research in the areas of quantitative methods, motivation, psychophysiology, language learning, and personality in *Psychological Bulletin, Journal of Educational*

Psychology, Organizational Behavior and Human Decision Processes, American Behavioral Scientist, Journal of Psychosomatic Research, Contemporary Educational Psychology, Journal of Research and Development in Education, Journal for the Education of the Gifted, and *Journal of Sport Behavior.* He is the author of *Human Factors* and contributes chapters to many books.

Alan Koenig is a senior research associate in the Center for the Study of Evaluation at the University of California Los Angeles. His research focuses on the design and evaluation of games and simulations that are used for training and instruction in both professional and academic settings. Alan holds a PhD in educational technology from Arizona State University, a bachelor of science in mechanical engineering from the University of Hartford, and a bachelor of arts in economics from the University of Connecticut.

Min Liu is professor of Instructional Technology (IT) at the University of Texas at Austin. She has been teaching courses on new media design, production, and research over 15 years. Her research interests center on the impact of new media technology on learning and the design of engaging and interactive learning environments for all age groups. She publishes widely in leading IT research journals and serves on a number of editorial/manuscript review boards of IT research journals. She is also active in professional organizations such as AACE, AERA, and ISTE. She has directed and managed both CD-ROM and Web based development projects, including award winning ones.

Renae Low (PhD) has published her research in the areas of text editing, modality, problem solving, and self-concept in *Journal of Educational Psychology, British Journal of Educational Psychology, The American Journal of Psychology, Journal of Research and Development in Education, Instructional Science, Journal for the Education of the Gifted.* She is a contributing author of *Handbook of Multimedia Learning* and other books.

Caroline R. Mahoney (PhD) is a research psychologist at the U.S. Army Natick Soldier Research, Development, and Engineering Center. She focuses on nutritional and dietary effects on cognition and behavior, spatial memory, motor control, attention, and human factors. Caroline received her PhD from Tufts University in experimental cognitive psychology and BA from Denison University.

Gina J. Mariano is currently a doctoral candidate in the educational psychology program in the Department of Learning Sciences and Technology at Virginia Tech, Blacksburg, VA. She is an associate editor of the *International Journal of Teaching and Learning in Higher Education* (IJTLHE). Her academic background includes a bachelor's degree in psychology and gerontology, and a master's degree in counseling psychology. Her research focus includes the investigation of knowledge transfer, knowledge application, working memory and long-term memory retrieval.

James H. Martin is a professor in the Department of Computer Science and the Department of Linguistics, and a fellow in the Institute of Cognitive Science at the University of Colorado at Boulder. He received a BS in computer science from Columbia University and a PhD in computer science from the University of California at Berkeley in 1988. He has over 70 publications in computer science and computational linguistics including the books *A Computational Model of Metaphor Interpretation* and *Speech and Language Processing.*

Stephen Reed is professor of Psychology and a member of the Center for Research in Mathematics and Science Education at San Diego State University. He was previously a member of the faculty at Case Western Reserve and Florida Atlantic University. He is primarily interested in applying research in cognitive psychology to the design of computer instruction to support visual thinking. His books include *Psychological Processes in Pattern Recognition, Word Problems: Research and Curriculum Reform, Thinking Visually,* and seven editions of *Cognition: Theory and Applications.*

Lloyd P. Rieber is a professor in the Department of Educational Psychology and Instructional Technology at the University of Georgia. He is interested in visualization, cognitive psychology, and constructivistic orientations to instructional design. His research focuses on using dynamic visualizations in the design of interactive learning environments. His most recent research is about the integration of computer-based microworlds, simulations, and games using play theory as the theoretical framework. He is now applying this research to support online learning environments and to help students with cognitive disabilities.

Wolff-Michael Roth is Lansdowne professor of applied cognitive science at the University of Victoria. As a research methodologist, he has a variegated method toolbox that he applies to interesting research questions pertaining to knowing, learning, identity, and emotion across the life in the areas of technology, mathematics, and science. Among his recent publication are *Doing Teacher-Research: A Handbook for Perplexed Practitioners* (Sense Publishers, 2007) and *Talking Science: Language and Learning in Science Classrooms* (Rowman & Littlefield, 2005).

Katharina Scheiter is an assistant professor in the Department of Applied Cognitive Psychology and Media Psychology at the University of Tuebingen, Germany. In her research she focuses on ways of designing and using educational technology as cognitive tools by linking basic cognitive psychology models of information processing to the design of multimedia and hypermedia learning environments. Recent projects deal with the effects of realism in dynamic visualizations on knowledge acquisition in the Natural Sciences, on ways of combining verbal and visual representations in multimedia learning, and on the affordances of representations in learner-controlled hypermedia environments. Dr. Scheiter's research has been funded by the Deutsche Forschungsgemeinschaft (DFG) and the Leibniz Gemeinschaft.

Florian Schmidt-Weigand, PhD studied psychology, mathematics, and linguistics at Philipps University Marburg and did her doctoral dissertation in psychology at Justus Liebig University Giessen. Dr. Schmidt-Weigand is currently a post-doc researcher at the Institute of Psychology, University of Kassel.

Craig E. Shepherd is an assistant professor in the University of Wyoming. His research focuses on the effects of Web-based tools used to promote inquiry and professional development on teachers at all stages of their careers. He earned his bachelors degree in psychology from Brigham Young University in 2002.

Rand Spiro is a professor of educational psychology at the Michigan State University. His research areas are knowledge acquisition in complex domains, hypermedia learning environments, multimedia case-based methods in professional education, biomedical cognition, and constructive processes in text comprehension and recall. A central part of his research involves the development and testing of theory-based hypermedia learning environments designed to promote cognitive flexibility.

Tamara Sumner is an associate professor at the University of Colorado at Boulder with a joint appointment between the Department of Computer Science and the Institute of Cognitive Science. Prior to joining the University of Colorado, Dr. Sumner served as a lecturer with the Knowledge Media Institute at The Open University in the UK. Dr. Sumner's research interests include human-computer interaction, design research, educational technology, and interactive scholarly publishing.

John Sweller is an Emeritus professor of Education at the University of New South Wales. His research is associated with cognitive load theory, an instructional theory based on our knowledge of human cognitive architecture. He initiated work on the theory in the early 1980's. Subsequently, "ownership" of the theory shifted to his research group at UNSW and then to a large group natural of international researchers. The theory is now a contributor to both research and debate on issues associated with human cognitive architecture, its links to evolution by selection, and the instructional design consequences that follow. It is one of the few theories to have generated a large range of novel instructional designs from our knowledge of human cognitive architecture.

Krista P. Terry is the director of Radford University's Technology in Learning Center and is an associate editor of the *International Journal of Teaching and Learning in Higher Education* (IJTLHE). Her academic background includes six years of higher education administration and leadership in the instructional design and technology area. She currently works with faculty in a training and development capacity to assist with the integration of technology into teaching and learning. Her research interests include a wide array of technology integration issues including the application and integration of new media technologies.

Paul Toprac is a Hart eCenter lecturer at the Southern Methodist University in the Guildhall, the premier graduate video game education program in the U.S. His dissertation work involved the design, development, and implementation of a digital game to help middle school students learn science. Prior to graduate school, Toprac was in the information technology industry for more than twenty years, where his roles ranged from CEO to executive director to product manager to consultant. Toprac holds a Bachelor's of Science in chemical engineering, a Master's of Business Administration, and a Doctor of Philosophy (instructional technology, curriculum and instruction, College of Education) from The University of Texas at Austin.

Marian J.A.J. Verhallen has worked in primary and special education and is currently working as a lecturer at the Centre for Learning Problems and Impairments of the Faculty of Social and Behavioural Sciences at Leiden University while completing her PhD research on the effect of living books on story understanding and language development of young children at risk.

Richard E. West is a doctoral candidate in the Educational Psychology and Instructional Technology Department at the University of Georgia. He studies the role of communities and collaborative relationships in learning and innovation, in both face-to-face and online settings. He also has worked as a mixed-methods evaluator in education, technology, and health care settings.

Eric Wiebe is an associate professor in the Department of Mathematics, Science, and Technology Education at North Carolina State University. Dr. Wiebe has focused much of his research on issues related to the use of technology in the instructional environment, with a particular emphasis on multimedia tools and techniques. Recent projects include a multi-year grant to help develop cutting edge research techniques in K-12 STEM education and a 3-year NSF project developing curricula using scientific and technical visualization in middle and high school. Dr. Wiebe is currently serving as a Senior Research Fellow at the Friday Institute at North Carolina State.

Philip H. Winne is professor and Canada Research Chair in the Faculty of Education, Simon Fraser University. He researches metacognition and self-regulated learning, specifically, how students monitor qualities of their study tactics, and how they use those evaluations to adapt old tactics and invent new ones. Winne and colleagues are currently developing nStudy, a leading edge educational technology for researching self-regulated learning and promoting student skills for learning. He co-edited the *Handbook of Educational Psychology* (2nd ed.) and the field-leading journal *Educational Psychologist* (2001-2005).

Timothy T. Yuen is a doctoral candidate in Instructional Technology Program at the University of Texas at Austin. His research interest is in multimedia-based cognitive tools and computer science education. Tim received his master's degree in computer science from the University of Southern California and a bachelor's degree in information and computer science from the University of California, Irvine.

Mingming Zhou is a PhD candidate and research assistant in the Educational Psychology Program, Faculty of Education, Simon Fraser University. Her research interests focus on exploring new methodologies to measure motivational constructs as well as how students use study tactics. She is currently coordinating the research project "nStudy," the successor of "gStudy" – educational software which helps learners learn more effectively and advances research in learning.

Lansdowne Professor, Applied Cognitive Science Lansdowne Professor, Applied Cognitive

Index